Readings in Comparative Health Law and Bioethics

Readings in Comparative Health Law and Bioethics

SECOND EDITION

Timothy Stoltzfus Jost

Carolina Academic Press
Durham, North Carolina

Library of Congress Cataloging-in-Publication Data

Jost, Timothy S.
Readings in comparative health law and bioethics / by Timothy Stoltzfus Jost. -- 2nd ed.
p. cm.
Rev. ed. of: Readings in comparative health law and bioethics / edited by Timothy Stoltzfus Jost, 2001
Includes bibliographical references and index.
ISBN-13: 978-1-59460-296-2 (alk. paper)
ISBN-10: 1-59460-296-4 (alk. paper)
1. Medical care--Law and legislation. 2. Comparative law. 3. Medicine, Comparative. 4. Ethics, Comparative. 5. Bioethics. I. Readings in comparative health law and bioethics. II. Title.

K3601.J67 2007
344.04'1--dc22 2007008986

Carolina Academic Press
700 Kent Street
Durham, NC 27701
Telephone (919) 489-7486
Fax (919) 493-5668
www.cap-press.com

Printed in the United States of America

Contents

Introduction

This book is a collection of annotated readings to be used for teaching comparative health law and bioethics.

While comparative health law is a relatively new field, this book is located within the tradition of the discipline of comparative law. The traditional concerns of comparative law have been to analyze, classify, and (to the extent possible) understand comparatively a foreign legal system as a whole. Traditionally, comparative law has concentrated on comparing continental European civil law systems with common law systems. It has also focused on private law. More recently, comparative law has attempted to apply new tools to comparative analysis—law and economics, feminist legal theory, critical legal theory, or postcolonial theory—to craft metatheories for understanding legal systems.

The task of understanding a foreign legal system as a whole is hard work, whatever approach one takes. One must be grounded in the culture and society of the country studied, which usually requires a knowledge of the country's language and some time spent on the ground. One must master procedural as well as substantive law. One must also distance one's self from one's own legal system. One must gain the ability to see one's own system as a foreign system.

This book stands in the tradition of micro, rather than macro, comparative law. It does not offer an understanding of other legal systems as a whole, but focuses rather on understanding how a wide variety of disparate legal systems deal with issues in a particular field—health care law. While this book attempts from time to time to describe the legal or societal context in which health care law is located in various countries, it does not pretend to present a complete picture of the legal systems of these countries. It also does not offer a metatheory that would make sense of the similarities and differences observed in health law in different legal systems.

The goals of this book are eminently pragmatic. It is my hope that readers will come to a better understanding of the health care law of their own jurisdiction through absorbing these materials. My assumption is that most users of these materials will be from the United States. I assume that many of these students will take an American health law course at some point. I also realize, however, that many students using this book will either be in American summer programs between their first and second year of law school, or in non-law school settings, and will not have taken an American health law course prior to using these materials. I do not see this as an impediment, as the textual notes (supplemented, of course, by the teacher's knowledge) should provide enough information about American health law to orient the novice.

Nonetheless, a primary purpose of these materials is to help American readers (as well as readers from other nations) to better understand their own health law. It is hoped that the reader will come to see how contingent; how culturally, politically, and historically-determined; and how dependent on the substantive, procedural, and evidence law of particular legal systems domestic approaches to various health law issues are. I hope that readers will better understand the possibility that there are very different solutions to the very difficult health law problems we face than the ones we commonly imagine. Finally, I hope that at those points in the reader's later career when an opportunity arises to influence health law or policy, the reader will remember the wealth of alternatives available beyond those that are obvious in the reader's particular system.

While this book is in part intended to inform health policy, it is not a book about comparative health policy. Many excellent books are available, both in the United States and elsewhere, about comparative health policy, health economics, and health politics. Though the first chapter of this book contains a rather lengthy section describing and analyzing health care systems, it is not the intent of this book to duplicate these sources. Rather, this book focuses on how law, legal systems, and legal institutions influence health care recipients, professionals, institutions, and systems. Thus, for example, this book is not so much concerned with how various health care systems ration care as it is with the role of the courts or of administrative agencies in health care rationing.

Because this is a book about health law, it is organized, not surprisingly, around the notion of rights. Whatever else law may be, it is generally understood as an attempt to articulate and protect rights. This book's four chapters deal with legal rights in different settings. The first chapter examines the concept of a human right to health care, established by international law, national constitutions, and domestic legislation. As a context for this discussion, and indeed for most of the rest of the book, this chapter also includes readings describing generally how health care systems are organized and function. This chapter also examines the right to health care in a particular setting—organ transplantation.

The second chapter deals with the rights of patients in their relationships with health care professionals and institutions. After a brief section introducing the notion of patients' rights, the topics of malpractice, alternatives to malpractice litigation, informed consent, confidentiality and rights to access medical records are examined.

The third chapter addresses bioethics—here understood as the right of patients to autonomous decision making and the limits that bound this right. This chapter examines abortion, assisted reproduction, and the right to die, including the right to assistance with suicide and euthanasia.

A brief chapter examines the interface between the rights of individuals and the interests of society in four contexts. First, it looks at the role of public health law in reconciling the rights of the individual and of the public in the context of the worldwide HIV-AIDS crisis. Second, it looks at the role of public health law in combating a different sort of empidemic—SARS. Third, it examines the attempts of various nations to limit tobacco use. Finally, it looks at issues that arise in health care research, where the interests of society in advancing knowledge sometimes come in conflict with the rights of the individual research subject.

Four final comments may be useful to understand this book. First, throughout the book I generally use the word "patient" to refer to recipients of health care. The word "patient" has increasingly become only one of many words used to describe persons who receive health care in the United States—including also consumer, beneficiary, member, resident, or recipient, to name a few. Patient has, indeed, sometimes taken on a negative connotation, describing one who passively receives health care as opposed to an active participant in the health care enterprise. The word is used here, however, for two reasons. First, it is still, even in the United States, the most specific word used to describe the person who receives health care from health care professionals and institutions. Second, it is the word that is used most widely throughout the world to describe recipients of health care. Given the international scope of this book, deference to international usage is perhaps appropriate.

Second, the reader will surely notice that, although this book resembles in many respects a traditional American law school casebook, the excerpts are much longer than would be found in most contemporary casebooks. It is for this reason that the book is entitled "*Readings* in Comparative Law and Bioethics." These lengthy excerpts are used for a reason. At the outset, it was noted that to do comparative law properly one should really know the language of the country one is studying, and spend time there observing the cultural context. While most readers of these materials will not have yet had the opportunity to do this for the range of the countries whose law is examined here, this book attempts at least to let the reader stay with one court or one scholar long enough to not simply catch a snippet of black-letter law, but also to observe how the particular author or country thinks about health law. For example, with respect to courts like the British House of Lords or Australian High Court, where multiple opinions are customary, a range of these are reproduced to give the reader a sense of the debate that characterizes these courts.

Third, the reader may observe that some of the writing deviates from standard American English. While we are very fortunate that English has become the world language, the English that others speak and write is not always that with which we are most comfortable. We can also learn, therefore, from seeing how others use the English language. This experience may also help us to remember a very important fact: just because others are speaking English does not mean that we can understand them (or they us). Often, really understanding what another is saying is hard work for us, even when the other seems to be speaking our language.

Fourth, some explanation of editing conventions may be helpful. First, cites, which were appropriately numerous in all sources, were in most instances omitted. Second, internal section titles and paragraph numbers were omitted from many sources. Third, ellipses (* * *) are inserted where text was omitted by the editor. Ellipses within a paragraph (or at its beginning or end) show that text was omitted from that paragraph. Centered ellipses between paragraphs show that a full paragraph or more of text was omitted. Brackets indicate additional explanatory text that has been added.

I am very grateful to the many authors and publishers who graciously allowed me to reprint their works in this text, often with no charge or at a reduced charge. The permissions table that follows lists their names. I am also grateful to Christopher Newdick and Herman Nys, who contributed original articles on the role of courts in rationing in the NHS and on assisted suicide and the right to die; Alain Garay, who assisted me in locating French sources; and Robert Leflar, Pierrick LeGoff, and Martine Jean who translated source materials for me. Finally, I would like to thank all of those who helped bring this work to fruition—Mark Hall, Barry Furrow, Rob Leflar, Norio Higuchi, Eleanor Kinney, Colleen Flood, Ted Marmor, Herman Nys, Eric Feldman, Margaret Lock, Kevin Outterson, Chris Newdick, Hank Greely, Andre den Exter, Larry Gostin, Naoki Ikegami, and Fran Miller; my Dean, Brian Murchison; the Frances Lewis Law Center; and Vera Mencer, my assistant.

Acknowledgments

Chapter 1: The Right to Health and Its Implementation

Eleanor D. Kinney, The International Human Right to Health: What Does This Mean for Our Nation and the World, 34 Indiana Law Review 1457, 1459–62, 1467–71 (2001), copyright © 2001, The Trustees of Indiana University. Reproduced with permission from the Indiana Law Review.

Karen Noelia Llantoy Huamán v. Peru, Human Rights Committee, Communication No. 1153/2003, 24 October 2005. Copyright © 2005 United Nations Publications Board. Used with permission.

Eleanor D. Kinney and Brian Alexander Clark, Provisions for Health and Health Care in the Constitutions of the Countries of the World, Cornell International Law Journal, vol. 37, pp. 285, 287, 289–90, 292–96, 298–301 (2004). Copyright © Cornell International Law Journal, 2004. Used with permission.

WHO, World Health Report 2000, pp. 11–13 (2000). Reprinted with Permission.

Timothy Jost, Why Can't We Do What They Do? National Health Reform Abroad, Journal of Law, Medicine and Ethics 432, 432–35 (2004). Copyright © 1999, American Society of Law, Medicine and Ethics. Reprinted with permission.

Theodore Marmor, Richard Freeman, and Kieke Okma, Comparative Perspectives and Policy Learning in the World of Health Care, 7 Journal of Comparative Policy Analysis, 331, 335–36, 339–43 (2005) Copyright © 2005, Journal of Comparative Policy Analysis. Used with permission..

Uwe E. Reinhardt, Reforming the Health Care System: The Universal Dilemma, 19 Am.J.L. & Med. 21, 21–27, 29, 31–36 (1994). Copyright © 1994, American Society of Law, Medicine and Ethics and Boston University School of Law. Reprinted with permission.

Carolyn Hughes Tuohy, Dynamics of a Changing Health Sphere: The United States, Britain, and Canada, 18 Health Affairs 114, 115–16, 118–120, 129–131 (May/June 1999). Copyright © 1999, Health Affairs, Published by Project Hope. Reprinted with permission.

George J. Annas & Frances H. Miller, The Empire of Death: How Culture and Economics Affect Informed Consent in the U.S., The U.K., and Japan, 20 Am.J.L. & Med. 357, 360–62, 377–81, 387–90 (1994). Copyright © 1994, American Society of Law, Medicine and Ethics, Boston University School of Law, Frances Miller and George Annas. Reprinted with permission.

Timothy Jost, ed. Health Care Coverage Determinations: An International Comparative Study. 240–44, 251–53. Copyright © 2005 Open University Press. Used with the kind permission of Open University Press

Colleen Flood, Mark Stabile and Carolyn Tuohy, What is In and Out of Medicare? Who Decides, from Just Medicare, 15, 16–17, 23–30. Copyright © University of Toronto Press, 2005. Used with the permission of the University of Toronto Press..

Christopher Newdick, Judicial Supervision of Health Resources Allocation—English Experience (2006). Copyright © 2006, Christopher Newdick. Used with permission.

Andre den Exter, Patient Mobility in the European Union, from Just Medicare, 331, 334–340. Copyright © University of Toronto Press, 2005. Used with the permission of the University of Toronto Press.

R. v. Secretary of State for Health, ex parte. Pfizer Ltd., Before the High Court (Queen's Bench Division) [1999]. Reprinted with permission of the Controller of Her Majesty's Stationary Office.

Act of 5 November 1997 on the Donation, Removal, and Trans-plantation of Organs, Bundesgesetzblatt, Part 1, 11 Nov. 1997, No. 74, pp. 2631–2639, as translated in World Health Organization, 49 Int. Dig. Health Leg. (2) 316 (1998). Reprinted with permission.

Bernard M. Dickens, Sev. S. Fluss, Ariel R. King, Legislation on Organ and Tissue Donation, in Organ and Tissue Donation for Transportation, 95, 100–04 (Jeremy R. Chapman, Mark Deierhoi and Celia Wight, ed. 1997). Copyright © 1997, Hodder Headline, Arnold Press. Reprinted with permission.

Margaret Lock, On Dying Twice: Culture, Technology, and the Determination of Death, in Margaret Lock, Alan Young and Alberto Cambrosio, ed., Living and Working with New Medical Technologies: Intersections of Inquiry, pp. 250–57 (2000)Copyright © Cambridge University Press (2000). Reprinted with permission of Cambridge University Press.

Chapter 2: The Rights of Patients in Relationship with Health Care Professionals and Institutions

World Health Organization, Regional Office for Europe, Copenhagen, European Health Reforms: Citizens' Choice and Patients' Rights, 11, 12–15, 17–19 (1996). Reprinted with permission.

World Health Organization, European Office, A Declaration on the Promotion of Patients' Right in Europe, 1994. Reprinted with permission.

Dieter Giesen. Medical Malpractice and the Judicial Function in Comparative Perspective, 1 Medical Law International, 3, 4–7 (1993). Copyright © 1993, A B Academic Publishers. Reprinted with permission.

Jean McHale, Medical Malpractice in England—Current Trends, 10 European Journal of Health Law 135, 135–41, 146–47 (2003). Copyright © 2003, Koninklijke Brill NV. Reprinted with permission.

Gerfried Fischer & Hans Lilie, Ärztliche Verantwortung im europäischin Rechtsvergleich, 17–21 (1999) (translated by Timothy S. Jost). Copyright © 1999, Carl Heymanns Verlag, KG. Reprinted with permission.

Law and Patient Safety in the United States and Japan, Robert B. Leflar, published as *Iryō anzen to hō no Nichibei hikaku,* 1323 Jurist 8, 14–18 (2006) (Tomoko Mise, trans.) Copyright © 2006, Mr. Michiyuki Nagasawa. Used by permission, Robert B. Leflar, Michiyuki Nagasawa, and Keiso Shobo Publishing, Co.

Lars H. Fallberg and Edgard Borgenhammer, The Swedish No Fault Patient Insurance Scheme, European Journal of Health Law, vol. 4, pp. 279, 279–284 (1997). Copyright © 1997, Kluwer Law International. Reprinted with permission.

Marie Bismark and Ron Paterson, No-Fault Compensation in New Zealand: Harmonizing Injury Compensation, Provider Accountability, and Patient Safety, Health Affairs, vol 25, 278, 278, 278–282, Jan./Feb. 2006. Copyright © 2006, Health Affairs, Published by Project Hope. Reprinted with permission.

Sidaway v. Bethlem Royal Hospital Governors and Others, [1985]. Reprinted with permission of the Controller of Her Majesty's Stationary Office.

Law and Health Care in Japan: The Renaissance of Informed Consent, by Robert B. Leflar, published as *Nihon no iryō to hō: Infōmudo konsento runessansu* (2002), pp. 125–146 (Michiyuki Nagasawa, translator.) Copyright © Robert B. Leflar, 2002. Used with permission.

Dieter Giesen, International Medical Malpractice Law, 341–355 (1980). Copyright © 1980, J.C.B. Mohr (Paul Siebeck) Tuebingen. Reprinted with permission.

Hank Leenen, Sjef Gevers, Genevieve Pinet, The Rights of Patients in Europe, 81–82, 96–97 (1995). Copyright © 1995, Kluwer Law International. Reprinted with permission.

Sabine Michalowski, Medical Confidentality and Medical Privilege—a Comparison of French and German Law, European Journal of Health Law, vol. 5, pp. 89, 89–91, 95–96, 97–99, 100–01, 102–03, 104–06 (1998). Copyright © 1998, Kluwer Law International. Reprinted with permission.

Frits W. Hondius, Protecting Medical a/nd Genetic Data, European Journal of Health Law, vol. 4, pp. 361, 378–384 (1997). Copyright © 1997, Kluwer Law International. Reprinted with permission.

UNESCO International Declaration on Human Genetic Data. Copyright © United Nations Publications Board. Used with Permission.

Chapter 3. The Patient's Right to Self-Determination and Competing Considerations.

Abortion Policies: A Global Review, United Nations, 1–2, 4–7 (2003). Copyright © United Nations Publications Board. Used with permission.

Joyce Outshoorn, The Stability of Compromise: Abortion Politics in Western Europe, in Abortion Politics: Public Policy in Cross-Cultural Perspective 145, 146–153 (Marianne Githens & Dorothy McBride Stetson, eds. 1996). Copyright © 1996, Routledge, Inc. Reprinted with permission

Kim Lane Scheppele, Constitutionalizing Abortion in Abortion Politics: Public Policy in Cross-Cultural Perspective 29, 38–42 (Marianne Githens & Dorothy McBride Stetson, eds. 1996). Copyright © 1996, Routledge, Inc. Reprinted with permission.

Kathryn Venturatos Lorio, The Process of Regulating Assisted Reproductive Technologies: What We Can Learn From Our Neighbors—What Translates and What Does Not, Loyola Law Review, vol. 45, 247, 247–66 (1999). Copyright © 1999, Loyola Law Review. Reprinted with permission.

Melanie Latham, Regulating the New Reproductive Technologies: A Cross-Channel Comparison, Medical Law International, vol. 3, pp. 89, 90–14, 106–11 (1998). Copyright © 1998, A B Academic Publishers. Reprinted with permission.

Regina (Quintavalle) v. Human Fertilisation and Embryology Authority, [2005]. Reprinted with permission of the Controller of Her Majesty's Stationary Office.

Herman Nys, Physician Involvement in a Patient's Death: A Continental European Perspective, Medical Law Review, vol. 7, 208 (1999). Copyright © 1999, Oxford University Press, and update, copyright ©2007, Herman Nys. Reprinted with permission.

Chabot, Supreme Court of the Netherlands, Criminal Chamber, 21 June 1994, no. 96.972, from John Griffiths, Alex Bood, and Haleen Weyers, Euthansia and the Law in the Netherlands, 329–38 (1998). Copyright © 1998, Amsterdam University Press. Reprinted with permission.

Chapter 4: The Rights of the Individual and the Interests of Society

John A. Harrington, AIDS, Public Health and the Law: A Case of Structural Coupling? European J. Health Law, vol. 6, pp. 213, 213–26 (1999). Copyright © 1999, Kluwer Law International. Reprinted with permission.

Peri H. Alkas, J.D. and Wayne X. Shandera, M.D. HIV and AIDS in Africa: African Policies in Response to AIDS in Relation to Various National Legal Traditions, 17 J. Legal Med. 527, 527–29, 538–43 (1996). Copyright © 1996, Taylor & Frances, Inc. Reprinted with permission.

Chenglin Liu, Regulating Sars in China: Law as an Antidote?, 4 Washington University Global Studies Review, 81, 82–101, 103–09, 115–17 (2005). This article was previously published in the Washington University Global Studies Law Review, volume 4, p. 81 (2005). Copyright © 2005. Chenglin Liu and Washington University Global Studies Law Review. Used with permission.

Jason W. Sapsin, Lawrence O. Gostin, Jon S. Vernick, Scott Burris, and Stephen P. Teret SARS and International Legal Preparedness. 77 Temple Law Review 155, 155–165, 167–68 (2004). Reproduced with the permission of Temple Law Review Volume 77, copyright © 2004 Temple University of the Commonwealth System of Higher Education.

Eric Feldman, The Culture of Legal Change: A Case Study of Tobacco Control in Twenty-First Century Japan, 27 Mich J. Int' L 743, 746–50, 769, 771–83, 797, 799, 803–04, 806, 815–17 (2006). Copyright © 2006, Michigan Journal of International Law. Used with permission.

Constance A. Nathason, *Liberte, Egalité, Fumée*: Smoking and Tobacco Control in France, reprinted by permission of the publisher from Unfiltered: Conflicts over Tobacco Policy and Public Health, edited by Eric A. Feldman and Ronald Bayer, pages 138, 143, 145, 149–150, 152, 153, 155, 159–160, Cambridge Mass.: Harvard University Press, Copyright © 2004 by the President and Fellows of Harvard College.

Erik Aibtek, Holy Smoke, No More? Tobacco Control in Denmark, reprinted by permission of the publisher from Unfiltered: Conflicts over Tobacco Policy and Public Health, edited by Eric A. Feldman and Ronald Bayer, pages 190–91, 193, 209, 215–216, Cambridge Mass.: Harvard University Press, Copyright © 2004 by the President and Fellows of Harvard College.

Timothy Stoltzfus Jost, The Globalizaton of Health Law: The Case of Placebo-based Research, American Journal of Law & Medicine, vol. 26, pp. 175–84 (2000). Copyright © 2000, American Society of Law, Medicine and Ethics and Boston University School of Law. Reprinted with permission.

Solomon R. Benatar, Towards Progress in Resolving Dilemmas In International Research Ethics, 32 Journal of Law, Medicine and Ethics 574, 574–75, 579–81 Winter 2004. Copyright © 2004, American Society of Law, Medicine and Ethics. Used with Permission.

Readings in Comparative Health Law and Bioethics

Chapter 1

The Right to Health and Its Implementation

A. The Right to Health in International Law

Is the right to health a fundamental human right? Should it be? If so, should it, alternatively, be called a right to health, to health care, or to health protection? What difference does it make what the right is called? What is the content of a right to health or health care? What ramifications does recognizing a right to health have? Against whom should such a right be enforceable? How should it be enforced? Should it include a guaranty of equal access to health care for all, or should disparities in health care access be tolerated?

The right to health, as well as a right of access to health care, is supported by international law and by regional conventions. Article 25 of the 1948 Universal Declaration of Human Rights provides:

> Everyone has the right to a standard of living adequate for the health and well-being of himself and of his family, including food, clothing, housing and medical care and necessary social services, and the right to security in the event of ... sickness, [and] disability....

Article 2 of the Declaration prohibits discrimination in the protection of the rights provided by the Declaration. Although the Universal Declaration is not a treaty, it is generally regarded as constituting international customary law.

The International Covenant on Economic, Social, and Cultural Rights (ICESCR) more clearly provides at Article 12:

> The States Parties ... recognize the right to everyone to the enjoyment of the highest attainable standard of physical and mental health.

The steps that signatories commit themselves to taking to implement this right include public health protection measures and also:

> The creation of conditions which would assure to all medical service and medical attention in the event of sickness.

Other provisions of the ICESCR (Art. 2(2)) again recognize the right to nondiscriminatory protection of the rights guaranteed by the Covenant.

The ICESCR has been signed by over ninety countries (not including the United States). The Covenant does not, however, create immediately binding legal obligations as does the companion Covenant on Civil and Political Rights, but rather obligates each State Party "to take steps ... to the maximum of its available resources, with a view to achieving progressively the full realization of the rights ... by all appropriate means, including legislative measures." Art 2.(1). Compliance with the Covenant is monitored by the United Nations Committee on Economic, Social and Cultural Rights, which receives periodic reports from signatory states, but the monitoring effort is under-resourced and largely ineffective. The language of the ICESCR is echoed in regional Human Rights Covenants, such as the American Declaration of the Rights and Duties of Man (Art. XI), the European Social Charter (Arts. 11 & 13), The European Convention on Human Rights and Biomedicine (Art. 3), and the African Charter on Human Rights (Art. 16).

A right that creates an obligation that is to be progressively achieved contingent upon the availability of resources is somewhat ephemeral. The legal enforceability and lexical primacy that is commonly thought to attend human rights does not seem to apply. Neither does such a right seem to focus exclusively on the relationship between individuals and states, as do most human rights. The right is even more problematic if it is articulated as a right to health, not health care. There are, of course, many factors that contribute to ill health that states can do little to influence.

The mere fact that a right requires positive action, rather than merely negative restraint, on the part of the state, however, does not render it less valid, or even less important. Many well established rights require positive protective action on the part of the state. Recognizing that a human right has a special claim on resources gives it a special dignity, and at least a rhetorical primacy. A conference convened to establish principles for implementation of the ICESCR concluded that it should be interpreted to mean that "State parties must at all times act in good faith to fulfill" these obligations, being "accountable both to the international community and to their own people for their compliance." The Limburg Principles on the Implementation of the International Covenant on Economic, Social and Cultural Rights, 9 *Human Rights Quarterly* 122 (1987).

Whatever else a right to health may mean, it should require that insofar as a state provides health protection or health care services, it should do so in a nondiscriminatory basis. A number of international covenants protecting special populations or addressing specific human rights issues reinforce this right to equal access to health protection and care. The International Convention on Rights of the Child recognizes "the right of the child to the enjoyment of the highest attainable standard of health and to facilities for treatment of illness and rehabilitation of health." Art 24(1). Discrimination in health care is also prohibited by the conventions on the Elimination of All Forms of Racial Discrimination (Art.5(e)(iv)); on Elimination of all Forms of Discrimination Against Women (Arts. 11(1)(f) & 12); and on the Protection of Migrant Workers and Their Families (Art. 28).

In fact, however the most important influence toward promoting access to health care at the international level may not be human rights covenants, but rather the primary international institution concerned with the promotion of health and health care, the World Health Organization.

The World Health Organization, a successor to the Parisian Office Internationale d'Hygiène Publique and the Health Organization of the League of Nations, was founded in 1946 as a specialized international organization to work together with the United Nations in the promotion of health. Its Constitution states:

> The enjoyment of the highest attainable standard of health is one of the fundamental rights of every human being without distinction of race, religion, political belief, economic or social condition. The objective of the World Health Or-

ganization shall be the attainment by all peoples of the highest possible level of health.

The WHO, however, pursues this objective through education and exhortation, and has no authority to compel compliance with this objective by member states. See, examining the World Health Organization in the context of international law, David P. Fidler, The Future of the World Health Organization: What Role for International Law?, 31 *Vand. J. Transnat'l L.* 1079 (1998).

The following recent article explores the ramifications of a right to health, as does the opinion of the Human Rights Committee which follows it:

The International Human Right to Health: What Does This Mean for Our Nation and World?

Eleanor D. Kinney, Indiana Law Review, vol. 34, pp. 1457, 1459–62, 1467–71 (2001)

* * *

In the 1960s, the UN sponsored the development of two international covenants that articulate the human rights recognized in the UN Universal Declaration of Human Rights. These two covenants are the International Covenant on Civil and Political Rights (ICCPR) and the International Covenant on Economic, Social and Cultural Rights (ICESCR).

The ICESCR—the so-called Economic Covenant—is the most important in terms of the right to health. Article 12 of ICESCR states that the right to health includes "the enjoyment of the highest attainable standard of physical and mental health." * * *

The UN Committee on Economic, Social and Cultural Rights has responsibility for the promotion, implementation and enforcement of this covenant. A human right to health is also recognized in numerous other international human rights authorities that establish prohibitions against government conduct that is detrimental to health. Such treaties include the International Convention on the Elimination of All Forms of Racial Discrimination of 1965, the Convention on the Elimination of All Forms of Discrimination against Women of 1979, and the Convention on the Rights of the Child of 1989.

The UN also has established several international agencies to promote economic and social development world wide. The World Health Organization (WHO) has a legislative capacity to make international health regulations in addition to its health promotion functions. The WHO constitution states a right to the "highest attainable standard of health" and defines health broadly as "a state of complete physical, mental and social well-being and not merely the absence of disease or infirmity."

In addition, regional international organizations have treaties and implementation bodies. The Inter-American system for the protection of human rights of the Organization of American States (OAS) is based on the OAS American Declaration of the Rights and Duties of Man and the OAS American Convention on Human Rights, among other instruments. Specifically, Article 11 of the American Declaration of the Rights and Duties of Man states "[e]very person has the right to the preservation of his health through sanitary and social measures relating to food, clothing, housing and medical care, to the extent permitted by public and community resources." The more recent Protocol of San Salvador specifies a human right to health in its interpretation of the OAS Convention on Human Rights. * * *

The Pan-American Health Organization (PAHO), located within WHO, promotes health in the Americas and implementation of these OAS instruments that recognize an international human right to health.

Also of interest, the 1993 Vienna Declaration and Programme of Action emphasizes the fundamental inter-relatedness of political and civil human rights and economic social and cultural human rights. The Vienna Declaration specifically provides:

> All human rights are universal, indivisible and interdependent and interrelated. The international community must treat human rights globally in a fair and equal manner, on the same footing, and with the same emphasis. While the significance of national and regional particularities and various historical, cultural and religious backgrounds must be borne in mind, it is the duty of States, regardless of their political, economic and cultural systems, to promote and protect all human rights and fundamental freedoms.

The Vienna Declaration has become a crucial principle in international human rights law recognizing the irreducible truth that all human rights must be recognized if specific human rights are to have concrete meaning. A look to the body of international treaties that comprise the corpus of human rights law at first glace seems promising. However, these treaties bind only those nations that ratify them. This situation is immediately disappointing with respect to the United States as the United States has not ratified many UN or OAS human rights treaties. Most importantly, the United States has signed but not ratified ICESCR and the two conventions on the rights of women and children. * * *

* * *

If there is a binding international human right to health, then how would it be defined and implemented? This is a challenge. In this effort, we should be imaginative. As lawyers, we tend to think of administrative regulation and enforcement as well as judicial recourse as the primary mechanisms for assuring the implementation of rights. However, these models may not be particularly appropriate or effective when we are talking about what, at least in the United States and many other nations, is essentially a right to health under international customary law.

Such legalistic visions of the right to health may also not be appropriate or effective as there is still some uncertainty about the content of the international human right to health. Indeed, getting a handle on the content of the right to health is a necessary first step to effective implementation. But this is no easy task. To have meaning, the content of the right to health must be essentially the same for all nations and people. Yet implementation is dependent on the resources, as well as cultures, of individual countries. How do we articulate the right to health in countries with vastly different economic resources and cultural traditions?

The UN Committee on International Economic, Social and Cultural Rights—the treaty body responsible for implementing and monitoring ICESCR—has published a General Comment 14 to ICESCR that outlines the content to the international right to health. This General Comment is extensive and quite specific and intended to apply to nations that have ratified the ICESCR. It addresses the content of the right to health and the implementation and enforcement of the right to health. It also provides remedies for individual parties who have been denied the human right to health.

General Comment 14 begins with some observations about the normative content of the right to health. Specifically, General Comment 14 states that "[t]he right to health is not to be understood as a right to be healthy" and that "[t]he right to health contains both freedoms and entitlements." The General Comment 14 specifies the freedoms and entitlements as follows:

> The freedoms include the right to control one's health and body, including sexual and reproductive freedom, and the right to be free from interference, such as the right to be free from torture, non-consensual medical treatment and experimentation. By contrast, the entitlements include the right to a system of health protection which provides equality of opportunity for people to enjoy the highest attainable level of health.

General Comment 14 then observes that the right to health extends

> not only to timely and appropriate health care but also to the underlying determinants of health, such as access to safe and potable water and adequate sanitation, an adequate supply of safe food, nutrition and housing, healthy occupational and environmental conditions, and access to health-related education and information, including on sexual and reproductive health.

These provisions of General Comment 14 indeed prescribe a broad and inclusive conception of the content of the human right to health.

General Comment 14 also provides that the health care system of a states party must have certain institutional characteristics to realize the right to health. These include the availability, accessibility, acceptability and quality of needed health care services and facilities. "Availability" means that the states party has sufficient facilities and services for the population given the country's state of development. Services include those that affect the underlying determinants of health, such as safe and potable drinking water. "Accessibility" to health care facilities and services include the four dimensions: non-discrimination, physical accessibility, economic accessibility (affordability), and information accessibility. "Acceptability" means that services and facilities must be respectful of medical ethics and culturally appropriate as well as being designed to respect confidentiality and improve the health status of those served. "Quality" means that services must also be scientifically and medically appropriate and of good quality.

General Comment 14 imposes three types or levels of obligations: the obligations to respect, protect and fulfill. The obligation to respect requires states parties to refrain from interfering directly or indirectly with the enjoyment of the right to health. The obligation to protect requires states parties to take measures that prevent third parties from interfering with article 12 guarantees. The obligation to fulfill requires states parties to adopt appropriate legislative, administrative, budgetary, judicial, promotional and other measures towards the full realization of the right to health. General Comment 14 also reaffirms that several "core" obligations have been established in prior international human rights instruments * * *.

General Comment 14 clearly addresses implementation. It imposes a duty on each states party "to take whatever steps are necessary to ensure that everyone has access to health facilities, goods and services so that they can enjoy, as soon as possible, the highest attainable standard of physical and mental health." Implementation requires adoption of "a national strategy to ensure to all the enjoyment of the right to health, based on human rights principles which define the objectives of that strategy, and the formulation of policies and corresponding right to health indicators and benchmarks." The national health strategy should also "identify the resources available to attain defined objectives, as well as the most cost-effective way of using those resources." The national health strategy and plan of action should "be based on the principles of accountability, transparency and independence of the judiciary, since good governance is essential to the effective implementation of all human rights, including the realization of the right to health."

General Comment 14 has extensive enforcement provisions and specifies violations of the right to health. The Comment explicitly provides that a states party which "is unwilling to use the maximum of its available resources for the realization of the right to health is in violation of its obligations under Article 12." Further, if resource constraints make compliance impossible, the states party "has the burden of justifying that every effort has nevertheless been made to use all available resources at its disposal in order to satisfy, as a matter of priority, the obligations outlined above."

General Comment 14 also specifies violations. For example, violations of the obligation to respect include "state actions, policies or laws that contravene the standards set out in Article 12 of the Covenant and are likely to result in bodily harm, unnecessary morbidity and preventable mortality." Violations of the obligation to protect include "failure of a State to take all necessary measures to safeguard persons within their jurisdiction from infringements of the right to health by third parties." Finally, violations of the obligation to fulfil include "failure of States parties to take all necessary steps to ensure the realization of the right to health."

Finally, General Comment 14 accords remedies to individual parties. Specifically, any person or group victim of a violation of the right to health should have access to effective judicial or other appropriate remedies at both national and international levels. All victims of such violations should be entitled to adequate reparation, which may take the form of restitution, compensation, satisfaction or guarantees of non-repetition. National ombudsmen, human rights commissions, consumer forums, patients' rights associations or similar institutions should address violations of the right to health.

General Comment 14 represents a significant step in delineating the international human right to state parties to the ICESCR. Yet, despite General Comment's specificity, as well as flexibility, the issue of how General Comment 14 will be interpreted, implemented and enforced in states parties at different stages of economic development and with markedly different cultures and values will still be a challenge. In sum, the content of the international right to health remains a tough issue.

* * *

Notes

Americans who are legally trained feel uncomfortable with the notion of rights that are on the one hand absolute human rights, and on the other that are to be implemented "progressively" as resources permit. Since positive rights (i.e. rights that support a claim for resources against the state) are almost invariably resource dependent, they present this problem. This is not to say that we do not recognize positive rights in the United States. Prisoners, for example, have a positive right to health care under the Eighth Amendment (*Estelle v. Gamble*, 492 U.S. 97 (1976)). Also, even negative rights, such as the freedoms of expression or religion, are not absolute under the United States' Constitutional system, and some rights, such as school desegregation, have been "progressively" realized. (Remember the "with all deliberate speed" language of the second *Brown v. the Board of Education* decision, 349 U.S. 294 at 300 (1955)).

It may be, however, that the notion of rights familiar to American law students is bound up with the way in which rights are customarily enforced in the United States. In the United States the primary institution for enforcing rights is the court system. Further, under the constitutional system of the United States, the courts, and in particular the Supreme Court, have final responsibility for interpreting the Constitution and the laws, and therefore can hold legislation or executive action to be unconstitutional as a violation of basic rights. While this model of judicial review is seen in many other countries, it is far from universal. In France, for example, laws passed by the National Assembly can be reviewed by a Constitutional Council, but only at the time the legislation is passed, and only at the request of the executive or a certain proportion of members of the legislature. England, on the other hand, has no written constitution as such and a strong tradition of legislative supremacy, though the courts tend to interpret legislation so as not to conflict with human rights, and England recognizes European human rights law. See Diana Brahams, UK: The Impact of European Human Rights Law, 356 *Lancet* 1433 (2000). Rights in other nations are often effectuated through means other than a court system—through complaint mechanisms; through human rights commissions; or through monitoring mechanisms (such as the United Nations Committee on Economic, Social and Cultural Rights which oversees compliance with the ICESC). These mechanisms offer far more flexibility in procedure and remedies, as well as the ability to conduct more wide-ranging fact-finding inquiries than are possible for a court. They may thus better suited for enforcing progressively realized, resource-dependent positive rights.

This is not to say, however, that health rights are never enforceable through litigation or proceedings that resemble litigation. The following decision of Human Rights Committee, the body of experts created under the International Covenant on Civil and Political Rights to enforce the terms of that Convention, represents one example of such proceedings.

Karen Noelia Llantoy Huamán v. Peru

Human Rights Committee, Communication No. 1153/2003, 24 October 2005

1. The author of the communication is Karen Noelia Llantoy Huamán, born in 1984, who claims to be a victim of a violation by Peru of articles 2, 3, 6, 7, 17, 24 and 26 of the International Covenant on Civil and Political Rights. She is represented by the organizations DEMUS, CLADEM and Center for Reproductive Law and Policy. * * *

2.1 The author became pregnant in March 2001, when she was aged 17. On 27 June 2001 she was given a scan at the Archbishop Loayza National Hospital in Lima, part of the Ministry of Health. The scan showed that she was carrying an anencephalic foetus.

2.2 On 3 July 2001, Dr. Ygor Pérez Solf, a gynaecologist and obstetrician in the Archbishop Loayza National Hospital in Lima, informed the author of the foetal abnormality and the risks to her life if the pregnancy continued. Dr. Pérez said that she had two options: to continue the pregnancy or to terminate it. He advised termination by means of uterine curettage. The author decided to terminate the pregnancy, and the necessary clinical studies were carried out, confirming the foetal abnormality.

2.3 On 19 July 2001, when the author reported to the hospital together with her mother for admission preparatory to the operation, Dr. Pérez informed her that she needed to obtain written authorization from the hospital director. Since she was under age, her mother, Ms. Elena Huamán Lara, requested the authorization. On 24 July 2001, Dr. Maximiliano Cárdenas Díaz, the hospital director, replied in writing that the termination could not be carried out as to do so would be unlawful, since under article 120 of the Criminal Code, abortion was punishable by a prison term of no more than three months when it was likely that at birth the child would suffer serious physical or mental defects, while under article 119, therapeutic abortion was permitted only when termination of the pregnancy was the only way of saving the life of the pregnant woman or avoiding serious and permanent damage to her health.

* * *

2.5 On 20 August 2001, Dr. Marta B. Rondón, a psychiatrist and member of the Peruvian Medical Association, drew up a psychiatric report on the author, concluding that "the so-called principle of the welfare of the unborn child has caused serious harm to the mother, since she has unnecessarily been made to carry to term a pregnancy whose fatal outcome was known in advance, and this has substantially contributed to triggering the symptoms of depression, with its severe impact on the development of an adolescent and the patient's future mental health".

2.6 On 13 January 2002, three weeks late with respect to the anticipated date of birth, the author gave birth to an anencephalic baby girl, who survived for four days, during which the mother had to breastfeed her. Following her daughter's death, the author fell into a state of deep depression. * * *

2.7 The author has submitted to the Committee a statement made by Dr. Annibal Faúdes and Dr. Luis Tavara, who * * * stated that anencephaly is a condition which is fatal to the foetus in all cases. Death immediately follows birth in most cases. It also endangers the mother's life. * * *

2.8 Regarding the exhaustion of domestic remedies, the author claims that this requirement is waived when judicial remedies available domestically are ineffective in the case in question, and she points out that the Committee has laid down on several occasions that the author has no obligation to exhaust a remedy which would prove ineffective. She adds that in Peru there is no administrative remedy which would enable a pregnancy to be terminated on therapeutic grounds, nor any judicial remedy functioning with the speed and efficiency required to enable a woman to require the authorities to guarantee her right to a lawful abortion within the limited period, by virtue of the special circumstances obtaining in such cases. She also states that her financial circumstances and those of her family prevented her from obtaining legal advice.

* * *

3.2 The author claims to have suffered discrimination in breach of article 3 of the Covenant [ensuring equal rights], in the following forms:

(a) In access to the health services, since her different and special needs were ignored because of her sex. In the view of the author, the fact that the State lacked any means to prevent a violation of her right to a legal abortion on therapeutic grounds, which is applicable only to women, together with the arbitrary conduct of the medical personnel, resulted in a discriminatory practice that violated her rights—a breach which was all the more serious since the victim was a minor.

(b) Discrimination in the exercise of her rights, since although the author was entitled to a therapeutic abortion, none was carried out because of social attitudes and prejudices, thus preventing her from enjoying her right to life, to health, to privacy and to freedom from cruel, inhuman and degrading treatment on an equal footing with men.

(c)Discrimination in access to the courts, bearing in mind the prejudices of officials in the health system and the judicial system where women are concerned and the lack of appropriate legal means of enforcing respect for the right to obtain a legal abortion when the temporal and other conditions laid down in the law are met.

3.3 The author claims a violation of article 6 of the Covenant [right to life]. She states that her experience had a serious impact on her mental health from which she has still not recovered. She points out that the Committee has stated that the right to life cannot be interpreted in a restrictive manner, but requires States to take positive steps to protect it, including the measures necessary to ensure that women do not resort to clandestine abortions which endanger their life and health, especially in the case of poor women. She adds that the Committee has viewed lack of access for women to reproductive health services, including abortion, as a violation of women's right to life, and that this has been reiterated by other committees such as the Committee on the Elimination of Discrimination against Women and the Committee on Economic, Social and Cultural Rights. The author claims that in the present case, the violation of the right to life lay in the fact that Peru did not take steps to ensure that the author secured a safe termination of pregnancy on the grounds that the foetus was not viable. She states that the refusal to provide a legal abortion service left her with two options which posed an equal risk to her health and safety: to seek clandestine (and hence highly risky) abortion services, or to continue a dangerous and traumatic pregnancy which put her life at risk.

3.4 The author claims a violation of article 7 of the Covenant. The fact that she was obliged to continue with the pregnancy amounts to cruel and inhuman treatment, in her view, since she had to endure the distress of seeing her daughter's marked deformities and knowing that her life expectancy was short. She states that this was an awful experience which added further pain and distress to that which she had already borne during the period when she was obliged to continue with the pregnancy, since she was subjected to an "extended funeral" for her daughter, and sank into a deep depression after her death.

* * *

3.6 The author claims a violation of article 17 [right to privacy], arguing that this article protects women from interference in decisions which affect their bodies and their lives, and offers them the opportunity to exercise their right to make independent decisions on their reproductive lives. The author points out that the State party interfered arbitrarily in her private life, taking on her behalf a decision relating to her life and reproductive health which obliged her to carry a pregnancy to term, and thereby breaching her right to privacy. She adds that the service was available, and that if it had not been for the interference of State officials in her decision, which enjoyed the protection of the law, she would have been able to terminate the pregnancy. * * *

3.7 The author claims a violation of article 24 [protecting the rights of children], since she did not receive the special care she needed from the health authorities, as an adolescent girl. Neither her welfare nor her state of health were objectives pursued by the authorities which refused to carry out an abortion on her. * * *

3.8 The author claims a violation of article 26 [equal protection], arguing that the Peruvian authorities' position that hers was not a case of therapeutic abortion, which is not punishable under the Criminal Code, left her in an unprotected state incompatible with the assurance of the protection of the law set out in article 26. The guarantee of the equal protection of the law implies that special protection will be given to certain categories of situation in which specific treatment is required. In the present case, as a result of a highly restrictive interpretation of the criminal law, the health authorities failed to protect the author and neglected the special protection which her situation required.

3.9 The author claims that the administration of the health centre left her without protection as a result of a restrictive interpretation of article 119 of the Criminal Code. She adds that the text of the law contains nothing to indicate that the exception relating to therapeutic abortion should apply only in cases of danger to physical health. But the hospital authorities had drawn a distinction and divided up the concept of health, and had thus violated the legal principle that no distinction should be drawn where there is none in the law. She points out that health is "a state of complete physical, mental and social well-being and not merely the absence of disease or infirmity", so that when the Peruvian Criminal Code refers to health, it does so in the broad and all-embracing sense, protecting both the physical and the mental health of the mother.

4. * * * The Committee * * * regrets that the State party has not supplied any information concerning the admissibility or the merits of the author's allegations. It points out that it is implicit in the Optional Protocol that States parties make available to the Committee all information at their disposal. In the absence of a reply from the State party, due weight must be given to the author's allegations, to the extent that these have been properly substantiated.

* * *

5.3 The Committee considers that the author's claims of alleged violations of articles 3 and 26 of the Covenant have not been properly substantiated, since the author has not placed before the Committee any evidence relating to the events which might confirm any type of discrimination under the article in question. * * *

* * *

6.2 The Committee notes that the author attached a doctor's statement confirming that her pregnancy exposed her to a life-threatening risk. She also suffered severe psychological consequences exacerbated by her status as a minor, as the psychiatric report of 20 August 2001 confirmed. The Committee notes that the State party has not provided any evidence to challenge the above. It notes that the authorities were aware of the risk to the author's life, since a gynaecologist and obstetrician in the same hospital had advised her to terminate the pregnancy, with the operation to be carried out in the same hospital. The subsequent refusal of the competent medical authorities to provide the service may have endangered the author's life. The author states that no effective remedy was available to her to oppose that decision. In the absence of any information from the State party, due weight must be given to the author's claims.

6.3 The author also claims that, owing to the refusal of the medical authorities to carry out the therapeutic abortion, she had to endure the distress of seeing her daughter's marked deformities and knowing that she would die very soon. This was an experience which added further pain and distress to that which she had already borne during the period when she was obliged to continue with the pregnancy. * * *The omission on the part of the State in not enabling the author to benefit from a therapeutic abortion was, in the Committee's view, the cause of the suffering she experienced. * * * Consequently, the Committee considers that the facts before it reveal a violation of article 7 of the Covenant [cruel and inhumane treatment]. In the light of this finding the Committee does not consider it necessary in the circumstances to made a finding on article 6 of the Covenant [right to life].

6.4 The author states that the State party, in denying her the opportunity to secure medical intervention to terminate the pregnancy, interfered arbitrarily in her private life. The Committee notes that a public-sector doctor told the author that she could either continue with the pregnancy or terminate it in accordance with domestic legislation allowing abortions in cases of risk to the life of the mother. * * * In the circumstances of the case, the refusal to act in accordance with the author's decision to terminate her pregnancy was not justified and amounted to a violation of article 17 of the Covenant.

6.5 The author claims a violation of article 24 of the Covenant, since she did not receive from the State party the special care she needed as a minor. The Committee notes the special vulnerability of the author as a minor girl. It further notes that, in the absence of any information from the State party, due weight must be given to the author's claim that she did not receive, during and after her pregnancy, the medical and psychological support necessary in the specific circumstances of her case. Consequently, the Committee considers that the facts before it reveal a violation of article 24 of the Covenant.

* * *

7. The Human Rights Committee, acting under article 5, paragraph 4, of the Optional Protocol to the Covenant, is of the view that the facts before it disclose a violation of articles 2 [which gives a right to enforce other rights], 7, 17 and 24 of the Covenant.

8. In accordance with article 2, paragraph 3 (a), of the Covenant, the State party is required to furnish the author with an effective remedy, including compensation. The State party has an obligation to take steps to ensure that similar violations do not occur in the future.

9. Bearing in mind that, as a party to the Optional Protocol, the State party recognizes the competence of the Committee to determine whether there has been a violation of the Covenant, and that, under article 2 of the Covenant, the State party has undertaken to ensure to all individuals within its territory and subject to its jurisdiction the rights recognized in the Covenant and to offer an effective and enforceable remedy when a violation is found to have occurred, the Committee wishes to receive from the State party, within 90 days, information about the measures taken to give effect to the present Views. The State party is also requested to publish the Committee's Views.

Note

Several excellent sources are available discussing international law obligations, including Judith Asher, *The Right to Health: A Resource Manual for NGOs* (2004), available at http://shr.aaas.org/pubs/rt_health/rt_health_manual.pdf; Rebecca Cook, Bernard Dickens and Mahmoud Fathalla, *Reproductive Health and Human Rights* (Clarendon Press, Oxford, 2003); Brigit C.A. Toebes, *The Right to Health as a Human Right in International Law* (Intersentia, Antwerp, 1999); *The Right to Health in the Americas.* (Pan American Health Organization, Washington DC 1989); Aart Hendriks, The Right to Health in National and International Jurisprudence, 5 *European J. Health L.* 389 (1998); Steven Jamar, The International Human Right to Health, 22 *So.U. L. Rev.* 1 (1994); and

Virginia A. Leary, The Right to Health in International Human Rights Law, 1 *Health & Hum. Rts.* 25 (1995).

B. The Right to Health in Constitutional Law

The constitutions of many countries also recognize a right to health or to health care. Note the different treatment of this subject in the constitutions of Spain, Switzerland and Brazil that follow:

Spanish Constitution, 1978

Article 43 [Health Protection, Sports, Leisure]

1. The right to health protection is recognized.

2. It is incumbent upon the public authorities to organize and watch over public health and hygiene through preventive measures and through necessary care and services. The law shall establish the rights and duties of all in this respect.

* * *

Swiss Constitution

Article 41 [Social Goals]

1. The Federation and Cantons will do what they can to complement personal responsibility and private initiative to assure that:

* * *

b. each person receives necessary care for his or her health.

* * *

3. The Federation and Cantons will pursue these social goals within the scope of their constitutional responsibilities and available resources.

4. No direct claim on state benefits shall be derived from these provisions relating to social goals.

Brazilian Constitution, 1998

Section II. Health

Article 196 [Health, Right of Assistance]

Health is the right of all persons and the duty of the State and is guaranteed by means of social and economic policies aimed at reducing the risk of illness and other hazards and at universal and equal access to all actions and services for the promotion, protection and recovery of health.

Article 197 [Public System, Private Nets]

Health actions and services are of public relevance and it is incumbent upon the Government to provide, pursuant to the law, for their regulation, supervision and control.

Such actions and services are to be carried out directly or through third parties and also by means of individuals or legal entities of private law.

Article 198 [Public Healthcare Guidelines]

(0) Public health actions and services are part of a regionalized and hierarchical network and constitute a single system organized according to the following guidelines:

I. decentralization with a single management in each government sphere;

II. full service, priority being given to preventive activities, without prejudice to assistance services;

III. participation of the community;

(1) The single health system is financed, * * *, with funds from the social security budget of the Republic, the States, the Federal District, and the Municipalities, in addition to other sources.

Article 199 [Private Enterprise]

(0) Health assistance is open to private enterprise.

(1) Private institutions may participate on a supplementary basis in the single health system, according to guidelines set forth by the latter, by means of public law contracts or agreements, preference being given to philanthropic and non-profit entities.

(2) The allocation of public funds to aid or subsidize private profit seeking institutions is forbidden.

(3) Direct or indirect participation of foreign companies or capital in Brazil's health assistance is forbidden, except in the cases foreseen in the law.

(4) The law establishes the conditions and requirements to allow the removal of human organs, tissues, and substances intended for transplantation, research, and treatment, as well as the collection, processing, and transfusion of blood and its by products, all kinds of sale being forbidden

---

What difference does the approach of these three constitutions make? The following excerpt analyzes constitutional approaches to guaranteeing health care.

Provisions for Health and Health Care in the Constitutions of the Countries of the World

Eleanor D. Kinney, Brian Alexander Clark, Cornell International Law Journal, vol. 37, pp. 285, 287, 289–90, 292–96, 298–301 (2004).

* * *

This Article reports findings of an empirical analysis of the provisions of the constitutions of the world that address health and health care. * * * The Article concludes that the national commitment to health and health care is not highly related to whether or not a nation's constitution specifically addresses health or health care * * *

* * * [W]e identified five types of constitutional provisions that addressed health and health care in national constitutions:

1. A statement of aspiration, stating a goal in relation to the health of its citizens.

2. A statement of entitlement, stating a right to health or health care or public health services.
3. A statement of duty, imposing a duty to provide health care or public health services.
4. A programmatic statement, specifying approaches for the financing, delivery or regulation of health care and public health services.
5. A referential statement, incorporating by specific reference any international or regional human rights treaties recognizing a human right to health or health care.

* * *

According to our criteria, 67.5% of the constitutions of the world have a provision addressing health or health care. In almost all of these constitutions, the provisions regarding health and health care are universal, rather than limited to particular groups. * * *

The fact that countries adopted their constitutions during different historical periods is a critical factor in determining whether the constitution addresses health or health care. Constitutions reflect the period of their formation as well as the level of the constitutional law development in other countries and international law at the time. Constitution making has occurred in specific periods of history—generally spawned by cataclysmic events affecting groups of nations in a particular geographic territory.

For purposes of this analysis, the basic periods of constitution making have been as follows: (1) England and its common law progeny, 1660s–present, including the United States; (2) European democratic states and constitutional monarchies, 1887–1960, including liberated nations after World War II in both the democratic West and the Communist Eastern Bloc; (3) emergence of new nations from former colonies in Africa, Asia, and the Middle East, 1945–1960; (4) the Latin American constitutional revolution, 1983–1994, replacing constitutions adopted in the 19th and 20th centuries following liberation from colonial rule; and (5) emergence of new democracies from the former Communist Bloc, 1989–present. During the last two periods, constitution making became something of a cottage industry among academics with the constitutions of many countries written in consultation with the same experts. Most of the constitutions were adopted after World War II. Indeed, only twenty-one constitutions adopted before World War II are currently in place and, of these, nine countries have substantially revised their constitutions since World War II. Of the twenty-one states, nine have provisions regarding health and health care in their constitutions, many of which were added when constitutions were revised after World War II.

It is clear that not all of the countries that have provisions regarding health and health care in their constitutions have in practice lived up to these mandates. Some of the most resounding constitutional commitments to health and health care are in poor countries with tenuous democracies. Haiti's constitution is exemplary of this phenomenon:

> Strengthen national unity by eliminating all discrimination between the urban and rural populations ... and by recognizing the right to progress, information, education, health, employment and leisure for all citizens.
>
> The State has the absolute obligation to guarantee the right to life, health, and respect of the human person for all citizens without distinction, in conformity with the Universal Declaration of the Rights of Man.

> The State has the obligation to ensure for all citizens in all territorial divisions appropriate means to ensure protection, maintenance and restoration of their health by establishing hospitals, health centers and dispensaries.

Many countries that devote extensive resources to assuring the health of and providing health care to their populations have no relevant provisions in their constitutions regarding health or health care. * * * Only three of the [twenty countries with highest per capita government expenditures for health care] * * * have provisions conferring an entitlement to health and/or imposing a duty on the state to provide health care. Thirteen countries have no provisions regarding health and health care in their constitutions.

* * *

The number or strength of constitutional provisions does not appear to have a determinative role in the amount of resources that countries spend for the health care of their populations. Specifically, countries that expressed the greatest constitutional commitment to health—evidenced by inclusion of both a statement of entitlement and duty]—had an average government per capita expenditure for health care of $308 in 2000. However, the same average for countries that had no provision regarding health or health care was $716.95. * * *

This finding is not surprising. There are many factors influencing government's decisions to finance programs promoting health and providing health care services. In addition, constitutions' national legal frameworks vary tremendously in at least three important ways. First, the general attitude toward the constitution influences the degree to which a population and the representative advocacy groups look to the constitution for resources and remedies for the promotion of health and health care. In some countries, the constitution is part of the political culture and is viewed as a source of protections, whereas in other countries, the population has little knowledge of the constitution and its potential for advancing legal and social protections. Second, the degree of legal remedies, such as judicial review, private rights of action and access to courts, and the opportunity to challenge policymakers who fail to implement or enforce constitutional provisions regarding health and health care, vary between the countries. Finally, many countries, particularly in the southern hemisphere and in other parts of the developing world, do not have the financial resources to devote to improving health or providing health care services.

* * *

The question of constitutional provisions' meaning is complex and has at least two dimensions. First is the actual content of the concepts of "health" and "health care." * * *

The second dimension of meaning refers to enforceability of the individual interest in health and health care. Customarily, lawyers and legal scholars think of the interests that constitute enforceable "rights" as the only interests with legal meaning. This view of rights as "trumps" in the Dworkian sense exposes the problematic distinction between social and economic rights on the one hand and civil and political rights on the other. Often these two groups of rights are characterized, respectively, as positive rights requiring affirmative state action and as negative rights requiring state abstention from specific conduct. This distinction quickly disappears when one considers that proper enforcement of so-called negative rights often implicates affirmative state action and that substantial implementation of positive rights may well result when the state refrains from conduct limiting access to existing services.

To be recognized and implemented, economic and social rights require affirmative state action, which creates the problem with their designation as "rights." The conventional understanding of rights is that, if violated, they assure legal remedies from courts or other authoritative adjudicative tribunals. Extant legal remedies are often tailored to addressing the denial of civil and political rights by governments or even private actors within the governments' jurisdiction. Under this more conventional understanding, if rights are without legal remedies, they are simply aspirational statements. Such rights, some argue, water down the concept of rights and rob it of its meaning and effectiveness.

There is a significant difference between remedies designed to prevent a government or regulated private party from acting in a certain way, such as curtailing civil rights, and a remedy intended to force a government or regulated party to provide a particular service. Specifically, the latter remedy implicitly asks the government or regulated private party to allocate resources as the legal remedy. Thus, in the act of granting the remedy, the adjudicator invariably steps into the role of policymaker regarding the allocation of resources, which is quintessentially a legislative function. This phenomenon poses the dilemma of who is best charged with making the policy call in this instance—the activist judge witnessing the deficiency, or the reluctant legislature facing the full panoply of national needs and state obligations.

* * *

A more useful observation about individual enforcement of economic and social rights is that the determination of their content involves facts and issues that are not appropriate for courts or other adjudicative tribunals to decide. * * *

Lon Fuller also addresses the use of adjudication in deciding policy issues. Policy concerns, such as the appropriate content of government programs to assure health care services and the allocation of budgetary resources, are "polycentric" issues that are least amenable to satisfactory adjudication. The resolution of polycentric issues inevitably involves multiple implications and trade-offs to accommodate various exigencies and constituencies. Their resolution involves making decisions about * * * "legislative facts," the accuracy or persuasiveness of which are not easily determined through adjudicative techniques.

However, conceiving of rights as only those interests that are enforceable in a court or adjudicative tribunal is a very narrow concept. Why do rights have to be legally enforceable in that manner for validation? A right might also include a policy imperative established by authoritative law such as a constitution, treaty, or other legal mandate. As such, the right as policy imperative requires bound states to take legislative action and array national budgetary priorities in ways that fulfill that policy imperative. * * * This idea is captured in the thoughtful observation of an Eastern European scholar, commenting on economic and social rights as human rights:

> To call social and economic rights "human rights" is not to make them automatically enforceable. Human rights should set standards and provide justification for moral claims to decent treatment, and should guide legislators in the implementation of legal rights.

* * *

The following case from the Indian Supreme Court represents one of the few instances in which a national supreme court has imposed obligations on government to effectuate a constitutional right to health.

Paschim Banga Khet Mazdoor Samity v. State of West Bengal

Supreme Court of India, AIR 1996 Supreme Court 2426

S.C. Agrawal and G.T. Nanavati, JJ.

S.C. Agrawal, J.:—In Pt Parmanand Katara v. Union of India (1989), this Court in the context of medico-legal cases, has emphasised the need for rendering immediate medical aid to injured persons to preserve life and the obligations of the State as well as doctors in that regard. This petition, filed under Article 32 of the Constitution raises this issue in the context of availability of facilities in Government hospitals for treatment of persons sustaining serious injuries.

Hakim Seikh [Petitioner No. 2] who is a member of Paschim Banga Khet Mazdoor Samity [Petitioner No. 1], an organisation of agricultural labourers, fell off a train at Mathurapur Station in West Bengal at about 7.45 P.M. on July 8, 1992. As a result of the said fall Hakim Seikh suffered serious head injuries and brain haemorrhage. He was taken to the Primary Health Centre at Mathurapur. Since necessary facilities for treatment were not available at the Primary Health Centre, the medical officer in charge of the Centre referred him to the Diamond Harbour Sub-Divisional Hospital or any other State hospital for better treatment. Hakim Seikh was taken to N.R.S. Medical College Hospital near Sealdah Railway Station, Calcutta at about 11.45 P.M. on July 8, 1992. The Emergency Medical Officer in the said Hospital, after examining him and after taking two X-ray prints of his skull recommended immediate admission for further treatment. But Hakim Seikh could not be admitted in the said hospital as no vacant bed was available in the Surgical Emergency ward and the regular Surgery Ward was also full. He was thereafter taken to Calcutta Medical College Hospital at about 12.20 A.M. on July 9, 1992 but there also he was not admitted on the ground that no vacant bed was available. He was then taken to Shambhu Nath Pandit Hospital at about 1.00 A.M. on July 9, 1992. He was not admitted in that hospital and referred to a teaching hospital in the ENT, Neuro Surgeon Department on the ground that the hospital has no ENT Emergency or Neuro Emergency Department. At about 2.00 A.M. on July 9, 1992 he was taken to the Calcutta National Medical College Hospital but there also he was not admitted on account of non-availability of bed. At about 8.00 A.M. on July 9, 1992 he was taken to the Bangur Institute of Neurology but on seeing the CT Scan (which was got done at a private hospital on payment of Rs.1310/-) it was found that there was haemorrhage condition in the frontal region of the head and that it was an emergency case which could not be handled in the said Institute. At about 10.00 A.M. on July 9, 1992 he was taken to SSKM Hospital but there also he was not admitted on the ground that the hospital has no facility of neuro surgery. Ultimately he was admitted in Calcutta Medical Research Institute, a private hospital, where he received treatment as an indoor patient from July 9, 1992 to July 22, 1992 and he had incurred an expenditure of approximately Rs 17,000/- in his treatment.

Feeling aggrieved by the indifferent and callous attitude on the part of the medical authorities at the various State run hospitals in Calcutta in providing treatment for the serious injuries sustained by Hamik Seikh the petitioners have filed this writ petition.

* * *

The Constitution envisages the establishment of a welfare State at the federal level as well as at the State level. In a welfare State the primary duty of the Government is to secure the welfare of the people. Providing adequate medical facilities for the people is an essential part of the obligations undertaken by the Government in a welfare State. The

Government discharges this obligation by running hospitals and health centres which provide medical care to the person seeking to avail those facilities. Article 21 imposes an obligation on the State to safeguard the right to life of every person. Preservation of human life is thus of paramount importance. The Government hospitals run by the State and the Medical Officers employed therein are duty bound to extend medical assistance for preserving human life. Failure on the part of a Government hospital to provide timely medical treatment to a person in need of such treatment results in violation of his right to life guaranteed under Article 21. In the present case there was breach of the said right of Hakim Seikh guaranteed under Article 21 when he was denied treatment at the various Governmental hospitals which were approached even though his condition was very serious at that time and he was in need of immediate medical attention. Since the said denial of the right of Hakim Seikh guaranteed under Article 21 was by officers of the State in hospitals run by the State, the State cannot avoid its responsibility for such denial of the constitutional right of Hakim Seikh. In respect of deprivation of the constitutional rights guaranteed under Part III of the Constitution the position is well settled that adequate compensation can be awarded by the court for such violation by way of redress in proceedings under Articles 32 and 226 of the Constitution. Hakim Seikh should, therefore, be suitably compensated for the breach of his right guaranteed under Article 21 of the Constitution. Having regard to the facts and circumstances of the case, we fix the amount of such compensation at Rs 25,000/-. A sum of Rs. 15,000/- was directed to be paid to Hakim Seikh as interim compensation under the orders of this Court dated April 22, 1994. The balance amount should be paid by respondent No. 1 to Hakim Seikh within one month.

We may now come to the remedial measures to rule out recurrence of such incidents in future and to ensure immediate medical attention and treatment to persons in real need.

* * *

[W]e are of the view that in order that proper medical facilities are available for dealing with emergency cases it must be that:

1. Adequate facilities are available at the Primary Health Centres where the patient can be given immediate primary treatment so as to stabilize his condition;

2. Hospitals at the district level and Sub-Division level are upgraded so that serious cases can be treated there;

3. Facilities for giving Specialist treatment are increased and are available at the hospitals at District level and Sub-Division level having regard to the growing needs;

4. In order to ensure availability of bed in an emergency at State level hospitals there is a centralised communication system so that the patient can be sent immediately to the hospital where bed is available in respect of the treatment which is required;

5. Proper arrangement of ambulance is made for transport of a patient from the Primary Health Centre to the District Hospital or Sub-Division hospital to the State hospital;

6. The ambulance is adequately provided with necessary equipment and medical personnel;

7. The Health Centres and the hospitals and the medical personnel attached to these Centres and hospitals are geared to deal with larger number of patients

needed emergency treatment on account of higher risk of accidents on certain occasions and in certain seasons.

It is no doubt true that financial resources are needed for providing these facilities. But at the same time it cannot be ignored that it is the constitutional obligation of the State to provide adequate medical services to the people. Whatever is necessary for this purpose has to be done. In the context of the constitutional obligations to provide free legal aid to a poor accused this Court has held that the State cannot avoid its constitutional obligation in that regard on account of financial constraints. The said observations would apply with equal, if not greater, force in the matter of discharge of constitutional obligation of the State to provide medical aid to preserve human life. In the matter of allocation of funds for medical services the said constitutional obligation of the State has to be kept in view. It is necessary that a time-bound plan for providing these services should be chalked out keeping in view the recommendations of the Committee as well as the requirements for ensuring availability of proper medical services in this regard as indicated by us and steps should be taken to implement the same.

The Union of India is a party to these proceedings. Since it is the joint obligation of the Centre as well as the States to provide medical services it is expected that the Union of India would render the necessary assistance in the improvement of the medical services in the country on these lines.

As regards the medical officers who have been found to be responsible for the lapse resulting in denial of immediate medical aid to Hakim Seikh it is expected that the State Government will take appropriate administrative action against those officers.

* * *

Note

The Indian courts have been particularly active in attempting to operationalize a right to health. In one case the High Court of Orissa ordered the state government to open a primary care center in a rural area to provide preventive services (*Mahendra Pratap Singh v. State of Orissa*, A.I.R. 1997 Ori. 37), while in another the Allahabad High Court held that hospital patients had the right to have access to medicine at night and at reasonable prices (*Prayag Vyapar Mandal v. State of Uttar Pradesh*, A.I.R. 1991, All. 1). See, discussing the right to health in India, Sheetel B. Shah, Illuminating the Possible in the Developing World: Guaranteeing the Human Right to Health in India, 32 *Vand.J.Transnat'l L.* 435 (1999). Other countries in which the Supreme or Constitutional Court has recognized an enforceable right to health care, including treatment for AIDS, include South Africa and Venezuela. See Lisa Forman, Ensuring Reasonable Health: Health Rights, the Judiciary, and South African HIV/AIDS Policy, 33 *J. L. Med. & Ethics* 711 (2005); Mary Ann Torres, The Human Right to Health, National Courts, and Access to HIV/AIDS Treatment: A Case Study from Venezuela, 3 *Chi. J Int'l L.* 105 (2002).

Constitutional Law need not only expand positive government obligations to provide health care, however. Human rights charters might also provide negative rights to be free from government interference in seeking private health care, as the following recent Canadian Supreme Court case illustrates.

Chaoulli v. Quebec (Attorney General)

2005 SCC 35 (Canada 2005)

1. Deschamps J.—Quebeckers are prohibited from taking out insurance to obtain in the private sector services that are available under Quebec's public health care plan. Is this prohibition justified by the need to preserve the integrity of the plan?

2. As we enter the 21st century, health care is a constant concern. The public health care system, once a source of national pride, has become the subject of frequent and sometimes bitter criticism. This appeal does not question the appropriateness of the state making health care available to all Quebeckers. On the contrary, all the parties stated that they support this kind of role for the government. Only the state can make available to all Quebeckers the social safety net consisting of universal and accessible health care. The demand for health care is constantly increasing, and one of the tools used by governments to control this increase has been the management of waiting lists. The choice of waiting lists as a management tool falls within the authority of the state and not of the courts. The appellants do not claim to have a solution that will eliminate waiting lists. Rather, they submit that the delays resulting from waiting lists violate their rights under the Charter of Human Rights and Freedoms ("Quebec Charter"), and the Canadian Charter of Rights and Freedoms ("Canadian Charter"). They contest the validity of the prohibition * * * on private insurance for health care services that are available in the public system. * * *

* * *

4. In essence, the question is whether Quebeckers who are prepared to spend money to get access to health care that is, in practice, not accessible in the public sector because of waiting lists may be validly prevented from doing so by the state. For the reasons that follow, I find that the prohibition infringes the right to personal inviolability and that it is not justified by a proper regard for democratic values, public order and the general well being of the citizens of Quebec.

5. The validity of the prohibition is contested by the appellants, George Zeliotis and Jacques Chaoulli. Over the years, Mr. Zeliotis has experienced a number of health problems and has used medical services that were available in the public system, including heart surgery and a number of operations on his hip. The difficulties he encountered prompted him to speak out against waiting times in the public health care system. Mr. Chaoulli is a physician who has tried unsuccessfully to have his home delivered medical activities recognized and to obtain a licence to operate an independent private hospital.* * *

6. The Superior Court dismissed the motion for a declaratory judgment * * *.

7. On the subject of s. 7 of the Canadian Charter, * * * Piché J.* * * was of the opinion that the purpose of the [the prohibition of private insurance contained in] the Hospital Insurance Act (HOIA) and the Health Insurance Act (HEIA) is to establish a public health system that is available to all residents of Quebec. The purpose of s. 11 HOIA and s. 15 HEIA [prohibiting the purchase of private medical insurance] is to guarantee that virtually all of Quebec's existing health care resources will be available to all residents of Quebec. In her opinion, the enactment of these provisions was motivated by considerations of equality and human dignity. She found no conflict with the general values expressed in the Canadian Charter or in the Quebec Charter. She did find that waiting lists are long and the health care system must be improved and transformed. In her opinion, however, the expert testimony could not serve to establish with certainty that a parallel health care system would solve all the current problems of waiting times and access.

* * *

11. The Court of Appeal dismissed the appeal * * *. According to Delisle J.A., the right affected by s. 11 HOIA and s. 15 HEIA is an economic right and is not fundamental to an individual's life. In addition, in his opinion, the appellants had not demonstrated a real, imminent or foreseeable deprivation. He was also of the view that s. 7 of the Canadian Charter may not be raised to challenge a societal choice in court. * * *

* * *

27. In the instant case, s. 7 of the Canadian Charter and s. 1 of the Quebec Charter have numerous points in common:

> Canadian Charter 7. Everyone has the right to life, liberty and security of the person and the right not to be deprived thereof except in accordance with the principles of fundamental justice.
>
> Quebec Charter 1. Every human being has a right to life, and to personal security, inviolability and freedom.

* * *

37. The appellant Zeliotis argues that the prohibition infringes Quebeckers' right to life. Some patients die as a result of long waits for treatment in the public system when they could have gained prompt access to care in the private sector. Were it not for s. 11 HOIA and s. 15 HEIA, they could buy private insurance and receive care in the private sector.

38. The Superior Court judge stated "that there [are] serious problems in certain sectors of the health care system" The evidence supports that assertion. After meticulously analysing the evidence, she found that the right to life and liberty protected by s. 7 of the Canadian Charter had been infringed. * * *

* * *

40. Dr. Daniel Doyle, a cardiovascular surgeon, testified that when a person is diagnosed with cardiovascular disease, he or she is "always sitting on a bomb" and can die at any moment. In such cases, it is inevitable that some patients will die if they have to wait for an operation. Dr. Doyle testified that the risk of mortality rises by 0.45 percent per month. The right to life is therefore affected by the delays that are the necessary result of waiting lists.

* * *

44. In the opinion of my colleagues Binnie and LeBel JJ., there is an internal mechanism that safeguards the public health system. According to them, Quebeckers may go outside the province for treatment where services are not available in Quebec. This possibility is clearly not a solution for the system's deficiencies. The evidence did not bring to light any administrative mechanism that would permit Quebeckers suffering as a result of waiting times to obtain care outside the province. The possibility of obtaining care outside Quebec is case specific and is limited to crisis situations.

* * *

46. Section 9.1 of the Quebec Charter sets out the standard for justification. It reads as follows:

> "9.1. In exercising his fundamental freedoms and rights, a person shall maintain a proper regard for democratic values, public order and the general well being of the citizens of Québec.

In this respect, the scope of the freedoms and rights, and limits to their exercise, may be fixed by law."

* * *

48. * * * First, the court must determine whether the objective of the legislation is pressing and substantial. Next, it must determine whether the means chosen to attain this legislative end are reasonable and demonstrably justifiable in a free and democratic society. For this second part of the analysis, three tests must be met: (1) the existence of a rational connection between the measure and the aim of the legislation; (2) minimal impairment of the protected right by the measure; and (3) proportionality between the effect of the measure and its objective. * * *

* * *

74. Even if it were assumed that the prohibition on private insurance could contribute to preserving the integrity of the system, * * * prohibiting insurance contracts is by no means the only measure a state can adopt to protect the system's integrity. * * * The regimes of the provinces where a private system is authorized demonstrate that public health services are not threatened by private insurance. It can therefore be concluded that the prohibition is not necessary to guarantee the integrity of the public plan.

* * *

78. In a number of European countries, there is no insurance paid for directly out of public funds. In Austria, services are funded through decentralized agencies that collect the necessary funds from salaries. People who want to obtain health care in the private sector in addition to the services covered by the mandatory social insurance are free to do so, but private insurance may cover no more than 80 percent of the cost billed by professionals practising in the public sector. The same type of plan exists in Germany and the Netherlands, but people who opt for private insurance are not required to pay for the public plan. Only nine percent of Germans opt for private insurance.

* * *

83. As can be seen from the evolution of public plans in the few OECD countries that have been examined in studies produced in the record, there are a wide range of measures that are less drastic, and also less intrusive in relation to the protected rights * * * A measure as drastic as prohibiting private insurance contracts appears to be neither essential nor determinative.

* * *

101. For these reasons, I would allow the appeal with costs throughout and would answer the questions relating to the Quebec Charter as follows:

Question 1: Does s. 11 of the Hospital Insurance Act, R.S.Q., c. A-28, infringe the rights guaranteed by s. 1 of the Quebec Charter? Answer: Yes.

Question 2: If so, is the infringement a reasonable limit prescribed by law as can be demonstrably justified in a free and democratic society under s. 9.1 of the Quebec Charter? Answer: No.

Question 3: Does s. 15 of the Health Insurance Act, R.S.Q., c. A-29, infringe the rights guaranteed by s. 1 of the Quebec Charter? Answer:Yes.

Question 4: If so, is the infringement a reasonable limit prescribed by law as can be demonstrably justified in a free and democratic society under s. 9.1 of the Quebec Charter? Answer: No.

McLachlin C. J.C. The Chief Justice, Major J.:

1102. We concur in the conclusion of our colleague Deschamps J. that the prohibition against contracting for private health insurance violates the Quebec Charter of Human Rights and Freedoms. On the argument that the anti-insurance provision also violates s. 7 of the Canadian Charter of Rights and Freedoms ("Charter"), we conclude that the provision impermissibly limits the right to life, liberty and security of the person protected by s. 7 of the Charter and has not been shown to be justified as a reasonable limit under s. 1 of the Charter.

103. The appellants do not seek an order that the government spend more money on health care, nor do they seek an order that waiting times for treatment under the public health care scheme be reduced. They only seek a ruling that because delays in the public system place their health and security at risk, they should be allowed to take out insurance to permit them to access private services.

104. The Charter does not confer a freestanding constitutional right to health care. However, where the government puts in place a scheme to provide health care, that scheme must comply with the Charter. * * *

* * *

106. The Canada Health Act, the Health Insurance Act, and the Hospital Insurance Act do not expressly prohibit private health services. However, they limit access to private health services by removing the ability to contract for private health care insurance to cover the same services covered by public insurance. The result is a virtual monopoly for the public health scheme. The state has effectively limited access to private health care except for the very rich, who can afford private care without need of insurance. This virtual monopoly, on the evidence, results in delays in treatment that adversely affect the citizen's security of the person. Where a law adversely affects life, liberty or security of the person, it must conform to the principles of fundamental justice. This law, in our view, fails to do so.

* * *

108. The government defends the prohibition on medical insurance on the ground that the existing system is the only approach to adequate universal health care for all Canadians. The question in this case, however, is not whether single-tier health care is preferable to two-tier health care. Even if one accepts the government's goal, the legal question raised by the appellants must be addressed: is it a violation of s. 7 of the Charter to prohibit private insurance for health care, when the result is to subject Canadians to long delays with resultant risk of physical and psychological harm? The mere fact that this question may have policy ramifications does not permit us to avoid answering it....

Binnier, Lebel JJ. (Dissenting):

* * *

166. The Quebec government views the prohibition against private insurance as essential to preventing the current single-tier health system from disintegrating into a de facto two-tier system. The trial judge found, and the evidence demonstrated, that there is good reason for this fear. * * *

* * *

176. It would be open to Quebec to adopt a U.S.-style health care system. No one suggests that there is anything in our Constitution to prevent it. But to do so would be contrary to the policy of the Quebec National Assembly, and its policy in that respect is shared by the other provinces and the federal Parliament. As stated, Quebec further takes

the view that significant growth in the private health care system (which the appellants advocate) would inevitably damage the public system. Our colleagues the Chief Justice and Major J. disagree with this assessment, but governments are entitled to act on a reasonable apprehension of risk of such damage. * * *

* * *

242. * * * We now propose to review briefly some of the evidence supporting the findings of the trial judge. * * *

* * *

248. The experience in other OECD countries shows that an increase in private funding typically leads to a decrease in government funding. At trial, Dr. Bergman explained that a service designed purely for members of society with less socio-economic power would probably lead to a decline in quality of services, a loss of political support and a decline in the quality of management.

* * *

249. The evidence suggests that parallel private insurers prefer to siphon off high income patients while shying away from patient populations that constitute a higher financial risk, a phenomenon known as "cream skimming". The public system would therefore carry a disproportionate burden of patients who are considered "bad risks" by the private market by reason of age, socio-economic conditions, or geographic location.

* * *

251. Reference has already been made to the U.S. health care system, which is the most expensive in the world, even though by some measures Americans are less healthy than Canadians. The existence of a private system has not eliminated waiting times. The availability, extent and timeliness of health care is rationed by private insurers, who may determine according to cost, not need, what is "medically necessary" health care and where and when it is to occur. Whether or not the private system in the U.S. is better managed is a matter of debate amongst policy analysts. The point here is simply that the appellants' faith in the curative power of private insurance is not borne out by the evidence put before the Court.

* * *

Note

For a thorough review and critique of the *Chaoulli* case in a national and international context, see Colleen Flood, Lorne Sossin and Kent Roach, eds., *Access to Care, Access to Justice: The Legal Debate Over Private Health Insurance in Canada* (2005).

C. The Organization of National Health Care Systems

While the right to health care is widely recognized, the manner in which it has been implemented varies dramatically from nation to nation. All nations, including the United States, have adopted some form of public insurance for a portion of their population (although most nations also have some form of private market for health care, including private health insurance). All nations also, obviously, have a health care delivery system to provide health care services. The variety of approaches to health care delivery and finance is endless. Nevertheless several common models for health care delivery and finance have emerged historically and became dominant.

This book is not primarily concerned with comparative health care organization and finance. Many books and articles written by experts in health policy, politics, and economics thoroughly explore this territory. Our focus is rather health law. It is difficult to understand health law, however, without some understanding of the context in which health law exists. This section and the one that follows provide a basic background in health care systems, and offer some basic tools of health policy analysis.

Two primary sources are presented here for introducing health systems. The first consists of excerpts the World Health Organization's *World Health Report 2000*, which ranked the world's health care systems with respect to three variables: contribution to improvement of health status; fairness in distribution of health care resources and costs; and responsiveness to expectations in regard to non-health matters such as respecting dignity, autonomy and confidentiality. Measured by these variables, the United States ranked 37, in the company with Costa Rica at 36 and Slovenia at 38. The low United States score was largely due to low health status measures and poor performance on fairness, as well as adjustment of the final score to reflect available health resources. France ranked first among all nations in overall performance. Although the methodology of the Report has been challenged, it is useful insofar as it takes a truly global view of health systems, both in its worldwide focus and in its emphasis on preventive and public health measures, as well as on curative care. An excerpt from this book included here explores the history of the emergence of different models of health care systems, illustrating the fact of their historical contingence and also of their rich variety. The second article describes the major models used for organizing health care delivery and provides some information as to the comparative performance of these systems.

World Health Report 2000

World Health Organization, pp. 11–13 (2000)

* * *

With rare exceptions, even in industrialized countries, organized health systems in the modern sense, intended to benefit the population at large, barely existed a century ago. Although hospitals have a much longer history than complete systems in many countries, few people living 100 years ago would ever visit one—and that remains true for many millions of the poor today. Until well into the 19th century they were for the most part run by charitable organizations, and often were little more than refuges for the orphaned, the crippled, the destitute or the insane. And there was nothing like the modern practice of referrals from one level of the system to another, and little protection from financial risk apart from that offered by charity or by small-scale pooling of contributions among workers in the same occupation.

Towards the close of the 19th century, the industrial revolution was transforming the lives of people worldwide. At the same time societies began to recognize the huge toll of death, illness and disability occurring among workforces, whether from infectious diseases which killed many thousands during the construction of the Panama Canal or from industrial accidents and exposures. Once it was realized that mosquitoes transmitted malaria and yellow fever, control of the insects' breeding-sites became part of prevention efforts that also translated into benefits for surrounding communities. In addition to the human costs, the toll of illness and death meant great losses in productivity. In response, company owners began providing medical services to treat their workers. * * *

About the same time, workers' health was becoming a political issue in some European countries, but for quite different reasons. Bismarck, Chancellor of Germany, reasoned that government take-over of labour unions' sickness funds would remove a source of their support at a moment when socialist workers' movements were gaining strength, and also increase workers' economic security. Thus, in 1883, Germany enacted a law requiring employer contributions to health coverage for low-wage workers in certain occupations, adding other classes of workers in subsequent years. This was the first example of a state-mandated social insurance model. The popularity of this law among workers led to the adoption of similar legislation in Belgium in 1894 and Norway in 1909. Until Britain followed suit in 1911, medical care for British wage-earners tended to be paid for by their subscriptions to trade unions or friendly societies, which in turn paid the providers. But only the worker, and not his family, had such coverage.

In the late 1800s, Russia had begun setting up a huge network of provincial medical stations and hospitals where treatment was free and supported by tax funds. After the Bolshevik revolution in 1917, it was decreed that free medical care should be provided for the entire population, and the resulting system was largely maintained for almost eight decades. This was the earliest example of a completely centralized and state-controlled model.

The influence of the German model began to spread outside Europe after the First World War. In 1922, Japan added health benefits to the other benefits for which workers were eligible, building on its tradition of managerial paternalism. In 1924, Chile brought all covered workers under the umbrella of a Ministry of Labour scheme. By 1935, a total of 90% of Denmark's population was covered by work-related health insurance. Social insurance was introduced in the Netherlands during the country's occupation in the Second World War.

Not least among its effects, the Second World War damaged or virtually destroyed health infrastructures in many countries and delayed their health system plans. Paradoxically, it also paved the way for the introduction of some others. Wartime Britain's national emergency service to deal with casualties was helpful in the construction of what became, in 1948, the National Health Service, perhaps the most widely influential model of a health system. The Beveridge Report of 1942 had identified health care as one of the three basic prerequisites for a viable social security system. The government's White Paper of 1944 stated the policy that "Everybody, irrespective of means, age, sex or occupation shall have equal opportunity to benefit from the best and most up-to-date medical and allied services available," adding that those services should be comprehensive and free of charge and should promote good health, as well as treating sickness and disease. New Zealand had already become, in 1938, the first country to introduce a national health service. Almost simultaneously, Costa Rica laid the foundation for universal health insurance in 1941. In Mexico, the Institute of Social Security and the Ministry of Health were both founded in 1943. * * *

In the immediate post-war period, Japan and the Soviet Union also extended their limited national systems to cover most or all of the population, as did Norway and Sweden, Hungary and other communist states in Europe, and Chile. As former colonies gained independence, they also tried to adopt modern, comprehensive systems with heavy state participation. India developed ambitious five-year development plans for a health system, based on the Bhore Report of 1946. The factors which made this period of system-building and expansion possible included realization of the power of the modern state, post-war movements towards reconciliation, stability and reconstruction, and collective solidarity stemming from the war effort. Newly acquired citizenship and the belief in a relatively effective and benevolent state which could promote development of all kinds led to a social and political environment in which "classical universalism," the concept of free access to all kinds of health care for all, could take root.

Today's health systems are modelled to varying degrees on one or more of a few basic designs that emerged and have been refined since the late 19th century. One of these aims to cover all or most citizens through mandated employer and employee payments to insurance or sickness funds, while providing care through both public and private providers. The earliest such social insurance systems usually evolved from small, initially voluntary, associations; later versions have sometimes been created *ex nihilo* by public action. Another, slightly more recent, model centralizes planning and financing, relying primarily on tax revenues and on public provision. Resources are traditionally distributed by budgets, sometimes on the basis of fixed ratios between populations and health workers or facilities. In a third model, state involvement is more limited but still substantial, sometimes providing coverage only for certain population groups and giving way for the rest of the populace to largely private finance, provision and ownership of facilities. Relatively pure examples, in which one or another model accounts for the bulk of resources or provision, are found mostly in rich countries; health systems in middle income countries, notably in Latin America, tend to be a mixture of two or even all three types.

* * *

Why Can't We Do What They Do? National Health Reform Abroad

Timothy Stoltzfus Jost, Journal of Law, Medicine and Ethics, vol. 32, pp. 432–35 (2004).

* * *

All other developed nations of the world [other than the United States], including developed countries in Western Europe, Asia, North and South America, and on the Pacific Rim, provide health care for all or most of their residents. Although private health insurance products are available for purchase on a voluntary basis in virtually every country, no other developed country relies on private insurance as does the United State to provide primary coverage for its population. All developed nations have recognized that voluntary private insurance cannot cover everyone, (as it does not in the U.S.) and have developed some form of public health insurance.

Two primary models can be found in the world: social insurance and national health insurance. Each term refers to a specific approach to the task of financing and organizing a nation's system for providing personal health care. The first, and older, model is social insurance, often called the Bismarck model after the German leader who established the first social health insurance system. The second, more recent, is the national health insurance model, often called the Beveridge model after Lord Beveridge who proposed this approach for the U.K. during World War II.

Chancellor Bismarck established the German social insurance system in 1883 in an attempt to turn back the tide of socialism that he feared would engulf Germany. Under the German system as it has developed, most citizens have an obligation to secure health insurance coverage, which in turn is paid for, usually by a deduction from earnings, on the basis of the insured's income rather than the insured's risk status or family size, in order to ensure affordability. In Germany the conceptual foundation of health insurance lies in a belief that members of a society have obligations to each other, a concept referred to as "solidarity," rather than in the belief that individuals are responsible only for themselves. This insurance obligation is effectuated through a system that collects the necessary revenues needed to sustain health care. Employers and employees each contribute a percentage of wages to social insurance funds; in turn, these funds provide health insurance for employees and their families. Most persons in Germany whose income falls below a certain level (46,350 Euros in 2004) must participate in this social health insurance program. Persons with incomes above this level are not required to participate, and many buy private insurance instead. However, about 60 percent of all of these upper income persons in fact participate in the public system because family coverage costs extra in the private system but not in the public, private insurance rates are risk-adjusted while social insurance rates are not, and persons who opt out of the social insurance system may not in most instances ever return.

Social insurance funds in Germany are not administered by the government, but rather by non-profit organizations, which are accountable to their members (and their members' employers). There are many of these funds, some tied to a particular employer, others occupation based, and still others locally-based. Thus employees of Mercedes or BMW would be insured through a company fund; farmers, miners or seamen are covered by special funds, and many people are insured through a general locally-based fund or through special funds that used to only cover white collar workers. All social insurance funds operate within a framework of laws, and all cover essentially the same services and charge similar (though not identical) premiums. In order to ensure the stability of the health funds—and thus the effectuation of a truly nationwide system—health plans that have younger and less costly members must transfer money through a risk-equalization scheme to the plans that have older and more expensive patients, but the plans also compete with each other for members and thus have some incentive to keep their premiums down.

Health insurers have traditionally paid hospitals on the basis of negotiated budgets, though Germany is moving toward payment on a diagnosis related group (DRG) basis. Physicians and dentists in Germany who furnish health care to plan members are organized into corporate bodies that resemble unions. In other words, while physicians and dentists are private businessmen, they negotiate with the health insurers collectively, much like an independent practice association would do in the U.S. In recent years these corporate entities have negotiated with social insurers for a fixed budget, which they have allocated among their members on a fee-for-service basis.

* * *

For each component of the health care sector (physician services, hospitals, pharmaceuticals, etc.) and in each region, budgets in Germany are established globally within a framework of "premium stability." This framework limits the rate of increase in social insurance premiums to the rate of increase in inflation generally and tends to ensure that practice style and practice choices evolve within a fundamental environment of overall health care spending control. * * *

The social insurance model created in Germany has been adopted in much of the world. Other central European countries, including Austria, Switzerland, France, Belgium, and the Netherlands have social insurance systems, as do many South American and Asian countries for at least part of their workforce. Many of the emerging democracies of Eastern Europe have also embraced the social insurance model. Part A of the U.S. Medicare program in most respects resembles a social insurance system. Though these systems vary in many important respects, in each one health insurance is financed primarily by payroll taxes or wage-based premiums, and services are purchased from independent health care providers who often are in private practice.

If the social insurance model was adopted by conservative governments to suppress the growth of socialism in the late 19th and early 20th century, the national health insurance model emerged from the triumph of socialism in Europe after World War II. The United Kingdom had adopted a limited social insurance system in 1911, but many people were excluded from it, and the U.K. emerged from WWII determined to provide health care as a right to its entire population. Access to health care would no longer depend on belonging to a social insurance plan (which was usually, in some sense, employment-related), but rather would be free at point-of-service to all residents. Thus, universal coverage was created independent of the economic or employment status of any individual.

The English NHS is financed through general revenue taxation. These funds are administered by local units called primary care trusts. These units purchase services from NHS hospital trusts, which are currently public corporations, as well as from general practitioners, who are private businessmen. These services are then provided to the general public, in most instances without cost, although co-payments are imposed for some things like drugs, and a few services—like most dental care—are provided mainly in the private sector.

The U.K., like many European countries, has a strong gatekeeper system. Every Briton has a general practitioner (GP), and a patient's first contact with the health care system is almost always with the GP. GPs still make house calls in the U.K., and the level of satisfaction with primary care in the U.K. is very high. Specialist services, including surgery, are only provided through hospitals and upon referral from a GP.

Many nations have adopted the national health insurance model of public health insurance in the past half century, although, again, in each nation the model looks somewhat different. Canada, Australia, the Scandinavian countries, Spain, Portugal, Italy, and some Latin American and Asian countries have national health insurance systems. Other countries, particularly less developed countries, provide services through public hospitals and clinics without necessarily developing a full and comprehensive national system of health care finance that would be essential to make such a network of services accessible to all persons. Our own Medicaid program, as well as our veterans', military, and Indian health services, resemble the "national health insurance" model, in that all use general revenue funds to pay for health services, but they are different in that their coverage is limited to certain narrowly delineated populations, which may even, as with Medicaid, vary from state to state.

In virtually all countries, voluntary private health insurance of the sort sold in the U.S. to both groups and individuals continues to exist, although it serves different functions in different countries. In some, such as Germany and the Netherlands, it covers wealthy people who are not covered by social insurance. In others, such as Canada, it covers services such as pharmaceuticals, which are not universally covered by public insurance. In yet others, such as France, it covers cost-sharing obligations, much like our own Medigap policies. In still others, such as the U.K. or Australia, it allows privately insured persons to jump the queue and get services faster or more conveniently than publicly insured patients.

Countries that have national health insurance programs cover all of their citizens and long-term residents, although in most countries individuals can choose to carry private insurance and obtain services privately. Some countries with social insurance funds, such as France or Austria, cover their entire populations as well. Others, however, such as Germany and the Netherlands, only require people whose income falls below a certain level to be part of the social insurance program. Although people with higher incomes can choose to be uninsured, few make this choice. In Australia, government subsidies are available that cover 30 percent of the cost of hospital care, while tax penalties are imposed on higher income persons who choose not to purchase private insurance. This results in about 43 percent of the population being privately insured for hospital care. In several of the southern European nations, many people choose to purchase care privately, even though everyone is covered by national health insurance, because they believe that they will get better care or more attention from their providers.

A number of countries apply means tests for determining coverage for certain services or for determining the applicability or level of cost-sharing. The Irish health care system is partially means tested: only low income holders of medical cards (about a third of the population) have free access to general practitioner services, and higher income people without medical cards must pay a co-payment for hospital and pharmacy services under some circumstances. In the U.K. where long-term nursing home care is primarily regarded as a social service, nursing homes are publicly funded only for those who do not have the means to pay privately. Pharmaceutical coverage in the U.K. is also means tested to the extent that the system waives required co-payments for low-income persons, although the government also waives co-payment for children, the elderly, and persons with certain chronic conditions. No developed nation other than the U.S., however, makes access to public health insurance depend totally on economic "medical dependency" (Medicaid), or on age and disability status (Medicare). And no other developed country has nearly as high a proportion of its population uninsured.

Social insurance and national health insurance programs vary somewhat in the benefits they offer. The Canadian health insurance program, for example, only requires the provinces to cover hospital, physician, and surgical dental services, though most provinces also cover pharmaceutical costs for at least some of their residents. Coverage in Australia is limited to hospital, physician, and pharmaceutical care. Most countries do not cover nursing home care or cover it as a social service rather than a health care service. In some countries some benefits that are nominally covered are in fact not generally available because of high cost sharing obligations, limited coverage, or lack of provider participation.

Though public finance of health care services is quite common in other countries, public provision of health care services is less universal. In most national health insurance countries, many health care services are furnished by private entities and health professionals in private practice. In few countries, for example, does the government directly employ primary care physicians or dentists. Pharmaceuticals and medical devices are generally produced by private manufacturers and sold through private pharmacies or medical equipment suppliers. In most national health insurance countries public hospitals are dominant, but in some countries private nonprofit or private hospitals also exist. Private hospitals are even more common in social insurance countries.

* * *

Notes

1. The health care systems of other nations continue to evolve. As of 2006, for example, the Netherlands has moved toward a managed competition model in which all residents are required to purchase insurance from competing private insurers, with part of the premium paid from a social insurance fund and part paid by the insured (with assistance for lower income residents from general revenue funds). Some Canadian provinces are considering a greater role for private insurance following the *Chaoulli* decision, but will continue to cover most health care through its general revenue-financed public system. England has dramatically increased public financing of health care in recent years and has had some success with addressing its chronic problem of wait lists. It has also turned to some extent to private finance of health care facilities, and is experimenting with pay-for-performance. Finally, Germany is considering whether to expand social insurance coverage or to rely in part on private insurance premiums, following the Dutch model. Current and comprehensive information on health care systems of European nations is available from the European Observatory on Health Systems and Policies. The Observatory's Health Systems in Transition (HiT) profiles currently cover about 50 countries, including "honorary European" countries like Australia, Canada, New Zealand, and Israel. See http://www.euro.who.int/observatory.

2. How might the role of legal institutions vary depending on whether health care systems are organized around a social insurance or national health service model? How will the role differ depending on whether services are provided by salaried or contracted providers? Are legal rights more important in systems that depend on private provision and finance, as in the United States, or on public finance or provision, as in Europe and much of the rest of the world?

3. The United States is obviously quite unusual on the world stage because of the extent of its reliance on private health insurance. Virtually every other nation has private health insurance, but usually it only allows persons wealthy enough to opt out of public health insurance program, insures services not covered by the social insurance program, or permits the insured person to "queue jump," i.e. to avoid the waiting lists found in the public system. In the United States private insurance, by contrast, is the primary means of health care finance for non-indigent non-elderly persons. It is important to realize, however, that we also have public health care systems in the United States, which today in fact fund nearly half of the nation's health care. Medicare, our program for the elderly and long-term disabled is a traditional social insurance program, funded through payroll taxes. Medicaid, our program for the poor, is financed through general revenues, and thus resembles more closely national health insurance programs of other countries.

D. Perspectives on Health Care Systems

This section opens the discussion of alternative economic, political, cultural approaches to variety in health care systems. As we will see throughout this book, economic, political, and cultural factors often help explain differences (and similarities) in the law between different countries. You have no doubt studied economics, sociology, anthropology, and political science in other contexts, but specific applications of these disciplines in the health care context will, it is hoped, prove useful. It will also broaden our knowledge and understanding of comparative health care systems. The first excerpt, from a distinguished group of health politics scholars, discusses generally the possibility of learning from comparative experience. The excerpts that follow, from prominent scholars in health economics, politics, and law, discuss varying perspectives on health care systems.

Comparative Perspectives and Policy Learning in the World of Health Care

Ted Marmor, Richard Freeman, and Kieke Okma, Journal of Comparative Policy Analysis, vol. 7, pp. 331, 335–37, 339–41 (2005).

* * *

The presumptions of * * * cross-national [health policy studies] are important to explore, even if briefly. One is that the outside observer can more easily highlight features of debates that are missed or underplayed by national participants. The other is that comparative commentary may bring some policy wisdom as well as illuminating asides about national debates. The common assumption is that cross-cultural observation, if accurate and alert, has some advantages. It brings a different, "foreign" and arguably illuminating perspective to the debate.

A similar rationale lies behind much of the enthusiasm for contemporary comparative policy studies. Welfare state disputes—over pensions and medical care most prominently—are undoubtedly salient on the public agendas of all industrial democracies. There is in fact a brisk trade in panaceas for the various (real and imagined) ills of welfare states. As will be obvious in later comments on the comparative literature, however, many cross-national investigations are not factually accurate enough to offer useful illumination, let alone policy wisdom. But, properly done, studies that compare what appear to be similar topics have two potential benefits not available to the policy analyst in a single nation inquiry.

First, how others see a problem, how options for action are set out and evaluated, how implementation is understood and undertaken—all offer learning opportunities even if the policy experiences of different polities are not easily transplantable as "lessons." Secondly, where the context is reasonably similar, comparative work has features of a quasi-natural experiment. So, for instance the adaptation of reference prices for pharmaceuticals in Germany and in the Netherlands—two countries with very similar institutional arrangements in health care—provides an interesting example of policy learning. The policy of reference pricing constrains drug outlays in the short term. But those gains are somewhat dissipated as the actors strategically adapt to the new policy reality.

* * *

Cross-national sources of information have proliferated to the extent that it has become almost impossible for a policy maker in any given country not to know something about what is going on elsewhere. But know what, exactly? What part can and should comparative policy analysis play in these debates? * * *

* * *

The paradox is that the post-1970 decades witnessed the rapid expansion of public policy research, of which a significant proportion claimed to provide comparisons across countries as a base for drawing lessons. But most of those studies, in fact, consisted of mere statistical and descriptive portraitures of health systems, ignoring the methodological issues of comparison. So the argument here underlines the truism that policy making and policy research are often—if not always—pursued with little reference to each other. Nevertheless, the question remains as why that truism should apply so fully in this particular, costly area of public policy: health care. Why are claims about system convergence so widespread in the face of persistent patterns of continuity in national models of health care?

The bulk of the ideological and fiscal debates about health reform took place within national borders, largely free from the spread of "foreign" ideas. To the extent that similar arguments arose cross-nationally, these mostly represented what might be described as "parallel thinking." That is to say, the common questioning of health policy reflects similarities in circumstances and problem definition. * * *

* * *

The emphasis in this part of the discussion is on the following, perhaps obvious, distinctions among the purposes comparative analysis in health policy can serve: learning about national health arrangements and how they operate, learning why they take the forms they do, and learning policy lessons from those analyses. While these distinctions should be obvious to scholars of the subject, much of the comparative commentary on health care neither clarifies the different modes of comparison nor addresses the difficulties of drawing policy lessons from the experience of other countries.

First, there is the goal of learning about health policy abroad. Comparative work of this sort can illuminate and clarify national arrangements without addressing causal explanation or seeking policy transplantation as aims. Its comparative element remains for the most part implicit: in reading (or writing) about them, we make sense of other systems by contrasting them with our own and with others we know about. The process of learning entails, which is obvious once noted: appreciation of what something is by reference to what it is like or unlike. This is the gift of perspective, which may or may not bring explanatory insight or lesson drawing.

The second fundamental purpose served by comparison is to generate causal explanations without necessarily seeking policy transplantation: that is, learning why policies develop as they do. Many of the historical and developmental studies of health care fall into this category. This approach uses cross-national inquiry to check on the adequacy of nation-specific accounts. Let us call that a defense against explanatory provincialism. What precedes policy making in country A includes many things, from legacies of past policy to institutional and temporal features, that "seem" decisive. How is one to know if a feature is decisive as opposed to simply present? One answer is to look for similar outcomes elsewhere where some of those factors are missing or configured differently. Another is to look for a similar configuration of precedents without a comparable outcome.

A third and still different approach is to treat cross-national experience as quasi-experimental. Here one hopes to draw lessons about why some policies seem promising and doable, promising but impossible, or doable but not promising. All of these approaches appear in the comparative literature. And, with the growth of such writing, there was widespread optimism about the promise of lesson drawing from comparative policy analyses. But is that optimism justified?

* * *

Offering new perspectives on problems and making factual adjustments in national portraits are not to be treated as trivial tasks. They are what policy craftsmen and women might well spend a good deal of time perfecting. * * *

An often cited advantage of comparative studies is that they serve as an antidote to explanatory provincialism. An example from North American health policy provides a good illustration of how and how not to proceed. Some policy makers and academics in North America regard universal health insurance as incompatible with American values. They rest their case in part on the belief that Canada enacted health insurance and the US has not because North American values are sharply different. In short, they attribute a different outcome to a different political culture in the US. In fact, the values of Canada and the United States, while not identical, are actually quite similar. Like siblings, differences are there, sure, but Canada's distribution of values is closer to that of the United States than any other modern, rich democracy. In fact, the value similarities between British Columbia and Washington State are greater than those between either of those jurisdictions and, say, New Brunswick or New Hampshire along the North American east coast. Similar values are compatible with different outcomes, which in turn draw one's attention to other institutional and strategic factors that distinguish Canadian from American experience with financing health care. One can imagine many other examples of such cautionary lessons, but the important point is simply that the explanatory checks are unavailable from national histories alone.

* * * Drawing lessons from the policy experience of other nations is what has financially supported a good deal of the comparative analysis available. The international organizations have this as part of their rationale. The WHO, as noted, is firmly in the business of selling "best practices." The OECD regularly produces extensive, expensive, hard to gather, statistical portraits of programs as diverse as disability and pensions, trade flows and the movement of professionals, education and health care. * * *

For now, it is enough to restate that learning about the experience of other nations is a precondition for understanding why change takes place, or for learning from that experience. Looking at the large and growing volume of comparative studies in health policy, we found that the vast majority of studies do not deliver on their claim to provide a sound base for drawing lessons from the experience of other countries. * * * [T]he majority of reports and studies available * * * provide, at best, a sound base for further analysis but hardly any ground for learning from experience abroad. The few studies that are based on more solid analysis * * * are less frequent, less wide in their geographical application and more modest in their claims about policy lessons.

* * *

Notes

1. Canada has been a favorite object of study for those who study comparative health care systems, not only because it is so accessible geographically, but also because Canada and the United States resemble each other in so many other respects. Indeed, the fact that the health care systems of the United States and Canada were so similar prior to the implementation of the Canadian Medicare system makes the subsequent history of the two countries look almost like a controlled experiment. During the health reform debates of the early 1990s, the Canadian experience was used effectively by both those who favored and opposed President Clinton's proposal for health care reform to argue their

points. Is this the "drawing lessons from" that Marmor has in mind? See, among many sources comparing the United States and Canadian experience, *National Health Care: Lessons for the United States and Canada* (Jonathan Lemco, ed., 1994); *The Canadian Health Care System: Lessons for the United States* (Susan Brown Eve, Betty Havens, and Stanley R. Ingman, eds., 1995).

2. Economics is a second lens through which health care systems can be viewed comparatively. Indeed, much of the literature on comparative health systems focuses on economic aspects. See, e.g. Elias Mossialos, et al., *Funding Health Care: Options for Europe* (2002); A. J. Culyer & J.P. Newhouse, *Handbook of Health Economics*, vols. 1A & 1B (2000); *Markets and Health Care: A Comparative Analysis,* (Wendy Ranade, ed., 1998); *Health Care and its Financing in the Single European Market* (R. Leidl, ed. 1998); *Fixing Health Budgets: Experience from Europe and North America* (Friedrich Wilhelm Schwartz, Howard Glennerster, Richard B. Saltman, eds., 1996); and *Implementing Planned Markets in Health Care: Balancing Social and Economic Responsibilities* (Richard B. Saltman and Casten von Otter, eds. 1995). The American law and economics movement has also championed the use of economics as a means of understanding law. See, for example, J. Mark Ramseyer and Minora Nakazato, *Japanese Law: An Economic Approach*, 66–74 (1999), attempting to explain Japanese malpractice law from a law and economics perspective.

The excerpt that follows brings an economic perspective to the study of health care systems:

Reforming the Health Care System: The Universal Dilemma

Uwe E. Reinhardt, 19 Am. J. L. & Med. 21, 21–27, 29, 31–36 (1994)

The human condition surrounding the delivery of health care is the same everywhere in the world: the providers of health care seek to give their patients the maximum feasible degree of physical relief, but they also aspire to a healthy slice of the gross national product ("GNP") as a reward for their efforts. Patients seek from health care providers the maximum feasible degree of physical relief, but, collectively, they also seek to minimize the slice of the GNP that they must cede to providers as the price for that care.

In other words, while there typically is a meeting of the minds between patients and providers on the clinical side of the health care transaction, there very often is conflict on the economic front. * * *

* * *

II. Controlling the Transfer of GNP to Providers

Society can control the total annual transfer of GNP to health care providers through the demand side of the health care market, the supply side, or both. Nations differ substantially in the mix of approaches they use. Their choice of cost-control policies hinges crucially on the social role that they ascribe to health care. The two extremes of the spectrum of views on this issue are:

1. Health care is essentially a private consumption good, whose financing is the responsibility of its individual recipient.

2. Health care is a social good that should be collectively financed and available to all citizens who need health care, regardless of the individual recipient's ability to pay for that care.

Canadians and Europeans have long since reached a broad social consensus that health care is a social good. Although their health systems exhibit distinct, national idiosyncracies, they share an obedience to that overarching, ethical precept.

Americans have never been able to reach a similarly broad political consensus regarding the point at which they would like their health care system to sit on the ideological spectrum that is defined by these two extreme views. Instead, American health policy has meandered back and forth between the two views, in step with the ideological temper of the time. During the 1960s and 1970s, the American health care system moved toward the social good end of the spectrum. On the other hand, during the 1980s, a concerted effort was made to move the system in the opposite direction. * * * This meandering between distinct, ethical precepts has produced contradictions between professed principles and actual practice that confuse and frustrate even the initiated in the United States.

Table 1 presents a menu of alternative approaches to financing and organizing health care. It makes explicit distinctions between the ownership of the health insurance mechanism and the production of health care. Almost all health care systems in the world fit into his grid, and most extend over more than one cell in the grid.

For example, the health systems of the United Kingdom and Sweden occupy primarily Cell A in Table 1, though private medical practices in the United Kingdom occupy Cell C. One may think of Cell A as socialized medicine in its purest sense because the production of health care is substantially owned by the government. Clearly, the health care system of the United States Department of Veterans Affairs also resides in Cell A, as does the bulk of the health care system for the United States armed forces.

Table 1 Alternative Mixes of Health Insurance and Health Care Delivery

	Collectivized (Socialized) Financing of Health Care			Direct Financing
		Private Health Insurance		
Production and Delivery	Government Financed Insurance	within a statutory framework	within an unregulated market	Out-of-pocket by Patients at Point of Service
Purely Government-Owned	A	D	G	J
Private Not-for-Profit Entities	B	E	H	K
Private For-Profit Entities	C	F	I	L
	The Canadian health system	The West German health system	The private portion of the American System	

The Canadian health care system occupies primarily Cells A, B, and C, as does the American federal Medicare program and the federal-state Medicaid program. Systems falling into Cells B and C represent government-run health insurance, not socialized medicine, because the delivery system is largely in private hands. This distinction between socialized insurance and socialized medicine is often lost on American critics of foreign health care systems.

Germany's health care system is best described by Cells D, E, and F. Health insurance in Germany is provided by a structured system of not-for-profit sickness funds that are privately administered, albeit within a federal statute that tightly regulates their conduct. This statutory health insurance system has evolved gradually over the span of 100 years and now covers eighty-eight percent of the population. The remainder is covered by private, commercial insurers more akin to commercial insurers in the United States. On the other hand, Germany's health care delivery system is a mixture of private and public, for-profit and not-for-profit, providers that is similar to the mix of providers found in the United States. In other words, the German health care system also does not represent socialized medicine, but socialized insurance.

As noted above, parts of the American health system fall squarely into Cell A. Others fall into Cells A, B, and C. Together, Cells A through C accounted for about forty-four percent of national health care spending in 1991. The rest of the system, its private sector, is spread from Cells G to L. * * *

A. The Approaches Used in Canada and Europe

As noted, Canadians and Europeans typically view health care as a social good. In these countries, it is anathema to link an individual household's health care financing contribution to the health status of that household's members. Health care in these countries is collectively financed, with taxes or premiums based on the individual household's ability to pay. Only a small, well-to-do minority—so far, less than ten percent of the population—opts out of collective social insurance in favor of privately insured or privately financed health care. Nevertheless, nearly ninety percent of the population typically shares one common level of quality and amenities in health care.

Control of health care costs in these countries is exercised partly by controlling the physical capacity of the supply side. The chief instrument for this purpose is formal regional health planning. Planning enables policymakers to limit the number of hospital beds, big-ticket technology (such as CT scanners or lithotripters), and sometimes even the number of physicians who are issued billing numbers under these nations' health insurance systems.

However, regulatory limits on the capacity of the health care system inevitably create monopolies on the supply side. To make sure that these artificially created monopolies do not exploit their economic power, these countries generally couple health planning on the supply side with stiff price and budgetary controls imposed on the demand side. Sometimes, price controls alone are deemed sufficient to control overall health spending. However, where the intent of price controls has been thwarted through rapid increases in the volume of health services rendered, these countries have imposed strictly limited global budgets on the health care systems as a whole, or upon particular segments (e.g., hospitals and doctors). Canada, for example, has long compensated its hospitals through pre-set global budgets. Similarly, West Germany now operates strict, state-wide expenditure caps for all physicians who practice within a state under nation's Statutory Health Insurance system. The United Kingdom and the Nordic countries budget virtually their entire health systems.

To implement their price and budget controls, Canada and the European countries tend to structure their health insurance systems so that money flows from third-party payers to health care providers through only one or a few large money-pipes. The "money-pipe" throughput is then controlled through formal negotiations between regional or national associations of third-party payers and associations of providers. The negotiated prices in these countries are usually binding on providers, who may not bill patients for extra charges above these prices. Although France permits extra billing within limits, most of these countries perceive unrestrained extra billing as a violation of the spirit of health insurance.

Remarkably, and in sharp contrast with the United States, Canada and Europe typically do not look to the individual patient as an agent of cost control. Usually, there is no significant flow of money from patient to provider at the time health services are received. Instead, most of these countries provide patients with comprehensive, universal first-dollar coverage for a wide range of services, including drugs (Canada covers drugs only for the poor). France does have co-payments at the point of service for all ambulatory care and hospital care, but not for certain high-cost illnesses. Furthermore, many French patients have supplemental private insurance to cover any co-payments.

One should not assume that Canada and the European nations eclipse patients from cost control because these nations' health policy analysts and policymakers lack the savvy of their American colleagues. American debates on health policy tend to characterize patients as "consumers" who are expected to shop around for cost-effective health care. One suspects that Canadians and Europeans are inclined to perceive patients as, for the most part, "sick persons" who should be treated as such. * * * [T]he distribution of health expenditures across a population tends to be highly skewed. In the United States, for example, only five percent of the population accounts for about half of all national health expenditures in any given year, and ten percent account for about seventy percent. The distribution of health expenditures in other countries is apt to present a similar pattern.

One must wonder whether the few individuals who account for the bulk of health care expenditures in any given year can actually act like regular "consumers" who shop around for cost-effective health care. Although cost sharing by patients can be shown to have some constraining effect on utilization for mild to semi-serious illness, it is unlikely to play a major role in the serious cases that appear to account for the bulk of national health care expenditures.

Where price and ability to pay cannot ration health care, something else must. Usually, in Canada and Europe, that non-price rationing device is a queue for elective medical procedures. At the extreme, some high-tech medical interventions, such as renal dialysis or certain organ transplantations, are simply unavailable to particular patients if the attending physician judges the likely benefits of intervention to be low. High-tech innovations are introduced rather cautiously in these nations, and only after intensive benefit-cost analysis. Therefore, at any given time, these nations' health care systems are likely to lag behind that in the United States in the degree to which a new medical technology has been adopted.

Finally, the tight control on overall outlays for health care tends to preclude the often luxurious settings in which health care is dispensed to well-insured patients in the United States. Atriums and gourmet dining in hospitals, or physician offices with plush carpets, are not common in Canada or Europe.

* * *

III. The Economic Footprints of These Approaches

It is generally agreed, both here and abroad, that the American entrepreneurial approach to health care has begotten one of the most luxurious, dynamic, clinically and organizationally innovative, and technically sophisticated health care systems in the world. At its best, the system has few rivals anywhere, though many health care systems abroad also have facets of genuine excellence. At its worst, however, it has few rivals as well.

A. The Cost of Health Care

Unfortunately, but perfectly predictably, the open-ended supply side of the American health care system, coupled with a financing system that looks to sick human beings (patients) as major agents of cost control, has led to perennial excess capacity in most parts of the country, and to large and rapidly growing costs. * * *

* * *

C. Styles of Rationing

The myth that, unlike other nations, America does not ration health care is just that, a myth. Americans do ration health care by price and ability to pay, sometimes in rather disturbing ways. Nations differ from one another not in whether they ration health care—all of them do somehow and in varying degrees—but in their style of rationing and their definition of that very term.

One rationing style is to limit physical capacity and use triage, based on medical judgment and the queue, to determine the allocation of artificially scarce resources among the population. That style of rationing is sometimes referred to as implicit rationing. The other style is to ration explicitly by price and ability to pay. It is the natural by-product of the so-called "market approach" to health care.

Implicit rationing predominates outside of the United States. In principle, the approach is thought to allocate health care strictly on the basis of medical need, as perceived and ranked by physicians. It is not known whether other variables, such as the patient's social status, ultimately enter the allocation decision as well. * * *

Many Americans believe that health care is not currently rationed in the United States. That belief seems warranted for well-insured patients who are covered by traditional, open-ended indemnity insurance and living in areas with excess capacity. For many of these patients, there seems to be virtually no limit to the use of real resources in attempts to preserve life or gain certainty in diagnosis.

On the other hand, persons who are less well-insured, uninsured, or covered by managed-care plans (including HMOs) do occasionally experience the withholding of health care resources strictly for economic reasons. In fact, in a recent cross-national survey, some 7.5 percent of the American respondents (the equivalent of eighteen million Americans) claimed that they had been denied health care for financial reasons. In Canada and the United Kingdom, fewer than one percent of the survey respondents made that claim.

Remarkably, the defenders of the American system, who are typically also vehement detractors of all foreign health systems, generally define rationing as only the withholding of health care from people who would have been able and willing to pay for such care with their own money. It is the nightmare of the well-to-do. Apparently, denial of health care to needy, uninsured patients who are unable to pay for that care is not viewed as rationing by these commentators because they have long countenanced it. How else can one explain these commentators' warnings that health care in, for example, the Canadian model would lead to rationing of health care, as if no American were ever denied needed or wanted health care?

* * *

IV. The Convergence of Health Care Systems

If one wished to paint with a very broad brush the evolution of health care policy during the past four decades in the industrialized world, one might describe it as a gradual shift from expenditure-driven financing of health care to budget-driven delivery of health care.

Under expenditure-driven financing, health care providers were allowed to do for patients whatever they saw fit and send the rest of society a bill at prices that seemed "reasonable." Typically, those presented with that bill paid without reservation. If they had reservations, they paid the bill nevertheless because they lacked the countervailing power present in normal markets without third-party payment. Naturally, under this open-ended approach, the supply side of the health sector became a rich economic frontier that attracted both the genius of private entrepreneurship and its relentless search for revenues.

Technological innovation flourished under this approach as the health sector stood an old adage on its head: instead of necessity being the mother of invention, invention became the mother of necessity. Once a technological innovation was at hand, its application was quickly deemed a "medical necessity" as long as it promised any additional benefits at all to the patient. * * *

Under the second approach, budget-driven health care delivery, society establishes some sort of prospective budget for health care and tells providers to do the best they can within that budget. Typically, the establishment of the overall budget has been rather arbitrary in practice, in the sense that the budget is tied to some arbitrary criterion—such as a fixed percentage of the GNP or a fixed annual growth rate. Ideally, this approach should lead policymakers to explore what additional benefits might be gained through incremental budget expansions, and to set the ultimate budget limits accordingly. In any event, however, the application of new medical technologies in this world will typically be subjected to rigorous benefit-cost analysis before payment for such technologies will be made out of the fixed budget. Merely demonstrating promised benefits is no longer sufficient and will not be accepted by those who would stand to lose from applications of novel technology within the given budget constraints.

As noted earlier, most of the industrialized world has already gone a long way toward budget-driven health care delivery, some (England and Sweden, for example) completely. The United States is the odd one out because it is only just beginning to move in that direction. * * *

* * *

At this time, the contrast between the current Canadian/European approach to resource allocation in health care and this newly emerging American approach is stark. Canadians and Europeans still appear to believe that the best way to control overall health spending is to: (1) constrain the physical capacity of the health system, (2) control prices, and, for good measure, (3) impose something as close as possible to global monetary budgets on the entire system. Within these constraints, however, they allow doctors and their patients considerable clinical freedom. In this way, the system will tend to maximize the benefits that are wrung out of the constrained set of real and financial resources. In other words, there is considerable trust in the medical establishment's willingness and ability to use the resources made available to it properly, without the need for day-to-day supervision. Direct comanaging of an ongoing patient-doctor relationship in the American model is still rather rare in Canada and Europe.

In contrast, the American proponents of managed competition believe that, by paying for everything that is beneficial, but denying payment for everything else, the nation can avoid setting an arbitrary global budget and will, in the end, devote the "right" percentage of GNP to health care. These proponents have considerable faith in the ability of ordinary consumers to choose wisely among the alternative cost-quality combinations that competing managed-care systems in the health care market offer. On the other hand, they have little faith in the ability or willingness of the individual physician to use scarce resources wisely in the treatment of patients; therefore, they would subject each doctor to constant statistical monitoring and hands-on supervision.

* * *

Notes

1. Uwe Reinhardt is one of the best known American health economists, though not perhaps the most conventional. Dr. Reinhardt was born and raised in Germany, and lived in Canada before moving to the United States. It is not surprising, therefore, that he sees the American health care system in a comparative perspective. This article was written in the context of the American debate on the Clinton health plan proposal in the early 1990s, so the data are somewhat dated. The issues, however, remain very current.

2. One striking impression that emerges from comparative health policy studies is the difference in the perspective of most American health economists and that of most health economists from other countries. Although Americans represent a wide range of interests and approaches, most begin with the position that market competition is good for society and government interference in markets—be it through regulation, tax subsidies, or social welfare programs—is on the whole not. Professor Reinhardt is in fact atypical in the extent to which he accepts government intervention in health care markets. More typical would be Mark Pauly (*Health Benefits at Work: An Economic and Political Analysis of Employment-based Health Insurance*, 1997); John Cogan, R. Glenn Hubbard, and Daniel Kessler (*Healthy, Wealthy, and Wise: Five Steps to a Better Health Care System*, 2005); or John Goodman, Gerald Musgrave and Devon Herrick (*Lives at Risk: Single-Payer National Health Insurance Around the World*, 2004). British, Canadian, and most continental European health economists, on the other hand, are more likely to accept (even embrace) an active government role in health care purchasing or provision. See, e.g. Robert Evans, The Fiscal Sustainability of Health Care in Canada, in *The Romanow Papers, Volume 1*, GP Marchildon, et al., eds., pp. 139–196 (2004). They are also more interested in making government programs work efficiently than in abolishing them. See, e.g. Cam Donaldson, et al., *Economics of Health Care Financing: The Visible Hand* (2004); Adam Oliver, The English National Health Service: 1979–2005, 14 *Health Econ.* S75 (2005).

Economic explanations of legal phenomena have been very influential in American legal scholarship over the past two decades. Other factors, however, such as politics and culture should not be ignored in understanding legal systems. The following excerpt of an article written by a prominent Canadian political scientist analyzes developments in the United States, Canada, and Britain from a political perspective:

Dynamics of a Changing Health Sphere: The United States, Britain, and Canada

Carolyn Hughes Tuohy, 18 Health Affairs 114, 115–16,118–120,129–131 (May/June 1999)

* * *

Framework for Analysis

This paper highlights two key dimensions of the decision-making system. The first relates to the balance of influence across key components of the politicoeconomic structure of interests—state actors, private finance, and health care professionals (principally the medical profession)—representing the key bases of power in the arena: authority, wealth, and skill, respectively. The second relates to the mix of mechanisms of social control that systematize and legitimize the relationships among these actors. In health care such mechanisms are typically threefold: the market, based on voluntary exchange; hierarchy, based on obedience to rules within a chain of command; and collegiality, based on subscription to a set of norms of behavior derived from a common knowledge base.

Different balances of influence imply the predominance of different lines of accountability. State actors, private financial interests, and professionals derive their influence from different sources and, accordingly, respond to different demands. In very broad terms, state actors function within systems in which those in command ultimately are dependent upon political support and therefore seek to accommodate a range of interests and opinions sufficient to maintain a coalition of support. Actors whose influence is based on access to private finance must respond to the demands of owners of private capital to realize rates of return comparable with those in other areas of investment. And professionals, who derive their influence from membership in the professional group, must maintain standing in the group by continuing to meet its evolving standards and norms.

* * *

The Distinctive Logic of the Three Systems

* * *

Britain's largely state financed system was founded upon an "implicit bargain" between the state and the medical profession under which the profession retained clinical autonomy to allocate resources within budgetary parameters established by the state. Collegial mechanisms of decision making were incorporated within structures of "hierarchical corporatism." The distinctive blend of hierarchy and collegiality that constituted NHS-style corporatism comprised two fundamental elements. First, it involved defined spheres of authority based on functional expertise, creating a set of parallel authority structures—some hierarchical, some collegial. Second, it brought these spheres together in hierarchical structures of "consensus management," which gave effective veto powers to the key functional groups (most notably, physicians) at each level of the hierarchy. These essential features persisted through two major NHS reorganizations, in 1974 and again in 1982.

Expectations regarding the roles of the various participants within these structures were fairly clear. Doctors, both general practitioners (GPs) and specialists, were to exercise their clinical judgment as independent professionals. GPs contracted independently with local "executive councils" and later with family practitioner committees to provide services on a modified capitation basis. Hospital consultants were salaried employees of the NHS, but their employment contracts were regional, not at the level of the operational unit (the hospital) in which they practiced. Consultants did not "report," then, to local managers, but rather formed self-governing, hospital-based medical staffs. Professional networks, not administrative rules, determined referral patterns from the "gatekeeper" GPs to the specialist consultants. Nurses performed within a hospital-based functional hierarchy dominated by the hospital matron. Here the administrative manager played the role of "diplomat" mediating across the various functional NHS authority centers and was always seen as being in service to, not in authority over, clinicians. Even when "general management" structures replaced "consensus management" following the Griffiths Report of 1983, these relationships remained essentially unchanged.

In Canada, more than perhaps any other nation in the late twentieth century, the health care system functioned according to the logic of an accommodation between the medical profession and the state. It was, in economic terms, the logic of an agency relationship in a bilateral monopoly. Under the terms of Canadian Medicare, provincial governments were the "single payers" for most medical and hospital services within a framework established by federal legislation: A single government plan in each province covered a comprehensive range of medical and hospital services, and no private insurance alternatives existed for coverage of those services. But provincial governments exercised their monopsony power in very gross terms. Decisions about the allocation of resources were made through negotiations with the monopoly providers of services, particularly with the medical profession. Those negotiating relationships left great discretion in the hands of the organized profession to govern the behavior of its members. The collegial mechanisms that permeated the system before Medicare, including independently constituted hospital medical staffs, were left in place. Medicare, moreover, was established on generous terms: The state provided universal coverage of medical and hospital services by essentially underwriting the costs of an existing system based on independent fee-for-service (FFS) medical practice and voluntary hospitals. * * *

As in Britain, the state developed a "second-level" agency relationship with the profession, which acknowledged the primacy of professional judgment in making decisions about the allocation of resources at the level of the clinical case, the professional practice, and the institution, within overall budgetary parameters established by the state. In Canada, however, because the state was a monopsonist but not an employer or even a contractor, the profession enjoyed even more formal autonomy. Medical fee schedules were negotiated at the provincial level between governments and medical associations. In all provinces but one these negotiations concerned only the aggregate percentage level of increase in fees, leaving the value of individual items in the schedule to be determined by the association itself. * * *

These arrangements made sense for both sides. The profession retained broad clinical autonomy and influence over the system as a whole, and the state kept budgetary control without incurring the transaction costs (or developing the capacity) to manage a very diffuse system. Furthermore, this accommodation retained the structures of health care delivery—private medical practices, free choice of physicians—to which Canadians were long accustomed and that were features of an extraordinarily popular system.

* * *

[The author proceeds to describe the health care system of the United States, and then discusses developments in all three systems during the 1990s.]

Lessons Drawn From the Three Systems

A review of the experience of the health care arenas of the United States, Britain, and Canada in the 1990s gives credence to the argument that each health care decision-making system has its own powerful logic, born of the intersection between the balance of influence and the mix of instruments in the system—a logic with particular implications for the pattern and the pace of change. In Britain the internal-market initiative [introduced by Margaret Thatcher in the 1990s] constituted an attempt to introduce a model with very high information costs (as necessary for writing specific contracts between independent units where various contingencies were possible) into a system with well-developed hierarchical and collegial networks for the exchange of information as deemed necessary. Within a budget-limited system, it is not surprising that actors would seek to economize on information costs by continuing to rely on established networks and relationships. Although the internal-market reforms of the NHS did bring about substantial change in the decision-making system, that change amounted largely to the introduction of explicit bargaining relationships between organized bodies of purchasers and providers—a form of voluntary exchange, but far from a competitive market.

In the United States the increasing price-consciousness of purchasers—which occurred somewhat later in the diffuse and heterogeneous U.S. mixed-market system than in state-financed systems in which costs were concentrated—ultimately limited the potential for cost shifting, required providers to minimize costs per case, broke the "alignment of incentives" between providers as professionals and providers as entrepreneurs, and led to the rise of for-profit, investor-owned entities in the entrepreneurial role. And in Canada provincial-level accommodations between the medical profession and the state that had served the purposes of both sides for two decades—affording physicians a high degree of individual and collective autonomy and allowing governments to maintain a highly popular system and to exercise broad budgetary control—persisted uneasily through the 1990s, even as they were threatened by the progressive tightening of their fiscal underpinnings.

These individual system logics are enlightening, and they remind us that the dynamics of systems need to be understood on their own terms. But two-way comparisons of these three cases also can generate some more generalizable propositions. Consider first the Canada/U.S. comparison. Two systems, almost identical in the 1960s, were set on different paths when Canada adopted universal hospital and medical care insurance and the United States adopted a program confined to the elderly and the poor. In particular, the collegial mechanisms that had permeated both systems prior to the adoption of governmental health insurance fared very differently. These mechanisms were elaborated in Canada as vehicles of profession/state collaboration but were supplanted in the United States by increasingly explicit forms of contracting (and, in some cases, hierarchical integration) with the rise of private MCOs.

The suggestion of this comparison—that collegial mechanisms and medical influence are better preserved in the context of a profession-state accommodation than in private markets—is reinforced by a comparison of Britain and Canada. Both of those nations, despite the very different organization of their publicly financed systems, were characterized by an "implicit bargain," a "second-level agency relationship" between the state and the medical profession with broadly similar terms: The state established broad budgetary parameters, and physicians were free to exercise clinical judgment in the allocation of resources within those parameters.

Finally, a comparison between Britain and the United States throws light on the implications of the "state/market" distinction in health care. The import of this paper has been to argue that "state" and "market" belong in fact to different dimensions of decision-making systems: The state is a set of actors; the market is a set of instruments. Placing "market-oriented" contracting instruments in the hands of state actors in Britain did not change those actors' lines of accountability. This meant that partisan and electoral considerations brought about direct political intervention. Even more importantly, it meant that the implementation of the reforms had to respect the need for state actors to maintain coalitions of support—coalitions that accorded a central role for the medical profession. In the United States, in contrast, private entrepreneurs in for-profit enterprises had to meet the demands of highly mobile investors for competitive rates of return, and their behavior drove the competitive dynamic of the system.

These differences between systems of public and private finance have at least two important corollaries. First, they explain the central role for the medical profession and for collegial mechanisms that is observed in systems of public finance. The foundational bargain between the state and the medical profession that characterizes systems of public finance can be seen as a logical component of such systems: An accommodation with the medical profession has been a significant component of the political coalitions of support that characterize state-financed systems.

A second implication of the fundamental difference between systems of public and private finance concerns the pace of change. The ease of exit for private investors, their quest for more profitable forms of organization in which to invest, and their attraction to entities that can demonstrate growth and expanding market share have driven rapid and volatile change in the industrial structure of health care delivery and financing in the United States and have given rise to a range of organizational innovation that is without parallel in systems dominated by public finance. In contrast, the need to maintain coalitions of political support moderated the pace and nature of change initiated by state actors in Britain and kept the basic features of the Canadian system remarkably constant, in an international perspective.

Notes

1. These themes are explored further in the Tuohy's book, *Accidental Logics* (1999).

2. Politics is always an important consideration in health care policy. Political considerations, for example, undoubtedly explain the difficulty that the United States has had with expanding health insurance coverage to the uninsured. The fear of socialism undoubtedly contributed to the extension of health coverage to workers in central Europe in the nineteenth century, while the triumph of socialism explains the creation of national health insurance systems in the middle of the twentieth. Politics, as Tuohy illustrates, involves not only national politics, but also politics within and among the professions, and between the professions and the state. See, further exploring these themes: Special Issue, Legacies and Latitude in European Health Policy, 30 *J. Health Pol., Pol'y & L.* Nos. 1 & 2 (2005); *Health Professions and the State in Europe* (Terry Johnson, Gerry Larkin, and Mike Saks, eds, 1995); David Wilsford, *Doctors and the State: The Politics of Health Care in France and the United States* (1991); and *Controlling Medical Professionals: The Comparative Politics of Health Governance* (George Freddi and James W. Bjorkman, eds., 1989). Though political positions often are based on economic considerations, they also often reflect cultural influences as well. The next excerpt discusses these considerations, which are explored later in the book as well.

The Empire of Death: How Culture and Economics Affect Informed Consent in the U.S., the U.K., and Japan

George J. Annas & Frances H. Miller 20 Am. J. L. & Med. 357, 360–62, 377–81, 387–90 (1994)

* * *

II. Culture and Medical Science

The definition of good medical care varies enormously from country to country. For example, German and French physicians for decades routinely prescribed government-financed "spa cures" for their patients. Such therapy choices would invite professional scorn, not to mention malpractice litigation, and would not be covered by insurance if prescribed by U.S. doctors. The international medical community often disagrees significantly about appropriate diagnosis and treatment. Most physicians are relatively ignorant, if not openly skeptical, about scientific findings reported from foreign countries.

At a more fundamental level, medical experts often frankly disagree about what constitutes disease. Many physical states defined and treated as worthy of medical intervention in the U.S., such as moderately elevated blood pressure, are considered unremarkable variations of the human condition elsewhere in the world. By way of contrast, low blood pressure is treated as a medical disorder in Germany while at the same time it is welcomed as a longevity indicator in both the U.S. and the U.K. American travelers becoming ill in foreign countries are often surprised to learn that 98.6° is not necessarily the gold standard for normal body temperature, notwithstanding what they have been led since childhood to believe. Far from being an "exact" science with commonly acknowledged definitional, diagnostic, and treatment principles, scientific uncertainty permeates medicine.

Professional cultural values also both overtly and subliminally prejudice medical practice, as do the cultural values imbedded in the particular society in which physicians practice their skills. Moreover, patients have culturally influenced attitudes of their own that affect their willingness to accept—as well as their response to receiving—medical therapy. * * *

The U.S. public has always been culturally predisposed toward action in the face of threatened adversity, medical or otherwise. Lynn Payer's masterful book *Medicine & Culture* * * * links the aggressive American approach toward medicine to the frontier spirit, and to Americans' deeply ingrained belief that "the main purpose of a man's life is to solve problems." For decades Americans have tolerated—if not encouraged—the delivery of superfluous medical services under the rubric of medical necessity, financed by cost-pass-through health insurance. * * *

Cost containment pressures are bringing home the lesson that medical necessity is actually a fluid notion, continually reconceived as scientific understanding, payment incentives, and culture evolve. Containing costs necessarily implies setting limits on health care expenditures, and cultural values are critical to determining where those limits will lie. * * *

[The authors use the example of informed consent doctrine to illustrate their theme of cultural differences, describing first the situation in the United States, where patient-centered informed consent is accepted in theory, if not always in practice; then the United Kingdom, where, as is demonstrated in chapter 2, medical custom dictates the extent of disclosure in informed consent cases; and Japan (also discussed in chapter 2), where doctors have until recently resisted disclosing information to their patients and often sought consent from the patient's family.]

IV. Culture, Choice and Health Resource Allocation

Patient knowledge advances personal autonomy; it elevates consent to medical treatment from a flak jacket merely protecting doctors from battery liability to an enhancement of patient sovereignty. * * * [N]ot all cultures place the same value on truth-telling and on an individual's ability to make fully informed choices, nor do they share the same fear of death. Informed consent legal doctrine reflects and shapes societal value choices, and thus it varies from country to country, and from time to time within countries.

* * *

Different cultures take differing official approaches to health resource allocation. Some countries rely primarily on governmental price and spending controls that affect everything from technology acquisition to hospital and physician reimbursement rates. For example, in the circumstances of tightly managed supply that exist in the U.K., primary care physicians assume powerful gatekeeping functions. These general practitioners must filter patient demand for medical services from clinical "need" for limited specialist and high technology care. This filter entails correspondingly narrower scope for individual choice. When medical choice is constrained by supply limitations, telling patients about potentially beneficial but economically unattainable therapy can be criticized as inhumane. However, such disclosure can also mobilize public opinion to challenge resource allocation inconsistent with societal values.

* * *

In countries officially dependent on gatekeeping like the U.K., informed consent doctrine not unsurprisingly favors professional rather than patient-oriented standards of disclosure, particularly with regard to treatment alternatives. Other cultures—most prominently the U.S.—prefer to let a more entrepreneurial market set the basic dimensions for health sector investment. U.S. informed consent law generally reflects support for market allocation mechanisms, and thus tends to expand the possibilities for patient choice through more thoroughgoing informed consent requirements.

But how can we explain Japan, where physicians are highly entrepreneurial and most hospitals and all clinics are privately owned, yet where the law supports keeping patients in the dark about diagnoses of serious illness? First, Japan does not impose the same budgetary controls that cap total health care spending in the U.K., although it regulates physician fees tightly and capped the number of hospital beds in 1985. It is dangerous for outsiders to generalize about any society, but cultural analysts from both Japan and America agree that in Japan individuality is deemed subservient to group needs and ideals. As a consequence, the proper role of the patient is to follow the instructions of the physician, who presumably has a superior understanding of the patient's illness and its significance.

Regardless of official government policy concerning health sector resource allocation, more or less flexibility concerning that policy usually exists within any society in practice. This flexibility is strongly influenced by the general cultural attitude toward death, and by what patients, health policy experts, and financiers actually know or believe about the availability and efficacy of medical services. * * *

* * *

Any country's health policy must continuously grapple with economic scarcity and with scientific, political, and cultural change. The successes and failures of other systems can be illuminating, but cultural attitudes toward medical information and other medical issues as well must be unearthed and understood if reform imported from other countries can succeed in new environments. Of course, societies and medical practitioners must grapple with the role of malpractice litigation in setting standards of care.

Customary medical practice, the standard against which a doctor's conduct is usually measured in a medical malpractice action, reflects the way resources are spent on care for individual patients in every culture. Since patients rarely refuse their doctors' recommendations for therapy, physician treatment preferences strongly influence the way societies allocate total health resources. But the concept of customary medical practice defies precise definition. What doctors actually do develops gradually over time as physicians adapt treatment to scientific advance, economic rewards and penalties, and more generalized legal and cultural incentives, especially a society's attitude toward death. * * *

* * *

V. Culture and Death

* * *

Ultimately a culture's view of death, and the role of medicine in preventing or postponing it, is at work when unpleasant or uncertain medical facts are not communicated to patients. In the U.S., for example, we usually seem to accept that prolonging life (at virtually any price) is a reasonable goal for medicine. Thus, procedures are introduced and utilized that offer hope of extending life without regard to cost, or even to the quality of the life prolonged. * * *

Our seemingly automatic use of technology to protract the dying process has spawned development of a clearly articulated legal right to refuse treatment. More than fifty state appeals court decisions and an opinion of the U.S. Supreme Court have affirmed this patient prerogative. In a country where still no right of access to basic health services exists, and where the major problem for approximately forty million Americans is obtaining any medical care outside hospital emergency departments, the development of such a right seems remarkable. The rallying cry of U.S. medical ethics has been focused more on the "right to die" than on the right to health care. We continue to debate physician-assisted suicide and euthanasia far more passionately than we debate the appropriate minimum benefit package. Americans rightly fear that doctors often ignore their wishes to refuse treatment, and to have proper medication for pain control near the end of life. Physician surveys consistently indicate that doctors routinely ignore patient wishes to end treatment, undermedicate for pain, and continue to see death as professional failure.

* * *

In countries like Japan and the U.K., which do not spend inordinate amounts of money on health care at the end of life, failure to discuss prognosis seems to be societally acceptable because death is not viewed as professional defeat. It is accepted as both natural and necessary by physicians and their patients alike. As Rihito Kamura has explained of Japan, "Death is an integral part of the Japanese cultural tradition. Most Japanese people resist the modern, technological death in which machines can supplant important rituals surrounding death and dying." Because members of these relatively more homogeneous societies share common perceptions about how much medical intervention is appropriate at the end of life, comprehensive discussion of treatment alternatives between doctor and patient seems less necessary.

In the more pluralistic U.S. society, however, there is less social consensus on the role of medicine toward the end of life, and physician biases toward more aggressive treatment may offend the value systems of many Americans. These people are going to great lengths, such as executing living wills, petitioning courts to terminate treatment, and committing suicide, to assert that merely prolonging the dying process is unacceptable to them.

* * *

Note

This text raises themes that will recur throughout this book. One of these is the tension between paternalism and autonomy. Whether a doctor decides what medical care a patient needs in his or her patient's best interest or the patient is able to choose what care he or she wants is to a considerable degree culturally determined. The choices that either or both may make are also influenced by cultural factors. The relationship between the individual and society, which in turn may influence the health care resources available to any individual, is also a cultural artifact. Perceptions of life, death, and even of tolerable pain, are also affected by culture. All of these factors are in turn reflected in the laws of particular jurisdictions. It is to law that we now again turn.

E. The Role of Legal Institutions in the Allocation and Rationing of Health Care Resources

As noted above, virtually all of the world's nations have acknowledged the existence of some sort of a right to health by establishing public systems for health care finance or provision. These systems are established by legislation. While this legislation establishes the framework for the administration of health care systems, questions often arise that require decisions applying or interpreting the law. These involve, for example, questions of eligibility, coverage of technologies or services, and payment amounts. In many instances these decisions are reviewable—by administrative review bodies, by the courts, or by international tribunals. The two readings that follow examine the role of legal institutions in determining what services get covered by public health programs.

Health Care Coverage Determinations: An International Comparative Study

Timothy Stoltzfus Jost ed., pp. 240–44, 251–53 (2005).

* * *

The answer to the question of who has standing to initiate a [technology] assessment [for determining coverage by public insurance programs] varies from country to country. In those countries where technology assessment is a necessary prerequisite to coverage, technology manufacturers or other sponsors usually have the opportunity to apply for coverage. This is true in the United States, Switzerland, Australia, and the Netherlands. Indeed, in the Netherlands, only manufactures have standing to request coverage. In Spain, Canada, the US, Australia, and England, requests for appraisals can come from other sources as well, including patients, providers or insurers. * * *

In Germany and Switzerland (and in Ontario, Canada, as to medical procedures), however, the corporatist institutions serve as gatekeepers to the technology assessment process. In Germany, a new technology cannot be covered out of hospital without a coverage determination, and the determination process can only be initiated by the sickness [health insurance] funds or by the insurance doctor's organizations. In Switzerland, by contrast, a new technology will be covered unless the application for coverage is contested by either the insurance fund or medical association. * * *

In most of our countries coverage determinations are usually reactive—appraisal bodies respond to a request for an assessment. Only in a few places, England, some of the Spanish regions, and to some extent in the US, is "horizon scanning" conducted proactively to identify new technologies that merit assessment.

The procedures followed by the various appraisal groups vary from highly structured to quite informal. The US Medicare process, for example, is a multistage process with time limits (not always strictly observed) at each step. * * *. The Australian MSAC [Medical Services Advisory Committee] and Spanish regional committee processes, by contrast, appear quite flexible. Most countries contemplate a multistep process, that usually involves a screening process to make sure the application is complete, review of the application by commission staff, review and recommendation by an expert committee, and preliminary and final coverage determinations. The process also sometimes involves the commissioning or acquisition of an external technology assessment. Provision may be made during the process for comments by the technology sponsor, or, in a few instances, as in the US or England, by the public.

* * *

Coverage processes in general seem to be investigational as opposed to adversarial in nature. An attempt is made, that is, to assess scientifically the proposed technology without a predisposition toward coverage or noncoverage, rather than requiring the proponent of a technology to meet a particular burden of proof in the face of opposition from a party contesting coverage. In some countries, notably Australia, the procedure is viewed as somewhat more adversarial, though the process is described in our Australian chapter as really more a process of bargaining.

Opportunities for appeal vary from country to country. The United States is most generous, offering several paths for appeal, and allowing challenges to the substance of coverage decisions, and not just to the procedures through which they were formulated. In Germany appeals to the Ministry are only available for procedural errors, while in the Netherlands an appeal can only be brought if there is new information with respect to the therapeutic value of the drug. Appeals in England are available only if NICE [the National Institute for Clinical Excellence] failed to act fairly or in accordance with its own procedures, the decision is perverse, or NICE exceeded its powers. Patients who are denied services in Ontario, or who face extraordinarily long waits, can appeal to an independent tribunal, the Health Services Appeal and Review Board.

In most countries coverage denials can be contested in court. In some countries these challenges can be brought by the applicant denied coverage, but in most countries a patient who needs a product or service has the right to appeal a coverage denial as well. In Germany and Switzerland cases involving coverage are quite common, though in Switzerland they rarely involve new technologies. In Australia and the Netherlands such litigation is apparently unusual and rarely successful. In the US Medicare system, appeals of individual technology coverage decisions are very common, but there are many layers of administrative review through which an appeal must wend its way before it judicial review becomes available, and thus judicial review is quite uncommon. There is no appellate review of the decisions of the Spanish regional technology assessment bodies. Even when formal judicial processes for appeal are not available, however, technology sponsors may still find a way to challenge a decision in court, as is demonstrated in the Canadian situation where Bristol-Myers Squibb sued (unsuccessfully) to block release of a report from the Canadian Coordinating Office for Health Technology Assessment arguing "negligent misstatement".

On the whole, the processes reviewed here are not very transparent. The most transparent is the American system, where assessment processes are tracked at each stage on the web, and opportunities for public comment are offered at several stages. England also seems to be moving toward a more transparent process, though comments are only accepted from invited participants in the process, who are often interested parties, such as technology sponsors, providers, or patient groups. By contrast, the German, Dutch, and Swiss processes take place largely behind closed doors. Reports are published, and comments are accepted at points in the process, but the decision making processes are not visible to the public. If anyone has access to information regarding an assessment process, it is usually the proponent. In Australia, the proponent of a technology, and only the proponent, has the right to comment on draft assessment papers. Similarly in Switzerland, only the applicant receives a written summary of the reasons supporting the Federal Department of Home Affairs coverage decision.

* * *

Most countries base coverage decisions on the criteria of efficacy, effectiveness, and medical necessity. These terms may be defined comparatively; i.e. a product or service may only be approved for coverage if it is as or more effective than existing technologies. In several countries there is a conscious effort to avoid the appearance of rationing, however, and all effective technologies will be covered. The authors of our German report, for example, report the findings of their own research which demonstrates that only effectiveness, and not cost, is considered in the German process. The United States has also been reluctant to embrace cost as a concern in coverage policy, though more expensive technologies get closer attention than less expensive technologies.

In some countries, however, there is more openness to consideration of economic concerns. This is clearly true in Australia, and will soon be true in the Netherlands. Even in Australia, however, imatinib (or GLIVEC® or GLEEVAC®) has been covered despite its high cost per case and a comparatively high cost-effectiveness ratio because it was the only drug available for treating CML [chronic myeloid leukemia] for some patients, * * * NICE in England also takes cost per QALY [quality-adjusted life year] into account in making coverage policy, though the experience in imatinib in England also demonstrates that cost is far from the only consideration taken into account in approving technologies for coverage. The purpose of a drug and distributional concerns are also important. * * *

* * *

When we look for overall lessons that can be drawn, then, from our comparative study of institutions and procedures and of how they have dealt with specific technologies, several emerge. First, despite widespread fears that technology assessment will lead to rationing, most countries still focus primarily on questions of effectiveness rather than on cost considerations. Only in Australia and England does cost seem to play a major and explicit role in making coverage determinations. Moreover, in England NICE only has authority to require coverage, its jurisdiction with respect to noncoverage decisions is strictly advisory, thus primary care trusts [which purchase health care in England] may be required to cover cost-effective technologies, but are not barred from covering technologies that are not cost effective. The drug approval process in the Netherlands is moving toward consideration of cost-effectiveness data, but it is not there yet, * * * Coverage evaluation in other countries focuses on effectiveness, or at most, on effectiveness in comparison to existing technologies.

Moreover, coverage assessment organizations seem quite willing to approve coverage for life-threatening, or even serious non-life-threatening, conditions, when there is some evidence of effectiveness of a breakthrough technology and no other technology adequate to treating the condition is otherwise available, as our case studies of imatinib and HBOT [hyperbaric oxygen therapy] demonstrate. The "rule of rescue" still plays a major role in technology approval. Finally, political considerations independent of science, can play a role in coverage processes, as is demonstrated by the Swiss experience with in vitro fertilisation.

Second, each of the technologies that were the subjects of our case studies are approved only for limited, specific indications. In some programs, like the US, technologies are also explicitly not covered for other specific indications. In other countries, technologies are implicitly not covered for indications for which they are not explicitly covered. Because technologies are only covered for particular indications, and sometimes when provided in particular settings by particular providers, however, coverage determination based on HTA [health technology assessment], which was supposed to result in macro-rationing, has in fact become micro-rationing. Coverage policy decisions often, that is, increasingly take the form of cost-effectiveness guidelines that resemble practice guidelines, rather than up or down determinations of what a public insurer will pay for.

Third, partial coverage tends to expand over time. Technology proponents denied tend to return with applications for coverage for additional indications, and thus coverage tends to expand to new indications. * * * Moreover, in several of our countries coverage expansion can take place de facto, without explicit approval, through doctor prescribing outside of approved indications, or through the use of existing codes to cover new technologies, albeit at a reduced price. In the end coverage assessment often has the effect of delaying rather than ultimately denying coverage.

Fourth, lack of hard scientific coverage does not necessarily block coverage expansion (but different countries reach different results). Indeed, on the whole, the results of the technology assessments from the various countries were quite consistent. The responses of the coverage assessment organizations, however, were not. * * * The fact that different countries reach different conclusions based on the same evidence suggests, of course, that the process is not wholly driven by scientific evidence, or, at least, that where evidence is open to varying interpretations, different countries place different weight of various aspects of that evidence reflecting different values.

Of course, in each of our countries coverage has also continued for existing technologies despite lack of hard scientific evidence supporting effectiveness. It is always easier to block expansion of coverage to new technologies than to remove existing technologies from coverage, a phenomena referred to by our Canadian authors as the "stickiness" of coverage.

Fifth, where agency procedures afford opportunity for public participation in the process, participants uniformly press for coverage. Where outsiders are permitted to apply for coverage, applications usually come from technology manufacturers, groups of providers or professionals who offer a new technology in their institutions or practices, or patient groups. When public hearings are held or public comments are solicited regarding technologies under consideration for coverage, these are also the groups that testify and comment. * * *

It is rare, on the other hand, that pressure is brought directly to bear on assessment agencies opposing coverage of any particular technology. Cost is, of course, a major consideration affecting all public insurance systems, and coverage organizations cannot help but be aware of it. Also, competitors may on occasion show up to contest exclusive coverage of one product to the exclusion of their products. * * * But except in rare instances, pressure is rarely directed at any particular product. * * *

* * *

What Is In and Out of Medicare? Who Decides?

Colleen Flood, Mark Stabile, and Carolyn Tuohy,
in Colleen Flood, ed., Just Medicare, pp. 15, 16–17, 23–30 (2005)

* * *

A Decision-Making Framework Grounded in the Canadian System

There have been many models put forward to guide decision-making about what should and should not be publicly funded both in Canada and internationally. However, these theoretical models have not been implemented in Canada or particularly successfully in any jurisdiction. In our view they suffer from being too general, too abstract, and divorced from messy local details. In particular, the existing models fail to take into account the political economy of particular systems. In any system of decision-making, considerations of values, resources, and information about costs and benefits are filtered through local structures and processes. As we discuss further below, in Canada, these structures and processes are characterized by accidents of history and by long-held accommodations between governments and the medical profession, inflexible and inadequate regulations and law, and the interaction of different stakeholders and interest groups.

Thus, before we can theorize about what processes and principles should be adopted we must understand how decisions are made now. The existing system will constrain what reforms are possible. For example, starting from the top, the overarching normative framework that governs it, the *Canada Health Act* (CHA), drives decision-making about what is in and what is out of Canadian Medicare. The CHA requires that provinces publicly fund all "medically necessary" hospital services and "medically required" physician services in order to receive federal funding. But, the CHA does not provide definitions of "medically necessary" or "medically required." Nor, in turn, does provincial legislation provide such definitions. How, then, do provinces determine which particular health care services to fund?

* * *

[The authors proceed to describe the role of the Physician Services Committee, a joint committee of the Ontario government and the Ontario Medical Association, which, among other things, recommends the listing and delisting of services to meet financial targets in Ontario, and of the medical directors of the provincial ministries of health, who decide which services to cover. They then proceed to discuss review of these decisions.]

The Health Services Appeal and Review Board

* * * [I]n most provinces, the only recourse from a decision not to fund a particular treatment or service is to seek relief in the general courts, either through judicial review or through a *Charter* challenge. Some relief may be obtained from appeal to an Ombudsman in the case of decisions made by the government or government-owned institutions (i.e., some psychiatric hospitals). The Ombudsman, however, intervenes as a last recourse; complainants have to first use all other complaints processes or means of appeal available to them before the Ombudsman will conduct an investigation. Quebec has a more generous system in that there is a Patient Ombudsman, charged with specifically investigating health complaints.

Three provinces (Ontario, Alberta, and British Columbia) have administrative tribunals to which the citizens thereof can bring (on limited grounds) an application to review a decision not to publicly fund a service or treatment. In Quebec, the Tribunal administrative du Québec hears appeals concerning health treatment or service coverage in Quebec as well as appeals from all administrative bodies in the province. Of all the specific tribunals Ontario's is the most active and has a broader mandate to review decisions but, as we discuss below, its discretion nonetheless remains limited.

* * *

The ability [in Ontario] to seek relief before an administrative tribunal rather than having to apply to the general courts offers the prospect of quicker, easier and cheaper recourse to justice. However, many who do appeal to the Ontario Board are disappointed to find that its discretion to review delisting or failure to list decisions is significantly constrained by the terms of the act and the regulations. For example, section 24 of the relevant regulations lists medical services that are specifically excluded from OHIP [Ontario Health Insurance Plan] coverage. These include: in subsection 24(1); services solely for the purposes of altering or restoring appearance (para. 10); treatment for a medical condition that is generally considered experimental (para. 17); in vitro fertilization, except in limited circumstances (para. 23); reversal of sterilization (para. 22); and the fitting and evaluation of hearing aids (para. 27). These services are not insured services (and thus, by a process of reverse engineering, are considered not "medically necessary" under the *Canada Health Act*). The Board has almost no discretion to reverse a decision not to publicly fund these services.

The Board does have some discretion with respect to access to out-of-country services. This occurs in two circumstances: when a citizen of Ontario requires unanticipated, emergency treatment while traveling, and/or when a citizen of Ontario secures prior approval to obtain treatment that is unavailable, or unavailable without significant delay, in the province. Most of the Board's discretion, and the most interesting decisions, revolve around the issue of pre-approved treatment.

* * *

The Courts

The role of the courts in determining the boundaries of Medicare is often overstated in the media and/or assumed to be much more significant than is actually the case. There are two main mechanisms by which the courts play a role in determining what is in and what is out of Medicare: judicial review through general administrative law and through *Charter* challenges. In general, plaintiffs are unsuccessful.

Faced with a challenge in administrative law, courts demonstrate their deference for determining what is in and out of Medicare, by reviewing decisions on the standard of "patent unreasonableness." This is the most deferential standard of review possible in administrative law, with the other possibilities being "reasonableness simpliciter" and "correctness" (the latter being the least deferential). For example, the only successful judicial review claim before the courts with regard to waiting times has been *Stein v. Québec (Régie de l'Assurance-maladie)*. In this case Mr. Stein waited months for surgery, even though his doctors warned that his life was in danger if he was not operated on within four to eight weeks. He was successful before the Quebec Superior Court in overturning the Quebec health insurance board officials' refusal to pay for his treatment in a New York hospital on the grounds that, given the facts of the case, the decision was patently unreasonable. Thus, the court was prepared to be very deferential to the Board's decision-making; however, even allowing for this very high standard of deference the court felt compelled to overturn the Board's decision. The courts will check the *rationality* of governmental decisions about what is in and out of Medicare, but to date have not held the government or other institutions to any higher standard.

* * *

With respect to *Charter* challenges, applicants have met with a similar lack of success. For example, the courts to date (with one exception) have not found that section 7 of the *Charter*, which guarantees life, liberty, and security of the person, entitles Canadians to publicly funded health care.

* * *

Most of the *Charter* challenges to limits on publicly funded health care are brought arguing section 15, the equality provision. Despite the absence of a *Charter* right to publicly funded health care, once a government elects to provide some publicly funded health care services, it must do so in compliance with the equality provisions of the *Charter*. Section 15(1) provides that "[E]very individual is equal before and under the law and has the right to the equal protection and equal benefit of the law without discrimination and, in particular, without discrimination based on race, national or ethnic origin, colour, religion, sex, age or mental or physical disability." However, even if discrimination is found under section 15(1), it may be "saved" by section 1 of the *Charter*, which provides that "the *Canadian Charter of Rights and Freedoms* guarantees the rights and freedoms set out in it subject only to such reasonable limits prescribed by law as can be demonstrably justified in a free and democratic society." Thus, a government may defend a finding that a particular policy or decision is discriminatory by pointing to the principles and processes that were followed in making it and arguing that although the needs of those discriminated against were considered, there were other countervailing needs or considerations that outweighed these concerns.

There have been a number of section 15 challenges that have grabbed attention. But between 1985 and 2002 of the thirty-three cases that have challenged health care policy, only eleven have been successful. More specifically, of the cases that have challenged policies limiting insured medical services only one has been upheld at the Supreme Court level. The successful case was in 1997, *Eidridge v. British Columbia* which was a claim by a deaf couple that they were discriminated against in contravention of theft section 15 rights by the failure of the British Columbian government (and more specifically a hospital) to fund interpretation services. The facts of this case were very compelling. The deaf woman was giving birth to twins and there were problems at the time of delivery. A nurse communicated to the mother through gestures that the heart rate of one of the babies had gone down. The twins were whisked away from the distressed women who did not know what was going on apart from a note being flashed at her with the word "fine" written thereon.

* * *

There are many issues that are raised by the court's review on *Charter* grounds of decisions not to publicly fund treatments. The first point to note is that only a very few patients have been successful. The expense and delay inherent in *Charter* litigation means that recourse to the *Charter* remains an unsatisfactory way to deal with *most* grievances and concerns that citizens have regarding access to health care services. Also, although the *Charter* can, in certain circumstances, address explicit rationing decisions by governments (for example, failing to fund a particular service or delisting a particular service), it has far less capacity to challenge the multitude of resource allocation decisions that are made in the health care system every day. In other words, although the *Charter* can protect against explicit governmental decisions that openly deny or prevent access to a particular treatment, most decisions are not explicit and have an indirect effect on access. Governments can eviscerate a health care system through underfunding so that services are available in theory although not in practice, and it is much harder to launch legal challenge against such methods of dilution. Second, it is important to note that *Charter* challenges are a one-way street, and they do nothing to counter the difficulty of *delisting* treatments and may, indeed, exacerbate the existing reluctance of decision-makers to formally delist treatments that are of relatively less benefit. However, given that the *Charter* as part of the *Constitution* is as clear a statement of agreed-upon public values as one is likely to find, the courts play a critical role in checking governmental decision-making, which increasingly emphasizes cost-effectiveness analysis and the objective of restraining government spending, that may unlawfully discriminate against marginalized and vulnerable groups of people. * * *

* * *

The Role of Law and Legal Institutions

Law and legal institutions can be both barriers and facilitators to an equitable and efficient health care system. For example, in Canada, the *Canada Health Act* gives primacy to hospital and physician services. Although the CHA has protected Canadians well through the years, it has skewed public resources towards hospital and physician services rather than community care, home care, public health, preventive care, drugs, and new technologies. Thus, while law can be a powerful force, entrenching values and protecting entitlements, it can also result in inflexibility and present barriers to reform if it fails to keep pace with changing technology, expectations, and health care needs.

* * *

Notes

1. Most nations provide some forum for review of improper administrative actions. The courts are usually available for this purpose, though in some nations a special forum exists that takes the place of, or supplements, the courts. France, for example, has a special tribunal, the Conseil d'Etat, for reviewing executive action—a function forbidden the courts. Other nations have complaint systems within the administrative agency, or health care ombudsmen with various jurisdictions. Where judicial review is available, courts are usually quite deferential to administrative agencies. This is especially true in England, as the article that follows illustrates.

2. In the United States, health insurers and managed care organizations often provide internal appeal procedures. Most states by statute also provide external review procedures. It is also possible for beneficiaries to sue their insurer or managed care organization for breach of contract if services or payment for services is denied. Under the law of several of the states, moreover, a beneficiary may sue in tort for bad faith breach of an insurance contract if the insurer or managed care organizations refusal was egregious. The federal Employee Retirement Income Security Act of 1974 (ERISA), however, preempts these remedies with respect to employee benefit plans. 29 U.S.C.A. §§1132(a), 1144(a). Since most Americans obtain health insurance through their employment, ERISA effectively means that they have no state court remedy when they are denied care or payment. The Supreme Court, however, has held that ERISA permits states to provide binding external review procedures for ERISA plans that are not self-insured. See *Rush Prudential HMO, Inc. v. Moran*, 536 U.S. 355 (2002). ERISA permits the recovery of benefits denied in federal court, but it does not permit recovery of extra-contractual damages or tort damages. See *Aetna Health, Inc. v. Davila*, 542 U.S. 200 (2004).

3. The reading notes that one means of challenging health care allocation decisions is through raising claims of discriminatory treatment. In the United States denials of access to health care are occasionally challenged on the grounds of discrimination. A few lawsuits have brought under Title VI, claiming race discrimination, and more recently under the Americans with Disabilities Act on the basis of disability discrimination. Another statute, the Emergency Medical Treatment and Active Labor Act, 42 U.S.C.A. §1395dd, more directly prohibits denial of emergency medical care to those who present at hospital emergency rooms requiring emergent care or in active labor, regardless of ability to pay. This statute also provides administrative means of enforcement. How effective has the strategy of prohibiting discrimination in the delivery of health care in the United States proved as a strategy for expanding access to health care?

The following essay, purpose-written for this text by an eminent scholar of the law of the National Health Services, describes the role of the courts in rationing within the N.H.S.

Judicial Supervision of Health Resource Allocation—English Experience (2006)

Christopher Newdick, University of Reading, UK.

Over the past five years, the UK's National Health Service (NHS) has enjoyed unparalleled increases in public funding. Having lagged behind its European neighbors for many years, the Labour government increased investment in health care from 2002 so that gross expenditure in UK public health is now broadly equivalent to that found elsewhere in the EU at 9.4% of GDP in 2007–08. In many ways the change has been significant. In the mid 1990s, for example, some patients could have waited as long as 18 months for treatment. Now the target for hospital treatment is 18 *weeks*. Impressive though these developments are, however, litigation and public anxiety about the NHS continues to increase. There are a number of reasons for this, familiar to other modern health care systems.

First, levels of chronic ill-health, for example, obesity-, alcoholism- and smoking-related diseases, continue to rise. Second, many new effective, but expensive, medicines are capable of treating long-term, chronic illness for which, previously, little could be done. Third, demographic changes mean that populations are growing older and require more medical care as they do so. Add to this the introduction of market principles into health care in the UK, which encourage patients to see themselves as "consumers" and require health suppliers (including privately owned hospitals) to compete for their custom; this too may drive up demand for care. All this means that the difficult decisions around health care resource allocation are as troublesome as ever.

This chapter, therefore, considers the legal principles governing patient claims to NHS resources. Many claims are brought by means of judicial review and the following considers the role of the courts in supervising the health care resource allocation process. The claim is normally brought against one of the 152 health authorities responsible for purchasing and organising NHS care in England. (Health authorities are called *primary care trusts* in England—even though they are also responsible for secondary (ie hospital) care.) We discuss judicial review in outline before applying the general principles to the special context of the NHS. We consider: (I) what is judicial review?, (II) the legality of rationing, (III) the reasonableness of rationing, and (IV) procedural propriety in the rationing process.

I. What is Judicial Review?

Judicial review has nothing to do with a claim for compensation. Its purpose is to "review" the decision of a public authority to see if it can be criticised. Courts in judicial review cannot impose solutions of their own because the statute imposes that duty on the public authority. The court can only "overturn" or "quash" the decision and refer it back to the decision-maker for re-consideration. Typically, for example, the authority may have failed to consider a relevant factor or failed to follow a procedure laid down by statute. In each case, the decision-maker has to take the decision again in the light of the court's observations. The grounds for judicial review are: (1) illegality, (2) irrationality, and (3) procedural impropriety (although there is substantial overlap between them). Let us outline each before applying them to the specific context of the NHS.

1. Illegality

The complaint of illegality is that the authority's decision transgresses the powers conferred upon it, e.g. it has done something it has no power to do, or failed to do something it is obliged to do. Public authorities, therefore, must be sensitive to the framework of laws surrounding their discretion and always pursue objectives consistent with their statutory functions. Although the theory is straightforward, the practice is more difficult because statutes and regulations are often expressed in imprecise terms which accommodate a range of meanings.

We should note, however, the logical priority as between statutes, regulations made within statutes, the common law and health service *policy*. First, the predominant sources of NHS law are statutes. Having been passed by Parliament, they are decisive and can modify the common law. Second, regulations, which derive their power from statutes, may not contradict or go beyond the boundary of the Act by which they have been created. Third, NHS *policy* has no legal force and must remain within the confines of the statutes, regulations and the common law.

2. Irrationality

The Courts have reserved for themselves the right to review public authority decisions which are unreasonable. In 1985, Lord Diplock said that the power to overturn an "unreasonable" decision:

> … applies to a decision which is so outrageous in its defiance of logic or of accepted moral standards that no sensible person who had applied his mind to the question to be decided could have arrived at it.

This is an extremely high hurdle. However, in *R v N and E Devon HA, ex p Coughlan* [1999] Lloyds Rep Med 306, the notion of "unreasonableness" was explained by Lord Woolf MR more widely. He said: "Rationality … has two faces: one is the barely known decision which simply defies comprehension; the other is a decision which can be seen to have proceeded by flawed logic." It is the second of these two notions which has become more prominent recently. Clearly, it gives the courts broader discretion to question the internal logic of the decision. The changed judicial attitude is striking and has led the courts to quash decisions which, previously, might have escaped scrutiny. Part of the reason for the change is the recent interest of the courts in obtaining satisfactory reasons for decisions. There is a clear trend of the courts insisting on greater openness, or transparency, in public authority decision-making.

3. Procedural Impropriety

Procedural impropriety covers a failure by a public authority to observe procedural rules that are expressly laid down by statute (and this might also give rise to action for *illegality*), or to observe the basic rules of natural justice. The requirement of procedural propriety runs throughout judicial review, but it is especially important when people are offered procedures to challenge decisions of a health authority with which they are not satisfied.

Let us now apply these general principles of illegality, irrationality and procedural impropriety, to the specific context of the NHS.

II. The *Legality* of NHS Rationing

To what extent do statutes and regulations control health authority decision-making? Put the other way, given the ethical difficulties of developing "fair" health care resource allocation policies, to what extent do health authorities retain discretion as to proper solutions? We consider the Secretary of State's duties: (1) to fund the NHS, (2) to promote a "comprehensive health service", (3) to fund GPs in primary care, (4) in connection with the National Institute for Health and Clinical Excellence (NICE) and (5) as regards EU law.

1. The Duty to Fund the NHS

The National Health Service Act 1977 imposes on the Secretary of State for Health a duty to pay health authorities sufficient funds to enable them to (a) the pay the salaries of those who provide NHS services and (b) cover the expenses incurred by arranging NHS services. Crucially, however, health authorities also have a corresponding statutory duty not to exceed their annual financial allocations and this is why there is tension within the system. Although many complain that we invest insufficient sums in the NHS, the matter is considered too "political" for judicial intervention. An analogous issue arose concerning expenditure guidance issued by the Secretary of State for the Environment to Local Authorities, which was challenged for being unreasonable. Rejecting the application, Lord Scarman said in *R v Secretary of State, ex p Nottinghamshire CC* [1986] AC 240:

> I cannot accept that it is constitutionally appropriate, save in very exceptional circumstances, for the courts to intervene on the ground of "unreasonableness" to

> quash guidance framed by the Secretary of State and by necessary implication approved by the House of Commons, the guidance being concerned with the limits of public expenditure by local authorities and the incidence of the tax burden ... these are matters of political judgment for him and for the House of Commons. They are not matters for the judges.

Thus, the overall level of funding devoted to the NHS is beyond the competence of the judges. Although Lord Scarman permits judicial intervention "in very exceptional circumstances", those circumstances exist more in legal theory than practical reality.

2. Duty to promote a "comprehensive health service"

A number of general statutory duties are imposed on the Secretary of State concerning the nature and extent of the service he, or she, must provide. The most broad-ranging is contained in sections 1 and 3 of the National Health Service Act 1977. Section 1 provides:

> (1) It is the Secretary of State's duty to continue the promotion in England and Wales of a comprehensive health service designed to secure improvement (a) in the physical and mental health of the people of those countries, and (b) in the prevention, diagnosis and treatment of illness, and for that purpose to provide or secure the effective provision of services in accordance with this Act.
>
> (2) The services so provided shall be free of charge except in so far as the making and recovery of charges is expressly provided for by or under any enactment, whenever passed.

Section 3 continues:

> It is the Secretary of State's duty to provide ... to such extent as he considers necessary to meet all reasonable requirements: (a) hospital accommodation; (b) other accommodation for the purpose of any service specified under this Act; (c) medical, dental, nursing and ambulance services; (d) such other facilities for the care of expectant and nursing mothers and young children as he considers are appropriate as part of the health service; (e) such facilities for the prevention of illness, the care of persons suffering from illness and the after-care of persons who have suffered from illness as he considers appropriate as part of the health service; [and] (f) such other services as are required for the diagnosis and treatment of illness.

We noted above the Secretary of State's duty to fund health authorities to arrange NHS services. It follows that, although these "duties" are imposed on the Secretary of State, their actual performance is delegated by statute to each of the 152 health authorities responsible for organizing NHS care at local level. Can the duties be enforced by individual patients? The Court of Appeal has said that the "duty" imposed by section 3 is relative, not absolute. In *ex parte Coughlan* (above) it said:

> First it will be observed that the Secretary of State's section 3 duty is subject to two different qualifications. First of all there is the initial qualification that his obligation is limited to providing the services identified to the extent that he considers that they are *necessary* to meet *all reasonable requirements*. In addition there is a qualification in that he has to consider whether they are appropriate to be provided as part of the health service ...
>
> The first qualification placed on the duty contained in section 3 makes it clear that there is scope for the Secretary of State to exercise a degree of judgment as

> to the circumstances in which he will provide the services ... When exercising his judgment he has to bear in mind the comprehensive service which he is under a duty to promote as set out in section 1. However as long as he pays due regard to that duty, the fact that the service will not be comprehensive does not mean that he is necessarily contravening either section 1 or section 3 ... a comprehensive health service may never, for human, financial and other resource reasons, be achievable ...
>
> In exercising his judgment the Secretary of State is entitled to take into account the resources available to him and the demands on those resources ... The [NHS] Act does not impose an absolute duty to provide the specified services. The Secretary of State is entitled to have regard to the resources made available to him under current government economic policy.

Thus, the 1977 Act confers broad discretion as to the manner in which a "comprehensive" health service is "promoted". However, it does cast a doubt in law over the economic theory of the quality adjusted life year (QALY) which recommends that resources be diverted to those who derive most benefit from them in terms of the length of time they will live thereafter and the extent of the improvement in their condition. Such a policy tends to exclude elderly patients and those with chronic, life-threatening diseases. If it impeded whole categories of patients from obtaining NHS care, it would probably offend the requirement that the service be comprehensive.

3. The Duty in Primary Care—The GP's Terms of Service

How do these considerations apply to general practitioners (GPs) in primary (or non-hospital) care? The duty to provide primary care is contained in regulations made under the 1977 Act. In connection with the duty to prescribe medicines, the General Medical Services (Contracts) Regulations 2004 (the "GMS" regulations) require that:

> A prescriber shall order any drugs or appliances which are needed for the treatment of any patient to whom he is providing treatment under these terms of service by issuing to that patient a prescription form.

These duties have remained largely intact since the inception of the NHS in 1948 and confer significant discretion on doctors. Note they require that the prescriber "shall" treat patients on the basis of clinical need. What does this mean? The only case to have considered this specific duty is *R v Secretary of State for Health, ex parte Pfizer* [1999] Lloyd's Rep Med 289, the "Viagra" case [reproduced below]. The Secretary of State was concerned at the resource implications of the drug becoming available to patients within the NHS. He alerted doctors and health authorities that he intended to place the drug on a related statutory "grey-list" of restricted medicines which should not generally be prescribed by GPs. However, before the required regulations had been approved by Parliament, the Secretary of State issued NHS *policy* instructing GPs not to prescribe Viagra.

This guidance was held to be illegal for contradicting the regulations. The court said: "The doctor must give such treatment as he, exercising the professional judgment to be expected from an average GP considers necessary and appropriate ... If a GP decides that a particular treatment is necessary, it must inevitably be appropriate...." The guidance in question trespassed upon the proper statutory responsibilities imposed on GPs by the GMS regulations. It would have been permissible for the Secretary of State to urge doctors to be cautious in using the drug, "but it must make it clear that the GP's clinical judgment is supreme." This confirms that specific statutory rights and duties may not be adjusted by executive *fiat*. If ministers of state wish to restrict those rights, they must do so through Parliament.

Exactly why there appears to be a *duty* to prescribe in primary care, but rationing is lawful in secondary care (see *ex p Coughlan* above) probably has more to do with history than common sense. Although it would be consistent with the 1977 Act to have the same system of priority setting in both primary and secondary care, the present favorable treatment of primary care patients was established in 1948 when the NHS was created. It would take a brave politician to try and reverse things now.

4. The National Institute for Health and Clinical Excellence (NICE).

There has long been concern in the NHS at "post-code rationing," i.e. that, since the 152 health authorities have statutory powers to promote the interests of their local communities, they may differ from one another in respect of the policies they adopt to do so. This can lead to post-code [ZIP code] differentials in which patients in differing health authorities do not always have equal access to the same treatments. NICE was created to reduce the prevalence of this phenomenon.

The statutory purpose of NICE is to recommend whether a new medicine or treatment should be used in the NHS having regard to "the promotion of clinical excellence and the effective use of available resources in the health service." Thus, it analyses and evaluates all the evidence concerning a treatment in order to advise whether it should be provided within the NHS. Its recommendations have been given special *mandatory* status by means of Secretary of State's "directions" (which have statutory force under the National Health Service Act 1977). Thus, a health authority

> ... shall, unless directed otherwise by the Secretary of State ... apply such amounts of the sums paid to it ... as may be required to ensure that a health intervention that is recommended by [NICE] in a Technology Appraisal Guidance is, from a date not later than three months from the date of the Technology Appraisal Guidance, normally available to be prescribed ...

Clearly, this removes from health authorities the discretion that otherwise exists in secondary care to decide resource allocation questions for themselves. In other words, failure to adhere to NICE would give grounds for judicial review in an action based on illegality.

Arguably, *substantive* rights of this nature are good for encouraging harmony in the NHS. But the impact of this "duty" may be to require health authorities to divert resources from one type of use to another. Within any system of finite resources, a focus on individualistic, consumer-based rights may conflict with notions of the public interest, solidarity and equality. We await a complaint by a patient whose treatment has been curtailed because NICE has required the resources necessary to provide it should be diverted to someone else.

5. The Impact of European Union (EU) Law.

Recent developments in EU law give further credence to the argument that patients are acquiring *substantive* health care rights. The underlying principle driving membership of the EU is that of freedom of movement—of goods, capital, labor and services. Free markets are said to generate benefits for consumers because they encourage efficiency and the best value for money. This freedom applies to private enterprise and prevents governments from introducing trade barriers to protect national commercial interests from competition. The question arises, should public *health* services be governed by the same rules so that patients have EU rights to obtain health care at public expense in other Member States of the EU?

For some time it was believed that such a principle did not extend to *public* services because national governments were entitled to preserve the solvency and integrity of their own health care systems. If people had a general right to travel in this way, it would be difficult to predict where and when demand would arise. This could cause inefficiencies and damage patient care. However, the case of *Watts v Bedfordshire PCT* (2006) ECJ, C-372/04 suggests that this is wrong. Mrs Watts required artificial hips and was put on an NHS waiting list which assured her of treatment within a year. Dissatisfied with having to wait so long, she obtained the necessary treatment in France, paid the bill and returned to present it for payment to her health authority. It refused to pay and the matter was taken to the European Court of Justice (ECJ) as raising a matter of EU law with respect to the right to freedom of movement of services.

The ECJ said that the principle of free movement of services does apply to public health care systems. However, in order to protect their solvency and integrity, the right is not unrestricted. It applies only when (a) the patient requires "normal" treatment of a kind that is supported by international medical science and (b) that treatment cannot be obtained at home without "undue delay." A moment's reflection reveals the difficulty of this approach. What treatments are "normal," which delays are "undue"? These unhelpful principles are now the responsibility of national courts to implement. This raises issues of *illegality* because EU law is automatically enforceable within each Member State. It is now for courts of judicial review to determine how to apply EU law to particular cases.

If courts become more sensitive to the needs of individuals than those of the community and encourage cross-border health care in the EU, the impact on health care will be inevitable. Finite resources diverted to one category of patients cannot be used for the treatment of others. In promoting this *individual-substantive* approach to health care rights, one doubts whether the ECJ has devoted sufficient attention to the those less articulate, less mobile patients (such as the elderly, disabled and mentally ill) who will tend to be adversely affected by it. An alternative response is to develop *community-procedural* rights to health care resource allocation and it is to this notion that we turn next.

III. The *Reasonableness* of Rationing—The Process of Priority Setting

There has been much movement in the case-law over the past 15 years on the willingness of the courts to scrutinize the "reasonableness" of NHS rationing. Before 1997, litigants for health service resources had slim prospects of success because courts felt unable to interfere with matters of NHS priorities. Since then, a more sympathetic response has developed. Courts now refer decisions back for reconsideration if they do not withstand scrutiny. This has created a more critical attitude to health authorities. Notice that each of the following cases arise in the context of secondary care where rationing is permissible. They were not subject to the particular laws governing primary (or GP) care, NICE, or EU law which have been discussed above. We look at the evolution of the law in two phases.

1. Passive non-intervention

Two cases illustrate a time in which the courts were reluctant to involve themselves in matters of resource allocation on the ground that, except in exceptional cases, it was beyond their competence to do so. In *R v Secretary of State, ex parte Walker* (1992) 3 BMLR 32 (decided in 1987) the health authority recognised that a premature baby required an operation to his heart. They were unable to perform the procedure because of a decision not to staff all the intensive care units in their neonatal ward. The plaintiff alleged that her baby had been denied the surgical care he needed in breach of the duty to promote a "comprehensive health service." Rejecting the application for judicial review, the court said:

> It is not for this court, or indeed any court, to substitute its own judgment for the judgment of those who are responsible for the allocation of resources. This court could only intervene where it was satisfied that there was a prima facie case, not only of failing to allocate resources in the way in which others would think that resources should be allocated, but of a failure to allocate resources to an extent which was … unreasonable.

Notwithstanding the pressing nature if this claim, the court felt unable to intervene. Notice, however, that this gives no indication of the threshold for knowing when a decision could be described as "unreasonable" and, therefore, when judicial intervention would be proper.

In *ex parte Walker*, there was no immediate danger to the baby and, had an emergency arisen, the hospital promised that the operation would be performed. By contrast, in *R v Central Birmingham Health Authority, ex parte Collier* (unreported, CA, 1988), a four year old boy was suffering from a hole in the heart. In September 1987, his consultant said that "he desperately needed open heart surgery" and placed the boy at the top of the waiting list, expecting that intensive care facilities would be made available within a month. Yet, by January 1988, the operation had still not been performed because no intensive care bed could be made available. The Court of Appeal was invited to order that, given that the boy would die unless the operation was performed, the operation should be carried out. It said, however, that:

> Even assuming that [the evidence] does establish that there is immediate danger to health … the legal principles to be applied do not differ from the case of Re Walker. This court is in no position to judge the allocation of resources by this particular health authority … there is no suggestion here that the hospital authority have behaved in a way which is deserving of condemnation or criticism. What is suggested is that somehow more resources should be made available to enable the hospital authorities to ensure that the treatment is immediately given.

This was beyond the competence of the court. Understandably, the court must be careful. If it diverts care to patient A, who will speak for patient B who is not party to the dispute but who may be affected by its outcome by having their care delayed, diluted, or denied? Nevertheless, the problem in *ex parte Collier* was that no one knew exactly why such urgent treatment had been refused, other than for general reasons concerning a shortage of specialist nurses. Counsel for the boy said, "it may be good reason or bad reason." And, in the absence of an explanation, the judge himself commented, somewhat forlornly: "No doubt the health authority would welcome the opportunity to deal with such matters so that they could explain what they are doing and what their problems are."

This is troubling because no one thought it appropriate to require explanation why he was not transferred to a hospital in (say) London, Nottingham, or Manchester. The case marks the low-point in judicial passivity in cases of this nature—indeed, it is a disgrace. The boy was effectively abandoned by the responsible health authority and the law could find no mechanism to assist him. Although a system of *community-procedural* rights was purportedly available, it was so weak as to be ineffective. It is not acceptable for the courts simply to shut their eyes in the face of such an application. In the light of the cases we discuss below, ex parte Collier should now be regarded as wrongly decided for the court's failure to scrutinise the reasons why he was not transferred elsewhere for treatment.

2. Increased Intensity of Judicial Review

From the mid 1990s there was a significant change of judicial attitude and it is here that we begin to see the development of more meaningful *community-procedural* rights in the NHS. The first indication of the change came in *R. v. Cambridge D.H.A., ex parte B* [1995] 2 All ER 129, although the case failed on its merits. A ten year-old girl with leukemia was refused remedial (as opposed to palliative) treatment that might have prolonged her life. Significantly, the High Court insisted on hearing exactly why such treatment could not be made available. The judge said:

> ... Merely to point to the fact that resources are finite tells one nothing about the wisdom, or ... the legality of a decision to withhold funding in a particular case ... Where the question is whether the life of a 10 year-old child might be saved, by however slim a chance, the responsible Authority must do more than toll the bell of tight resources. They must explain the priorities that have led them to decline to fund the treatment.

In the light of *ex parte Collier*, this was dramatic! That same afternoon, however, the case was taken the Court of Appeal. The reasons for denial of care were explained in more detail and a different view was taken. The Court of Appeal heard that (i) the treatment was untested and "experimental", (ii) its prospects of success were small, i.e. between 1% and 4% overall, (iii) it would have debilitating side-effects which, given her prospects, were not in her best interests, and (iv) given her prospects, the total cost of £75,000 could not be justified. The unanimous clinical view of the doctors was that the procedure should not be carried out and the health authority confirmed that the decision had been taken in the light of "all the clinical and other relevant matters ... and not on financial grounds." The Court of Appeal reversed the judgment of the High Court. It said:

> Difficult and agonizing judgments have to be made as to how a limited budget is best allocated to the maximum advantage of the maximum number of patients. That is not a judgment the court can make. In my judgment, it is not something that a health authority ... can be fairly criticised for not advancing before the court.

Thus, although there was the possibility of some benefit, it was insufficient to justify treatment; given her poor prospects, it would not have been in her best interests. The case is significant. First, the judgment of the High Court contrasts with the previous cases and indicates changing judicial attitudes. Secondly, although the Court of Appeal said it would not insist on evidence of the health authority's resource allocation policies (the "macro"-issues), it certainly heard why this *particular* patient had been denied care (the "micro"-issue). Indeed, had persuasive evidence not been produced, the High Court's judgment might have been affirmed. This marks the start of the trend toward *intensive* judicial review of NHS cases.

Two years later, *R v NW Derbyshire HA, ex parte Fisher* [1997] 8 Med LR 327 was the first NHS rationing case to succeed against a health authority in judicial review. The HA refused to purchase beta interferon for patients suffering from multiple sclerosis. One of the authority's reasons for the refusal was that there was insufficient funding to provide treatment to everyone who needed it. Therefore, deserving cases referred at the end of the year would be denied treatment because the funds would have been exhausted by patients seen earlier. This, it said, was so unfair that it would be better to refuse treatment to everyone. The judge was wholly unpersuaded by this argument and granted judicial review on grounds of irrationality. He said:

> If correct it would be a reason for refusing to make any expensive treatment available in almost all circumstances. When deciding whether to prescribe treatment to a patient a clinician has to have regard to many factors including the resources available for that treatment and the needs of and likely benefit to that patient as compared with other patients who are likely to be suitable ... It is absurd to suppose that before any patient is prescribed any expensive treatment a survey must be made of all patients who are, or might be, in need of the same treatment in the area.

The case was referred back for reconsideration (and the treatment was provided). Similarly, in *R v NW Lancashire HA, ex parte A, D and G* (2000) 53 BMLR 148 the applicants suffered from "gender identity dysphoria" and requested trans-gender surgery. The Authority accepted that the condition was an illness, but adopted a policy which allocated low priority to procedures it considered clinically ineffective. It refused to pay for the surgery and the applicants sought judicial review. The health authority explained that it had limited financial resources and could not afford to fund all services of proven clinical effectiveness. In order to serve all those for whom the authority was responsible, it had to make hard choices. This is why, it said, transsexual surgery was given low-priority relative to other treatments.

In principle, the court approved the process of priority setting. It agreed that health authorities should give greater priority to life-threatening illnesses than to others less demanding of medical intervention and that the precise weighting of priorities was for each local health authority to decide. Special policies should be developed for doing so; "indeed, it might well be irrational not to have one ..." Any such policy would normally place treatment of transsexualism lower in its scale of priorities than, say, cancer or heart disease or kidney failure. Thus:

> in establishing priorities—comparing the respective needs of patients suffering from different illnesses and determining the respective strengths of their claims to treatment—it is vital: for (1) an authority accurately to assess the nature and seriousness of each type of illness, (2) to determine the effectiveness of various forms of treatment for it and (3) to give proper effect to that assessment and that determination in the application of its policy.

Nevertheless, on the facts of this case, the court reversed the Health Authority's decision to deny treatment. In reality, it said, the Authority had closed its mind to the possibility of providing transsexual surgery in any circumstances. It had adopted a blanket ban which ignored the doctors who supported the treatment, or whether the patients had exceptional circumstances which justified making care available. Thus, the decision failed to withstand scrutiny and was referred back to be taken again (and, again, the treatment was made available).

These cases illustrate the increased willingness of the courts to scrutinise the reasonableness of rationing decisions. Although this *community-procedural* approach leaves the ultimate decision to health authorities, it insists on fair procedures and where the interests of the patient are sensitive (as in the transsexuals' case) the review will be especially intense. This provides an interesting contrast with the *individual-substantive* response discussed above.

IV. *Procedural Propriety*—Process of Consultation

Should the public be involved in the important questions of health care resource allocation, for example, on the configuration of local services, whether hospital wards should be closed, or whether pediatric, geriatric, orthopedic, cancer, or mental health services should have priority over others? Government attaches increasing importance to public involvement in the process of NHS policy-making. The NHS is sometimes seen as the laboratory in which "public participation" in health care decision-making is being tested as a mechanism for resolving these sensitive questions. Thus, the Health Act 2001 imposes on NHS bodies an obligation that persons to whom services are provided are involved and consulted on:

> (a) the planning of the provision of those services, (b) the development and consideration of proposals for changes in the way those services are provided, and (c) decisions made by that body affecting the operation of those services.

And the Court of Appeal said in *ex parte Coughlan*, that all consultations, whether statutory, or voluntary, must be genuine and avoid the appearance of a sham:

> To be proper, consultation [1] must be undertaken at a time when proposals are still at a formative stage; [2] must include sufficient reasons for particular proposals to allow those consulted to give intelligent consideration and an intelligent response; [3] adequate time must be given for this purpose; [4] the product of consultation must be conscientiously taken into account when the ultimate decision is taken.

For example, *ex parte Daniels* (1994) 19 BMLR 67 a health authority closed a unit in London in which a child suffering from cancer was receiving bone-marrow treatment and offered the same care in Bristol instead. The Court of Appeal agreed that the unit had been closed without the required consultation (under regulations in force at the time). The same occurred in 2006 when a health authority proposed to enter a private contract with United Health Care Ltd to provide its primary care services. The failure to consult over the matter flawed the decision which was referred back to the authority to be taken again in the light of a proper consultation. Of course, the same conclusion is still available, but it must be made on the basis of a genuine consultation.

On the other hand, the duty to consult could be used to frustrate all progress. What, for example, if the process of consultation itself generates fresh ideas which lead to new proposals which were not originally consulted upon? Does this require a new consultation? Where would the process end? Recently, the High Court expressed concern that too sensitive a trigger to consult could ossify the entire system. Therefore, further consultation is not required unless "there is a fundamental difference" between the two.

Often, the duty to consult will not provide clear answers. Communities contain dozens of single-interest groups all presenting their own agenda, which may conflict with one another. There is nothing necessarily *democratic* about pressure-group politics. What about those whose views are not heard? Is there a danger of giving way to those who shout loudest? Consultation provides information, but it cannot replace the duty of decision-makers to make decisions for the community as a whole. They must weigh and balance public opinion, but the difficult decisions still remain. Indeed, care must be taken that those who are not represented by articulate groups continue to have their interests considered.

V. Conclusion

We can trace the evolution of law and judicial review in these cases in three stages. First, until the 1990s, "passive" judicial review offered patients very little hope of success in litigation. Second, thereafter, the courts became more intensive in their examination of cases and it is reasonable to speak in terms of coherent *procedural* rights. Such rights do not give access to specific resources because they (a) balance *community* interests in the equation and

(b) defer (albeit in a critical sense) to the discretion of public authorities in doing so. This process has been enhanced by the statutory duty on health authorities to consult patients and the public about the planning, development and reconfiguration of local services.

Thirdly, especially in respect of NICE and the impact of EU law, the movement has been toward the creation of *substantive-individual* rights. There is some superficial attraction in this approach. However, as we noted, in any health service constrained by scarce resources (ie all public, or private insurance-based systems) it is problematic. If it promotes the claims of individuals without regard to the community as a whole, there is a danger of diverting scarce resources to vocal and mobile patients and ignoring those who are inarticulate and poorly represented. History suggests that elderly, disabled and mentally ill patients are the first to suffer in such a regime. Although this may be something that resonates more in Europe than the different health care environment of the US, for any public policy interested in promoting fairness and reducing inequality in health care, this is undesirable.

Note

Among a number of excellent sources on NHS law are Professor Newdick's book, *Who Should we Treat?—Rights, Rationing and Resources in the N.H.S.* (2005); C. Newdick, Public Health Ethics and Clinical Freedom, 14 *J. Cont. Health Law and Policy* 335 (1998); and Diane Longley, *Health Care Constitutions* (1996) (which also looks at the law in Canada and New Zealand).

Professor Newdick mentions the growing importance of European Community law in member countries. This role is analyzed further in the excerpt that follows, as well as by the *Pfizer* case referred to in Professor Newdick's article, which follows the excerpt, and which also addresses domestic British law.

Patient Mobility in the European Union

Andre den Exter, Just Medicare, 331, 334–340 (2006)

EC Internal Market Law and Access to Health Care

* * *

The free movement provisions are relevant not only to health professionals, but also to patients. Free movement is not restricted to "workers," and relatives, tourists, and other categories of EU citizens can also make an appeal to benefit from this provision. Article 22 of *Coordination regulation 1408/71 (Regulation 1408/77),* in conjunction with article 39, entities cross-border workers to access the health care system in the country of residence; emergency care in case of temporary residence abroad; and care abroad that is pre-authorized by the patient's insurer or the competent (national) health authority. *Regulation 1408/71* aims to coordinate the different social security systems in the member states, but the free movement of patients remains problematic. A major problem with cross-border health care is how to regulate and finance it. Some member-states fear an influx of patients from those member-states that lack facilities and/or provide lower-quality care. Rulings from the European Court of Justice, simplifying cross-border health care, have only strengthened this fear.

The regulation of patient mobility is provided for in article 22 of *Regulation 1408/71.* Although member-state authorities are authorized to define the conditions for entitlements, an overrestricted interpretation of article 22(1)(a) would "cause a significant obstacle to the freedom of movement of persons whose conditions necessitate continuous and regular medical treatment such that they will be likely to require immediate benefits in the event of a stay in the territory of another member-state." Regulating patient mobility requires an adequate authorization policy adopted by (secondary) law, that includes the relevant procedures to be used when citizens incur health care in another member-state.

Since precedents set in *Decker* and *Kohll,* the ECJ has been confronted with a growing number of cases questioning the legitimacy of preauthorization, in view of internal market principles. In the joint case of *Smits* and *Peerbooms,* Mrs Smits suffers from Parkinson's disease. The Dutch social insurance fund *(Ziekenfonds)* refused reimbursement for specific multidisciplinary hospital treatment costs that she incurred in a German clinic. Unlike in Canada, the Dutch equivalent of Medicare is comprised of several social insurance providers. Justifying its decision, the social insurer in question said that satisfactory and adequate treatment for Parkinson's disease was available in the Netherlands and that the specific clinical treatment offered in Germany provided no additional advantage. Thus, it was deemed not "medically necessary" that Mrs Smits undergo treatment at the German clinic.

The second claimant, Mr Peerbooms, fell into a coma after a road accident. He was transferred to a hospital in the Netherlands and then transferred, in a vegetative state, to the university clinic in Innsbruck, Austria, where he received special intensive therapy using neurostimulation. In the Netherlands that technique was considered experimental and to be used only in certain circumstances. Pursuant to guidelines in effect in the Netherlands, Mr Peerbooms would not have qualified for such experimental treatment because of his age. Thus, his sickness insurance fund refused to pay the costs of his treatment.

In both cases, the ECJ had to make a determination based on the preauthorization rule, and whether such a rule in the particular circumstances constituted a barrier to the freedom to provide services. In contrast to *Decker* and *Kohll* (dealing with non-hospital care within a reimbursement system), *Smits/Peerbooms* concerned access to hospital care services for which the sickness fund had not contracted, and which, within the Netherlands, is provided on a "benefit-in-kind" basis. The Court agreed that sickness funds should not be exposed to the cost of hospital services for which they have not contracted. However, the preauthorization condition, as applied by the authorities in the Netherlands, was criticized for its potentially discriminatory effect. In the Netherlands, the general legal rule under which the costs of medical treatment are covered is in instances where the treatment is found to be "normal in the professional circles concerned." This expression, however, is open to a number of interpretations, depending in particular on whether what is "normal" is considered as such in Dutch medical circles (this narrow interpretation being favoured by the national court in the Netherlands). In contrast, the ECJ decided that to allow only treatment that is habitually carried out on national territory, and based on scientific views prevailing in national medical circles and which determine what is or is not "normal," does not offer sufficient guarantees to patients that the treatment guidelines in place are objective, non-discriminatory, known in advance, and not used arbitrarily. Moreover, such a focus on national conceptions of "normal" will make it likely that Dutch providers will always be preferred in practice. The ECJ found that where treatment is sufficiently tried and tested by international medical science, refusal of the prior authorization cannot be justified. Further, to satisfy the "normal" criterion, a member-state "must take into consideration all the relevant available information, including, in particular, existing scientific literature and studies, the authorized opinions of specialists and the fact that the proposed treatment is covered or not covered by the sickness insurance system of the member-state in which the treatment is provided."

From this case, it became clear that member-states must apply the pre-authorization procedure consistently and that patients cannot be denied health care abroad arbitrarily (that is, there have to be nondiscriminatory, transparent procedures and appeal mechanisms). For patients entitled to benefit-in-kind services, such as in the Dutch system, this ruling means that it should be just as easy to receive medical treatment from a foreign non-contracted provider as it is to obtain it from a non-contracted provider in the country of insurance. As such, the ECJ's interpretation of communal pre-authorization conditions creates new opportunities for extended access to health care abroad.

Subsequent to *Smits/Peerbooms,* the ECJ ruled on two more or less identical situations in the Dutch mixed case of *Müller-Fauré/Van Riet.* Here, the Court consolidated and clarified its previous reasoning on prior authorization, at least concerning inpatient hospital care. However, the Court also confirmed that there are several reasons that may justify requiring prior authorization where social health insurance funds cover benefits provided in another member-state. These reasons include: the protection of public health in as much as the system of agreements is intended to ensure that there are high-quality, balanced medical and hospital services open to all; to guarantee the financial balance of the social security system; and, finally, to enable managing authorities to control expenditures for, and the planning of, health care services. The Court noted that concerns regarding undermining the financial balance of the social security system were particularly valid vis-à-vis hospital care. In the case of hospital services, according to the ECJ, it is well known that to ensure sufficient access to a wide range of hospital services and to contain costs, careful planning is required regarding the number of hospitals, their geographic distribution, the mode of their organization, and the equipment with which they are provided. Nonetheless, the conditions attached to the grant of authorization must be justified and satisfy the requirement of proportionality, and such a prior authorization scheme must likewise be based on a procedural system that is easily accessible and capable of being challenged in judicial or quasi-judicial proceedings.

With respect to outpatient (non-hospital) health care, however, as in *Müller-Fauré* (that is, dental care), the Court was not convinced that abolishing prior authorization would have a system-undermining effect. According to the Court, "there was no evidence that indicated that the removal of the prior authorization requirement for that type of care would give rise to patients travelling to other countries in such large numbers, despite linguistic barriers, geographic distance, the cost of staying abroad and lack of information about the kind of care provided there, and that the financial balance of the social security system would be seriously upset." Therefore, applying the free movement principles, in case of non-hospital services, there was no justification for requiring prior authorization.

Consequences for Patients and Member States

* * *

First, the Court's rulings enable patients to search for non-hospital services that are not available in their home country or, if available, are not available in a timely fashion. One should keep in mind, however, that without prior authorization, social health insurance providers are still fully entitled to reimburse only costs up to the maximum amount applicable in the claimant's country of residence. For that reason, the Court did not consider the removal of the administrative prior authorization condition to be a serious threat to the financial balance of the social security system, since it had to bear the cost of treatment when received in the patient's home country anyway. Patients seeking non-hospital care in other EU nations without prior authorization must bear any additional costs above and beyond the relevant tariff provided for in their own country.

The ECJ has specified the conditions that member-states must meet when restricting citizens' claims on social security (including health care) entitlements abroad. Although the individual rulings seem prima facie clear, general conclusions on the effects on cross-border care in the EU, as such, are much less so given that social security systems vary by country. Nonetheless, one can derive some general conclusions relevant to member-states. First, it has now been established that medical services fall within the scope of the EC Treaty provision on free movement of services, even hospital services. Consequently, national social security rules cannot be used to exclude implementation of the free-movement provision. This applies to insurance arrangements, such as those in the Netherlands, that provide benefits in kind, but also to hospital services provided by a national health service such as exists in Canada. The U.K. government unsuccessfully attempted to exempt its National Health Service from the ambit of Article 50 of the EC Treaty since the NHS provides services directly rather than reimbursing the cost of services received. The ECJ noted "that a medical service does not cease to be a provision of services because it is paid for by a national health service or by a system providing benefits-in-kind."

Second, the ECJ has also, on occasion, made explicit that EU law does not undermine the power of the member-states to organize their respective social security systems. In the absence of harmonization at the EU level, each member-state may pass legislation pursuant to which citizens have a right or duty to be insured with a social security scheme, and, second, the conditions for entitlement to benefits. Moreover, it is not incompatible with EU law for a member-state to establish, with a view towards achieving its aim of limiting costs, a negative list excluding certain products or services from reimbursement. It follows that EU law cannot, in principle, have the effect of requiring a member-state to extend the list of medical services paid for by its social insurance system.

Nonetheless, in exercising its powers, the member-state must not disregard EU law. It follows from this that the list of insured medical treatments must be drawn up in accordance with objective criteria, which are known in advance, and without reference to the origin of the service (non-discrimination). In the Netherlands, the health insurance system is not based on a pre-established list of types of treatment for which payment will be guaranteed; rather the legislature has enacted a general rule providing that all costs of medical treatment will be assumed provided that the treatment is "normal in the professional circles concerned." It is thus largely up to the discretion of the social health insurers to decide which types of treatment satisfy that condition; however, in applying that criterion, these insurers must now interpret it on the basis of what is sufficiently tried and tested by *international* medical science. This may mean that where a certain treatment has sufficiently been tried and tested by international science, authorization by the sickness fund could not be refused on the grounds that it is not presently provided in the Netherlands. The only justifiable reason for refusal of authorization would be where, given the need to maintain an adequate supply of hospital care and to ensure the financial stability of the sickness insurance system, the "same or equally effective treatment can be obtained without undue delay" at a contracted provider.

* * *

Third, as mentioned above, the larger public interest in maintaining a sustainable social insurance system may be accepted as justifying barriers to freedom to provide medical services in the context of a hospital infrastructure. Member-states need to determine whether their respective national rules can be legitimately justified in the light of such *overriding* reasons. In accordance with settled case law, *it* is necessary to ensure that they do not exceed what is objectively necessary for the given purpose and that the same result cannot be achieved by less restrictive rules. As determined in *Muller-Fauré/Van Riet,* these requirements apply regardless of the type or nature of the health care system (for example, whether a social insurance system as in the Netherlands or a national health service as in the United Kingdom).

* * *

R. v. Secretary of State for Health, ex parte Pfizer Ltd.

Before the High Court (Queen's Bench Division) [1999]
3 C.M.L.R. 875 , 51 B.M.L.R. 189

Collins, J.

Viagra is the trade name of a drug developed by the applicants, Pfizer Ltd, called Sildenafil. It is the only drug licensed for the treatment of erectile dysfunction (ED) (that is to say a man's inability to achieve or to maintain an erection so as to undertake satisfactory sexual activity) which is taken orally. There are many causes of ED. It may result from physical injury, for example trauma to the spinal cord, from surgery, such as that for prostate cancer, from disease, such as diabetes, from psychological problems or from natural causes such as ageing. There are a number of other treatments available, but all have material shortcomings, either because they have unpleasant side effects or are not particularly effective. Viagra is undoubtedly the most desirable treatment now available for ED, although some sufferers cannot use it, if, for example, they are receiving medication for heart trouble.

Sildenafil was discovered in the applicant's laboratories in Sandwich, but Viagra itself is manufactured for the European market in France from bulk Sildenafil supplied from Ireland. It attracted the attention of the media following its receipt of a marketing authorisation in the United States in March 1998. But in January 1998 a monograph was published by the National Prescribing Centre and issued to all NHS Trusts and Health Authorities putting them on notice that Sildenafil had the potential for considerable impact once it received its marketing authorisation within the European Union. That authorisation was expected in the Autumn of 1998. The potential financial impact was stated thus:

> It is difficult to determine the impact of this drug as prevalence data are scarce. Assuming that between 1,000 and 2,000 men per 100,000 population may have long term complete erectile dysfunction and that 25 per cent of them received one treatment per week at £10 per treatment. the cost would be between £125,000 to £200,000 per 100,000 population per annum. This market would develop over time and costs would increase significantly if use became more widespread.

The actual cost of the drug is somewhat less than was then anticipated, but the evidence before me suggests that some 1.8 million men suffer complete and some 8 million partial ED. Thus the cost to the NHS of Viagra will be tens of millions of pounds per annum unless some restrictions are placed on its use.

Viagra * * * enhances the body's natural response to sexual stimulation and is effective regardless of the cause of the existing lack of response. ED itself can be highly distressing to those who suffer from it and may lead to depressive illness, loss of self esteem and loss of confidence and may have serious effects upon personal relations. It is not an aphrodisiac and according to the evidence presented on behalf of the applicants cannot enhance a man's libido or sexual performance if he does not suffer from ED. The Department's evidence has pointed to the lack of any clinical trial to confirm that, but has not sought to challenge the applicants' expert medical evidence that that is indeed so. However, there were real and understandable fears that, once Viagra received the marketing, * * * there would be an enormous pressure on GPs to prescribe it. Furthermore, it was feared, and the fear was reasonable, that the media interest and the resultant perception of the advantages and effect of Viagra would encourage a recreational use of the drug. Since GPs are usually dependent on the word of the patient that he is suffering from ED and there are no independent means of verifying the patient's assertions, extensive prescribing and so considerable expenditure by the NHS on the drug to the detriment of other use of resources was feared.

In the summer of 1998, the respondents began to take positive steps to prepare for the impact of Viagra when it was licensed as was then anticipated in the late autumn of that year. On 14 July 1998 there was a debate in the House of Commons in the course of which the Minister of State, Mr Alan Milburn, stated that the Standing Medical Advisory Committee (SMAC) had been asked to develop guidance for the NHS on the role of Viagra. * * *

SMAC is a body set up under the provisions of the National Health Service Act 1977 as amended to advise the Secretary of State and the Central Health Services Council on medical matters. * * * There are at present 32 members of SMAC. All are distinguished and knowledgeable in their particular field of medicine and advice given by SMAC is regarded as authoritative, broad-based and independent. * * *

* * *

At a meeting on 29 July, SMAC decided to set up a working group to consider the issue because it was agreed that the matter needed careful consideration. * * * It was not then certain when the marketing authorisation was likely to be granted (it being generally anticipated that an authorisation would be approved) and it was hoped that SMAC would be able to produce its final report before then. In fact, the authorisation was granted somewhat earlier than expected on 15 September 1998 by the European Medicines Evaluation Agency, on which the United Kingdom is represented, and that authorisation entitled the applicants to market Viagra throughout the Union.

Following the meeting of 29 July, Professor Johnson wrote to Baroness Hayman, who by then had succeeded Baroness Jay as Minister, stating:

> Should the drug be licensed before [the working group can advise], SMAC would recommend that Sildenafil should not be routinely prescribed until it has finalised its advice on the clinical circumstances in which such prescribing would be appropriate: and we should be happy for the Department, at that time, to draw this recommendation to doctors' attention.

On 8 September a meeting of the Working Party took place. By then it was apparent that Viagra was about to receive its marketing authorisation and SMAC had been requested by the Department to change the wording of the interim advice. The new wording, which Professor Johnson thought did not change the substance of the original advice, was promulgated in Circular 1998/158 dated 16 September 1998, in these terms:

* * *

> As you may know, Sildenafil (Viagra) is in the process of receiving marketing authorisation from the European Commission.
>
> The potential availability of this drug raises issues about the priority which should be given to the treatment of erectile dysfunction under the NHS.
>
> Ministers are considering these issues in the light of available information about Sildenafil, including seeking the further views of scientific and clinical advisers, and the manufacturer.
>
> Ministers will be considering all the advice and information they receive and will be drawing up substantive policy proposals within the next few weeks. As an interim measure. Standing Medical Advisory Committee has advised that doctors should not prescribe Sildenafil. Health authorities are also advised not to support the provision of Sildenafil at NHS expense to patients requiring treatment for erectile dysfunction, other than in exceptional circumstances which they should require be cleared in advance with them.
>
> I would stress that this is interim guidance only, and should not be taken as implying that Ministers have made decisions relating to the nature and extent of any future availability of this drug as part of NHS services.

The Circular contains, under its title, the words "material which is for guidance only and aims to share good practice on a particular issue". * * * The lawfulness of this Circular is challenged in these proceedings.

* * *

The governing Act is the National Health Services Act 1977. Section 1 lays upon the Secretary of State the general duty to continue to promote a comprehensive health service and effective services, which "shall be free of charge except insofar as the making and recovery of charges is expressly provided for by or under any enactment, whenever passed." Section 3 enjoins the Secretary of State to provide, inter alia, medical services "to such extent as he considers necessary to meet all reasonable requirements". * * * Suffice it to say that there is no specific power in the Secretary of State to issue directions the effect of which is to prevent a drug from being prescribed either wholly or partially. * * *

The relevant regulations are the National Health Service (General Medical Services) Regulations 1992. Regulation 3, so far as material, provides:

> (1) The arrangements with doctors for the provision of general medical services ... shall include arrangements for the provision of:
>
> (a) all necessary and appropriate personal medical services of the type usually provided by general practitioners.
>
> (2) The arrangements to which paragraph (1) refers shall incorporate the terms of service set out in Schedule 2 and Schedules ... 10 and 11 ... shall have effect for the purposes of paragraphs ... 44(1), 44(2) ... respectively of the terms of service.

Schedule 2 contains the following relevant paragraphs:

* * *

> 12(1). Subject to paragraphs 3 ... and 44, a doctor shall render to his patients all necessary and appropriate medical services of the type usually provided by general medical practitioners.
>
> 43(1). Subject to paragraph 44, a doctor shall order any drugs or appliances which are needed for the treatment of any patient to whom he is providing treat-

> ment under these terms of service by issuing to that patient a prescription form, and such a form shall not be used in any other circumstances.
>
> 44(1). In the course of treating a patient to whom he is providing treatment under those terms of service, a doctor shall not order on a prescription form a drug or other substance specified in Schedule 10 to these Regulations but may otherwise prescribe such a drug or other substance for that patient in the course of that treatment.
>
> (2). In the course of treating such a patient a doctor shall not order on a prescription form a drug specified in an entry in column 1 of Schedule 11 of these Regulations unless [certain exeptions are met] * * *

* * *

Schedule 10 contains a long list of drugs and substances for which the NHS will not pay. It is largely made up of items such as patent remedies, drugs which are no more effective than cheaper (often generic) alternatives, substances such as sun creams, hair tonics and vitamin supplements and the occasional drug, for example temazepam capsules, which has proved to have been misused and which has no unique positive benefits. Schedule 11 is designed for drugs which, for example, are needed for the treatment of particular conditions but which can be used for others where there are cheaper and equally effective alternatives. Alterations to the lists in the two Schedules require an amending Statutory Instrument. [Under British law a statutory instrument is delegated legislation made by a body under powers given it by Parliament.]

The Regulations do not indicate the basis upon which drugs or substances should be "black listed" in Schedules 10 or 11. One public announcement of criteria was by the then Secretary of State, Mr Kenneth Clarke in March 1985 (dealing with a precusor to the 1992 Regulations) when he said this:

> It follows that the criterion for including drugs in the schedule of medicinal products and other substances not to be available on NHS prescription from 1 April 1985 was that, on expert advice, they had no clinical or therapeutic advantage over other, cheaper, drugs in the categories of antacids, laxatives, analgesics for mild to moderate pain, cough and cold remedies, bitters and tonics, vitamins and benzodiazepine sedatives and tranquillisers. Drugs prescribable only for specified conditions—at present only one, Clobazam for epilepsy—are those which have more than one distinct therapeutic use and which meet this criterion for at least one of those uses but do not meet it for all of them.

* * *

There are no cheaper drugs which are equally effective and so those criteria do not apply to Viagra. However Mr Pannick Q.C. [representing Pfizer] rightly concedes that the Secretary of State is entitled to include Viagra in Schedule 11 because of resource implications following the likely cost of allowing it to be freely prescribed. On 7 May 1999, the Friday before the Monday on which this application came before me, the Secretary of State issued a circular indicating that he proposed to make regulations on 1 July 1999 to limit the prescription of all treatments for ED on the NHS to men who suffered it as a result of various specified causes or who were receiving treatment (which, of course, would have been other than by Viagra) before 14 September 1998. These proposals were anticipated following a consultation which commenced on 21 January 1999.

I should add that, as the wording of paragraph 44 makes clear, doctors can prescribe Viagra privately, provided that they do not breach paragraphs 40 or 42. There was, according to Professor Johnson, particular concern that it would prove extremely difficult, if not impossible, to claw back the position if SMAC's eventual advice was to the effect that there should be some restrictions on prescribing Viagra. Patients might receive treatment which would have to cease. Further, SMAC felt there was a danger of different approaches by GPs and Health Authorities to the pressures on them and the resource implications stemming from the availability of Viagra which might lead to the undesirable practice of what is dubbed "post-code prescribing", i.e. different treatment in different areas. There were also concerns that ED was a condition which relied upon self reporting by the men affected and often no objective criteria were available to test the existence or the severity of the condition. Furthermore, there were stories of misuse by young men who believed the drug could enhance their sexual performance.

In due course, SMAC gave its final advice, once the Working Party had concluded its deliberations, on 9 November 1998. Its conclusions were as follows:

> (i) SMAC recognises that the aim of prescribing Sildenafil is to correct the distressing condition of erectile dysfunction so that sexual function returns towards normal. In common with many treatments available under the NHS this improves quality of life, but does not save or prolong it:
>
> (ii) provided that Sildenafil is prescribed only to patients who have the medical condition of erectile dysfunction, SMAC sees no medical reason why it should not be available on the NHS in accordance with the terms of the summary of product characteristics in the marketing authorisation: nor why it should not be prescribed by GPs with referral to hospital specialists where appropriate:
>
> (iii) SMAC suggests that Ministers should consider the priority to be given to all methods of managing erectile dysfunction within the NHS relative to treatments for other conditions, but that any decision should take into account equity of access as well as availability of resources. Doctors will need clear Government support and national guidance;
>
> (iv) once Ministers have decided in principle on the prescribing of Sildenafil. SMAC would be happy if so requested to prepare appropriate clinical guidance for doctors.

Thus there was in SMAC's view no medical bar to the prescribing of Viagra and GPs were considered perfectly competent to decide whether a particular patient should be treated with it.

* * *

Advice or guidance promulgated by a public authority may be the subject of judicial review if it contains an error of law. This is particularly so if it is likely to be acted upon by those it addresses: * * *

It is clear that, for very understandable and proper reasons, the Secretary of State was concerned that Viagra would prove to have a significantly adverse effect on the resources of the NHS. The Press Release which accompanied the Circular quoted him as stating "doctors are advised not to prescribe Viagra nor Health Authorities support the provision by NHS Trusts of the drug at NHS expense, until further notice". It was therefore hardly surprising that the press reported the Circular as a "ban" on Viagra. Indeed, Mr Moran, the chairman and managing director of the applicants, deposes without contradiction that he understands that the Secretary of State had personally briefed one of the journalists who used the terminology "a ban". * * *

The advice was initially very effective and its effect was exacerbated because, since Viagra was not "blacklisted" in Schedule 11, it could not be prescribed privately to their patients by NHS GPs. The respondent's own evidence shows that between September and December 1998 an average of only 108 NHS prescriptions for Viagra were issued each week across the country. In the light of the feared rush to obtain the drug, that is a clear indication that the advice was largely effective. The "exceptional circumstances" referred to in the Circular were never specified, although no doubt the proposals put out to consultation on 21 January 1999 gave from that date some indication of when Viagra should be prescribed. * * *

All this, which I have summarised very briefly, enables Mr Pannick to submit that the purpose and effect of the Circular was indeed to deter GPs from carrying out their statutory duties under their Terms of Service. He submitted that paragraph 43 imposed a duty on a GP to prescribe a drug if he was satisfied the patient had a clinical need for it. Paragraph 43 in my judgment does not impose a duty to prescribe a drug. It is dealing with the mechanism to enable a patient to receive a drug if the doctor decides that that drug should be used to treat the patient. * * * The doctor must give such treatment as he, exercising the professional judgment to be expected from an average GP, considers necessary and appropriate. * * *

The very fact that the advice in the Circular comes from SMAC is likely to make GPs respect it the more and thus to follow it. Mr Pannick has attacked the reasons given for imparting it, castigating them as irrational. I do not think that attack succeeds. I should hesitate long before branding the views on medical matters of eminent practitioners to be irrational. In any event, whether the reasons be good or bad cannot affect the lawfulness of the Circular if its purpose and effect is to cause GPs to act contrary to their professional obligations and contrary to their duty as reflected in paragraph 12(1).

* * * Mr Pannick accepted that advice could be given in strong terms to deter the prescribing of Viagra, but it must make clear that the GPs' clinical judgement is supreme. In essence, the advice should have been reasoned, at least so that GPs knew why they should only prescribe Viagra sparingly. To state in bald terms that Viagra should not be prescribed save in (undefined) exceptional circumstances is tantamount to telling the recipients of the advice to follow it. They cannot know how their professional judgement should be influenced by the advice. In my judgement, the evidence confirms that this was intended to be acted upon by GPs independently of whether in their professional judgement a patient needed treatment for ED and so should have the better such treatment available, namely Viagra. Thus I am satisfied that the Circular was, and is, unlawful in terms of domestic law.

* * *

I must now turn to consider European law.

Mr Pannick submits that the Circular is contrary to the law of the European Union in two respects. First, it amounts to a measure having equivalent effect to a quantitative restriction within the meaning of Article 30 of the E.C. Treaty (now, after amendment. Article 28 E.C.). That Article reads:

> Quantitative restrictions and measures having equivalent effect shall, without prejudice to the following provisions, be prohibited between Member States.

Article 28 is qualified by Article 36 of the E.C. Treaty (now, after amendment, Article 30 E.C.), which, so far as material, reads:

> The provisions of Article 28 ... shall not preclude prohibitions or restrictions on imports, exports or goods in transit justified on grounds of ... the protection of

> health and life of humans ... Such prohibitions or restrictions shall now. however, constitute a means of arbitrary discrimination or a disguised restriction on trade between Member States.

The submission is made possible because Viagra is the only remedy for ED which is singled out and has restrictions placed upon it. It is imported from another Member State and so there is discrimination against it which amounts to a quantitative restriction upon it. * * *

I have already discussed the purpose of the Circular and it undoubtedly has had a very considerable effect upon the sales of and the imports from another Member State of the product. Thus I have no doubt that the Circular constitutes a measure within the meaning of Article 28, and if its effect is to restrict or to be capable of restricting Community trade, it is unlawful.

Miss Baxendale [representing the Secretary of State for Health] submits that, whether or not it is a measure, the Circular cannot contravene Article 28 because the restriction of a particular product under a national health system is outside Article 28. * * * [In evaluating this argument, the court refers to a case, Case 238/82, *Duphar BV and Others v. Netherlands.*] That case concerned measures in the Netherlands which were akin to our Schedules 10 and 11 whereby restrictions where placed on the ability of some products to be paid for under the Dutch National Health Scheme. Such measures are prima facie discriminatory, but that will not render them unlawful under Article 28 provided that two conditions are fulfilled. The core of the judgment of the Court is contained in paragraph [22] which reads:

> The answer to the first question should therefore be that provisions adopted within the framework of a compulsory national health care scheme with the object of refusing insured persons the right to be supplied, at the expense of the insurance institution, with specifically named preparations are compatible with Article 30 of the Treaty if the determination of the excluded medicinal preparations involves no discrimination regarding the origin of the products and is carried out on the basis of objective and verifiable criteria, such as the existence on the market of other, less expensive products having the same therapeutic effect, the fact that the preparations in question are freely marketed without the need for any medical prescription, or are products excluded from reimbursement for reasons of a pharmaco-therapeutic nature justified by the protection of public health, and provided that it is possible to amend the list whenever compliance with the specified criteria so requires.

The Court then goes on to make the point that if the conditions set out are not met, the measure in question cannot be justified within Article 36 if its primary objective is budgetary "inasmuch as it is intended to reduce the operating costs of a sickness insurance scheme." It seems to me that it might be argued that the intention to reduce operating costs can itself be justified in non economic terms because of the effect on the ability to provide other treatment if Viagra costs too much. It is clear from what was said when the Circular was introduced that the respondent was speaking in purely economic terms, but that was because of the effect on the ability of the Health Service to provide for others and so the health of the nation could be adversely affected. Thus, although there was discrimination against Viagra, I am persuaded that the measure was justified under Article 30.

The second transgression of European law lies, submits Mr Pannick, in a breach of the Directive 89/105 * * *. It requires that there be publicity given to the criteria to be applied in measures to restrict or exclude any particular products for the obvious reason that manufacturers should know in advance what is the likely marketing fate of any product. As would be expected, the purpose behind the Directive is to ensure that there is no distortion or hindrance of intra-Community trade in medicinal products which cannot be justified or falls outside the *Duphar* conditions.

* * *

Articles 6 and 7 deal with positive and negative listing respectively. * * *

> Article 7
>
> The following provisions shall apply if the competent authorities of a Member State are empowered to adopt decisions to exclude individual, or categories of, medicinal products from the coverage of its national health insurance system (negative lists)
>
> 1. Any decision to exclude a category of medicinal products from the coverage of the national health insurance system shall contain a statement of reasons based upon objective and verifiable criteria and be published in an appropriate publication.
>
> 2. Before the date referred to in Article 11(1). Member States shall publish in an appropriate publication and communicate to the Commission the criteria which are to be taken into account by the competent authorities in deciding whether or not to exclude an individual medicinal product from the coverage of the national health insurance system.
>
> 3. Any decision to exclude an individual medicinal product from the coverage of the national health insurance system shall contain a statement of reasons based on objective and verifiable criteria. Such decisions. including. if appropriate, any expert opinions or recommendations on which the decisions are based, shall be communicated to the person responsible, who shall be informed of the remedies available to him under the laws in force and the time limits allowed for applying for such remedies.
>
> 4. Within one year of the date referred to in Article 11(1). the competent authorities shall publish in an appropriate publication and communicate to the Commission a list of the individual medicinal products which have been excluded from the scope of its health insurance system. This information shall be updated at least every six months.

* * *

It seems to me that there has been a continuing breach of Article 7.2. No doubt, the criteria can be updated from time to time, but, so far as I am aware, there has been no "publication in an appropriate publication" * * * and no communication to the Commission except in individual cases. However, more importantly, there was no compliance with Article 7.3. The applicants complained from the outset that they had been given no "reasons based on objective and verifiable criteria" and no opinions or recommendations (save for the bold statement in the Circular) were vouchsafed to them. The Directive sets out requirements (and domestic law is to the same effect) which are to be complied with before the blacklisting of a product can take place. It cannot be correct to bypass those requirements, which are there to safeguard the applicants' rights, and to restrict the product's marketing without complying with them.

It follows that I am satisfied that there was a breach of the transparency Directive.

Notes

1. Following its loss in this litigation, the Secretary of State for Health repromulgated its Viagra regulations, following proper procedures and publication requirements. A challenge to the new regulations was rejected, with the Court of Appeal holding that the government had complied with transparency requirements and that the criteria it applied were a political decision to be made by the Secretary. *Pfizer v. Secretary of State for Health* [2003] 1 C.M.L.R. 19.

2. The introduction of Viagra in 1998 posed a host of health law and policy problems for health care systems throughout the world. Its extraordinarily widespread potential use, its high cost, and its potential for abuse, raised issues for many health care systems. In Japan it raised another issue. Until very recently, oral contraceptives, which have been available for almost four decades, have not been approved for use by women in Japan. As is discussed further in chapter 3 below, this has contributed to a very high abortion rate. While opposition has been based in part on health reasons (concern about adverse cardiovascular effects), it has also been driven by concerns that widespread use of contraceptives would contribute to a decline in sexual morality, an increase in sexually transmitted disease, and a falling birth rate. Opposition to oral contraceptive approval has also been led by physicians who perform abortions (whose fees were estimated to total $400 million annually), and those who profit from the sale of condoms. While approval of oral contraceptives was repeatedly delayed in Japan, approval of Viagra came in March or 1999, only a half year following approval application, and without Japanese clinical trials. Women and the media protested a double standard of evaluating the health risks of drugs that affect sexual functioning for men and women, as Viagra also has the potential of significant side-effects. In June of 1999, a few months later, the use of oral contraceptives was finally approved. See Aya Goto, Michael R. Reich, and Iain Aitken, Oral Contraceptives and Women's Health in Japan, 282 *JAMA* 2173 (1999).

3. European Union law and European human rights law, and the institutions that interpret and enforce them, the European Court of Justice and the European Court of Human Rights, have the potential of affecting quite radically the right to health care in European nations. These institutions offer in nations without traditions of judicial review both the possibility of rights superior to legislative enactments or executive action and the availability of extra-national fora for challenging these rights.

The EC Treaty protects not only the free movement of patients and of products such as drugs, but also the free movement of professionals within member states, therefore in general, one EU member nation (e.g. Great Britain), cannot refuse to license professionals from another country (e.g. Italy). The qualifications that professionals must meet to be licensed (or to be recognized as specialists), however, vary from country to country, and thus complex issues arise as to whether the qualifications recognized by one country must be recognized by another, and what minimal qualifications must be met. The EU has put a great deal of effort into working out these issues. See Hervey and McCale, *Health Law and the European Union* 189–236 (2004). EU free trade and competition law also constrains the ability of European states to regulate private insurance, which poses problems for countries like the Netherlands that are trying to integrate private insurance into their social insurance programs. See Timothy Jost, Diane Dawson, and André den Exter, The Role of Competition in Health Care: A Western European Perspective, 31 J. *Health Pol., Pol'y & L.* 687 (2006); André den Exter, Blending Private and Social Health Insurance in the Netherlands: Challenges Posed by the EU, in Colleen Flood, Kent Roach and Lorne Sossin, *Acccess to Care, Access to Justice,* 257 (2005). Finally, the European Medicines Evaluation Agency, mentioned in the *Pfizer* opinion, provides a Europe-wide agency for approving the marketing of drugs.

Even beyond the borders of Europe, free trade law constrains the ability of countries to control their own health care systems. See Tracy Epps and David Schneiderman, Opening Medicare to Our Neighbors or Closing the Door on a Public System? International Trade Law Implications of *Chaoulli v. Quebec,* in Flood, Roach and Sossin, 369. The role of international trade law has become particularly controversial when the intellectual property rights of pharmaceutical companies have been asserted to maintain high prices and have thus limited access in developing countries. It is discussed further in chapter 4. See Roxanne Mykitiuk and Michelle Dagnino, The Agreement on Trade-Related Aspects of Intellectual Property Rights and Its Implications for Health Care, in Colleen Flood, *Just Medicare, What's In, What's Out, How We Decide,* 309 (2006).

F. Removing Barriers to the Exercise of the Right to Health: Access to Transplantable Organs

Although the most significant barriers to access to health care in most countries are financial, some medical resources are in short supply regardless of the availability of funding. The classic example of this is transplantable organs. In every country on earth where organ transplantation is available, the pool of potential recipients exceeds the supply. In response to this shortage, many countries have adopted legislation to attempt to increase the supply of transplantable organs. The form that this legislation takes varies dramatically from country to country, depending on cultural, religious, political, and legal factors. In some countries, however, these factors have led to the imposition of severe limitations on organ transplantation, or, in some instances to a total ban.

Most countries that permit organ transplantation have adopted legislation to address potential problems and abuses. See World Health Organization, *Legislative Responses to Organ Transplantation* (1994), cataloging this legislation. Issues commonly addressed include consent to removal of organs, determination of death, allocation of transplantable organs, confidentiality, and quality control. Cadaver organs are generally treated differently than organs from living donors. Germany adopted legislation dealing with organ transplantation in 1997, making its statute one of the most recent. Excerpts from the legislation follow:

Act of 5 November 1997 on the Donation, Removal, and Transplantation of Organs

Bundesgesetzblatt, Part 1, 11 Nov. 1997, No. 74, pp. 2631–2639, as translated in World Health Organization, 49 Int. Dig. Health Leg. (2) 316 (1998)

Part One: General provisions

1.(1) The present Act applies to the donation and the removal of human organs, parts of organ or tissues (organs) for the purpose of transplanting them to other persons as well as to the transplanting of such organs and including the preparation of these measures. Furthermore, it shall also apply to the prohibition of trade in human organs.

(2) The present Act shall apply neither to blood and marrow nor to embryological and fetal organs and tissues.

2.(1) The competent authorities according to *Land* [State] law, the Federal authorities within the framework of their competence, in particular the Federal Centre for Health Education as well as the statutory health insurance funds shall, on the basis of the present Act, educate the population as to the possibilities existing for organ donation, the prerequisites for organ removal and the significance of organ transplantation. They should also keep readily available cards with which the willingness to donate organs can be documented (organ donor cards) along with suitable educational material. The statutory health insurance funds and the private health insurance companies shall make such material available to those persons insured with them who have reached the age of 16, at regular intervals, asking them to declare themselves willing to donate their organs.

(2) Any person who submits a declaration of donation can consent to the removal of an organ pursuant to Section 3, can refuse such removal or can delegate the taking of the decision to a person of their trust mentioned therein by name (declaration of donation). The declaration may restrict the donation to specific organs. Both the consent and the delegation of the decision can be declared from the age of 16, the refusal from the age of 14.

(3) The Federal Ministry for Health may issue ordinances, subject to the consent of the *Bundesrat* [Federal Council, i.e. the German senate], delegating to an agency the function of storing the declaration of donation at the request of the person making the declaration and of furnishing information to persons entitled to such information (organ donation registry). The stored personal data may only be used to determine the admissibility of the removal of an organ pursuant to Section 3 or Section 4, from the person by whom the declaration was made.

* * *

Part Two: Removal of organs from deceased donors

3.(1) The removal of organs is, unless otherwise stipulated in Section 4, admissible only in cases where:

1. the organ donor has consented to the removal;
2. the death of the organ donor has been determined according to rules which comply with state-of-the-art medical standards;
3. the intervention is performed by a physician.

(2) The removal of organs is inadmissible in cases where:

1. the person whose death has been determined had objected to the removal;
2. the final, irreversible cessation of all function of the cerebrum, the cerebellum, and the brain stem is not determined according to rules of procedure which comply with state-of-the-art medical standards before the organ is removed from the donor.

(3) The physician shall inform the donor's next-of-kin of the intended organ removal. The former shall record the course and scope of the organ removal operation. The next-of-kin shall have the right to examine such records. The latter shall be entitled to call in a person who enjoys their confidence.

4.(1) In cases where the physician who is supposed to remove the organ has neither written evidence of consent nor written evidence of objection by the potential donor, the latter's next-of-kin shall be asked whether he or she is aware of a declaration of donation on the part of the potential donor. If the next-of-kin has no knowledge of such a declaration either, removal under the provisions set forth in Section 3, paragraph 1, numbers 2 and 3, as well as paragraph 2 of that Section shall only be admissible if a physician has informed the next-of-kin about a possible organ removal and has obtained his or her consent. In making the decision, the next-of-kin shall respect the presumed wishes of the potential donor. The physician shall inform the next-of-kin of this requirement. The latter may agree with the physician that his or her consent may be withdrawn within a specific, agreed deadline.

(2) Within the meaning of this Act, next-of-kin are, in the following order of priority:

1. the spouse;
2. children of full age;
3. the parents or, in so far as the potential donor was a minor at the time of death and the custody for his or her person was exercised at that time by only one parent, by a guardian or curator, then the person exercising this custody;
4. sisters and brothers of full age; and
5. grandparents.

Next-of-kin are only authorized to make a decision pursuant to paragraph 1 if personal contact between the former and the potential donor existed in the two years preceding the potential donor's death. * * * A person of full age who has evidently had an especially intimate personal relationship with the potential donor until the latter's death shall be of equal rank to the next-of-kin; such a person shall be on a par with the next-of-kin.

(3) In the event that the potential donor had delegated the decision regarding organ removal to a specific person, this person shall take the place of the next-of-kin.

* * *

5.(1) The determination of death pursuant to Section 3, paragraph 1, number 2 and paragraph 2, number 2 shall always be made by two physicians qualified for this purpose who have examined the donor independently of one another. By way of derogation from sentence 1, the examination and finding to that effect by one physician shall be sufficient to constitute the determination of death pursuant to Section 3, paragraph 1, number 2, if the final irreversible cessation of the heart and the circulation has taken place and more than three hours have elapsed since that time.

(2) The physicians involved in the examinations pursuant to paragraph 1 may participate neither in the removal, nor in the transplanting of the organs belonging to the donor. Nor may they be bound by the instructions of a physician involved in these measures.

* * *

6.(1) The removal of organs and any other measures taken in connection with that procedure must be performed in a manner which respects the dignity of the donor while observing the physician's duty to take due care.

(2) The donor's body shall be presented for burial in a dignified condition. Prior to this, the next-of-kin shall be given the opportunity to view the body.

* * *

Part Three: Removal of organs from living donors

8.(1) The removal of organs from a living person shall only be admissible if:

1. the person

   (*a*) is of full age and capable of giving informed consent;

   (*b*) has been informed pursuant to paragraph 2, sentence 1, and has consented to the removal;

   (*c*) is considered suitable as a donor according to medical judgement and is exposed to no foreseeable risk beyond that of the operation nor is likely to suffer any serious damage to his or her health other than the direct results of the organ removal;

2. the transplantation of the organ to the envisaged recipient is suited, according to medical opinion, to saving a person's life or to curing a serious disease, preventing it from worsening or alleviating the resulting complaints;

3. a suitable organ from a donor pursuant to Section 3 or Section 4 is not available at the time when the organ removal takes place; and

4. the intervention is performed by a physician.

Beyond this, the removal of organs which cannot regenerate is only admissible for the purpose of transplanting to relatives of the first or second degree, spouses, fiancés, or other persons with whom the donor obviously entertains an especially intimate personal relationship.

(2) The donor shall be informed by a physician about the type of intervention, its scope and the possible, also indirect, repercussions and delayed sequelae of the intended organ removal for his or her health, the organ transplant's expected chances of succeeding, as well as other facts which are evidently of importance to him or her with respect to the organ donation.

(3) The removal of organs from a living donor may only be performed after the organ donor and the recipient have declared themselves willing to participate in medically recommended post-operative care. A further condition is that the Commission responsible according to *Land* legislation has given an expert opinion on whether there are real, substantiated grounds to suppose that the person's consent to the organ removal is not being given freely or that the organ is the object of the trade prohibited under Section 17. The Commission shall be comprised of a physician, who is involved neither in the removal nor in the transplanting of organs, nor is bound by the instructions of a physician who is involved in such measures, a person who is qualified to exercise the functions of a judge, as well as a person who is experienced in psychological matters. Further details, especially those governing the composition of the Commission, the procedure and financing shall be regulated by *Land* law.

Part Four: Removal, allocation, and transplantation of specific organs

9. Transplantation of the heart, kidneys, liver, pancreas, and intestines may only be performed in transplantation centres authorized for this purpose. If these organs have been removed from donors pursuant to Section 3 or Section 4 (organs which are subject to allocation), it shall only be admissible to transplant them if they are allocated by an allocation agency acting in accordance with the provisions contained in Section 12. If organs which are subject to allocation are removed within the territorial scope of the present law, it shall, furthermore, only be admissible to transplant them if the removal has been performed in accordance with the provisions contained in Section 11.

* * *

10.(2) The transplantation centres are required to:

1. draw up waiting lists of those patients accepted for a transplant along with the particular necessary for organ allocation pursuant to Section 12, to decide without delay about a patient's acceptance for an organ transplant and his or her placement on the waiting list and to inform the attending physician thereof, as well as of the removal of a patient from the waiting list;
2. base the decision regarding placement on the waiting list on rules which reflect the current state of medical knowledge, especially the necessity of an organ transplant and its chances of success;

* * *

Part Six : Provisions containing prohibitions

17.(1) It is forbidden to trade in organs which are intended to be used in the treatment of patients. Sentence 1 shall not apply to:

1. the payment or acceptance of an appropriate compensation for the measures necessary to achieve the objective of the treatment regime especially for the removal, preservation, the further processing including measures to prevent infection, the storage and transport of the organs; * * *

* * *

Notes

1. Proposed amendments to the 1997 German organ transplantation statute were pending in the federal legislature as this book went to press. The primary effect of these amendments would be to expand the statute to cover tissue and cell as well as organ transplantation, and to regulate tissue the quality and security of transplantation and transplantation organizations. The amendments statute also address transplantation of organs and tissue from fetuses and embryos, bone marrow transplantation, and autologous transplantation. The provisions reproduced here, however, are not substantially altered.

2. The primary reason why Germany delayed accepting organ transplantation was opposition to accepting the concept of brain death. Traditionally death was determined by the absence of respiration and blood circulation, but solid organs degenerate quickly once the body ceases to be oxygenated. For this reason, widespread transplantation of cadaver organs required acceptance of the concept of brain death, as defined in section 3(2)2 of the legislation. There has been, however, and continues to be widespread opposition to the concept of brain death in Germany. This opposition is based in part on religious and philosophical concerns about reducing life to mental functioning, but also reflects Germany's uneasiness with the history of Nazi murders of mentally handicapped persons and, perhaps, with concern about excessive medical paternalism. See Bettina Schoene-Seifert, Defining Death in Germany, in Stuart J. Younger, Robert M. Arnold, and Renie Schapiro, *The Definition of Death, Contemporary Controversies*, 257 (1999).

3. The German statute is typical in outlawing the sale of organs. This provision is consistent with the Resolution of the World Health Organization (WHA42.5) on preventing the purchase and sale of human organs; Guiding Principles 5, 6, 7, and 8 of the World

Health Organization on Human Organ Transplantation (1991); Article 9 of Resolution (78) 29 of the Council of Europe dealing with organ transplantation; and the legislation of many countries. Article 21 of the Additional Protocol to the Convention on Human Rights and Biomedicine on Transplantation of Organs and Tissues of Human Origin, for example, provides:

Article 21—Prohibition of financial gain

> 1. The human body and its parts shall not, as such, give rise to financial gain or comparable advantage.
>
> The aforementioned provision shall not prevent payments which do not constitute a financial gain or a comparable advantage, in particular:
>
> – compensation of living donors for loss of earnings and any other justifiable expenses caused by the removal or by the related medical examinations;
>
> – payment of a justifiable fee for legitimate medical or related technical services rendered in connection with transplantation;
>
> – compensation in case of undue damage resulting from the removal of organs or tissues from living persons.

4. Despite the widespread prohibition, indeed criminalization, of organ sales, rumors of such sales persist in many countries. There have been, for example, persistent allegations that are routinely harvested in the Peoples Republic of China from persons who are executed and are subsequently sold. Allegedly, from 2000 to 3000 organs are obtained from prisoners in China per year, some of which are sold to overseas customers for up to U.S. $30,000 for the transplant operation. See Cesar Chelala, Prospect of Discussions on Prisoners' Organs for Sale in China, 350 *Lancet* 1307 (1997); BBC News, *Organ Sales Thriving in China*, 27 Sept. 2006.

Most alleged organ sales involve sellers from developing nations. There are obvious issues of equity involved here. Are developed nations denying developing nations a source of wealth by prohibiting sales, or are they legitimately protecting the citizens of these nations from over-reaching by the wealthy of the earth? One particular issue is whether organ sales in developing nations are truly voluntary. In addition to the allegations regarding China, there have been occasional media reports noting the involvement of organized criminal elements in the trafficking of organs in developing countries. Among the most gruesome reports are those involving the harvesting of organs from street children who are kidnaped and killed for this purpose. Should individuals from countries that strictly regulate organ transplantation be subject to prosecution in their own country if they travel to other countries to purchase organs for transplantation?

5. Donations by living donors obviously raise important questions of consent and concerns of possible duress or compulsion. How does the German legislation address these issues? What additional safeguards should be considered? Why are additional safeguards needed if consent to transplantation is voluntary and informed? Should donations to family members be favored or disfavored by law? Should it be permitted to conceive children to serve as potential donors for their siblings who need organs?

6. There is a particular concern with living organ donation by incompetents or minors. The WHO Guiding Principles (3 and 4) prohibit such donations, as would the Council of Europe Recommendation No. R(79), Article 9. Other nations, however, permit donations by minors or incompetents, with appropriate substitute consent, and subject to procedural safeguards. See David Price and Hans Akveld, Living Donor Organ Trans-

plantation in Europe: Re-evaluating its Role, 5 *European J. Health L.* 19, 36–37 (1998); Thomas Gutmann and Bernhard Gerok, *International Legislation in Living Organ Donation, in Procurement, Preservation and Allocation of Vascularized Organs* (G.M. Collins, et. al, eds., 1997). The provisions of the Council of Europe, Convention on Human Rights and Biomedicine on this topic are as follows:

Chapter VI — Organ and tissue removal from living donors for transplantation purposes

Article 19 — General rule

1 Removal of organs or tissue from a living person for transplantation purposes may be carried out solely for the therapeutic benefit of the recipient and where there is no suitable organ or tissue available from a deceased person and no other alternative therapeutic method of comparable effectiveness.

2 The necessary consent * * * must have been given expressly and specifically either in written form or before an official body.

Article 20 — Protection of persons not able to consent to organ removal

1 No organ or tissue removal may be carried out on a person who does not have the capacity to consent * * *.

2 Exceptionally and under the protective conditions prescribed by law, the removal of regenerative tissue from a person who does not have the capacity to consent may be authorised provided the following conditions are met:

i there is no compatible donor available who has the capacity to consent;

ii the recipient is a brother or sister of the donor;

iii the donation must have the potential to be life-saving for the recipient;

iv the authorisation [by a duly appointed representative] has been given specifically and in writing, in accordance with the law and with the approval of the competent body;

v the potential donor concerned does not object.

The Additional Protocol provides further:

Article 9—General rule

Removal of organs or tissue from a living person may be carried out solely for the therapeutic benefit of the recipient and where there is no suitable organ or tissue available from a deceased person and no other alternative therapeutic method of comparable effectiveness.

Article 10—Potential organ donors

Organ removal from a living donor may be carried out for the benefit of a recipient with whom the donor has a close personal relationship as defined by law, or, in the absence of such relationship, only under the conditions defined by law and with the approval of an appropriate independent body.

Article 11—Evaluation of risks for the donor

Before organ or tissue removal, appropriate medical investigations and interventions shall be carried out to evaluate and reduce physical and psychological risks to the health of the donor.

The removal may not be carried out if there is a serious risk to the life or health of the donor.

* * *

6. The German law says relatively little about allocation of organs once they are harvested. A recent study of allocation practice in Germany and in Western Europe finds that allocation practices vary considerably from center to center, and often involve a fair bit of discretion. While medical criteria and place in the queue are important factors, their relative weight varies from place to place, and other criteria, including controversial social criteria, may come into play. See Volker H. Schmidt, Selection of Recipients for Organs in Transplant Medicine, 23 *J. Med. and Phil.* 50 (1998).

7. With respect to cadaver organs, most nations follow either an express consent (opt-in) or a presumed consent (opt-out) model. These models are discussed in the following excerpt:

Legislation on Organ and Tissue Donation

Bernard M. Dickens, Sev. S. Fluss, Ariel R. King in Organ and Tissue Donation for Transplantation, 95, 100–04 (Jeremy R. Chapman, Mark Deierhoi and Celia Wight, eds. 1997).

* * *

Where legislation expressly allows post-mortem recovery of transplantable materials, it tends to fall into one of two general legislative patterns, namely "express consent" or "opting-in/contracting-in" legislation, and "presumed consent" or "opting-out/contracting-out" or implied consent legislation. The former are more traditional, and remain common for instance in Anglo-Saxon influenced jurisdictions. The latter are becoming more prevalent in especially Western European countries. They are frequently favoured by transplantation advocates because they may facilitate recovery of transplantable organs and also present the enterprise of cadaveric organ recovery and transplantation as a benefit society may legitimately promote.

Express consent legislation permits individuals before death, or family members after death, to donate cadaveric materials, as an expression of altruism and autonomy. It may suggest, however, that donation is an exceptional act, and that the norm is that bodies are buried intact. Presumed consent legislation treats cadaveric materials as a public asset, but permits individuals who object to their own or deceased family members' materials being removed to prohibit recovery. The right to withhold permission preserves personal autonomy, but it may require individuals who object to recovery of material to identify themselves to health or other public authorities, to place their personal religious or other convictions on record, and to declare that they decline to contribute an asset to the public.

Express consent laws may be reinforced by legal provisions that require health personnel or facilities to ask eligible individuals whether they are willing to do so. These are often described as "required request" laws.

Express consent laws

Early legislation that permitted donation of materials for transplantation after death was limited to recovery of corneas, the first human body part to become transplanted on a significant scale. Legislation now commonly empowers individuals to approve in advance post-mortem acquisition of any body materials, and also permits specified family members of a deceased person to consent to recovery, provided that the deceased when living had not expressed disapproval. Further, when patients apparently close to death have not consented to materials being recovered post mortem for transplantation but have not objected to this prospect, and physicians or other attendants cannot request their consent because they are unconscious or not able to form or express a choice, physicians or others may discuss recovery of materials with their relatives before death. Any consent that appropriate family members give prior to death, to posthumous removal of material, can be acted on as promptly as possible when death occurs, to maximize utility of recovered materials.

A legal concern is how clearly a person must express his consent to posthumous donation, and how that consent should be recorded. The common practice to attach a general and brief donation card to another significant document, particularly a vehicle driver's licence, may tend to exclude those ineligible to hold such a document. * * * In many countries and cultures, however, this form of consent to donation may also exclude women where it is not usual for women to hold relevant documents. Where organizations have been formed to promote post-mortem donation, they may produce separate donation forms or cards that are easily available and give assistance in applying any legislated or other provisions for the recording of such donation.

A comparable legal concern in posthumous organ donation is recording refusal of consent. Legislation usually empowers surviving family members to approve removal of materials for transplantation from bodies of deceased relatives who left no evidence that they did not wish their bodies to be used in this way. Evidence would exist in a prohibitive religious faith, in burial instructions incompatible with organ removal, and, of course, in clearly communicated disapproval of donation. A communication to a family member or a health or other service provider who proves not to be available when death unexpectedly occurs, and a request for posthumous donation made to another available person ineligible to consent, may fail to achieve its purpose. Accordingly, while express consent legislation requires donors to take the initiative to declare donation in some suitable way, it also requires people who do not want their organs to be removed after death on consent of their family members to demonstrate their refusal in a way that reasonably anticipates the usually unforeseeable circumstances of their deaths.

Legislation often declares that a family member eligible to consent commits no offence if he or she consents in good faith to posthumous recovery of materials from a deceased person who had in life expressed an objection of which the consenting family member is unaware. Similarly, a hospital or other facility involved in removing or transplanting materials on such consent incurs no legal liability, provided that its relevant officers and staff had no independent evidence of the deceased person's objection. A procedure should be in place in a facility that recovers organs after death to ensure that any patients' objections are adequately recorded. * * *

Legislation frequently provides that a person's competent declaration of post-mortem donation is legally sufficient to empower appropriate authorities to recover materials for transplantation. This is not an invariable rule, and for instance in Denmark, Italy, Sweden and Norway removal of materials is unlawful on the deceased person's earlier consent if relatives object to it for reasons of their own. Additional consent of family members is usually not required, however, since normally they have no legal power of veto. Despite this legal reassurance, however, there is considerable evidence that many health care personnel will not take materials on deceased persons' declarations when family members object.

Accommodation of family members' objections may be a dysfunction of a legislated rule that is sound in itself. Legislation usually provides that determination of a potential donors' death and surgical removal of materials shall be performed by physicians who have no commitment to or involvement with a prospective recipient. The provision is designed to preclude any conflict of interest in diagnosis of death and in management of the patient in the process and aftermath of death. However, personnel involved with such potential donors tend to remain engaged with their family members following death, and committed to family members' successful management of bereavement and grief. When surgery on the deceased to recover materials would cause distress to family members and obstruct their recovery from mourning, hospital personnel may consider it preferable not to undertake the surgery. "Wastage" of recoverable materials may be considered necessary for surviving family members' well-being.

* * *

Presumed consent laws

A number of countries, predominantly in Western Europe, have enacted legislation that authorizes removal of materials from cadavers unless in life the deceased had expressed an objection, and thereby opted out of automatic liability to posthumous removal of bodily materials for transplantation. In France, for example, Law No. 94-654 of 29 July 1994 on the donation and use of elements and products of the human body * * *, includes detailed provisions (introduced into the Public Health Code) that are based on this approach as shown in Articles L. 671-7 and L. 671-8.

* * * That decree prescribes that persons who wish to prohibit organ removal after their death may formulate the prohibition in any manner, and a hospital licensed to remove organs from dead bodies may record a prohibition at any time in a special register. If a person is incapable of expressing views, any indication found on his or her person, among his or her personal effects or elsewhere, that suggests that he or she would prohibit the removal of organs following death must be entered in the register. Anyone who can testify that a hospitalized person is opposed to organ removal after death must enter a substantiated statement to this effect in the register. Physicians responsible for recovery of cadaveric organs must, if not already aware of a prohibition, ensure that there is no prohibition in the register and ensure that the deceased was not a minor nor mentally incompetent. If the deceased was a minor or mentally incapable, organs may be removed only on written authorization of the deceased's legal representative before or possibly following the deceased person's death.

Details of the central concept expressed in the French legislation differ among countries. In Belgium, for instance, the law of 13 June 1986 on the removal and transplantation of organs provides in section 10(1) that:

> Organs and tissues for transplantation, and for the preparation of therapeutic substances ... may be removed from the body of any person recorded in the Register of the Population or any person recorded for more than six months in the Aliens Register, unless it is established that an objection to such a removal has been expressed.
>
> It shall be a requirement, in the case of persons other than those mentioned above, that they have explicitly expressed their consent to the removal.

Capable persons aged 18 years and over may object, but so also may a younger person who is capable of objection or, during his or her lifetime, a close relative living with the youth may record the youth's opposition to posthumous removal of organs and/or tissues. Legal representatives, guardians or closest relatives of mentally incapable persons may express objection during such persons' lifetimes. Objections to posthumous removal of materials made by capable persons or on their behalf must be signed and dated, and transmitted to the Data Processing and Information Centre of the Ministry of Public Health and Family Affairs.

It may be questionable under civil liberties and privacy legislation whether persons who object to posthumous organ recovery, perhaps on religious grounds, should be required to record this fact in governmental registers. Giving such information to hospital authorities is less objectionable, since knowledge of this nature permits hospitals to treat patients and their dead bodies according to patients' religious requirements, for instance concerning dietary practices and notifications and procedures on death.

Notes

1. Organ donation in the United States is governed by state law. With respect to most organs, express consent is required for donation, though family consent is usually permitted. Under the 1987 Uniform Anatomical Gifts Act, the coroner or medical examiner may also consent to removal of organs from a person in his or her custody if there is no indication that the person would have objected and the family cannot be found. Under federal law, and the laws of many states, a health care provider must request donation of a viable organ. Finally, federal law, and the laws of many states, prohibit the sale of organs. 42 U.S.C.A. §274(e).

2. Studies show that presumed consent countries do have higher rates of donation than express countries, although the difference is not large. In virtually all presumed consent countries, however, the family is consulted before organs are harvested. (Austria is the clearest exception.) A recent careful study, however, concludes that more important than the approach the country takes to consent are other factors, such as the wealth of a country, the incidence of auto accidents, and, most importantly, the organization of the transplant system. Kieran Healy, Do Presumed-Consent Laws Raise Organ Procurement Rates, 55 *DePaul L. Rev.* 1017 (2006). The latter factor seems to explain much of the success of Spain and Italy, which have dramatically expanded procurement in recent years. Presumed consent laws may also create, or alternatively express, a societal climate more hospitable to donation. Studies tend to show that the public in countries without presumed consent laws oppose them, while the public of countries with such laws are not bothered by them. See Paul Michielsen, Informed or Presumed Consent Legislative Models, in *Organ and Tissue Donation for Transplantation*, 344 (Jeremy R. Chapman, Mark Deierhoi and Celia Wight, eds. 1997).

The practical manifestations of various approaches to organ transplantation in widely differing cultural settings is illustrated by the following reading by an anthropologist who has extensively studied organ transplantation in Japan.

On Dying Twice: Culture, Technology and the Determination of Death

Margaret Lock, in Margaret Lock, Alan Young and Alberto Cambrosio, ed., Living and Working with New Medical Technologies: Intersections of Inquiry, pp. 250–57 (2000)

* * *

Tomoko Abe, a Japanese pediatrician employed for many years in a hospital that specializes in neurological disorders, has spent considerable energy during the past decade working with the grassroots movement in Japan against the legalization of brain death as the end of life. In discussing her position with me at one of our several meetings, she emphasized that the concept of brain death was created primarily for the purpose of facilitating organ transplants. She is emphatic that when a dying person is understood as the focus of both a concerned family and a caring medical team, then it is difficult to interpret brain death as the demise of an individual. Her opinion is derived, Abe states, from reflection on her own subjective feelings as a pediatrician: "The point is not whether the patient is conscious or unconscious, but whether one *intuitively* understands that the patient is dead. Someone whose color is good, who is still warm, bleeds when cut, and urinates and defecates, is not dead as far as I am concerned. Of course I know that cardiac arrest will follow some hours later—but I think even more significant is the transformation of the warm body into something that is cold and hard—only then do the Japanese really accept death." When asked why this is so, Abe replies that "it's something to do with Buddhism, I suppose, I'm not really a Buddhist but it's part of our tradition." Abe is completely opposed to organ transplants that are dependent on brain dead donors, and also has strong reservations about living related organ donations.

In 1985, the Japanese Ministry of Health and Welfare published guidelines for the diagnosis of brain death. The Ministry report is explicit, however, that "death cannot be judged by brain death" and it makes no claims to having any legal clout. Nevertheless, the diagnosis is frequently applied, and by 1987, 70 percent of the larger hospitals and university centers in Japan were making use of it, although patients were almost without exception maintained on ventilation even after the diagnosis "because relatives cannot accept the reality and medical personnel fear legal repercussions if they insist on discontinuing cardiopulmonary care."

The three decades of debate and confusion about brain death in Japan *apparently* reached closure on 17 June 1997 when the Japanese government passed a bill just moments before parliament was dissolved for the year end recess. The bill, which became law in October 1997, is a compromise, however, and the long dispute over whether brain death represents human death remains unresolved because ambiguity is built into the wording of the new law. This states that organs may be retrieved from a patient diagnosed as brain dead provided that the patient (at least fifteen years of age) has left written consent to be a donor, and that the family does not overrule the declared wish of the patient. Consent should be obtained from *all* relatives who lived with the deceased, including grandparents and grandchildren, if appropriate. Caution is advised with patients who are mentally handicapped. If no advanced directives exist, then a brain dead patient will continue to receive medical care after such a diagnosis is made, until such time as the family and medical team agree to terminate treatment and turn off the ventilator, often several days after brain death is diagnosed.

In other words, brain death is legally recognized only for those patients who have made it clear that they wish to donate organs. For potential organ donors, the legal time of death is when brain death is confirmed. For all other patients, brain dead or not, it is when the heart stops beating. If organs are removed from the body, then this must be noted on the death certificate. The Act also stipulates that medical expenses for patients who continue to be ventilated after a diagnosis of brain death will be reimbursed through the health insurance system, "for the time being." The current law is subject to revision after three years. The law has been described as a "typically confusing Japanese compromise" by many commentators in Japan. Under the new bill, physicians are not required by law to make routine requests for organs from the relatives of brain dead patients, nor can they be required by hospital administrators to do so. Initiation of inquiries about donation is thus left entirely up to the family.

Over the past thirty years, charges of murder have been laid against more than twenty doctors for procuring organs from brain dead, or purportedly brain dead patients. These charges were for the most part made by citizen activist groups, some of them led by physicians such as Tomoko Abe. Earlier this year all outstanding legal cases were dropped, and the assumption is that these decisions will facilitate the institutionalization of organ transplants using brain dead donors. However, despite the new law, to date not a single transplant has been performed making use of a brain dead donor. * * *

A vast literature exists, mostly in Japanese, commenting on why there has been so much resistance to the recognition of brain death in Japan. There is no consensus, and explanations range from historical prohibitions about the dissection of human bodies, concerns about the souls of the dead, corruption in the Japanese medical system, to a lack of trust in doctors in tertiary care institutions, caused especially because the idea of informed consent is not fully recognized in Japan. All of these arguments have some validity, but Japan is a complex, pluralistic society about which sweeping generalizations cannot be made (even though many commentators are tempted to do so). Despite the thirty-year impasse about brain death, public opinion polls have shown for several years now that approximately 50 percent of people in Japan think of brain death as the end of human life, a figure that is not very different from those obtained from polls in North America.

Among the fifteen Japanese intensivists whom I interviewed, the majority of whom were neurosurgeons, I did not find anyone who took such an extreme position as Abe, although her sentiments and those of others who think as she does (including many physicians), are well known among the Japanese public because they have made numerous television appearances and published widely on the subject. Like the North American intensivists, all of the physicians with whom I talked believe that brain death is an irreversible condition, provided that no errors have been made, but that a brain dead body is not dead. * * *

Although I conducted interviews in the year before the law was implemented, I would be surprised if the neurosurgeons working in departments of emergency medicine in Japan have changed their practices very much. Their position, even though they are not in principle in opposition to organ donation, is that it is inappropriate to declare brain death and then abruptly ask the family about donation. If the family does not raise the question of donation independently, as they rarely do (although this is changing a little since the passing of the new law), then the matter will not be discussed. There is, therefore, no haste, no pressure, and no need for an accurate diagnosis. This situation remains even after the enactment of the law in most clinical settings because, aside from a relatively small number of designated, university hospitals, other hospitals are still not legally able to procure organs, and thus far a lack of cooperation among hospitals continues to be the usual state of affairs. Given the discursive background and the history of legal suits in connection with brain death in Japan, it might be assumed that doctors would tend to practice "defensive medicine" and that this would therefore account for their reluctance to approach families about donation. While there is some validity to such an interpretation, it is grossly oversimplified in my opinion, and underestimates to what extent doctors are active participants in their own cultural milieu.

Among the neurosurgeons interviewed, they all agree that they "more or less" follow the Takeuchi Criteria, that is, the standards set out by the Ministry of Health and Welfare in 1985 for determining brain death. However, several of them added comments to the effect, "we don't always make the diagnosis, even when we suspect brain death. We often guess, which is much easier for the patient and the family." What is implied is that, in severe cases, the attending neurosurgeon will do one or more clinical tests, on the basis of which he comes to the conclusion that the patient is either brain dead or very close to it. He then informs the family that their relative is *hobo nôshi no jotai* (almost brain dead), or alternatively that the situation looks *zetsubôteki* (hopeless). Despite the prognosis, the ventilator is not turned off until the family requests it, often several days after the diagnosis.

One physician commented, "perhaps this is unique to Japan, but we believe that it is best to tell the family that we are continuing to do our best for their relative even though brain death is 'approaching,' rather than to say as they do in America, 'the patient is brain dead, here are the test results, we are going to terminate all care.'" This same neurosurgeon went on to state that usually, once he is convinced of brain death, he will "gradually reduce the treatment," meaning that no more medications are administered, and that the amount of oxygen being delivered from the ventilator is reduced. In his own mind nothing more can be done for the patient, but this neurosurgeon continues catering to what he believes are legitimate family desires.

Another neurosurgeon commenting on the actions of his colleagues said that "brain death is a kind of "end stage," in other words, there is nothing more that we can do for the patient, but we are ambivalent because brain death is not human death. * * *

A neurosurgeon with more than fifteen years of clinical experience said that he would never approach a family about donation, nor does he turn off the ventilator until the family requests it. This doctor reminded me that an extended family is often involved, and that if even one distantly related uncle telephones to say that he does not want the ventilator stopped, then it remains in place. * * * This same doctor insists that he has recently been getting firmer with families who stubbornly refuse to accept that the situation is hopeless. However, he never tells families that their relative is dead, simply that their condition is irreversible, and that they can no longer breathe on their own. Among those specialists who were interviewed, only one emergency medicine doctor, a man who had worked for several years in America, believes that families should be told firmly that their relative is dead once brain death is diagnosed.

Of the four Japanese nurses whom I interviewed, in common with the neurosurgeons, none of them evinced any difficulty with turning down the supply of oxygen from the ventilator once it was clear to the medical staff that brain death was close. Nevertheless, as one nurse insisted, for the family a brain dead relative always remains alive. Like several of the doctors, the nurses insisted that "life" and "death" are not fully medical matters, and family sentiments must be considered. Further, they argued that although moral and ethical issues in connection with the brain dead are not the same as for the living, brain dead patients remain in a "micro world" of their own where "something continues to exist."

In complete contrast to the responses given in North America by medical professionals, although there is an acute sensitivity about the ambiguous nature of a living cadaver, no one in Japan described the shell of a body remaining once the person or the soul departs. There are three reasons for this, I think. One is that clinicians do not think it is appropriate to persuade families that their relative is no longer alive; second, although many of the doctors stated clearly that for them once consciousness is permanently lost a patient is as good as dead, they do not believe that most families think as they do. "Traditional" medical knowledge in Japan holds that life is diffused throughout the body in the substance of *ki* (*ch'i*, in Chinese), and it is assumed as a result that most Japanese are not willing to equate a permanent loss of consciousness with death; third, surveys have shown that in Japan a good number of families remain concerned about tampering with the newly deceased who will eventually attain immortality as ancestors, and therefore deserving of special respect. * * *

Japanese have never been overly concerned by something resembling a Cartesian dichotomy, nor is the concept of unique, clearly bounded individuals in whom rights are unequivocally invested part of their recent heritage, although both these topics are extensively debated in Japan today. Among fifty Japanese I have talked to, only one-third locate the "center" of their bodies in the brain; the others, of varying ages, selected *kokoro* as the center, a very old metaphorical concept that represents a region in the thorax where "true" feelings are located.

The idea of individual rights is currently gaining a serious foothold in Japan, but has to battle against the still powerful flow of tradition in which an individual is conceptualized as residing at the center of a network of obligations, so that personhood is constructed out-of-mind, beyond body, in the space of ongoing human relationships. "Person" in Japan remains, for perhaps the majority, a dialogical creation, and what one does with and what is done to one's body are by no means limited to individual wishes. Moreover, self-determination is often thought of as essentially selfish. * * *

In North America, for intensivists, a brain dead body is alive, but no longer a person, whereas in Japan, such an entity is both living and a person, at least for several days after a declaration of brain death. Because, in the Japanese case, a social identity of brain dead patients remains intact, a brain dead body cannot be easily made into an object and commodified, but continues to be invested with "human rights." In North America, in contrast, a brain dead body takes on a cadaver-like status, deserving of the respect given to the dead, and, with family cooperation, is available for commodificaiton, on the assumption that the procured organs will be transformed into the "gift of life." While these differing discursive backgrounds do not determine what happens in clinical settings, they nevertheless contribute profoundly to the way in which clinical signs and symptoms are interpreted and then acted upon. * * *

In North America a cultural anesthesia has prevailed, the dominant position was institutionalized with little trouble by powerful mediators in the medical world, backed up by the law, and given the stamp of approval of the Catholic Church. What few disputes arose were refocused by medicine and the media onto the heroics of organ transplants, an act deemed to promote social affiliation. In Japan the Medical world blundered. The infamous case of 1969 that resulted in a murder charge being laid against the physician, and others similar to it that followed, exposed corruption in medicine. Japanese lawyers were immediately opposed to recognition of brain death, religious bodies remained virtually silent, and the media for the most part participated in a campaign to bring down the profession they have repeatedly described as arrogant. Culturally shared ideas about dying and the importance of family involvement in the determination of death have been mobilized in Japan and put to use for political ends in creating these arguments, but these same ideas are also acted out at the clinical level, where preservation of family affiliation is usually given precedence over any promotion of the donation of organs to unknown others.

One other major difference between Japan and North America is that in North America those individuals who choose not to cooperate with the donation of the organs of their relatives tend to be thought of as aberrant. Organ donation is thoroughly normalized and, aside from the perennial concern about sales of organs, it is assumed that organ procurement and transplants should be promoted worldwide. In Japan, by contrast, there is a reflexivity and caution about these practices, caused not simply by the internal national difficulties that have arisen with these procedures, but also by an awareness that ideas about altruism, human relations and human solidarity, personhood, and autonomy are cultural constructs. * * *

Note

In the previous sections variations among the law of the studied nations was largely explainable in terms of differences in political ideology and economic and social policy. With these materials on organ transplantation, new factors come into play, cultural and religious differences. Though most nations of the world now recognize freedom of religious belief to some extent, many nations still officially recognize and favor a particular religion. In others a religion, not officially established, is so predominant in society as to have an important influence on the law. What difference, if any, does it make that a law is based on religion, rather than on politics or economic policy?

Chapter 2

The Rights of Patients in Relationship with Health Care Professionals and Institutions

A. Patients' Rights

Although historically the relationship between health care professionals and patients has been paternalistic, most western countries now recognize at least in principle the notion of patients' rights. This chapter explores the most important of these rights: the right to receive competent care, the right to consent to medical treatment, the right to confidential treatment of health information, and the right of access to medical information. We begin our treatment of this material with a general discussion of the recognition of patients' rights in Europe, followed by the articulation of patients' rights formulated by two international bodies: the World Health Organization's European Region and the World Medical Association.

Citizens' Choice and Patients' Rights

World Health Organization, Regional Office for Europe, Copenhagen,
European Health Care Reforms,
Lars Fallberg, Chapter One, Patients' Rights, 11, 12–15 (1996).

* * *

The rights of patients and patient-centred care are concepts which are now stressed in almost every European country. Some have come farther than others. This status has to do with new factors such as culture, organization of health care, financing, legal traditions, power of actors, etc. The use of "push" principles are of interest in the sense that laws and normative rules have to influence and change a traditional, well-rooted health care system. This is influenced to a large extent by "paternalistic" views. The other side of the change process is that of patients. They have been, and are to a large extent obedient. In order to change this attitude, terminology such as "health consumers" and "users" are being used as an alternative for "patients." The use of such terminology is, however, criticized by some patient organizations as well as by groups of health care personnel.

Patient organizations are somewhat afraid that "strong" groups and individuals will gain more from such a change in terminology. It is reminiscent of market terminology, with negative connotations. This is partly supported by an analysis of Norwegian health care legislation where persons with certain diagnoses have legal entitlements to care within six months. It seems natural that the more severe diagnosis a patient has, the earlier he or she will receive treatment, provided the treatment is likely to succeed. An analysis of patients waiting for treatments of various kinds illustrates that psychiatric patients were "parked" on the lowest level without any entitlements whatsoever. A conclusion is that "patients' rights" have to be closely and continuously monitored and altered. A risk is that weak groups will tend to be forgotten in relation to more articulate citizens with well defined diagnoses.

In order to describe the development of patients' rights, it is necessary to have a "common language." For some people, patients' rights are related to legal rights where the key question is whether the right is enforceable in court or not. * * * In general, it is fair to say that patient rights are a combination of legislation and principles including ethical guidelines for different professional groups. The judicial part of the term includes civil rights for patients, material procedural as well as and duties for health care personnel, often interpreted as "rights" for patients. Principles on patients' rights are based on general agreements, consensus and the will to live up to agreed principles.

Depending on tradition and culture, the two patients' rights tools are used differently in various countries. The idea of general principles related to more defined forms of care guarantee is used in the Nordic countries. The principles are often national and improved in the County Council or municipality depending on regional conditions. Similar to the Nordic approach is that of the national patient charter, used in the UK. The Patient Charter, however, contains more defined principles, partly replacing similar legal provisions. The aim is to set a national minimum level of care and treatment.

Patient Charters are also used by East European countries as an effective way to promote the rights of patients. Civil legislation is perhaps most commonly used in the northern European countries. The general principle is to let patients choose and provide legal provisions in order to safe keep rights. Regardless of whether legislation, guidelines or principles are used to promote the situation of patients, it has to be used in consensus with all parties involved in providing health services.

* * *

The Nordic countries (Denmark, Finland, Iceland, Norway and Sweden) are characterized by administrative legislation which emphasizes the duties of the physicians and other professional groups rather than the rights of patients. Even if they are two sides of the same coin, there is a fundamental difference in that professional legal duties can not be enforced by patients, contrary to legal rights. The rights of various kinds which are expressed in health legislation are largely related to patient autonomy and access to information. There is no tradition of any considerable extent of civil court procedures. However, it is possible to seek compensation via the tort system. In all Nordic countries except Iceland there is some kind of "No fault patient insurance scheme" where patients are financially compensated for injuries received through health care services. The schemes are implemented in law or as an agreement between care providers and the state. The investigation regarding injuries is free of charge to the patient and is made by a patient insurance association. * * * Special legal (civil) entitlements to care are not to be found in Scandinavia. However, there is a tradition to use "principal documents" or "care guarantees" quasi rights. They give patients access to health care within a set time frame under certain circumstances, for defined illnesses and within the frame of available government resources. There are usually no sanctions when the obligation is not fulfilled, but the time limits are generally respected by health care providers and hospitals. Some Swedish County Councils have additional "rights" which compensate the patient when, for example, the doctor is more than 30 minutes late for an appointment.

Scandinavian medical associations are traditionally powerful in health policy. Their declared ambition is to work in favour of empowered patients. The influence of the many hundred patients organizations is acknowledged by the governments from which they receive considerable financial support. The major organizations are often heard when there is a patient related bill in the Parliament. There is no tradition of private fund-raising in Scandinavian patient organizations, * * *.

Northern Europe except the Nordic countries (Netherlands, Germany, Belgium, Luxembourg) have a similar organization for health care: as various forms of competing sickness funds and a choice of hospital organizations. This means a market influenced health care system where what in Germany is called *Krankenkasse* acts as purchaser and financier of health services. The legislation empowers patients somewhat differently in these countries. In the Netherlands patients' rights are implemented by legislation as well as by principal documents. In the Act on Medical Treatment Contracts from 1995 the objective is to strengthen the legal position of patients and the law compares to an ordinary tenancy agreement or employment contract. In Germany the rights of patients are not emphasized in the same way, which to some extent may depend on a strong medical profession with, as it seems, a relatively paternalistic view. The most active patient organizations are to be found in the Netherlands where patient perspectives play an important role, based on a strong consumer organizations representing over two million consumers.

In the United Kingdom the national Patients' Charter has had a major impact on public awareness of the performance of health care providers. It was launched in 1991 as a management tool for improving standards. It is described as part of an overall trend to improve the quality of health services and give more value to the views of patients and carers. The charter does not include any entitlements to health care and can be described as a statement of fundamental principles. The national Patients' Charter outlined ten "rights" and nine national standards such as the right to register with a general practitioner, to information, to be treated with dignity, etc. As an effect of this "charterism," several care providers have adopted local charters with various kinds of principles, originating, however, from the national charter. Yet the legal right of individuals to health care service, enforceable in court, is not emphasized in the United Kingdom. In general, the objective is to set a minimum standard throughout the country with local improvements.

Patient organizations and self-help groups in the United Kingdom receive little financial support from the government. Fund-raising is necessary and the financial frames of these organizations' activities are often narrow. The day-to-day work in the organizations is active and several of them provide a range of services to members as well as non-members. The hot-lines are popular and some organizations, such as the British Diabetic Association, help its members to get cheap insurance etc.

In southern Europe (Portugal, Italy, Greece, Spain) patients and consumers have a broad range of rights and principles. Health care provides and national authorities are active in developing and promoting various charters for patients rights. Legislation also explicitly provides citizens with certain rights. However, due to financial reasons, culture etc. these rights are not linked to sanctions if not fulfilled. The consequence of this is that existing rights are not fully taken advantage of by patients, nor are they respected by care providers and others.

Former socialist block countries (Hungary, Rumania, Russia, Lithuania) had for decades organized their health care services in a centralized way with practically no regard for the rights of patients. If there were any in the previous systems, they existed on paper and were rarely implemented in practice. However, recent developments have made these countries aware of the importance of patient centred care and the empowerment of patients. In order to keep pace with other European countries, several former East European countries are working on patients' right legislation and patients' rights charters, etc. Characteristic of this development is that the ambitions of politicians and legislators do not fit together economic resources and health services practice. One illustrative example is Lithuania. In 1994 the Health System Law was adopted. It contained a few citizens' rights such as a right to choose health care facility and health care provider, a right to information about ones' health status, a right to certain medical services, etc. Because of a wide gap between ambitions and primary conditions, the law had to be altered and the ambitions lowered one year later.

In other cases, ambitious declarations on the rights of patients have been made but have not reached the individual citizen. Behind these high ambitions is the pressure from other European countries to hasten the process of democratisation.

* * *

World Medical Association Declaration on the Rights of the Patient

Adopted by the 34th World Medical Assembly, Lisbon, Portugal, September/October 1981, and amended by the 47th General Assembly Bali, Indonesia, September 1995

Preamble

The relationship between physicians, their patients and broader society has undergone significant changes in recent times. While a physician should always act according to his/her conscience, and always in the best interests of the patient, equal effort must be made to guarantee patient autonomy and justice. The following Declaration represents some of the principal rights of the patient which the medical profession endorses and promotes. Physicians and other persons or bodies involved in the provision of health care have a joint responsibility to recognize and uphold these rights. Whenever legislation, government action or any other administration or institution denies patients these rights, physicians should pursue appropriate means to assure or to restore them.

In the context of biomedical research involving human subjects—including non therapeutic biomedical research—the subject is entitled to the same rights and consideration as any patient in a normal therapeutic situation.

Principles

1. Right to medical care of good quality

a. Every person is entitled without discrimination to appropriate medical care.

b. Every patient has the right to be cared for by a physician whom he/she knows to be free to make clinical and ethical judgements without any outside interference.

c. The patient shall always be treated in accordance with his/her best interests. The treatment applied shall be in accordance with generally approved medical principles.

d. Quality assurance always should be a part of health care. Physicians, in particular, should accept responsibility for being guardians of the quality of medical services.

e. In circumstances where a choice must be made between potential patients for a particular treatment which is in limited supply, all such patients are entitled to a fair selection procedure for that treatment. That choice must be based on medical criteria and made without discrimination.

f. The patient has the right of continuity of health care. The physician has an obligation to cooperate in the coordination of medically indicated care with other health care providers treating the patient. The physician may not discontinue treatment of a patient as long as further treatment is medically indicated, without giving the patient reasonable assistance and sufficient opportunity to make alternative arrangements for care.

2. Right to freedom of choice

a. The patient has the right to choose freely and change his/her physician and hospital or health service institution, regardless of whether they are based in the private or public sector.

b. The patient has the right to ask for the opinion of another physician at any stage.

3. Right to self-determination

a. The patient has the right to self-determination, to make free decisions regarding himself/herself. The physician will inform the patient of the consequences of his/her decisions.

b. A mentally competent adult patient has the right to give or withhold consent to any diagnostic procedure or therapy. The patient has the right to the information necessary to make his/her decisions. The patient should understand clearly what is the purpose of any test or treatment, what the results would imply, and what would be the implications of withholding consent.

c. The patient has the right to refuse to participate in research or the teaching of medicine.

* * *

6. Procedures against the patient's will

Diagnostic procedures or treatment against the patient's will can be carried out only in exceptional cases, if specifically permitted by law and conforming to the principles of medical ethics.

7. Right to information

a. The patient has the right to receive information about himself/herself recorded in any of his/her medical records, and to be fully informed about his/her health status including the medical facts about his/her condition. However, confidential information in the patient's records about a third party should not be given to the patient without the consent of that third party.

b. Exceptionally, information may be withheld from the patient when there is good reason to believe that this information would create a serious hazard to his/her life or health.

c. Information must be given in a way appropriate to the local culture and in such a way that the patient can understand.

* * *

8. Right to confidentiality

a. All identifiable information about a patient's health status, medical condition, diagnosis, prognosis and treatment and all other information of a personal kind, must be kept confidential, even after death. Exceptionally, descendants may have a right to access to information that would inform them of their health risks.

b. Confidential information can only be disclosed if the patient gives explicit consent or if expressly provided for in the law. Information can be disclosed to other health care providers only on a strictly "need to know" basis unless the patient has given explicit consent.

c. All identifiable patient data must be protected. The protection of the data must be appropriate to the manner of its storage. Human substances from which identifiable data can be derived must be likewise protected.

9. Right to Health Education

Every person has the right to health education that will assist him/her in making informed choices about personal health and about the available health services. The education should include information about healthy lifestyles and about methods of prevention and early detection of illnesses. The personal responsibility of everybody for his/her own health should be stressed. Physicians have an obligation to participate actively in educational efforts.

10. Right to dignity

a. The patient's dignity and right to privacy shall be respected at all times in medical care and teaching, as shall his/her culture and values.

b. The patient is entitled to relief of his/her suffering according to the current state of knowledge.

c. The patient is entitled to humane terminal care and to be provided with all available assistance in making dying as dignified and comfortable as possible.

* * *

A Declaration on the Promotion of Patients' Rights in Europe, 1994

World Health Organization, European Office

* * *

In the treatment of patients' rights, a distinction should be made between social and individual rights. Social rights in health care relate to the societal obligation undertaken or otherwise enforced by government and other public or private bodies to make reasonable provision of health care for the whole population. What is reasonable in terms of the volume and range of services available and the degree of sophistication of technology and specialization will be dependent on political, social, cultural and economic factors. Social rights also relate to equal access to health care for all those living in a country or other geopolitical area and the elimination of unjustified discriminatory barriers, whether financial, geographical, cultural or social and psychological.

Social rights are enjoyed collectively and are relative to the level of development of the particular society; they are also in some measure subject to political judgement regarding priorities for development in a society.

In contrast, individual rights in patient care are more readily expressed in absolute terms and when made operational can be made enforceable on behalf of an individual patient. These rights cover such areas as the integrity of the person, privacy and religious convictions. Although this text does address social rights, the main focus is on individual rights. * * * The intention is not to create new rights but to apply them in one coherent, comprehensive statement to the field of patients and health care. For similar reasons the text does not address general rights, obligations and liabilities, which are covered by the statutes and case law of each country.

The Rights of Patients

1. *Human rights and values in health care*

The instruments cited in the Introduction [i.e. the international conventions listed in Chapter 1 Section A above] should be understood as applying also specifically in the health care setting, and it should therefore be noted that the human values expressed in the instruments shall be reflected in the health care system. It should also be noted that where exceptional limitations are imposed on the rights of patients, these must be in accordance with human rights instruments and have a legal base in the law of the country. It may be further observed that the rights specified below carry a matching responsibility to act with due concern for the health of others and for their same rights.

1.1 Everyone has the right to respect of his or her person as a human being.

1.2 Everyone has the right to self-determination.

1.3 Everyone has the right to physical and mental integrity and to the security of his or her person.

1.4 Everyone has the right to respect for his or her privacy.

1.5 Everyone has the right to have his or her moral and cultural values and religious and philosophical convictions respected.

1.6 Everyone has the right to such protection of health as is afforded by appropriate measures for disease prevention and health care, and to the opportunity to pursue his or her own highest attainable level of health.

2. *Information*

2.1 Information about health services and how best to use them is to be made available to the public in order to benefit all those concerned.

2.2 Patients have the right to be fully informed about their health status, including the medical facts about their condition; about the proposed medical procedures, together with the potential risks and benefits of each procedure; about alternatives to the proposed procedures, including the effect of non-treatment; and about the diagnosis, prognosis and progress of treatment.

2.3 Information may only be withheld from patients exceptionally when there is good reason to believe that this information would without any expectation of obvious positive effects cause them serious harm.

2.4 Information must be communicated to the patient in a way appropriate to the latter's capacity for understanding, minimizing the use of unfamiliar technical terminology. If the patient does not speak the common language, some form of interpreting should be available.

2.5 Patients have the right not to be informed, at their explicit request.

2.6 Patients have the right to choose who, if anyone, should be informed on their behalf.

2.7 Patients should have the possibility of obtaining a second opinion.

2.8 When admitted to a health care establishment, patients should be informed of the identity and professional status of the health care providers taking care of them and of any rules and routines which would bear on their stay and care.

2.9 Patients should be able to request and be given a written summary of their diagnosis, treatment and care on discharge from a health care establishment.

3. *Consent*

3.1 The informed consent of the patient is a prerequisite for any medical intervention.

3.2 A patient has the right to refuse or to halt a medical intervention. The implications of refusing or halting such an intervention must be carefully explained to the patient.

3.3 When a patient is unable to express his or her will and a medical intervention is urgently needed, the consent of the patient may be presumed, unless it is obvious from a previous declared expression of will that consent would be refused in the situation.

* * *

3.7 In all other situations where the patient is unable to give informed consent and where there is no legal representative or representative designated by the patient for this purpose, appropriate measures should be taken to provide for a substitute decision making process, taking into account what is known and, to the greatest extent possible, what may be presumed about the wishes of the patient.

3.8 The consent of the patient is required for the preservation and use of all substances of the human body. Consent may be presumed when the substances are to be used in the current course of diagnosis, treatment and care of that patient.

3.9 The informed consent of the patient is needed for participation in clinical teaching.

3.10 The informed consent of the patient is a prerequisite for participation in scientific research. All protocols must be submitted to proper ethical review procedures. Such research should not be carried out on those who are unable to express their will, unless the consent of a legal representative has been obtained and the research would likely be in the interest of the patient.

* * *

4. *Confidentiality and Privacy*

4.1 All information about a patient's health status, medical condition, diagnosis, prognosis and treatment and all other information of a personal kind must be kept confidential, even after death.

4.2 Confidential information can only be disclosed if the patient gives explicit consent or if the law expressly provides for this. Consent may be presumed where disclosure is to other health care providers involved in that patient's treatment.

4.3 All identifiable patient data must be protected. The protection of the data must be appropriate to the manner of their storage. Human substances from which identifiable data can be derived must be likewise protected.

4.4 Patients have the right to access to their medical files and technical records and to any other files and records pertaining to their diagnosis, treatment and care and to receive a copy of their own files and records or parts thereof. Such access excludes data concerning third parties.

4.5 Patients have the right to require the correction, completion, deletion, clarification and/or updating of personal and medical data concerning them which are inaccurate, incomplete, ambiguous or outdated, or which are not relevant to the purposes of diagnosis, treatment and care.

4.6 There can be no intrusion into a patient's private and family life unless and only if, in addition to the patient consenting to it, it can be justified as necessary to the patient's diagnosis, treatment and care.

4.7 Medical interventions may only be carried out when there is proper respect shown for the privacy of the individual. This means that a given intervention may be carried out only in the presence of those persons who are necessary for the intervention unless the patient consents or requests otherwise.

4.8 Patients admitted to health care establishments have the right to expect physical facilities which ensure privacy, particularly when health care providers are offering them personal care or carrying out examinations and treatment.

5. *Care and Treatment*

5.1 Everyone has the right to receive such health care as is appropriate to his or her health needs, including preventive care and activities aimed at health promotion. Services should be continuously available and accessible to all equitably, without discrimination and according to the financial, human and material resources which can be made available in a given society.

5.2 Patients have a collective right to some form of representation at each level of the health care system in matters pertaining to the planning and evaluation of services, including the range, quality and functioning of the care provided.

5.3 Patients have the right to a quality of care which is marked both by high technical standards and by a humane relationship between the patient and health care providers.

5.4 Patients have the right to continuity of care, including cooperation between all health care providers and/or establishments which may be involved in their diagnosis, treatment and care.

5.5 In circumstances where a choice must be made by providers between potential patients for a particular treatment which is in limited supply, all such patients are entitled to a fair selection procedure for that treatment. That choice must be based on medical criteria and made without discrimination.

5.6 Patients have the right to choose and change their own physician or other health care provider and health care establishment, provided that it is compatible with the functioning of the health care system.

5.7 Patients for whom there are no longer medical grounds for continued stay in a health care establishment are entitled to a full explanation before they can be transferred to another establishment or sent home. Transfer can only take place after another health care establishment has agreed to accept the patient. Where the patient is discharged to home and when his or her condition so requires, community and domiciliary services should be available.

5.8 Patients have the right to be treated with dignity in relation to their diagnosis, treatment and care, which should be rendered with respect for their culture and values.

5.9 Patients have the right to enjoy support from family, relatives and friends during the course of care and treatment and to receive spiritual support and guidance at all times.

5.10 Patients have the right to relief of their suffering according to the current state of knowledge.

5.11 Patients have the right to humane terminal care and to die in dignity.

6. *Application*

6.1 The exercise of the rights set forth in this document implies that appropriate means are established for this purpose.

6.2 The enjoyment of these rights shall be secured without discrimination.

6.3 In the exercise of these rights, patients shall be subjected only to such limitations as are compatible with human rights instruments and in accordance with a procedure prescribed by law.

6.4 If patients cannot avail themselves of the rights set forth in this document, these rights should be exercised by their legal representative or by a person designated by the patient for that purpose; where neither a legal representative nor a personal surrogate has been appointed, other measures for representation of those patients should be taken.

6.5 Patients must have access to such information and advice as will enable them to exercise the rights set forth in this document. Where patients feel that their rights have not been respected they should be enabled to lodge a complaint. In addition to recourse to the courts, there should be independent mechanisms at institutional and other levels to facilitate the processes of lodging, mediating and adjudicating complaints. These mechanisms would, inter alia, ensure that information relating to complaints procedures was available to patients and that an independent person was available and accessible to them for consultation regarding the most appropriate course of action to take. These mechanisms should further ensure that, where necessary, assistance and advocacy on behalf of the patient would be made available. Patients have the right to have their complaints examined and dealt with in a thorough, just, effective and prompt way and to be informed about their outcome.

Notes

1. The World Medical Association is an association of the world's doctors, represented by the medical associations of the various nations. The World Health Organization is the official organ of the United Nations for dealing with health issues. The European Regional Office in Copenhagen has been a leader in encouraging the protection of patients' rights.

2. Compare and contrast these two patients' rights statements. On the surface they are very similar. Compare, however, their different specifications of the information neces-

sary for informed consent, of rights to medical records, of abandonment or discharge. Look at the order in which rights are presented. Who are the audiences to which these statements are addressed? Who are the constituents whom these statements serve?

3. How should patients' rights be enforced? What form of enforcement is contemplated by the WMA patients' rights statement? What form of enforcement do the WHO guidelines suggest? Statements of patients' rights are found both in legislation and professional codes. The former emphasizes the rights of patients, the latter the duties of professionals. What difference does it make which approach is taken? Several countries, most notably the United Kingdom, have adopted "Patient Charters"—statements of patient rights that are not specifically subject to judicial enforcement. What would be the benefit of this approach?

4. In many countries patient advocacy and self-help groups, often disease specific, play an important role in realizing rights. In some countries, such as the Scandinavian countries, these groups receive public support. In other countries, such as the U.K., they engage extensively in fund-raising activities (most conspicuously operating used clothing stores). A coalition of patients' rights organizations, the Active Citizenship Network, has drafted a European Charter of Patients' Rights (2002) and monitors compliance by European countries with this charter. See Allessandro Lamanna, Giovanni Moro and Melody Ross, *Citizens' Report on the Implementation of the European Charter of Patients' Rights* (2005), http://www.activecitizenship.net/documenti/patients_rights/ACN%20Working%20Paper.pdf. The rights included in this charter include the

- right to prevention,
- right to access (including financial and physical access)
- right to information,
- right to free choice,
- right to consent,
- right to privacy and confidentiality,
- right to respect of patients' time,
- right to the observance of quality standards,
- right to safety,
- right to innovation,
- right to avoid unnecessary suffering and pain,
- right to personalized treatment (with attention to diversity),
- right to complain, and
- right to compensation.

How and why does this list of rights differ from those set out above?

5. Many countries (and in particular countries with national health services) have ombudspersons or special administrative bodies charged with receiving, investigating, and resolving patient complaints. The first edition of this book included a section examining the operation of these mechanisms, but this section was dropped to make room for other topics. What advantages might administrative complaint mechanisms provide over compensation systems, usually administered through the courts? What weaknesses might they have compared to judicial remedies?

6. In the United States, federal patients' rights legislation exists only for nursing home residents (See 42 U.S.C.A. §§1395i-3(d); 1396r(d)). However, the Joint Commission on

Accreditation of Healthcare Organizations, which accredits virtually all hospitals in the United States, includes patients' rights requirements among its accreditation requirements. Many hospitals have patients' rights statements as well. Some states also have patients' rights statutes or regulations. Unless a breach of patients' rights by an institution amounts to malpractice and results in serious injury, however, enforcement of patients' rights is difficult.

In a number of nations, recipients of medical care are increasingly referred to as "consumers" rather than patients. "Consumer-driven" health are is a current fad in the United States in particular. See Timothy Jost, *Health Care at Risk: A Critique of the Consumer-Driven Movement* (2007). What difference does it make whether patients are considered to be patients or consumers? Consider the following.

Citizens' Choice and Patients' Rights

World Health Organization, Regional Office for Europe, Copenhagen, European Health Care Reforms, 17–19 (1996)

In some cultures the use of the word "health care consumer" is becoming more and more common. In the Netherlands and the UK, consumers of care and patients are almost synonymous. In the Netherlands, consumer and patient organizations are joined in the same federation and with the same general objectives. This is not the case in most other European countries. Although the word "consumer" is occasionally used in many countries, it remains controversial to some. It is seen as a market oriented approach without connection to the "empathy" which is so important in health services. Relations between health care providers and patients may touch upon existential questions with a high emotional content.

However, some patient organizations see the health consumer concept and the consumer movement as an opportunity to empower patients and to increase patients' influence. The Swedish Diabetes Federation, for instance, is undergoing change towards a more consumer oriented approach. This mirrors a more concerned and demanding citizen who wants explanations, quality information and to be a subject, not an object, in encounters with physicians, nurses and other professional groups. To distinguish between a traditional patient role and the role of consumers of health care, the following table can be an illustration.

Table 3 - Differences between being a patient or a consumer

The Role of Patients	The Role of Consumers
Patience	Activity
Dependence	Integrity
Weak Position	Equality
Lack of Freedom	Mobility, freedom of choice
To be represented by experts	To represent oneself
Unawareness of quality	Awareness of quality
Unawareness of costs	Awareness of costs

The political decision makers' efforts to empower patients varies from vague political principles and statements, to legal rights, where the individual can enforce his or her care in court. In countries where politicians and health care professionals long have been the one and only guarantee of patients' interests, the system is criticized for its inability to give sufficient care to weak patient groups. However, in countries with a legal tradition of strong individual rights, the present development is more in harmony with its traditions.

* * *

An analysis published by the Swedish Institute for Health Economics in Lund demonstrates that citizens' attitudes to care, treatment and health care personnel is largely related to age. As a rules principle, citizens largely wanted to be involved in decisions about the health care services to be provided. Citizens above 40 years of age see the choice of general practitioners as most important. Younger citizens, however, were of the opinion that the choice between doctor and hospital is equally important. The study also shows a difference between citizens with higher versus lower education. Young, well educated citizens are less in favour of saying that the level of competence in hospitals and with respect to physicians is so high that it does not matter where to go in case of need. Only 17% of persons below 30 wanted to leave the physician to decide alone in medical matters.

Only 6% of the interviewees believed that physicians in general are so competent that it is irrelevant by whom to be treated. However, there is a difference between old and young. The latter prefer to believe that competence in general is sufficiently high. Factors related to competence such as education, speciality, experience and disciplinary warnings is what is most asked for. Young citizens in particular do not hesitate to make demands of the physician and to ask for criteria in order to judge their competence.

B. The Right to be Free from Medical Negligence

1. Civil Liability

In most countries of the world, medical professionals and institutions can be held responsible through civil litigation for injuries that their negligent errors cause to their patients. In common law countries this obligation is generally imposed under the common law of tort, or, more specifically, the law of medical negligence. In civil law countries, liability is imposed under civil code provisions addressing the law of obligations. Liability could be based on delict, the civil law equivalent of tort. But in many jurisdictions it is more likely to be based on contract law. The doctor-patient relationship is primarily contractual, and the doctor who injures a patient may be held liable for breach of this contractual obligation. The contract is seen as one of means rather than result, however—the doctor is not liable for a bad result, as through breach of warranty, but rather for failing to use the proper means in dealing with the case, as is demonstrated by the following case:

Cour de Cassation of France

1st Civil Chamber, Decision of 25 February 1997 (translated by Pierrick LeGoff)

On the motion to overrule the decision of the Court of Appeals, the following was decided:

Whereas, according to the facts established in the judgement rendered by the judges of the Court of First Instance, Mr. Mazoyer, surgeon, performed surgery at the Engene

Andre clinic on September 15, 1987, on Mr. Goenvic, a civil servant working for the city of Lyon. The surgery was performed under local anesthesia and was intended to eliminate a carotid fistula by the use of an inflatable and releasable balloon. While the balloon was being put in place, it became evident that it was necessary to modify the position of the balloon by deflating it. This could only be done by piercing the balloon; therefore the surgeon attempted to retrieve the balloon.

During this procedure, the deflated balloon detached itself from the carrying catheter and entered into the internal carotid artery. From there, it entered into the mid cerebral artery which became obstructed. This resulted in an emiplegia (paralysis of the right side of the body) even though the patient was immediately transported to a neurological hospital and underwent surgery intended to unblock the artery. M. Goenvic and his employer have initiated litigation against Mr. Mazoyer, the clinic, and the clinic's insurer to recover compensation for the damage suffered. Based on the report issued by two medical experts and the contrary report issued by three other medical experts, the Court of Appeals of Lyon (decision of 10 November 1994) rejected the compensation claim on the ground that neither medical malpractice nor defective medical equipment were present, and that the incident suffered by Mr. Goenvic was to be viewed as the materialization of a risk inherent in any surgery.

Whereas, the city of Lyon and Mr. Goenvic have filed a motion to overrule the decision rendered by the Court of Appeals of Lyon arguing i) that the surgeon who uses a device to be placed inside the body of the patient is bound by an "obligation of result" as far as the safety of the patient is concerned and ii) that having concluded that there was a problem with the balloon used by the surgeon, since it could not be deflated during the normal course of the surgery and had detached itself from the carrying catheter, the Court of Appeals should have decided that Mr. Mazoyer did not comply with the "obligation of result" concerning the safety of his patient, and did not need to investigate further whether the balloon was affected by a defect. According to the plaintiffs, it would follow therefrom that the Court did not draw the conclusions it should have in the light of article 1147 of the Civil Code.

Whereas, however, a surgeon who places a device in a patient is only bound by an "obligation of means". Whereas, further, the Court of Appeals, having due regard to the reports of the medical experts, concluded i) that in view of the pathology of the patient, the medical procedure used was not only justified but also was the best one under the current state of medical knowledge, ii) that the equipment used was free from any defect and iii) that the surgeon had checked the equipment prior to its use in the particular case by testing the balloon. The surgeon therefore took all standard precautions recommended in the medical field for such situations. Based again on the experts' views, the Court of Appeals concluded further that no medical malpractice was committed at the time of placing the balloon or during its retrieval. The Court of Appeals added further i) that the medical treatment had been performed in a conscientious manner and in compliance with the current state of knowledge of medical science and ii) that the method used for the retrieval of the balloon was sensible. As a result, the Court of Appeal, by concluding that no mistake had been made in the preparation, performance and follow-up of the surgery gave a proper legal justification for its decision. The motion to overrule this decision is therefore rejected.

Note

Article 1147 referred to in the decision is part of the Civil Code section on damages to be paid for failure to comply with an obligation. It is the article on the basis of which the distinction between "obligation of result" and "obligation of means" has been developed. This Article states: "Even if he acted in good faith, the obligor is liable to pay damages if there is either a failure to perform or a delay in the performance of the obligation, unless the obligor is able to prove that such failure or delay was due to a reason beyond his control."

Whether the obligation owed the patient is based on tort or contract, however, in most jurisdictions its content is quite similar to that found in the case above—professionals and institutions are held to a standard of reasonable conduct defined with reference to the conduct of professionals of similar specialty or training. The court must turn to medical experts for evidence of the appropriate standard of care. As the following excerpt from Dieter Giesen points out, national courts do differ in their interpretation and application of this standard, with the English and Scottish courts affording professionals more deference than other common law courts or continental courts under the classic *Bolam* doctrine.

Medical Malpractice and the Judicial Function in Comparative Perspective

Dieter Giesen. 1 Medical Law International, 3, 4–7 (1993)

* * *

It is proposed, in the course of this article, to expose and elaborate upon these central concerns of the law [of malpractice] through a comparative study of the rules of liability developed by a number of major legal systems. A comparative analysis will enable us to look beyond the particular and to ascertain the basic legal conception of the role of doctors in the provision of health care. This analysis will not reveal a wholly uniform picture of applicable legal rules and we will see that there exist considerable differences between the relevant legal rules in Britain and those in other common law and civil law jurisdictions. It is our intention to show that the position in England and Scotland is inconsistent with the legal *régime* governing all other professions, with the standards expected of doctors in all other member states of the European Community, as well as in the major common law jurisdictions, and, perhaps most fundamentally, with the central function of the law in all democratic societies. * * * Put briefly, courts in most common law and in all civil law countries take, to varying degrees, a patient-centred approach to the imposition of liability for medical malpractice and this approach is a necessary function of the role of the courts as protectors of citizens in the exercise of their fundamental and constitutionally guaranteed rights.

Objective Standards in Treatment and Diagnosis

An examination of the standards imposed by the law of England and Scotland upon doctors in the performance of their therapeutic and diagnostic functions and of the role of expert medical evidence in determining such standards will show the regrettably *isolated* and notably *deferential* attitude of judges in those jurisdictions. The standard of care which is expected of doctors in all common law countries is that laid down by McNair J in the landmark English case of *Bolam v. Friern Hospital Management Committee.* According to this test a defendant doctor will not be held liable if he conformed to the standard of an *ordinary skilled man* exercising and professing to have that particular skill which the defendant held himself out as possessing. This standard does not require perfection of the doctor in the performance of his tasks, nor does it make of him the guarantor of a successful outcome to the patient's course of treatment. As long as doctors act in accordance with the practice of a *responsible body of medical practitioners* they will not incur a legal obligation to compensate the disappointed patient.

It is obvious, however, that the so-called *Bolam* test cannot be applied without the testimony of *expert medical witnesses* to assist in determining what exactly the prevalent practice or practices are in the area of treatment or diagnosis under review. Perhaps due to the admitted complexity of medical evidence, but perhaps also because of the exalted status of the medical profession in the eyes of the judiciary, decisions in England and Scotland betray an unusual deference to doctors' interests. Thus, in Scotland the *Bolam* test was interpreted to imply that a defendant will not be held liable unless " ... he has been proved to be guilty of such failure as *no doctor* of ordinary skill would be guilty of if acting with ordinary care." This minimalist approach clearly reduces the scope for judicial evaluation of the differing practices of the profession in any given field. The plaintiff patient's position of relative weakness at trial is exacerbated when the ruling of the Court of Session is read in conjunction with the decision of the House of Lords in the case of *Maynard v. West Midlands Regional Health Authority*. There, Lord Scarman, * * * rejected the trial judge's finding of negligence. The latter had found that although the defendant doctor had complied with the practice of a considerable body of medical professionals there was an alternative course of treatment which was in his view preferable to that in fact taken. Lord Scarman held, however, that " ... a judge's preference for one body of distinguished professional opinion to another also professionally distinguished is not sufficient to establish negligence." This ruling seems to indicate that expert medical evidence enjoys *virtually conclusive status* in the law of England and Scotland. If so, British medical professionals are privileged beyond their colleagues in the rest of the developed World and also by comparison with members of other professions in the United Kingdom.

Comparison shows the *singularity* of the British position. While accepting that recourse to expert evidence will be necessary in deciding professional negligence cases, courts elsewhere have consistently and emphatically stated that the role of the expert witness is always subordinate to the discharge of what is *ultimately and exclusively a judicial function*, namely that of determining legal standards of care. As it was put in a leading Australian case if a court merely followed " ... the path apparently pointed by expert evidence with no critical consideration of it and the other evidence, it would abdicate its duty to decide, on the evidence whether in law a duty existed and had not been discharged." Similarly courts in civil law countries have clearly rejected the unquestioning adoption by the law of expert medical evidence. Such evidence merely provides a factual basis for the application of wholly *legal* standards.

In most legal systems the test of liability is, therefore, not merely a descriptive summary of various widespread professional practices. Rather, it involves the application, by the judiciary, of *an objective, normative standard of care*. This crucial objective aspect of the legal standard is indeed made explicit even in the aforementioned *Bolam* test, which requires that the medical practice adhered to by the doctor has been that of a *responsible* body of medical men. Thus, English and Scottish judges are empowered and indeed obliged to evaluate even the most commonly followed approaches to treatment and diagnosis and in doing so to determine their reasonableness and legal acceptability. In the light of this necessarily critical process of evaluation, it is obvious that doctors cannot be allowed to set their own standards of conduct. In the words of the High Court of Ontario, courts reserve to themselves the power " ... to strike down substandard approved practice when common sense dictates such a result. *No profession is above the law* and the courts on behalf of the public have a critical role to play in monitoring and precipitating changes where required in professional practices." In this regard it may be noted that it is all too often overlooked by critics of contemporary medical malpractice law that an objective standard is applied to all other defendants including those who are members of the other major professions.

It has frequently been made clear that *any* failure to meet the standard of care required by law will constitute actionable negligence. Thus, even in England earlier claims, chiefly made by Lord Denning, that mere errors of clinical judgement were not accountable for at law were decisively rejected by the House of Lords in its decision in *Whitehouse v. Jordan.* Lord Fraser said that "[m]erely to describe something as an error of judgement tells us nothing about whether it is negligent or not ... If the [error] is one which would not have been made by a reasonably competent man professing to have the standard and type of skill that the defendant held himself out as having, and acting with ordinary care, then it is negligent. If on the other hand, it is an error that a man acting with ordinary care, might have made, then it is not negligence." It is thus no defence for a doctor to claim that his *culpa* was only *levissima.* Similarly, the attempts of legal commentators in Germany to develop an altogether exceptional margin of permissible error for doctors have foundered for lack of judicial support. Thus, a plaintiff has a right to recover damages for injuries caused, not just by gross negligence, but by *any deviation* from the standard of care and skill *which the law expects of doctors* in the discharge of their professional duties.

Because the legal standard should necessarily be an objective one, no allowance can be made for the particular subjective inadequacies or lack of experience or qualifications of a doctor who *holds himself out* to a patient as being competent to perform a particular medical procedure. In the case of *Wilsher v. Essex Area Health Authority* the English Court of Appeal was faced with a claim that the standard of care expected of a doctor inexperienced in a given field should be modified downwards. A putative public interest in enabling doctors to "learn on the job" was advanced in support of this contention. However, a majority of the court *rejected any notion of a duty tailored to the actor,* which it held, has no place in the law of tort. The reasons for this decisive rejection go to the heart of the role of the law in regulating the doctor-patient relationship. In Lord Justice Mustill's words, "... it would be a false step to subordinate the legitimate expectation of the patient that he will receive from each person concerned with his care a degree of skill appropriate to the task which he undertakes to an understandable wish to minimize the psychological and financial pressures on hard-pressed young doctors." Furthermore, it is widely held that patients have a right to expect that hospitals and other medical centres will provide a level of care consistent with that which they hold themselves out to the public as possessing. This imposes legal obligations on those who manage such institutions, not just in relation to technical facilities and equipment, but also in relation to the level of skill and competence of medical staff.

It may thus be concluded that courts in most jurisdictions seek to ensure the *uniform and coherent protection of patients rights.* This is achieved through the application of an objective standard of care which precludes the consideration of variable subjective factors which would render the patient's exercise of his rights unacceptably contingent. It is for this reason also that the case law makes clear that the ascertainment and application of this standard is essentially a matter of *normative evaluation,* which it is uniquely the function of the courts to engage in. These, it is submitted, are central features of the judicial protection of individual rights in any state based on the rule of law. Unfortunately, we have seen that the injured patient coming before the courts of England and Scotland cannot expect such clear and consistent protection of his or her substantive and procedural rights.

The reading that follows provides more recent information on the English law of medical malpractice. Does the law remain as unique as it is represented to be in the Giesen reading?

Medical Malpractice in England—Current Trends

J.V. McHale, European Journal of Health Law vol 10, pp. 135, 135–41, 146–47 (2003)

Malpractice litigation in England is increasing apace. But while the number of claims have steadily increased over the last decade litigants have in practice met with rather mixed success in bringing such actions. * * *

While the establishment of a duty can be regarded in the majority of situations as being comparatively unproblematic other elements of the malpractice action have imposed far more difficult burdens upon litigants—notably in relation to the standard of care and causation. Nonetheless in recent years there has been some evidence that judicial attitudes have been altering and with this has come an enhanced willingness to scrutinise clinical practice. Lord Woolf has commented that

> "until recently the courts treated the medical profession with excessive deference, but recently the position has changed. In my judgment it has changed for the better."

But to what extent has Lord Woolf s optimism proved to be justified and indeed why did he suggest that things had changed? Woolf identifies a number of factors which can be seen as contributing to this change. First, that the courts are today less deferential to authority. Second, the courts are becoming increasingly conscious that claims were routinely unsuccessful. Third, the move towards a rights-based society. Fourthly, what is termed the "automatic presumption of beneficence" has been impacted by a number of notable scandals regarding the medical profession and that judicial confidence in the medical profession has thus diminished. Fifthly, the fact that in other jurisdictions the medical profession was coming under greater judicial scrutiny. Sixthly, the malpractice crisis which was developing showed only too clearly that the hospitals and professions could not themselves be relied upon to resolve claims. Seventhly, the increase in number of cases of ethical complexity going to court which could not be regarded in terms of "clinical judgment". Eighthly, the impact of the Human Rights Act 1998 which enables the English courts to interpret law consistently with the European Convention of Human Rights.

* * *

The English law of medical malpractice and the standard of care has traditionally been rooted in the case of *Bolam v Friern Hospital Management Company.* In this case McNair J stated that

> "A doctor is not guilty of negligence if he has acted in accordance with a practice accepted as proper by a responsible body of medical men skilled in that particular act."

He went on to say

> "A doctor is not if he is acting in accordance with such a practice merely because there is a body of opinion taking a contrary view."

The standard applied to the individual doctor is objective. Over time the *Bolam* test was interpreted by the courts in a different manner than the approach taken to actions concerning other professionals. Brazier and Miola have noted that while in relation to other professionals the courts were prepared to scrutinise expert evidence in reaching a decision, in contrast with regard to medical negligence the courts have stood back and judicial decision making militated in favour of providing a broad degree of discretion to clinical decision making. In the years that followed the courts confirmed where there was a disagreement between different bodies of clinical opinion then the court could not "cherry pick" between them. Even in a situation in which the body of professional practice is very small in number, for example, 4 or 5 out of 250 specialists the court was still prepared to accept its opinion. Although there was some judicial scepticism the "hands off approach" largely remained. * * *

* * *

However in 1997 the House of Lords in the case of *Bolitho v City of Hackny Health Authority* made statements which have been interpreted to suggest that today there is indeed greater judicial willingness to scrutinise the opinion expressed by the body of professional practice. The facts in this case concerned a two year old child who was being treated for breathing difficulties. On one day he suffered two instances of acute shortness of breath. On both occasions the ward sister sent for a doctor, but no doctor attended. Later that day he suffered respiratory and cardiac arrest and while he was resuscitated he suffered severe brain damage consequent upon cardiac arrest. An action was brought. It was alleged that failure to attend was actionable in negligence. Evidence was given to the effect that even had a doctor had attended brain damage would still have arisen because the doctor would not have intubated the patient. On appeal the House of Lords were concerned to address the issues as to whether the *Bolam* test was applicable in relation to causation. While normally, as we shall see below, the causation test would not be referable to *Bolam* the situation which arose in this case related to an omission to act. Even if the doctor had attended the result would not have been intubation. Thus in such a situation the *Bolam* test was relevant to ascertain whether the doctor on attending should have made the decision to intubate this child.

The second issue before the court was the extent to which they could scrutinise the medical evidence provided. The House of Lords held that the courts did have the power to scrutinise such medical evidence. Lord Browne Wilkinson stated that

> "In particular where there are questions of assessment of the relative risks and benefits of adopting a particular medical practice, a reasonable view necessarily presupposes that the relative risks and benefits have been weighed by the experts in forming their opinions. But if in a rare case, it can be demonstrated that the professional opinion is not capable of withstanding logical analysis, the judge is entitled to hold that the body of opinion is not reasonable or responsible. I emphasis that in my view it will be very seldom right for a judge to reach the conclusion that views genuinely held by a competent medical expert are unreasonable."

This judgment was initially heralded as the beginning of a brave new dawn of judicial interventionism, that *Bolitho* was the "new *Bolam*". Kennedy and Grubb have commented that

> "Experts will have in the future, "to look to their metal" as the court will require more than sincerely held views: they will require defensible views."

But the pioneering potential of the judgment has been questioned by some academic commentators. On the issue of expert evidence for example Keown argued that "it is not clear whether medical opinion may be disregarded only if it is not logical." Brazier and Miola have argued that the impact of this judgment was in effect to restore English law to the original limits of the judgment of McNair J in *Bolam*. They commented that

> "While the medical experts are to be required, in rare cases to justify their opinions on logical grounds, there still appears to be a prima facie presumption that non-doctors will not be able fully to comprehend the evidence. This leads inexorably to a conclusion that the evidence cannot after all be critically evaluated by a judge."

Has such scepticism been vindicated through the application of judicial reasoning? We now first consider the impact of a perceived willingness to scrutinise clinical decision making in relation to negligence actions in relation to two notable decisions, *Marriot v West Midland Health Authority* and *Pearce v United Bristol NHS Trust* the area of consent to treatment.

The boundaries of *Bolitho* were explored subsequently in 1999 in the case of *Marriot v West Midlands Health Authority.* Marriott suffered head injuries after a fall at his home. While initially taken to hospital and X-rayed he was discharged the next day. However his condition did not improve. Eight days after the discharge his general practitioner paid a home visit. While neurological tests were undertaken at that stage no abnormalities were found. A further four days later he was admitted to hospital when his condition worsened. During the operation which was undertaken it was found that he had suffered a fracture of the skull and internal bleeding. Ultimately he suffered paralysis and a speech disorder. An action was brought against the Health Authority which alleged that first the initial discharge was negligent as was the general practitioner who should have referred him back to the hospital during the home visit.

On the issue of the liability of the general practitioner the issue was as to whether the tests undertaken by the general practitioner who attended the patient were adequate and would have thus as a consequence have averted the subsequent deterioration in his condition. Should he have at that stage immediately referred the patient back to hospital?

At first instance the judge noted that there was a dispute in medical evidence from the experts as to whether the patient should have been referred to the hospital. She held that

> "Furthermore whilst a Court must plainly be reluctant to depart from the opinion of an apparently careful and prudent general practitioner I have concluded that if there is a body of professional opinion which supports the course of leaving a patient who has some 7 days previously sustained a severe head injury at home in circumstances where he continues to complain of headaches drowsiness etc and where there continues to be a risk of an intracranial lesion which could cause a sudden and disastrous collapse, then such an approach is not reasonably prudent. It may very well be that if in the vast majority of cases the risk is very small. Nevertheless, the consequence if things go wrong are disastrous to the patient."

The decision was appealed. One of the defendants' arguments was that the judge had been wrong to discount the evidence adduced by the expert witness for the defence. In the Court of Appeal Beldam LJ made reference to the words of Lord Browne Wilkinson in *Bolitho.* He commented that while the risk of a lesion was small nonetheless the judge was entitled to hold that in these circumstances as she found them it would not be a reasonable exercise of general practitioner's discretion to leave the patient at home rather than to refer the patient to hospital where further diagnostic facilities were available. Interestingly while another member of the Court of Appeal, Pill J, agreed on the facts of the case he stated that in his view the *Bolitho* point did not actually arise as the medical evidence simply pointed in one direction.

Nonetheless he went on to say that

> "If contrary to my view, it was necessary for the plaintiff to rely on the principle that, in some circumstances, a judge is entitled to form her own view upon the logic of medical evidence introduced to provide a benchmark, I agree with the analysis by Beldam J on this issue."

Commenting on this case Jones stated that

> "The importance of *Bolitho* lies in the now explicit requirement to undertake a logical analysis of that evidence before characterising it as responsible, rather than relying upon the eminence or the number of the experts expressing the particular view. But the qualifying comments of Lord Browne-Wilkinson and the actual decision on the facts of *Bolitho* would depend upon how the lower courts and in particular the trial judge, responded to the shift in emphasis that it appeared to herald."

Mason, McCall Smith and Laurie have commented that here judicial scrutiny was going one step further.

> The judge was effectively dismissing the evidence of *both* sides; the courts opinion suggests that the result might have been different had she chosen one expert's evidence in preference to the other rather than substitute her own analysis."

They even suggest that *Marriott* may be shifting again the boundaries of judicial scrutiny from a "logic" test to that of "reasonableness". However while *Marriott* provided further optimism for the view that there might be enhanced judicial scrutiny of clinical decision making, subsequent case law has not conclusively vindicated the initial enthusiasm. Although in some cases a *Bolitho* type approach has been evidenced, in others *Bolam* orthodoxy has held sway. A further example of judicial criticism of clinical decision making arose in *Penney v East Kent HA*.

This case concerned screening for cervical cancer. Three women were wrongly informed that their tests were negative. Although the existence of false positives and negatives is a normal part of the screening process and thus of itself not indicative necessarily of negligence nonetheless in this case it was held that given this they should not have definitively classed the slides as negative. Pepitt J at first instance, with whom the Court of Appeal agreed, held that in his opinion it fell outside *Bolam* because all the experts agreed that the screener of the slides was wrong here to class it as negative. But he went on to say that even were *Bolam* applicable classification as negative was "illogical". This can however as has been noted be regarded as an exceptional case on its facts. Space here precludes further detailed examination of the case law. As Mason, McCall Smith and Laurie comment

> "while the courts are increasingly determined to see that the *Bolam* principle is not extended, they still have an innate reluctance to abandon it in respect of medical opinion: there is a sense that *Bolitho,* although welcome, is being used mainly in a 'back-up' position. What seems certain is that *Bolam* can no longer be regarded as impregnable."

Despite the perceived limitations of the impact of *Bolitho* with regard to medical malpractice actions, as many commentators have already noted it has in principle much broader implications across a range of areas. This is because the *Bolam* test has been utilised as the basis of decision making regarding the incompetent patient by the House of Lords in *Re F* and with consequent further discussion in relation to end of life decision making in cases such as *Airedale NHS Trust v Bland.* Nonetheless while this is the case in theory *Bolitho* seems not to have led to any radical change by itself Although there is some evidence generally that the court may be willing to take a more extensive approach to best interests in treatment decisions nonetheless this is arguably linked to a broader policy shift regarding such decision making and considerations of human rights.

* * *

There is undoubtedly a proliferation of malpractice litigation in the UK . Post *Bolitho* there was considerable speculation as to the extent to which enhanced judicial scrutiny of clinical decision-making would be manifest. But to what extent has the situation radically altered? Writing in 2000 Brazier and Miola commented that "no flood of judgments ruling expert evidence to be logical and indefensible should be expected." While in some respects Lord Woolf's optimism has been supported by developments in health care law generally through enhanced judicial involvement through the Human Rights Act 1998, in relation to clinical malpractice actions an overview of cases post *Bolitho* would suggest that the situation has not significantly changed. While the courts have indicated that they are in principle prepared to take a "harder look" at clinical decision making the problematic nature of clinical negligence actions has militated against success in the vast majority of cases. The adversarial system with its scope for conflicting medical opinion does place the courts essentially at the behest of clinical judgment. While the proposals by Lord Woolf for reform of the civil justice system suggested enhanced use of a single court appointed experts the difficulty of taking such an approach in clinical negligence actions meant that this was not ultimately pursued. The courts may be less willing to "rubber-stamp" but the reality is that the judiciary still allows the medical profession a wide margin of appreciation in very many cases—although and perhaps ironically in one of the historically most difficult issues that of causation the courts do seem to be taking a broader approach which may be more cognisant of patient rights.

Notes

1. If the English and Scottish courts are more deferential to medical judgment than are the courts of other countries, why should this be so? Might it have something to do with the nature of health care delivery in England and Scotland? Might it say something about the medical profession in these countries?

2. In fact hospital doctors in England will rarely be personally responsible for malpractice judgments. Under NHS indemnity, in place since 1990, NHS hospitals are responsible for all judgments against doctors practicing in NHS hospitals. Does it make sense to talk about defensive medicine in these circumstances? What motivation would doctors have to practice defensively?

3. Obviously, malpractice litigation is problematic for health services when they are providing treatment under severe resource constraints. Might the possibility of bringing malpractice litigation be even more important, however, in these circumstances than in traditional fee-for-service medicine? Why have a number of states adopted laws providing for liability for managed care organizations at the same time states have been cutting back on liability of doctors and hospitals under traditional medical malpractice litigation?

4. Throughout much of the world it is believed that medical negligence litigation has run amok in the United States. Prof. Gerard Memeteau begins his discussion of the law of medical negligence in France in the *World Encyclopedia of Medical Law* entry on civil medical liability by commenting on the emotive content of this subject for physicians, "who imagine that the country will be invaded by the kind of uncontrolled malpractice suits which appear to prevail in the USA," and then later notes that, "even in the USA", medical liability is founded on fault (para. 236, 242).

In fact, it is generally believed that the standard of care in the United States is set by the customs of the health care professions. See Furrow, et al., *Health Law Hornbook*, 265 (2nd ed. 2000). This would place the United States in fact among the more deferential jurisdictions of England and Scotland. But is it in fact true, or is the standard in care increasingly set by judges or juries? See Philip Peters, The Role of the Jury in Modern Malpractice Law, 87 *Iowa L. Rev.* 902 (2002); Philip Peters, The Quiet Demise of Deference to Custom: Malpractice Law at the Millennium, 57 *Wash. & Lee L. Rev.* 163 (2000).

5. The most significant differences found in medical negligence litigation among various nations are arguably not found in the standard of care applied by the courts, but rather in the nature of the legal system in which the standard is applied. The legal context in which medical negligence litigation takes place in the United States—plaintiff representation on a contingent fee basis, proof by experts put forth by the parties, trial by jury, and loser bears only his or her own legal costs—leads, some have argued, to excessive litigation and results in excessive verdicts for plaintiffs. The contrary regime found in most civil law countries—representation of plaintiffs only on a fee-basis, loser pays winner's costs, trial by judge, and testimony by experts appointed by the court—makes it more difficult, arguably, for plaintiffs to bring and win cases. Indeed, historically this context has supported a conspiracy of silence under which medical professionals allegedly refused to testify against each other.

In recent years, however, courts in continental Europe have become more hospitable to malpractice plaintiffs. A major path through which this has come to be is alteration of the burden of proof. The following excerpt discusses the burden of proof under German law.

Medical Responsibility in Comparative European Law

Gerfried Fischer & Hans Lilie, 17–21 (1999) (translated by Timothy S. Jost)

* * *

The malpractice claim of the patient is based upon the existence of a negligent medical error, damages, and a causal relationship between the two. In most legal systems, and in particular those of Western Europe, it is necessary to prove all three requirements. To the contrary, several of the socialist countries (and, still today, the states of the former Yugoslavia) are of the view that a treating institution must prove the absence of fault, that is, of liability. A corresponding reversal of the burden of proof was also contemplated by Art. 1, paragraph 2, of guidelines proposed by the EU Commission, under which one who provided a service would be obligated to establish his lack of liability. Art. 1, paragraph 3, concretized this rule to the effect that in judging liability the court should take into account that one who provides a service must under normal and foreseeable conditions guaranty the safety of the recipient of the service. The extent to which this alteration of the burden of proof extends not just to the question of liability, but also to the issue of objective breach of duty—that is malpractice—is contested.

1. Decreasing the burden of proof through prima-facie proof.

Internationally, the most common device for lowering the burden of proof is the doctrine of prima-facie proof. Where the kind of injury the patient suffers is typically, according to medical experience, attributable to a medical error, there is an actual presumption that the injury was caused by such an error. It is then the responsibility of the doctor to rebut this presumption. This rule is found in German, Austrian, Swiss, French, Dutch, Italian, Spanish and Portuguese law. It is related to the Anglo-American doctrine of res ipsa loquitur. While this doctrine is often compared to the prima facie proof rule, their operation is different. To rebut the prima facie proof the doctor must only show the possibility of a divergent, atypical course of events having occurred, not that this course of events in fact took place. By contrast, under res ipsa loquitur liability depends on a "balance of the probabilities." The Defendant must prove that a contrary explanation was at least as probable, or more probable, than that proposed by the plaintiff. The application of the res ipsa loquitur doctrine, that is, lessens the burden of proof to a greater extent than the prima facie evidence rule. On this basis, however, in English and Scottish law, in comparison to the law of many American jurisdictions, there is a great reluctance to apply this rule, with its customary effects. To the contrary, however, one can observe recently a tendency to impose on defendants at least an obligation to provide the patient with greater information, and thus to expand the presumption of liability. The continental European law with its presumptions is more in line with the German prima-facie proof doctrine, although relationships with both doctrines can be shown. This is true, for example, for the Italian law, which, in recent legal interpretation, has developed a presumption under which an injury caused by a simple, low-risk procedure is evidence of negligence, which must rebutted by the doctor's proof of careful conduct.

Typical of this area are particular groups of cases, such as cases involving the leaving behind of foreign objects during operations. The German legal doctrine here inclines toward a presumption of medical error, which the doctor must disprove by showing that he exercised appropriate security measures or encountered exceptional circumstances in the operation. The positions of Austria, Spain and the Netherlands are similar, while the legal doctrine of France, without regard to the particular circumstances, assumes a "*faute virtuelle*." To the contrary in England there is a decision, currently still accepted as authoritative, that declined to apply res ipsa loquitur where a swab was left behind.

To the contrary, the rule applied in recent English decisions in another group of cases involving anesthesia incidents corresponds to the German doctrine. A third group of cases involves infections that follow from injections. In France and Switzerland such infections are prima face evidence of the lack of safety measures, that is, of negligence. The French Cour de Cassation extended this presumption in a decision from May 1996 to infections incurred during a surgery in an operating theater. In Germany, as far as I can see, to this point, the plaintiff's case is only established if he can prove the absence of sterilization, that is, careless treatment.

2. Lessening of the burden of proof under gross negligence.

In Germany, it is long-established that upon the establishment of gross medical error the burden of proof is reversed. The doctor or hospital must prove that the error is not responsible for the death or injury of the patient. A similar clear rule exists perhaps in Norway. In England, the House of Lords imposed on an employer, who had neglected health safety measures and thereby had dramatically increased the risk of skin disease, the burden to prove that the plaintiff-employee's disease was not the result of the lack of precautions. This has been interpreted in a recent lower court decision as supporting a reversal of the burden of proof for a physician's breach of duty that raised the risk of danger. However, the Court of Appeals as well as the House of Lords have rejected a general alternation of the burden of proof in the case of *Wilsher v. Essex A.H.A.*, as has the leading text on English medical law. In the countries (in particular France and Switzerland) that have already accepted liability for damages for loss of a chance, the likelihood of success increases with the seriousness of the medical error, so that there is obviously no need for an alternation of the burden of proof as exists in Germany. In Italy, to the contrary, the degree of deviation from the customary treatment relates to the presumption based on prima facie proof. The Cassation court has in a decision from Nov. 16, 1988 expressly confirmed an earlier decision which held that where simple, low risk, procedures which customarily have positive results in fact injure the patient's health, the court can presume that they were carried out negligently.

3. Lowering of the Burden of proof through faults in documentation

The most significant difficulty of proof for the patient lies in the fact that the course of conduct, the negligence of which must be shown, does not lie in the patient's area of control and understanding, but rather in that of the doctor. The right, recognized in many jurisdictions, to examine the doctor's medical notes and records can assure the patient access to the necessary information only when all important events are recorded therein. If this is to protect the patient in the event of injury, the doctor or hospital must suffer from a failure in the documentation, in particular through a change in the burden of proof. This is, in fact, not only the position of the German, but also of the Dutch, Norwegian, Austrian, Portuguese, and possibly also the Swiss law. In these jurisdictions, this rule based upon the difficulty of proof is not so developed as in the German legal doctrine (and the Austrian doctrine that follows it). German doctrine permits a lessening of the burden of proof corresponding to the extent of failure of documentation up to a reversal of the burden. The highest German civil court has held, however, that the diminution of the burden of proof only applies for the proof of negligence, and applies to proof of causality of damages only where the failure of documentation suggests gross negligence.

Notes

1. Why might the burden of proof altering rules be very important when the judge relies on a single medical expert, often chosen with assistance from a local medical association, as was traditionally the case in civil law countries? In many countries, an alleged "conspiracy of silence", in which expert witnesses rarely testify that the defendant has breached the standard of care, has at various times in the past made (and still in some countries makes) malpractice litigation all but impossible.

2. Though the burden-shifting doctrines of prima facie proof and gross negligence look very similar, they, in fact, play rather different roles. Prima facie evidence works backwards from a bad outcome, difficult to understand in the absence of negligence, to presume a breach of the standard of care, even absent express proof of negligence. Gross negligence works forward from obviously negligent conduct to presume that the negligence caused a subsequent bad result. Why might the "gross negligence" doctrine largely obviate the need of a "loss of a chance" doctrine, as the reading suggests? How does the prima facie evidence rule compare to the American doctrine of res ipsa loquitur?

3. The *Journal of Law, Medicine, and Ethics* from the Fall of 2005 includes a symposium on comparative malpractice law, which includes Dean Harris and Chien-Chang Wu, Medical Malpractice in the People's Republic of China: The 2002 Regulation on Handling Medical Accidents, 33 *J. L. Med & Ethics* 456 (2005) and Fiona Tito Wheatland, Medical Indemnity Reform in Australia: "First Do No Harm," 33 *J. L. Med. & Ethics* 429 (2005).

2. Criminal Liability

While civil liability is the standard legal approach to addressing medical negligence in the United States, other countries rely more on criminal sanctions, as is illustrated by the following reading, which also compares more generally malpractice claiming behavior and approaches to patient injury taken in the United States and Japan.

Law and Patient Safety in the United States and Japan

Robert B. Leflar, published as *Iryō anzen to hō no Nichibei hikaku,* 1323 Jurist 8, 14–18 (2006) (Tomoko Mise, trans.)

* * *

Despite the lack of data about nonjudicial medical injury dispute resolution in Japan and the merely partial availability of such data in the U.S., tentative comparisons based on reasonable factual hypotheses are possible. Even supposing the invisible part of the iceberg of medical injury claims in Japan is very large, for example ten times the number of cases filed in court, that would still leave the number of medical injury claims in Japan, adjusted for population, considerably *below* the number of claims in the United States. It is unknown what proportion of nonjudicial claims in Japan results in compensation, but it is reasonable to suppose that the percentage of successful claims is not radically different in Japan and the U.S. This leads to the tentative conclusion that if, as the U.S. data demonstrate, only a small minority of Americans suffering injuries from medical mistakes receive compensation, the proportion of Japanese medical error victims who receive compensation is likely to be smaller still.

A multitude of institutional, social, and cultural factors could be offered to explain the apparent disparity in medical injury claims frequency between Japan and the United States. The scholarly debate over the reasons for differences between the two societies in litigation behavior is a long and extensive one, and it is not the purpose of this paper to review those reasons exhaustively. It may be helpful, however, to identify and evaluate a few factors of particular importance in the medical injury context.

Among "cultural" reasons that have been offered for differences between American and Japanese claiming behavior, one is the greater historical prevalence of *jō-ge kankei* [hierarchical relationship] in Japan than in the United States, with Japanese patients' greater deference to their physicians deterring patients from bringing claims. To the extent that explanation may have been persuasive in the past, it is now less persuasive in this era of widespread questioning and distrust of the Japanese medical profession.

A second partially "cultural" reason for the small number of medical injury claims in Japan, no doubt, is the medical profession's historical secrecy concerning its mistakes. Patients suffering preventable injury have simply lacked the means of obtaining the information to support claims of malpractice. That secrecy, however, is by no means unique to Japan; the American medical profession has also hidden the facts about error from its patients, probably to an equivalent degree. In both nations, however, considerations of professional ethics and liability avoidance appear, in the past few years, to be leading to significantly higher levels of honesty toward patients. It is difficult to attribute much of the difference between American and Japanese patients' claiming behavior to the "cultural" ground of differences in levels of candor between American and Japanese medical practitioners.

More persuasive, to this writer at least, than the "cultural" explanations for differences in claiming behavior are *institutional* reasons that have rendered it somewhat less difficult for medical error victims to engage the legal system in the United States than in Japan. One of these institutional factors is simply the greater availability of attorneys experienced in medical malpractice in the U.S. Although the number of Japanese attorneys handling medical malpractice cases is increasing, it is a small cadre indeed in comparison with the regiments of medical malpractice specialists practicing in the United States. The expected growth in the number of attorneys admitted to practice in Japan will narrow the gap only gradually, since considerable specialized training is necessary before an attorney gains the competence to practice successfully in the medical injury field.

Another institutional reason is that the traditional structures of plaintiffs' attorney compensation in the two countries have been more friendly to victims of serious medical error in the United States than in Japan. There are several respects in which the attorney compensation structure has been more plaintiff-friendly in the U.S. The first is the threshold barrier: in contrast to the substantial up-front retainers (*chakushukin*) traditionally required from clients in Japan, plaintiffs' attorneys in the United States operate on a pure contingency-fee basis, so that patients with strong cases but limited financial resources can obtain representation without the obstacle of a substantial initial payment.

A second respect in which the attorney compensation structure is more plaintiff-favorable in the United States is that the contingency fee system provides higher rewards to plaintiffs' attorneys, making it economically possible for an attorney to take on a wider range of medical injury cases and still receive a reasonable reward for time and money invested in preparing them. * * *

* * * In Japan, by contrast, traditionally the attorney's fee has been limited to 10–15% of the amount collected from the defendants, with various adjustments. This difference in plaintiff attorney rewards has no doubt created a considerable difference in case screening philosophies in plaintiff-oriented law firms. A case involving high preparation expense, uncertain chance of success, but large potential damages, might be accepted by a plaintiff's firm in the United States but refused by a law office in Japan, both making decisions in accordance with rational calculations of probable returns to the firm.

A third respect in which legal rules have traditionally been structured to favor American plaintiffs and disfavor Japanese plaintiffs is in the question of access to the patient's medical records. Information about what occurred during the patient's course of treatment is a *sine qua non* of a plaintiff's cause of action. * * * In Japan, until recently, patient access to medical records was strongly resisted by medical providers. The only way that patients interested in obtaining the facts about what had happened to them could be sure of gaining access to that information was by filing a *shoko hozen* [evidence preservation] action, which typically would cost ¥200,000 to ¥400,000 [currently $2,000 to $4,000.]. This cost barrier constituted an additional obstacle to the bringing of medical malpractice claims.

Both of these initial cost barriers to obtaining legal representation may be diminishing in Japan. Attorney compensation structures have become more flexible since the bar associations recognized their non-mandatory nature. For example, some attorneys specializing in medical malpractice offer potential clients the option of a lower retainer fee (*chakushukin*) and a higher percentage of the ultimate judgment or settlement as a contingency fee. The recent recognition that patients have a right of access to their own medical records eliminates the need for a *shoko hozen* action in some cases. But the fact remains that the compensation structure for plaintiffs' attorneys is more conducive to the filing of high-value, difficult-to-prove cases in the United States than it is in Japan.

* * *

A major point of difference between Japan and the United States in the way in which the legal system regulates medical quality is the vastly greater role of criminal law in Japan. The uproar over the arrest earlier this year of an obstetrician in Fukushima indicates the sensitivity of the issue to Japanese medical professionals. * * * American physicians and hospitals do not share that concern. I would offer two types of reasons for this critical difference: one from the perspective of the structure of criminal law in the two nations, and the other from the perspective of functional political theory.

First, the structures of the criminal laws are different in Japan and the U.S. In Japan, the standard charge brought by prosecutors against medical personnel under the Criminal Code is "professional *negligence* causing death or injury." This crime, derived like most of the Criminal Code from the German penal code, has no specific equivalent in Anglo-American jurisprudence. The few convictions in medical cases in recent years in the U.S. almost all involve charges of a higher level of *mens rea*: intent or recklessness. In Japan, mere negligence is enough. A second charge occasionally brought by prosecutors is the failure to report unnatural deaths (*ijōshi*) to police. This ground for criminal prosecution as a means of sanctioning medical error is likewise unknown in American law.

The second chief reason for the importance of criminal law in Japan has to do with functional political theory. * * * [H]istorically professional self-regulation and peer review in Japanese medicine have been weak. Hospital accreditation has been optional, not mandatory. Administrative sanctions against physicians committing serious malpractice were extremely rare. The civil law system, until recently, has operated largely beneath the radar level of most physicians' attention. When the realization that medical error is remarkably common burst upon the Japanese public's consciousness several years ago, organized medicine was caught napping, the health ministry was unprepared, and the civil law system's ability to respond had its institutional limits. For want of other adequate mechanisms of public accountability, police and prosecutors stepped into the breach, employing the statutory weapons at their disposal. Whatever the drawbacks of reliance on the criminal law as a regulator of medical practice—and those drawbacks are serious—prosecutions in the high-profile cases in the first years of this century did serve as a wake-up call to the health ministry and the medical profession. The Japanese criminal justice system, its workings spotlighted by the media, in effect has been filling an accountability vacuum.

* * *

Note

Although criminal liability for medical error is certainly possible in common law jurisdictions, (see Alexander McCall Smith, Criminal Negligence and the Incompetent Doctor, 1 *Med. L. Rev.* 336 (1993)), it is much more common in civil law countries. In a number of civil law countries a criminal prosecution may be brought in tandem with a civil action, the criminal prosecution being initiated by the civil plaintiff. A civil plaintiff may want to initiate a criminal complaint for a variety of reasons. It may provide the plaintiff easier access to the medical records (which can be obtained by subpoena) or to an expert opinion on the case. It may put additional pressure on the defendant to settle. A favorable criminal judgment may effectively be *res judicata* in the civil proceeding (though this may also mean that a finding of innocence in a criminal proceeding may bar a civil proceeding).

The criminal law of civil law countries generally recognizes criminal liability for medical professionals who cause bodily harm to their patients under certain circumstances. These include treatment without consent, treatment by personnel who are not properly licensed, treatment lacking a therapeutic justification, or treatment that is not medically indicated. In some jurisdictions (Austria for example), the conduct must also cause a serious injury to the patient.

Under French law, for example, the conduct that a physician undertakes with respect to a patient is considered to be interference with a human being, which can only be justified if it is within the scope of the physician's duties as prescribed by the state. The physician's duty is to undertake only therapeutic actions, including diagnosis, treatment and prevention. Moreover, a physician's actions can be considered criminal if they are done without consent. This understanding of the obligation of the physician to act therapeutically has led to special legislation to justify research, in vitro fertilization, abortions, and other conduct that is not strictly speaking therapeutic. Memeteau, *World Encyclopedia of Medical Law*, para. 271–283. See generally, Gerfried Fischer and Hans Lilie, *Ärztliche Verantwortung im europäischen Rechtsvergleich*, 83–96 (1999).

3. Administrative Proceedings

Most countries also have disciplinary tribunals that can hear complaints against health care professionals for improper or unethical conduct. In most nations these tribunals rarely address competency issues. An exception may be the Netherlands, where disciplinary courts exist for the various health care professions, formed generally of two lawyers and three professionals. These courts investigate complaints and hold hearings at which the complainant and doctor may appear. They then issue decisions, which must impose a sanction if they find that the professional is guilty. These decisions often remain private, though they can be made public if the proceeding was open to the public, or if the court otherwise decides that the decision should be made public. Sanctions ranging from warning to loss of license to practice are possible. These decisions may be appealed to a Central Medical Disciplinary Court in the Hague, composed of three lawyers and two professionals. Some consider these tribunals an inadequate substitute for civil or criminal proceedings, as they permit doctors to pass on their colleagues in secrecy, though others believe that the confidentiality of these proceedings leads to greater candor. See Fischer & Lilie, supra at 88, 94–95, 286–87.

4. "No Fault" Alternatives to Negligence Litigation

A great deal has been written in recent years with respect to replacing the medical malpractice scheme currently found in the United States with a "no-fault" scheme. Patient injury compensation schemes currently exist in New Zealand, in the Scandinavian countries, and in France. A description of the operation of the Swedish scheme, with commentary on the New Zealand scheme, follows:

The Swedish No Fault Patient Insurance Scheme

Lars H. Fallberg and Edgard Borgenhammer, European Journal of Health Law, vol. 4, pp. 279, 279–284 (1997)

The NFPI [No Fault Patient Insurance scheme] came into effect in 1975, being the first of its kind in any country. It includes damages caused to patients in government owned hospitals as well as in government administered primary care. Dentistry is also covered. Private hospitals, which are rare in Sweden, have a similar insurance. In 1997 the Swedish NFPI was implemented in law, the Patient Insurance Law, requiring all health care providers to be insured. The Pharmaceutical Insurance, however, is still a voluntary agreement largely financed by the Pharmaceutical companies. Since the No Fault Patient Insurance Scheme and the Patient Insurance Law has more or less the same content, the common abbreviation NFPI will be used when referring to both systems in the following.

Before the introduction of NFPI in 1975, an average of only ten cases per year, in this country of about nine million inhabitants, had been compensated. This number can be compared with the number of cases compensated for in the early 1990s: several thousand per year.

How did the NFPI get started? Were experiences from the Southern hemisphere of importance? New Zealand is sometimes referred to as a source of inspiration, as an insurance act was introduced there in 1974. However, this act is limited to medical accidents, no matter where and how they occur. It does not include, e.g., a situation where a patient has received treatment on the basis of an erroneous diagnosis. The Swedish NFPI thus differs from the accident insurance in New Zealand also in its scope.

According to a Harvard report, the scheme in New Zealand did not originate from the eye of a malpractice storm. The same can be said about the Swedish NFPI. Few malpractice claims were made at the time of the inception of the scheme. The one in New Zealand appeared as an appendage to dramatic changes in compensation law that swept the country in the early 1970s. A major reason behind the introduction of NFPI in Sweden was the ambition to increase the number of patients receiving compensation for injuries due to clinical mistakes. A problem facing patients at that time was to prove negligence from the physician in charge. Several private bills had been introduced and duly opposed before 1975 in Parliament. One basis for the opposition was the considerable technical and principal difficulties which would arise if a law had to specify the exact distinction between liability and unavoidable consequences. Professional negligence and malpractice are negatively loaded words which tend to create a defensive attitude. Therefore, the ambition was to avoid them.

There emerged a desire from both the national government and the health services providers to abandon the traditional principle of liability based on malicious intent and negligence. The ambition was to replace it by a system in which greater attention was given to the injured person's need for compensation, seen in relation to the damage. * * *

A significant difference between Sweden and New Zealand in this respect is that the Swedish NFPI does not require the patient to contact his or her physician in order to file a complaint with the insurance. The patient in Sweden only has to lodge a claim to a NFPI company. The overall climate of co-operation between health care personnel and patients has, however, the effect that a majority of the complaints are filed after voluntary consultation with a physician or nurse. In several cases this takes place on their initiative. The rejection rate on claims from the start in 1975 up to 1994 is 60 per cent. A corresponding figure mentioned for New Zealand is four per cent.

Until December 31, 1993, the NFPI was handled by a consortium consisting of four major Swedish insurance companies. Then it was decided that the consortium should end its activities in order not to limit competition, in line with Sweden's membership in the European Union. A consequence is that health care providers can sign separate agreements with different insurance companies.

* * *

Three other Nordic countries have followed with similar NFPIs: Finland in 1987, Norway in 1988 and Denmark in 1992. In Finland, Denmark and Sweden the systems have become part of the law. Norway has a NFPI based on voluntary agreements. Belgium has shown interest in a similar system but no implementation has so far taken place.

* * *

Protection for the injured person is assured by a claims process which as a principle is free of charge for the patient. If a patient is not satisfied with the decision of the insurance consortium, he or she can turn to the next level, which is the Patient Injury Board. If the patient still is not satisfied, and if the claim is considered reasonable, the patient can turn to arbitration, which the patient has to pay herself.

The purpose with a No Fault Insurance scheme differs to some extent from one culture to another. One reason behind a growing interest in, e.g., the USA, is the high cost of malpractice suits. * * *

Another reason is that only a fraction of the total number of injuries which occur in health care are reported and, thereby, analyzed in a systematic way. It is likely that about one per cent of all hospitalised patients are treated negligently in a way that results in injury to them. But only one out of eight who are injured by negligence is filing a lawsuit. The patient in the USA encounters problems in finding sufficient evidence for a decision on compensation by court. Here, a NFPI scheme could possibly simplify the compensation procedure. In many cases it is difficult to get expert opinions from physicians against a colleague or to find witnesses against a physician. The possibility of learning from patient complaints and thereby, hopefully, avoiding future negative events is important. The more valid the correspondence is between on the one hand incidents or damages and on the other hand complaints and compensations, the greater are the chances for the system to learn. The number of unrecorded cases should be as low as possible. The assumption is that in a system with NFPI, openness between patients and health professionals is more developed.

The necessity of developing and maintaining a positive relation between health services personnel and the patient should be emphasised. In a system where one does not have to pinpoint a particular professional as having been negligent in order to get compensation, the likelihood for a constructive dialogue is higher. The right to compensation is especially important for unexpected and unforeseen injuries, or at least those considered improbable by the physician.

The NFPI is an insurance with the purpose of covering responsibility in a "quasi-contractual" relationship between care provider and patient. The starting point is that the insurance shall cover injuries related to health care services. However, a number of specific conditions have to be met for financial compensation.

> A general condition for compensation is that the undesirable outcome has been worse than the one that would have resulted from the disease itself, or that the outcome has turned out to be other than would reasonably have been expected, if properly treated. Examples are severe invalidity or death. A precondition for compensation is the existence of a casual connection between the injury and the treatment provided.

Compensation is also given:

> when technical equipment has produced faulty data in examining a patient, or when the physician has not interpreted or observed symptoms of illness or analyzed data in accordance with manifested practice; for infection injuries, unless caused by unclean bodily areas of the patient; and for an accidental injury to the patient in relation to care or depending on non adequate standard of equipment used in therapy, diagnosis, rehabilitation or care.

Protection for the injured person is assured by a claims process which as a principle is free of charge for the patient. A demand for compensation has to be put to the health care provider or to the insurance consortium within three years from the time of knowledge of the injury. Another limit is that the claim has to be forwarded within ten years from the treatment which caused the injury. The amounts paid are relatively small, which must be seen in the context of the general provisions of the welfare state. The maximum amount of compensation is at present 2,922,885 ECU for each occasion, independent of the number of persons, and 584,477 ECU per person [The ECU was the predecessor of the Euro]. Only personal physical injuries, and psychological injuries caused by a physical damage, are covered by the insurance.

When a patient is not satisfied with the decision of the insurance company he or she may turn to the Patient Injury Board (PIB) which consists of six members. Three of the members shall represent the interest of patients and the fourth shall have medical knowledge; in reality, being a physician. The two other members are appointed by the County Councils. The PIB comes up with a recommendation which the NFPI can, but does not have to, follow. If the decision by the insurance company is not changed and the patient wants to appeal, she may turn to a court of arbitration. However, the last alternative, and in fact the only way to appeal the decision by the NFPI, is not free of charge, and has to be financed by the patient herself. Since the start of the NFPI an increasing number of more than 3,000 complaints have been handled by the Patient Injury Board. The present figure is about 500 cases per year. The number of appeals to the court of arbitration is 10–15 annually, rapidly increasing.

Since the introduction of the NFPI there have been about 100,000 complaints. Approximately forty per cent of these have resulted in financial compensation of one kind or another. The total cost for the insurance during its twenty years of existence is estimated at roughly 175,373,134 ECU. Up to the year 1993 the amount that has been paid out in compensation exceeded 93,532,338 ECU. The difference has largely to do with the fact that a good number of cases are yet not cleared.

Compensation for bodily defects and harm accounts for 38 per cent of the amounts, followed by compensation for expenses, 18 per cent, for loss of income 17 per cent, for inconvenience 15 per cent, and pain and suffering 12 per cent.

What are the weaknesses of a NFPI? Is there a risk that physicians and other health personnel become so well protected that they lack incentive to improve their competence? Can issues related to quality of skill be neglected? And are the possibilities of learning from reports to NFPI fully utilised?

It is likely that one of the factors that have contributed to the profound interest in total quality among physicians and hospital owners in the USA is the risk for being brought to court. A study from a Swedish hospital showed that as many as one third of surgical patients got an infection of some kind or another during their hospital stay. The use of antibiotics for prophylactic purposes is probably more offensive in the American hospital than in the Swedish one, for good and bad. Further education for health services professionals is in a state of mess in many countries, and probably not worse in Sweden than in the USA. The possibilities for learning from systematised studies regarding NFPI complaint are in no way fully utilised in Sweden. But the potential is there, waiting for creative research to be conducted. In all there are more than 30 national registers on health services quality. But they are at large not available for patients or potential patients as a support for their "rational decision making."

Another area where more research is needed is in the field of justice in the process of appeal. The PIB only gives recommendations per case. In order to appeal patients have to turn to an arbitration board. Due to the fact that the NFPI does not allow financial support in case of appeal, the process may be very expensive and long.

A key problem that must be dealt with in establishing a medical injury compensation scheme is defining the compensable event. Obviously it is not practical to compensate a patient every time his or her health takes a turn for the worse following medical treatment. At least a causal relationship between the treatment and the injury must be established, but even that may not be enough. It may also be advisable, for example, to require that the injury be serious, or that it be unexpected, or that it result directly from the treatment. On the other hand, if a scheme is so limited that it only covers injuries caused by negligence, it begins to resemble the tort system it was meant to replace. The patient compensation system of New Zealand has struggled with this problem since its inception. Its latest solution is discussed in the following reading.

No-Fault Compensation in New Zealand: Harmonizing Injury Compensation, Provider Accountability, and Patient Safety

Marie Bismark and Ron Paterson, Health Affairs, vol 25, 278, 278–282, Jan./Feb. 2006

In 1974 New Zealand adopted a government-funded system for compensating people with personal injuries (operated by the Accident Compensation Corporation, or ACC), replacing its former tort-based system. A generation of New Zealanders has now grown up knowing the ACC as the primary method of dealing with personal injury claims, including medical injuries, and avoidance of litigation is widely regarded as a social gain. Reforms in 2005 removed the final fault element from the compensation criteria for medical injuries, making it a true no-fault system.

* * *

New Zealand's compensation system arose not in response to concerns about medical malpractice but through farsighted workers' compensation reforms. A Royal Commission, established in 1967, concluded that accident victims needed a secure source of financial support when deprived of their capacity to work. Skeptical of the ability of a liability-based system to provide such support, the commission recommended no-fault compensation for personal injury. At around the same time, the United States, Australia, and the United Kingdom also debated the merits of no-fault compensation, but the idea of a comprehensive approach to injury by accident failed to gain traction.

In the New Zealand system, injured patients receive government-funded compensation through the ACC. In exchange, they give up the right to sue for damages arising out of any personal injury covered by the accident compensation legislation. This prohibition applies even when a person chooses not to lodge a claim or is not entitled to compensation. It remains possible to bring actions for exemplary damages, but the courts have found that not even gross negligence warrants such damages unless there is some element of conscious or reckless conduct.

Historically, health care–related injuries have made up 0.05 percent of all claims made to the ACC, * * *. Under the original legislation, personal injury by accident included "medical, surgical, dental or first aid misadventure," without further definition. At the time, claims against health professionals were uncommon, and for several years doctors remained uncertain about the extent to which the specter of liability had been removed.

In 1992, the concepts of *medical error* and *medical mishap* were formally introduced into the ACC legislation. *Medical error* was defined as the failure to observe a reasonable standard of care and skill—civil negligence by another name. Before 2002 medical error could not be attributed to an organization; this focus on individual error, combined with the threat of disciplinary action, hindered open communication and delayed compensation, as doctors sought to challenge error findings.

The second category, *medical mishap*, was defined as a rare (occurring in less than 1 percent of cases) and severe (disability or prolonged hospitalization) adverse consequence of properly given treatment. The *mishap* concept allowed recovery for non-negligent injuries and accounted for the majority of accepted claims. Yet the definition was a clumsy one, with the rarity and severity criteria criticized for being confusing and arbitrary. * * *

Criticisms of the compensation criteria—particularly the inconsistency between *medical error* and the no-fault basis of the wider ACC system—prompted an interagency review in 2002. The review found overwhelming support for new coverage criteria and almost no suggestion of returning to a right to sue * * * .

Consequently, on 1 July 2005, *medical mishap* and *medical error* were replaced with a new concept of *treatment injury*. This change broadened coverage to include all personal injuries suffered while receiving treatment from health professionals. A causal link between treatment and injury is still required. Injuries that are a necessary part or ordinary consequence of treatment (such as chemotherapy hair loss) are not covered. Clarification of what constitutes "a necessary part" will be critical. As before, there is no coverage where the injury is solely the result of resource allocation decisions.

A key objective of the change is to encourage health professionals to assist injured patients to make claims earlier, thereby facilitating timely provision of ACC assistance. Claimants are informed about the availability of independent processes for resolving concerns about the quality of care, and the ACC is required to report any "risk of harm to the public" to the responsible authority. A new Patient Safety team analyzes claims data and works with the health sector and researchers to help improve patient safety.

The ACC system is one of the simplest in the world for patients to navigate, and although the eligibility criteria have changed, the decision-making process remains much the same. Claims are decided in the ACC's national claims unit, based on information provided by patients and their providers, and advice from independent clinical advisers. Straightforward claims can be processed in weeks, with a statutory requirement for decisions to be made within nine months. Historically, the ACC has accepted around 40 percent of all claims. Dissatisfied claimants may request a review of the decision, and if this fails, they have a right of court appeal.

The ACC is financed through general taxation and an employer levy. A fixed award schedule means that claimants with similar disabilities receive similar compensation. Entitlements fall into four categories. (1) *Treatment and rehabilitation* includes the cost of pharmaceuticals, disability aids, child care, home modifications, and vocational retraining. Most treatment costs are already covered by New Zealand's universal health care system. (2) *Compensation for loss of earnings* includes weekly compensation of 80 percent of the claimant's earnings at the time of injury, up to a set maximum. (High earners can purchase additional first-party income protection insurance.) Weekly compensation was the most important driver of compensation costs during 1992–2003. (3) *Lump-sum compensation*—a onetime payment of up to US$70,000 to compensate for permanent impairment resulting from an injury—is paid in addition to any other ACC entitlements. (4) *Support for dependents* takes the form of a funeral grant and a survivor's grant paid to surviving spouses and children under age eighteen.

No-fault systems have the potential to compensate many more patients than malpractice litigation can, but depending on compensation criteria, level of awards, and social context, this need not result in greatly increased costs. Accurately estimating the long-term costs of the New Zealand system is difficult, with uncertainty about future claim rates, changes in life expectancy, and innovations in health care. To date, compensation for medical injuries has cost around US$29 million per year. As in the United States, the most costly claims involve neurological injury to infants: fewer than 7 percent of claims yet more than 16 percent of spending.

The ACC expects that following the 2005 reforms, the number of compensation claims will go up by 50 percent, and many more claims will be successful. However, most of the new claims will involve minor, temporary injuries, which were previously ineligible for compensation. The reforms are expected to cost an additional US$5 million a year.

Four main factors have contributed to the system's affordability. First, New Zealanders benefit from a strong social security system. Injured patients, like everyone else, receive free hospital care and subsidized pharmaceuticals. * * * Thus, New Zealand's public health and welfare systems cover many of the damages that would be at issue in a U.S. medical malpractice claim, leaving the ACC with a much smaller compensation burden.

Second, compensation awards are generally lower and more consistent than under a malpractice equivalent. As described above, economic losses are compensated according to a fixed schedule, and compensation for noneconomic losses is available only for permanent disabilities.

Third, the New Zealand experience suggests that even under such a system (which includes a legal duty of open disclosure), most entitled patients never seek compensation, and many may be unaware that they have even suffered an adverse event. Peter Davis and colleagues have estimated that the ratio of potentially compensable events to successful claims is around thirty to one.* * *

And finally, the New Zealand system does not incur large legal and administrative costs. The system has been very cost-effective, with administrative costs absorbing only 10 percent of the ACC's expenditures compared with 50–60 percent among malpractice systems in other countries.

Many U.S. commentators have expressed concern that a "no-fault" compensation system equates to a "no-accountability" medico-legal system. * * * Between 1972 and 1994 such criticisms had some legitimate foundation, because the abolition of the right to sue did leave a lacuna in systems of medical accountability. However, in the late 1980s a major inquiry at a leading teaching hospital forced New Zealand to consider this accountability function and recommended the establishment of a Health and Disability Commissioner to restore balance to the system.

The commissioner promotes patients' rights and provides accountability where care has not been provided with reasonable care and skill. As the following case study shows, complaints are resolved using patient advocacy, mediation, or investigation, as appropriate. The actions of organizations and individuals are considered, and the commissioner acts as a gatekeeper to disciplinary proceedings in serious cases. Complaints are used as a "window of opportunity" to improve health services, and lessons learned through complaint investigations are widely disseminated.

> A general practitioner referred his patient for mammography of a breast lump and told her he would contact her if there were any problem. Thirteen weeks later (after two phone calls from his patient), the doctor obtained the mammography report and told his patient the results were abnormal. The patient complained to the commissioner, who found that the doctor had failed to provide care of an appropriate standard. The commissioner recommended that the medical center implement a system for follow-up of test results.
>
> In light of this and other cases that involved physicians' failure to follow up test results adequately, the commissioner drew attention to the topic in a medical journal. This led to debate by general practitioners and the development and implementation of pilot guidelines for improving follow-up of test results.

Despite the recent reforms, four major concerns about the ACC system remain unresolved. First, many observers believe that levels of ACC compensation are inadequate, particularly in comparison with tort jurisdictions. This is especially a problem for patients—usually women and the elderly—who are not in paid employment at the time of the injury and thus are unable to claim earnings-related compensation.

Second, compensating treatment injuries, while excluding most other illnesses from the ACC system, is bound to produce tensions, because ACC assistance is generally higher than that received from the health and welfare systems. This is particularly troubling in the area of birth abnormalities, such as cerebral palsy, in which babies with similar needs could be eligible for very different kinds of support.

Third, the ACC system has been criticized for its duplication of processes following an adverse event. In response, the ACC has strengthened interagency relationships with police, coroners, the health and disability commissioner, and other regulatory bodies, to reduce unnecessary overlap.

Finally, although the system is structured to support efforts to improve patient safety, the potential gains are still a long way from being fully realized. After thirty years of the ACC and nine years of independent complaint resolution, New Zealand hospitals appear no safer (or more dangerous) than those in other Western countries. * * * Although the recent reforms are expected to bolster efforts to create a culture of learning, the task of making health care safer is daunting and will not be achieved through medico-legal reform alone.

Notes

1. France is the country that has most recently established a form of no-fault compensation. In 2002, France created a kind of "no-fault" compensation system. People who are seriously injured in medical accidents can file a claim with a compensation board. This board then compensates the injured party. The board next determines fault, as best I can understand, and if the provider is found at fault it (or, as a practical matter, its insurer) must pay. Otherwise, the patient is paid from a compensation fund. The system is thus fault-based from the perspective of the provider, no-fault from the perspective of the patient. The system only applies, however, to serious injuries. See, Simon Taylor, Note, Clinical Negligence Reform: Lessons from France? 52 *Int. & Comp. L. Q.* 737 (2003).

2. Many believe that the United States is not well served by its medical malpractice system. Health care professionals hate it because they view it as random and devastating in its effects. They also fear the shame and psychological stress that malpractice litigation brings and the career consequences that can follow from even nuisance settlements being reported to the National Practitioner Data Bank. Injured patients, on the other hand, are unlikely to recover except for the most severe injuries, and then must share much of the recovery with their attorneys. Transaction costs are very high, with considerably less than half of the money paid in malpractice insurance premiums ending up with injured patients. Our fault-based system also does not seem to have been very effective in deterring medical error.

For all of these reasons, the idea of a no fault compensation system has long interested American legal academics, leading to a considerable volume of comparative scholarship considering the Scandinavian and New Zealand approaches. See, e.g. Stephen Todd, Privatization of Accident Compensation: Policy and Politics in New Zealand, 39 *Washburn L.J.* 404 (2000); David M. Studdert, et al., Can the United States Afford a "No-Fault" System of Compensation for Medical Injury? 60 *Law & Contemp. Probs.* 1 (1997); Patricia M. Danzon, The Swedish Patient Compensation System: Myths and Realities, 14 *Int'l Rev. L. & Econ.* 453 (1994).

These readings, however, illustrate the difficulty of establishing a no-fault system. If fault is not the basis of recovery, what is? It is difficult to define otherwise the event that precipitates compensation, unless one is prepared to compensate all adverse events related to health care, a very expensive proposition. Other problems have also deterred the adoption of no-fault to deal with medical error in the United States, not the least of which is the likelihood that many more iatrogenic injuries would be compensated under a no-fault system than are now compensated under our fault-based system, leading to much higher costs. To date, only Virginia and Florida have adopted limited no-fault system for dealing with babies who are brain damaged at birth. See David M. Studdert, Lori A. Fritz, Troyen A. Brennan, The Jury is Still In: Florida's Birth-Related Neurological Injury Compensation Plan After a Decade, 25 *J. Health Pol. Pol'y & L.* 499 (2000); Randall R. Bovbjerg & Frank A. Sloan, No-Fault for Medical Injury, Theory and Evidence, 67 *U.Cin.L. Rev.* 53 (1998).

3. Why might it be easier to adopt a no-fault compensation system in a country like the Scandinavian countries where social insurance covers most health and accident costs in any event?

4. For an exercise in examining how different treatment injuries are compensated under various compensation systems, see Peter Davis, et al., Modeling Eligibility for

National Systems of Compensation for Treatment Injury, 31 *J. Health Pol., Pol'y & L.* 295 (2006).

C. The Right to Consent to Treatment

1. The Standard of Disclosure

It has long been accepted law virtually everywhere that the provision of medical treatment without consent is a battery, resulting in civil damages. In most of the world, moreover, the law has gone further, recognizing that consent to a medical procedure is not effective unless that medical professional has provided the patient with information relative to the nature of the procedure, its risks and alternatives. The development of this legal doctrine, often referred to as the right to "informed consent" has varied from country to country, however. In particular, a number of issues have arisen with respect to the application of the doctrine.

The first set of materials below discusses the standard to be applied in informed consent cases for determining the scope of disclosure. The initial case, *Sidaway*, is still the leading British case, though it has been subjected to a great deal of critical commentary. See, Murray Earle, The Future of Informed Consent in British Common Law, 6 *European J. Health L.* 235 (1999); Michael A. Jones, Informed Consent and Other Fairy Stories, 7 *Med. L. Rev.* 103 (1999); P.D.G. Skegg, English Medical Law and "Informed Consent": An Antipodean Assessment and Alternative, 7 *Med. L. Rev.* 135 (1999). It represents the traditional approach, still applied in many United States jurisdictions, which defines the duty to disclose with reference to professional practice—the standard of disclosure is that followed by reasonable practitioners. The second case, *Rogers v. Whitaker*, an Australian High Court case, represents the position taken by Australia, Canada, many United States jurisdictions, and most civil law countries, that the physician's obligation to disclose is measured by the patient's need to know. A third excerpt discusses the recent developments in Japan, a country with very different medical and legal traditions.

Sidaway v Bethlem Royal Hospital Governors and others

[1985] 1 AC 871, [1985] 1 All ER 643, [1985] 2 WLR 480, 1 BMLR 132
(House of Lords, 1985)

The plaintiff, Amy Doris Sidaway, appealed with leave of the Court of Appeal against the decision of that court dismissing her appeal against the decision of Skinner J on 19 February 1982 whereby he dismissed the appellant's action against the first respondents, the Board of Governors of the Bethlem Royal and Maudsley Hospitals, and the second respondents, Coutts & Co and Mrs Valda Helen Falconer, the executors of the estate of Murray A Falconer deceased, for damages for personal injury suffered by the appellant as a result of an operation carried out on her by Mr Falconer while employed by the first respondents. The facts are set out in the opinion of Lord Scarman.

Panel Lord Scarman, Lord Diplock, Lord Keith of Kinkel, Lord Bridge of Harwich, and Lord Templeman

Lord Scarman. [Note: Some commentators characterize Lord Scarman's opinion as a dissent. Although he agrees with the other Lords as to the result, his reasoning is very different.]

My Lords, the state of the evidence in this case compels me to the conclusion that the appellant has not made out a case of negligence against her surgeon, the late Mr Murray A Falconer. * * *

* * * The issue is whether Mr Falconer failed to exercise due care (his skill was not challenged) in the advice which he gave his patient when recommending an operation. * * * Whatever be the correct formulation of the applicable law, the issue cannot be settled positively for or against the doctor without knowing what advice, including any warning of inherent risk in the operation, he gave his patient before she decided to undergo it and what was his assessment of the mental, emotional and physical state of his patient. The trial judge derived no help on these two vital matters from the evidence of the appellant. Mr Falconer was not an available witness, having died before trial, and the medical records afforded no sure guide on either matter. Regrettable though a "non-proven" verdict is, it is not, therefore, surprising. Where the court lacks direct evidence as to the nature and extent of the advice and warning (if any) given by the doctor and as to his assessment of his patient the court may well have to conclude that the patient has failed to prove her case.

* * *

This is an appeal by the plaintiff, Mrs Sidaway, from the dismissal by the Court of Appeal of her appeal from the judgment of Skinner J given on 19 February 1982 whereby he dismissed her action for damages in respect of the personal injuries which she suffered as a result of a surgical operation performed on her by a neuro-surgeon on 29 October 1974. The first defendants are the governing body of the Maudsley Hospital, where she was treated and where she underwent the operation. The second defendants are the executors of Mr Falconer, the distinguished neuro-surgeon who advised and performed the operation. * * * Mrs Sidaway does not allege negligence in the performance of the operation. Her case is that she was not informed of a risk inherent in the operation, that the risk materialised with the result that she suffered, and continues to suffer, serious personal injury, and that, had she been warned, she would not have consented to the operation. Damages are agreed at £67,500 subject to liability.

The case is plainly of great importance. It raises a question which has never before been considered by your Lordships' House: has the patient a legal right to know, and is the doctor under a legal duty to disclose, the risks inherent in the treatment which the doctor recommends? If the law recognises the right and the obligation, is it a right to full disclosure or has the doctor a discretion as to the nature and extent of his disclosure? And, if the right be qualified, where does the law look for the criterion by which the court is to judge the extent of the disclosure required to satisfy the right? Does the law seek guidance in medical opinion or does it lay down a rule which doctors must follow, whatever may be the views of the profession? There is further a question of law as to the nature of the cause of action. Is it a cause of action in negligence, i.e. a breach of the duty of care, or is it based on a breach of a specific duty to inform the patient which arises not from any failure on the part of the doctor to exercise the due care and skill of his profession but directly from the patient's right to know?

Before attempting to answer these questions it is necessary to set out the facts of the case. At once a formidable difficulty arises. Mr Falconer was dead before the trial. The judge was not prepared to accept Mrs Sidaway's evidence that he gave no warning. The judge was, therefore, without any direct evidence as to the extent of the warning given. Further, the judge lacked evidence which Mr Falconer alone could have given as to his assessment of his patient with especial reference to his view as to what would be the effect on her of a warning of the existence of a risk, albeit slight, of serious personal injury arising from the operation however skilfully and competently it was performed. Such being the limitations on the availability of critically important evidence, I confess that I find it surprising that the trial judge felt able to reach the detailed findings as to the extent of the warning given which are a striking feature of his judgment. There is, however, no appeal against his findings and I have no doubt that your Lordships' House must proceed on the basis of the facts as found. * * *

Mrs Sidaway was 71 years of age at the time of the trial in 1982. She was severely disabled by a partial paralysis resulting from her operation. The relationship of doctor and patient between Mr Falconer and herself had been long-standing prior to the operation. * * *

Mr Falconer annually reviewed his patient's progress between 1960 and 1970. In 1973 he wrote to Mrs Sidaway asking how she was. She replied, complaining of very persistent pain "in the right arm and shoulder", which was the same area as before, and now also of pain in the left forearm. Mr Falconer saw her in the early months of 1974. After some delays, she was admitted to hospital on 11 October 1974. Her pain in the mean time had got progressively worse.

On admission Mrs Sidaway was thoroughly examined by Dr Goudarzi, a junior member of Mr Falconer's team. On 17 October she underwent a myelogram which revealed a partial block at the level of the C4/5 disc space, a posterior ridge in the same area which appeared to have, at least in part, a bony structure, and a narrowing of the subarachnoid space in the same area. Mr Falconer diagnosed that pressure on a nerve root was the cause of her pain and decided to operate. * * *

* * *

It was common ground between all the neuro-surgeons who gave evidence that the operation involved specific risks beyond those inherent in all operations under general anaesthetic. * * *

The two specific risks of injury were (1) damage to a nerve root in the area of the operation and (2) damage to the spinal cord either by direct contact or by some interference, which might be slight and of short duration or very much more serious, of the radicular arteries running through a foramen. The risk of either sort of damage occurring was not great: one surgeon estimated the degree of risk at between 1% and 2%. But, if either risk materialised, the injury could be severe. Mr Uttley, the distinguished surgeon called on behalf of Mrs Sidaway, said that the possible effects of the damage ranged from a sensation of pins and needles in the hand to paraplegia, i.e. a partial paralysis. * * * [The witnesses] distinguished between the two categories of specific risk, the effect of damage to a nerve root being in all probability that the operation would fail to relieve and might increase pain, while damage to the spinal cord might cause a partial paralysis. The risk of damage to the spinal cord was, however, in their opinion less than 1%.

There is no challenge to the judge's findings (1) that Mr Falconer's diagnosis was correct, (2) that his recommendation in favour of operative treatment was one which he could reasonably and properly have made to his patient and (3) that he performed the operation with due care and skill.

The issue between the parties arises solely in respect of the warning, if any, which Mr Falconer gave his patient of the specific risks inherent in the operation. * * *

Mrs Sidaway consented to the operation. She signed the usual consent form, in which she declared that the nature and purpose of the operation had been explained to her by Dr Goudarzi. Dr Goudarzi confirmed that he had given her this explanation but he made it clear in his evidence that he would have left warning of the risks to Mr Falconer. And we know from the hospital records that Mr Falconer saw his patient before he operated. It would have been his practice to give a warning but a finding as to what warning he gave faces the formidable difficulty to which I have already referred, that Mr Falconer was not available to give evidence. Nevertheless, the judge, while refusing to accept Mrs Sidaway's evidence that she was given no warning, made the following findings on the balance of probabilities. He said:

> On the evidence ... the probabilities are that ... on the day before the operation he [Mr Falconer] followed his usual practice ... it is probable that he explained the nature of the operation [to his patient] in simple terms ... As to the risks, I think it is probable that he mentioned the possibility of disturbing a nerve root and the consequences of doing so, but I am satisfied that he did not refer to the danger of cord damage or to the fact that this was an operation of choice rather than necessity.

The medical witnesses were agreed that they would give a patient some warning of the specific risks involved before performing an operation of this kind. They would explain the nature and purpose of the operation, and that there was a small risk of untoward consequences and of an increase of pain instead of relief. Mr Uttley would go further: he would warn of the possible risk of some weakness of the legs resulting from the operation. Two answers in his cross-examination were of great importance. When asked whether he would question the judgment of a surgeon that it was not in his patient's interest to frighten her by talking about death or paralysis, he replied, "Not at all" and he agreed that such a judgment would be in accordance with a practice accepted as proper by a responsible body of competent neuro-surgeons. * * * Their view may be summarised as being that the extent of the warning is a matter for medical judgment with especial importance attached to the doctor's assessment of his patient

This being the state of the evidence, the question for the House is whether the omission by Mr Falconer to warn his patient of the risk inherent in the operation of damage to the spinal cord with the possible result of a partial paralysis was a breach of duty owed by him to his patient. The duty of a doctor to warn was considered in *Bolam v Friern Hospital Management Committee*, where it was treated as one to be answered within the context of the duty of care and skill owed by a doctor to his patient. * * *

* * *

The *Bolam* principle may be formulated as a rule that a doctor is not negligent if he acts in accordance with a practice accepted at the time as proper by a responsible body of medical opinion even though other doctors adopt a different practice. In short, the law imposes the duty of care but the standard of care is a matter of medical judgment. The *Bolam* principle has been accepted by your Lordships' House as applicable to diagnosis and treatment: It is also recognised in Scots law as applicable to diagnosis and treatment * * *.

But was the judge correct in treating the "standard of competent professional opinion" as the criterion in determining whether a doctor is under a duty to warn his patient of the risk, or risks, inherent in the treatment which he recommends? * * * The implications of this view of the law are disturbing. It leaves the determination of a legal duty to the judgment of doctors. Responsible medical judgment may, indeed, provide the law with an acceptable standard in determining whether a doctor in diagnosis or treatment has complied with his duty. But is it right that medical judgment should determine whether there exists a duty to warn of risk and its scope? It would be a strange conclusion if the courts should be led to conclude that our law, which undoubtedly recognises a right in the patient to decide whether he will accept or reject the treatment proposed, should permit the doctors to determine whether and in what circumstances a duty arises requiring the doctor to warn his patient of the risks inherent in the treatment which he proposes.

The right of "self-determination", the description applied by some to what is no more and no less than the right of a patient to determine for himself whether he will or will not accept the doctor's advice, is vividly illustrated where the treatment recommended is surgery. A doctor who operates without the consent of his patient is, save in cases of emergency or mental disability, guilty of the civil wrong of trespass to the person. He is also guilty of the criminal offence of assault. The existence of the patient's right to make his own decision, which may be seen as a basic human right protected by the common law, is the reason why a doctrine embodying a right of the patient to be informed of the risks of surgical treatment has been developed in some jurisdictions in the United States of America and has found favour with the Supreme Court of Canada. Known as the "doctrine of informed consent", it amounts to this: where there is a "real" or a "material" risk inherent in the proposed operation (however competently and skilfully performed) the question whether and to what extent a patient should be warned before he gives his consent is to be answered not by reference to medical practice but by accepting as a matter of law that, subject to all proper exceptions (of which the court, not the profession, is the judge), a patient has a right to be informed of the risks inherent in the treatment which is proposed. The profession, it is said, should not be judge in its own cause or, less emotively but more correctly, the courts should not allow medical opinion as to what is best for the patient to override the patient's right to decide for himself whether he will submit to the treatment offered him. It will be necessary for the House to consider in this appeal what is involved in the doctrine and whether it, or any modification of it, has any place in English law.

The appellant's first submission is that, even if (which she does not accept) the *Bolam* principle determines whether a warning of risk should or should not be given, the facts found establish liability. * * * It is not possible to hold that the appellant has shown negligence in the *Bolam* sense on the part of Mr Falconer in advising or treating her. His decision not to warn her of the danger of damage to the spinal cord and of its possible consequences was one which the medical witnesses were agreed to be in accordance with a practice accepted as proper by a responsible body of opinion among neuro-surgeons. * * * There is no evidence to justify an inference that this careful and compassionate man (the history of the case, which I have related, shows that he merited both adjectives) would have failed to consider what was in the best interests of his patient. He could well have concluded that a warning might have deterred her from agreeing to an operation which he believed to be the best treatment for her.

The appellant's second submission is that she has a cause of action which is independent of negligence in the *Bolam* sense. The submission is based on her right to decide for herself whether she should submit to the operation proposed. In effect, she invokes the transatlantic doctrine of informed consent.

The doctrine is new ground in so far as English law is concerned. * * *

* * *

* * * [T]he *Bolam* principle does not cover the situation. The facts of this very case expose its limitation. Mr Falconer lacked neither care for his patient's health and well-being nor professional skill in the advice and treatment which he offered. But did he overlook or disregard his patient's right to determine for herself whether or not to have the operation? Did he fail to provide her with the information necessary for her to make a prudent decision? There is, in truth, no evidence to answer these questions. Mrs Sidaway's

evidence was not accepted and Mr Falconer was dead. Assume, however, that he did overlook this aspect of his patient's situation. Since neither his advice nor his treatment could be faulted on the *Bolam* test, his patient may have been deprived of the opportunity to exercise her right of decision in the light of information which she, had she received it, might reasonably have considered to be of importance in making up her mind. On the *Bolam* view of the law, therefore, even if she established that she was so deprived by the lack of a warning, she would have no remedy in negligence unless she could also prove that there was no competent and respected body of medical opinion which was in favour of no warning. Moreover, the tort of trespass to the person would not provide her with a remedy, for Mrs Sidaway did consent to the operation. Her complaint is that her consent resulted from ignorance of a risk, known by the doctor but not made known by him to her, inherent in the operation. Nor would the law of contract offer her a sure way forward. Medical treatment, as in her case, is frequently given today under arrangements outside the control of the law of contract.

One point is clear, however. If failure to warn of risk is actionable in English law, it must be because it is in the circumstances a breach of the doctor's duty of care in other words, the doctor must be shown to be negligent. English law has not accepted a "no fault" basis for the liability of a doctor to compensate a patient for injury arising in the course of medical treatment. If, however, the *Bolam* principle is to be applied to the exclusion of any other test to advice and warning, there will be cases in which a patient who suffers injury through ignorance of a risk known to the doctor has no remedy. Is there any difficulty in holding that the doctor's duty of care is sufficiently extensive to afford a patient in that situation a remedy, if as a result she suffers injury or damage? I think not. The root principle of common law negligence is to "take reasonable care to avoid acts or omissions which you can reasonably foresee would be likely to injure your neighbour." If it be recognised that a doctor's duty of care extends not only to the health and well-being of his patient but also to a proper respect for his patient's rights, the duty to warn can be seen to be part of the doctor's duty of care.

It is, I suggest, a sound and reasonable proposition that the doctor should be required to exercise care in respecting the patient's right of decision. He must acknowledge that in very many cases factors other than the purely medical will play a significant part in his patient's decision-making process. The doctor's concern is with health and the relief of pain. These are the medical objectives. But a patient may well have in mind circumstances, objectives and values which he may reasonably not make known to the doctor but which may lead him to a different decision from that suggested by a purely medical opinion. The doctor's duty can be seen, therefore, to be one which requires him not only to advise as to medical treatment but also to provide his patient with the information needed to enable the patient to consider and balance the medical advantages and risks alongside other relevant matters, such as, for example, his family, business or social responsibilities of which the doctor may be only partially, if at all, informed.

I conclude, therefore, that there is room in our law for a legal duty to warn a patient of the risks inherent in the treatment proposed, and that, if such a duty be held to exist, its proper place is as an aspect of the duty of care owed by the doctor to his patient. I turn, therefore, to consider whether a duty to warn does exist in our law and, if it does, its proper formulation and the conditions and exceptions to which it must be subject.

[Judge Scarman proceeded to discuss American and Canadian precendents recognizing the law of informed consent.]

* * *

In my judgment the merit of the propositions enunciated in *Canterbury v Spence* is that without excluding medical evidence they set a standard and formulate a test of the doctor's duty the effect of which is that the court determines the scope of the duty and decides whether the doctor has acted in breach of his duty. This result is achieved, first, by emphasis on the patient's "right of self-determination" and, second, by the "prudent patient" test. If the doctor omits to warn where the risk is such that in the court's view a prudent person in the patient's situation would have regarded it as significant, the doctor is liable.

The *Canterbury* propositions do indeed attach great importance to medical evidence, though judgment is for the court. First, medical evidence is needed in determining whether the risk is material, i.e. one which the doctor should make known to his patient. * * * And, second, medical evidence would be needed to assist the court in determining whether the doctor was justified on his assessment of his patient in withholding the warning.

My Lords, I think the *Canterbury* propositions reflect a legal truth which too much judicial reliance on medical judgment tends to obscure. In a medical negligence case where the issue is as to the advice and information given to the patient as to the treatment proposed, the available options and the risk, the court is concerned primarily with a patient's right. The doctor's duty arises from his patient's rights. If one considers the scope of the doctor's duty by beginning with the right of the patient to make his own decision whether he will or will not undergo the treatment proposed, the right to be informed of significant risk and the doctor's corresponding duty are easy to understand, for the proper implementation of the right requires that the doctor be under a duty to inform his patient of the material risks inherent in the treatment. And it is plainly right that a doctor may avoid liability for failure to warn of a material risk if he can show that he reasonably believed that communication to the patient of the existence of the risk would be detrimental to the health (including, of course, the mental health) of his patient.

Ideally, the court should ask itself whether in the particular circumstances the risk was such that this particular patient would think it significant if he was told it existed. * * * The law, however, operates not in Utopia but in the world as it is and such an inquiry would prove in practice to be frustrated by the subjectivity of its aim and purpose. The law can, however, do the next best thing, and require the court to answer the question, what would a reasonably prudent patient think significant if in the situation of this patient? The "prudent patient" cannot, however, always provide the answer for the obvious reason that he is a norm (like the man on the Clapham omnibus), not a real person and certainly not the patient himself. Hence there is the need that the doctor should have the opportunity of proving that he reasonably believed that disclosure of the risk would be damaging to his patient or contrary to his best interest. This is what the Americans call the doctor's "therapeutic privilege". Its true analysis is that it is a defence available to the doctor which, if he invokes it, he must prove. On both the test and the defence medical evidence will, of course, be of great importance.

* * *

My conclusion as to the law is therefore this. To the extent that I have indicated, I think that English law must recognise a duty of the doctor to warn his patient of risk inherent in the treatment which he is proposing and especially so if the treatment be surgery. The critical limitation is that the duty is confined to material risk. The test of materiality is whether in the circumstances of the particular case the court is satisfied that a reasonable person in the patient's position would be likely to attach significance to the risk. Even if the risk be material, the doctor will not be liable if on a reasonable assessment of his patient's condition he takes the view that a warning would be detrimental to his patient's health.

Applying these principles to the present case, I ask first: has the appellant shown the risk of damage to the spinal cord to have been a material risk? The risk was slight, less than 1% but, if it were to materialise, it could result in severe injury. It was for the appellant, as plaintiff, to establish that the risk was so great that the doctor should have appreciated that it would be considered a significant factor by a prudent patient in the appellant's situation deciding whether or not to have the operation. * * * After an anxious consideration of the evidence I do not find it possible to say that it has been proved that Mr Falconer failed in his duty when he omitted, as we must assume that he did, to warn his patient of the risk of injury to the spinal cord.

* * *

Lord Diplock

* * * Inevitably all treatment, medical or surgical, involves some degree of risk that the patient's condition will be worse rather than better for undergoing it. Statistically, the chances of any risk of the proposed treatment going awry at all may be small, but, particularly if surgery is involved * * * it is never totally absent and the degree of possible worsening involved may cover a whole spectrum of disabilities from mild occasional discomfort to what might justify the epithet "catastrophic". All these are matters which the doctor will have taken into consideration in determining, in the exercise of his professional skill and judgment, that it is in the patient's interest that he should take the risk involved and undergo the treatment recommended by the doctor.

There is no evidence in the instant case that the patient asked the neuro-surgeon a single question about whether there were any risks involved in undergoing the operation that he was proposing for her, or, if there were, what were the consequences of those risks or the chances of their occurring. So there are eliminated from our consideration matters of clinical judgment of the neuro-surgeon as to how to conduct a bilateral discussion with the patient in terms best calculated not to scare her off from undergoing an operation which, in the exercise of the paramount duty of care he owed to her individually to exercise his skill and judgment in endeavouring to heal her, he is satisfied that it is in her interests to undergo despite such risks as may be entailed.

Likewise, we do not know, * * * what risks the neuro-surgeon did mention to the patient.

* * *

What we do know, however, and this is in my view determinative of this appeal, is that all the expert witnesses specialising in neurology (including the patient's own expert witness, Mr Uttley, who would not himself have undertaken a similar operation without waiting a period of time, after October 1974, to see what developed as to the persistence of the patient's pain) agreed that there was a responsible body of medical opinion which would have undertaken the operation at the time the neuro-surgeon did and would have warned the patient of the risk involved in the operation in substantially the same terms as the trial judge found on the balance of probabilities the neuro-surgeon had done, i.e. without specific reference to risk of injuring the spinal cord.

My Lords, it is the very paucity of facts in evidence that makes it possible, in my view, to treat this appeal as raising a naked question of legal principle. * * * For the last quarter of a century the test applied in English law whether a doctor has fulfilled his duty of care owed to his patient has been that set out in the summing up to the jury by McNair J in *Bolam v Friern Hospital Management Committee.* * * *

The *Bolam* test is far from new; its value is that it brings up to date and re-expresses in the light of modern conditions in which the art of medicine is now practised an ancient rule of common law. The original rule can be traced to the maxim *spondet peritiam artis et imperitia culpae adnumeratur*. It goes back to the origin of assumpsit it applied to all artificers and was firmly founded in "case" (*moderniter* negligence) although it may be of interest to note that as long ago as 1767 in *Slater v Baker* * * * a suggestion that where injury was caused by surgery the form of action lay in trespass vi et armis was rejected with scant sympathy by the Court of King's Bench.

The standard of skill and judgment in the particular area of the art of medicine in which the doctor practised that was called for by the expression *peritia* was the standard of ordinary skill and care that could be expected to be shown by a doctor who had successfully completed the training to qualify as a doctor, whether as general practitioner or as consultant in a speciality if he held himself out as practising as such, as the case might be. But, unless the art in which the artificer claims to have acquired skill and judgment is stagnant so that no improvement in methods or knowledge is sought (and of few is this less true than medicine and surgery over the last half-century), advances in the ability to heal resulting from the volume of research, clinical as well as technological, will present doctors with alternative treatments to adopt and a choice to select that treatment * * * that is in their judgment likely at the time to prove most efficacious or ameliorating to the health of each particular patient committed to their care.

* * * The merit of the *Bolam* test is that the criterion of the duty of care owed by a doctor to his patient is whether he has acted in accordance with a practice accepted as proper by a body of responsible and skilled medical opinion. There may be a number of different practices which satisfy this criterion at any particular time. These practices are likely to alter with advances in medical knowledge. * * *

In English jurisprudence the doctor's relationship with his patient which gives rise to the normal duty of care to exercise his skill and judgment to improve the patient's health in any particular respect in which the patient has sought his aid has hitherto been treated as a single comprehensive duty covering all the ways in which a doctor is called on to exercise his skill and judgment. * * *

My Lords, no convincing reason has in my view been advanced before your Lordships that would justify treating the *Bolam* test as doing anything less than laying down a principle of English law that is comprehensive and applicable to every aspect of the duty of care owed by a doctor to his patient in the exercise of his healing functions as respects that patient. What your Lordships have been asked to do, and it is within your power to do so, is to substitute a new and different rule for that part only of the well-established test as comprises a doctor's duty to advise and warn the patient of risks of something going wrong in the surgical or other treatment that he is recommending.

The juristic basis of the proposed substitution, which originates in certain state court jurisdictions of the United States of America and has found some favour in modified form by the Supreme Court of Canada, appears to me, with great respect, to be contrary to English law. Its foundation is the doctrine of "informed consent" which was originally based on the assumption made in the United States Court of Appeals, District of Columbia Circuit, in *Canterbury v Spence* * * * that prima facie the cause of action in a case of surgery was trespass to the person unless "informed consent" to the particular battery involved in the surgical operation could be proved. From a period long before American independence this, as I have pointed out, has never been so in English law. The relevant form of action has been based in negligence, i e in assumpsit, alone.

The Supreme Court of Canada, after some initial vaccilation, rejected trespass to the person, i.e. battery, as the cause of action in cases of surgery but endeavoured to transfer the concept of "informed consent" to a patient's cause of action in negligence, into which, in my opinion, it simply cannot be made to fit. Consent to battery is a state of mind personal to the victim of the battery and any information required to make his consent qualify as informed must be relevant information either actually possessed by him or which he is estopped from denying he possessed, because he so acted towards the defendant as to lead to the latter reasonably to assume the relevant information was known to him. There is no room in the concept of informed consent for the "objective" patient (as he is referred to at one point by the Supreme Court of Canada) to whom the doctor is entitled, without making any inquiry whether it is the fact or not, to attribute knowledge of some risks but not of others. * * *

My Lords, I venture to think that in making this separation between that part of the doctor's duty of care that he owes to each individual patient, which can be described as a duty to advise on treatment and warn of its risks, the courts have misconceived their functions as the finders of fact in cases depending on the negligent exercise of professional skill and judgment. In matters of diagnosis and the carrying out of treatment the court is not tempted to put itself in the surgeon's shoes; it has to rely on and evaluate expert evidence, remembering that it is no part of its task of evaluation to give effect to any preference it may have for one responsible body of professional opinion over another, provided it is satisfied by the expert evidence that both qualify as responsible bodies of medical opinion. But, when it comes to warning about risks, the kind of training and experience that a judge will have undergone at the Bar makes it natural for him to say (correctly) it is my right to decide whether any particular thing is done to my body, and I want to be fully informed of any risks there may be involved of which I am not already aware from my general knowledge as a highly educated man of experience, so that I may form my own judgment whether to refuse the advised treatment or not.

No doubt, if the patient in fact manifested this attitude by means of questioning, the doctor would tell him whatever it was the patient wanted to know but we are concerned here with volunteering unsought information about risks of the proposed treatment failing to achieve the result sought or making the patient's physical or mental condition worse rather than better. The only effect that mention of risks can have on the patient's mind, if it has any at all, can be in the direction of deterring the patient from undergoing the treatment which in the expert opinion of the doctor it is in the patient's interest to undergo. To decide what risks the existence of which a patient should be voluntarily warned and the terms in which such warning, if any, should be given, having regard to the effect that the warning may have, is as much an exercise of professional skill and judgment as any other part of the doctor's comprehensive duty of care to the individual patient, and expert medical evidence on this matter should be treated in just the same way. The *Bolam* test should be applied.

I agree with your Lordships that this appeal should be dismissed.

Lord Bridge of Harlock

* * *

Broadly, a doctor's professional functions may be divided into three phases: diagnosis, advice and treatment. In performing his functions of diagnosis and treatment, the standard by which English law measures the doctor's duty of care to his patient is not open to doubt. "The test is the standard of the ordinary skilled man exercising and professing to have that special skill." * * * The test is conveniently referred to as the *Bolam* test. In *May-*

nard's case Lord Scarman, with whose speech the other four members of the Appellate Committee agreed, further cited with approval the words of the Lord President (Clyde) in *Hunter v Hanley:*

> In the realm of diagnosis and treatment there is ample scope for genuine difference of opinion and one man clearly is not negligent merely because his conclusion differs from that of other professional men ... The true test for establishing negligence in diagnosis or treatment on the part of a doctor is whether he has been proved to be guilty of such failure as no doctor of ordinary skill would be guilty of if acting with ordinary care ...

* * *

The important question which this appeal raises is whether the law imposes any, and if so what, different criterion as the measure of the medical man's duty of care to his patient when giving advice with respect to a proposed course of treatment. It is clearly right to recognise that a conscious adult patient of sound mind is entitled to decide for himself whether or not he will submit to a particular course of treatment proposed by the doctor, most significantly surgical treatment under general anaesthesia. This entitlement is the foundation of the doctrine of "informed consent" which has led in certain American jurisdictions to decisions and, in the Supreme Court of Canada, to dicta on which the appellant relies, which would oust the *Bolam* test and substitute an "objective" test of a doctor's duty to advise the patient of the advantages and disadvantages of undergoing the treatment proposed and more particularly to advise the patient of the risks involved.

There are, it appears to me, at least theoretically, two extreme positions which could be taken. It could be argued that, if the patient's consent is to be fully informed, the doctor must specifically warn him of all risks involved in the treatment offered, unless he has some sound clinical reason not to do so.

* * *

At the other extreme it could be argued that, once the doctor has decided what treatment is, on balance of advantages and disadvantages, in the patient's best interest, he should not alarm the patient by volunteering a warning of any risk involved, however grave and substantial, unless specifically asked by the patient. I cannot believe that contemporary medical opinion would support this view, which would effectively exclude the patient's right to decide in the very type of case where it is most important that he should be in a position to exercise that right and, perhaps even more significantly, to seek a second opinion whether he should submit himself to the significant risk which has been drawn to his attention. I should perhaps add at this point, although the issue does not strictly arise in this appeal, that, when questioned specifically by a patient of apparently sound mind about risks involved in a particular treatment proposed, the doctor's duty must, in my opinion, be to answer both truthfully and as fully as the questioner requires.

[A discussion of *Canterbury* ensued.]

I recognise the logical force of the Canterbury doctrine, proceeding from the premise that the patient's right to make his own decision must at all costs be safeguarded against the kind of medical paternalism which assumes that "doctor knows best". But, with all respect, I regard the doctrine as quite impractical in application for three principal reasons. First, it gives insufficient weight to the realities of the doctor/patient relationship. A very wide variety of factors must enter into a doctor's clinical judgment not only as to what treatment is appropriate for a particular patient, but also as to how best to communicate to the patient the significant factors necessary to enable the patient to make an informed decision whether to undergo the treatment. The doctor cannot set out to educate the patient to his own standard of medical knowledge of all the relevant factors involved. He may take the view, certainly with some patients, that the very fact of his volunteering, without being asked, information of some remote risk involved in the treatment proposed, even though he describes it as remote, may lead to that risk assuming an undue significance in the patient's calculations. Second, it would seem to me quite unrealistic in any medical negligence action to confine the expert medical evidence to an explanation of the primary medical factors involved and to deny the court the benefit of evidence of medical opinion and practice on the particular issue of disclosure which is under consideration. Third, the objective test which *Canterbury* propounds seems to me to be so imprecise as to be almost meaningless. If it is to be left to individual judges to decide for themselves what "a reasonable person in the patient's position' would consider a risk of sufficient significance that he should be told about it, the outcome of litigation in this field is likely to be quite unpredictable.

* * *

Having rejected the *Canterbury* doctrine as a solution to the problem of safeguarding the patient's right to decide whether he will undergo a particular treatment advised by his doctor, the question remains whether that right is sufficiently safeguarded by the application of the *Bolam* test without qualification to the determination of the question what risks inherent in a proposed treatment should be disclosed. The case against a simple application of the *Bolam* test is cogently stated by Laskin CJC, giving the judgment of the Supreme Court of Canada in *Reibl v Hughes*:

> To allow expert medical evidence to determine what risks are material and, hence, should be disclosed and, correlatively, what risks are not material is to hand over to the medical profession the entire question of the scope of the duty of disclosure, including the question whether there has been a breach of that duty. * * *

I fully appreciate the force of this reasoning, but can only accept it subject to the important qualification that a decision what degree of disclosure of risks is best calculated to assist a particular patient to make a rational choice whether or not to undergo a particular treatment must primarily be a matter of clinical judgment. It would follow from this that the issue whether non-disclosure in a particular case should be condemned as a breach of the doctor's duty of care is an issue to be decided primarily on the basis of expert medical evidence, applying the *Bolam* test. But I do not see that this approach involves the necessity "to hand over to the medical profession the entire question of the scope of the duty of disclosure, including the question whether there has been a breach of that duty". * * * But, even in a case where, as here, no expert witness in the relevant medical field condemns the non-disclosure as being in conflict with accepted and responsible medical practice, I am of opinion that the judge might in certain circumstances come to the conclusion that disclosure of a particular risk was so obviously necessary to an informed choice on the part of the patient that no reasonably prudent medical man would fail to make it. The kind of case I have in mind would be an operation involving a substantial risk of grave adverse consequences, as for example the 10% risk of a stroke from the operation which was the subject of the Canadian case of *Reibl v Hughes*. In such a case, in the absence of some cogent clinical reason why the patient should not be informed, a doctor, recognising and respecting his patient's right of decision, could hardly fail to appreciate the necessity for an appropriate warning.

In the instant case I can see no reasonable ground on which the judge could properly reject the conclusion to which the unchallenged medical evidence led in the application of the *Bolam* test.

* * *

I would dismiss the appeal.

Lord Templeman

* * *

In my opinion a simple and general explanation of the nature of the operation should have been sufficient to alert Mrs Sidaway to the fact that a major operation was to be performed and to the possibility that something might go wrong at or near the site of the spinal cord or the site of the nerve root causing serious injury. If, as the judge held, Mr Falconer probably referred expressly to the possibility of damage to a nerve root and to the consequences of such damage, this warning could only have reinforced the possibility of something going wrong in the course of a delicate operation performed in a vital area with resultant damage. In view of the fact that Mr Falconer recommended the operation, Mrs Sidaway must have been told or could have assumed that Mr Falconer considered that the possibilities of damage were sufficiently remote to be ignored. Mrs Sidaway could have asked questions. If she had done so, she could and should have been informed that there was an aggregate risk of between 1% and 2% of some damage either to the spinal cord or to a nerve root resulting in injury which might vary from irritation to paralysis. But to my mind this further information would only have reinforced the obvious, with the assurance that the maximum risk of damage, slight or serious, did not exceed 2%. Mr Falconer may reasonably have taken the view that Mrs Sidaway might be confused, frightened or misled by more detailed information which she was unable to evaluate at a time when she was suffering from stress, pain and anxiety. A patient may prefer that the doctor should not thrust too much detail at the patient. * * *

On the assumption that Mr Falconer explained that it was necessary to remove bone and free a nerve root from pressure near the spinal cord, it seems to me that the possibility of damage to a nerve root or to the spinal cord was obvious. The operation was skilfully performed but by mishap the remote risk of damage to the spinal cord unfortunately caused the disability from which Mrs Sidaway is now suffering. However much sympathy may be felt for Mrs Sidaway and however much in hindsight the operation may be regretted by her, the question now is whether Mr Falconer was negligent in the explanation which he gave.

In my opinion, if a patient knows that a major operation may entail serious consequences, the patient cannot complain of lack of information unless the patient asks in vain for more information or unless there is some danger which by its nature or magnitude or for some other reason requires to be separately taken into account by the patient in order to reach a balanced judgment in deciding whether or not to submit to the operation.

* * *

I do not subscribe to the theory that the patient is entitled to know everything or to the theory that the doctor is entitled to decide everything. The relationship between doctor and patient is contractual in origin, the doctor performing services in consideration for fees payable by the patient. The doctor, obedient to the high standards set by the medical profession, impliedly contracts to act at all times in the best interests of the patient. No doctor in his senses would impliedly contract at the same time to give to the patient all the information available to the doctor as a result of the doctor's training and experience and as a result of the doctor's diagnosis of the patient. An obligation to give a patient all the information available to the doctor would often be inconsistent with the doctor's contractual obligation to have regard to the patient's best interests. Some information might confuse, other information might alarm a particular patient. Whenever the occasion arises for the doctor to tell the patient the results of the doctor's diagnosis, the possible methods of treatment and the advantages and disadvantages of the recommended treatment, the doctor must decide in the light of his training and experience and in the light of his knowledge of the patient what should be said and how it should be said. At the same time the doctor is not entitled to make the final decision with regard to treatment which may have disadvantages or dangers. Where the patient's health and future are at stake, the patient must make the final decision. The patient is free to decide whether or not to submit to treatment recommended by the doctor and therefore the doctor impliedly contracts to provide information which is adequate to enable the patient to reach a balanced judgment, subject always to the doctor's own obligation to say and do nothing which the doctor is satisfied will be harmful to the patient. When the doctor himself is considering the possibility of a major operation the doctor is able, with his medical training, with his knowledge of the patient's medical history and with his objective position, to make a balanced judgment whether the operation should be performed or not. If the doctor making a balanced judgment advises the patient to submit to the operation, the patient is entitled to reject that advice for reasons which are rational or irrational or for no reason. The duty of the doctor in these circumstances, subject to his overriding duty to have regard to the best interests of the patient, is to provide the patient with information which will enable the patient to make a balanced judgment if the patient chooses to make a balanced judgment. A patient may make an unbalanced judgment because he is deprived of adequate information. A patient may also make an unbalanced judgment if he is provided with too much information and is made aware of possibilities which he is not capable of assessing because of his lack of medical training, his prejudices or his personality. Thus the provision of too much information may prejudice the attainment of the objective of restoring the patient's health. * * * At the end of the day, the doctor, bearing in mind the best interests of the patient and bearing in mind the patient's right to information which will enable the patient to make a balanced judgment, must decide what information should be given to the patient and in what terms that information should be couched. The court will award damages against the doctor if the court is satisfied that the doctor blundered and that the patient was deprived of information which was necessary for the purposes I have outlined. In the present case on the judge's findings I am satisfied that adequate information was made available to Mrs Sidaway and that the appeal should therefore be dismissed.

Appeal dismissed.

Notes

1. The Appellate Committee of the House of Lords is the United Kingdom's highest court. It includes the Lord Chancellor and the Lords of Appeal in Ordinary, and is composed only of professional members of the House of Lords chamber of Parliament, who are generally former distinguished barristers and judges. House of Lords opinions look unfamiliar to American law students because there is no opinion of the Court. Rather, each Lord issues his own written opinion, speaking only for him or herself. One can, of course, determine who won a case, but there is often no single *ratio decidendi* for a decision.

2. Does the House of Lords in *Sidaway* consider recipients of medical care to be patients or consumers? How complete is its faith in the competency of medical science? Is this decision simply attributable to a primitive medical paternalism, or might there be more going on here? See Frances H. Miller, Denial of Health Care and Informed Consent in English and American Law, 18 *Am.J.L. & Med.* 37 (1992).

Rogers v. Whitaker

109 A.L.R. 625, 67 A.L.J.R. 47 (1992) (High Court of Australia)

Judgment: Mason CJ, Brennan, Dawson, Toohey and McHugh JJ.

The appellant, Christopher Rogers, is an ophthalmic surgeon. The respondent, Maree Lynette Whitaker, was a patient of the appellant who became almost totally blind after he had conducted surgery upon her right eye. The respondent commenced proceedings against the appellant for negligence in the Supreme Court of New South Wales and obtained judgment in the amount of $808,564.38. After an unsuccessful appeal to the Court of Appeal of New South Wales, the appellant now appeals to this court.

There is no question that the appellant conducted the operation with the required skill and care. The basis upon which the trial judge, Campbell J, found the appellant liable was that he had failed to warn the respondent that, as a result of surgery on her right eye, she might develop a condition known as sympathetic ophthalmia in her left eye. The development of this condition after the operation and the consequent loss of sight in her left eye were particularly devastating for the respondent as she had been almost totally blind in her right eye since a penetrating injury to it at the age of nine. Despite this early misfortune, she had continued to lead a substantially normal life: completing her schooling, entering the workforce, marrying and raising a family. In 1983, nearly 40 years after the initial injury to her right eye and in preparation for a return to the paid workforce after a three year period during which she had looked after her injured son, the respondent decided to have an eye examination. Her general practitioner referred her to Dr Cohen, an ophthalmic surgeon, who prescribed reading glasses and referred her to the appellant for possible surgery on her right eye.

The respondent did not follow up the referral until 22 May 1984 when she was examined by the appellant for the first time. The appellant advised her that an operation on the right eye would not only improve its appearance, by removing scar tissue, but would probably restore significant sight to that eye. At a second consultation approximately three weeks later, the respondent agreed to submit to surgery. The surgical procedure was carried out on 1 August 1984. After the operation, it appeared that there had been no improvement in the right eye but, more importantly, the respondent developed inflammation in the left eye as an element of sympathetic ophthalmia. Evidence at the trial was that this condition occurred once in approximately 14,000 such procedures, although there was also evidence that the chance of occurrence was slightly greater when, as here, there had been an earlier penetrating injury to the eye operated upon. The condition does not always lead to loss of vision but, in this case, the respondent ultimately lost all sight in the left eye. As the sight in her right eye had not been restored in any degree by the surgery, the respondent was thus almost totally blind.

In the proceedings commenced by the respondent, numerous heads of negligence were alleged. Campbell J rejected all save the allegation that the appellant's failure to warn of the risk of sympathetic ophthalmia was negligent and resulted in the respondent's condition. While his Honour was not satisfied that proper medical practice required that the appellant warn the respondent of the risk of sympathetic ophthalmia if she expressed no desire for information, he concluded that a warning was necessary in the light of her desire for such relevant information. The Court of Appeal dismissed all grounds of the appellant's appeal from the judgment of $808,564.38 on both liability and damages; the court also dismissed a cross-appeal by the respondent on the question of general damages. * * *

Neither before the Court of Appeal nor before this court was there any dispute as to the existence of a duty of care on the part of the appellant to the respondent. The law imposes on a medical practitioner a duty to exercise reasonable care and skill in the provision of professional advice and treatment. That duty is a "single comprehensive duty covering all the ways in which a doctor is called upon to exercise his skill and judgment" * * *.

The standard of reasonable care and skill required is that of the ordinary skilled person exercising and professing to have that special skill, in this case the skill of an ophthalmic surgeon specialising in corneal and anterior segment surgery. As we have stated, the failure of the appellant to observe this standard, which the respondent successfully alleged before the primary judge, consisted of the appellant's failure to acquaint the respondent with the danger of sympathetic ophthalmia as a possible result of the surgical procedure to be carried out. The appellant's evidence was that "sympathetic ophthalmia was not something that came to my mind to mention to her".

The principal issue in this case relates to the scope and content of the appellant's duty of care: did the appellant's failure to advise and warn the respondent of the risks inherent in the operation constitute a breach of this duty? The appellant argues that this issue should be resolved by application of the so-called *Bolam* principle, * * *.

[The Court proceeded to discuss the application of *Bolam* in *Sidaway*.]

* * *

One consequence of the application of the *Bolam* principle to cases involving the provision of advice or information is that, even if a patient asks a direct question about the possible risks or complications, the making of that inquiry would logically be of little or no significance; medical opinion determines whether the risk should or should not be disclosed and the express desire of a particular patient for information or advice does not alter that opinion or the legal significance of that opinion. The fact that the various majority opinions in *Sidaway*, for example, suggest that, over and above the opinion of a respectable body of medical practitioners, the questions of a patient should truthfully be answered (subject to the therapeutic privilege) indicates a shortcoming in the *Bolam* approach. The existence of the shortcoming suggests that an acceptable approach in point of principle should recognise and attach significance to the relevance of a patient's questions. Even if a court were satisfied that a reasonable person in the patient's position would be unlikely to attach significance to a particular risk, the fact that the patient asked questions revealing concern about the risk would make the doctor aware that this patient did in fact attach significance to the risk. Subject to the therapeutic privilege, the question would therefore require a truthful answer.

In Australia, it has been accepted that the standard of care to be observed by a person with some special skill or competence is that of the ordinary skilled person exercising and professing to have that special skill. But, that standard is not determined solely or even primarily by reference to the practice followed or supported by a responsible body of opinion in the relevant profession or trade. Even in the sphere of diagnosis and treatment, the heartland of the skilled medical practitioner, the *Bolam* principle has not always been applied. Further, and more importantly, particularly in the field of non-disclosure of risk and the provision of advice and information, the *Bolam* principle has been discarded and, instead, the courts have adopted the principle that, while evidence of acceptable medical practice is a useful guide for the courts, it is for the courts to adjudicate on what is the appropriate standard of care after giving weight to "the paramount consideration that a person is entitled to make his own decisions about his life".

In *F v R*, which was decided by the Full Court of the Supreme Court of South Australia two years before Sidaway in the House of Lords, a woman who had become pregnant after an unsuccessful tubal ligation brought an action in negligence alleging failure by the medical practitioner to warn her of the failure rate of the procedure. The failure rate was assessed at less than 1% for that particular form of sterilisation. The court refused to apply the *Bolam* principle. King CJ said:

> The ultimate question, however, is not whether the defendant's conduct accords with the practices of his profession or some part of it, but whether it conforms to the standard of reasonable care demanded by the law. That is a question for the court and the duty of deciding it cannot be delegated to any profession or group in the community.

King CJ considered that the amount of information or advice which a careful and responsible doctor would disclose depended upon a complex of factors: the nature of the matter to be disclosed; the nature of the treatment; the desire of the patient for information; the temperament and health of the patient; and the general surrounding circumstances. His Honour agreed with the following passage from the judgment of the Supreme Court of Canada in *Reibl v Hughes* :

> To allow expert medical evidence to determine what risks are material and, hence, should be disclosed and, correlatively, what risks are not material is to hand over to the medical profession the entire question of the scope of the duty of disclosure, including the question whether there has been a breach of that duty. Expert medical evidence is, of course, relevant to findings as to the risks that reside in or are a result of recommended surgery or other treatment. It will also have a bearing on their materiality but this is not a question that is to be concluded on the basis of the expert medical evidence alone. The issue under consideration is a different issue from that involved where the question is whether the doctor carried out his professional activities by applicable professional standards. What is under consideration here is the patient's right to know what risks are involved in undergoing or forgoing certain surgery or other treatment.

The approach adopted by King CJ is similar to that subsequently taken by Lord Scarman in *Sidaway* and has been followed in subsequent cases. In our view, it is correct.

Acceptance of this approach does not entail an artificial division or itemisation of specific, individual duties, carved out of the overall duty of care. The duty of a medical practitioner to exercise reasonable care and skill in the provision of professional advice and treatment is a single comprehensive duty. However, the factors according to which a court determines whether a medical practitioner is in breach of the requisite standard of care will vary according to whether it is a case involving diagnosis, treatment or the provision of information or advice; the different cases raise varying difficulties which require consideration of different factors. Examination of the nature of a doctor-patient relationship compels this conclusion. There is a fundamental difference between, on the one hand, diagnosis and treatment and, on the other hand, the provision of advice or information to a patient. In diagnosis and treatment, the patient's contribution is limited to the narration of symptoms and relevant history; the medical practitioner provides diagnosis and treatment according to his or her level of skill. However, except in cases of emergency or necessity, all medical treatment is preceded by the patient's choice to undergo it. In legal terms, the patient's consent to the treatment may be valid once he or she is informed in broad terms of the nature of the procedure which is intended. But the choice is, in reality, meaningless unless it is made on the basis of relevant information and advice. Because the choice to be made calls for a decision by the patient on information known to the medical practitioner but not to the patient, it would be illogical to hold that the amount of information to be provided by the medical practitioner can be determined from the perspective of the practitioner alone or, for that matter, of the medical profession. Whether a medical practitioner carries out a particular form of treatment in accordance with the appropriate standard of care is a question in the resolution of which responsible professional opinion will have an influential, often a decisive, role to play; whether the patient has been given all the relevant information to choose between undergoing and not undergoing the treatment is a question of a different order. Generally speaking, it is not a question the answer to which depends upon medical standards or practices. Except in those cases where there is a particular danger that the provision of all relevant information will harm an unusually nervous, disturbed or volatile patient, no special medical skill is involved in disclosing the information, including the risks attending the proposed treatment. Rather, the skill is in communicating the relevant information to the patient in terms which are reasonably adequate for that purpose having regard to the patient's apprehended capacity to understand that information

In this context, nothing is to be gained by reiterating the expressions used in American authorities, such as "the patient's right of self-determination" or even the oft-used and somewhat amorphous phrase "informed consent". The right of self-determination is an expression which is, perhaps, suitable to cases where the issue is whether a person has agreed to the general surgical procedure or treatment, but is of little assistance in the balancing process that is involved in the determination of whether there has been a breach of the duty of disclosure. Likewise, the phrase "informed consent" is apt to mislead as it suggests a test of the validity of a patient's consent. Moreover, consent is relevant to actions framed in trespass, not in negligence. Anglo-Australian law has rightly taken the view that an allegation that the risks inherent in a medical procedure have not been disclosed to the patient can only found an action in negligence and not in trespass; the consent necessary to negative the offence of battery is satisfied by the patient being advised in broad terms of the nature of the procedure to be performed.

* * * The law should recognise that a doctor has a duty to warn a patient of a material risk inherent in the proposed treatment; a risk is material if, in the circumstances of the particular case, a reasonable person in the patient's position, if warned of the risk, would be likely to attach significance to it or if the medical practitioner is or should reasonably be aware that the particular patient, if warned of the risk, would be likely to attach significance to it. This duty is subject to the therapeutic privilege.

The appellant in this case was treating and advising a woman who was almost totally blind in one eye. As with all surgical procedures, the operation recommended by the appellant to the respondent involved various risks, such as retinal detachment and haemorrhage infection, both of which are more common than sympathetic ophthalmia, but sympathetic ophthalmia was the only danger whereby both eyes might be rendered sightless. Experts for both parties described it as a devastating disability, the appellant acknowledging that, except for death under anaesthetic, it was the worst possible outcome for the respondent. According to the findings of the trial judge, the respondent "incessantly" questioned the appellant as to, amongst other things, possible complications. She was, to the appellant's knowledge, keenly interested in the outcome of the suggested procedure, including the danger of unintended or accidental interference with her "good", left eye. * * * She did not, however, ask a specific question as to whether the operation on her right eye could affect her left eye.

The evidence established that there was a body of opinion in the medical profession at the time which considered that an inquiry should only have elicited a reply dealing with sympathetic ophthalmia if specifically directed to the possibility of the left eye being affected by the operation on the right eye. While the opinion that the respondent should have been told of the dangers of sympathetic ophthalmia only if she had been sufficiently learned to ask the precise question seems curious, it is unnecessary for us to examine it further, save to say that it demonstrates vividly the dangers of applying the *Bolam* principle in the area of advice and information. The respondent may not have asked the right question, yet she made clear her great concern that no injury should befall her one good eye. * * *

For these reasons, we would reject the appellant's argument on the issue of breach of duty.

Although the appellant's notice of appeal challenges the confirmation by the Court of Appeal of the trial judge's finding that the respondent would not have undergone the surgery had she been advised of the risk of sympathetic ophthalmia, counsel for the appellant made no submissions in support of it. There is, therefore, no occasion to deal with this ground of appeal.

For the foregoing reasons, we would dismiss the appeal.

Notes

1. Notice how the Australian High Court draws on British and Canadian, as well as Australian, precedents in reaching its decision. In notes edited out, it also cited repeatedly *Canterbury v. Spence,* 464 F.2d 772 (D.C.Cir. 1972), a leading American authority. What vision of the common law does this evidence? Is this vision shared by courts in the United States? Is it appropriate, given the different histories and cultural contexts of the various common law countries?

2. Does the British House of Lords in *Sidaway* seem to focus on the doctor's duty while the Australian High Court in *Rogers* focuses on the patient's rights? What difference does this make? What different vision of the professional-patient relationship does it evidence?

3. See, discussing this case, Don Chalmers and Robert Schwartz, *Rogers v. Whitaker* and Informed Consent in Australia: A Fair Dinkum Duty of Disclosure, 1 *Med. L. Rev.* 139 (1993).

Law and Health Care in Japan: The Renaissance of Informed Consent

by Robert B. Leflar, published as *Nihon no iryō to hō: Infōmudo konsento runessansu* (2002), pp. 125–146 (Michiyuki Nagasawa, trans.)

The reception of the doctrine of informed consent into the previously hostile environment of Japanese medicine has followed an unusual course. As in all other countries, the general progression has been from an entrenched medical paternalism toward a degree of patient participation in shaping the course of care, at least in some clinical settings. But in Japan's case, that progression has been marked by uncommon features linked in atypical fashion with specific aspects of Japanese society. * * *

Patients' rights issues, once obscure, have risen to the level of an important daily topic in the Japanese media. This increased attention devoted to patients' rights is partly attributable to a significant change over the past few years in power relations within Japanese society in general. *Tōmeisei* (transparency) is one of the catchwords of political reform movements in Japan, linked to the opening up of political and social processes that previously were tightly controlled. * * * The movement for informed consent and patients' rights in the previously tightly controlled world of Japanese medicine connects with the spirit of transparency.

The reception of informed consent principles into Japanese medicine is also significant as a chapter in the fascinating study of the adaptation of Western concepts to the specific needs, structures, and rhythms of Japanese society. The word "reception" is used here in a particular and slightly technical way, to evoke the reception of European law into Japan. German and French law, to a certain extent, formed a convenient framework or skeleton for the sinews, as it were, of the Japanese codes, so that the law in action could be adapted to the needs of society, and employed in the service of the interests of those with the capability of invoking it. In a similar way, though in a smaller arena, the idea of informed consent, imported into Japan mainly from Germany and North America, is providing a framework within which contests for control of the directions of Japanese health care are, in part, being played out.

For illustrative purposes, this paper first sets out several stereotypes about paternalistic Japanese medicine, contrasted with supposedly autonomy-oriented North American medical practice styles. Like many stereotypes, these are perhaps exaggerated versions of typical events. Overstated though they may be, however, the stereotypes will allow the drawing of sharp contrasts to recent developments in Japan. Second, the paper presents six examples of ways in which traditional paternalistic attitudes and legal structures are changing in Japan * * *

There follow several stereotypical images of the god-like doctor in the white coat, *hakui no kami*:

The doctor sees his patients for three minutes each after their three-hour wait, dictating the patients' courses of treatment, without giving them any choices or indeed any explanations whatever. (Some "*kamikaze* doctors" have been known to see 100 patients per day. The stereotype applies more to larger hospitals with high reputations than to neighborhood clinics.)

1. The doctor prescribes half a dozen different drugs at every patient visit, again without explanation of their names, purposes, contraindications, cautions, or—if the drugs are experimental—of their investigational nature. (Typically the drugs would be purchased at the doctor's own clinic rather than at a pharmacy; the more drugs the doctor prescribes, the greater his income.)
2. In case of a diagnosis of cancer, the doctor covers up the diagnosis from the patient and enlists the patient's family in the deception, in order to keep the patient from losing all hope and lapsing into a decline or committing suicide.
3. The doctor views any request by the patient for information about the treatment course as an impudent intrusion into medical matters. (A patient's request to

look at his or her own medical records would be considered a rupture of the relationship of trust between doctor and patient, and the likely precursor to a lawsuit.)

These kinds of images have fueled the patients' rights movement in Japan.

One could contrast that set of images with the contrary stereotype of the North American physician who, in pursuit of the ethical principle of preserving patients' individual autonomy, carefully gives her patients a full picture of their condition, discusses all reasonable medical alternatives with them, and bases her caregiving on their idiosyncratic choices, rational or otherwise. That image may be medicine in the eyes of some bioethicists, but it is not medicine as it is actually practiced, nor is it really medicine in the eyes of the law. In fact * * * the vast majority of American patients in most cases do not question their doctors' judgment, whether couched in terms of suggestions or "doctor's orders." United States law is actually rather flexible in its attitude toward the principle of informed consent. * * * There are relatively few successful lawsuits in the United States based on alleged violations of informed consent alone; usually informed consent claims are merely "background music" for a malpractice suit.

Whatever the traditional value differences between Western and Japanese medical practice may be, we are now witnessing a gradually accelerating convergence between the two, with regard to some aspects of patients' rights. This accelerating convergence centers on recognition by the medical profession, the media, the courts, and an increasing number of the population of some concept of informed consent—or to use the Japanese phrase, "*infōmudo konsento*," an expression adopted for lack of any satisfactorily analogous phrase in the Japanese language. This convergence is demonstrated by the following six examples.

Example # 1: The Organ Transplantation Law

After almost thirty years of intense nationwide debate, the Japanese Diet (parliament) finally enacted the Organ Transplantation Law in 1997, granting limited legislative recognition to the concept of brain death. * * *

* * * [I]ncorporation of the informed consent principle was central to the political compromise that enabled the law's enactment. Under the act, informed written consent on the part of both the donor (in the form of a donor card) and the donor's family is necessary before organs can be taken. Moreover, brain death is considered the end of life only when the donor has given advance written consent to employment of the statutorily specified brain death criteria. In effect, the donor selects the legal criteria to be applied to the determination of his or her own death.

* * *

Example # 2: Strengthening of Patients' Rights in Clinical Drug Trials

In response to publicity surrounding alleged abuses in clinical trials of investigational drugs, the Ministry of Health and Welfare in 1998 put into effect more stringent Good Clinical Practice rules, and in 1999 further strengthened their implementation. (Another reason for these rules was to bring Japan into conformity with the patients' rights aspects of the international harmonization of pharmaceutical standards, which is a precondition for Japanese drug companies to obtain licenses to sell their drugs in the vast markets of North America and Europe.) The revised rules have a new fundamental provision: patients' welfare and safety have priority over scientific and social benefit. Among the features of these rules is a requirement that patients give their written consent to participation, after being informed of the known risks and benefits of the drug to be tested.

The new rules seem to have teeth: their enforcement is having a significant impact on hospital practices. * * *

Moreover, a trial court in March 2000 found in favor of the spouse of a patient who died after having been given an experimental drug. The patient had ovarian cancer, and a standard treatment for that type of cancer was available. But the physician told neither the patient nor her husband about the existence of the standard treatment, or that the drug being administered was in the investigational stage. (The physician engaged in other questionable activities as well, such as giving dosages beyond those called for in the protocol and entering fraudulent data into the patient's records.) The court found that the patient's informed consent rights had been violated, that the violation was a legal cause of her death since she might have been saved by the standard treatment, and awarded a sum of the equivalent of more than US $300,000. The physician's acts took place before the strengthened Good Clinical Practice rules went into effect. The decision therefore confirms that the Japanese Civil Code provides independent informed consent protections for research subjects.

Example # 3: Disclosure of Cancer Diagnoses

A steadily increasing majority of Japanese would prefer to be told if they are diagnosed with cancer—76%, according to an autumn 2000 public opinion poll. Responding to this preference, many physicians are changing their previous practice of concealing the truth from their cancer patients. A recent well-designed study comparing current practices at a rural medical school hospital in Western Japan with previous practices in both Japan and the United States concluded:

> A dramatic shift toward more frequent cancer disclosure similar to the change seen in the United States appears to be occurring in Japan. Over a brief four-year span [1991–1995] the percentage of physicians who report a usual policy of cancer disclosure has tripled.... [W]here there was once a fixed rule against cancer disclosure, there is now tolerance for exceptions.

This study noted that unlike Western countries in which disclosure of a cancer diagnosis is near-universal, Japanese physicians are practicing *selective* disclosure based on consideration of a range of patient-specific factors, including whether the patient wanted to be told. Among the physicians queried, two-thirds reported they themselves were likely to change their policy and tell more patients in the future.

On the other hand, almost one-third of the doctors in this study stated that they are less likely to disclose a cancer diagnosis to the patient when the family opposes disclosure, even if the patients themselves ask for the truth. * * * These results suggest a considerable residual role for traditional family-based decisionmaking, even when it conflicts with patients' own assertions of individual preference.

Example # 4: Judicial Movement Toward Recognition of Patients' Rights: The Jehovah's Witness Transfusion Case

A decision in February 2000 by the Supreme Court of Japan recognized one important aspect of a patient's right of autonomous health care decisionmaking: the right to accurate advance information about physicians' treatment intentions concerning life-and-death decisions during surgery, enabling the patient to reject the proposed treatment if she chooses.

The patient, a Jehovah's Witness of unquestioned decisional capacity, was diagnosed as having a large malignant liver tumor requiring surgery. In preoperative consultations with her surgeons, the patient requested that the surgery be carried out absolutely without the use of a blood transfusion, even if she were to die. She offered the written release from liability typical of surgical procedures on Jehovah's Witnesses. The surgeons proceeded with the operation without explicitly agreeing to her request, instead giving reassurances that they would avoid the use of blood "according to our doctors' conscience" (i.e., to the extent possible). During the operation, in fact, the patient lost an unusual amount of blood. Fearing that she might go into shock, the surgeons did transfuse her. The operation was a success, by medical standards: the patient lived for five years, instead of the expected twelve months. The patient learned of the transfusion only after a hospital employee later leaked the story to a journalist. The patient sued for psychological injury.

The Tokyo District Court granted judgment for the defendants, on the ground that the physicians' employment of a transfusion to save the patient's life, despite their understanding of her contrary wishes, was "socially proper" because "a human life is of sublime value" and "a doctor is under the obligation to do his best to save the life of his patients." That was the expected outcome under traditional principles of the Japanese Civil Code, which recognized informed consent in theory but granted physicians wide discretion in construing the scope of the emergency exception. However, the Tokyo High Court reversed, and likewise, the Supreme Court of Japan concluded that the doctors had committed an unlawful act. The Court observed that the doctors knew the patient had a firm determination to refuse a blood transfusion under any circumstances based on her religious belief. The Court stated that the doctors should have explained to her the hospital's policy that they would give a blood transfusion if it were to become necessary to save her life. They should have let her make the decision whether she would undergo the surgery at that hospital or not. Failure to do so infringed on her personal rights. * * *

* * *

Example # 5: Government Initiatives for Recognition of Patients' Rights

The Ministry of Health, Labor, and Welfare and its predecessor agency, the Ministry of Health and Welfare (MHW), have been moving at a measured pace for several years toward incorporating aspects of informed consent into Japanese medical practice. A Ministry-sponsored Study Commission on Informed Consent issued an extensively publicized report in 1995 that advocated the widespread diffusion of the informed consent principle through Japanese medicine. The rhetoric of the Commission's report did not focus on the need to protect patients' rights; rather, it said the main purpose of informed consent, "Japanese-style," is to improve doctor-patient relations, and thereby advance the quality of care (contrary to the litigious United States system). A main purpose of the report was to make informed consent more palatable to medical professionals, by emphasizing its therapeutic aspects.

Rhetoric is only part of any package of persuasion. In 1996 MHW added a dose of financial incentives by slightly modifying the point-fee system at the heart of Japan's price-controlled health care financing system. This modification initially allowed physicians to be reimbursed for providing specific written information, accompanied by an oral explanation, to patients at the time of hospitalization. The information to be provided includes the patient's disease, the treatment plan, and the planned duration of hospitalization. If the patient cannot understand the explanation, or if full disclosure of the diagnosis is considered inappropriate (for example because of a bleak prognosis), the explanation may be provided to the family instead of the patient. Additionally, at the time of discharge, the physician can receive an additional reimbursement for informing the patient and the family about the post-discharge treatment plan and issues that require attention after discharge. MHW recently revised the fee schedule to encompass the assumption that the specified information *would* be provided to patients as a standard requirement; if the information is not shown to be provided, a deduction is now assessed from the physician's standard reimbursement.

This new policy does not explicitly provide for the communication to patients of all the elements of information that are required by informed consent theory as propounded by Western medical ethics, or even as recognized by Japanese courts. Moreover, the documentation requirement for physician reimbursement purposes may be easily fulfilled—so easily that full reimbursement may be successfully claimed even though the information exchange is superficial at best. Still, the new policy does at least provide an impetus toward fuller doctor-patient communication.

Related to the trend toward disclosure of cancer diagnoses, but with a goal broader in scope, is the movement for patients' right of access to their own medical records. Traditionally, the only means of obtaining these records was to file a legal action (*shōko hozen*). However, many forward-looking physicians and clinics have recently adopted policies allowing patients routine access to information about their own medical status.

The health ministry has been supporting this idea. In standard fashion, MHW organized a Study Commission on the Use of Medical Charts and Information. The Commission's report, issued in 1998, rejected the option of nonbinding guidelines for physicians and hospitals to follow on records access issues. The Commission recommended instead that the Medical Services Law and related laws be amended to provide that, with the exception of cases in which there would clearly be an adverse effect on treatment, health care providers would have the duty to provide medical records to the patient on request. * * *

On medical records access as on treatment information, the health ministry supplemented its rhetoric with the power of the purse. Provision of medical charts to the patient now entitles the hospital to a modest reimbursement from the health insurance system.

Example # 6: The Response of the Medical Profession

The Japanese medical profession has long recognized that something called "informed consent" was inevitably going to make its way into medical practice. Acknowledging its legitimacy, but aiming to preserve the profession's autonomy and position, the medical establishment (chiefly represented by the Japan Medical Association, or JMA) has been striving to control the direction in which the concept of informed consent is defined in medical practice and in law—leaving ample room for physician discretion. To that end, the JMA has always opposed any attempt to codify the informed consent concept in the Japanese Civil Code.

As one would expect, then, when MHW issued its report favoring codification of patients' right of access to their medical charts, the JMA criticized the report severely. But in 1999, the doctors' organization reversed its position. The JMA declared that in principle, as a matter of medical ethics, patients should have access to their own medical records created from January 1, 2000. * * *

* * *

Notes

1. Two of the fundamental principles of bioethics are beneficence and autonomy. The Japanese practice of informed consent historically gave little scope for autonomy. Was it based on beneficence? Is autonomy being exercised if the family, rather than the individual, is the decision making unit, as was often the case traditionally in Japan and still is in some other cultures? What has motivated the change in Japanese informed consent practice?

2. The Leflar reading notes that traditionally Japanese doctors were known for dispensing large number of pills. It seems that throughout the world, patients routinely expect and doctors routinely provide, medication. Indeed, the United States seems to be an outlier in spending a smaller proportion of total health care expenditures on pharmaceuticals than most other countries. In many countries, moreover, a significant proportion of drugs that are prescribed have no proven efficacy. Why is the provision of drugs so common? What difference does it make whether drugs are dispensed (i.e. provided directly by the doctor) or prescribed (i.e. provided by a pharmacy at the doctor's order)? Dispensing is relatively uncommon in the United States, but has been common in Japan, although changes in the payment system to encourage prescribing and discourage dispensing have made prescribing more common.

3. Japan's law is based on an adapted model of the German civil code, yet the law of informed consent has developed very differently in Japan than in Germany. In particular, the therapeutic privilege, recognized in most other countries, has been interpreted much more generously in Japan. Does law shape culture as much as culture shapes law? Does law change culture or do changes in culture change law?

4. One of the pleasures of comparative law is to experience the exotic in other legal cultures. The *Sidaway* decision and the traditional Japanese practice of informed consent certainly seem exotic to the American observer. What are the benefits, and risks, of experiencing the exotic in other legal cultures? See Nathaniel Berman, Aftershocks: Exoticization, Normalization, and the Hermeneutic Compulsion, 1997 *Utah L. Rev.* 281.

2. The Problem of Causation

In the United States the informed consent doctrine has in fact rarely resulted in judgments for plaintiffs because many courts have followed the position of the D.C. Circuit in *Canterbury v. Spence*, 464 F.2d 772 (D.C. Cir. 1972) on causation. Under this authority, a plaintiff has not suffered from a failure to disclose unless the patient would have declined the treatment that resulted in harm, and thus avoided injury, had the withheld information been disclosed. The *Canterbury* court, however, worried about the doctor falling victim to patient hindsight, held that causation could be shown only if a prudent person in the patient's position would have declined treatment if suitably informed. 464 F.2d at 790–91. *Canterbury* applied, that is, an objective test for determining causation. A moment's reflection, however, suggests that it will rarely be possible to prove that a reasonable patient would have declined treatment unless the treatment itself was unreasonable (or experimental). Thus, a patient who undergoes a procedure without sufficient information will rarely be able to recover for lack of informed consent unless the proposed treatment was itself unreasonable.

As the following excerpt from Dieter Giesen's monumental treatise on medical negligence shows, this position is rejected by continental legal systems, which apply a subjective test, looking to what the particular patient would have done. Many courts go even further, moreover, requiring the defendant to show that the patient would have accepted treatment were the information provided. The case of *Chappel v. Hart,* which follows, represents a common law court applying a subjective standard.

International Medical Malpractice Law

Dieter Giesen, 341–355 (1980)

* * *

According to the Civil Law, causation between the physician's failure to discharge his duty of disclosure and the resulting damage is sufficient to establish both contractual and/or delictual liability. Where personal injury is caused by unconsented-to medical procedures, the physician causing the damage has the burden of proving that his acts were legal and covered by a valid consent based on a proper exercise of his duty of disclosure. Consent is a defence throughout the law of delict, and, like all other defences in that branch of the law, must always be raised and substantiated by the defendant. However, by implication, before a defendant can obtain a legally acceptable consent, he must first have rendered to his patient such information as to enable him to appreciate the nature and significance of the proposed procedure, available alternatives, anticipated results, and the risks that may ensure, and if called upon, show to the satisfaction of the court that he did so. As usual, courts will be the final arbiter. Where it is established that the disclosure malpractice did not cause the injury because the patient would in any case have submitted to it, then at least according to German and Swiss law, the plaintiff's case comes to a quick end. Since the basis of the physician's liability is his negligent failure properly to discharge his duty of care and disclosure, there is no need for the patient to go on to establish that the physician reckoned with or negligently disregarded the damage thereby caused.

At Common Law, the position is somewhat different. As far as the tort of battery is concerned, the patient does not have to prove either causation or damage in order to establish a cause of action (although causation is, however, relevant to the recovery of compensatory damages). But actions in trespass are now rather restricted and, after cases such as *Cobbs v. Grant*, *Canterbury v. Spence*, *Reibl v. Hughes*, or *Chatterton v. Gerson* and *Hills v. Potter* are, except for the more extreme cases of an invalid (vitiated) consent, probably beyond recall outside this narrowly confined area. In both the law of contract and the remainder of the law of torts, it normally is the patient who must prove both causation and damage, especially in negligence actions.

In the tort of negligence, where substandard disclosure practices and the question of the patient's consent are at issue, Common Law courts apply different tests of causation. They may apply a subjective test, as in England or New Zealand, and ask what *this* plaintiff patient would have decided had he been informed of the risk which was in fact concealed. Alternatively, as in Canada and the United States, they may apply an "objective" test of "what a prudent [or reasonable] person in the patient's position would have decided if suitably informed of all perils bearing significance." Finally, they may apply a "combined test," now slowly emerging in Canada in what could be called the post-*Reibl* case law, consisting of considerations both of what this particular patient, and a reasonable patient in that patient's position, would have decided.

In all these cases, the causal relationship between the physician's failure of disclosure and the injury to the patient's health "arises only if it is established that, had revelation been made, consent to treatment would not have been given." Much will, of course, depend on which "test" is being used; if treatment turns out to be unsuccessful, the patient certainly will sometimes be sorely tempted to say that, had he been told of the risks, he would not have chosen to undergo the treatment proposed, or, as in cases like *Thake v. Maurice* or a similar German decision, would have taken the necessary precautions or steps to avoid the damage now incurred.

a) Where an objective test of causation is applied, "it is not enough ... for the Court to be convinced that the plaintiff would have refused the treatment if he had been fully informed; the Court must *also* be satisfied that a reasonable patient, in the same situation, would have done so." This astonishing proposition apparently arises from the fear "that every patient who becomes a plaintiff will insist that he would have foregone the operation if he had been properly warned." The objective test can thus be interpreted "as a method of protecting doctors from unwarranted claims." Several important North American decisions have firmly rejected the subjective test on this basis.

But it is "unclear how justice is advanced by wilfully closing your eyes to evidence of what the patient actually would have done in those cases where the reasonable patient test fails." Courts which apply a subjective test have had to come to grips with the problem of embittered patients; patients must not be modeled to fit the law but the law must rather be organized in a way which sufficiently protects the patient's right of self-determination, including his or her idiosyncracies.

According to Professors Hart and Honoré, the adoption of an "objective" test can also be seen "as a *pis aller* resorted to because direct evidence of the patient's probable reaction is unlikely to be reliable." It may be questioned, however, why an assessment of what the "reasonable" patient might have done in the real patient's position should in any way be more reliable as a test, than what a patient with hindsight knowledge of subsequent events and developments, says he would have done. At least the *real* patient's credibility can be evaluated by sensitive courts whereas that of "this excellent but odious character" the prudent reasonable but imaginary model of near-perfection on the Clapham omnibus cannot or, at least, adds to the problems of evaluating a hypothetical case those of evaluating a hypothetical fellow and his hypothetical reactions.

As has been said with apposite irony by Lord Diplock in the *Sidaway* case, courts which measure a patient's right of self-determination by the yardstick of "reasonableness," pay no more than lip service to the concept. In the words of the German Federal Supreme Court, "no one has the right to set himself up as judge and decide in what circumstances another person would reasonably be prepared to sacrifice his bodily integrity in order to recover from illness." As has been stated by the New Zealand Court of Appeal in a well-known case, every patient has "[a] right to decline operative investigation or treatment however unreasonable or foolish this may appear in the eyes of his medical advisers."

This right of self-determination is not legally protected only to the extent and standards of what *others* think is reasonable. Every adult patient of sound mind is legally free to decide for *any* reason that appeals to him and has a right to be taken seriously; he also "has a right to be wrong." The causation hurdle for the plaintiff in informed consent or substandard disclosure cases remains formidable enough, but it would indeed be ironical if the courts, by applying a fallacious "objective" patient test, were to take away with one hand the greater fairness given to the patient with the other in abandoning the medical professional standard of disclosure in favour of a principally patient-based informational needs test. This should itself be sufficient to exclude "objective" tests from any further consideration as a test of causation.

b) Furthermore, it is submitted that the "objective" test is, quite apart from what the late Chief Justice of Canada propounded in *Reibl v. Hughes*, *not* in itself a test of causation at all.

First, there is the serious problem inherent in the "objective" test of "causation," that there can be more than just one "reasonable" decision in any given situation. Each of two mutually exclusive choices can be regarded as reasonable in the sense that a reasonable man might equally choose either. Thus, the *post Canterbury* and *Reibl* cases fail to allow for the possibility of a decision to decline and a decision to accept being equally reasonable.

Secondly, as has been convincingly argued by Professor Robertson,

> [t]he only way in which the objective test can operate as a test of causation is if there is added to it the presumption that the plaintiff would have acted in the same way as a reasonable person. By applying this presumption, a causal link is established between the defendant's negligence and the plaintiff's injury. Moreover, for the objective test to apply as the sole test of causation in informed consent cases, this presumption must be regarded as irrebuttable. Thus, evidence that the plaintiff, if properly informed, would still have agreed to the treatment, even though a reasonable person would not have done so, must be regarded as irrelevant.

Accordingly, it has been concluded that the "objective" test is in fact not operating as a test of causation; rather, it is performing primarily "an evidentiary function in that it provides a test of the credibility and reliability of the plaintiff's own testimony that he would have declined the treatment if he had been informed of the risks." Thus, it operates to dispose of altogether unreasonable claims. Professor Robertson concludes, therefore, that "to satisfy the objective test the plaintiff does not have to establish that a reasonable man *would have* declined the treatment. Instead, it is sufficient if the plaintiff establishes that his decision to forego the treatment would have been reasonable in the sense that it is a decision which a reasonable man might well have reached in similar circumstances."

However, it is submitted that the "reasonable" man still figures too prominently in this proposition for it to work as a test of causation. As was aptly emphasized by Cox J in the recent South Australian case of *Gover v. State of South Australia*: "At any rate the basic causation principle governing actions in negligence plainly supports, in my opinion, the subjective test."

It should be noted that English, New Zealand and also perhaps Australian courts and judges still adhere to a subjective test, as do some American jurisdictions and most courts in Civil Law countries. It is significant that, in evidential circumstances much more favourable to the plaintiff patient than at Common Law outside the field of trespass, the German Federal Supreme Court, although it has similarly warned of the dangers of hindsight, still adheres to a subjective test which accepts that a patient may be as unreasonable to himself as he wishes as long as he is an adult person and of sound mind. Even the most unreasonable conduct is protected by the law as the right of self-determination also includes, within the boundaries of *boni mores*, the right to be what others may look upon as "objectively" unreasonable.

In a more recent summary, the German Federal Supreme Court spoke once again in favour of a clearly subjective test of causality:

First, since every bodily invasion not validly consented to was *a priori* illegal, the onus was on the defendant physician to justify his intervention by proving a valid consent and, as a logical precondition to the consent's validity, a legally acceptable discharge of his duty of disclosure and information. The facts to prove this were peculiarly within the knowledge of the health care providers whose duty it was to document such consent appropriately and to satisfy a court of law that a legally acceptable consent had in fact been obtained from the patient as alleged by the defendant. To prove negligence (and by implication also a substandard disclosure practice) would actually also at Civil Law be for a plaintiff to establish, but as an indispensable precondition which determines whether the *consent* of an adult person of sound mind allegedly obtained really was valid, and not vitiated by unacceptable disclosure practices (or practices to keep silent), it had to be established by the defendant who wants to avail himself of the *defence* of consent. * * * As the German Federal Supreme Court re-emphasized, it was up to the defendant physician to prove that there had been acceptable consent, not on the patient to show there had been none.

Secondly, it was admissible, both according to German and Swiss law, to allow the defendant physician to show that, alternatively, this particular patient would have undergone the procedure proposed even if he had been properly informed.

But thirdly, the onus was again on the defendant physician to show this, and courts, as a general rule had to apply very strict standards for this proof to succeed "lest the right of the patient to receive proper disclosure is being undermined."

Fourthly,

> most importantly, it is not sufficient for a physician to show that disclosure of the inherent risks would not have deterred a reasonable patient from submitting to the operation. The patient's right of self-determination, which is meant to be protected by the physician's legal duty of disclosure, extends to decisions which according to medical judgment appear to be indefensible. However, this Court has repeatedly emphasized that patients, when claiming damages for breach of duty of disclosure, may also have their own obligation to substantiate their allegation [that they would not have consented had they been informed]. Such obligations exist at least where the reasons adduced for refusing treatment are not altogether comprehensible in the light of the specific facts of the case, where the patient is suffering from a serious condition which could be treated by an established therapy with favourable prospects of success and at low risk. In such cases it is for the patient to furnish some plausible reason why he would have refused to be treated had he known the risks in advance. It is true, again, that the patient's personal reasons for this refusal must be respected. No generalizing yardstick is allowed: not that of a reasonable patient, and even less so that of medical judgment. But the reasons to be adduced by the patient must be such as to enable the court to be satisfied that the patient, had he received proper disclosure as to the risks, would have been faced—from his *own* perspective—with a real conflict which now makes his hypothetical refusal at *that* time appear to be plausible and not simply dictated by hindsight. Only in this way can the patient's right to receive appropriate disclosure be shielded against arising from forensic considerations.

If the patient is required by the court to substantiate or make plausible why he would not have submitted to the treatment had he been properly informed, he need not do so by reference to a total refusal of treatment. The patient may, for instance, allege that, had he been properly informed, he would not have submitted to the treatment at all, or not at that particular time, or without first obtaining a second opinion, or that he would have chosen to undergo the procedure not by that particular physician or surgeon but a more specialized one, or would have opted for a better equipped or more highly specialized hospital, such as a university clinic with all its additional facilities. Once the court finds that *from the patient's point of view* a decision not to undergo treatment would have been plausible *at the time*, it is again incumbent on the defendant physician to prove the contrary. He may do so, for instance, by showing that the same incident or accident resulting in the damage now complained of would have occurred in any event at a later time, or even had the patient been treated by a more specialized physician, or in a better equipped or more specialized university institution. But "lest the patient's right of self-determination be undermined," Civil Law has only rarely accepted this proof.

Further, various courts have made it clear beyond doubt that the physician's onus of proof cannot be met by proving that the procedure proposed was medically indicated and that the patient would therefore have consented to it. It is also inadmissible to allege that the patient would nevertheless have consented on the basis of medical experience with the average patient, or because the greater number of patients would have done so. * * *

In view of the widely-accepted difficulties of proof facing the plaintiff patient in a Common Law medical malpractice action, it is hardly helpful to confine his recourse to the action of battery (where at least he is relieved of the onus of proving causation and damage in establishing a cause of action) to cases where consent is totally absent or where treatment is extended beyond the scope of consent given. If a trespass to the patient's body is committed by medical intervention not covered by valid consent, then to refer any failure to disclose material risks, however serious, to negligence rather than battery, is to assert that the quality of disclosure can never affect the validity of consent outside the narrow field of misrepresentation and actual fraud.

If it is true that the patient's interest in bodily integrity, self-determination and patient choice commands protection not only against intentional invasions by an unauthorized operation or treatment but also against a negligent invasion by his physician's dereliction or substandard discharge of his duty to adequately disclose, then the true test is whether the procedure proposed was validly consented to or not. If the protectional needs of the patient are the same, namely freedom from non-consensual bodily invasion, then it appears quite unreasonable to maintain artificial procedural differences which can only be explained in terms of legal history. Judicial efforts in medical malpractice law to make sense of the old distinctions between battery and negligence once again highlight the difficulties experienced by some Common Law countries in adapting their traditional range of torts to modern exigencies and in avoiding entrapment in conflicting strains of authority.

Instead of emphasizing the important role of the tort of battery in the vindication of constitutional rights, some courts have obstructed use of the action by the patient in need of such protection, on the basis that the moral opprobrium which "battery" connotes, renders it an undesirable remedy in this context. Such decisions, however, fail to recognize that outside the battery action evidential problems may defeat the broad justice of the patient's general case. The patient has come out the loser from the changes in the law effected by decisions such as *Cobbs v. Grant*, *Hopp v. Lepp*, *Reibl v. Hughes*, or *Chatterton v. Gerson*, *Hills v. Potter*, *Freeman v. Home Office* and the like, and impressive scholarly efforts at restructuring the issues of consent in medical malpractice cases show clearly how much additional light needs to be shed in the dark of the re-opened graves from which the old forms of action, buried long ago, continue to rule.

It should also be noted in this context that it is rather problematic to create new and extremely doubtful judicial distinctions in the medical malpractice field between consent to the basic nature and character of the treatment on the one hand (battery issue) and to "collateral risks" (negligence issue). This amounts to a distortion of an ordinary understanding of consent as covering the procedure in its entirety, and will often "defeat our normal, reasonable expectations." Untenable distinctions at war with a natural usage of language should give way to an example set by the uniform law of delict which comprizes both intentional and unintentional infringements of the right of bodily integrity and, at least in this context, has no difficulties in applying to all delictual and contractual actions the same definitions and principles.

* * *

In other words, this time from the Swiss Federal Court, the risks normally borne by the patient as to what happens to him if he submits to medical treatment, *shift* to the physician who negligently fails to discharge a duty of disclosure which would have enabled the patient to make his own final decision either to accept the risks or to forego the treatment proposed. It is submitted here that this legal reasoning can and should also be applied to Common Law medical malpractice actions for substandard disclosure practices.

a) Encouraging cases from England and elsewhere hold that the plaintiff discharges his burden of proof by showing that the defendant's conduct has materially contributed to the risk to which he is exposed. The leading case, *McGhee v. National Coal Board*, can further be interpreted to hold that in cases of negligent omission (and this includes all cases of negligent disclosure practices when in the court's view more should have been disclosed than actually was), causation can be established, and compensation awarded, for the loss of a chance. In this case, the House of Lords held that it was sufficient for a plaintiff to show that the defendant's breach of duty made the risk of injury more probable, even though it was uncertain whether it was the actual cause. As was emphasized by an English writer in this context, Michael A. Jones, this case is indeed remarkable since, "logically, it appears as though the plaintiff has succeeded without actually proving that the defendants caused him any injury—what the defendants did merely increased the risk of injury." But the reasoning would appear to be sound enough, as will be seen from the following statement from Lord Wilberforce in the *McGhee* case:

> From the evidential point of view, one may ask, why should a man who is able to show that his employer should have taken certain precautions, because without them there is a risk, or an added risk of injury or disease, and who in fact sustains exactly that injury or disease, have to assume the burden of proving more: namely, that it was the addition to the risk, caused by the breach of duty, which caused or materially contributed to the injury? In many cases, of which the present is typical, this is impossible to prove, just because honest medical opinion cannot segregate the causes of an illness between compound causes. And if one asks which of the parties, the workman or the employers, should suffer from this inherent evidential difficulty, the answer as a matter of policy or justice should be that it is the creator of that risk who, *ex hypothesi*, must be taken to have foreseen the possibility of damage, who should bear its consequences.

b) On this basis it appears to be clear that negligent failure to disclose a material risk of proposed treatment necessarily increases the likelihood of the patient's deciding to undergo the treatment and thus of losing a chance to decline it, and it is an impressive argument that the fundamental nature of the patient's right to make his own decision in the full or appropriate knowledge of all relevant facts and risks justifies applying the *McGhee* principle with regard to medical liability for loss of a chance to decline treatment.

This principle, now elaborated in two more recent English cases of medical negligence, *MacLennan* and *Hotson*, and praised by a distinguished Canadian authority on the law of torts as having much to commend it, would enable the plaintiff patient to succeed in cases where the nondisclosure substantially reduced the likelihood of his declining the treatment and thus avoiding the ensuing injury.

* * *

In other words, where a physician falls below the legally acceptable standard of disclosure, and injury occurs which that duty to disclosure was designed to prevent, he will have the burden of proving that he was not in fact negligent. The plaintiff's lost chance of making his own informed and final decision would be regarded as an injury *per se* giving rise to liability under *McGhee* or, alternatively, the violation of the patient's right to make an informed decision could be regarded as an injury in itself which would permit a court to view the loss of the chance to decline the proposed treatment simply as an item of damage flowing from that injury, and thus to award damages in accordance with well-settled general principles in personal injury actions. As was stated by Mr. Justice Bayda (now CJ) of the Saskatchewan Court of Appeal, when embracing the *McGhee* decision of the House of Lords, "if causation is overwhelmingly difficult to prove or impossible to prove then it is a matter of public policy or justice that it is the creator of the risk who should be put to the trouble of hurdling the difficulty or bearing the consequences," and not the victim.

Notes

1. Dieter Giesen had appointments both at the Free University of Berlin and at Oxford and had a thorough understanding of both the civil and common law. Is his observation correct that the problems common law countries experience in dealing with causation in informed consent cases stem from the common law writs, in particular from the relationship between trespass and trespass on the case; between battery and negligence? If we think of the right to consent to medical treatment as a basic human right, then why would we ever apply an objective, reasonable-patient, rather than a subjective, this-patient, test in determining whether proper consent had been given? Do we rely on negligence law because accusing a doctor of battery seems too extreme? Once we start thinking in terms of negligence, can we escape the application of "reasonableness" in evaluating behavior? Does the civil law escape this quandary?

2. Note the role of allocation of the burden of proof in the German law of informed consent. It is far easier to win an informed consent case in Germany than in the United States, in large part because the burden rests largely on the defendant medical professional to establish proper consent. The fact, of course, that the patient can win if it is established that the withheld information could have caused a "real conflict" in the patient as to which course of action to pursue, also makes it much easier for the patient to win than in many juridictions in the United States, where it must be proved that a reasonable patient would have declined the proffered treatment.

Chappel v. Hart

Contract

195 CLR 232, [1998] HCA 55,156 A.L.R. 517 [2 September 1998]
(High Court of Australia)

Judges: Gaudron, McHugh, Gummow, Kirby & Hayne, JJ

[The opinion of Gaudron J.is omitted.]

McHugh J.[dissenting].

* * *

The plaintiff's claim must fail. This follows from her failure to prove that there was open to her an alternative course of action which would have reduced the inherent chance of a perforation and consequent onset of mediastinitis and damage to the recurrent laryngeal nerve. The highest that her case can be put is that the defendant's failure to warn her resulted in her having the procedure at an earlier date and no doubt at a different place with a different surgeon than would have been the case if the defendant had carried out his duty and warned her. On the evidence, the carrying out of the procedure by the defendant on the day and at the place did not increase the risk of injury involved in the procedure. That being so, the defendant's failure to warn did not materially contribute to the plaintiff's injury. Her claim that a causal connection existed between that failure and her injury must be rejected.

On the view that I take of the case, it is of no relevance that, if she had been warned, another surgeon would have performed the procedure and that the chance of her suffering damage to the laryngeal nerve in that procedure was very remote. Perforation of the oesophagus with consequential mediastinitis and inflammation resulting in damage to the laryngeal nerve is such a rare event that it is close to a certainty that the plaintiff would have avoided mediastinitis and consequential damage to the laryngeal nerve if another surgeon had performed the procedure.

* * *

However, it is also close to a certainty that neither mediastinitis nor damage to the laryngeal nerve would have occurred if the defendant had performed the operation on some other day or even at some different hour on that day. * * *

To hold the defendant liable on the basis that if the plaintiff had been given a warning of the risk of mediastinitis occurring she would have avoided that condition is simply to apply the "but for" test, * * *. If, as the result of the defendant warning the plaintiff about the risk of perforation, the plaintiff had sought out another surgeon who had operated and accidentally perforated the plaintiff's oesophagus with consequent mediastinitis, only the most faithful adherents to the "but for" test would argue that the defendant's warning had caused the perforation and mediastinitis. To so argue would seem an affront to common sense. Similarly, with great respect to the learned judges in the courts below, it seems contrary to common sense to conclude that the defendant's failure to warn caused or materially contributed to him perforating the plaintiff's oesophagus on this occasion. From a common sense point of view, the cause of the perforation and the consequent mediastinitis was the examination of the oesophagus with a rigid endscope, an examination which carried with it an inherent risk of perforation.

The plaintiff also sought to rely on an alternative case that she lost the chance of having the procedure performed without a perforation occurring. However, this is not a case concerned with "loss of a chance". * * * Her relationship with the defendant gave her a legal right to have her condition examined, diagnosed and treated with reasonable care and skill by the defendant and to be informed and advised by him of any material risk inherent in the proposed procedure. But nothing in that relationship required the defendant to provide opportunities of the kind to which I have just referred. The damage that the plaintiff suffered was physical injury, not loss of a chance or opportunity. That being so, her claim stands or falls according to whether the physical injury that she suffered was causally connected for legal purposes with the defendant's failure to warn.

The appeal must be allowed.

Gummow J.

* * *

In the present case, the obtaining of adequate advice as to the risks involved was a central concern of Mrs Hart in seeking and agreeing to undergo the surgical procedure in question. It would, in the circumstances of the case, be unjust to absolve the medical practitioner from legal responsibility for her injuries by allowing decisive weight to hypothetical and problematic considerations of what could have happened to Mrs Hart at the hands of some other practitioner at some unspecified later date and in conditions of great variability.

* * *

The appeal should be dismissed with costs.

Kirby J.

This is yet another appeal concerned with the difficult topic of causation.

Establishing a causal connection between an alleged wrongdoer's conduct or default and the harm complained of is a pre-condition to the legal liability to pay damages. But, as Professor Dieter Giesen has observed, establishing a causal connection between medical negligence and the damage alleged is often the most difficult task for a plaintiff in medical malpractice litigation (as, indeed, in other negligence actions). Judges in common law countries can take only the smallest comfort from the fact that determining what caused an injury, for the purposes of legal liability, is also regarded as a most difficult task by the courts of civil law countries. Like courts of the common law, those courts have searched for principles to provide a "filter to eliminate those consequences of the defendant's conduct for which he [or she] should not be held liable". The search sets one on a path of reasoning which is inescapably "complex, difficult and controversial". * * *

There are no easy solutions to these problems. This is apparent from the many cases concerned with causation in the context of medical negligence coming before final and other courts of appeal in England, Canada, the United States of America, and Australia. It is further illustrated by the division of opinions in this case, Gaudron J and Gummow J favouring the dismissal of the appeal, McHugh J and Hayne J being in favour of allowing it. * * *

* * * Mrs Beryl Hart [the respondent] underwent an operation performed by Dr Clive Chappel [the appellant]. He was, and is, a medical practitioner and an ear, nose and throat specialist. The purpose of the operation, from Mrs Hart's point of view, was to relieve a long period of difficulty she had experienced in swallowing, eating and digestion, as well as with soreness of the throat. Radiological examination revealed pharyngeal diverticular and associated narrowing of the adjacent oesophagus. Dr Chappel suspected the presence of a pharyngeal pouch in which food could become caught. He proposed a procedure known as a Dohlman's operation.

Unfortunately, the operative procedure perforated Mrs Hart's oesophagus. This set in train the escape of an infection (mediastinitis) which, in turn, compromised one of her laryngeal nerves. This, in its turn, severely affected her voice. It resulted in her premature retirement from a position as principal education officer. Mrs Hart sued Dr Chappel for negligence and breach of contract. At the trial in the Supreme Court of New South Wales, Donovan AJ upheld her claim. He awarded her $172,500.61 damages. Dr Chappel and Mrs Hart both appealed to the Court of Appeal. He contended that no damages should have been awarded. She argued that the damages were inadequate. The Court of Appeal dismissed both appeals. Dr Chappel now appeals to this court. * * *

* * *

Mrs Hart's claim against Dr Chappel was limited to a complaint that he had failed to warn her adequately, or at all, of the dangers involved in the operation: specifically, that there was a danger that her voice could be compromised by the complications which, in fact, occurred. A claim that Dr Chappel had conducted the operation negligently, although initially pleaded, was not supported by evidence and was abandoned at the trial.

* * *

The aetiology of the damage to Mrs Hart's laryngeal nerve was not in doubt. It required the coincidence of three events: (1) the operative tear to the oesophagus; (2) an escape of bacteria from the oesophagus; and (3) consequential impingement of the resulting infection upon the nearby right vocal cord causing paralysis and damage. Each of these preconditions was accepted to be very rare. A tear could occur * * * once in every 20, 30 or 40 operations. Usually, it resulted in nothing more than the "escape of a few bubbles of air". The complication of mediastinitis that occurred in this case was "very rare indeed".* * * However, it was a recognised possibility. Once a patient asked a question about that possibility, he or she was entitled to have an accurate and candid answer so that the patient could make an informed decision about the surgery. For Mrs Hart, the consequences were important and they were large.

The condition which originally took Mrs Hart to Dr Chappel was "relentlessly progressive". Surgery was the "only relief" for it. Without surgery there would not only be soreness and difficulty in swallowing but the danger that food might become caught in the throat needing emergency attention. It was therefore accepted that, even if Mrs Hart had been warned of the danger of damage to her voice, she would eventually have undergone an operation on her throat. In any such operation the slight risk would exist of the kind that followed Dr Chappel's procedure. Mrs Hart did not dispute this. Dr Chappel conceded that, if the surgery had in fact been postponed and carried out at a different time, "[i]n all likelihood [Mrs Hart] would not have suffered the random chance of injury" to her vocal cord. This represented nothing more than acceptance that such injury was an extremely rare occurrence. * * *

Mrs Hart swore that if she had been told by Dr Chappel of the risks to her voice she would not have gone ahead with the operation by him. She would have sought further advice. She would have wanted the operation performed by the most experienced person available. * * * The primary judge accepted that Mrs Hart was a witness of truth. Her claim must therefore be assessed on the footing that, with the warning that the law required Dr Chappel to give her, she would not have gone ahead with the operation when she did. She would thus not in fact have suffered the damage which ensued.

Dr Chappel contended that, in the foregoing facts, Mrs Hart was not entitled to recovery. The random chance of complications could just as easily have struck during an operation at a later time and place and conducted by a different surgeon. In the absence of proof of negligence in the performance of the operation, his accepted failure to warn Mrs Hart had not caused her damage. Mrs Hart, armed with the decisions below, contended that she had established sufficient facts to demonstrate a causal connection and to retain her damages.

To answer the problem presented by the appeal, it is useful to collect a number of propositions, established by authority, relevant to a case such as the present:

A practical question: The starting point is to remember the purpose for which causation is being explored. It is a legal purpose for the assignment of liability to one person to pay damages to another. It is not to engage in philosophical or scientific debate, still less casuistry.

* * *

The law allocates responsibility by a process which at once determines the entitlement of the particular plaintiff and sets the standards of conduct that may be expected of other persons in positions analogous to the defendant. The law's concern is entirely practical. * * * Where a breach of duty and loss are proved, it is natural enough for a court to feel reluctant to send the person harmed (in this case a patient) away empty handed. However, such reluctance must be overcome where legal principle requires it. It must be so not only out of fairness to the defendant but also because, otherwise, a false standard of liability will be fixed which may have undesirable professional and social consequences.

A common sense approach: Causation is essentially a question of fact. It is to be resolved as a matter of common sense. This means that there is usually a large element of intuition in deciding such questions which may be insusceptible to detailed and analytical justification. * * * Yet, a losing party has a right to know why it has lost and should not have its objections brushed aside with a reference to "common sense", at best an uncertain guide involving "subjective, unexpressed and undefined extra-legal values" varying from one decision-maker to another. Nevertheless, despite its obvious defects, the common sense test has been embraced by this court as a reminder that a "robust and pragmatic approach" to such questions is the one most congenial to the common law.

The "but for" consideration: If, but for the negligent act or omission, the actual damage suffered by a plaintiff would not have occurred, it will often be possible, as a practical matter, to conclude the issue of causation in the plaintiff's favour. Similarly, where the damage would probably have happened anyway, it will often be possible to conclude that the act or omission was not the cause for legal purposes. In this sense, the "but for" test, so qualified, remains a relevant criterion for determining whether the breach of duty demonstrated is a cause of the plaintiff's damage. However, it is not the exclusive test. Nor is it sufficient on its own to demonstrate the causal link for legal purposes. It is a mistake to read this court's cautionary words about the "but for" test as an expulsion of that notion from consideration where the question of causation is in contest. * * * The court has simply added the warning that it is necessary to temper the results thereby produced with "value judgments" and "policy considerations". This qualification has been expressed lest a party, shown to have been in breach of duty, is forever thereafter to be liable for every misfortune that follows in time whatever the breach demonstrated and however irrelevant it may appear to the damage which ensued. * * *

The plaintiff's legal onus: It is elementary to say that it is a pre-condition to recovery of damages for an established breach of a legal duty that the onus is upon the plaintiff to prove that the breach alleged was the cause of the damage shown. It is important to keep separate the questions of liability and the calculation of damages. Where, as in this case, a plaintiff relies on a claim in contract, proof of breach of that contract will entitle the plaintiff to nominal damages at least. For recovery of compensation beyond nominal damages in contract, the plaintiff must prove that the breach was the cause of the damage. This is as true of a claim based on the tort of negligence as of one framed in contract. In this sense, the legal burden of proving causation is, and remains throughout the proceedings, upon the plaintiff. It is not an insubstantial burden. In some medical contexts it has even been described as Herculean. * * * The reasons include the imprecision of, and uncertainty about, some medical conditions; the progressive nature of others; the complexity of modern medical practice and technology; and the fact that some mistakes, serious enough in themselves, have no untoward results which can properly be attributed to them. In the present case, Dr Chappel argued that he fell into the last stated class of exemption. The recognised difficulties of causation for plaintiffs in medical negligence cases have occasionally given rise to legal devices designed to lighten their burdens. * * *

Displacing apparent causation: In certain circumstances, the appearance that there is a causal connection between the breach and the damage, arising from the application of the "but for" test and the proximity of the happening of the damage, has been displaced by a demonstration that:

(a) the happening of the damage was purely coincidental and had no more than a time connection with the breach;

(b) the damage was inevitable and would probably have occurred even without the breach, for example, by the natural progression of an undetected, undiagnosed or unrevealed condition, or because the condition presented a life threatening emergency which demanded instant responses without time for the usual warnings and consents;

(c) the event was logically irrelevant to the actual damage which occurred;

(d) the event was the immediate result of unreasonable action on the part of the plaintiff; or

(e) the event was ineffective as a cause of the damage, given that the event which occurred would probably have occurred in the same way even had the breach not happened.

Reinforcing the duty to warn: In judging the performance of a health care or other professional, the law does not require perfection. It recognises the variability of professional skills. * * * However, the requirement to warn patients about the risks of medical procedures is an important one conducive to respect for the integrity of the patient and better health care. In Australia, it is a rigorous legal obligation. Its rigour was not challenged in this appeal. It must be accepted that, by establishing the requirement to warn patients of a risk to which they would be likely to attach significance, or of which they should reasonably be aware, the law intends that its obligations be carefully observed. Breaches must be treated seriously. Because in some cases the failure to warn would have no, or no relevant, consequences, proof of a breach will not of itself be sufficient to establish an entitlement to damages for every harm that thereafter occurs to the patient. To reason in such a way would involve the logical fallacy of *post hoc ergo propter hoc*. The plaintiff's legal obligation to show the causal connection remains throughout the proceedings.

Accepting subjective intentions: In considering the suggested consequences of a failure on the part of a medical practitioner to advise a patient about the risks of a particular procedure, courts in Australia have adopted a "subjective" approach which has regard to what the particular patient's response would have been had proper information been given. A contrary (objective) approach, having regard to the response of a reasonable person in the patient's situation, was not urged in this case, although it has found favour in Canada and the United States of America. The subjective criterion involves the danger of the "malleability of the recollection" even of an upright witness. Once a disaster has occurred, it would be rare, at least where litigation has commenced, that a patient would not be persuaded, in his or her own mind, that a failure to warn had significant consequences for undertaking the medical procedure at all (where it was elective) or for postponing it and getting a more experienced surgeon (as in this case). Yet, these dangers should not be overstated. Tribunals of fact can be trusted to reject absurd, self-interested assertions. Where such a conclusion is reached the case will rarely come before an appellate court. The present appeal must be approached on the footing accepted by the primary judge. This was that, if she had been warned, Mrs Hart would not have had the operation, not have suffered the physical injuries which then ensued and would have sought a more experienced surgeon when the time for operation eventually came.

Shifting the evidentiary onus: One means of alleviating the burden cast by law on a plaintiff to establish a causal relationship between the breach and the damage concerns the evidentiary onus. * * * Once a plaintiff demonstrates that a breach of duty has occurred which is closely followed by damage, a prima facie causal connection will have been established. It is then for the defendant to show, by evidence and argument, that the patient should not recover damages.

* * *

Valuing a lost chance: A further way in which, in some circumstances, the difficulties of causation for a plaintiff are alleviated is by treating the plaintiff's loss as a "loss of a chance". In cases in which this approach is permissible, it may allow evaluation of the plaintiff's loss in terms of comparing the chances of suffering harm (given the breach which has occurred) against those that would have existed (if the breach is hypothesised away). * * * It is clearly laid down by the authority of this court that, in some circumstances, a plaintiff may recover the value of a loss of a chance caused by a wrongdoer's act or omission. The approach also has some judicial support in the context of medical negligence in England, Canada and the United States. A number of commentators favour this approach because of the failure of orthodox reasoning to do justice to some patients' losses and because it invites a more empirical calculation of loss, with the use of statistics which might offer outcomes that are more accurate and fair to all concerned. On the other hand, the weight of judicial opinion in England and Canada and some academic writing appears to be critical of the application of the loss of a chance theory to cases of medical negligence. In part this is because, where medical negligence is alleged, "destiny ... [has] taken its course", arguably making an analysis by reference to chance inappropriate or unnecessary in the view of the critics of this approach. Alternatively, the loss of a chance calculation has been criticised on the ground that it would discard common sense, undermine the plaintiff's onus of proving the case and submit the law to the "paralysis" of statistical abstractions.

Discounting damages: If it is established that damage was caused by the breach alleged, it remains to calculate the amount of compensation recoverable. It is then proper to reduce any damages which a defendant should pay for the harm it has caused to a proper proportion actually attributable to its breach. If, independently of the breach on the part of a defendant, the evidence shows that the plaintiff would have suffered loss, the damages may be reduced by reference to the estimate of the chances that this would have occurred. * * * Dr Chappel argued that, even if he had given the requisite warning to Mrs Hart, and she had postponed the procedure and later undergone an operation by a more experienced surgeon, there was still the same random chance that she would have suffered the complications that occurred; neither more nor less. Mrs Hart argued that the true comparison was between the loss that had in fact occurred to her and the concededly small risk that such loss would have happened at the postulated postponed operation. She resisted any reduction in her damages, submitting that a chance of injury in a postponed operation was minuscule, i.e. "speculative" in the sense described by this court.

The application of the foregoing principles to the facts of this case, as now established, presents difficult puzzles upon which reasonable minds may differ; as indeed they have. The strongest arguments for Dr Chappel, as it seems to me, are those which lay emphasis upon a logical examination of the consequences which would have flowed had he not breached his duty to warn his patient. Dissecting the facts in that way affords a powerful argument which would banish from consideration the events which in fact occurred in the operation which he carried out. All that would have happened, had he given the requisite warning, would have been a change in the timing of the operation and of the identity of the surgeon. For Dr Chappel, these were irrelevant changes as the evidence showed that, whenever the operation was performed and whoever did it, the tripartite chances which had to combine to produce the misfortune which Mrs Hart suffered were extremely rare. There was thus an equivalence of unlikelihood. They were risks inherent in the procedure, not wholly avoidable even by the most skilful and experienced of surgeons. In the view which Dr Chappel urged of the case, Mrs Hart was left with nothing more than the time sequence. To burden a surgeon, in whose actual performance no fault could be found, with civil liability for randomised chance events that followed the surgery would not be reasonable. It would penalise him for chance alone. It would do nothing to establish a superior standard in the performance of the work of surgeons generally.

For a time I was attracted to Dr Chappel's arguments. Ultimately, I have concluded against them. The "common sense" which guides courts in this area of discourse supports Mrs Hart's recovery. So does the setting of standards which uphold the importance of the legal duty that was breached here. This is the duty which all health care professionals in the position of Dr Chappel must observe: the duty of informing patients about risks, answering their questions candidly and respecting their rights, including (where they so choose) to postpone medical procedures and to go elsewhere for treatment.

* * *

* * * This was an unusual case where the patient was found to have made very clear her concerns. The practicalities are that, had those concerns been met as the law required, the overwhelming likelihood is that the patient would not, in fact, have been injured. So much was eventually conceded. In such circumstances, common sense reinforces the attribution of legal liability. It is true to say that the inherent risks of injury from rare and random causes arise in every surgical procedure. A patient, duly warned about such risks, must accept them and their consequences. Mrs Hart was ready to accept any general risks of the operation of which she was warned. However, she declined to bear the risks about which she questioned the surgeon and received no adequate response. When those risks so quickly eventuated, common sense suggests that something more than a mere coincidence or irrelevant cause has intervened. This impression is reinforced once it is accepted that Mrs Hart, if warned, would not have undergone the operation when she did.

Although no statistical or other evidence was called to demonstrate that recourse to a more experienced surgeon would necessarily have reduced the risk of the kind of injury that occurred (and while some risk was unavoidable), intuition and common sense suggest that the higher the skill of the surgeon, the less is the risk of any perforation of the oesophagus into the mediastinum. * * * And without perforation (already a rare occurrence) the second and third events necessary to produce paralysis of the vocal cords in a patient like Mrs Hart (occurrences even more rare) would not occur.

Once Mrs Hart showed the breach and the damage which had immediately eventuated, an evidentiary onus lay upon Dr Chappel to displace the inference of causation which thereupon arose. He failed to do so. Nor, in my view, causation being established, did he prove that Mrs Hart would have been exposed to the same, or substantially the same, possibilities of like injury if she had postponed the procedure and had it done by someone more experienced, as was her right. On the contrary, the evidence demonstrated that the chances of her receiving such injury in any other operation were minuscule. * * *

To the complaint that Professor Benjamin [an expert witness in the case] (or his equivalent) could not possibly undertake every Dohlman's operation (any more than the most skilful barrister can appear for every client) the answer comes back. This was not an ordinary patient. It was an inquisitive, persistent and anxious one who was found to have asked a particular question to which she received no proper answer. Had a proper answer been given, as the law required, it was found that she would not have undergone the operation at the hands of Dr Chappel when she did. It is virtually certain, then, that she would not have suffered mediastinitis at all. She therefore adequately proved causation. Dr Chappel did not displace the inferences to which her evidence gave rise. Nor was it shown that the damages to which she was entitled should be reduced on the footing that they would have occurred in any event.

As to the question of loss of a chance, Dr Chappel, by leave, added a ground of appeal to assert that Mrs Hart's damages should have been assessed in those terms. * * * At trial, the only claim for damages, which she had asserted, was in respect of the physical injury done to her vocal cords and its sequelae. She neither pleaded, nor sought to prove, a case expressed in terms of a loss of a chance. * * * The case is therefore not one in which an entirely new perspective should be adopted at such a late stage. * * * [T]his case must be approached on the footing that the loss suffered by Mrs Hart was that claimed: physical injury and its consequence—nothing more.

The appeal should be dismissed with costs.

Hayne J.

* * *

In my view, the only connection between the failure to warn and the harm the respondent has suffered is that but for the failure to warn she would not have been in harm's way. The appellant's conduct did not affect whether there would be pathogens present in the respondent's oesophagus when the procedure was carried out; his conduct did not affect whether the pathogens that were present would, in all the circumstances, produce the infection which they did; his conduct did not affect whether that infection would damage the laryngeal nerve as it did. Of course, he manipulated the instrument which perforated the oesophagus but he did so without negligence.

* * *

The law of negligence is intended to compensate those who are injured as a result of departures from standards of reasonable care. It is not intended to compensate those who have received reasonable care but who may not have had the best available care. To hold that the appellant's failure to warn the respondent of the risks of the operation caused her to lose the chance of the best available care would depart from that fundamental premise of the law of negligence.

* * *

The respondent did not establish that she had suffered damage as a result of the appellant's negligence. The claim having been framed in breach of contract and breach having been established, she is, of course, entitled to nominal damages but, in my view, to no more. I would allow the appeal.

Appeal dismissed with costs.

Notes

1. While *Chappel v. Hart* disavows the loss of a chance doctrine, is it not in fact applying it? Was not the patient's injury in fact the loss of an opportunity to have the surgery done by a more expert surgeon and thus to avoid the risk that eventuated? Does the court not hint at this in its consideration of damages?

2. A recent British case, *Chester v. Afshar* [2004] 4 All. E.R. 587, similarly involved a patient who, not having been warned of the small possibility of significant motor and sensory disturbance resulting from a spinal operation, had the operation and suffered the disability. The House of Lords, in a 3 to 2 decision, held for the patient, with the majority reasoning that had Miss Chester been warned she would have had surgery on a different day and would have faced only a very small chance of being injured. Subsequently in a later missed diagnosis case (*Gregg v. Scott* [2004] 1 A.C. 134) a majority of the House of Lords panel rejected the application of the loss of a chance doctrine to find causation. Can the two cases be reconciled? See Sarah Green, Coherence of Medical Negligence Cases: A Game of Doctors and Purses, 14 *Med. L. Rev.* 1 (2006).

2. An American case suggests a different approach to the problem presented by *Chappel v. Hart.* In *Johnson v. Kokemore,* 545 N.W.2d 409 (1996), a plaintiff who was severely injured by a surgery was permitted to recover damages under an informed consent claim against a surgeon who had failed to disclose that he had little experience with the particular surgery and that the mortality and morbidity rates for the particular surgery would be much worse if the surgery was performed by him than they would be if the surgery were performed by a more experienced surgeon. The court dealt with the problem of physician-specific risks, therefore, as a standard or care rather than as a causation issue.

D. Rights to Control Over Patient Information

1. Confidentiality and Secrecy

Health care involves of necessity the collecting, processing, and storage of information. Indeed, a very important aspect of health care provision—the diagnosis—is itself information and its accuracy is dependent on the ability of the medical professional to collect accurate information. Much of the information involved in health care delivery is highly sensitive, pertaining to mental stability, or sensitive diseases, or sexual activity. Casual revelation of such data can be very harmful to the patient. Protecting the confidentiality of medical information is, therefore, of great importance. This issue has, moreover, become even more pressing in the modern context in which medical data has become part of vast electronic data banks.

In most medical traditions physicians have long honored an ethical obligation to keep confidences. This is reflected in many legal systems in statutes or ethical codes requiring the keeping of secrets. The first reading that follows discusses the relationship between the right to confidentiality and the duty of secrecy, and the reflection of both under European law. A second reading contrasts the obligation to keep secrets under French and German law.

The Rights of Patients in Europe

Hank Leenen, Sjef Gevers, and Genevieve Pinet, 81–82, 96–97 (1995)

5.4 Discussion [Privacy and Protection of Data]

The rights to privacy and secrecy are interrelated. Both are intended to protect citizens (and thus patients) from disclosure of data that they have to provide in the context of medical assistance. The modern concept of privacy originates to a large extent from secrecy. Secrecy covers the relationship between the patient and the doctor, but the rules for this relationship no longer suffice for personal health data stored in data banks and administered by third parties. New rules had to be developed to protect such data, and to cover their storage and administration, access and provision to third parties. From the individual point of view, data in data banks are difficult to control. This is the more important because decisions concerning the individual are made on the basis of these data. Moreover, third parties have an interest in personal medical data, and data processed in automated systems are liable to access by more people than medical files under the supervision of a doctor. Data processing also raises problems of confidentiality.

The right of access must also be seen in connection with privacy. It is one of the instruments used by the individual to control personal data. In addition, many countries grant the right to correct inexact or inaccurate data. In several countries, a patient can require the erasure or destruction of data that are incomplete, incorrect or irrelevant or whose collection, recording, communication or storage is prohibited. This right is restricted by provisions in the Netherlands and Sweden, but patients in Sweden can appeal to an administrative court if their requests are refused.

The protection of personal data is regulated by administrative provisions and by the recognition of individual rights. An example of strict regulation of the recording of data is found in the Belgian draft bill that requires the written consent of the patient for the automatic processing of medical data, to third parties without the patient's written consent.

The regulation of privacy by administrative law does not exclude civil law from playing a role. The contractual relationship provides for legal action when a violation of privacy has caused harm.

Access to personal health data by third parties is regulated in a way rather similar to the exceptions to secrecy * * * and sometimes by the same rules. For example, the consent of the patient allows the release of data concerning him or her. The patient's consent to the communication of data to the health personnel involved in treatment is mostly presumed. Moreover, access to personal medical data can be determined by legislation. In many but not all countries, the health inspectorate has the authority to investigate personal data and files. In addition, some data communication is accepted in connection with payment for medical services by social security or health insurance schemes.

Several kinds of rules are adopted on the transmission of data for research purposes. In Belgium and Luxembourg, for instance, such data must be anonymous. Some countries (such as Denmark) do not require the patient's consent to the provision of data, but regulations require that the user be licensed and the data not be traceable to individuals. In the Netherlands, the communication of data without consent is allowed only under certain conditions.

The need for legislation on privacy has been widely recognized in Europe. This recognition relates mainly to the privacy of data, but the privacy concept also applies to the administration of medical procedures and the stay in the hospital or other establishment. In one Scandinavian country, the protection of hospitalized patients is regarded as covered by the penal code provisions. Some of these countries also have special regulations for patients in nursing homes and similar institutions.

* * *

6.3 Discussion [Secrecy]

While privacy is regulated by administrative provisions and the recognition of patients' rights, the legal form of secrecy is somewhat different. Secrecy is often formulated as a legal duty of the health professional, a duty that has a long history in tradition and law. Nowadays professional secrecy is primarily regarded and often described in legislation as the right of the patient to confidentiality. This right is also seen to arise from the contractual relationship between patient and doctor.

One of the reasons for making professional secrecy a legal duty of health professionals is to exempt them fully or partially from giving testimony in court proceedings. Moreover, professional secrecy serves the interests of both the individual patient and the public, because access to medical assistance in general would be hampered when patients could not trust the doctor to keep confidential the very personal data they have to reveal in the context of medical treatment.

As confidentiality is a patient's right in all countries, the passing of secret data to a third party must be authorized by the patient. In addition, the law can break the rule of confidentiality. In some countries, conflicting duties are accepted to allow the transmission of secret data to a third person. The doctor must then find a solution in each case, according to the facts and circumstances. When such a case comes before a court, the court then judges whether, given the facts of the case, the doctor could reasonably have decided to break confidentiality. In other countries, the legislator or a code of conduct guides the doctor in this conflict of duties. For instance, the Code of Medical Conduct in Monaco allows the disclosure of confidential information to the patient's relatives only in so far as necessary to carry out the treatment or to avoid contagion. The Law relating to the Practice of Medicine in Poland releases the doctor from the obligation to keep secrecy when the keeping of the secret would endanger the health or life of a patient or the people surrounding him or her.

Countries differ as to whether the patient's consent allows or forces the doctor to speak. In the latter case, the secret is regarded as fully within the hands of the patient; in the former, aspects of public interest in keeping the secret, regardless of the patient's request, are taken into account.

The consent of the patient is sometimes less voluntary than it may appear. For instance, when applying for social security benefits, an insurance policy or a job, the patient is almost forced to give information during the medical examination in order to achieve his or her goal. Privacy as to medical data in such situations can be breached more than reasonably necessary for the judgement at stake; this can motivate the legislator to intervene. Other types of medical screening (for example, of schoolchildren and of people seeking permission for long-term residence in a foreign country) can help to erode medical confidentiality. It must be added that some types of screening, for example, of foreigners, are not carried out in the interest of the examiner but rather in other interests.

Notes

1. In the United States, confidentiality of medical records has historically been addressed through a patchwork of state statutes, which often are limited to particular professions or institutions. Regulations issued under the Health Insurance Portability and Accountability Act of 1996 and found at 45 C.F.R. Parts 160 and 164 attempt to address the issue comprehensively, at least for health plans and providers. The regulations establish a principle of confidentiality of individually identifiable health information, but include many complicated exceptions. On recent developments in British law, see Paula Case, Confidence Matters: The Rise and Fall of Informational Autonomy in Medical Law, 11 *Med. L. Rev.* 208 (2003).

2. Under American law the right to privacy (as traditionally understood as a right to be left alone) is distinguished from the right to protection of confidentiality of medical data. See *Humphers v. First Interstate Bank of Oregon*, 298 Or. 706, 696 P.2 527 (1985). European use of the term "privacy" is closer to our concept of confidentiality.

Medical Confidentiality and Medical Privilege— A Comparison of French and German Law

Sabine Michalowski, European Journal of Health Law, vol. 5, pp. 89, 89–91, 95–96, 97–99, 100–01, 102–03, 104–06 (1998)

* * *

1. Scope of medical confidentiality

In French law, the physician is under a contractual duty to maintain medical confidentiality. In addition, the code of professional ethics also imposes on the physician an obligation to medical confidentiality. However, the discussion of the duty to maintain medical confidentiality mainly focuses on the relevant provisions of the criminal code (Code Pénal), as in French law, a breach of the duty to medical confidentiality is a criminal offence.

> "The disclosure of any secret information by a person who is the depository of such information because of his/her social position or profession or on the grounds of a temporary office or mission, will be punished with imprisonment of one year and a fine of 100,000 F."

* * *

Even though the members of the medical profession are no longer expressly listed as being under an obligation to maintain medical confidentiality, they belong to the category of persons who are depositories of confidential information on the grounds of their status or their profession. * * *

For Article 226-13 criminal code to apply, different requirements have to be fulfilled. First, the revelation must refer to information confided in a person in connection with his/her social position or profession or on the grounds of a temporary office or mission. The obligation to maintain medical confidentiality is not limited to what the patient has confided in the physician, but rather also includes everything the physician hears, sees or observes in the course of the exercise of his/her profession. This extension of the protection of medical confidentiality seemed necessary for various reasons. First, it seemed appropriate to protect confidential patient information in cases in which the patient had not expressly shared his/her secret with the physician, but the physician had still, on the grounds of his profession, obtained confidential information concerning his/her patient. The Cour de Cassation, for example, had to decide a case in which a physician who happened to be at the site of a road accident applied first aid to an accident victim and later submitted the medical certificate regarding the victim's injuries to the police. According to the court, the physician had violated his duty to maintain confidentiality. Even though the patient did not confide anything in the physician, the physician had obtained knowledge referring to the patient's health, thus the patient's intimate sphere, because of his profession. * * * The criminal offence of a revelation of confidential information does neither require any damage done to the patient, nor the intent to cause the patient harm.

With regard to the scope of protection awarded to medical confidentiality, German law is rather similar to French law. In German law, the physician is under a contractual duty to maintain medical confidentiality and the code of professional ethics imposes a similar duty on the physician. In addition the breach of medical confidentiality is a criminal offence. S.203 German criminal code states as follows:

> "(A) A person who, without authorisation, discloses a secret of another, namely a secret that belongs to the private sphere of life or a company or business secret, that was confided in him or the knowledge of which he obtained in his capacity as
>
> 1. physician, dentist, veterinary, pharmacist ...
>
> 2. professional psychologist in the possession of an academic degree that is recognised by the state ... will be punished with imprisonment of up to one year or with a fine."

For the criminal offence of breach of medical confidentiality to be fulfilled, in German law, similar to French law, the information must be a secret, and it must have come to the knowledge of the physician in the course of his/her profession. No distinction is made between the protection of express confidences made by the patient and observations the physician makes in the exercise of his/her profession.

Different from the situation in France, however, in Germany, the principle of medical confidentiality receives constitutional protection. Article 2(1) (freedom of self-determination), and 1(1) (respect for human dignity) Basic Law (*Grundgesetz*) have been interpreted by the German Federal Constitutional Court as protecting the individual's right to a private and intimate sphere free from state intrusion and as protecting the right of the individual to decide autonomously whether or not to reveal intimate facts.

* * *

3. Medical confidentiality—an absolute duty?

An important feature of the French approach to medical confidentiality is the frequently promoted concept of the "general and absolute" nature of medical confidentiality and the consequences of this concept for the application of medical confidentiality in French law. The formula of the "general and absolute" nature of the principle of medical confidentiality is mainly promoted by criminal courts. The Chambre Criminelle of the Cour de Cassation has for example stated in its decision of 22 December 1966 that the duty to maintain confidentiality, established and sanctioned by Article 378 old criminal code to guarantee the confidence necessary for the exercise of certain professions, is imposed on physicians as a duty in relation with their function, that it is general and absolute and that no one can relieve the physician from it. French courts have made it clear that the notion of "no one" includes the patient him/herself, * * *. The patient therefore does not have the right to relieve the physician from his/her duty to medical confidentiality.

Several arguments are listed in favour of this approach. Cambaldieu, for example, promotes the view that even though there can sometimes be good and even imperative reasons for revealing the secret, it is still true that every exception bears the risk that the duty will be annihilated. He continues that a case by case rather than an absolute approach would have the inconvenience of blurring the content of the duty to maintain confidentiality, and he concludes that it is preferable to declare the obligation to be general and absolute as this concept, though being rigid and inflexible, nevertheless has the merit not only to be based on tradition and precedents, but also to regulate the behaviour in a precise manner. It has also been argued that a relativist concept of medical confidentiality is dangerous for the physician, because it leaves the physician with a choice of whether or not to reveal the secret; if this choice does not find the approval of his/her judges, he/she risks a conviction and disciplinary sanctions. Accordingly, it was argued that the physician who finds him/herself confronted with a criminal provision must know where he/she stands and needs a rule that leaves no room for doubts.

Those who reject the theory of the absolute nature of medical confidentiality allege that this theory, instead of protecting the patient, rather backfires and ultimately turns the secret against the patient. This view is mainly based on the fact that the courts use this formula to deny the patient any possibility to relieve the physician from the obligation even where a disclosure lies in the patient's interests, * * *. Promoters of this attitude argue that the relative nature of the medical secret is confirmed by legislation imposing on the physician a duty to disclose certain sensitive health information, for example with regard to venereal diseases. If exemptions are possible, it is argued, the secret cannot be absolute.

The French approach of the "general and absolute" nature of medical confidentiality seems unique. Not even in countries, such as Germany and the United States, in which the principle of medical confidentiality is rooted in the Constitution can this attitude be encountered, as both countries, based on slightly different consideration, adhere to the view that medical confidentiality must be balanced against other interests and can therefore under certain circumstances be outweighed by overriding interests of the public or of third parties, a principle which applies to all constitutionally protected individual rights. In Germany, this view is so unanimously accepted that the possibility of an absolute and general nature of the principle of medical confidentiality is not even considered.

4. Medical confidentiality and the physician as a witness in court

* * *

As the obligation created by Article 109 code of criminal procedure expressly provides an exemption for those who are under an obligation to maintain professional confidentiality, it seems clear that Article 109 code of criminal procedure does not impose on the physician an obligation to give testimony in court with regard to confidential patient information. But it is still not clear whether this means that the physician is not allowed to give testimony, or whether it only means that the physician, while under no obligation to give testimony, can choose to do so and will then be exempt from his/her duty of medical confidentiality under Article 226-13 criminal code. Article 109 code of criminal procedure is mostly interpreted so as to prohibit any testimony that might violate the obligation to maintain medical confidentiality. As Article 109 code of criminal procedure exempts the physician from the obligation to give testimony, while Article 226-13 criminal code does not provide for an exemption in the case of testimony in court, the legislator has clearly demonstrated how to solve the conflict between the two competing duties. According to this interpretation, a physician who decides to give testimony in court will thereby commit the criminal offence of Article 226-13 criminal code, unless, exceptionally, a legal justification in his/her favour applies. Some suggest that this conclusion is also supported by caselaw, though it must be said that there are no cases directly on this point. Rather, the existing case-law refers to the question whether the physician has the right or even the obligation to give testimony if the patient has consented to the revelation of confidential information. In that situation, the courts took the stance that it was up to the physician to choose which obligation to fulfil in the particular case. Given the rather narrow scope of this case law, it is thus not at all clear whether the courts would give the physician a choice between giving testimony or maintaining medical confidentiality where the patient has not consented to the revelation.

In Germany, the situation is somewhat different. First, even though everybody is in principle under an obligation to appear, swear an oath and give testimony when called as a witness, a disregard of this obligation does not amount to a criminal offence. With regard to physicians, German law expressly provides for medical privilege, as s.53 German code of criminal procedure states that:

> "(1) Also entitled to refuse testimony are ...
>
> 3.... physicians, dentists, pharmacists and midwifes about what has been confided in them or what came to their knowledge in this capacity."

Thus, German law has resolved the conflict possibly arising between the duty to maintain medical confidentiality and the duty to give testimony in court by giving the physician the right to refuse to give testimony when called as a witness in criminal proceedings. As s.53 code of criminal procedure awards the right to refuse to testify, the unanimous opinion is that s.203 criminal code, the crime of breach of confidentiality, also applies to testimony in court. The fact that a physician discloses confidential information in the court room can, therefore, not in itself justify a breach of confidentiality. To see whether the physician, when exercising the choice between testifying and refusing to testify, will thereby commit a criminal offence, one has to refer to general principles of criminal law, which means that the breach of medical confidentiality will constitute a criminal offence, unless a legal justification applies.

At first sight, the German approach seems close enough to that adopted by the predominant opinion in France, given that in both legal systems, the physician is under conflicting duties. * * * However, there is also a fundamental difference. The legal debate, or at least the relevant case-law in France, mainly refer to cases in which the patient has consented to the revelation of his/her confidential details, and it is then discussed whether the physician under these circumstances has the choice between maintaining confidentiality or giving testimony. According to the predominant French view, the patient's consent has no legal relevance. As the duty to medical confidentiality is seen by many, including the criminal courts, as an absolute obligation from which the patient cannot dispense the physician, a conflict exists even where the patient has given consent to the revelation. In Germany, on the other hand, the patient's consent to disclosure automatically voids the physician's right to choose, as s.53(2) code of criminal procedure expressly removes the physician's right to refuse to testify in court. No conflict therefore exists, once the patient has given consent to the revelation, as the physician is then under the unequivocal obligation to testify. Rather, a conflict presupposes that the patient withheld his/her consent to disclosure. This seems consistent from the German perspective, as the physician in German law is only under a duty to maintain medical confidentiality as long as the patient has not authorised disclosure. It can thus be seen that the different concepts of medical confidentiality, i.e., absolute as opposed to relative nature of the principle, lead to a different perception of the conflict of interests and, accordingly, to different solutions.

4.2 Defence rights of the physician

A special problem arises if the physician is accused of professional irregularities and wants to testify about confidential patient information to exonerate him/herself. In such a case, we are no longer merely concerned with a conflict between the interest in medical confidentiality and the general public interest in establishing the truth in criminal proceedings. Rather, in addition to the latter, the physician's interest in the unobstructed exercise of his/her defence rights must also be taken into account when undertaking a balancing exercise.

Given the importance of the defence rights as fundamental human rights, there is wide agreement in France that the physician's defence rights outweigh the interest in medical confidentiality. In a case in which a physician was accused of medical malpractice leading to the death of a patient, and where the physician submitted photos to the court that he had taken in the course of the medical examination and which were useful for his defence, the court has for example held that:

> "one cannot deny defence rights to anybody, and this fundamental freedom cannot be limited by the principles relating to medical confidentiality."

* * *

It is surprising that the solutions offered to resolve the conflict of interests seem detached from the theories of the absolute or relative nature of medical confidentiality. In particular the courts seem to have left the theoretical foundation of the medical secret behind when allowing for the physician's defence rights to outweigh the obligation to maintain medical confidentiality, though an absolute duty.

In respect of the physician's defence rights when he/she is accused in criminal proceedings, the legal discussion in Germany is very similar to the French debate. The predominant opinion argues that the physician's disclosure of confidential patient information in such a situation will be justified under the necessity defence, as a balancing of medical confidentiality, on the one hand, and the physician's defence rights, on the other hand, will clearly lead to a prevalence of the latter. A minority opinion, however, for reasons more or less similar to those forwarded in France, suggests severe restrictions of the physician's defence rights.

* * *

4.4 Effects of the patient's consent

Situations can arise in which a physician is called as a witness and in which the patient consents to the revelation of his/her confidential medical information by the physician in court. The patient may be the accused and want to prove certain medical facts beneficial to his/her defence, or the patient is the victim and may want the physician to give testimony regarding his/her injuries, or the patient may be neither the accused nor a victim, but medical information concerning this patient can still be important for the outcome of the case and the patient might want it to be available to the court through the testimony of his/her physician. The question thus arises whether the patient can validly relieve the physician from his/her obligation to medical confidentiality so as to enable the physician to give testimony with regard to confidential patient information without being subjected to the punishment laid down in Article 226-13 criminal code.

In France, the opinions with regard to the effect of the patient's consent are split, and the views very much depend on whether medical confidentiality is seen as an absolute or as a relative obligation. In French criminal law, consent of the victim normally does not provide a legal justification for a criminal offence. The reason behind this is that criminal law is not intended to directly safeguard individual interests, but rather aims at maintaining the social and public order, even though this may indirectly promote individual interests. However, in respect of a criminal offence protecting interests that are at the free disposition of the victim, the victim's consent omits one of the constituent elements of the crime, so that the criminal offence cannot be committed where the victim has consented to it. Thus, if medical confidentiality were at the free disposition of the patient, the patient's consent could have the effect of omitting one constituent element of the offence of Article 226-13 criminal code. If, on the other hand, medical confidentiality were not at the free disposition of the patient, the patient's consent could not relieve the physician from the obligation to medical confidentiality, and a physician, revealing confidential patient information with the patient's consent would still be guilty of the criminal offence under Article 226-13 criminal code.

The attitude of the criminal courts is clear:

> "The duty to maintain confidentiality, established and sanctioned by Article 378 to guarantee the confidence necessary for the exercise of certain professions, is imposed on physicians as a duty in relation with their position, it is general and absolute and no one can relieve the physician from it."

The criminal courts do not make any distinction between cases in which the patient is accused in criminal proceedings and calls the physician as a defence witness, and all other cases including those in which the patient is the victim of a criminal offence.

* * *

And in yet another decision in which a physician was called as a defence witness and in which the accused patient had consented to the physician's testimony about confidential medical facts, the Cour de Cassation stated that:

> "The court cannot determine for the physician in which cases the revelation of confidential information is appropriate. Consent of the accused cannot be seen as a justification taking away the criminal nature of a revelation of confidential information. The refusal of the instance court to force a physician called as a defence witness by the accused to give testimony with regard to confidential information referring to the accused, when the physician invoked medical privilege, was a correct application of the law. The principle that medical confidentiality is general and absolute ... applies to everybody without any distinction between witnesses of the prosecution and witnesses of the defence."

Thus, in this decision, the Cour de Cassation again confirmed the principle of the general and absolute nature of the medical secret, and inferred from this principle that medical confidentiality cannot be at the disposition of the patient, so that the patient cannot validly relieve the physician from this obligation. More importantly, however, the first sentence of the quote could be read as giving the physician a choice to decide whether or not to give testimony in a situation in which the patient has consented to a revelation of his/her confidential medical information and even requested the revelation for his/her defence. Thus, the court seemed to indicate that a revelation would under these circumstances not be regarded as a violation of the principle of medical confidentiality, but that the decision whether or not to give testimony was rather exclusively in the hands of the physician.

Legal scholars approving of this case law and trying to explain the reasoning behind it argue that as the protection of medical confidentiality is not exclusively based on the interests of the patient, it follows that the patient cannot have the right to relieve the physician from an obligation that is imposed on him/her in the public interest. If the obligation to medical confidentiality exists in the public interest of protecting the confidence of the public in the secrecy of the medical profession, it does not seem appropriate that the patient can relieve the physician from his/her obligation to maintain confidentiality, as potential patients could be worried when seeing a physician reveal confidential patient information in court. But how then can it be explained that the physician is given the choice between maintaining confidentiality and disclosure? It must certainly be more worrying for patients if it is left to the physician to decide whether or not to disclose information.

Another argument supporting the view that the patient's consent cannot relieve the physician from his/her duty to maintain confidentiality is that valid consent must be informed and freely given. Therefore, one can only validly relieve someone from a duty of confidentiality with regard to a secret the content of which one knows perfectly well; but sometimes, for humanitarian reasons, the physician will not reveal the whole truth to the patient so that the patient who relieves the physician from his/her duty to confidentiality can then not fully appreciate the range of his consent. But this problem could be avoided if the physician, when relieved by his/her patient from the duty to maintain medical confidentiality, interpreted this authorisation as only referring to that what is known to the patient.

Yet another worry of the opponents of the patient's right to relieve the physician from his/her obligation to maintain medical confidentiality is that if the accused patient had such a right, it would follow that a patient's refusal to consent to a revelation could raise suspicions regarding his/her guilt. As a consequence, a patient might feel forced into waiving his/her right to medical confidentiality and allow a revelation just to avoid negative conclusions courts could draw from his/her reluctance to consent to disclosure. Others, admitting this risk, demand that the courts and the law ensure that the patient be free from any pressure to consent to a revelation of his/her medical secrets. They suggest that in situations where the patient is the accused, only the patient him/herself but not the prosecution should have the right to call the physician as a witness. To deny the accused patient the right to call the physician as a witness, it is argued, would be a violation of his/her defence rights. If, on the other hand, the prosecution or a third party could call the physician as a witness, this would subject the patient to an inadmissible dilemma: either to refuse consent to the revelation, which could give rise to suspicions on the part of the judge or the jury, or to relieve the physician from the secret to avoid this risk, thus exposing him/herself to a revelation of confidential information which was covered by a promise of secrecy. It is submitted that the problem could be solved by clarifying that the patient's right not to consent to a revelation of confidential medical information by his/her physician is guaranteed by the right to silence, and that no negative conclusions may be drawn from the exercise of said right.

A totally different argument brought forward is that even if as a result of the patient's consent, the criminal offence of breach of confidence disappeared and the confidant, if he decided to speak, could not be penalised, consent would nevertheless not free the physician from the moral duty to medical confidentiality. The supporters of the view that this moral dilemma justifies the physician's refusal to give testimony submit that only the physician, in accordance with his/her conscience, can judge whether or not to give testimony, and that, as a consequence, the patient's consent cannot force the confidant into a breach of his/her silence. When called upon to give testimony, the physician must assess the patient's interests according to his/her conscience; if his/her testimony conforms with these interests, the physician should give testimony under the twofold condition that free and voluntary consent of the patient is given and that in the given case medical confidentiality exclusively promotes a private interest; in the opposite case, the physician has to remain silent. However, the whole argument seems dubious. The possible moral dilemma evoked here seems to stem from a very paternalistic view of the physician's role, as it implies that the physician knows better than the patient what the patient's interests are.

* * *

The civil chamber of the Cour de Cassation as well as the Conseil d'Etat allow the revelation if the patient has given consent. To prove medical facts in these courts, the patient can either produce a medical certificate or call the physician as a witness who then does not have the right to hide behind medical confidentiality.

From a comparative perspective, it must be noted that the approach adopted by French criminal courts seems rather unique, and that the attitude of the French civil and administrative courts is more in line with the solutions adopted in other legal systems. In Germany, for example, it is generally accepted that the patient can relieve the physician from the obligation to medical confidentiality. It is therefore well-established that a revelation of confidential information with the patient's consent does not amount to the criminal offence of breach of confidentiality (s. 203 German criminal code). German law goes even further in stating in s.53(2) German code of criminal procedure that the physician's right to refuse to give testimony in criminal court with regard to confidential patient information disappears if the patient has consented to the disclosure. Thus, as soon as the patient has given consent to the disclosure of confidential medical facts in court, the physician has no choice but rather must testify. The arguments underpinning this principle are comparable to those provided by French civil and administrative courts and part of the French legal doctrine. It is felt that nobody, neither the patient, nor the physician or even the public can have an interest in the physician's silence about confidential facts which concern the private sphere of a patient who does not want these facts to remain secret. With regard to the concern that the patient's consent might not be fully informed, as it is possible that the physician kept certain facts from the patient, some suggest that valid consent should presuppose that the physician informs the patient about the extent of the information he/she will testify about. The Higher Regional Court of Hamburg argued, however, that it must be sufficient that the physician indicates the possibility that the patient might not be aware of the full extent of the physician's knowledge. If the patient then still consents to the disclosure, this consent is valid.

* * *

Notes

1. Should a right to protection of secrecy be treated separately from the right to protection of privacy or confidentiality? Does the notion of secrecy perhaps have more to do with the ethical duties of professionals; that of privacy with the human rights of patients? Does the French position, in particular, represent a more traditional, ethical duty, approach while the German approach is more rights oriented?

2. In the case of *Plon (Societe) v. France*, 58148/00 [2004] ECHR 200 (18 May 2004), the European Court of Human Rights held that an injunction entered by a French court blocking the publication of a book by the private physician of French President François

Mitterand after Mitterand's death (disclosing that the President had concealed from the public the fact that he was dying of cancer) violated Article 10 of the European Convention of Human Rights which protects freedom of expression. The Court held that the public interest in the information outweighed concerns of protecting medical confidentiality under the circumstances.

Several international bodies have addressed issues of the privacy of medical data and in particular of genetic information. These issues are addressed in the readings that follow: a Recommendation of the Council of Europe, a brief excerpt of a reading discussing that recommendation, an International Declaration by UNESCO on genetic data, and an Icelandic Supreme Court decision.

Recommendation No. R (97) 5 of the Committee of Ministers to Member States on the Protection of Medical Data (1997)

Council of Europe—Committee of Ministers

1. Definitions

For the purposes of this recommendation:

- the expression "personal data" covers any information relating to an identified or identifiable individual. An individual shall not be regarded as "identifiable" if identification requires an unreasonable amount of time and manpower. In cases where the individual is not identifiable, the data are referred to as anonymous;
- the expression "medical data" refers to all personal data concerning the health of an individual. It refers also to data which have a clear and close link with health as well as to genetic data;
- the expression "genetic data" refers to all data, of whatever type, concerning the hereditary characteristics of an individual or concerning the pattern of inheritance of such characteristics within a related group of individuals.

It also refers to all data on the carrying of any genetic information (genes) in an individual or genetic line relating to any aspect of health or disease, whether present as identifiable characteristics or not.

* * *

2. Scope

2.1. This recommendation is applicable to the collection and automatic processing of medical data, unless domestic law, in a specific context outside the health-care sector, provides other appropriate safeguards.

2.2. A member state may extend the principles set out in this recommendation to cover medical data not processed automatically.

3. Respect for privacy

3.1. The respect of rights and fundamental freedoms, and in particular of the right to privacy, shall be guaranteed during the collection and processing of medical data.

3.2. Medical data may only be collected and processed if in accordance with appropriate safeguards which must be provided by domestic law.

In principle, medical data should be collected and processed only by health-care professionals, or by individuals or bodies working on behalf of health-care professionals. Individuals or bodies working on behalf of health-care professionals who collect and process medical data should be subject to the same rules of confidentiality incumbent on health-care professionals, or to comparable rules of confidentiality.

Controllers of files who are not health-care professionals should only collect and process medical data subject either to rules of confidentiality comparable to those incumbent upon a health-care professional or subject to equally effective safeguards provided for by domestic law.

4. Collection and processing of medical data

4.1. Medical data shall be collected and processed fairly and lawfully and only for specified purposes.

4.2. Medical data shall in principle be obtained from the data subject. They may only be obtained from other sources if in accordance with Principles 4, 6 and 7 of this recommendation and if this is necessary to achieve the purpose of the processing or if the data subject is not in a position to provide the data.

4.3. Medical data may be collected and processed:

a. if provided for by law for:

- i. Public health reasons; or
- ii. Subject to Principle 4.8, the prevention of a real danger or the suppression of a specific criminal offence; or
- iii. Another important public interest; or

b. if permitted by law:

- i. For preventive medical purposes or for diagnostic or for therapeutic purposes with regard to the data subject or a relative in the genetic line; or
- ii. To safeguard the vital interests of the data subject or of a third person; or
- iii. For the fulfilment of specific contractual obligations; or
- iv. To establish, exercise or defend a legal claim; or

c. If the data subject or his/her legal representative or an authority or any person or body provided for by law has given his/her consent for one or more purposes, and in so far as domestic law does not provide otherwise.

4.4. If medical data have been collected for preventive medical purposes or for diagnostic or therapeutic purposes with regard to the data subject or a relative in the genetic line, they may also be processed for the management of a medical service operating in the interest of the patient, in cases where the management is provided by the health-care professional who collected the data, or where the data are communicated in accordance with principles 7.2 and 7.3.

Genetic data

4.7 Genetic data collected and processed for preventive treatment, diagnosis or treatment of the data subject or for scientific research should only be used for these purposes or to allow the data subject to take a free and informed decision on these matters.

4.8. Processing of genetic data for the purpose of a judicial procedure or a criminal investigation should be the subject of a specific law offering appropriate safeguards.

The data should only be used to establish whether there is a genetic link in the framework of adducing evidence, to prevent a real danger or to suppress a specific criminal offence. In no case should they be used to determine other characteristics which may be linked genetically.

4.9. For purposes other than those provided for in Principles 4.7 and 4.8, the collection and processing of genetic data should, in principle, only be permitted for health reasons and in particular to avoid any serious prejudice to the health of the data subject or third parties. However, the collection and processing of genetic data in order to predict illness may be allowed for in cases of overriding interest and subject to appropriate safeguards defined by law.

5. Information of the data subject

5.1. the data subject shall be informed of the following elements:

a. the existence of a file containing his/her medical data and the type of data collected or to be collected;

b. the purpose or purposes for which they are or will be processed;

c. where applicable, the individuals or bodies from whom they are or will be collected;

d. the persons or bodies to whom and the purposes for which they may be communicated;

e. the possibility, if any, for the data subject to refuse his consent, to withdraw it and the consequences of such withdrawal;

f. the identity of the controller and of his/her representative, if any, as well as the conditions under which the rights of access and of rectification may be exercised.

* * *

5.3. Information for the data subject shall be appropriate and adapted to the circumstances. Information should preferably be given to each data subject individually.

5.4. Before a genetic analysis is carried out, the data subject should be informed about the objectives of the analysis and the possibility of unexpected findings.

6. Consent

6.1. Where the data subject is required to give his/her consent, this consent should be free, express and informed.

6.2. The results of any genetic analysis should be formulated within the limits of the objective of the medical consultation, diagnosis or treatment for which consent was obtained.

* * *

7. Communication

7.1. Medical data shall not be communicated, unless on the conditions set out in this principle and in Principle 12.

7.2. In particular, unless other appropriate safeguards are provided by domestic law, medical data may only be communicated to a person who is subject to the rules of confidentiality incumbent upon a health-care professional, or to comparable rules of confidentiality, and who complies with the provisions of this recommendation.

7.3. Medical data may be communicated if they are relevant and:

a. if the communication if provided for by law and constitutes a necessary measure in democratic society for:

i. public health reasons; or

ii. the prevention of a real danger or the suppression of a specific criminal offence; or

iii. another important public interest; or

iv. the protection of the rights and freedoms of others; or

b. if the communication is permitted by law for the purpose of:

i. the protection of the data subject or a relative in the genetic line;

ii. safeguarding the vital interests of the data subject or a third person; or

iii. the fulfilment of specific contractual obligations; or

iv. establishing, exercising or defending a legal claim; or

c. if the data subject or his/her legal representative, or an authority, or any person or body provided for by law has given his/her consent for one or more purposes, and in so far as domestic law does not provide otherwise; or

d. Provided that the data subject or his/her legal representative, or an authority, or any person or body provided for by law has not explicitly objected to any non-mandatory communication, if the data have been collected in a freely chosen preventive, diagnostic or therapeutic context, and if the purpose of the communication, in particular the provision of care to the patient or the management of a medical service operating in the interest of the patient, is not incompatible with the purpose of the processing for which they were collected.

8. Rights of the data subject

Rights of access and of rectification

8.1. Every person shall be enabled to have access to his/her medical data, either directly or through a health-care professional or, if permitted by domestic law, a person appointed by him/her. The information must be accessible in understandable form.

8.2. Access to medical data may be refused, limited or delayed only if the law provides for this and if:

a. this constitutes a necessary measure in a democratic society in the interests of protecting state security, public safety, or the suppression of criminal offences; or

b. knowledge of the information is likely to cause serious harm to the data subject's health; or

c. the information on the data subject also reveals information on third parties or if, with respect to genetic data, this information is likely to cause serious harm to consanguine or uterine kin or to a person who has a direct link with this genetic line; or

d. the data are used for statistical or for scientific research purposes where there is clearly no risk of an infringement of the privacy of the data subject, notably the possibility of using the data collected in support of decisions or measures regarding any particular individual.

8.3. The data subject may ask for rectification of erroneous data concerning him/her and, in case of refusal, he/she shall be able to appeal.

Unexpected findings

8.4. The person subjected to genetic analysis should be informed of unexpected findings if the following conditions are met:

a. domestic law does not prohibit the giving of such information;

b. the person himself has asked for this information;

c. the information is not likely to cause serious harm:

i. to his/her health; or

ii. to his/her consanguine or uterine kin, to a member of his/her social family, or to a person who has a direct link with his/her genetic line, unless domestic law provides other appropriate safeguards.

Subject to sub-paragraph a, the person should also be informed if this information is of direct importance to him/her for treatment or prevention.

9. Security

9.1. Appropriate technical and organisational measures shall be taken to protect personal data—processed in accordance with this recommendation—against accidental or illegal destruction, accidental loss, as well as against unauthorised access, alteration, communication or any other form of processing.

* * *

12. Scientific research

12.1. Whenever possible, medical data used for scientific research purposes should be anonymous. Professional and scientific organisations as well as public authorities should promote the development of techniques and procedures securing anonymity.

12.2 However, if such anonymisation would make a scientific research project impossible, and the project is to be carried out for legitimate purposes, it could be carried out with personal data on condition that:

a. the data subject has given his/her informed consent for one more research projects; or

b. when the data subject is a legally incapacitated person incapable of free decision, and domestic law does not permit the data subject to act on his/her own behalf, his/her legal representative or an authority, or any person or body provided for by law, has given his/her consent in the framework of a research project related to the medical condition or illness of the data subject; or

c. disclosure of data for the purpose of a defined scientific research project concerning an important public interest has been authorised by the body or bodies designated by domestic law, but only if:

i. the data subject has not expressly opposed disclosure; and

ii. despite reasonable efforts, it would be impracticable to contact the data subject to seek his consent; and

iii. the interests of the research project justify the authorisation; or

d. the scientific research is provided for by law and constitutes a necessary measure for public health reasons.

12.3. Subject to complementary provisions determined by domestic law, health-care professionals entitled to carry out their own medical research should be able to use the medical data which they hold as long as the data subject has been informed of this possibility and has not objected.

* * *

12.5. Personal data used for scientific research may not be published in a form which enables the data subjects to be identified, unless they have given their consent for the publication and publication is permitted by domestic law.

Protecting Medical and Genetic Data

Frits W. Hondius, European Journal of Health Law, vol. 4, pp. 361, 381–82 (1997).

* * *

The most noteworthy step taken by the drafters of Recommendation No. R (97) 5 was to include genetic data under the concept of "medical data," thereby renouncing the idea of two parallel recommendations. There is no doubt that genetic data are personal data, albeit common to more than one individual. The latter trait is covered by Article 8 of the European Human Rights Convention which enshrines both privacy and family life, the privacy sphere of the individual and the intimate link he has with other persons close to him.

Recommendation No. R (97) 5 has innovated by introducing in addition to the traditional legal subjects, *i.e.* the data subject and "others" (or "third parties"), a new intermediate category of "co-subjects," persons also concerned, *i.e.* those belonging to his genetic line, a line which is constituted by genetic similarities resulting from procreation and shared by two or more individuals.

* * *

* * * [O]ne of the subjects on which the CDBI [the Council of Europe's bioethics expert committee] is at present elaborating a protocol is research. The draft for this protocol contains a Chapter VII "Confidentiality" on which consultations are taking place with the data protection experts, the CJPD [the Council of Europe data protection expert committee]. It appears that the latter committee is beginning to have second thoughts about whether it had been right in lumping medical and genetic data together under the Recommendation No. R (97) 5. The possibility should not be excluded that in the near future the genetics part of that recommendation will be split off into a separate instrument.

An improvement of Recommendation No. R (97) 5 as compared with its 1981 predecessor is that it deals with medical information used not only for strictly medical purposes (prevention, diagnosis and therapy) but also for other purposes such as insurance, criminal justice, immigration control or employment. There is concern about such information getting out of hand, about social stigmas attached to it, as well as about the possibility of information carriers being encoded without the foreknowledge of the data subjects. Providing data protection on such information is the duty of the users in those other fields of application—police, insurance etc. However in order to avoid such data getting lost in a regulatory no man's land, Principle 2.1 declares the Recommendation applicable unless sufficient other safeguards are provided for outside the health-care sector.

Principles 3 and 4 contain exhaustive rules on the question *who may collect and process medical data* and for what purpose. Principle 3.2 starts from the premise that it is the health care staff which runs itself the information systems and that the entrusting of data processing to non-health care staff is now an exception to this rule, a reversal of what was considered normal in 1981.

Principle 5 contains the classical elements of the passive "*right to know*." The data subject has the right to know what medical data concerning him are on record and there is a corresponding duty to inform him. However, the Recommendation does not indicate on whom that duty rests. Nor has the Recommendation taken into account the "right *not* to know" which is recognised by Article 10 (2) of the Oviedo Convention. The only concession which the Recommendation makes to the "right not to know" can be construed *a contrario* from Principle 8.4 concerning unexpected findings, which may be communicated only if the data subject has asked for such information. Unexpected findings may reveal not only traditional health information but also other kinds of sensitive information such as the existence of a hitherto unknown member of the biological family or the fact that someone who was supposed to belong to it, does not.

* * *

Notes

1. The Council of Europe should not be confused with the European Union. The Council deals primarily with human rights and security issues rather than economic concerns, and includes virtually all of the states of Europe. Its conventions have different legal status in different countries. Quite clearly its recommendations on data privacy anticipate implementing domestic legislation in member states. The Council of Europe has become increasingly involved in the health law area, with its most important pronouncement probably being the Convention on Human Rights and Biomedicine, signed on April 4, 1997 in Oviedo Spain (referred to in the reading as the Oviedo Convention). The Convention (parts of which are reproduced at various points in this book) deals with a wide variety of issues, including right to privacy of and access to medical information, that should result in substantial uniformity of protection of these rights in Europe. With respect to the issue of privacy, Article 10(1) of the Convention states:

> Everyone has the right to respect for private life in relation to information about his or her health.

2. Why is the requirement of informing the data subject of collection and communication handled separately from the issue of consent? To what extent, indeed, is consent relevant to the collection and communication of medical data?

3. Should genetic data be treated the same as other medical data? Alternatively, should it be dealt with completely separately? The Recommendations seem to treat it as medical data, but as a special type of medical data. A number of American states also have special laws protecting genetic privacy. See discussing the issue of genetic privacy, John A. Robertson, Privacy Issues in Second Stage Genomics, 40 *Jurimetrics J.* 59 (1999). See, arguing against "genetic exceptionalism," Lawrence O Gostin & James G. Hodge, Jr., Genetic Privacy and the Law: An End to Genetic Exceptionalism, 40 *Jurimetrics J.* 21 (1999).

4. When would it be appropriate under 8.2.c. or 8.4.c to withhold genetic data from data subjects? What is the problem which these provisions address?

5. The UNESCO Universal Declaration on the Human Genome and Human Rights states at Article 5c that:

> The right of every individual to decide whether or not to be informed of the results of genetic examination and the resulting consequences should be respected.

Why would a person want not to be informed of genetic information? See Graeme T. Laurie, In Defence of Ignorance: Genetic Information and the Right not to Know, 6 *Medical Law Int.* 119 (1999). See also, discussing the UNESCO Declaration, Noelle Lenoir, Universal Declaration on the Human Genome and Human Rights: The First Legal and Ethical Framework at the Global Level, 30 *Colum. Hum. Rts. L. Rev.* 537 (1999). More recently, UNESCO has issued a declaration explicitly addressing genetic data, which, together with the Human Genome declaration, is one of the two U.N. declarations on bioethics issues.

UNESCO International Declaration on Human Genetic Data

16 October 2003

* * *

Article 1 — Aims and scope

(a) The aims of this Declaration are: to ensure the respect of human dignity and protection of human rights and fundamental freedoms in the collection, processing, use and storage of human genetic data, human proteomic data and of the biological samples from which they are derived, referred to hereinafter as "biological samples", in keeping with the requirements of equality, justice and solidarity, while giving due consideration to freedom of thought and expression, including freedom of research; to set out the principles which should guide States in the formulation of their legislation and their policies on these issues; and to form the basis for guidelines of good practices in these areas for the institutions and individuals concerned.

* * *

(c) The provisions of this Declaration apply to the collection, processing, use and storage of human genetic data, human proteomic data and biological samples, except in the investigation, detection and prosecution of criminal offences and in parentage testing that are subject to domestic law that is consistent with the international law of human rights.

* * *

Article 3 — Person's identity

Each individual has a characteristic genetic make-up. Nevertheless, a person's identity should not be reduced to genetic characteristics, since it involves complex educational, environmental and personal factors and emotional, social, spiritual and cultural bonds with others and implies a dimension of freedom.

Article 4 — Special status

(a) Human genetic data have a special status because:

(i) they can be predictive of genetic predispositions concerning individuals;

(ii) they may have a significant impact on the family, including offspring, extending over generations, and in some instances on the whole group to which the person concerned belongs;

(iii) they may contain information the significance of which is not necessarily known at the time of the collection of the biological samples;

(iv) they may have cultural significance for persons or groups.

(b) Due consideration should be given to the sensitivity of human genetic data and an appropriate level of protection for these data and biological samples should be established.

Article 5 — Purposes

Human genetic data and human proteomic data may be collected, processed, used and stored only for the purposes of:

(i) diagnosis and health care, including screening and predictive testing;

(ii) medical and other scientific research, including epidemiological, especially population-based genetic studies, as well as anthropological or archaeological studies, collectively referred to hereinafter as "medical and scientific research";

(iii) forensic medicine and civil, criminal and other legal proceedings, taking into account the provisions of Article 1(c);

(iv) or any other purpose consistent with the Universal Declaration on the Human Genome and Human Rights and the international law of human rights.

Article 6 — Procedures

(a) It is ethically imperative that human genetic data and human proteomic data be collected, processed, used and stored on the basis of transparent and ethically acceptable procedures. States should endeavour to involve society at large in the decision-making process concerning broad policies for the collection, processing, use and storage of human genetic data and human proteomic data and the evaluation of their management, in particular in the case of population-based genetic studies. This decision-making process, which may benefit from international experience, should ensure the free expression of various viewpoints.

(b) Independent, multidisciplinary and pluralist ethics committees should be promoted and established at national, regional, local or institutional levels * * *. Where appropriate, ethics committees at national level should be consulted with regard to the establishment of standards, regulations and guidelines for the collection, processing, use and storage of human genetic data, human proteomic data and biological samples. They should also be consulted concerning matters where there is no domestic law. Ethics committees at institutional or local levels should be consulted with regard to their application to specific research projects.

* * *

(d) It is ethically imperative that clear, balanced, adequate and appropriate information shall be provided to the person whose prior, free, informed and express consent is sought. Such information shall, alongside with providing other necessary details, specify the purpose for which human genetic data and human proteomic data are being derived from biological samples, and are used and stored. This information should indicate, if necessary, risks and consequences. This information should also indicate that the person concerned can withdraw his or her consent, without coercion, and this should entail neither a disadvantage nor a penalty for the person concerned.

Article 7 — Non-discrimination and non-stigmatization

(a) Every effort should be made to ensure that human genetic data and human proteomic data are not used for purposes that discriminate in a way that is intended to infringe, or has the effect of infringing human rights, fundamental freedoms or human dignity of an individual or for purposes that lead to the stigmatization of an individual, a family, a group or communities.

* * *

Article 10 — The right to decide whether or not to be informed about research results

When human genetic data, human proteomic data or biological samples are collected for medical and scientific research purposes, the information provided at the time of consent should indicate that the person concerned has the right to decide whether or not to be informed of the results. This does not apply to research on data irretrievably unlinked to identifiable persons or to data that do not lead to individual findings concerning the persons who have participated in such a research. Where appropriate, the right not to be informed should be extended to identified relatives who may be affected by the results.

Article 11 — Genetic counselling

It is ethically imperative that when genetic testing that may have significant implications for a person's health is being considered, genetic counselling should be made available in an appropriate manner. Genetic counselling should be non-directive, culturally adapted and consistent with the best interest of the person concerned.

* * *

Article 14 — Privacy and confidentiality

* * *

(b) Human genetic data, human proteomic data and biological samples linked to an identifiable person should not be disclosed or made accessible to third parties, in particular, employers, insurance companies, educational institutions and the family, except for an important public interest reason in cases restrictively provided for by domestic law consistent with the international law of human rights or where the prior, free, informed and express consent of the person concerned has been obtained provided that such consent is in accordance with domestic law and the international law of human rights. The privacy of an individual participating in a study using human genetic data, human proteomic data or biological samples should be protected and the data should be treated as confidential.

(c) Human genetic data, human proteomic data and biological samples collected for the purposes of scientific research should not normally be linked to an identifiable person. Even when such data or biological samples are unlinked to an identifiable person, the necessary precautions should be taken to ensure the security of the data or biological samples.

(d) Human genetic data, human proteomic data and biological samples collected for medical and scientific research purposes can remain linked to an identifiable person, only if necessary to carry out the research and provided that the privacy of the individual and the confidentiality of the data or biological samples concerned are protected in accordance with domestic law.

(e) Human genetic data and human proteomic data should not be kept in a form which allows the data subject to be identified for any longer than is necessary for achieving the purposes for which they were collected or subsequently processed.

Article 15 — Accuracy, reliability, quality and security

The persons and entities responsible for the processing of human genetic data, human proteomic data and biological samples should take the necessary measures to ensure the accuracy, reliability, quality and security of these data and the processing of biological samples.* * *.

* * *

Article 17 — Stored biological samples

(a) Stored biological samples collected for purposes other than set out in Article 5 may be used to produce human genetic data or human proteomic data with the prior, free, informed and express consent of the person concerned.* * *

* * *

Article 19 — Sharing of benefits

(a) In accordance with domestic law or policy and international agreements, benefits resulting from the use of human genetic data, human proteomic data or biological samples collected for medical and scientific research should be shared with the society as a whole and the international community. In giving effect to this principle, benefits may take any of the following forms:

(i) special assistance to the persons and groups that have taken part in the research;

(ii) access to medical care;

(iii) provision of new diagnostics, facilities for new treatments or drugs stemming from the research;

(iv) support for health services;

(v) capacity-building facilities for research purposes;

(vi) development and strengthening of the capacity of developing countries to collect and process human genetic data, taking into consideration their specific problems;

(vii) any other form consistent with the principles set out in this Declaration.

(b) Limitations in this respect could be provided by domestic law and international agreements.

* * *

Article 22 — Cross-matching

Consent should be essential for the cross-matching of human genetic data, human proteomic data or biological samples stored for diagnostic and health care purposes and for medical and other scientific research purposes, unless otherwise provided for by domestic law for compelling reasons and consistent with the international law of human rights.

* * *

Note

The attempt to create a comprehensive database of clinical medical information regarding the population of Iceland for genomics research raised particularly controversial data privacy issues. The project was to be carried out by a private company with the authority of the government of Iceland. Icelanders were presumed to consent to inclusion in the medical database unless they specifically opted out. Although assurances were given that the privacy of information would be protected, given the small population of Iceland, the proposal raised significant privacy issues.

Ragnhildur Guthmundsdóttir vs. The State of Iceland

Icelandic Supreme Court, 27 November 2003

* * *

The Appellant referred the case to the Supreme Court on 29 April 2003, calling for a reversal of the refusal of the Medical Director of Health to her request of 16 February 2000 to the effect that information from the medical records of her father, Guthmundur Ingólfsson, who died on 12 August 1991, should not be transferred into the Health Sector Database. The Appellant furthermore calls for the Court's recognition of her right to prohibit the transfer of the above information into the database.

* * *

The Health Sector Database Act No. 139/1998 entered into force on 30 December 1998. According to Article 1 of the Act, the purpose of the Act is to authorise the creation and operation of a centralised database of non-personally identifiable health data, with the aim of increasing knowledge for the purpose of improving health and health services. * * * Article 7 of Act No. 139/1998 contains instructions on the authorisation of the licensee to obtain data derived from the medical records of health institutions and self-employed health service workers. However, according to Article 8, persons who do not want information on them to be entered into the database can prevent this by a notification to the Medical Director of Health. Article 10 of the Act contains instructions concerning the utilisation of the database, including the purpose, restrictions and supervision, Article 11 provides for the obligation of confidentiality of the employees of the licensee and contractors in his service, * * *.

The Minister of Health and Social Security issued Government Regulation No. 32/2000 on a Health-Sector Database on 22 January 2000. On the same date, the Minister issued a license to Íslensk Erfthagreining ehf. for the creation and operation of the Health Sector Database. * * *

The guardian of the Appellant, who was born in 1985, wrote a letter to the Medical Director of Health on 16 February 2000, with an enclosed notification in the Appellant's name requesting that information contained in her father's medical records should not be transferred to the Health Sector Database. Furthermore, the request was made that the genealogical or genetic information on the Appellant's father should not be transferred into the database. The Medical Director of Health replied by a letter dated 21 February 2001. Reference was made, inter alia, to the fact that Act No. 139/1998 contained no direct provisions on the right of the relatives of a deceased person to prevent information about him/her being transferred into the Health Sector Database. However, in the commentary attached to the legislative Bill which eventually passed into law it had been stated that it was not the intention that people should be able to refuse the transfer of information on their deceased parents into the database. * * *

Following receipt of the reply of the Medical Director of Health, the Appellant initiated these proceedings on 30 April 2001. * * *

Based on information that emerged in the course of proceedings before the Supreme Court, the compilation of the Health Sector Database has not yet started. There is, furthermore, some doubt that this will happen. The documents of the case do not reveal that formal measures for the preparation of the database have advanced significantly since the operating license was issued on 22 January 2000 to Íslensk Erfthagreining ehf. and the annexes to the license referred to above were ready.

According to the principles of Icelandic law, the personal rights of individuals lapse on their death insofar as legislation does not provide otherwise. * * * The Appellant cannot, therefore, exercise the right provided for in this statutory provision as her deceased father's substitute.

As stated in the appealed judgement, the Appellant bases her legitimate interest in the case partly on the fact that she has a personal interest in preventing the transfer of data from her father's medical records to the Health Sector Database, as it is possible to infer, from the data, information relating to her father's hereditary characteristics which could also apply to herself. * * * [T]he argument of the Appellant is accepted that, for reasons of personal privacy, she may have an interest in preventing information of this sort about her father from being transferred into the database, and therefore her right to make the claims that she is making in the case is admitted.

* * *

According to Paragraph 1 of Article 7 of Act No. 139/1998, it is permitted, with the approval of health institutions or self-employed health service workers, to provide data processed from medical records to the holder of an operating licence for a health sector database for transfer into the database. * * * Personal identifiers must be encrypted by means of one-way coding, * * * before the information is transferred into the database, in order to ensure that the licensee's staff only work with non-personally identifiable data. * * *

Article 10 of Act No. 139/1998 provides that data recorded in the Health Sector Database, or obtained by processing in the database, may be used to develop new or improved methods of achieving better health, prediction, diagnosis and treatment of diseases, to seek the most economic ways of operating health services, and to produce public health reports. The licensee is authorised to process data in the database from the medical records therein, provided that data are processed and connected in such a way that they cannot be traced to identifiable individuals. The obligation is imposed on the licensee to develop methods and protocols that meet the requirements of the Data Protection Authority in order to ensure protection of privacy in connecting data from the Health Sector Database, from a database of genealogical data, and from a database of genetic data. It is stated specifically in the provision that no information on individuals must be given, and this shall be ensured by means which include access restrictions. Also, the licensee is not permitted to provide direct access to data in the database. * * * The committee [Committee on the Operation of the Database] is moreover responsible for monitoring all queries and processing of information from the database and also for reporting regularly to the National Bioethics Committee on all queries processed in the database and the sources of the queries. Moreover, Paragraph 3 of Article 12 of the Act provides for the obligation of the Minister to issue a regulation on an multidisciplinary ethics committee to evaluate licensee's research and queries to the database. According to the Act, the committee's evaluation must show that there are no scientific or ethical grounds for preventing the study in question from being carried out or for preventing the queries from being processed. * * *

As may be inferred from the above, extensive information is entered into medical records on people's health, their medical treatment, lifestyles, social circumstances, employment and family. They contain, moreover, a detailed identification of the person that the information concerns. Information of this kind can relate to some of the most intimately private affairs of the person concerned, irrespective of whether the information can be seen as derogatory for the person or not. It is unequivocal that the provisions of Paragraph 1 of Article 71 of the Constitution apply to information of this kind and that they guarantee protection of privacy in this respect. To ensure this privacy the legislature must ensure, inter alia, that legislation does not result in any actual risk of information of this kind involving the private affairs of identified persons falling into the hands of parties who do not have any legitimate right of access to such information, irrespective of whether the parties in question are other individuals or governmental authorities.

Article 7 of Act No. 139/1998 opens the possibility of a private entity, who is neither a medical institution nor a self-employed health service worker, obtaining information from medical records without the explicit consent of the person whom the information concerns. Although this alone does not necessarily, in and of itself, violate the provisions of Paragraph 1 of Article 71 of the Constitution, the legislature, having regard to all of the above, must take steps, in the establishment of a rule of this kind, to ensure to the furthest extent that the information cannot be traced to specific individuals. The District Court, * * * concluded that the so-called one-way encryption * * * could be carried out so securely as to render it virtually impossible to read the encrypted information. This conclusion has not been contested successfully in the course of the proceedings before the Supreme Court. It should be noted, however, that Act No. 139/1998 provides no guidance as to what information from medical records must be encrypted in this manner prior to transfer into the Health Sector Database or whether certain information contained in the medical records relating to the personal identity of the patient will not be transferred. * * *

* * *

Individual provisions in Act No. 139/1998 refer repeatedly to the fact that health information in the Health Sector Database should be non-personally identifiable. * * * The achievement of this stated objective is far from being adequately ensured by the provisions of statutory law. Owing to the obligations imposed on the legislature by Paragraph 1 of Article 71 of the Constitution to ensure protection of privacy, as outlined above, this assurance cannot be replaced by various forms of monitoring of the creation and operation of the Health Sector Database, monitoring which is entrusted to public agencies and committees without definite statutory norms on which to base their work. Nor is it sufficient in this respect to leave it in the hands of the Minister to establish conditions in the operating licence or appoint other holders of official authority to establish or approve rules of procedure concerning these matters, * * *.

Article 8 of Act No. 139/1998 permits those who so wish to issue binding instructions to the effect that information about them should not be transferred from medical records into the Health Sector Database. * * * It has been recognised above that the Appellant may herself have an interest in preventing the transfer of information from her father's medical records into the Health Sector Database because of the risk that inferences could be made from such information which could concern her private affairs. Based on the above, it is impossible to maintain that the provisions of Act No. 139/1998 will adequately ensure, in fulfilment of the requirements deriving from Paragraph 1 of Article 71 of the Constitution, attainment of the objective of the Act of preventing health information in the database from being traceable to individuals. * * *

* * *

In light of this, and taking into account the principles of Icelandic legislation concerning protection of privacy, the Court recognises the right of the Appellant in this respect. Her court claims in this regard are therefore upheld. * * *

Notes

1. See discussing the Iceland project, George Annas, Rules for Research on Human Genetic Variation—Lessons from Iceland, 343 *New. Eng. J. Med.* 1830 (2000); Henry T. Greely, Iceland's Plan for Genomics Research: Facts and Implications, 40 *Jurimetrics J.* 153 (2000); Oddny Mjöll Arnardóttir, Davíd Thór Björgvinsson, Vidar Már Matthíasson, The Icelandic Health Sector Database, 6 *European J. Health L.* 307 (1999); Henriette D.C.

Roscam Abbing, Central Health Database in Iceland and Patient's Rights, 6 *European J. Health L.* 363 (1999).

2. DeCODE, the private company given the contract for managing the Iceland genetic database has apparently not gone forward with the project, although the reaons might be as much economic as legal. Other countries are, however, also attempting to build large genetic databases. According to Professor Henry Greely, The best existing example of very large, very broad genotype and phenotype database is in the UK (which will cover about 500,000 people). Estonia has done a pilot project for about 10,000 people and is looking for financing to cover one million. Taiwan expects to start a 200,000 person database in the near future.

2. Access to Medical Records

If a patient has a right to control access to medical information, it would seem obvious that the patient should have access to that information. Traditional notions of medical paternalism, concerns about the sensitivity of medical data, and proprietary attitudes towards medical records, however, have long limited the access of patients to their records. This is changing in many parts of the world (and has, by and large, changed in the United States). In common law countries, however, the change has often come by statute rather than by court decision. Though the Canadian Supreme Court decision below recognizes a far ranging right of access to medical information, the Australian High Court decision that follows it rejects general access to records. These cases are important, not only because of their conclusion with respect to medical records, but also because of their characterizations of the physician-patient relationship.

McInerney v. MacDonald

[1992] 2 Can. S.C.R. 138, 93 D.L.R. (4th) 415 (Canadian Supreme Court)

Panel: La Forest, L'Heureux-Dube, Gonthier, Stevenson* and Iacobucci JJ.

* Stevenson J. took no part in the judgment.

La Forest, J.—The central issue in this case is whether in the absence of legislation a patient is entitled to inspect and obtain copies of his or her medical records upon request.

Facts

The facts are simple. The appellant, Dr. Elizabeth McInerney, is a medical doctor who is licensed to practise in New Brunswick. The respondent, Mrs. Margaret MacDonald, was her patient. Before her consultations with Dr. McInerney, Mrs. MacDonald was treated by various physicians over a period of years. On Dr. McInerney's advice, Mrs. MacDonald ceased taking thyroid pills previously prescribed by other physicians. She then became concerned about her medical care before consulting Dr. McInerney, and wrote the latter requesting copies of the contents of her complete medical file. The doctor delivered copies of all notes, memoranda and reports she had prepared herself but refused to produce copies of consultants' reports and records she had received from other physicians, stating that they were the property of those physicians and that it would be unethical for her to release them. She suggested that Mrs. MacDonald contact the other physicians for release of their records.

An application was then made on behalf of Mrs. MacDonald to the New Brunswick Court of Queen's Bench for an order directing Dr. McInerney to provide a copy of her entire medical file relating to Mrs. MacDonald. Turnbull J. granted the application. The appeal to the Court of Appeal of New Brunswick was dismissed, * * *.

* * *

The appellant raises two issues in this appeal:

1. Are a patient's medical records prepared by a physician the property of that physician or are they the property of the patient?

2. If a patient's medical records are the property of the physician who prepares them, does a patient nevertheless have the right to examine and obtain copies of all documents in the physician's medical record, including records that the physician may have received which were prepared by other physicians?

The current position of the medical profession with respect to the right of patients to information in their medical records is reflected in the policy statement of the Canadian Medical Association published in 1985:

> The Canadian Medical Association (CMA) regards medical records as confidential documents, owned by the physician/institution/clinic that compiled them or had them compiled. Patients have a right to medical information contained in their records but not to the documents themselves. The first consideration of the physician is the well-being of the patient, and discretion must be used when conveying information contained in a medical record to a patient. This medical information often requires interpretation by a physician or other health care professional. Other disclosures of information contained in medical records to third parties (eg. physician-to-physician transfer for administrative purposes, lawyer, insurance adjuster) require written patient consent or a court order. * * *

I am prepared to accept that the physician, institution or clinic compiling the medical records owns the physical records. This leaves the remaining issue of whether the patient nevertheless has a right to examine and obtain copies of all documents in the physician's medical records. The majority of the Court of Appeal based the patient's right of access on an implied contractual term. While it may be possible to pursue the contractual route in the civil law system, I do not find it particularly helpful in the common law context. Accordingly, I am not entirely comfortable with the approach taken by the Court of Appeal. However, I do agree that a patient has a vital interest in the information contained in his or her medical records.

Medical records continue to grow in importance as the health care field becomes more and more specialized. As L. E. Rozovsky and F. A. Rozovsky put it in *The Canadian Law of Patient Records* (1984), * * *

> The twentieth century has seen a vast expansion of the health care services. Rather than relying on one individual, a physician, the patient now looks directly and indirectly to dozens and sometimes hundreds of individuals to provide him with the services he requires. He is cared for not simply by his own physician but by a veritable army of nurses, numerous consulting physicians, technologists and technicians, other allied health personnel and administrative personnel.

While a patient may, in the past, have relied primarily upon one personal physician, the trend now tends to favour referrals to a number of professionals. Each of the pieces of information provided by this "army" of health care workers joins with the other pieces to form the complete picture. As the number and use of specialists increase, the more difficult it is for the patient to gain access to that picture. If the patient is only entitled to obtain particular information from each health care provider, the number of contacts he or she may be required to make may become enormous. The problem is intensified when one considers the mobility of patients in modern society.

Medical records are also used for an increasing number of purposes. This point is well made by A. F. Westin, *Computers, Health Records, and Citizen Rights* (1976).

> As to medical records, when these were in fact used only by the physician or the hospital, it may have been only curiosity when patients asked to know their contents. But now that medical records are widely shared with health insurance companies, government payers, law enforcement agencies, welfare departments, schools, researchers, credit grantors, and employers, it is often crucial for the patient to know what is being recorded, and to correct inaccuracies that may affect education, career advancement or government benefits.

* * *

When a patient approaches a physician for health care, he or she discloses sensitive information concerning personal aspects of his or her life. The patient may also bring into the relationship information relating to work done by other medical professionals. The policy statement of the Canadian Medical Association cited earlier indicates that a physician cannot obtain access to this information without the patient's consent or a court order. Thus, at least in part, medical records contain information about the patient revealed by the patient, and information that is acquired and recorded on behalf of the patient. Of primary significance is the fact that the records consist of information that is highly private and personal to the individual. It is information that goes to the personal integrity and autonomy of the patient. * * * [S]uch information remains in a fundamental sense one's own, for the individual to communicate or retain as he or she sees fit. * * * In sum, an individual may decide to make personal information available to others to obtain certain benefits such as medical advice and treatment. Nevertheless, * * * he or she has a "basic and continuing interest in what happens to this information, and in controlling access to it".

A physician begins compiling a medical file when a patient chooses to share intimate details about his or her life in the course of medical consultation. The patient "entrusts" this personal information to the physician for medical purposes. * * * [T]he relationship between physician and patient is one in which "trust and confidence" must be placed in the physician. This statement was referred to with approval by LeBel J. * * * who himself characterized the physician-patient relationship as "fiduciary and confidential", * * *

In characterizing the physician-patient relationship as "fiduciary", I would not wish it to be thought that a fixed set of rules and principles apply in all circumstances or to all obligations arising out of the doctor-patient relationship. * * * [N]ot all fiduciary relationships and not all fiduciary obligations are the same; these are shaped by the demands of the situation. A relationship may properly be described as "fiduciary" for some purposes, but not for others. That being said, certain duties do arise from the special relationship of trust and confidence between doctor and patient. Among these are the duty of the doctor to act with utmost good faith and loyalty, and to hold information received from or about a patient in confidence. When a patient releases personal information in the context of the doctor-patient relationship, he or she does so with the legitimate expectation that these duties will be respected.

The physician-patient relationship also gives rise to the physician's duty to make proper disclosure of information to the patient. The appellant concedes that a patient has a right to be advised about the information concerning his or her health in the physician's medical record. In my view, however, the fiducial qualities of the relationship extend the physician's duty beyond this to include the obligation to grant access to the information the doctor uses in administering treatment. * * *

Certain textbooks and case law go further and assert that the patient has a "proprietary" or "property" interest in the medical records. For example, Meagher et al., supra, write:

> In the absence of an agreement, a doctor or hospital owns the records of the patient, but the patient is considered to have a property interest in the medical information contained in the record, with a right of access to it, but not to its possession.

* * *

A similar sentiment is expressed in the American text by R. D. Miller, *Problems in Hospital Law.* The author has this to say,

> The medical record is an unusual type of property because physically it belongs to the hospital and the hospital must exercise considerable control over access, but the patient and others have an interest in the information in the record. One way of viewing this is that the hospital owns the paper or other material on which the information is recorded, but it is just a custodian of the information. * * *

I find it unnecessary to reify the patient's interest in his or her medical records and, in particular, I am not inclined to go so far as to say that a doctor is merely a "custodian" of medical information. The fiduciary duty I have described is sufficient to protect the interest of the patient. The trust-like "beneficial interest" of the patient in the information indicates that, as a general rule, he or she should have a right of access to the information and that the physician should have a corresponding obligation to provide it. The patient's interest being in the information, it follows that the interest continues when that information is conveyed to another doctor who then becomes subject to the duty to afford the patient access to that information.

There is a further matter that militates in favour of disclosure of patient records. As mentioned earlier, one of the duties arising from the doctor-patient relationship is the duty of the doctor to act with utmost good faith and loyalty. If the patient is denied access to his or her records, it may not be possible for the patient to establish that this duty has been fulfilled. As I see it, it is important that the patient have access to the records for the very purposes for which it is sought to withhold the documents, namely, to ensure the proper functioning of the doctor-patient relationship and to protect the well-being of the patient. * * *

Disclosure is all the more important in our day when individuals are seeking more information about themselves. It serves to reinforce the faith of the individual in his or her treatment. The ability of a doctor to provide effective treatment is closely related to the level of trust in the relationship. A doctor is in a better position to diagnose a medical problem if the patient freely imparts personal information. The duty of confidentiality that arises from the doctor-patient relationship is meant to encourage disclosure of information and communication between doctor and patient. In my view, the trust reposed in the physician by the patient mandates that the flow of information operate both ways. * * *

* * * Indeed, H. E. Emson observes that the practice of giving patients their own records "has been said to improve patient understanding, cooperation and compliance". In this sense, reciprocity of information between the patient and physician is prima facie in the patient's best interests. It strengthens the bond of trust between physician and patient which, in turn, promotes the well-being of the patient.

While patients should as a general rule, have access to their medical records, this policy need not and, in my mind, should not be pursued blindly. The related duty of confidentiality * * * is absolute unless there is some paramount reason that overrides it. For example, "there may be cases in which reasons connected with the safety of individuals or of the public, physical or moral, would be sufficiently cogent to supersede or qualify the obligations prima facie imposed by the confidential relation". Similarly, the patient's general right of access to his or her records is not absolute. The patient's interest in his or her records is an equitable interest arising from the physician's fiduciary obligation to disclose the records upon request. * * * If the physician reasonably believes it is not in the patient's best interests to inspect his or her medical records, the physician may consider it necessary to deny access to the information. But the patient is not left at the mercy of this discretion. When called upon, equity will intervene to protect the patient from an improper exercise of the physician's discretion. In other words, the physician has a discretion to deny access, but it is circumscribed. It must be exercised on proper principles and not in an arbitrary fashion. * * *

I hasten to add that, just as a relationship may be fiduciary for some purposes and not for others, this characterization of the doctor's obligation as "fiduciary" and the patient's interest in the records as an "equitable interest" does not imply a particular remedy. Equity works in the circumstances to enforce the duty. This foundation in equity gives the court considerable discretion to refuse access to the records where non-disclosure is appropriate.

In my view, the onus properly lies on the doctor to justify an exception to the general rule of access. Not only is the information in some fundamental sense that of the patient; the doctor has primary access to it. * * * To some extent, what the documents contain is a matter of speculation for the patient. Consequently, there is a marked disparity in the ability of each party to prove its case. The burden of proof should fall on the party who is in the best position to obtain the facts.

If a physician objects to the patient's general right of access, he or she must have reasonable grounds for doing so. Although I do not intend to provide an exhaustive analysis of the circumstances in which access to medical records may be denied, some general observations may be useful. I shall make these in a response to a number of arguments that have been advanced by the appellant and in the literature for denying a patient access to medical records. These include: (1) disclosure may facilitate the initiation of unfounded law suits; (2) the medical records may be meaningless; (3) the medical records may be misinterpreted; (4) doctors may respond by keeping less thorough notes; and (5) disclosure of the contents of the records may be harmful to the patient or a third party.

* * *

Denial of access may actually encourage unfounded law suits. If a law suit is started, a patient can generally obtain access to his or her records under rules of civil procedure relating to discovery of documents. Thus, if a patient strongly wishes to see his or her records, one way of achieving this result is to commence an action before ascertaining whether or not there is a valid basis for the action.

The arguments that the records may be meaningless or that they may be misinterpreted do not justify non-disclosure in the ordinary case. If the records are, in fact, meaningless, they will not help the patient but neither will they cause harm. It is always open to the patient to obtain assistance in understanding the file. * * *

The concern that disclosure will lead to a decrease in the completeness, candour and frankness of medical records, can be answered by reference to the obligation of a physician to keep accurate records. A failure to do so may expose the physician to liability for professional misconduct or negligence. It is also easy to exaggerate the importance of this argument. Certainly physicians may become more cautious in what they record, but it cannot be assumed as a natural consequence that this will detrimentally affect the standard of care given to the patient. Generally I doubt that the quality of medical records will be measurably affected by a general rule allowing access to the patient. * * *

Non-disclosure may be warranted if there is a real potential for harm either to the patient or to a third party. This is the most persuasive ground for refusing access to medical records. However, even here, the discretion to withhold information should not be exercised readily. Particularly in situations that do not involve the interests of third parties, the court should demand compelling grounds before confirming a decision to deny access. * * * Non-disclosure can itself affect the patient's well-being. If access is denied, the patient may speculate as to what is in the records and imagine difficulties greater than those that actually exist. In addition, the physical well-being of the patient must be balanced with the patient's right to self-determination. Both are worthy of protection. In short, patients should have access to their medical records in all but a small number of circumstances. In the ordinary case, these records should be disclosed upon the request of the patient unless there is a significant likelihood of a substantial adverse effect on the physical, mental or emotional health of the patient or harm to a third party.

* * *

Since I have held that the tangible records belong to the physician, the patient is not entitled to the records themselves. Medical records play an important role in helping the physician to remember details about the patient's medical history. The physician must have continued access to the records to provide proper diagnosis and treatment. Such access will be disrupted if the patient is able to remove the records from the premises. Accordingly, the patient is entitled to reasonable access to examine and copy the records, provided the patient pays a legitimate fee for the preparation and reproduction of the information. Access is limited to the information the physician obtained in providing treatment. It does not extend to information arising outside the doctor-patient relationship.

Appeal dismissed.

Breen v. Williams

4 A.L.D. 481, 186 C.L.R. 71 (High Court of Australia, 6 Sept. 1996)

Judges: Brennan, CJ, Dawson, Toohey, Gaudron, McHugh, and Gummow, JJ.

Dawson and Toohey JJ. [The opinion of Dawson and Toohey appears after the opinion of Brennan, C.J., in the original, but is moved in front of it here because it contains the statement of facts.]

In 1977 the appellant had a bilateral augmentation mammoplasty which involved the insertion of a silicone implant in each of her breasts. Thereafter she developed bilateral breast capsules. In 1978 she consulted the respondent, who is a plastic surgeon, but not the plastic surgeon who performed the implant. The respondent advised the appellant that the capsules should be compressed and he performed that operation. The appellant experienced severe pain and, after two further consultations with her, the respondent operated and performed a bilateral capsulotomy. The appellant has not consulted the respondent since that operation, although she corresponded with him in 1983 over matters unrelated to this appeal.

In 1984 another doctor, Dr McDougall, diagnosed a lump in the appellant's left breast as silicone gel which had leaked from the breast implant. As a result, he performed a partial mastectomy upon the appellant. Since then she has had further corrective surgery on her left breast and has had the right silicone breast implant replaced. These operations were not performed by the respondent.

The appellant became interested in litigation in the United States by way of a class action against the manufacturer of the breast implants claiming that they were defective. In that litigation she was given the opportunity to "opt in" to a settlement which had been given conditional approval by a United States court. It appears that it was a condition of opting in that the appellant do so before 1 December 1994 and that she file with the United States court copies of medical records in support of any claim which she wished to make. The appellant sought to have access to the medical records kept by the respondent in her case and maintains that she did so both to secure advice whether she should opt in to the United States settlement and to comply with the condition imposed should she decide to do so. She also maintains that she has a right of access to the medical records to ensure that she has all information relating to her health at her disposal which will, in turn, ensure that she is able to make decisions regarding her future treatment.

The appellant could have secured access to the medical records by compulsory court process. It would appear that an order for discovery of the records was within the equitable jurisdiction of the Supreme Court of New South Wales. Another procedure was by way of letters rogatory. These were obtained from the United States court by several litigants in her position and orders were made by the Supreme Court of New South Wales compelling the production of medical records to the court in aid of the United States proceedings. The appellant did not avail herself of this procedure because, she said, the time available was too short. Instead, she commenced this action in the Supreme Court of New South Wales claiming a declaration that she is entitled to access to the medical records kept by the respondent in relation to herself. * * * The appellant also sought an order that the respondent allow her access to her medical records to examine them and obtain copies of the information contained in them.

Those records were not in evidence but the trial judge, Bryson J, found by inference that they comprised * * * [the defendant's handwritten notes, as well as other records].

* * * For practical purposes, the relief sought by the appellant related in the end to the respondent's handwritten notes and it was upon these that argument centred.

Of these the respondent said:

> The handwritten notes ... are prepared and maintained by me, along with the other documents described above in the belief that such records belong to me and are private to me ... [S]ome of these records will contain information supplied to me in confidence by family and friends of the patient in circumstances where I have been told by such persons that they do no[t] wish the patient to be aware of their communications with me. Often the information I receive from such sources is what I would regard as sensitive and confidential, and I would not wish to divulge my knowledge of it or source unless I judged it necessary to do so in the interest of the patient. In some cases because of the state of mind or health of the patient these records will contain information the disclosure of which in my judgment might be detrimental to the patient's well being if disclosed at all or if disclosed without full explanation. Because these

> notes are prepared by me in the belief that they will remain private to me, they often contain conclusions, commentary and musing which might well be different in form and substance if the notes were prepared by me in the knowledge that the patient was entitled to a copy of my records. I would be concerned that these notes and some of the other records maintained by me might, at least in some cases, cause confusion and unnecessary worry and stress to patients if they were made available to them without adequate explanation. Finally, in part, these notes contain information which relates solely to the business and administration of my practice and not to aspects of the treatment and management of my patients.

On 4 August 1993 the appellant's solicitors wrote to the respondent requesting copies of the appellant's medical records, not a medical report. By a letter dated 10 August 1993 the respondent replied to the appellant herself, saying:

> As [your solicitors] well know, it is a longstanding legal tradition in this country that such records are the doctor's property, an aide memoire to his treatment of the patient, and may only be released on production of a court subpoena.
>
> Accordingly the advice which I have received from my medical defence legal advis[e]rs is that this situation still holds, but that they would be very happy for me to release your records, were you to supply me with a document which would release me from any claim that might arise in relation to my treatment of you.

Despite the reference in that letter to a claim against the respondent, the appellant has not sought, nor does she seek, to make any claim against the respondent based upon his default. Had she commenced proceedings upon that basis she would have been entitled to discovery of her medical records in the ordinary course. Nevertheless, the appellant was not prepared to give the undertaking sought by the respondent's insurers and sought access to her medical records as of right.

During the trial of the appellant's action, the respondent made an open offer to provide a report in writing to the appellant about the contents of her medical records, excluding his correspondence with the New South Wales Medical Defence Union and with the appellant's solicitors. * * *. The trial judge found that the appellant did not wish to have a report such as that offered by the respondent and thus regarded himself as not called upon to consider whether the respondent's readiness to provide a report was reasonable or extended sufficiently far to satisfy any contractual duty which the respondent might have to provide a report.

Notwithstanding the purposes which the appellant asserted for wanting access to her medical records, her claim was that, in general, any patient is entitled to require from a treating doctor copies of all records relating to that patient for whatever purpose the patient has in mind. * * *

* * *

However, the appellant conceded that the right which she asserted must be subject to qualification. She accepted that "a doctor may withhold information where disclosure would be adverse to the patient's interests" and referred to this as the "therapeutic privilege".

The trial judge refused the appellant the relief which she sought. She appealed to the New South Wales Court of Appeal which, by a majority (Mahoney and Meagher JJA; Kirby P dissenting), dismissed the appeal. It is from the order of the Court of Appeal that the appellant now appeals to this court.

* * *

Proprietary right of interest

The appellant's contention is * * * that the information contained in the records can be separated from the records themselves and it is in the information that the appellant has a proprietary right or interest entitling her to access to the records. But there can be no proprietorship in information as information, because once imparted by one person to another, it belongs equally to them both. It is true, that equity acts to protect confidential information and the degree of protection afforded makes it appropriate to describe it as having a proprietary character, but that is not because property is the basis upon which protection is given. It is because of the effect of that protection. In this case, while the information provided by the appellant to the respondent was no doubt confidential, there is no question of any abuse by the respondent of that confidence and there is no property in that information in any sense upon which the appellant might base the right which she asserts.

* * *

Fiduciary duty

Whilst duties of a fiduciary nature may be imposed upon a doctor, they are confined and do not cover the entire doctor-patient relationship. Thus a doctor is under a duty to protect the confidentiality of information given by a patient. And the doctor-patient relationship is such that any substantial benefit received by the doctor from a patient (other than proper remuneration) is presumed to be the result of undue influence with the doctor bearing the onus of rebutting the presumption. Whether these aspects of the doctor-patient relationship are properly to be described as fiduciary may be a matter of debate. For example, in *Moorgate Tobacco Co Ltd v Philip Morris Ltd (No 2)*, Deane J saw the protection afforded by equity to confidential information as something separate from a wider fiduciary duty arising from the general nature of a relationship. Similarly, academic writers have classified the doctrine of undue influence as standing apart from a more general fiduciary doctrine. But the debate is not worth pursuing in the present context because it is plain that the appellant relies upon a wider fiduciary relationship between her and the respondent as giving rise to a duty on the part of the respondent to afford her access to her medical records.

The difficulty in dealing with the appellant's contention is that the law has not, as yet, been able to formulate any precise or comprehensive definition of the circumstances in which a person is constituted a fiduciary in his or her relations with another. There are accepted fiduciary relationships, such as trustee and beneficiary, agent and principal, solicitor and client, employee and employer, director and company, and partners, which may be characterised as relations of trust and confidence. In *Hospital Products Ltd v United States Surgical Corp* Mason J said:

> The critical feature of these relationships is that the fiduciary undertakes or agrees to act for or on behalf of or in the interests of another person in the exercise of a power or discretion which will affect the interests of that other person in a legal or practical sense. The relationship between the parties is therefore one which gives the fiduciary a special opportunity to exercise the power or discretion to the detriment of that other person who is accordingly vulnerable to abuse by the fiduciary of his position. The expressions "for", "on behalf of", and "in the interests of" signify that the fiduciary acts in a "representative" character in the exercise of his responsibility.

* * * It is not the case that whenever there is "a job to be performed", and entrusting the job to someone involves reposing substantial trust and confidence in that person, a fiduciary relationship arises. But it is of significance that a fiduciary acts in a representative character in the exercise of his responsibility.

A doctor is bound to exercise reasonable skill and care in treating and advising a patient, but in doing so is acting, not as a representative of the patient, but simply in the exercise of his or her professional responsibilities. No doubt the patient places trust and confidence in the doctor, but it is not because the doctor acts on behalf of the patient; it is because the patient is entitled to expect the observance of professional standards by the doctor in matters of treatment and advice and is afforded remedies in contract and tort if those standards are not observed and the patient suffers damage.

Equity requires that a person under a fiduciary obligation should not put himself or herself in a position where interest and duty conflict or, if conflict is unavoidable, should resolve it in favour of duty and, except by special arrangement, should not make a profit out of the position. The application of that requirement is quite inappropriate in the treatment of a patient by a doctor or in the giving of associated advice. There the duty of the doctor is established both in contract and in tort and it is appropriately described in terms of the observance of a standard of care and skill rather than, inappropriately, in terms of the avoidance of a conflict of interest. It has been observed that what the law exacts in a fiduciary relationship is loyalty, often of an uncompromising kind, but no more than that. The concern of the law in a fiduciary relationship is not negligence or breach of contract. Yet it is the law of negligence and contract which governs the duty of a doctor towards a patient. This leaves no need, or even room, for the imposition of fiduciary obligations. Of course, fiduciary duties may be superimposed upon contractual obligations and it is conceivable that a doctor may place himself in a position with potential for a conflict of interest—if, for example, the doctor has a financial interest in a hospital or a pathology laboratory—so as to give rise to fiduciary obligations. But that is not this case.

* * *

The appellant relied upon the decision of the Canadian Supreme Court in *McInerney v MacDonald*, in which La Forest J, delivering the judgment of the court, held that a patient is entitled to reasonable access to examine and copy the doctor's records. * * * In basing the duty upon a fiduciary relationship, La Forest J was giving expression to the view that it is the duty of the doctor to act with "utmost good faith and loyalty". Such a duty hardly fits with the undoubted duty of a doctor in this country to exercise reasonable skill and care in the giving of treatment and advice. It is, perhaps, reflective of a tendency, not found in this country, but to be seen in the United States and to a lesser extent Canada, to view a fiduciary relationship as imposing obligations which go beyond the exaction of loyalty and as displacing the role hitherto played by the law of contract and tort by becoming an independent source of positive obligations and creating new forms of civil wrong. But, with respect, that is achieved by assertion rather than analysis and, while it may effectuate a preference for a particular result, it does not involve the development or elucidation of any accepted doctrine. There is no foundation in either principle or authority in this country, however different the position may be in Canada, for the conclusion reached by La Forest J that:

> information about oneself revealed to a doctor acting in a professional capacity remains, in a fundamental sense, one's own. The doctor's position is one of trust and confidence. The information conveyed is held in a fashion somewhat akin to a trust. While the doctor is the owner of the actual record, the information is

> to be used by the physician for the benefit of the patient. The confiding of the information to the physician for medical purposes gives rise to an expectation that the patient's interest in and control of the information will continue.

It should be observed in relation to that passage that the court was not concerned in that case, as we are not in this, with a patient's right to information. It was concerned with access to the actual records containing the information, notwithstanding that in places the passage appears to regard "information" as interchangeable with "the actual record".

In England, s 3 of the Access to Health Records Act 1990 (UK) gives a prima facie right of access to health records by the individuals to whom they relate and other persons, but s 5(1) provides:

> Access shall not be given under section 3(2) above to any part of a health record:
>
> (a) which, in the opinion of the holder of the record, would disclose:
>
> (i) information likely to cause serious harm to the physical or mental health of the patient or of any other individual; or
>
> (ii) information relating to or provided by an individual, other than the patient, who could be identified from that information; or
>
> (b) which was made before the commencement of this Act.

That Act was passed as a result of the decision of the European Court of Human Rights in *Gaskin v United Kingdom* which held that the refusal to allow access by the applicant to certain health records was in breach of his right to respect for his private and family life under Art 8 of the European Convention for the Protection of Human Rights and Fundamental Freedoms 1950.

In *R v Mid Glamorgan Family Health Services* the Court of Appeal upheld a decision by Popplewell J dismissing an application by a patient for access to his medical records. Popplewell J was of the view that there had been no breach of Art 8 because the respondent had offered to make available the records (which predated the 1990 Act) to an independent medical adviser who might judge whether the information was likely to cause harm to the applicant or anyone else. However, he reached "the clearest possible conclusion" that at common law there was no right of access by the applicant to records pre-existing the Access to Health Records Act. In the Court of Appeal Nourse LJ (with whom the other members of the Court agreed) referred in his judgment to the well-known passage in the speech of Lord Templeman in *Sidaway v Governors of Bethlem Royal Hospital* in which he said:

> I do not subscribe to the theory that the patient is entitled to know everything nor to the theory that the doctor is entitled to decide everything. The relationship between doctor and patient is contractual in origin, the doctor performing services in consideration for fees payable by the patient. The doctor, obedient to the high standards set by the medical profession impliedly contracts to act at all times in the best interests of the patient. No doctor in his senses would impliedly contract at the same time to give to the patient all the information available to the doctor as a result of the doctor's training and experience and as a result of the doctor's diagnosis of the patient. An obligation to give a patient all the information available to the doctor would often be inconsistent with the doctor's contractual obligation to have regard to the patient's best interests. Some information might confuse, other information might alarm a particular patient. Whenever the occasion arises for the doctor to tell the patient the results of the doctor's diagnosis, the possible methods of treatment and the advantages and dis-

advantages of the recommended treatment, the doctor must decide in the light of his training and experience and in the light of his knowledge of the patient what should be said and how it should be said.

* * *

For these reasons, we would dismiss the appeal.

Brennan CJ.

The circumstances which give rise to the issues in this appeal are set out in other judgments. The appellant, who has been a patient of the respondent medical practitioner, claims a legal right to reasonable access to the records kept by the respondent with respect to the appellant and a right to inspect and/or copy those records. Subject to certain admitted exceptions, the appellant submits that that right is enforceable by declaration and injunction. The right is submitted to be based variously on contract, property and fiduciary duty. In my view, none of these bases gives any support to the appellant's claim. * * *

* * *

Contract

In the absence of special contract between a doctor and a patient, the doctor undertakes by the contract between them to advise and treat the patient with reasonable skill and care. The consideration for the undertaking may be either a payment, or promise of payment, of reward or submission by the patient, or an undertaking by the patient to submit, to the treatment proposed. A duty, similar to the duty binding on the doctor by contract, is imposed on the doctor by the law of torts. The advice and treatment required to fulfil either duty depends on the history and condition of the patient, the facilities available and all the other circumstances of the case.

The provision of advice and treatment with reasonable skill and care may not exhaust the duty of the doctor. Unless the contract between doctor and patient is especially restricted, the doctor's obligation is to maintain or improve the health of the patient generally and to use reasonable skill and care in doing so, even though the advice or treatment required on a particular occasion is in a specialist field or is to be provided only on that occasion or for a limited time. * * *

In some situations, there may be a duty to provide to the patient, or to the patient's nominee, information which the doctor has acquired in the course or for the purpose of advising or treating the patient. That is information received or otherwise acquired by the doctor pursuant to an authority given—expressly or impliedly—by the patient for the purpose of enabling the doctor to perform the doctor's contractual duty to maintain or improve the health of the patient generally. Absent the patient's permission, the doctor must not use that information for any other purpose. When the future medical treatment or physical or mental well-being of a patient might be prejudiced by an absence of information about the history or condition or treatment of the patient on an earlier occasion, the doctor who has acquired that information for the benefit of the patient's health must make it available to avoid or diminish that prejudice. Such an obligation is implied by the doctor's acceptance of the patient's authority under the contract to obtain that information. The authority is given in order to benefit the patient's health generally; the authority must be accepted and acted upon for the same purpose. As the obligation is implied, it can be excluded by express provision.

The obligation is not unqualified. As it arises from and is conditioned by the doctor's duty to benefit the patient's health generally, the obligation falls to be discharged only when the patient's health would or might be prejudiced by refusing to make the information available. And, as the service of making the information available is not ordinarily covered by the fee paid for advice or treatment, the doctor is entitled to a reasonable reward for the service.

For these reasons, I would hold that information with respect to a patient's history, condition or treatment obtained by a doctor in the course or for the purpose of giving advice or treatment to the patient must be disclosed by the doctor to the patient or the patient's nominee on request when (1) refusal to make the disclosure requested might prejudice the general health of the patient, (2) the request for disclosure is reasonable having regard to all the circumstances, and (3) reasonable reward for the service of disclosure is tendered or assured. A similar duty may be imposed on the doctor by the law of torts * * *.

An undertaking to provide information is one thing; a duty to give the patient access to, and to permit the patient to copy, the doctor's records is another. The doctor's duty to provide information not only can be discharged, but in some circumstances ought to be discharged, without allowing the patient to see the doctor's records. Where that duty can be performed without giving the patient access to the doctor's records, there is no foundation for implying any obligation to give that access. * * *

The appellant argued for an implied term in the contract between the appellant and respondent that the respondent would act in the appellant's "best interests", even to the extent of testifying for her in litigation. The propounded "best interests" obligation was said to encompass an obligation to give a patient access to the doctor's records. The term implied in the ordinary contract does not go so far. It is limited by the subject matter to which the contract relates, namely, benefiting the health of the patient.

* * * In the present case, it is not suggested that access to the respondent's records is needed for any therapeutic reason. Nor could such a suggestion be made. The respondent made an open offer to provide a report in writing relating to the history, physical examination findings, investigation results, diagnosis, proposed management plan, treatment or advice furnished to the appellant. That offer, if accepted and if fulfilled, would have discharged any obligation that might have arisen by implication from the contract between the parties. The offer was not accepted, the appellant contending not for a right to be informed but for a right of access to the doctor's records. As the contract between the appellant and respondent was wholly effective without any term entitling the appellant to access to the respondent's records and requiring the respondent to give that access, there is no foundation for implying such a term. Accordingly, the first basis of the appellant's claim fails.

Property

The appellant concedes that the property in the records as chattels is in the respondent. The concession is rightly made. Documents prepared by a professional person to assist the professional to perform his or her professional duties are not the property of the lay client; they remain the property of the professional. In the light of that principle, it is not easy to see what relevance the law of property has to the supposed right of the appellant to access to the respondent's records. If (as it was put during argument) the respondent is said to have no proprietary right that would entitle him to refuse access, the question whether the appellant has a right to be given access still remains. On that approach, the supposed right (if any) must find some basis other than property. But even on that approach, the argument is flawed. Absent some right to require, or the exercise of some power to compel, production of a document for inspection, its owner is entitled by virtue of the rights of ownership to refuse to produce it. As for copying, where the professional person is the owner of the copyright, he or she has the sole right to copy or to permit the copying of the document.

If the approach is that a right to access and to copy arises because the information contained in the records is proprietary in nature, the approach mistakes the sense in which information is described as property. * * *

* * *

Equity might restrain the respondent from disclosing without authority any information about the appellant and her medical condition that is contained in the respondent's records and, in that sense, it might be arguable that that information is the property of the appellant. Even if such a description were correct—and it is not necessary to consider that question—the description would provide no foundation for the existence of a right to access and to copy enforceable in equity. * * * There is no obligation in conscience requiring the respondent to open his records to inspection and copying by the appellant. Whichever approach is taken to the relevance of the law of property, it fails to provide any basis for the appellant's claim.

Fiduciary Duty

Fiduciary duties arise from either of two sources, which may be distinguished one from the other but which frequently overlap. One source is agency; the other is a relationship of ascendancy or influence by one party over another, or dependence or trust on the part of that other. Whichever be the source of the duty, it is necessary to identify "the subject matter over which the fiduciary obligations extend". It is erroneous to regard the duty owed by a fiduciary to his beneficiary as attaching to every aspect of the fiduciary's conduct, however irrelevant that conduct may be to the agency or relationship that is the source of fiduciary duty.

As Mason J said in *Hospital Products Ltd v United States Surgical Corp*: "it is now acknowledged generally that the scope of the fiduciary duty must be moulded according to the nature of the relationship and the facts of the case."

* * *

What is the nature of the doctor-patient relationship? Generally there is no relationship of agency. But the relationship of doctor and patient is one where the doctor acquires an ascendancy over the patient and the patient is in a position of reposing trust in the doctor. Such a relationship casts upon the doctor the onus of proving that any gift received from the patient was given free from the influence which the relationship produces. But in this case the doctor has received no gift; he has taken no step to procure an advantage for himself. Nor has he taken any advantage of his ascendancy over his patient or of her trust in him. His refusal to give access to his records does not deny his patient a benefit to which the patient was entitled either by reason of his position as the appellant's medical adviser and provider of medical treatment or by reason of the trust she reposed in him to provide medical treatment. In Canada, the Supreme Court has held that the relationship between doctor and patient casts on the doctor a fiduciary duty to provide the patient with access to his or her medical records: *McInerney v MacDonald*. But in this respect the notion of fiduciary duty in Canada does not accord with the notion in the United Kingdom. Nor, in my opinion, does the Canadian notion accord with the law of fiduciary duty as understood in this country. There is simply no fiduciary relationship which gives rise to a duty to give access to or to permit the copying of the respondent's records. There is no relevant subject matter over which the respondent's fiduciary duty extended.

* * *

The appeal should be dismissed.

Gaudron and McHugh JJ.

* * *

Australian courts have consciously refrained from attempting to provide a general test for determining when persons or classes of persons stand in a fiduciary relationship with one another. * * *

As the law stands, the doctor-patient relationship is not an accepted fiduciary relationship in the sense that the relationships of trustee and beneficiary, agent and principal, solicitor and client, employee and employer, director and company and partners are recognised as fiduciary relationships. In Hospital Products, Mason J pointed out that in all those relationships "the fiduciary acts in a 'representative' character in the exercise of his responsibility". But a doctor is not generally or even primarily a representative of his patient.

However, the categories of fiduciary relationship are not closed, and the courts have identified various circumstances that, if present, point towards, but do not determine, the existence of a fiduciary relationship. These circumstances, which are not exhaustive and may overlap, have included: the existence of a relation of confidence; inequality of bargaining power; an undertaking by one party to perform a task or fulfil a duty in the interests of another party; the scope for one party to unilaterally exercise a discretion or power which may affect the rights or interests of another; and a dependency or vulnerability on the part of one party that causes that party to rely on another.

Some aspects of the doctor-patient relationship exhibit characteristics that courts have used to find a fiduciary relationship. For example, from the most mundane consultation with a general practitioner through to the most complicated surgical procedure by a specialist surgeon, a patient is invariably dependent upon the advice and treatment of his or her doctor. Patients also invariably confide intimate personal details about themselves to their doctors. In some circumstances, the dependency of the patient or the provision of confidential information may make the relationship between a doctor and patient fiduciary in nature. But that does not mean that their relationship would be fiduciary for all purposes. * * *

* * * In the present case, if Dr Williams owed a fiduciary duty to Ms Breen, the duties and obligations which arose from their fiduciary relationship could only come from those aspects of the relationship which exhibited the characteristics of trust, confidence and vulnerability that typify the fiduciary relationship. They could only attach in respect of matters that relate to diagnosis, advice and treatment.

A consideration of the fundamental obligations of a fiduciary shows that Dr Williams owed no fiduciary duty to Ms Breen to give her access to the records that he had created. The law of fiduciary duty rests not so much on morality or conscience as on the acceptance of the implications of the biblical injunction that "[n]o man can serve two masters". Duty and self-interest, like God and Mammon, make inconsistent calls on the faithful. Equity solves the problem in a practical way by insisting that fiduciaries give undivided loyalty to the persons whom they serve * * *.

* * *

In the present case, there was no breach of fiduciary duty in the conditional denial of access because there was no pre-existing duty on the part of Dr Williams to give access to the records.

* * *

The right of access claimed by Ms Breen is not one given by the contract between her and Dr Williams. Nor can it arise from any undertaking, express or implied, by Dr Williams to act as the representative of Ms Breen because no such undertaking was given. Moreover, the contract between the parties gives her no right to or interest in the medical records. They remain the property of Dr Williams. Furthermore, a fiduciary duty that Dr Williams would always act in Ms Breen's best interests, which is the foundation of the claim of a fiduciary obligation to provide access to the records, would conflict with the narrower contractual and tortious duty to exercise reasonable care and skill in the provision of professional advice and treatment that Dr Williams undertook.

In addition, Dr Williams is the owner of the copyright in the records. By federal law, ownership of the copyright gives Dr Williams a number of exclusive proprietary rights including the right to reproduce the records in any material form. He is the beneficial owner of those rights. He does not hold them on trust for Ms Breen. In the absence of an undertaking, express or implied, on the part of Dr Williams to allow her to copy the records, it is difficult to see how Ms Breen could be allowed to copy the records even if she had a right of access to the records.

In our view, there is no basis upon which this court can hold that Dr Williams owed Ms Breen a fiduciary duty to give her access to the medical records. She seeks to impose fiduciary obligations on a class of relationship which has not traditionally been recognised as fiduciary in nature and which would significantly alter the already existing complex of legal doctrines governing the doctor-patient relationship, particularly in the areas of contract and tort. * * *

Fiduciary duties should not be superimposed on these common law duties simply to improve the nature or extent of the remedy.

Dr Cashman [the appellant's lawyer] relied strongly on the decision of the Supreme Court of Canada in *McInerney v MacDonald* to support his contention that Dr Williams owed Ms Breen a fiduciary duty to give her access to the medical records.

* * *

[T]he Canadian law on fiduciary duties is very different from the law of this country with respect to that subject. One commentator has recently pointed to the "vast differences between Australia and Canada in understanding of the nature of fiduciary obligations". One significant difference is the tendency of Canadian courts to apply fiduciary principles in an expansive manner so as to supplement tort law and provide a basis for the creation of new forms of civil wrongs. The Canadian cases also reveal a tendency to view fiduciary obligations as both proscriptive and prescriptive. However, Australian courts only recognise proscriptive fiduciary duties. This is not the place to explore the differences between the law of Canada and the law of Australia on this topic. With great respect to the Canadian courts, however, many cases in that jurisdiction pay insufficient regard to the effect that the imposition of fiduciary duties on particular relationships has on the law of negligence, contract, agency, trusts and companies in their application to those relationships. * * *

In this country, fiduciary obligations arise because a person has come under an obligation to act in another's interests. As a result, equity imposes on the fiduciary proscriptive obligations—not to obtain any unauthorised benefit from the relationship and not to be in a position of conflict. If these obligations are breached, the fiduciary must account for any profits and make good any losses arising from the breach. But the law of this country does not otherwise impose positive legal duties on the fiduciary to act in the interests of the person to whom the duty is owed. If there was a general fiduciary duty to act in the best interests of the patient, it would necessarily follow that a doctor has a duty to inform the patient that he or she has breached their contract or has been guilty of negligence in dealings with the patient. That is not the law of this country.

* * *

The appeal should be dismissed.

[Opinion of Gummow, J. omitted.]

Notes

Patients in Australia now have a general right to have access to and to copy their medical records, subject to certain exceptions (for example, to protect the privacy of third parties) under the Privacy Amendment (Private Sector) Act, 2000. See National Privacy Principles, http://www.privacy.gov.au/publications/npps01.html.

2. Note the role that equity and the concepts of beneficial ownership in trust and fiduciary obligations play in these cases. For one thing, they make it possible to think about patients having an interest in their medical information, even though both courts accept that the legal ownership of the records rests in the physicians. The trust idea, of course, grows out of the medieval division between the English courts of law and Chancery, and has no exact equivalent in the civil law. In this instance, the common law has a means of flexibility not available in the civil law.

3. The notion of the fiduciary nature of the doctor/patient relationship has often played a key role in American decisions. The *Canterbury* decision, discussed in the preceding section, and American cases following it, relied in part on this relationship. The judges in *Breen* accept that a doctor has a fiduciary obligation not to take advantage of a patient financially, even if they reject the argument as a means to gain access to patient records. This obligation forms the basis of American prohibitions against bribes and kickbacks and self-referrals in American fraud and abuse law. See Barry R. Furrow et al., *Health Law Hornbook*, 637ff (2nd ed. 2000). Though fraud and abuse is an issue in other countries, it lacks elsewhere the political saliency that it enjoys in the United States. Why should this be true?

4. Note the rather different understanding of the notion of fiduciary that is found in these two cases. *McInerney* sees the doctor as being a fiduciary with respect to the patient, but describes the patient as a consumer. Does not the notion of a consumer assume an at-arms-length relationship, a relationship of reciprocity—rather than a relationship of dependence? *Breen* rejects the fiduciary analogy, because the relationship between doctor and patient, though characterized in part by ascendancy and dependancy, is not one of representation. The duty owed by the doctor to the patient, therefore, is one of skill and competence (based in tort and contract), not of fiduciary loyalty. *Breen* seems to take

a more paternalistic approach to the doctor/patient relationship, but in the end refuses to impose paternal obligations on the doctor.

5. The European Council Convention on Human Rights and Biomedicine embraces a principle of access to medical information, so this issue should become less contested in Europe. See Article 12(2), a principle that would be binding in the U.K. As recently as 1995, however, the British Court of Appeal rejected a claim of access to medical records. *R. v. Mid Glamorgan Family Health Services*, 1 All.E.R. 356 [1995], as noted in the Dawson and Toohey opinion.

Chapter 3

The Patient's Right to Self-Determination and Competing Considerations

A. Abortion

There are few legal issues that provoke such heated debate in the United States as abortion. This is true in many other countries as well, but certainly not in all. In some countries, as in the United States, the opposition to abortion is based on religious convictions, and thus the debate raises issues pertaining to the relationship between a dominant religion and the state. The Irish Constitution, for example, specifically recognizes a right to life in the unborn, and attempts to weaken the opposition of the Irish state to abortion have been vigorously opposed by the Catholic church. In Poland, another state in which the Catholic church is very influential, the permissive 1956 law adopted under the Communist regime, which permitted abortion because of "difficult living conditions," was replaced after the fall of Communism with a much more restrictive law. The Catholic states of southern Germany have led the opposition to liberalization of the German abortion laws. In Belgium a stalemate that had existed for two decades between a parliament that wanted to liberalize one of the most restrictive abortion laws in Europe and a devout Catholic king who would have no part of it was broken in 1990 when parliament suspended the king's reign for one night to allow the law to go into effect. In Iran, a law that liberally permitted abortion, adopted under the Shah, was replaced after the 1979 revolution with a law that made abortion illegal except where necessary to save the life of the pregnant woman. In Japan, in which Buddhism, Confucianism, and Shintoism are all influential, Shinto promotion of reproduction has contributed in part to a legal ban on birth control pills, in place until 1999, which in turn contributed to a high rate of abortion as a birth control method. See, discussing the Japanese situation, Sara Walsh, Liquid Lives and Liquid Laws: The Evolution of Abortion Law in Japan and the United States, 7 *Int'l Legal Persp.* 187 (1995); Evy F. McElmeel, Legalization of the Birth Control Pill in Japan will Reduce Reliance on Abortion as the Primary Method of Birth Control, 8 *Pac.Rim. L. & Pol'y J.* 681 (1999).

In some countries population policy plays a more important role than religion in determining abortion laws, although the two are often, as in Japan, interrelated. The most rigorous ban on abortion in modern history was probably found in Romania, where the Ceauşescu regime in the 1960s adopted a strong pro-natal policy, declaring the fetus the property of the state, and vigorously prosecuting abortion. Women were examined monthly at their place of work to identify pregnancies, and women who had an illegal abortion were subject to two years in prison and were denied medical care if the abortion was botched and the woman refused to identify the abortionist. In other countries, such as Russia, abortion has been used as a relatively inexpensive means of birth control, though with high costs in terms of maternal life and health. Under China's one-child policy, abortion on demand is not only permitted, but encouraged. Abortion is paid for by the state, and the woman who receives it is given fourteen days of paid sick leave for a first-trimester abortion, thirty days for a later abortion.

In many developing countries abortion practice, if not policy, is driven by economic considerations. Where both conventional birth control and additional children are unaffordable, abortion (or infanticide) remains the most viable alternative when more primitive approaches to birth control fail. If legal abortions are unaffordable (where laws require abortions to be done in hospitals or done by licensed physicians, for example), illegal abortions become common. Making safe and effective contraception widely available, therefore, may be the most effective means of discouraging abortion in these countries. In some countries, however, abortion is also used as a means of sex selection, which often is in turn driven by economic reasons, as boys are more likely to be able to provide security to their parents in old age. India permits abortion, but outlaws abortion for selection of sex, though the law is apparently widely violated. See Azim A. Khan Sherwani and M. Minhajul Haq, Illegal Abortion and Women's Reproductive Health, 3 *Med. L. Int'l.* 223 (1998). The readings that follow further examine abortion law and policy throughout the world.

Abortion Policies: A Global Review

United Nations, 1–2, 4–7 (2003)

* * *

Although abortion is commonly practised throughout most of the world and has been practised since long before the beginning of recorded history, it is a subject that arouses passion and controversy. Abortion raises fundamental questions about human existence, such as when life begins and what it is that makes us human. Abortion is at the heart of such contentious issues as the right of women to control their own bodies, the nature of the State's duty to protect the unborn, the tension between secular and religious views of human life and the individual and society, the rights of spouses and parents to be involved in the abortion decision, and the conflicting rights of the mother and the foetus. Also central to the subject of abortion is one of the most highly controversial social issues of all, sexuality. * * *

* * *

* * * [T]he legal provisions governing abortion in many countries are not always conveniently located within one text. The most common place in which such provisions appear is a country's criminal code or criminal laws relating to offences against persons, for abortion has, at least in the last two centuries, been considered a criminal offence of a highly serious nature. However, with the movement during the last half of the twentieth century to liberalize abortion laws, this is no longer invariably the case; consequently, legal provisions on abortion can be found in a variety of places. Some countries have incorporated liberalized abortion provisions into their criminal codes. Others have enacted special abortion laws that are separate from criminal codes. Thus it is possible for a criminal code to prohibit abortions, while a law on abortion will describe the circumstances under which abortions are allowed. In still other countries, public health codes or medical ethics codes may contain special provisions that clarify how to interpret an abortion law. For example, a medical ethics code may specify the circumstances under which it is ethically acceptable for a physician to perform an abortion. In a final group of countries, mostly common-law countries (see below), abortion may not be governed by a specific law, but by a court decision. In a few cases, the existence of multiple texts, each with con-

flicting provisions, can make it difficult to determine the exact nature of the law and policy concerning abortion in a specific country.

* * *

* * * Most common law countries, other than the United States, have abortion laws that are based on various English laws and court decisions. Some take as their model the Offences Against the Person Act of 1861. Under this Act it was prohibited "unlawfully" to use any means to procure an abortion either for oneself or for another person or unlawfully to supply means for that end, and the prescribed punishment was imprisonment. Originally, this Act was interpreted as prohibiting all abortions, except those performed on the grounds of necessity, in order to save the life of the pregnant woman. Other countries follow the English court decision, *Rex* v. *Bourne*, in which it was held that abortions performed for serious physical or mental health reasons would not be considered "unlawful" under the 1861 Act. Still other countries have looked to the British Abortion Act of 1967, which sets forth broad health, foetal impairment, and socio-economic indications for abortions, in general until the twenty-fourth week of pregnancy.

The abortion laws of many civil law countries are based on the abortion provisions of the French Napoleonic Code of 1810, the 1939 French version of that Code or the 1979 abortion law of France. Under the 1810 Napoleonic Code, any person who by any means procured the abortion of a pregnant woman was punished with imprisonment, as was a pregnant woman who procured her own abortion, although it was understood that an abortion could be performed when necessary to save the life of the pregnant woman. To the provisions of the 1810 Code, the 1939 French Penal Code added language specifically allowing an abortion to be performed to save the life of the pregnant woman. The 1979 Law allows a woman who is in a state of distress to have an abortion performed on request during the first ten weeks of pregnancy after she undergoes counselling and waits a week, and later in pregnancy on other serious grounds. In contrast to the common law system, court interpretations of these laws play a minor role.

Unlike the situation in either the common law or civil law countries, no single abortion text or court case can be identified as the model for most modern Islamic abortion laws. The Quran and the *sunnah*, the two primary sources of Islamic law, do not deal specifically with abortion. Moreover, until recently, Islamic criminal laws were not always codified. Consequently, Islamic law adopts a number of approaches towards abortion, depending upon which of the five major schools of Islamic law is followed. In general, the attitude of Islamic law towards abortion is dependent upon whether the abortion is performed before ensoulment, the time at which a foetus gains a soul. This is most often viewed as occurring 120 days into a pregnancy, but is also interpreted as occurring at 40 days. Some schools permit abortion for justifiable reasons before ensoulment, while others generally prohibit it at all points of pregnancy. All schools, however, allow abortion at any time during pregnancy in order to save the life of the pregnant woman. In contrast to the situation under both common law and civil law, the punishment for abortion under classic Islamic law is payment of a sum of money to the relatives of the foetus. The amount of payment depends upon the stage of pregnancy reached at the time of the abortion. * * *

Owing to the different treatments of abortion in these three legal systems, a number of ambiguities arise in interpreting specific indications for abortion, making any comparison challenging. The most widely accepted indication for abortion—to save the life of the pregnant woman—provides a good example. Broadly speaking, this indication is valid in two categories of countries: those with abortion laws that specifically mention it and those with laws in which it is not mentioned but is inferred from the general criminal-law principles of necessity. In the latter, an abortion, although considered illegal, can be performed on the rationale that it is necessary to preserve a greater good, the life of the pregnant woman.

In practical terms, these two situations differ substantially. In the first, a physician contemplating the performance of an abortion is able to point to a specific legal provision authorizing such an act and be reasonably certain that he or she was acting within the law. In the second, no such certainty exists, only a general principle that could be raised as a defence if the physician were prosecuted for performing an illegal abortion. It would then be a matter for a court to determine after a trial. The result is that in the latter case, a physician would in general exercise much more caution in determining whether to perform an abortion to save the life of the pregnant woman.

A similar situation arises with respect to laws that permit an abortion to be performed to preserve the health of a pregnant woman. An important distinction holds between countries with laws that specifically state that an abortion is allowed to preserve the health of a pregnant woman and countries in which a court or courts have, through their interpretation of a law that lacks specific provisions, allowed such an abortion to take place. In the former, a physician can be reasonably certain of acting within the law; again, in the latter, he or she might have to rely on a court decision as a defence in criminal proceedings. * * *

Additional ambiguities are connected with the health indication for abortion. One is that a number of countries use the term "health" in their abortion laws without specifying what it encompasses. Thus it is unclear whether they intend abortions to be allowed in cases of threat to mental and physical health or only physical health. * * * The question arises as to whether health should be interpreted as historically understood or in the light of current thinking. Similarly, unless a country specifies that the threat must be serious or grave or permanently disabling, it is unclear what degree of threat to health is intended.

Other terms referring to health are even more ambiguous. Some countries allow abortions for "therapeutic" purposes or permit abortions for the purpose of "medical or surgical treatment." Others provide that the threat to health by continuation of the pregnancy must be greater than the threat posed by its termination. Statistically, during the first trimester, a pregnancy is always a greater threat to health than its termination; it is therefore difficult to determine how to interpret this phrase. A literal interpretation would allow abortion under most circumstances. Given such a lack of clarity in the laws, the designation of a country as allowing abortions for health purposes can cover a wide variety of situations. These range from allowing abortion only in cases that threaten permanent and serious damage to physical health, to cases that threaten mental health owing to socio-economic distress, to the case of "medical or surgical treatment", which is essentially abortion on request. Unless the issue has been the subject of litigation in the courts, or a target of significant legal analysis of the nature of the threat in legal commentaries, it is difficult to ascertain exactly what the circumstances must be to justify an abortion.

Procedural requirements to establish the presence of an indication for abortion are also a factor in determining the exact nature of an indication for abortion. In the context of the indication of health, it may be necessary for two or three physicians to attest to the threat to health. A great deal of difference exists between this and the situation in which the physician who is willing to perform the abortion is the only judge of whether the indication is present. In the context of abortions performed in cases of pregnancy due to rape or incest, a variety of mandated procedures also prevail. In some countries, the incident of rape or incest must be reported to police or judicial authorities, while in others the pregnant woman must only reasonably believe that the pregnancy was the result of rape or incest. Some specify no procedural requirements or, conversely, require a judicial determination that the pregnancy was the result of rape or incest. Such differences again produce a significant variation on the nature of the indication of pregnancy due to rape or incest in various countries.

The terminology employed under Islamic law presents another formidable challenge in comparing abortion laws. The principles underlying Islamic law differ fundamentally from those of common and civil law, which have at the most basic level a Western orientation; it is therefore difficult to compare laws under the two systems. An example of this problem involves the notion under Islamic law that the crime of abortion is punished not by imprisonment and government-imposed fines, but by the payment of compensation by the perpetrator of the crime to the relatives of the victim of the crime. In the context of abortion, this is entirely foreign to Western law. The problem is also illustrated in the definition of the stages of pregnancy. While Western law does recognize different stages of pregnancy, in present-day law they are almost exclusively defined by weeks of gestation; under Islamic law they can be defined in more descriptive terms such as "the lump," "something that clings," "ensoulment," or "the forming of organs and limbs".

Beyond these conceptual challenges, determining whether the written law or policy of a country conforms to the practice observed or inferred remains a major problem. In many countries where the performance of abortions is generally illegal, statistics indicate that large numbers are being carried out, most of them illegally, with few prosecutions. Of the approximately 50 million abortions carried out every year in the world, estimates place the number performed illegally at 40 per cent. In these countries, law enforcement authorities ignore or tolerate the performance of illegal abortions or even unofficially license clinics for that purpose. A number of factors are responsible for this situation. Among these are the ease with which abortions can be performed, the lack of will or resources to prosecute, particularly in the light of more pressing social needs, and the clandestine nature of the procedure. In some countries where abortion is technically legal, access to authorized facilities and personnel may be limited, or resources to pay for the abortion may be lacking, resulting in more illegal abortions. In a few cases, although abortion is authorized, the Government may not have issued regulations allowing the law to be effectively implemented. In all of these situations, legal action is rarely taken except in the most egregious cases, usually involving the death of a pregnant woman. In some countries, the indifference to abortion is so great that most of those performing abortions or enforcing laws do not know what the provisions of the law actually are. The advent of new scientific developments such as RU 486, the so-called "abortion pill", which makes abortion even easier to perform without the need for special facilities, will in all probability only increase the gap between law and practice.

Note

In no country is abortion totally banned, even in Ireland and Iran a woman can obtain an abortion where necessary to save her life. On the other hand, in no country is abortion totally permitted. Even in Russia abortion is only available until twenty-eight weeks from conception, and after twelve weeks a justification must be given, though the grounds are very liberal. In China abortion is restricted in the last trimester. See generally, describing the law of abortion worldwide, Albin Eser and Hans-Georg Koch, *Abortion and the Law: From International Comparison to Legal Policy* (2005). Also, describing the law in Africa,

Charles Ngwena, An Appraisal of Abortion Laws in Southern Afria from a Reproductive Rights Perspective, 32 *J. Law, Med. & Ethics* 708 (2004). In many countries compromises have been reached for permitting, but regulating abortion, that have remained relatively stable. The state of the law in Western Europe is discussed in the following excerpt:

The Stability of Compromise: Abortion Politics in Western Europe

Joyce Outshoorn, 145, 146–153 in Abortion Politics: Public Policy in Cross-Cultural Perspective (Marianne Githens & Dorothy McBride Stetson, eds. 1996)

* * *

The Western European abortion situation is relatively stable (Table 1 gives the dates of the Western European abortion reforms). From Table 1 it can be observed that the high tide of the Western European abortion reform occurred in the period from 1970 to 1986. In that period, too, early reformers in Sweden and Denmark readjusted their legislation to guarantee women's control over abortion. France, where the abortion reform was first enacted as a provisionary measure, confirmed the reform in 1979. With the coming to power there of the left-wing coalition in 1982, the final reform took place, ensuring financial support by national insurance for women having abortions. In the mid-eighties only Ireland and Belgium (and the minor states of Monaco and Malta) had failed to liberalize their legislation, leaving intact very restrictive statutes dating back to the nineteenth century. After twenty years of debate, Belgium finally revised its abortion laws in 1990. * * * Ireland has stuck to its extremely conservative position, enforcing the existing prohibitive legislation by constitutional amendment in 1983. With the legal tangles around several Irish and European Court cases, the Maastricht Treaty, and the 1992 referendum, however, the first cracks are beginning to appear in the hitherto impenetrable Irish edifice. In Spain, further reform is pending; the Spanish government sent a new bill to parliament in June 1994 that aims at extending the grounds for abortion.

Table 1 Abortion in Western Europe: Year of Reform

Nation	Year
Switzerland	1942
Sweden	1960, 1967
Britain	1967
Denmark	1970, 1975
Finland	1970
Austria	1974
Iceland	1975
France	1975, 1979, 1982
Germany (West)	1976
Luxembourg	1978
Italy	1978
Greece	1978, 1986
Norway	1978, 1979
Netherlands	1981
Ireland	1983, 1992
Portugal	1984
Spain	1986
Belgium	1990

Until German Unification in 1990, no European nation, except for Ireland, had changed its laws in a more restrictive direction. Prior to unification, West Germany had reformed modestly in 1976, allowing abortion on a limited number of grounds, while East Germany had had an abortion-on-request law. After much controversy, the German parliament finally passed a very restrictive abortion bill in 1995. It allows for abortion until twelve weeks if a woman's mental or physical health is seriously endangered and has a small loophole for social grounds. Counseling for each woman is compulsory with the explicit aim of dissuading her from her intention to have an abortion.

For the purposes of comparison, several authors have endeavored to draw up a topology of laws. Most classifications distinguish term models from indication models. Term models have a time limit; up to a certain time, usually twelve weeks, abortion is permitted on request, with or without special requirements, after which another regime is operative, usually only allowing abortion for health reasons or in the case of deformity of the fetus. Term models also differ as to whether they set an upper time limit; several nations have no time limit if health reasons are involved. Sometimes it is hard to distinguish term models from indication models, as some term models allow abortion on request if the woman is in a "state of distress" (France) or in an "untenable emergency situation," which can only be alleviated by an abortion (the Netherlands, Belgium); this is a stipulation close to an indication, enacted with the intent of pacifying parliamentary opponents of abortion law reform.

Indication models allow for abortion on a number of grounds. These can be medical grounds (with attendant debates about whether this also covers mental health), or they can take into account damage to the fetus, or allow for socioeconomic problems. They usually also include cases of pregnancy after rape and incest. "Narrow" types only allow medical indications; the "broader" ones will include the socioeconomic grounds. Much earlier reform in Europe started off as an indication type of law; but generally speaking over the course of time these reforms have proved unworkable. They were not liberal enough to satisfy the demands for reform from the emerging women's movement and the more radical "traditional reformers" such as various family planning and sexual reform groups. Moreover, indications lead to continual controversy over the interpretation of what constitutes a permissible reason for an abortion, resulting in considerable inequality before the law, which undermines the law's legitimacy. Britain, with its very early 1967 Abortion Act, is a clear case in point. Like much early abortion legislation, it was only meant to be a limited reform, allowing doctors to perform abortion without running the risk of prosecution. An indication model was drawn up, leaving the decision and interpretation firmly in hands of the medical profession. Paradoxically, Britain today has one of the most restrictive regimes in Western Europe, a long cry from the day when women from all over Europe traveled there for an abortion which they could not obtain under their own country's law.

Generally speaking, term models are more liberal than indication models, but further analysis is needed to establish whether abortion on request is possible, how indications are interpreted, and whether women have decent access to an abortion. In addition, the crucial question of control cannot be read off from the above topology. Who actually decides about an abortion? The woman herself, or a doctor or even two doctors? In case of indication types of laws, it will be the doctor (and sometimes, as in Britain, Switzerland, and West Germany before 1993, two doctors) interpreting the permitted indications, in which case women are placed in a dependent position and have to plead their case. Term models score quite well in terms of control up to the time limit, after which the doctors also take over, defining the exceptions allowed under the law. The clauses in the law about the actual decision are often (deliberately) ambiguous, not explicitly allowing an abortion on request, but not ruling it out either. Despite such clauses, in countries like Ice-

Abortion in Practice

Table 2 Type of Abortion Legislation in Western Europe

Term Model *(Up to 12 Weeks)*	**Indications** *(Broad)*	**Indications** *(Narrow)*	*Illegal*
Austria	Britain	Portugal	Ireland
Belgium	Finland	Spain	Malta
Denmark	Italy	Germany	Monaco
France	Switzerland		
Greece			
Luxembourg			
Netherlands			
Norway			
Sweden			

land, Finland (with an indication model!), and the Netherlands, abortion on request is the normal situation. If a woman states she is in a situation of distress because of the pregnancy, and abortion is the only way out of this state of distress, the doctor accepts this and will limit his or her intervention to checking to ensure that the woman is not being coerced into the abortion by her partner or parents. Only in Sweden (since the amendments of 1975), Denmark (since the 1973 revision of its legislation), and Norway (the 1979 revision) is abortion on request explicitly written into the statutes.

One should bear in mind, though, that legislation is only half the story when examining whether women can obtain abortions on request and in how far they actually have access to abortion facilities. It is generally accepted that the availability of proper medical services and financial support are crucial in going beyond mere *de jure* provision. The differences in access for women in various Western European nations to abortion facilities therefore vary more than just by what the legal provisions may lead one to believe.

From the work of Ketting and van Praag, in which they compared nine Western European nations and the United States, one can derive several barriers to free abortion. First of all, there is the law itself. Does it allow for abortion on request or is the woman seeking an abortion dependent on others such as medical doctors? Does the framing of the law specify indications? Are there time limits after which abortion is not permitted? Is there a compulsory waiting period between approaching a doctor and the actual medical operation? Is registration of the operation required by statute? Is a second opinion of another doctor required? Is parental consent required in the case of minors? The consent of the father of the fetus is not required in any Western European statute. Is counseling required? Is advice on "solutions" other than abortion obligatory? Does it specify where abortions have to take place, for instance, only in hospitals?

Second, barriers to access can be found in the implementation of the legislation. This mainly revolves around the question of whether sufficient hospitals, clinics, and doctors willing to perform abortions are available. Institutional factors such as different hospital systems, the possibility to set up private clinics, and the presence of trained personnel are key factors here. Of extreme importance are the attitudes of hospital and clinic boards and personnel. Most European laws allow for a conscience clause, i.e., that personnel can refuse help in abortion cases for reasons of conscience. Doctors are not always obliged to refer the woman seeking an abortion to a more cooperative colleague; and sometimes these colleagues do not exist. Because of such limitations, in Roman Catholic regions and nations it has proved much more difficult to implement reform legislation. In the seventies, this factor was important in accounting for differences between nations. Relatively liberal laws in France were circumvented by conservative Catholic doctors and nursing staff, but the situation improved after the 1982 reform, which was also an attempt to compel hospitals to provide services. Availability remains a crucial problem in Spain and Portugal after their very limited reforms. Even women who fall under the cases delineated by the law have considerable difficulty in obtaining professional help. Needless to say, clandestine abortions continue to flourish: for Spain, estimates are around 70,000 a year; for Portugal, no figures are available.

Interregional discrepancies within nations can also be accounted for by this factor. Germany has had a North-South split in availability for years: the conservative Catholic Lander of Bavaria and Baden-Württemberg applied the 1976 regulation in the strictest manner possible, while in the northern (and Protestant) cities of Bremen and Hamburg facilities for abortion are widely available. In Italy abortion has remained inaccessible for poorer women from the rural South and in those areas where the Catholic Church has managed to retain control of the hospital services. In Austria, the Vienna district with its big-city secular tradition provides good facilities, in contrast to the rural and conservative districts of Tyrol and Salzburg. French-speaking Belgians found their way into clinics in their own part of the country, traditionally the industrialized and more secularized area, while Dutch-speaking Belgian women crossed over the Dutch border for their abortions for years through lack of similar facilities and an active prosecution policy in Flanders.

Because of these differences a lively traffic, often called "abortion-tourism" by anti-abortionists, has always been part of the European landscape. Before the major reforms of the seventies, Dutch women traveled to London, Austrians to Yugoslavia, and Scandinavians to Poland. From 1972 onward West Germans traveled to the Netherlands, as did the Belgians, the French, and the Spanish. The Irish are still traveling to England. One of the reasons that the incumbent government party, the Christian Democrats in Germany, was keen to develop one new federal law as part of the unification treaty was to prevent West German women traveling into the former Eastern Länder, where a term-law was operative since 1972, making abortion on request accessible for women until the twelfth week of pregnancy.

Although it can be argued that this abortion traffic can work as a safety valve, taking pressure off the necessity for reform, which has demonstrably been the case in Belgium, it is more likely that it has promoted the speed of the reforms. Countries were very much aware of what was going on across the border, and although authorities did try to interfere with women crossing over, in due course they also became convinced that the traffic could only be stopped by reform in their own countries. It also meant that abortion reform was not something distant or abstract happening in a totally different culture, but something going on right on your own doorstep. For this reason, the early reforms of Sweden and Britain had an impact going far beyond the material effect of allowing women from abroad to obtain an abortion. It brought home to other nations' political elites the issue that reform could not be avoided altogether.

At the stage of implementation, the monitoring of the law can provide barriers for women seeking an abortion. Usually the text of the law is in need of interpretation, giving doctors and women some leeway in how the abortion decision is taken. If, however, some form of registration is required of this process, doctors can be called to account for their interpretation. Through this channel, public prosecutors can restrict the workings of the law and limit access. This has been very much the case in Germany, where occasional prosecutions in the South kept doctors towing the line. In Spain a doctor was recently jailed for performing abortions, which, according to the prosecution and the court, were only made possible by his too-liberal reading of the indications allowed under Spanish law.

Finally, the cost of abortion is a potential barrier. In the early period of reform especially, when doctors often had to take risks to perform abortions, fees were high and only more affluent women were able to obtain a medically safe abortion. Today, fees are still high when abortion is taboo and not openly discussed, or when more abortions are *de jure* illegal, as in Portugal, Spain, and also in Switzerland. * * * The demand for the inclusion of abortion in a national health insurance scheme has therefore always been part of the demands of both the women's movements and the various reform groups. It also has been a concern shared by Western Europe's many socialist parties, who have included state funding in their party platforms. Reform groups providing abortion facilities in private clinics have always had reserve funds providing financial assistance to those women who could not afford to pay. They also kept their prices at an acceptable level. Once abortion became legalized, it also became possible to regulate abortion fees and put a rein on doctors' tendencies to use their monopoly to set prices at a profitable level. In most European nations today, national health insurance covers the cost of an abortion on condition of it being performed under the terms of its national legislation. This is not the case in Austria, however. In Britain, abortion is only refunded if it is done in one of the hospitals of the National Health Service, but only about half of all abortions are actually performed there. Half of all women go to private clinics and pay themselves. This is not only due to the long waiting lists of the National Health Service, but also because these abortions fall under the terms of the 1967 Abortion Act with its paternalistic treatment of women, requiring the consent of two doctors and their assessment of the indications as final.

Given the different barriers, it is very difficult to make an assessment of the access of women to abortion facilities and the *de facto* control over abortion decisions. On the basis of their extensive 1983 study of nine Western European states, Ketting and van Praag defined Sweden as the nation allowing women the greatest degree of self-determination, with Denmark and Austria as second, and the Netherlands, France, and Italy in third place. Assessment is difficult, however, as the weighing of the various factors operating in the matter of self-determination can hardly be done by objective indicators. In Ketting and van Praag's assessment, regional differences were not taken fully into account. This become apparent by looking at Austria and Italy, who end up high in this hierarchy, while both countries are characterized by a poor geographic spread of facilities. Traveling for an abortion is both a financial and psychological burden for women and does form a real barrier in a number of cases (especially for young women and poorer women).

Abortion rates are not good indicators of women's access to abortion facilities. They also do not say much about the effectiveness of abortion legislation. They do reflect several other extremely important indicators for women's health, which indirectly contribute to their self-determination. Low abortion figures indicate the level of knowledge about the availability and use of contraceptives and the presence of medical provisions and the level of sex education. * * * Henshaw and Morrow indicate that the Netherlands has the lowest abortion rate in the world, less than half of the English rate and one-fourth of the Danish and Swedish rate. It can also be noted that countries with a very low abortion rate, such as the Scandinavian nations and the Netherlands, also have the most liberal abortion regimes in Western Europe and probably in the world. This fact can be attributed to the widespread use of contraceptives and an open climate around sexuality and sex education at all schools. A careful assessment of the degree of self-determination for women in Western Europe today would therefore show that all Scandinavian countries and the Netherlands rate at the top. Falling below the average would be Germany, Britain, Italy, and drawing up the rear Spain, Portugal, and Ireland.

* * *

Notes

1. The reading mentions term and indication model abortion laws. Some authors, however, have noted a third model, the "counseling model" or "conflict (emergency)-oriented discourse model." See Eser & Koch, 298; Sjef Gevers, Abortion Legislation and the Future of the "Counseling Model," 13 *Eur. J. Health L.* 27 (2006). Under this model, the law establishes grounds (such as an emergency) under which an abortion is legal, but leaves the decision as to whether such grounds exist to the woman. She must make a careful decision, however, and to be open to being counseled. What are the advantages and disadvantages of this model?

2. Although religion seems to be a key factor in determining abortion policy, the religiosity of a country is not always directly related to the legal status of religion in that country. The United States, for example, prohibits the establishment of religion in its Constitution, while Great Britian has an established church. Politics in the United States, however, have been far more influenced by religious conviction than has been the case in Britain. This is quite evident in abortion policy. In Germany every state has its established church, yet only in the Catholic states of the south, Bavaria and Baden-Württemburg, has religion played a major role in abortion politics.

3. Economic facts are among the most important barriers to abortion in the world as a whole. Many women who would prefer to have an abortion simply cannot afford to have safe and legal abortions, or to travel to a region or country where abortions are available. In some instances, however, economic interests may lead to higher abortion rates. The long delay in the approval of oral contraceptives in Japan (until 1999), has been attributed in part to the power of the $400 million abortion industry.

4. The law of abortion has been constitutionalized to a greater extent than any other health law issue. In the following 1988 decision, the Canadian Supreme Court, for example, held the Canadian Criminal Code provisions on abortion to violate the pregnant woman's rights under the Canadian Bill of Rights and the Canadian Charter of Rights and Freedoms:

R. v. Morgentaler

(1988) 1 Can. S.C.R. 30, 44 D.L.R. (4th) 385, Supreme Court of Canada

Dickson C.J. and Beetz, Estey, McIntyre, Lamer, Wilson and La Forest JJ.

Dickson C.J. [Lamer J. concurring—] The principal issue raised by this appeal is whether the abortion provisions of the Criminal Code infringe the "right to life, liberty and security of the person and the right not to be deprived thereof except in accordance with the principles of fundamental justice" as formulated in s. 7 of the Canadian Charter of Rights and Freedoms. * * *

* * *

The Canadian Charter of Rights and Freedoms

> [Sec.] 1. The Canadian Charter of Rights and Freedoms guarantees the rights and freedoms set out in it subject only to such reasonable limits prescribed by law as can be demonstrably justified in a free and democratic society.
>
> [Sec.] 7. Everyone has the right to life, liberty and security of the person and the right not to be deprived thereof except in accordance with the principles of fundamental justice.

* * *

The three appellants are all duly qualified medical practitioners who together set up a clinic in Toronto to perform abortions upon women who had not obtained a certificate from a therapeutic abortion committee of an accredited or approved hospital as required by s. 251(4). The doctors had made public statements questioning the wisdom of the abortion laws in Canada and asserting that a woman has an unfettered right to choose whether or not an abortion is appropriate in her individual circumstances.

Indictments were preferred against the appellants charging that they conspired with each other between November 1982 and July 1983 with intent to procure the miscarriage of female persons, using an induced suction technique to carry out that intent, contrary to s. 423(1)(d) and s. 251(1) of the Criminal Code.

Counsel for the appellants moved to quash the indictment or to stay the proceedings before pleas were entered on the grounds that s. 251 of the Criminal Code * * * infringed ss. 2(a), 7 and 12 of the Charter, and was inconsistent with s. 1(b) of the Canadian Bill of Rights [a federal statute that antedated the Charter]. The trial judge, Parker A.C.J.H.C., dismissed the motion, and an appeal to the Ontario Court of Appeal was dismissed. The trial proceeded before Parker A.C.J.H.C. and a jury, and the three accused were acquitted. The Crown appealed the acquittal to the Court of Appeal and the appellants filed a cross-appeal. The Court of Appeal allowed the appeal, set aside the verdict of acquittal and ordered a new trial. The Court held that the cross-appeal related to issues already raised in the appeal, and the issues were therefore examined as part of the appeal.

* * *

Section 7 of the Charter

In his submissions, counsel for the appellants argued that the Court should recognize a very wide ambit for the rights protected under s. 7 of the Charter. Basing his argument largely on American constitutional theories and authorities, Mr. Manning submitted that the right to "life, liberty and security of the person" is a wide-ranging right to control one's own life and to promote one's individual autonomy. The right would therefore include a right to privacy and a right to make unfettered decisions about one's own life.

In my opinion, it is neither necessary nor wise in this appeal to explore the broadest implications of s. 7 as counsel would wish us to do. I prefer to rest my conclusions on a narrower analysis than that put forward on behalf of the appellants. I do not think it would be appropriate to attempt an all encompassing explication of so important a provision as s. 7 so early in the history of Charter interpretation. The Court should be presented with a wide variety of claims and factual situations before articulating the full range of s. 7 rights. I will therefore limit my comments to some interpretive principles already set down by the Court and to an analysis of only two aspects of s. 7, the right to "security of the person" and "the principles of fundamental justice".

A. Interpreting Section 7

The goal of Charter interpretation is to secure for all people "the full benefit of the Charter's protection". To attain that goal, this Court has held consistently that the proper technique for the interpretation of Charter provisions is to pursue a "purposive" analysis of the right guaranteed. A right recognized in the Charter is "to be understood, in other words, in the light of the interests it was meant to protect".

* * *

With respect to the second part of s. 7, in early academic commentary one of the principal concerns was whether the reference to "principles of fundamental justice" enables the courts to review the substance of legislation. *In Re B.C. Motor Vehicle Act*, Lamer J. noted that any attempt to draw a sharp line between procedure and substance would be ill-conceived. He suggested further that it would not be beneficial in Canada to allow a debate which is rooted in United States constitutional dilemmas to shape our interpretation of s. 7

> We would, in my view, do our own Constitution a disservice to simply allow the American debate to define the issue for us, all the while ignoring the truly fundamental structural differences between the two constitutions.

* * *

I have no doubt that s. 7 does impose upon courts the duty to review the substance of legislation once it has been determined that the legislation infringes an individual's right to "life, liberty and security of the person". The section states clearly that those interests may only be impaired if the principles of fundamental justice are respected. Lamer J. emphasized, however, that the courts should avoid "adjudication of the merits of public policy". In the present case, I do not believe that it is necessary for the Court to tread the fine line between substantive review and the adjudication of public policy. * * * [I]t will be sufficient to investigate whether or not the impugned legislative provisions meet the procedural standards of fundamental justice. First it is necessary to determine whether s. 251 of the Criminal Code impairs the security of the person.

B. Security of the Person

The law has long recognized that the human body ought to be protected from interference by others. At common law, for example, any medical procedure carried out on a person without that person's consent is an assault. Only in emergency circumstances does the law allow others to make decisions of this nature. * * * "Security of the person", in other words, is not a value alien to our legal landscape. With the advent of the Charter, security of the person has been elevated to the status of a constitutional norm. This is not to say that the various forms of protection accorded to the human body by the common and civil law occupy a similar status. "Security of the person" must be given content in a manner sensitive to its constitutional position. The above examples are simply illustrative of our respect for individual physical integrity. Nor is it to say that the state can never impair personal security interests. There may well be valid reasons for interfering with security of the person. It is to say, however, that if the state does interfere with security of the person, the Charter requires such interference to conform with the principles of fundamental justice.

The appellants submitted that the "security of the person" protected by the Charter is an explicit right to control one's body and to make fundamental decisions about one's life. The Crown contended that "security of the person" is a more circumscribed interest and that, like all of the elements of s. 7, it at most relates to the concept of physical control, simply protecting the individual's interest in his or her bodily integrity.

Canadian courts have already had occasion to address the scope of the interest protected under the rubric of "security of the person". * * * The Ontario Court of Appeal has held that the right to life, liberty and security of the person "would appear to relate to one's physical or mental integrity and one's control over these ..."

* * * In *Mills*, Lamer J. * * * stressed the close connection between the specific rights in ss. 8 to 14 and the more generally applicable rights expressed in s. 7 * * *:

> ... security of the person is not restricted to physical integrity; rather, it encompasses protection against "overlong subjection to the vexations and vicissitudes of a pending criminal accusation" ... These include stigmatization of the accused, loss of privacy, stress and anxiety resulting from a multitude of factors, including possible disruption of family, social life and work, legal costs, uncertainty as to the outcome and sanction.

* * *

I note also that the Court has held in other contexts that the psychological effect of state action is relevant in assessing whether or not a Charter right has been infringed. * * *

* * *

The case law leads me to the conclusion that state interference with bodily integrity and serious state-imposed psychological stress, at least in the criminal law context, constitute a breach of security of the person. It is not necessary in this case to determine whether the right extends further, to protect either interests central to personal autonomy, such as a right to privacy, or interests unrelated to criminal justice.

I wish to reiterate that finding a violation of security of the person does not end the s. 7 inquiry. Parliament could choose to infringe security of the person if it did so in a manner consistent with the principles of fundamental justice. The present discussion should therefore be seen as a threshold inquiry and the conclusions do not dispose definitively of all the issues relevant to s. 7. With that caution, I have no difficulty in concluding that the encyclopedic factual submissions addressed to us by counsel in the present appeal establish beyond any doubt that s. 251 of the Criminal Code is prima facie a violation of the security of the person of thousands of Canadian women who have made the difficult decision that they do not wish to continue with a pregnancy.

At the most basic, physical and emotional level, every pregnant woman is told by the section that she cannot submit to a generally safe medical procedure that might be of clear benefit to her unless she meets criteria entirely unrelated to her own priorities and aspirations. Not only does the removal of decision-making power threaten women in a physical sense; the indecision of knowing whether an abortion will be granted inflicts emotional stress. Section 251 clearly interferes with a woman's bodily integrity in both a physical and emotional sense. Forcing a woman, by threat of criminal sanction, to carry a foetus to term unless she meets certain criteria unrelated to her own priorities and aspirations, is a profound interference with a woman's body and thus a violation of security of the person. Section 251, therefore, is required by the Charter to comport with the principles of fundamental justice.

Although this interference with physical and emotional integrity is sufficient in itself to trigger a review of s. 251 against the principles of fundamental justice, the operation of the decision-making mechanism set out in s. 251 creates additional glaring breaches of security of the person. The evidence indicates that s. 251 causes a certain amount of delay for women who are successful in meeting its criteria. In the context of abortion, any unnecessary delay can have profound consequences on the woman's physical and emotional well-being.

More specifically, in 1977, the Report of the Committee on the Operation of the Abortion Law (the Badgley Report) revealed that the average delay between a pregnant woman's first contact with a physician and a subsequent therapeutic abortion was eight weeks. Although the situation appears to have improved since 1977, the extent of the improvement is not clear. * * *

* * *

These periods of delay may not seem unduly long, but in the case of abortion, the implications of any delay, according to the evidence, are potentially devastating. The first factor to consider is that different medical techniques are employed to perform abortions at different stages of pregnancy. The testimony of expert doctors at trial indicated that in the first twelve weeks of pregnancy, the relatively safe and simple suction dilation and curettage method of abortion is typically used in North America. From the thirteenth to the sixteenth week, the more dangerous dilation and evacuation procedure is performed, although much less often in Canada than in the United States. From the sixteenth week of pregnancy, the instillation method is commonly employed in Canada. This method requires the intra-amniotic introduction of prostaglandin, urea, or a saline solution, which causes a woman to go into labour, giving birth to a foetus which is usually dead, but not invariably so. The uncontroverted evidence showed that each method of abortion progressively increases risks to the woman.

The second consideration is that even within the periods appropriate to each method of abortion, the evidence indicated that the earlier the abortion was performed, the fewer the complications and the lower the risk of mortality. * * * Even more revealing were the overall mortality statistics evaluated by Drs. Cates and Grimes. They concluded from their study of the relevant data that:

> Anything that contributes to delay in performing abortions increases the complication rates by 15 to 30%, and the chance of dying by 50% for each week of delay.

* * *

It is no doubt true that the overall complication and mortality rates for women who undergo abortions are very low, but the increasing risks caused by delay are so clearly established that I have no difficulty in concluding that the delay in obtaining therapeutic abortions caused by the mandatory procedures of s. 251 is an infringement of the purely physical aspect of the individual's right to security of the person. * * *

The above physical interference caused by the delays created by s. 251, involving a clear risk of damage to the physical well-being of a woman, is sufficient, in my view, to warrant inquiring whether s. 251 comports with the principles of fundamental justice. However, there is yet another infringement of security of the person. It is clear from the evidence that s. 251 harms the psychological integrity of women seeking abortions. A 1985 report of the Canadian Medical Association, * * * emphasized that the procedure involved in s. 251, with the concomitant delays, greatly increases the stress levels of patients and that this can lead to more physical complications associated with abortion. * * *

* * *

In summary, s. 251 is a law which forces women to carry a foetus to term contrary to their own priorities and aspirations and which imposes serious delay causing increased physical and psychological trauma to those women who meet its criteria. It must, therefore, be determined whether that infringement is accomplished in accordance with the principles of fundamental justice, thereby saving s. 251 under the second part of s. 7.

Although the "principles of fundamental justice" referred to in s. 7 have both a substantive and a procedural component, I have already indicated that it is not necessary in this appeal to evaluate the substantive content of s. 251 of the Criminal Code. My discussion will therefore be limited to various aspects of the administrative structure and procedure set down in s. 251 for access to therapeutic abortions.

In outline, s. 251 operates in the following manner. Subsection (1) creates an indictable offence for any person to use any means with the intent "to procure the miscarriage of a female person". Subsection (2) establishes a parallel indictable offence for any pregnant woman to use or to permit any means to be used with the intent "to procure her own miscarriage". The "means" referred to in subs. (1) and (2) are defined in subs. (3) as the administration of a drug or "other noxious thing", the use of an instrument, and "manipulation of any kind". The crucial provision for the purposes of the present appeal is subs. (4) which states that the offences created in subss. (1) and (2) "do not apply" in certain circumstances. * * *

The procedure surrounding the defence is rather complex. A pregnant woman who desires to have an abortion must apply to the "therapeutic abortion committee" of an "accredited or approved hospital". Such a committee is empowered to issue a certificate in writing stating that in the opinion of a majority of the committee, the continuation of the pregnancy would be likely to endanger the pregnant woman's life or health. Once a copy of the certificate is given to a qualified medical practitioner who is not a member of the therapeutic abortion committee, he or she is permitted to perform an abortion on the pregnant woman and both the doctor and the woman are freed from any criminal liability.

* * *

* * * In order to understand the true nature and scope of s. 251, it is necessary to investigate the practical operation of the provisions. The Court has been provided with a myriad of factual submissions in this area. One of the most useful sources of information is the Badgley Report. The Committee on the Operation of the Abortion Law was established by Orders-in-Council P.C. 1975-2305, -2306, and -2307 of September 29, 1975 and its terms of reference instructed it to "conduct a study to determine whether the procedure provided in the Criminal Code for obtaining therapeutic abortions is operating equitably across Canada". * * *

The Badgley Report contains a wealth of detailed information which demonstrates, however, that many of the most serious problems with the functioning of s. 251 are created by procedural and administrative requirements established in the law. For example, the Badgley Committee noted, that:

> ... the Abortion Law implicitly establishes a minimum requirement of three qualified physicians to serve on a therapeutic abortion committee, plus a qualified medical practitioner who is not a member of the therapeutic abortion committee, to perform the procedure. * * *
>
> Of the 1,348 civilian hospitals in operation in 1976, at least 331 hospitals had less than four physicians on their medical staff. In terms of the distribution of physicians, 24.6 percent of hospitals in Canada did not have a medical staff which was large enough to establish a therapeutic abortion committee and to perform the abortion procedure.

* * *

The Powell Report reveals another serious difficulty with s. 251 procedures. The requirement that therapeutic abortions be performed only in "accredited" or "approved" hospitals effectively means that the practical availability of the exculpatory provisions of subs. (4) may be heavily restricted, even denied, through provincial regulation. In Ontario, for example, the provincial government promulgated O. Reg. 248/70 under The Public Hospitals Act. This regulation provides that therapeutic abortion committees can only be established where there are ten or more members on the active medical staff. A minister of health is not prevented from imposing harsher restrictions. * * *

A further flaw with the administrative system established in s. 251(4) is the failure to provide an adequate standard for therapeutic abortion committees which must determine when a therapeutic abortion should, as a matter of law, be granted. Subsection (4) states simply that a therapeutic abortion committee may grant a certificate when it determines that a continuation of a pregnancy would be likely to endanger the "life or health" of the pregnant woman. It was noted above that "health" is not defined for the purposes of the section. * * *

* * *

[The Bagley Report also concluded:]

> There has been no sustained or firm effort in Canada to develop an explicit and operational definition of health, or to apply such a concept directly to the operation of induced abortion. In the absence of such a definition, each physician and each hospital reaches an individual decision on this matter. How the concept of health is variably defined leads to considerable inequity in the distribution and the accessibility of the abortion procedure.

Various expert doctors testified at trial that therapeutic abortion committees apply widely differing definitions of health. For some committees, psychological health is a justification for therapeutic abortion; for others it is not. Some committees routinely refuse abortions to married women unless they are in physical danger, while for other committees it is possible for a married woman to show that she would suffer psychological harm if she continued with a pregnancy, thereby justifying an abortion. * * *

> The [Badgley] report, and other evidence adduced in support of this motion, indicates that each therapeutic abortion committee is free to establish its own guidelines and many committees apply arbitrary requirements. Some committees refuse to approve applications for second abortions unless the patient consents to sterilization, others require psychiatric assessment, and others do not grant approval to married women.

* * *

The combined effect of all of these problems with the procedure stipulated in s. 251 for access to therapeutic abortions is a failure to comply with the principles of fundamental justice. * * * One of the basic tenets of our system of criminal justice is that when Parliament creates a defence to a criminal charge, the defence should not be illusory or so difficult to attain as to be practically illusory. The criminal law is a very special form of governmental regulation, for it seeks to express our society's collective disapprobation of certain acts and omissions. When a defence is provided, especially a specifically-tailored defence to a particular charge, it is because the legislator has determined that the disapprobation of society is not warranted when the conditions of the defence are met.

* * *

I conclude that the procedures created in s. 251 of the Criminal Code for obtaining a therapeutic abortion do not comport with the principles of fundamental justice. It is not necessary to determine whether s. 7 also contains a substantive content leading to the conclusion that, in some circumstances at least, the deprivation of a pregnant woman's right to security of the person can never comport with fundamental justice. Simply put, assuming Parliament can act, it must do so properly. For the reasons given earlier, the deprivation of security of the person caused by s. 251 as a whole is not in accordance with the second clause of s. 7. It remains to be seen whether s. 251 can be justified for the purposes of s. 1 of the Charter.

Section 1 Analysis

Section 1 of the Charter can potentially be used to "salvage" a legislative provision which breaches s. 7. * * * A statutory provision which infringes any section of the Charter can only be saved under s. 1 if the party seeking to uphold the provision can demonstrate first, that the objective of the provision is "of sufficient importance to warrant overriding a constitutionally protected right or freedom", and second, that the means chosen in overriding the right or freedom are reasonable and demonstrably justified in a free and democratic society. This second aspect ensures that the legislative means are proportional to the legislative ends. In *Oakes*, the Court referred to three considerations which are typically useful in assessing the proportionality of means to ends. First, the means chosen to achieve an important objective should be rational, fair and not arbitrary. Second, the legislative means should impair as little as possible the right or freedom under consideration. Third, the effects of the limitation upon the relevant right or freedom should not be out of proportion to the objective sought to be achieved.

The appellants contended that the sole purpose of s. 251 of the Criminal Code is to protect the life and health of pregnant women. The respondent Crown submitted that s. 251 seeks to protect not only the life and health of pregnant women, but also the interests of the foetus. On the other hand, the Crown conceded that the Court is not called upon in this appeal to evaluate any claim to "foetal rights" or to assess the meaning of "the right to life". I expressly refrain from so doing. In my view, it is unnecessary for the purpose of deciding this appeal to evaluate or assess "foetal rights" as an independent constitutional value. Nor are we required to measure the full extent of the state's interest in establishing criteria unrelated to the pregnant woman's own priorities and aspirations. What we must do is evaluate the particular balance struck by Parliament in s. 251, as it relates to the priorities and aspirations of pregnant women and the government's interests in the protection of the foetus.

Section 251 provides that foetal interests are not to be protected where the "life or health" of the woman is threatened. Thus, Parliament itself has expressly stated in s. 251 that the "life or health" of pregnant women is paramount. The procedures of s. 251(4) are clearly related to the pregnant woman's "life or health" for that is the very phrase used by the subsection. [T]he aim of s. 251(4) is "to restrict abortion to cases where the continuation of the pregnancy would, or would likely, be injurious to the life or health of the woman concerned, not to provide unrestricted access to abortion." I have no difficulty in concluding that the objective of s. 251 as a whole, namely, to balance the competing interests identified by Parliament, is sufficiently important to meet the requirements of the first step in the *Oakes* inquiry under s. 1. I think the protection of the interests of pregnant women is a valid governmental objective, where life and health can be jeopardized by criminal sanctions. Like Beetz and Wilson JJ., I agree that protection of foetal interests by Parliament is also a valid governmental objective. It follows that balancing these interests, with the lives and health of women a major factor, is clearly an important governmental objective. * * *

I am equally convinced, however, that the means chosen to advance the legislative objectives of s. 251 do not satisfy any of the three elements of the proportionality component of *R. v. Oakes*. The evidence has led me to conclude that the infringement of the security of the person of pregnant women caused by s. 251 is not accomplished in accordance with the principles of fundamental justice. It has been demonstrated that the procedures and administrative structures created by s. 251 are often arbitrary and unfair. The procedures established to implement the policy of s. 251 impair s. 7 rights far more than is necessary because they hold out an illusory defence to many women who would prima facie qualify under the exculpatory provisions of s. 251(4). In other words, many women whom Parliament professes not to wish to subject to criminal liability will nevertheless be forced by the practical unavailability of the supposed defence to risk liability or to suffer other harm such as a traumatic late abortion caused by the delay inherent in the s. 251 system. Finally, the effects of the limitation upon the s. 7 rights of many pregnant women are out of proportion to the objective sought to be achieved. Indeed, to the extent that s. 251(4) is designed to protect the life and health of women, the procedures it establishes may actually defeat that objective. * * *

I conclude, therefore, that the cumbersome structure of subs. (4) not only unduly subordinates the s. 7 rights of pregnant women but may also defeat the value Parliament itself has established as paramount, namely, the life and health of the mother * * * State protection of foetal interests may well be deserving of constitutional recognition under s. 1. Still, there can be no escape from the fact that Parliament has failed to establish either a standard or a procedure whereby any such interests might prevail over those of the woman in a fair and non-arbitrary fashion.

Section 251 of the Criminal Code cannot be saved, therefore, under s. 1 of the Charter.

* * *

[The concurring opinion of Beetz and Estey, JJ. is ommitted.]

McIntyre, J. (dissenting) [with Le Forest J. concurring]

* * *

The judgment of my colleague, Wilson J., is based upon the proposition that a pregnant woman has a right, under s. 7 of the Charter, to have an abortion. The same concept underlies the judgment of the Chief Justice. He reached the conclusion that a law which forces a woman to carry a foetus to term, unless certain criteria are met which are unrelated to her own priorities and aspirations, impairs the security of her person. That, in his view, is the effect of s. 251 of the Criminal Code. He has not said in specific terms that the pregnant woman has the right to an abortion, whether therapeutic or otherwise. In my view, however, his whole position depends for its validity upon that proposition and that interference with the right constitutes an infringement of her right to security of the person. It is said that a law which forces a woman to carry a foetus to term unless she meets certain criteria unrelated to her own priorities and aspirations interferes with security of her person. If compelling a woman to complete her pregnancy interferes with security of her person, it can only be because the concept of security of her person includes a right not to be compelled to carry the child to completion of her pregnancy. This, then, is simply to say that she has a right to have an abortion. It follows, then, that if no such right can be shown, it cannot be said that security of her person has been infringed by state action or otherwise.

* * *

The proposition that women enjoy a constitutional right to have an abortion is devoid of support in the language of s. 7 of the Charter or any other section. While some human rights documents, such as the American Convention on Human Rights, 1969 (Article 4(1)), expressly address the question of abortion, the Charter is entirely silent on the point. It may be of some significance that the Charter uses specific language in dealing with other topics, such as voting rights, religion, expression and such controversial matters as mobility rights, language rights and minority rights, but remains silent on the question of abortion which, at the time the Charter was under consideration, was as much a subject of public controversy as it is today. Furthermore, it would appear that the history of the constitutional text of the Charter affords no support for the appellants' proposition. * * *

* * *

* * * It follows then, in my view, that the interpretive approach to the Charter, which has been accepted in this Court, affords no support for the entrenchment of a constitutional right of abortion.

As to an asserted right to be free from any state interference with bodily integrity and serious state-imposed psychological stress, I would say that to be accepted, as a constitutional right, it would have to be based on something more than the mere imposition, by the State, of such stress and anxiety. It must, surely, be evident that many forms of government action deemed to be reasonable, and even necessary in our society, will cause stress and anxiety to many, while at the same time being acceptable exercises of government power in pursuit of socially desirable goals. The very facts of life in a modern society would preclude the entrenchment of such a constitutional right. * * * In the interests of public health and welfare, governments must have and exercise the power to regulate, control—and even suppress—aspects of the manufacture, sale and distribution of alcohol and drugs and other dangerous substances. Stress and anxiety resulting from the exercise of such powers cannot be a basis for denying them to the authorities. At the present time there is great pressure on governments to restrict—and even forbid—the use of tobacco. Government action in this field will produce much stress and anxiety among smokers and growers of tobacco, but it cannot be said that this will render unconstitutional control and regulatory measures adopted by governments. Other illustrations abound to make the point.

To invade the s. 7 right of security of the person, there would have to be more than state-imposed stress or strain. A breach of the right would have to be based upon an infringement of some interest which would be of such nature and such importance as to warrant constitutional protection. This, it would seem to me, would be limited to cases where the state-action complained of, in addition to imposing stress and strain, also infringed another right, freedom or interest which was deserving of protection under the concept of security of the person. For the reasons outlined above, the right to have an abortion—given the language, structure and history of the Charter and given the history, traditions and underlying philosophies of our society—is not such an interest. * * *

* * *

I would only add that even if a general right to have an abortion could be found under s. 7 of the Charter, it is by no means clear from the evidence the extent to which such a right could be said to be infringed by the requirements of s. 251 of the Code. In the nature of things that is difficult to determine. The mere fact of pregnancy, let alone an unwanted pregnancy, gives rise to stress. The evidence reveals that much of the anguish associated with abortion is inherent and unavoidable and that there is really no psychologically painless way to cope with an unwanted pregnancy.

It is for these reasons I would conclude, that save for the provisions of the Criminal Code, which permit abortion where the life or health of the woman is at risk, no right of abortion can be found in Canadian law, custom or tradition, and that the Charter, including s. 7, creates no further right. * * *

* * *

Wilson, J.

* * *

With all due respect, I think that the Court must tackle the primary issue first. A consideration as to whether or not the procedural requirements for obtaining or performing an abortion comport with fundamental justice is purely academic if such requirements cannot as a constitutional matter be imposed at all. If a pregnant woman cannot, as a constitutional matter, be compelled by law to carry the foetus to term against her will, a review of the procedural requirements by which she may be compelled to do so seems pointless. Moreover, it would, in my opinion, be an exercise in futility for the legislature to expend its time and energy in attempting to remedy the defects in the procedural requirements unless it has some assurance that this process will, at the end of the day, result in the creation of a valid criminal offence. I turn, therefore, to what I believe is the central issue that must be addressed.

* * *

The idea of human dignity finds expression in almost every right and freedom guaranteed in the Charter. Individuals are afforded the right to choose their own religion and their own philosophy of life, the right to choose with whom they will associate and how they will express themselves, the right to choose where they will live and what occupation they will pursue. These are all examples of the basic theory underlying the Charter, namely that the state will respect choices made by individuals and, to the greatest extent possible, will avoid subordinating these choices to any one conception of the good life.

Thus, an aspect of the respect for human dignity on which the Charter is founded is the right to make fundamental personal decisions without interference from the state. This right is a critical component of the right to liberty. * * *

* * *

The question then becomes whether the decision of a woman to terminate her pregnancy falls within this class of protected decisions. I have no doubt that it does. This decision is one that will have profound psychological, economic and social consequences for the pregnant woman. The circumstances giving rise to it can be complex and varied and there may be, and usually are, powerful considerations militating in opposite directions. It is a decision that deeply reflects the way the woman thinks about herself and her relationship to others and to society at large. It is not just a medical decision; it is a profound social and ethical one as well. Her response to it will be the response of the whole person.

* * *

It seems to me, therefore, that in a free and democratic society "freedom of conscience and religion" should be broadly construed to extend to conscientiously-held beliefs, whether grounded in religion or in a secular morality. Indeed, as a matter of statutory interpretation, "conscience" and "religion" should not be treated as tautologous if capable of independent, although related, meaning. Accordingly, for the state to take sides on the issue of abortion, as it does in the impugned legislation by making it a criminal offence for the pregnant woman to exercise one of her options, is not only to endorse but also to enforce, on pain of a further loss of liberty through actual imprisonment, one conscientiously-held view at the expense of another. It is to deny freedom of conscience to some, to treat them as means to an end, to deprive them, as Professor MacCormick puts it, of their "essential humanity". * * *

* * *

Notes

1. The *Morgentaler* case was decided soon after the adoption of the Canadian Charter of Rights and Freedoms, which only became effective in 1982, and is one of the early cases interpreting the Charter. Note how it does so with an eye towards the jurisprudence of the United States, carefully trying to avoid the pitfalls into which the United States Supreme Court has stumbled. It avoids recognizing an explicit right to privacy for example, and stresses the difference between "fundamental justice" and "due process." Note, however, that its step-by-step "test" requirement, looks very similar to United States Supreme Court interpretation of Constitutional Law in its abortion cases.

2. The German Constitutional Court, and the Hungarian Constitutional Court have invalidated liberal abortion laws because of their impact on the right to life of the fetus. These decisions are discussed in the excerpt that comes next, followed by excerpts from the most recent Hungarian Constitutional Court decision, which reviewed the legislation adopted after the first Court decision discussed in the reading.

Constitutionalizing Abortion

in Abortion Politics: Public Policy in Cross-Cultural Perspective, Kim Lane Scheppele, 29, 38–42 (Marianne Githens & Dorothy McBride Stetson, eds. 1996)

* * *

Germany

In the early 1970s, as a number of European countries were liberalizing their laws on abortion to allow the procedure under a wider array of circumstances, the German Bundestag considered a series of statutes designed to liberalize abortion in what was then West Germany. The existing law, enacted originally in 1871, provided criminal penalties for any abortion, with the exception of those carried out to save the life or health of the mother. After much deliberation and a confusing set of Parliamentary votes, the Bundestag in 1974 passed the most liberal of several bills under simultaneous consideration. The new law allowed abortion in the first twelve weeks of pregnancy without restriction. After twelve weeks, abortions could be performed up to 22 weeks to save the life or health of the woman, or to abort a fetus suffering from an incurable injury to its health. Right after the passage of the statute, 193 Bundestag members who had voted against it (particularly those from various Christian-based political parties) and the governments of six German *Länder* filed suit in the Constitutional Court to challenge its constitutionality.

The Court's ruling, *The Abortion Decision*, announced on February 25, 1975, struck down the newly passed reform statute for being in violation of the German Basic Law (the Constitution), particularly Article 2, Paragraph 2, Sentence 1, which declares, "Everyone shall have a right to life." This "everyone," according to the Court, includes the fetus from the fourteenth day after conception when "life, in the sense of historical existence of a human individual, exists, according to definite biological-physiological knowledge." The Court found that "the security of human existence against encroachments by the state would be incomplete if it did not also embrace the prior step of 'completed life,' unborn life." This obligation to protect unborn human life exists even against the mother, the Court continued, even though the mother possesses her own right to life and the right to the free development for her personality. But rights, short of a right to life, were not without limits, the Court concluded.

The state must express its condemnation of abortion through its laws, the Court said, and must "reawaken and, if required, to strengthen the maternal duty to protect" the fetus. This does not mean that the pregnant woman can never get an abortion, only that she has to have serious enough reasons to get an abortion so that the infringements on her rights outweigh those to the unborn child in the particular instance. If the pregnant woman's life is at risk, or if her health would be infringed by continuing the pregnancy, then these would be good enough reasons to get an abortion. If the pregnant woman found herself in a desperate situation, then, this too would be an acceptable circumstance in which to get an abortion. But the obligation of the state to protect unborn life would require it "to offer counseling and assistance with the goal of reminding pregnant women of the fundamental duty to respect the life of the unborn, to encourage her to continue the pregnancy and—especially in cases of social need—to support her through practical measures of assistance." The liberal abortion law was struck down.

Returning to the drawing board, the Bundestag passed another reform statute, this one criminalizing abortion, except in situations where the pregnant women's life or health was in danger, where the fetus was substantially deformed, or to "avert the danger of a distress which is so serious that the pregnant woman cannot be required to continue the pregnancy and cannot be averted in any other way she can reasonably be expected to bear." The statute also required mandatory counseling and a three-day waiting period after the counseling before the abortion could be performed. This revised statute was upheld by the European Commission on Human Rights in a challenge brought under the European Convention. But in practice, the decentralized form of the law's practical operation allowed doctors in the Catholic areas of Germany to deny abortions to many women, while doctors in other parts of the country performed something close to abortion on demand.

With one of the most restrictive abortion laws in Europe, West Germany found another challenge to its abortion policy when East and West were united in 1990. In contrast to the relatively restrictive law in the West, East Germany had a liberal law on abortion in force, allowing an abortion in the first twelve weeks of pregnancy without restriction, nearly identical to the law that the Constitutional Court had struck down in 1975. In the hastily drafted unification agreement, which ran to some 900 pages, the two parts of the new Germany were able to agree to common regulations on a vast array of policies—but they could not agree on a uniform law on abortion. At the last minute, negotiators agreed to leave each law intact in its own territory, with an agreement to draft a new abortion law before two years were out. In advance of the deadline, on June 27, 1992, the Bundestag voted by a 357 to 284 margin in favor of a statute that would allow abortion without restriction within the first three months of pregnancy, but only if the woman first underwent counseling and then waited three days before having the procedure. At the time, it looked as if the proponents of the liberal law of the East had prevailed.

Within days of its passage, however, 249 Bundestag members, primarily from the Christian parties, challenged the statute in the Constitutional Court. After several publicly announced delays in the final date of its decision and public challenges to two of the judges who had well-known ties to various pro-life groups, the Court announced *Abortion II* on May 28, 1993. The decision upheld part of the statute while striking down other parts.

The reasoning of the Constitutional Court in the second abortion case is striking, because it opens up a wholly different way of thinking about state responsibility for enforcing rights. At first, the justices appeared to follow the decision of 1975. In fact, the Court substantially modified its earlier ruling while giving lip-service to continuity, just as the American Supreme Court did in the *Casey* decision. While the Federal Constitutional Court had said in 1975 that the German state must use the criminal law to fulfill its obligation to protect unborn life, the 1993 case softened that strong requirement by saying that such criminal law provisions, though still required, did not have to be accompanied by criminal punishment. Thus, the unification law was unconstitutional insofar as it *decriminalized* abortion—but constitutional in saying that the state could substitute "normative counseling" for criminal punishment as a way of fulfilling its obligations to protect fetuses. The 1993 decision required that abortion remain a criminal offense under German law for those cases that still fell outside the Court's 1975 list of acceptable circumstances, but normative counseling that was designed to persuade the woman to have the child could be used instead of criminal sanctions to reduce the number of actual abortions that German women would have. The state did not have to require that women give reasons for getting abortions or to have their personal circumstances subject to scrutiny by third persons, leaving the decision about whether to have an abortion fully in the woman's hands in the first trimester. And the woman could choose to follow the law or not, but the state did not have to inquire or act further.

In practice, then, this meant both that abortion restrictions in the West were greatly eased compared with the previous situation and that women in the East now had to undergo counseling they had not previously had to encounter. But there was a hitch in all this for women seeking abortions. While under both previous laws all approved abortions were paid for by state health insurance, under the new ruling the state must limit funding of abortions. Since some of the abortions that women will get under the new ruling will be illegal (though not punishable) and the government has no way to tell which abortions are legal and which are not, the Court ruled that the state need not pay for *any* of the abortions that women get, unless the woman's life or health is threatened or she is too poor to pay at all.

Finding that both the woman and the fetus had constitutionally protectable rights in its second decision as well as in its first, the Federal Constitutional Court of Germany designed a regime of legal regulation that avoided criminal sanctions while still requiring a state role in providing non-neutral information and advice for women seeking abortions.

Hungary

Compared with most of the states under the influence of the former Soviet Union, Hungary had a relatively restrictive abortion law prior to the establishment of a constitutional rule-of-law state in 1989. Women seeking abortions had to go before medical committees that could and did inquire into the personal details of their lives before giving permission for abortions. Only women over age thirty-five or women who had at least two children were exempted from this procedure, which many women found humiliating and intrusive.

Hungary's new Constitution—a heavily amended version of the Stalinist Constitution of 1949—went into effect on October 23, 1989, and on January 1, 1990, the new Hungarian Constitutional Court opened for business. One of the first petitions that the Court received was from a group of Catholic law professors from Miskolc called Pacem in Utero, urging on the Court the view that the fetus had a qualified right to life under the new Hungarian Constitution.

While the Court wrestled with this question, a major public debate over abortion took place in Hungary. Strongly pro-life views were aired for the first time, and small and embattled groups of feminists argued in favor of women's rights of self-determination. The Parliament wanted to avoid the question and managed to do so until a ruling of the Constitutional Court in December 1991.

In its long opinion, the Court held that the existing legal regulations on abortion violated the Hungarian Constitution because they necessarily implicated fundamental human rights. The fetus might have a right to life under the Hungarian Constitution, the Court said; but the woman carrying the fetus surely had a constitutional right to self-determination. But rather than reason from these statements directly through to conclusions about what the abortion law should look like concretely, the Court said only that the Parliament had to pass a formal law instead of allowing abortion to be governed by regulations of the welfare ministry (formerly the ministry of health). Within broad parameters that required only that the Parliament take both the rights of the woman and the potential rights of the fetus into account, the Court suggested that it might be possible for the state to meet its constitutional obligations to protect human life and the self-determination rights of women in many ways.

Did the fetus have a right to life protected by the Hungarian Constitution? This question, the Court said, "cannot be resolved by constitutional interpretation." It was instead, according to the Court, a matter of political judgment, to be exercised by the Parliament within broad constitutional parameters. Here, too, the legislature had several options. It could grant the fetus legal personhood, like that given to a corporation, personhood that did not necessarily come with the full complement of rights required by the protection of human dignity. Or, the legislature might provide only general background protection for the survival of human life in general, which would mean that the state would not have to intervene in every individual case to protect a specifically threatened fetus. In this way, the regulation of abortion could be like the laws for the protection of workplace safety or the protection of the environment—generally supportive of healthy conditions without guaranteeing a specific standard to every specific individual. Or the legislature could find that the fetus was a person with full rights to life and dignity. But if the legislature determined that the fetus was a person on an equal par with the woman carrying it, then this would require the logical consequences that the fetus would have stronger claims than the woman, since the right to life was stronger than the right to self-determination. Leaving the decision to the Parliament, the Court hinted that it would revisit the question and consider the balance of rights after the new law was passed.

In 1992, the Hungarian Parliament passed a new abortion law that took effect at the start of 1993. The new law reads like many western European laws, with abortion formally criminalized, allowing exceptions for a variety of circumstances that include a woman's difficult social conditions. The law stopped short of granting the fetus a right to life, but requires informational (not normative) counseling to inform the woman both about state programs designed to assist her with childraising and also about birth control. * * *

* * *

Notes

1. Would the German "counseling model" approach of criminalizing abortion but not imposing sanctions (other than normative counseling) work as a compromise in the United States? Why does it work in Germany? The notion of crime without punishment (like those of rights to health not corresponding to any duties imposed on particular persons, or of professional duties not enforceable by individual patients) seem odd from the United States perspective. Do these approaches, however, solve problems that are intractable within our normal way of dealing with legal rights and remedies?

2. A 1998 German Constitutional Court decision struck down portions of a Bavarian law further restricting abortion rights, in part because the state legislation was preempted by federal law, but also because portions of the law restricting the proportion of practice income that a doctor could earn from abortions, limiting the practice of abortion to doctors possessing certain qualifications without providing transitional regulations for those already practicing in the area, and prescribing the content of doctor/patient communications regarding abortion, violated Article 12 of the German Constitution which protects the freedom of the professions. See Bundesverfassungsgericht, Nr. 117, Oct 27, 1998.

3. See also, discussing the German situation, Albin Eser and Hans-Georg Koch, *Abortion and the Law: From International Comparison to Legal Policy* (2005); Nanette Funk, Abortion Counseling and the 1995 German Abortion Law, 12 *Conn. J. Int'l L.* 33 (1996); D.A. Jeremy Telman, Abortion and Women's Legal Personhood in Germany: A Contribution to the Feminist Theory of the State, 24 *N.Y.U. Rev. L. & Soc. Change* 91 (1998); Albin Eser, Abortion Law Reform in Germany in International Comparative Perspective, 1 *European J. of Health L.* 15 (1994); and Udo Werner, The Convergence of Abortion Regulation in Germany and the United States: A Critique of Glendon's Rights Talk Thesis Abortion Regulation in Germany & the U.S., 18 *Loy.L.A. Int'l & Comp. L. J.* 571 (1996)

4. Very rarely (Ireland is an exception) is the fetus afforded full status as a human being and full protection of human rights law. What are the legal consequences of recognizing the fetus as a person? How does the Hungarian Constitutional Court case, reproduced below, address the question of the personhood of the fetus?

Decision 48/1998 (XI. 23.) AB

Hungarian Constitutional Court, pages 1–21, 23, 26–28 (1998).

* * *

The Constitutional Court establishes that it is not unconstitutional to enact an Act of the Parliament permitting abortion in case the pregnant woman is in a situation of serious crisis. However, the legislature may only dispense, in a constitutional way, with the examination of the existence of a serious crisis situation if, at the same time, it establishes provisions creating adequate counterbalance with a view to protecting foetal life.

The Constitutional Court establishes that the concept and the application criteria for a situation of serious crisis may only be defined in an Act of the Parliament; the lack of such a definition may not be substituted for either in statute of a lower level, or by way of judicial interpretation.

* * *

The Constitutional Court rejects the petitions seeking to establish the unconstitutionality of, and to annul Section 6 para. (1) item d) and Section 6 para. (2) item b) of the Act on the Protection of the Foetus. Similarly, the Constitutional Court rejects the petitions claiming the unconstitutionality of the entire Act on the Protection of the Foetus based on the lack of an explicit definition in the Act on the legal status of the foetus, the lack of a declaration in the Act on the legal subjectivity of the foetus, and the lack of provisions in the Act on the foetus' rights * * *.

The Constitutional Court rejects the petition proposing that the Constitutional Court decide whether or not the foetus is a human.

* * *

According to Section 6 para. (1) item d) of the Act on the Protection of the Foetus, abortion may be procured until the 12th week of pregnancy if the pregnant woman is in a situation of serious crisis. Almost all the petitioners challenged the above provision, arguing that—taking into account Section 12 para. (6) defining the concept of a situation of serious crisis—it practically allows unrestricted abortion. In this context, one of the petitioners claimed the unconstitutionality of Section 9 para. (3) of the Implementing Decree, by which the existence of a situation of serious crisis is verified by the statement of the pregnant woman seeking abortion, and the staff member of the Family Protection Service has no discretionary powers concerning the contents and the validity of her representation.

One of the petitioners claimed the unconstitutionality of Section 6 para. (2) item b) of the Act on the Protection of the Foetus allowing to extend the time limit for procuring abortion to the 18th week of pregnancy if the pregnant woman did not realise her pregnancy earlier due to a medical error or a health-related cause beyond her scope of responsibility, or if exceeding the 12th week of pregnancy was caused by the default of a healthcare institution or an authority.

Some of the petitioners challenged the entire Act on the Protection of the Foetus as unconstitutional, claiming that—contrary to its title—it does not contain any concrete provision on the protection and the rights of the foetus, and it does not declare the legal subjectivity of the foetus. Therefore, one of the petitioners asked the Constitutional Court to decide whether or not the foetus is a human.

The petitioners referred to several provisions of the Constitution including Article 54 para. (1) (the right to life and human dignity), Article 8 para. (1) (the obligation of the State to protect fundamental human rights), Article 66 para. (2) (mothers shall receive State support and protection before and after the birth of the child), Article 70/D (the right to physical and mental health), and Article 70/E (the right to social security). Similarly, all of the petitioners referred to Decision 64/1991 (XII. 17.) AB of the Constitutional Court (ABH 1991, 297; hereinafter: the "Decision of the Constitutional Court") concerning the former regulations on abortion. The petitioners claimed that when adopting the regulations in force, the legislature had not complied with the constitutional requirements specified in the Decision of the Constitutional Court.

* * *

The following provisions of the Act on the Protection of the Foetus and of the Implementing Decree are examined in the present decision:

* * *

Act on the Protection of the Foetus:

> SECTION 6 para. (1) Abortion may be procured until the 12th week of pregnancy if

a) it is justified by a cause seriously endangering the pregnant woman's health;
b) it is medically probable that the foetus suffers from a serious deficiency or any other damage;
c) the pregnancy is the result of a criminal act, and
d) the pregnant woman is in a situation of serious crisis.

* * *

SECTION 12 para. (6) A situation of serious crisis is one which causes physical or mental breakdown or a subsequent impossible situation in social terms, thus endangering the healthy development of the foetus. The pregnant woman verifies the existence of the situation of serious crisis by signing the application form.

* * *

In the Decision of the Constitutional Court, Council of Ministers Decree on abortion, Decree of the Minister of Social Affairs and Healthcare on the implementation thereof, and the provisions of Act II of 1972 on Healthcare authorising that regulation be done in a decree were declared unconstitutional and annulled by the Constitutional Court * * *. The Constitutional Court established that abortion must in each case be regulated on the level of an Act of the Parliament. By regulating abortion, the legislature decides, at the same time, on the legal subjectivity of the foetus—and this may only be done in an Act of the Parliament. The Constitutional Court did not examine the contents of the annulled provisions. However, it pointed out constitutional boundaries which—subject to the legislature's decision concerning the legal capacity of the foetus—limited the possibilities of regulating abortion in a constitutional way.

* * *

It was established in the Decision of the Constitutional Court that * * * with regard to abortion, regulation on the level of an Act of the Parliament is required because in each case where abortion is regulated, a statement on the status of the foetus in terms of fundamental rights must be made. For the same reason, regulations affecting the mother's right to self-determination and her right to health must in each case be provided for in an Act of the Parliament.

* * *

The Constitutional Court establishes that by adopting the Act on the Protection of the Foetus, the Parliament formally met the requirements specified in the Decision of the Constitutional Court, and therefore, the unconstitutional situation is deemed to be terminated in this respect.

In the Decision of the Constitutional Court, it was explained in detail that when regulating abortion, the legislator (or the constituent body) must decide on the preliminary question of whether or not the foetus is a human and, at the same time, a subject of law, i.e. whether the legal concept of man should include the foetal phase back to conception. The Constitutional Court established that the provisions of the Constitution do not contain any express rule regarding the legal subjectivity of the foetus, nor can it be determined by interpreting the Constitution. It does not follow from the Constitution that the foetus must be recognised as a subject of law or that it is legally impossible to accord it as a human.

* * *

According to Article 2 paragraph (1) of the [European] Convention [on the Protection of Human Rights and Fundamental Freedoms], "Everyone's right to life shall be protected by law. No one shall be deprived of his life intentionally (...)". When interpreting the words of the Convention, one may face the same problem as in the case of Article 54 para. (1) of the Constitution, namely, whether it can be stated beyond any doubt that the term "everyone" * * * obligatorily covers the foetus as well; in other words, does the Convention protect the foetus' right to life the same way as in the case of a man born. The practice of the European Human Rights Commission has been consistent in addressing this issue in several concrete cases: it has, namely, not taken a stand. In the Case X v United Kingdom it stated concerning Article 2 paragraph (1) of the Convention the following: "It seems that the term "everyone" cannot be applied to an unborn child". It was added in the decision that even if supposing that the provision concerned secured for the foetus the right to life from the moment of conception, this right may be restricted—including by abortion—in order to protect the mother's life and health. * * * Therefore, in the opinion of the Commission, the Member States have certain discretion on the basis of the Convention in regulating abortion.

* * *

The Constitutional Court establishes that—although the Act on the Protection of the Foetus does not contain an explicit provision on the legal subjectivity of the foetus—the Act in question regarding abortion expresses the implicit opinion of the Parliament on the foetus not being a human in legal terms. * * *

However, the lack of granting legal subjectivity for the foetus does not mean that foetal life is not protected by the Constitution. As explained in the Decision of the Constitutional Court, the foetus must enjoy protection—which is not absolute—resulting from the right to life (Article 54 para. (1) of the Constitution), to be secured by the State for conceived human life during its formation. This protection is not questioned by the Act on the Protection of the Foetus and, in line with the above concept, the legislator stated in the Preamble of the Act that "foetal life which starts in the moment of conception must be respected and protected" and repeated it in the text of the legal norm in the following form: "the foetus formed by the unification of an ovum and a spermatozoon, and developing in the womb, as well as the pregnant woman must be supported and protected." * * *

* * *

As stated in the Decision of the Constitutional Court, if the legislature or the body adopting the Constitution decides that the foetus is not a human from a legal point of view, i.e. a subject of law under Article 56 of the Constitution, and therefore, does not have the right to life and dignity, then—in accordance with the Constitution—it is not only possible but inevitable for the State to protect foetal life together with determining and considering other values defined in, and protected by, the Constitution against the mother's right to self-determination, and her other fundamental rights.

It is reinforced by the Constitutional Court that according to Article 54 para. (1) and Article 8 para. (1) of the Constitution, the protection of human life is "the primary obligation of the State". The State's duty to "respect and protect" these fundamental rights is not exhausted by the duty not to encroach on them, but incorporates the obligation to ensure the conditions necessary for their realisation. * * *

* * *

For the individual, the subjective right to life serves to ensure his/her own life. However, the duty of the State based on the right to life goes beyond its obligation not to violate the individual's subjective right to life and to employ its legislative and administrative measures to protect this right, but it must protect human life in general and the conditions thereof. The protection of human life cannot be limited to the protection of the life of men born and having legal subjectivity. Human life is a continuous process starting in the moment of conception. Primarily as legal subjectivity is regarded, certain sections of the life of the same individual human being are, however, qualified by the legislation in force in a different manner as permitted rather than made obligatory by the Constitution. The State's duty of protecting life is qualitatively different from aggregating the right to life of individuals; it is "human life" in general, and consequently, human life as a value that is the subject of protection. Hence, the State's objective and institutionalised duty to protect human life extends to lives which are in their formation. This duty, in contrast with the right to life, is not absolute. This is why the legislature may consider other rights—such as the mother's right to health or self-determination—against it.

* * *

For the above balancing act, the Constitutional Court may only designate the constitutional boundaries of the freedom of the legislature wherein the law must lie; and alternatively, it can establish an unconstitutional omission of legislative duty if the legislature has failed to extend the constitutionally required minimum protection either to the mother's right or to the foetus' life. Accordingly, if the foetus' legal capacity is not recognised, the legislature—when called upon to designate conditions authorising abortion—may not ignore the sometimes conflicting rights and obligations determining the contents of regulation: this way, it must weigh both the woman's right to self-determination, to life and to physical integrity as well as the State's duty to protect life—including foetal life—that follows from the right to life.

A complete ban on abortion would, therefore, be unconstitutional. It would likewise not be constitutional if regulations would favour exclusively the mother's right to self-determination. The State has a duty to protect human life from the moment of conception, and hence, the mother's right to self-determination cannot prevail alone even in the earliest stages of pregnancy. This objective duty to protect life means that the State may not constitutionally permit unjustified abortion. Justification is especially necessary in the case of abortion as the State's duty to safeguard human life does not serve the purpose of averting or minimising anonymous statistical risks but concerns the wilful termination of individual human lives being formed. * * *

* * * The State's objective duty to protect life has the same status when applied to the protection of conceived individual human life. As explained in the Decision of the Constitutional Court, the above circumstances do not require that the foetus be declared a special subject of law, * * *. Nevertheless, it is pointed out by the Constitutional Court that the special significance of foetal life to be protected under the State's duty to protect life may, in other legal systems, be reflected in the establishment of individual fundamental rights as "the human dignity of unborn human life" and "the unborn man's own right to life". For example, the German Federal Constitutional Court established that the foetus has its own individual right to life.

According to the petitions, the Parliament did not act in compliance with the Constitution when * * * the legislature allowed abortion to be procured if the pregnant woman is in a situation of serious crisis, and * * * the existence of a situation of serious crisis may be justified exclusively by the pregnant woman's declaration, without any control by another person. * * *

* * *

The pregnant woman's "situation of serious crisis" is a criterion used in the legal systems of several countries when regulating abortion, although it may have different meanings and functions. It can be established in general that the situation of serious crisis is practically a concrete application of the condition of proportionality to the particular statutory definition of abortion. If a legal system—as most of the European legal systems—applies the State's obligation to protect foetal life or—exceptionally—the foetus' own right to life, which can nevertheless be restricted by the mother's right to self-determination, restricting the protection of foetal life by the mother's right becomes proportionate on the ground of assuming that bearing the child, i.e. enforcing the protection (in other legal systems: the right) of the foetus, would put a burden on the pregnant woman which is far bigger than the usual burden of pregnancy, and this way, the continuation of pregnancy cannot be expected from the woman. In a broad sense, all classically accepted indications are "situations of serious crisis": medical and ethical indications as far as the mother and genetic-teratological ones as far as the foetus are concerned. However, in a narrow sense, the term "situation of crisis" is a social indication, which is a more recent concept subject to many debates. * * * [T]he *state of the pregnant woman* is in the focus and the enforcement of *her right* is justified by the "situation of serious crisis" *in conflict* with the "right" or the constitutionally protected legal status of the foetus. * * *

The American law approaches in a different way the conflict between the pregnant woman and the foetus. There, for the last two decades, the mother's right to decide on abortion in the first trimester of pregnancy has been accepted as a constitutional right [(Roe v. Wade, 410 U.S. 113 (1973)]. However, it became clear by 1992 that due to changes first occurring a decade ago, the State's right to intervene into the mother's right to privacy in the foetus' interest should be accepted even in the first trimester. Although no majority opinion has been accepted concerning the constitutional standard of intervention, a concept that seems to correspond to the "situation of serious crisis" is presented in the opinions of three judges: restrictions by the State cannot unduly burden the woman's freedom of decision. Thus, the function of undue burden is exactly the opposite as in Europe: it is not the exceptional burden of pregnancy why a woman cannot be expected to perform the obligation—that would normally result from the "foetus' right to life" or the State's duty to protect foetal life—of bearing the foetus and giving birth to the child, but her constitutionally protected freedom of decision is protected from being "unduly" restricted by the State. It is the concept of "undue burden" that limits (constitutionally allowed) intervention by the State, including consultations aimed at preventing abortion, useless medical examinations etc. * * *

In the Hungarian law—similarly to other European legal systems using the concept of a situation of serious crisis, the theoretical basis of which is different from the American approach to abortion—the seriously critical state of the pregnant woman, as an independent indication, must qualify the state of the pregnant woman whose situation may justify derogation from the protection of the foetus. * * *

* * *

According to Section 12 para. (6) of the Act on the Protection of the Foetus, in case of a pregnant woman, a situation of serious crisis is one which causes physical or mental breakdown or a subsequent impossible situation in social terms, *thus* endangering the healthy development of the foetus. * * *

To the alternative criteria of physical or mental breakdown or a subsequent impossible situation in social terms, the Parliament must have added as a conjunctive condition the resulting endangerment of the healthy development of the foetus in order to render more stringent the criteria for a situation of serious crisis and—supposedly—to harmonise it with the principle contained in the Act at the beginning of the chapter on abortion, specifying that abortion may only be procured in case of endangerment, under the conditions laid down in the Act (Section 5). The conditions (Section 6) then take into account the endangerment of both the mother and the foetus. When defining the situation of serious crisis, the Act represents the endangerment of both of them.

However, as the definition of a situation of serious crisis puts the conditions into not only a conjunctive relation, but a relation of cause and effect as well, the endangerment of the healthy development of the foetus becomes the decisive feature in an indication the essence and the aim of which as well as its constitutional acknowledgement may only be justified by circumstances in the mother's life demanding disproportionate sacrifice.* * * This construction of cause and effect results in further logical contradictions. As already pointed out by the Constitutional Court, the mother being in a situation of serious crisis is the reason for restricting the State's duty to protect foetal life: therefore, these two aspects must be weighed against each other; the mother's rights and the State's duty to protect foetal life restrict each other.

The protection of foetal life may only exceptionally be restricted with reference to the endangerment of the foetus' health—a cause not related to the mother. This, of course, requires the verification of a serious foetal damage under strictly controlled medical circumstances. * * * Serious foetal disability is accepted by the law as a legitimate indication of abortion because, on the one hand, the law is aimed at protecting the foetus from the burdens of disabled life in the future * * * and, on the other hand, it is not expected from the mother to bear the mental and physical burdens caused by the disability of her child. Therefore, in case of a genetic indication, the mother's situation of serious crisis is not the cause, but a result of the foetus' genetic disorder. Nevertheless, the statutory definition of the situation of serious crisis turns this relationship upside down.

* * *

Based on the above, the Constitutional Court establishes that the first sentence of Section 12 para. (6) of the Act on the Protection of the Foetus is contrary to the principle of legal certainty, thus violating Article 2 para. (1) of the Constitution, while due to its further deficiencies it does not meet the State's obligation to protect foetal life either, and therefore, it violates Article 54 para. (1) of the Constitution as well.

However, it is necessary to examine the statutory definition of a situation of serious crisis, as a legitimate indication, in the context of all the legal criteria of abortion, as it is not applied in itself and the criteria of its enforcement together with its wider legal environment give rise to further important constitutional concerns. According to Section 12 para. (6) of the Act on the Protection of the Foetus, the pregnant woman verifies the existence of a situation of serious crisis by signing the application form. According to Section 9 para. (3) of the Implementing Decree, the staff member of the Family Protection Service—who is in charge of verifying the statutory indication of abortion—has no discretionary powers concerning the contents and the validity of her representation.

* * *

It is a fact that in the law of many European countries, there has been a shift from the objective and professionally controlled social indication to a subjective and uncontrollable "general situation of crisis" based on a statement by the pregnant woman. The most significant shift may be seen in the German Federal Constitutional Court's decisions on abortion adopted between 1975 and 1993 and the resulting changes in legislation . The first decision allowed the legislature to declare that the pregnant woman may not be expected to continue pregnancy in case it represents an extreme burden similar to the weight of a state seriously endangering the pregnant woman's life or health, which is another legitimate indication of abortion. The existence of this indication of abortion, called a general state of emergency or social indication, had to be verified. However, the decision of 1993 and the amendments of the Act that followed it in 1995 expressly renounce verification of the indication by a third party, and what is more, it is not necessary to reveal the mother's identity during the obligatory consulting session.* * *

A similar indication has been introduced by the Belgian Act on Abortion in 3 April, 1990. Accordingly, abortion is legitimate in the first 12 weeks of pregnancy if there is a state of emergency and it is the firm will of the pregnant woman to have an abortion. However, as stated in the reasoning of the draft of the Act, there is practically no difference between these two conditions: the woman's determined and constant reluctance to have a child is, in fact, the state of emergency. * * *

* * *

It is only a decision made by the Polish Constitutional Court in 1997 that follows a contrary approach. Accordingly, allowing abortion on the basis of the pregnant woman's financial or social difficulties violates the principle of proportionality of constitutional values. As stated in the reasoning of the decision, in the conflict of protecting the woman's interests on the basis of her subjective evaluation of the situation and the right to life, the latter has primacy.

* * *

It has been constantly stated by the Constitutional Court that among the rights to be weighed against the State's duty to give increased protection to foetal life, the mother's right to self-determination—as part of the right to human dignity—is the most important one. Undoubtedly, revealing details of the situation of crisis and having it assessed by a third party violate the woman's privacy and may in some cases violate her right to human dignity as well. Any violation of the above fundamental rights may only be evaluated in the context of abortion, where it collides with the State's duty to protect foetal life. * * * [I]ndeed, it is constitutionally required to have a balance in the mutually restrictive relationship between the woman's right to self-determination and the State's duty to protect life.

It was only in the United States where the right to privacy was applied (for a certain period of time) as a constitutional ground for the right to abortion, with no other right or state interest aimed at the protection of the foetus raised against it in the first trimester.* * *

Contrary to the interpretation of the American Constitution, according to the Constitutional Court it follows ab ovo from the Constitution of Hungary that—if the legal subjectivity of the foetus is not acknowledged by the law—the woman's right to dignity and privacy must be weighed against the State's duty to protect foetal life. It is always the State's life protecting duty—in the present case, protection from the wilful termination of an individual foetal life—which must be weighed against the woman's rights. In the conflict of the above rights and duties, obliging the woman by the law to give details on her situation of serious crisis does not qualify as a disproportionate restriction of the woman's right to privacy and dignity. * * *

* * *

Instituting a general indication of crisis and waiving the assessment of the case practically result in applying the deadline method, i.e. allowing abortion in the first 12 weeks at the pregnant woman's request without any further condition or discretion. * * * Maintaining the statutory requirement of a serious, disproportionate, extraordinary, unbearable etc. situation of crisis in the field of legitimate causes of abortion—as the most important and in constitutional terms most sensitive point of the former legal regulation of abortion—is aimed at demonstrating that the State, at least in principle and on constitutional grounds, does not give a free way to abortion, an act acknowledged by the law only in exceptional cases: abortion may only be legally implemented in case there is a serious conflict related to conscience or to a personal situation of life, and if the woman's rights to life, health and self-determination are violated to a great extent.

* * *

If the right to verify the situation of crisis is waived by the law, other means are to be found to remedy the protection lost. In the international practice, the State's acknowledging a situation of serious crisis means a shift in the focus of protection from expressly banning and punishing abortion to regulating the circumstances thereof.

* * *

Section 12 para. (6) of the Act on the Protection of the Foetus and Section 9 para. (3) of the Implementing Decree—examining the norms themselves—are unconstitutional on the basis of the foregoing.

* * * [I]t is incompatible with the State's duty to protect foetal life to have the situation of serious crisis verified simply by the pregnant woman's signing the application form * * * the staff member of the Family Protection Service—who is in charge of verifying the statutory indication of abortion—has no discretionary powers concerning the contents and the validity of her representation. Such provisions themselves cannot secure for the foetus the level of minimum protection required by the constitutional interpretation of the Constitutional Court, and in fact, they do not secure any protection, as the regulation is concerned with the mother's right to self-determination only. * * * Consequently, the legislature has failed to comply with the constitutional criteria specified in the Decision of the Constitutional Court for the case of the Parliament not acknowledging the legal subjectivity of the foetus.

* * *

The Criminal Code in force specifies abortion as a crime against life, physical integrity and health. Performing abortion on the foetus of another person is a criminal act. * * * [T]he legislature considered it unnecessary to expressly declare that permitted abortion performed personally, or on order, by the pregnant woman is not a criminal offence.

* * *

* * * [L]egal certainty (Article 2 para. (1) of the Constitution) requires that one could prove the existence of a particular circumstance exceptionally excluding the unlawful nature of an act which is dangerous to the society, and therefore, punishable in principle, and such an exception must be verified by the court or another competent institution. If abortion is allowed on the basis of a situation of serious crisis, the staff member of the institution concerned, i.e. the Family Protection Service, may only complete the form authorising abortion, but his or her right to verify the existence of the cause regarding the contents or truthfulness of the representation specifying the cause is expressly withdrawn by the law: in essence, the right to establish the cause excluding unlawfulness is allocated by the Act on the Protection of the Foetus and the Implementing Decree solely to the pregnant woman requesting abortion. As a consequence, Section 12 para. (6) of the Act on the Protection of the Foetus and Section 9 para. (3) of the Implementing Decree violate the principle of legal certainty in the context of Section 169 of the CC.

All this shall not mean that the State may not take certain cases of abortion out of the scope of criminal punishment, with reference either to the lack of actual endangerment of the society and the lack of unlawfulness (e.g. abortion based on medical or ethical indication), or to the supposed inefficiency of criminal punishment, where the State wishes to use other means to perform its constitutional duty of protecting life.* * *

The Constitutional Court points out that in the law of several countries that also dispense with controlling the indication of a situation of serious crisis, this case no longer falls under the statutory definition of the criminal offence of abortion. (In the Netherlands, Belgium and Germany, the Acts on abortion themselves or the parallel modification of criminal legislation have amended the statutory definition of the criminal offence of abortion by omitting abortion performed without specifying the reasons therefor.)

* * *

The Constitutional Court establishes that Section 9 of the Act on the Protection of the Foetus assigns a merely informative task to the staff member of the Family Protection Service. After receiving the application for abortion, the staff member shall inform the pregnant woman on the statutory conditions of abortion [paragraph 1(a)], then on the financial allowances and benefits in kind available in case the child is born, as well as on the institutions offering support, the conditions of adoption, the circumstances, the method and the dangers of abortion, the medical institutions that perform abortion, and finally, the methods of contraception proposed personally to the woman concerned. According to paragraph 2, after giving the above information, the staff member shall complete the appropriate application form to be signed by the applicant [as a verification of the situation of serious crisis in line with Section 12 para. (6)], and at the same time, he or she designates the institution chosen to perform the abortion. According to the Implementing Decree, in addition to the above information service, the Family Protection Service shall have administrative tasks only (Sections 9 and 10). * * * Finally, according to Section 15 of the Act on the Protection of the Foetus, it is banned to advertise or propagate abortion, institutions performing abortion, and tools or substances that may be used for abortion. In contrast, according to Section 2 of the Act on the Protection of the Foetus, elementary and secondary-level educational institutions have the duty of instruction on the value of health and human life, a healthy way of life, a responsible relationship between man and woman, family life meeting human standards, and contraceptive methods that are not detrimental to health; at the same time, the State supports the publication and the presentation in the mass media of brochures that serve the purpose of protecting foetal life.

The Constitutional Court establishes that the provisions of the Act on the Protection of the Foetus and of the Implementing Decree referred to before are not suitable for remedying the unconstitutional situation caused by the provisions of the Act. The pregnant woman's personality rights, and in particular, her right to self-determination may have primacy over the right to life and the State's obligation to protect foetal life only in exceptional cases when there is a conflict arising from the mother's rights being seriously endangered. In case the enforcement of such rights is allowed by the law to as great an extent as provided by the Act on the Protection of the Foetus when regulating the situation of serious crisis, foetal life, too, must be protected by firm and effective provisions in order to re-establish the constitutional balance. * * *

* * *

After the nullification of Section 12 para. (6), with Section 6 para. (1) item d) remaining in force, the Act on the Protection of the Foetus may only comply with the requirements—already established in the Decision of the Constitutional Court—resulting from Article 8 para. (2) of the Constitution as far as the level of regulating the indication of a situation of serious crisis is concerned if the contents of the concept of a situation of serious crisis and the respective application criteria are regulated on the level of an Act of the Parliament.

* * *

Dissenting opinion by Dr. Tamás Lábady, Judge of the Constitutional Court

* * *

All abortions violate the right to life. The State must use the tools of legislation, information, training and education in acting against abortion. The legal norms and the constitutional concept of the State should not suggest that such a tolerated phenomenon is in line with the values and the human image of the Constitution. * * *

In my opinion, a more severe constitutional requirement should have been specified in the decision of the Constitutional Court — even on the grounds of its concept — for the objective protection of the right to life, taking into account the individuality of foetal life, i.e. the fact that each and every foetal life is the origin of an individual and irreproducible human life. Therefore, the State must—in addition to cutting the "statistical risk" of abortion—work on letting all foetuses be born without any discrimination.

Notes

1. Another country that has struggled with the constitutionality of abortion is Ireland. The Eighth Amendment to the Irish Constitution, adopted in 1983, recognizes a right to life in the unborn. This provision was adopted in part, apparently, to forestall the application of European human rights and community law to preempt Irish statutes prohibiting abortion. After a widely publicized 1992 case in which a fourteen year old girl who had been raped by her friend's father was enjoined from leaving Ireland to get an abortion (a decision eventually reversed by the Irish Supreme Court, though on grounds that left the right to travel very unclear), Ireland adopted by referendum two new constitutional amendments. Amendments 13 and 14 to the Irish Constitution recognized the right of women to travel abroad to have an abortion, and to receive within Ireland information about the availability of abortions abroad. In 1995, the Irish parliament adopted a statute that permitted the dissemination of information respecting abortion, but prohibited the distribution of information that would counsel or advocate abortion, and forbade professionals within Ireland from arranging abortions elsewhere. The Irish Supreme Court subsequently upheld this statute against attacks from both those who opposed and those who supported abortion rights. See Patrick Hanafin, Reproductive Rights and the Irish Constitution: From Sanctity of Life to Sanctity of Autonomy? 3 *European J. Health L.* 179 (1996); Keith S. Koegler, Ireland's Abortion Information Act of 1995, 29 *Vand.J.Transnat'l L.* 117 (1996); Bryan Mercurio, Abortion in Ireland: An Analysis of the Legal Transformation Resulting from Membership in the European Union, 11 *Tul. J. Int'l & Comp. L.* 141 (2003). An attempt in 2002 to amend the Irish Constitution to outlaw abortion except when necessary to save the life of the mother (other than by threat of suicide) was narrowly defeated. Under Irish law, however, human life begins at implantation, thus the "morning after" pill or the use of coils is not specifically illegal. See Simon Mills and R.A.J. Spence, *Clinical Practice and the Law,* 287–89 (2002).

2. A number of countries have also adopted laws prohibiting or severely restricting research involving human embryos, recognizing that embryos are potential human life. The Council of Europe, Convention on Human Rights and Biomedicine provides:

Article 18—Research on embryos *in vitro*

1 Where the law allows research on embryos *in vitro*, it shall ensure adequate protection of the embryo.

2 The creation of human embryos for research purposes is prohibited.

See, discussing the impact of this provision, Jennifer Gunning, Article 18 of the European Biomedicine Convention: What Impact on Assisted Reproduction, 6 *European J. Health L.* 165 (1999). For a multination study, see Albin Eser, Hans-George Koch, Carola Seith, editors, *International Perspectives on the Status and Protection of the Extracorporeal Embryo* (2007).

B. Assisted Reproduction

Since in vitro fertilization first became possible in the late 1970s, developed nations have had to confront the question of whether and to what extent to regulate the availability and terms and conditions of assisted reproduction. In fact, many nations even before this time regulated artificial insemination, which has been available at least since the 18th century. Not surprisingly, national responses to assisted reproduction have varied considerably. As reproductive technology has continued to develop, its legal status has continued to evolve, although legal developments have not always kept pace with technological change.

As the following excerpts illustrate, most countries permit some forms of assisted reproduction. Other forms, most notably commercial surrogacy and cloning are generally prohibited where addressed. Assisted reproduction is normally regulated, however, rather than prohibited. Topics addressed by law or regulation include licensing of facilities that offer this service, requirements for fully informed consent of recipients, provisions of rules for determining parentage, restrictions on commercialization, and protection of the confidentiality of donors. A separate question in many countries is whether public health insurance will pay for assisted reproduction technology. A number of countries that permit assisted reproduction do not finance it because of its cost.

The primary consideration driving assisted reproduction policy is a concern for assisting families with fertility problems. A common concern, however, is whether assisted reproduction should be limited to situations involving infertility, or whether it should also be available to single women or homosexuals who are not otherwise infertile, but prefer not to procreate naturally. Most countries limit the availability of assisted reproduction to infertile women or couples (or to situations where natural reproduction would risk passing on genetic disorders), but in a few countries, a broader policy favoring reproductive autonomy would permit assisted reproduction in other situations. One policy consideration that counsels restrictions on assisted reproduction is a concern for avoiding increased risks of genetic abnormalities, present in some forms of assisted reproduction. Screening of sperm is also common to avoid transmission of HIV or other diseases. Concern for protection of human life, or potential human life, present in gametes and embryos, also affects policy. Some states, for example, limit the storage of embryos. Concern for potential children also grounds recipient screening policies that consider the age, mental health, and character of potential parents. Another issue is the potential problems posed by multiple births, which are common with some forms of artificial reproduction. The relative weight given to these various concerns in different countries, and the varying ways in which these concerns affect different reproductive technologies, results in a range of regulatory approaches.

The following two excerpts describe assisted reproduction regulation. The first presents a worldwide overview of assisted reproduction regulation, the second focuses on two contrasting states, the United Kingdom and France.

The Process of Regulating Assisted Reproductive Technologies: What We Can Learn from Our Neighbors—What Translates and What Does Not

Kathryn Venturatos Lorio, Loyola Law Review, vol. 45, 247, 247–66 (1999).

* * *

Perhaps the initial step in attempting to formulate a governmental response to these new reproductive techniques is to articulate the reasons why the government should intervene in such a private area of human behavior. * * *

A primary goal may be to protect society from egregious harm and, ancillary to that, to provide for future generations. Although it may be difficult to agree on what is egregious, at least there may be a consensus that whatever its incarnation, it should be avoided. Also, there might be acknowledgment that despite the ways children are conceived or gestated, the best interest of all children should be a primary concern. Further, regardless of whether the intentions or modes of behavior of the participants in these reproductive endeavors are sanctioned, society should promote the safety and health of its people, if, for no other reason, than to avoid having the society as a whole provide care for the participants. Realistically, because of the strong incentive to procreate, people will continue to avail themselves of the new reproductive techniques. Thus, some societal response is necessary in order to set predictable legal parameters for these couples and/or individuals.

* * *

[C]ountries * * * vary in their ideological orientation to the new procreation techniques. One author notes that nations approach the subject of eligibility for use of artificial reproductive technologies from either a "child-oriented" perspective or a "parent-oriented" perspective. Of course, even that distinction is arguably value-laden as to what is best for the child in a "child-oriented" perspective. Interestingly, the "child-oriented" approach is generally more conservative in nature, viewing access to artificial reproductive technologies within the context of the traditional creation of a family. In contrast, the "parent-oriented" perspective is more liberal, focusing on the rights of individuals who avail themselves of the new techniques.

Adopting a more "child-oriented" perspective, most jurisdictions which speak to the subject restrict the use of the new artificial reproductive techniques to either married couples or those unmarried couples living in a "committed" or "stable" relationship. When states address the question of sexual orientation, there is generally either a limitation to, or a recommendation that, the couples be heterosexual. Notably, the Law Reform Commission of Canada in its Medically Assisted Procreation Working Paper, approaching the issue from a "parent-oriented" perspective, recommended no discrimination based on family, marital status, or sexual orientation.

Another restriction which some countries place on candidates seeking to avail themselves of the technologies is that the patients either be infertile, often evidenced by proof that other medical treatment has previously failed to yield a conception, or that the techniques are being sought to avoid the risk of transmission of a serious genetic disease. Generally, the requirement of showing avoidance of a genetically transmitted disease has also been imposed if a couple wishes to use the techniques for purposes of sex selection.

Presumably in an effort to mirror the more traditional family, some countries also limit women to their child-bearing years, specifying 45 or 50, with Great Britain allowing for an extension to the age of 55 under special circumstances. Notably, no age restriction was indicated for males, despite the fact that life expectancies are higher for women than men.

Public health requirements typical in other nations limit the administration of these processes to licensed physicians and usually restrict their performances to authorized facilities. Additionally, extensive record-keeping and informed consent documentation is commonly mandated. Additionally, psychological counseling and full disclosure of legal and medical ramifications are frequently required.

Artificial insemination is accepted in most nations, perhaps due somewhat to the fact that it is the oldest means of artificial procreation, having first been used on humans in 1790. Most jurisdictions recognize the resulting child as legitimate if the husband of the mother consents to the insemination. As with new techniques in general, most nations permit the use of artificial insemination by married couples or those in a committed relationship. Generally, the question of homosexual use is not addressed or, where addressed, is rejected. Other limitations include proof of infertility as required in France, and in some cases, an indication that other solutions, medical or otherwise, have been exhausted. For example, in Italy a couple must also indicate that adoption was not available after a six-month wait. In Sweden, the character of the potential parents is also taken into consideration.

A number of jurisdictions require the screening or quarantine of sperm for a minimum period to avoid transmission of the HIV virus or other diseases. Denmark stands out in its availability for use of fresh unscreened sperm. Many other jurisdictions have set limits on the number of uses of the same sperm donor in order to avoid incestuous unions. Notably, Iceland, being such a small nation, requires that sperm used for insemination in Iceland be imported from Denmark.

In most nations, sperm donors are not paid. Payment is prohibited in France and actually outlawed in Germany. Travel and other expenses of donors may be paid in some countries, whereas payment beyond expenses is permitted in Japan and Russia, although the payment is quite modest in the latter. In New Zealand, payment has not even been an issue due to the fact that most donors there do so on a voluntary basis.

The question of anonymity of the donor is not uniformly answered. Anonymity is traditional in Spain and Latin America, and protected in France. It is viewed as "self-evident" in Australia, Israel, New Zealand, Norway, and the republic of South Africa. While most cautiously guard the identity of the donor, some nations permit the release of some vital health information to the children, and Switzerland has a constitutional article which guarantees a person access to data relating to his descent. Opponents of such disclosure argue that it deters donors from participating in the programs.

In other countries, there are additional requirements for donors. In France, the process of artificial insemination is viewed somewhat as a gift given from one couple to another. In addition to requiring that the donor already have at least one child, the consent to the donation by the donor's partner is required. A similar consent by the donor's wife is required in South Africa.

In vitro fertilization with the gametes of the couple desiring to raise the child is generally permitted. Even in Egypt, which forbids artificial insemination donor, in vitro fertilization with the gametes of the couple is allowed. Differences abound on the question of how many eggs to fertilize within one given cycle and, in some nations, ancillary questions as to time limits on cryopreservation and the use of any "spare" embryos are addressed. Some countries forbid research on the embryos; others permit it for specified medical purposes, and others allow research but forbid later implantation of any embryos which were subjected to research.

The use of donor gametes presents more controversy, often resulting in reproductive tourism, as couples travel from their homes with restrictive laws to other nations which are more liberal in their approach. As mentioned above, donation of sperm in the context of artificial insemination is generally permitted. However, one nation, Austria, although allowing sperm donation in that context, forbids it in the context of in vitro fertilization.

The donation of eggs is not as generally accepted, although many countries permit it as a last resort when other medical intervention has failed to produce a child or where the risk of transmission of a genetic abnormality is great. Again, there is no consensus as to the use of donated embryos, although the sale of embryos is uniformly viewed as unacceptable.

The sole procedure that has elicited almost uniform disapproval is that of surrogate motherhood. Sanctions imposed extend from criminal penalties for violations, as provided in Germany, to non-enforceability of surrogate contracts, as in the United Kingdom. Commercial surrogacy is uniformly prohibited with some nations providing for criminal sanctions against the brokers.

Another procedure that has not met with approval, although not as generally as surrogate motherhood, is posthumous conception. Most of the legislation which deals with the subject prohibits the use of the sperm of a deceased man. However, some countries also address the newer issue of use of the eggs of a deceased woman or the use of embryos when one member of the couple dies. The Law Reform Commission of Canada in its Medically Assisted Procreation Working Paper recommended that any children born as a result of post-mortem use of gametes or embryos not be permitted to inherit unless the decedent contributor specifically so provided in his or her will.

In reviewing the regulations collectively, certain patterns tend to emerge. Some countries are quite restrictive and prohibitive in their approach to the new reproductive techniques. Germany and, to a lesser extent, Austria are examples of this. One author, positing historical reasons for this approach, suggests that this is an effort to distance the country from various reproductive abuses that took place during World War II.

Less restrictive and, as one author classifies it, a "cautious regulatory" approach, is illustrated by the 1994 legislation in France and by the regulations advanced by the Scandinavian countries of Denmark, Sweden, and Norway.

The United Kingdom and the Netherlands exemplify what is often referred to as the "liberally" regulated countries. Characterized as more fragmented and regulated as the need arises, the English system possesses its own Statutory Licensing Authority to deal with public law matters such as licensing and medical standards but is less restrictive as to private matters.

Finally, a number of countries are labeled as "laissez faire" in their approach, having minimal, if any, legislation. These include Italy and Greece. One author suggests that "soft" rules are more appropriate for these nations because they allow for a "peaceful coexistence of a plurality of divergent moral views." A less formal structure, void of strict prohibitions which would be quite difficult to enforce, would be more conducive to these cultures.

* * *

Regulating the New Reproductive Technologies: A Cross-Channel Comparison

Melanie Latham, Medical Law International, Vol. 3, pp. 89, 90–14, 106–11 (1998)

* * *

The questions needing answers in relation to assisted conception and to the status of the embryo tend to be the same across a large part of the developed world. In Britain and in France the developments in medicine have proceeded at a similar pace. Both countries have been at the forefront of progress. The answers offered by the two Parliaments to the dilemmas posed by that progress have, however, in some respects been markedly different. The process of legislating to regulate assisted conception proved to be much more problematic in France than in Britain. The outcome in the three key areas of the debate namely controlling access to assisted conception, defining parenthood and defining the status of the embryo, reveals fundamental divisions between understandings of law and culture in these two major European states. * * *

II. The Road to Law: Pragmatism Versus Principle

* * *

This task would appear to have been much more pragmatically dealt with in Britain. The original findings of the Warnock Committee, published in 1984, formed the basis of the relatively small number of government-sponsored publications which followed, namely the Green Paper of 1986, the White Paper of 1987, and ultimately the Human Fertilisation and Embryology Act 1990, which provided statutory regulations governing donor insemination (DI), *in vitro* fertilisation (IVF), and embryo research.

The French "bioethics laws" of 1994 had a longer and more arduous genesis. Numerous government bodies examined the issue in the course of the 1980s and into the early 1990s. * * * Though often of a different nature or political persuasion these bodies reached very similar conclusions based on pre-existing Code law and medical ethics and advocated that NRT [new reproductive technology] treatment be given only within a framework of consent, anonymity, non-commercialisation and the parental undertaking of a particular couple or "*projet parental.*" Two government decrees were issued in 1988 (88-327 and 88-328) and one law passed in 1991 on sperm donation. Three government bills were published in 1992.

Unfortunately the establishment of the many advisory bodies of the 1980s only served to forestall legislation for numerous reasons. Firstly, though in England Royal Commissions and the genre have been used on occasions to study social issues, such institutions as the Braibant and Lenoir Commissions were unusual and unfamiliar in France. * * *

Secondly, the reports published by these various bodies were legal firsts for France. They were ambitious and far-reaching, involving lengthy and in-depth interest group consultation. * * *

Thirdly, the French legal system is a finely balanced codified system which attempts to cater for all eventualities before they arise. In cases before the courts the law is applied rather than interpreted and is meant to be read as a coherent whole. Any change to the law thus has the potential to upset that balance which has discouraged legal commentators from endorsing change. NRTs law would have had repercussions for this balance especially as the medicine behind it appeared to be continually throwing up new legal quandaries that needed to be resolved. Moreover, codified law necessitated a parliamentary and public consensus that on NRTs proved difficult to obtain. * * *

Finally, fundamental to any legal solution sought by commissions in France was the need to take account of the numerous far reaching legal principles upon which French law was based, particularly in relation to human rights, and therefore inherent in any legal framework set up to deal with NRTs. The legal principles which formed the foundation of the Braibant Report in 1989, for example, and which have been enumerated by successive commissions, were: the right to respect of one's body, *"droit au respect de son corps"*; consent before the use or handling of one's body, *"nul ne peut porter atteinte à l'intégrité du corps humain sans le consentement de l'intéressé"*; the special nature of human parts and organs such that they cannot be assimilated to other heritable goods, *"les organes et les produits du corps humain ne peut faire l'objet d'un droit patrimonial"*; the dignity of a dead or living person; the respect of existing family structures; the right to treatment; the right to a private life; freedom of research; the protection of the human race.

The French overcame these obstacles and finally passed three separate statutes on bioethics in July 1994. The first to be passed, on 1st July, related to the use of information held on computer about patients involved in NRTs and research. * * * The second Statute related to the respect to be accorded to the human body as regards donation surrogacy, and genetic research and thus made additions to the Civil Code. The third Statute related to donation and use of the human body and its parts, regulated assisted conception and prenatal diagnosis, embryo research and gene therapy, and made additions to the Public Health Code. In this article I will refer to the Statute on respect of the human body (94-653) and the Statute on donation and assisted conception (94-654), respectively.

III. Access to Assisted Reproductive Techniques

Several different kinds of patients are now turning to artificial techniques to assist them in their quest for a child. Some of these patients may be infertile, others may be seeking to avoid passing on a genetic disorder to their offspring, and yet others may not want to engage in heterosexual sex. An important issue for these patients has been access to the new technologies. Patients who do not fit with accepted ideas of parenthood have been refused treatment according to strict and often questionable criteria which could dash any hopes they had for a family and nullify their past efforts. These criteria have led critics, such as feminists, to pose questions such as who controls access to NRTs? Who has the right to set criteria whereby single and lesbian women are excluded from NRT treatment? Such regulation is especially questionable when nature does not prevent single or lesbian women from becoming mothers.

Since the early 1980s in both Britain and France an increasing number of clinics providing medically assisted procreation have sprung up, both in the public and private sectors, providing IVF and DI. Neither British nor French patients who go to these clinics in search of medical help to conceive are completely free to pick and choose the services on offer, however. The British and French establishments have seen fit to limit and regulate such access. * * *

Section 13(5) of the Human Fertilisation and Embryology Act 1990 requires that the welfare of the child be taken into account when assessing suitability for all licensed treatment "including the need of that child for a father." This has, however, been charitably interpreted by the Human Fertilisation and Embryology Authority (HFEA). In its Code of Practice it has therefore alleviated any threat to single mothers to be, to some extent, by accepting that there might not be a husband or partner, and allowing centres to consider, in such a case, "whether there is anyone else within the prospective mother's family and social circle who is willing and able to share the responsibility for meeting those needs and for bringing up, and maintaining and caring for the child." However, the relevance of the need for a father at all is questionable.

Part 3 of the Code of Practice lists long and detailed guidance for centres to follow when taking account of the welfare of the child. Some of these are perhaps unnecessary considering the efforts potential parents put into infertility treatment, for example, commitment to bring up a child or the ability to meet the needs of the child. Others are certainly of a social nature, such as patients having had children removed from their care or evidence of a previous or relevant conviction. Who should make the final decision based on such criteria? Can such decisions be left to the medical personnel involved, even assisted by an ethics committee? Even GPs and "any individual, authority or agency" are to be asked their opinion as to the suitability of parents, and account taken of the fact that a patient has not consented to this. Even those services not requiring a licence need to use criteria for their donors, for example, if the insemination following sperm donation is to take place in a licensed clinic. Donors of embryos must be having treatment themselves. Moreover, though the prospective parents under review have the opportunity to give their views and to meet objections, their "assessors" include any person at the clinic who has come into contact with them and confidential information from an outside source can also be discussed with the medical team involved.

Access to IVF has been limited further by the attitude of the British government to health service provision. Local health authorities have limited resources. A low priority has thus been given to an illness that is not life-threatening and whose treatment can be extremely costly. As a result of this assisted conception treatment in Britain is provided to a large extent on a private basis and there are only two clinics wholly funded by the NHS. The cost of one IVF treatment cycle (collection of eggs plus fertilisation and transfer to mother) has been estimated at over a thousand pounds and a live birth (ie. after a number of treatment cycles) at several thousand pounds. Many couples are having to remortgage their homes to pay for treatment.

Clinics providing IVF and DI in Britain have followed criteria to determine access to treatment that are usually based on age, medical history, duration of infertility, and likelihood of success. In NHS clinics, criteria have been even more stringent in order to limit spending. By way of example, the criteria at the NHS funded IVF Unit at St. Mary's Hospital in Manchester in 1984 and 1985 included that the couple be in a stable relationship, childless and resident within the area covered by the Regional Health Authority, with a limit set on treatment cycles to three per couple. The 1990 Act does not indicate how a review of a decision to refuse licensed treatment services to a woman or couple might be brought. It is obligatory, however, to establish and use an ethics committee to oversee the management of individual cases.

One obvious avenue of redress for women or couples refused treatment is to seek judicial review of a clinic's decision to refuse treatment. * * * Their prospects of success in the courts are slim. First, the courts have consistently declined to force health providers to re-order their general priorities for treatment. Second, so far, attempts by individuals to upset clinics' judgments at to their suitability for treatment have been unsuccessful. * * * A significant amendment to the HFEA Code of Practice in December 1995 was the emphasis on the age of the patient and their "likely future ability to look after or provide for a child's needs." In *R. v. Sheffield Health Authority, ex, p. Seale* Auld J. upheld an age bar of 37 preventing older women from being afforded IVF. Only a judgment no reasonable clinic could possibly arrive at in *rationing its resources* would be struck down, he said. The woman reported in 1994 as complaining of a treatment refusal based on her husband already having a child by a previous marriage would have been unlikely to find comfort in the courts. The British patient is required by law to submit to an assessment of suitability for parenthood. In the private sector that assessment may well be minimal. Within the NHS, rationing of resources has meant that poorer patients may be ruled out of contention for treatment unless they are part of a conventional heterosexual couple, young and have no other children by their current or prior relationship.

The French position on access is very different. The law imposes stringent rules excluding from access to treatment any patients who do not seek treatment as a heterosexual couple seeking to replicate a conventional nuclear family structure. But if patients meet that standard the methods of funding treatment ensure that poverty is no bar to access. French patients may only be treated within a *"projet parental"* (parental undertaking). All treatment must be given in the spirit of a particular couple's undertaking to be a parent. Under article 8 of the Statute on donation and assisted conception assisted reproductive techniques or a created embryo can only be used to help a couple have a child or to prevent the transmission to that child of a particularly serious illness. This man and woman must not only be alive at the time of any treatment cycle, but also of procreating age (pre-menopausal), married or cohabiting for more than two years, and giving their annual written, informed consent beforehand to embryo transfer or artificial insemination. An embryo can only be created to satisfy that particular couple's use of a treatment cycle to achieve a conception, gestation and then a child. Each couple is entitled to four treatment cycles or five years of treatment. As a general rule couples undergoing treatment may only use one donated gamete, rather than both. In exceptional circumstances, an embryo can be donated to a couple undergoing treatment by another such couple who have tried NRT without success. Both members of the donating couple must give written consent to donation of what is in effect "their" embryo, whether the original gametes were donated or not.

In addition to the *"projet parental"* being introduced by the 1994 Statutes, the final part of article 8, which deals with counselling, also serves to make life more difficult for French patients trying to gain access to treatment. Under the 1990 Act in Britain counselling has to be provided to all patients receiving treatment in a licensed clinic. Patients themselves, particularly in Britain, have campaigned for this to be introduced in clinics in order for the more difficult aspects of treatment to be discussed, such as the low success rates, the invasive surgery, and the psychological problems associated with "failure." In France counselling was not taken up until Parliamentary debate took place in the run-up to the passing of the 1994 Statutes themselves. Unfortunately for patients the French form of "counselling" is a double edged sword. The purpose of these sessions is to inform the couple of the low success rates, the difficulties of treatment, the law, and what treatments involve. Their other purpose, however, is to verify the motivation of the couple and to inform them of the possibilities of adoption. A month waiting-period must then follow, which can be lengthened by a doctor, before written confirmation that treatment is to be allowed. This form of "counselling" in France might just serve to deter couples, rather than help them in their decision-making or even contribute to an informed consent, especially those who do not fit the ideal model of parents-to-be.

French legislators appear to be emphasising the protection of the interests of the child through the *"projet parental."* Successive government reports since the mid-1980s in France have argued that access *should* be limited, that treatments should be therapeutic and for consenting infertile heterosexual couples only. The Braibant Report in 1989, for example, underlined its support for the nuclear family and pointed to *"toutes les études psychologiques, sociologiques"* as evidence for the need of a child for a family. It argued that the NRT child had a fundamental right to a father and mother from conception, just like a normally conceived child. Though single women are able to adopt in France the Report argued that society should not seek to create one parent families or babies abandoned at birth. It decided that NRTs should only be available to consenting, infertile, heterosexual stable couples or those with a transmissable genetic disease. When the French Senate consulted the British HFEA, on the issue of access to single and lesbian women in 1992, it was dismayed to hear that the Authority saw no fundamental difficulty in providing treatment to such women when nature did not discriminate in this way and when there was no guarantee that a stable, heterosexual couple would be good parents.

However, couples deemed to enjoy the requisite *"projet parental"* status will be able to be treated regardless of income for in France treatment for "sterility" is fully reimbursed by the State, as infertility treatment is categorised as a "cure" for infertility or sterility, and sterility is explicitly seen as an "illness." * * * The French government undertakes an expenditure of approximately 200,000 francs (£24,000) for every couple—at great expense to the public purse.

The cultural difference underlying this generosity is the twentieth century predisposition of the French State towards pronatalism. This is accepted wisdom in France across the political spectrum and has played an important part in all reproductive policy there since the turn of the century, influencing law and policy, for example, on contraception and abortion. Unlike its British counterpart, the French State is no stranger to expensive financial attempts to encourage its citizens to have more children.

Legislators have emphasised the interests of the child rather than the parents in both France and Britain, but in different ways. The French have done this through formally preventing single parents or non-heterosexuals from having access to any assisted conception treatment and having this written into the law. However, if a French woman applying for treatment is in a heterosexual stable relationship, even if she already has a child, whether related to her or not, but does not have the means to obtain treatment privately, she is almost guaranteed assisted conception treatment. A * * * woman of limited resources who would not fit with strict UK NHS, criteria would be likely to have a much easier time in France, as the French bioethics laws allot less discretion to the clinician or to a resident ethics committee and fund assisted conception treatments much more generously. In the UK a woman on the brink of menopause by the time she applies for treatment is unlikely to receive treatment. In France a woman in her late thirties may be legally entitled to treatment but may not be able to find a clinic protective of its success rates that is willing to treat her. A woman in her forties may therefore find access actually easier in the UK as long as she can pay for it.

IV. Defining Parenthood: Filiation, Law and the Artificial Family

Legislators faced with the growing demand for medically assisted conception have attempted to formulate regulations for what is in essence a growing medical industry. But this particular industry has thrown up a series of thorny ethical issues. In the area of donor insemination, the gamete used to create an embryo is invariably, by necessity, donated, and donated anonymously. The genetic parent of the resulting child will therefore be different to the eventual social parent who takes the child home. The practice of gamete donation thus raises many questions. If somebody's sperm or ovum can be given to another person in this way what is the nature of humanity or humanness? What is a family? Who is the true parent of the child? Should children be told that their genetic parent is not their social parent? Do donors need to remain anonymous?

Gametes may well have a special status because they are of human origin. They also contain genetic material. For some they also hold special meaning because they are part of the procreation of a new life, and are helping another person to create this new life. For most of us, then, human gametes are distinct from other human body parts and from non-human gametes and merit the particularly restrictive provisions governing their use, the resulting offspring, and their "parents." It could be argued that the donation of gametes objectifies them and assimilates them to property. However, the stipulation in both countries for informed consent before donation underlines that the law holds donors to be social persons, and gametes to be more than a mere clump of cells. Legislators have to some extent assured their humanity in this way.

Section 13(6) of the 1990 Act in England therefore requires that consent is required, after the opportunity for counselling has been given, from donors of sperm, eggs and embryos, before the latter can be used for treatment, donation, storage, or research. To ensure their informed consent, donors of gametes (or embryos) must be told, *inter alia*, about the possible uses their gametes may be put to and their legal status as parents. Under section 12(e) donors may not be paid at all and may only have their expenses reimbursed up to £15 or treatment in kind, though the HFEA is currently considering whether payment should be prohibited.

The issue of whether a human could donate his or her own body part, and if s/he could consent to that, has been much more of a philosophically problematical issue for French lawyers and ethicists. Particular problems were raised for French academic lawyers, as legislation had to deal with important principles which had existed in the Civil Code since the 1789 Revolution, and which impinged on donation. Firstly, there was the principle of the"*liberté de disposer de soi*"—the freedom and privacy to do what one likes with one's own body. More significant was the"*indisponibilité du corps*" or unavailability of the body which became a principle of law after 1789 when the higher authority of the Church was replaced by that of man himself, and the superior status of the soul by the body itself. Having gained in importance and status, the body could not be commercialised, contracted, enslaved, separated, or tampered with in classical civil law and private law—it was not a thing,"*une chose*" under Article 1128 of the Civil Code. Following codified law therefore, any products of human origin could not be bought or sold, nor could the human donors or their inheritors profit from their production, although the donors could be informed of the intended use. The only exceptions to commercialisation of human products were if they were for therapeutic or diagnostic purposes (not cosmetic), or very small in size, such as genes produced by naturally sourced micro-organisms (which have been patentable in Europe since the 1960s).

The bulk of gamete donation law in France is dealt with by the 1994 Statute on donation and assisted conception. Article 10 reaffirms the regulations pertaining to donor insemination which have operated under self-regulation by the largest, and government-approved, donation body, the *Centre d'Etudes et de Conservation de Sperme* (CECOS), in relation to consent before donation, anonymity, and a ban on payment. Most importantly, and on this the regulations in France on donation contrast with our own, gametes may only be donated from one set couple to another: a donor must now be a father or mother in a couple and have the written consent of their partner to donation. The partner of a gamete donor has as much right to revoke their consent as the donor themselves, at any time before fertilisation. Once an embryo is created the embryo "belongs" to a particular couple having treatments. In Britain, by contrast, centres are only advised to encourage donors to obtain their partners' consent. Prior to the passing of the 1994 Statutes a handful of French clinics carried out insemination and did not follow these CECOS-inspired rules.

The fact that informed consent was included in the French law is especially noteworthy and underlines the French attitude to the inherent humanness of gametes. * * * The fact that informed consent, along with the strict rules governing donation in France, were included in the 1994 Statutes underlines both the seriousness with which this issue was taken there, and that this has been used as a method for solving the problems pertaining to the humanity of gametes and the legal repercussions of that, sitting alongside the strict rules of the *"projet parental."*

* * * The use of donor gametes has thrown up such difficult philosophical questions as what constitutes a family and who is the true parent of a donated gamete? Various new regulations have been introduced which attempt to clarify parenthood in relation to them and give a firm, clear legal basis to who exactly is the parent of an NRT child, bearing in mind the various situations that can arise. In both countries legislators have instigated the rule that a donor can never be the parent where the donation and treatment are carried out in a licensed clinic and the donor appropriately consents and remains anonymous. The legal parents of the NRT child are set out as soon as treatment begins: a "child" belongs to one set of parents rather than any other from before its conception at the time of gamete selection, the exception to this rule being in the use of surrogacy. The use of donor "parents" have turned long established and accepted rules on filiation or parenthood in France upside down as biological "facts" are no longer as tenable.

On the question of motherhood rules have been identical on either side of the channel since 1990. Under section 27 of the 1990 Act and article 374 of the French Civil Code the woman who gives birth to the child is considered to be its mother. This applies whatever the genetic makeup of the child, in other words whether or not the original ovum was genetically the product of the birth mother. This rule has had to be instigated in regulations governing NRTs because the use of donation has resulted in an anomaly, which could not have existed previously, whereby a woman who gave birth was not necessarily the genetic mother of that child. The child could be the product of a donated ovum or a donated embryo. The birth mother in France, however, has had the ability to remain anonymous since the eighteenth century. This became accepted practice as it was thought that a woman who did not want a child, or to be seen to have given birth to an illegitimate child, might seek to destroy it either at birth or before. This method was used to enable such a woman to give birth with impunity, with the state then taking charge of the child and seeking to have it adopted. Such a child in France would then be legally motherless in the same sense that its birth certificate would not acknowledge any woman by name as its mother.

Section 28 of the 1990 Act applies to NRT fatherhood in Britain. Section 28(2) reenacts the provision in section 27 of the Family Law Reform Act 1987 whereby the husband is presumed to be the father of any child his wife gives birth to, unless he can prove that he did not consent at the time of treatment. Section 28(3) extends this to partners within unmarried couples, where they are seeking treatment together and the male partner is infertile. There is no requirement to seek consent but it is normal practice. Under Section

29(4) if the husband or partner does consent only he is the father. If he does not he may accept later that the child is his. Under Schedule 3 of the Act the donor is never the father if the donation and treatment are carried out in licensed clinics and if the donor appropriately consents. This can therefore in theory lead to legally fatherless children where the husband or partner proves he has not consented.

* * *

[In France] Article 10 of the 1994 Statute on respect of the human body refers specifically to filiation in the case of donation. None is established between a donor and offspring. Laws on filiation in France previously applied only to men, as the law on birth mothers has existed for almost two centuries. Although ova donation is less important numerically than sperm donation, perhaps due to the much more invasive procedure it necessitates, its introduction has meant that both fatherhood and motherhood are now contestable where NRTs have been used. The new regulations of the 1994 Statutes therefore apply to donors of both sexes, and therefore to women for the first time. These rules relate to a male donor in a couple who have used donated sperm, and a female donor in a couple who have used donated ova alongside the husband's sperm (otherwise they would be using a donated embryo which in France is a much more contested procedure, see below). Under the new law, once either a man or a woman in a couple has consented to the use of a donor, filiation cannot be contested unless it can be proven that the child is not a result of NRTs (and is the result of intercourse outside the couple), in which case the father still has to pay for the child's upkeep if that couple separate and the woman gains custody of the child.

The filiation rules in France now differentiate between NRT and non-NRT children. The non-NRT child's filiation depends upon its genetic make-up and biological origins at the time of its conception, if its fatherhood is brought into question in court. Parenthood of the NRT child is dependent on who gave birth to it, who was the legal partner of that woman at the time of birth, and whether the correct procedure was carried out for consent in a licensed clinic.

In both countries then, legally fatherless children can be created where the husband or partner proves he has not consented. In France a legally parentless child can also be created if its mother also gives birth anonymously.

V. Anonymity, Consent and Postmortem Insemination

It would appear then that informed consent has been introduced in both countries as a precaution against conflict around the question of fatherhood and to ensure agreement about treatment between a couple using a donor. This is further reinforced by the legal stipulation that donors must remain anonymous. In this way there is no question of their being held to be the parents of the NRT child produced. Psychological studies on adopted children have shown the value of telling children the truth about their origins and adopted children have been given the right to such information. In practice, however, it would appear that parents of NRT children do not intend telling those children the truth. Should children be told that their genetic parent is not their social parent? Do donors need to remain anonymous? Many donors themselves would wish to remain anonymous and not have any relationship or given inheritance rights to children resulting from their donation.

Under the 1990 Act (s. 13(2)) licensed centres must keep records of the users of their services: the donors' names; the child's name; which services were used; and the names of those whose consent was required (for 50 years). Under Section 31(4)(b) information will be available to the 18-year-old NRT child, or younger and planning to marry, after counselling. This does not force parents to inform their children but will avoid consanguineous marriage, as the two people are entitled to information on whether or not they are related. Section 31(4)(a) provides that any information the Authority decides to give may include identifying information. * * *

The idea of there being a right to know genetic and personal information in parliamentary debates in Britain was based on a European Court of Human Rights case, *Gaskin v. UK*. This held that article 8 of the European Convention, demanding respect for the private life of an individual, required that all people should be able to establish details of their identity as individual human beings.

No such challenges have been made to French law. Article 2 of the 1994 Statute on donation and assisted conception therefore goes further than the English law and ensures complete anonymity to donors. This means that children born as a result of donated gametes would never be able to know their genetic identity or their natural parents. Under article 10 of this Statute non-identifying information may be given to children resulting from donation only on the grounds of therapeutic necessity and subject to clinical discretion. * * *

In order to cement the relationship of the social father, it has been decided in England that the child will have no claims on the biological father and will only have access to the most meagre information on him, and in France that there will be complete anonymity. This contrasts with laws on adoption, whereby adoptees have access to information on their mothers, something that has been accepted as necessary to the children concerned. Despite the conclusions of psychologists, legislators have seen fit to prevent the NRT child from knowing its genetic parents, or even, in France, its genetic identity. It would appear then that parents and legislators alike would rather not respect their child's "right to know" and are instead respecting the rights of parents. * * *

* * *

VI. Embryos and Personhood

The use of medically assisted conception from the 1980s has meant that gametes can live outside the human body for the first time. As we have seen, the storage and donation of these human genetic products have raised questions regarding humanness and parenthood in relation to their insemination. NRTs have also provided methods whereby these gametes can go on to be fertilized outside the body. An individual human thus begins its life in a Petri dish. But is this oocyte or "preembryo" the same as the person born some nine months later? Or does it have a status separate from other people? Should such status mean the law should guarantee preservation of the embryo in all circumstances? Is the embryo equivalent to a "thing"? Does the embryo then belong to people as other property does?

Legislators in each country have dealt with the issue of the classification of the embryo as a person or thing in crucially different ways. The pragmatism of the common law has enabled the English to avoid having to classify the nature of the embryo. For example, the 1990 Act affords civil liability to the child damaged as a result of treatment. * * * It provides for damages if a child is born disabled as a result of an act or omission following the selection, keeping or use of gametes or embryos or if there has been negligence or a breach of statutory duty to one or both parents, and/or which if injury had occurred would have given rise to liability. The defendant must be liable in tort to one or both parents. * * * Following *R v. Tait*, where a five-month-old foetus was not a person for the purposes of the Offences Against the Person Act 1861, an embryo cannot be a person.

Moreover, the Court of Appeal in 1994 reaffirmed that under English law the foetus (or embryo) was not a separate person from its mother, but was rather one of two things: either an integral part of its mother, or in coexistence with its mother, in other words "Not-One-But-Not-Two." Both approaches were compatible with the Abortion Act 1967 which permitted women, on public policy grounds to allow clinicians to harm their foetuses. Such questions were left unclear by the 1990 Act, however.

French legislators have been hard pressed to formulate guidelines for NRTs, not only with the difficulties of amending Codes and having to formulate law for new types of medical technologies, but also because French law is based on Christian tradition which makes it a sacrilege to own or sell or commercialise the body, even one's own body. Under French law, therefore, the embryo must be categorized as a person or as a thing. As in England, embryos in France have rights as people that are contingent on being born and being viable which means that women's rights outweigh them. They have a right to inherit, to not be murdered, and to damages after birth. Pre-embryo rights are even less than those of the foetus or new-born.

Under section 14 of the 1990 Act in England a licence is required from the HFEA (renewable after ten years) for the storage of gametes or embryos or both. Under this section gametes may be stored for ten years, and embryos for five years. In 1991 regulations were published which allowed the statutory storage period for sperm to be extended beyond ten years for men under 45 whose fertility was likely to become impaired after medical treatment, to allow them subsequently to have children with their partner.

* * * Under article 9 of the 1994 [French] Statute on donation and assisted conception, embryos must now be destroyed if they have been stored for five years and have been "abandoned" by the couple undergoing treatment as part of a "*projet parental*" due to their lack of agreement or consent as to the fate of the embryos, or due to their disappearance, or to an end to their status as a couple, and a receiving couple to whom to donate their embryos cannot be found. There is a difference in status, therefore, between those embryos which were put into storage after the implementation of the 1994 laws and those already in storage at this time. The latter are due for destruction after the five year limit. Their fate will be decided when the laws come up for their scheduled re-examination in 1999. Debates in France in this year will almost certainly reflect those which took place in Britain during the summer of 1996.

On the issue of embryo donation the 1990 Act in England authorises donation after the appropriate counselling and consent, with the embryo being "allowed to perish" when no consent can be procured. The ensuing child is considered in law as that of the recipient couple subject to the requirements of sections 27 and 28 regarding the birth mother, the consent of the father, whether married or not, and providing the child is not then adopted. As with gamete donation, the embryo donor remains anonymous and does not have any rights in the child. Succession rights begin at birth, not at fertilisation.

Since the early 1980s in France government bodies have been in favour of strict limits on embryo donation arguing that it should not be commercialised and should involve the consent of donor and recipient and be part of a "*projet parental.*" Under the 1994 Statute on donation and assisted conception, embryo donation, as with storage, is only available as part of a "*projet parental.*" Once an embryo has been created in France, the control over its fate as regards storage or donation passes from the gamete provider to the couple having treatment as part of a parental undertaking, and passes from one such couple to another such couple, if donated. This contrasts with the power of gamete providers under the 1990 Act in England to vary their consent to embryo storage. Article

8 of the French Statute on donation and assisted conception stipulates guidelines to follow in situations when the couple do not use their own embryo. In exceptional circumstances both partners may give written consent to donate their stored embryo, anonymously, to a particular couple for whom ART without a donor and as part of a *"projet parental"* has already been unsuccessful. The criteria of the receiving couple are to be checked to see whether they can offer to any resulting child suitable familial, educational, and psychological conditions. It should be borne in mind that these strict criteria on embryo donation have been put in place when only a handful of embryos are actually made available for donation each year.

Under article 9 of the French Statute on donation and assisted conception, after the death of one of the "parents" of a stored embryo, the survivor is to be asked by a judge to donate their embryo(s). The consent of the deceased parent to donation after his or her death is not necessary as donation to another couple is within the spirit of the law. However, if the survivor does not consent to donation, the embryo(s) must be destroyed after five years' storage. This could create a rather unfortunate situation, where for example, a French widow who has gone through the difficult experience of infertility treatment and then the death of her partner, is then faced with the choice of donating the resulting embryos to another couple or seeing them destroyed. Indeed, this was confirmed in a French case on 9th January 1996 at the Cour de Cassation.

On the whole the 1994 laws in France appear to try to protect the embryo more forcefully than the 1990 Act in relation to donation whereby an embryo must be donated from one couple to another, and in relation to research whose regulation is considerably more strict to the extent that basic research would appear to have been completely outlawed. As with the other legal issues raised by the new techniques of assisted conception, in France constitutional principles have complicated the legislating process for Parliamentarians. The idea of embryo storage has also created fierce legal debate in France due to the question of whether you can destroy or dispose of abandoned frozen embryos as if they were things rather than humans. Again the constitutional idea of a human never legally being construed as a thing impinges on this law. Academic lawyers have concluded that the issue has not been solved by the 1994 laws. This question led to a referral to the Constitutional Court to decide on the constitutionality of embryo storage, disposal and research. * * *

A comparison of the English and French responses to the question of embryo status, particularly in relation to research, leads to the conclusion that the embryo is a good deal more valued and protected under French law than English. This "value" does not mean, however, that the value of the embryo is closer to that of the born child in France. Personhood is dependent on birth and viability in both countries.

* * *

Notes

1. The House of Commons Select Committee on Science and Technology recently recommended that assisted reproduction be largely deregulated, given that assisted reproduction has become standard medical practice and its regulation infringes on private decisions. See Shelia Mclean, De-Regulating Assisted Reproduction: Some Reflections, 7 Med. L. Int. 233 (2006); Jacqueline Laing and David Oderberg, Artificial Reproduction, the "Welfare Principle", and the Common Good, 13 Med. L. Rev. 328 (2004). As of this writing, however the U.K. legislation has not changed.

2. The problem of assisted reproduction represents a new and growing class of legal issues—instances where a major breakthrough in scientific or medical research or technology leaves the law playing catch-up. These situations present an ideal opportunity to turn to comparative law and policy, since a number of nations must simultaneously solve the same problem. In fact, it has become common for European nations to hold conferences or to appoint commissions to consider how other nations are approaching such problems. This is all the more necessary in Europe because such issues increasingly involve European law. See, e.g. *R. v. Human Fertilisation and Embryology Authority, ex parte Blood*, Court of Appeal (Civil Division), [1997] 2 All. ER 687 (considering whether wife could take frozen sperm of deceased husband to Belgium to receive fertility treatment prohibited under British law).

3. Why do persons who wish to use new reproductive technologies have to meet requirements as to their suitability for parenting that would be considered to violate basic human and constitutional rights nearly everywhere if they were imposed on natural parents? Such requirements are much less common in the United States, at least as a matter of law. In the United States access to artificial reproduction is not regulated by law, though clinics that provide such services may have their own screening criteria. Why are screening requirements imposed in the United Kingdom and France?

4. Austria, Germany and Switzerland have recently considered adopting the French provision for anonymous birth, but only Austria has accepted it. Barbara Willenbacher, Legal Transfer of French Traditions? German and Austrian Initiatives to Introduce Anonymous Birth, 18 *Int.J.L.& Pol'y & Fam.* 343 (2004). The French provision for anonymous birth was challenged in 2002 in *Odievre v. France* before the European Court of Human Rights by a woman born of an anonymous birth who claimed that denying her knowledge of her identity violated her right to private life. The Court held, 10 to 7, that the mother's interest in privacy and the state's interest in discouraging abortion and protecting life outweighed the child's interest in knowing her identity. Nadine Lefaucheur, The French "Tradition" of Anonymous Birth, the Lines of Argument, 18 *Int'l J. L. & Pol'y & Fam.* 319 (2004). Sweden is one of the few countries in which offspring conceived through artificial insemination have a right to know the identity of the donor. See, considering the attitudes of donors towards this law, K.R. Daniels, H.L. Ericsson and I.P. Burn, The Views of Semen Donors Regarding the Swedish Insemination Act 1984, *3 Med. L. Int.* 117 (1998)

5. Italy is identified in the Lorio article as taking a "laissez faire" approach to assisted reproduction. In 2004, however, Italy passed one of the world's most restrictive statutes on the subject. Under the new law, medically-assisted reproduction methods can only be used when an adult heterosexual couple is infertile and it is otherwise impossible to eliminate the cause of infertility. The law prohibits heterologous insemination, prohibits the creation of more embryos than are needed for a single implantation cycle (three), and prohibits cryo-preservation of embryos. The law also prohibits preimplantation diagnosis. Severe fines are provided for those who violate the statute. A. Conti, P. Delbon, Medically-Assisted Procreation in Italy, 24 *Med. & L.* 163 (2005). The German law is also quite conservative, banning egg donation and surrogacy, preimplantation testing, fertilization of more eggs than can be implanted in a single cycle, or implanting more than three embryos. See John A. Robertson, Reproductive Technology in Germany and the United States: An Essay in Comparative Law and Bioethics, 43 *Colum. J. Transnat'l L.* 189 (2004). What policies motivate these restrictive laws?

6. Earlier in these materials, notably in our discussion of informed consent, we took note of the problems the common law confronts in dealing with issues not read-

ily conforming to the classification of torts offered by the common law writs. Here, however, we see the common law, with its practical orientation, having an easier time addressing new legal problems than the French civil law, with its well established categories of persons and things. A civil code is supposed to address all problems comprehensively, and thus must sometimes go through uncomfortable adjustments when new issues arise.

7. Note that the problem of assisted reproduction, unlike many of the problems we have heretofore confronted, is essentially a problem for elites. For most persons living in most countries on earth, in vitro fertilization and embryo transplants are simply unaffordable luxuries.

8. See also, discussing the English situation, in addition to sources cited earlier, Renate Gertz, et al., Developments in Medical Law in the United Kingdom in 2005 and 2006, 13 *Eur. J. Health L.* 143 (2006); Margaret Brazier, Regulating the Reproduction Business? 7 *Med. L. Rev.* 166 (1999); Michael Freeman, Does Surrogacy Have a Future After Brazier? 7 *Med. L. Rev.* 1 (1999); Lynn Hagger, The Role of the Human Fertilisation and Embryology Authority, 3 *Med. L. Int.* 1 (1997); Ian Mccallister, Modern Reproductive Technology and the Law: Surrogacy Contracts in the United States and England, 20 *Suffolk Transnat'l L. Rev.* 303 (1996); Robert L. Stenger, The Law and Assisted Reproduction in the United Kingdom and United States, 9 *J.L & Health* 135 (1995); and Kristina Stern, The Regulation of Assisted Conception in England, 1 *Eur. J. Health L.* 53 (1994). See, discussing further developments in France regarding research involving embryos, Melanie Latham, The French Parliamentary Guidelines of May 1997: Clarification or Fudge, 3 *Med. L. Int.* 235 (1998).

9. See, discussing legal regulation of assisted reproduction in other countries, Aaron Fahrenkrog, A Comparison of International Regulation of Preimplantation Genetic Diagnosis and a Regulatory Suggestion for the United States, 15 *Transnat'l L. & Contemp. Probs.* 757 (2006); Jennifer Gunning, Regulation of Assisted Reproductive Technology: A Case Study of Japan, 22 *Med. & L.* 751 (2003); Andreas S. Voss, The Right to Privacy and Assisted Reproductive Technologies: A Comparative Study of the Law of Germany and the U.S., 21 *N.Y.L. Sch. J. Int'l & Comp. L.* 229 (2002); Trees A.M. te Brakke, Regulation of Assisted Reproductive Technology in the Netherlands, 35 *Tex. Int'l L.J.* 93 (2000); George P. Smith, Assisted Reproduction: A Comparative Analysis, 8 *B.U. Int'l L. J.* 21 (1990); Calum MacKellar, Legal Regulations in Europe and Deryck Beyleveld, The Moral and Legal Status of the Human Embryo, in *In Vitro Fertilisation in the 1990s*, 247, 265 (Elisabeth Hildt & Dietmar Mieth, eds, 1998); and Anita Stuhmcke, Surrogate Motherhood: The Legal Position in Australia, 2 *J. L. & Med.* 116 (1994).

The intensive Regulation of assisted reproduction in the U.K. gives rise to litigation involving fascinating and complex ethical issues dealt with privately in the U.S., as the following case illustrates.

Regina (Quintavalle) v. Human Fertilisation and Embryology Authority

House of Lords, [2005] UKHL 28, [2005] 2 A.C. 561 (2005)

* * *

This was an appeal, by leave of the House of Lords, by the claimant, Josephine Quintavalle, on behalf of Comment on Reproductive Ethics, against the judgment of the

Court of Appeal allowing an appeal by the defendant, the Human Fertilisation and Embryology Authority ("the authority") from the order of Maurice Kay J quashing, by way of judicial review, the decision in principle made by the authority, dated 13 December 2001, to allow HLA typing in order to test an embryo for tissue compatibility with an affected sibling, pursuant to section 11 of the Human Fertilisation and Embryology Act 1990.

* * *

Lord Hoffmann

My Lords, Zain Hashmi is a little boy, now aged six, who suffers from a serious genetic disorder called beta thalassaemia major. His bone marrow does not produce enough red blood cells and in consequence he is often very poorly and needs daily drugs and regular blood transfusions to keep him alive. But he could be restored to normal life by a transplant of stem cells from a tissue compatible donor.

The problem is to find compatible tissue which Zain's immune system will not reject. The chances of finding a compatible donor who is not a sibling are extremely low. Even in the case of siblings, the chances are only one in four. None of Zain's three elder siblings is compatible. In addition, the donor must be free of the same disorder. That lengthens the odds even more. Zain's mother, Mrs Hashmi, has twice conceived in the hope of giving birth to a child whose umbilical blood could provide stem cells for Zain. Once the foetus was found to have beta thalassaemia major and she had an abortion. On the second occasion she gave birth to a child whose tissue turned out not to be compatible.

There is a way to save the Hashmi family from having to play dice with conception. * * * In vitro fertilisation ("IVF") has enabled many couples who could not achieve natural fertilisation to have children. More recently, it has become possible to perform a biopsy upon the newly fertilised IVF embryo and remove a single cell to test it for genetic disorders. This is called pre-implantation genetic diagnosis ("PGD"). It provides a woman with information about the embryo proposed to be implanted in her body so that she may decide whether or not to proceed. Mrs Hashmi, for example, would have been spared having to have her foetus carrying beta thalassaemia major aborted if the embryo had been created by IVF and the disorder diagnosed by PGD.

Still more recently, and so far only in the United States, it has become possible to use the same single cell biopsy technique to test for tissue compatibility. This involves examination of the human leukocyte antigens ("HLA") and is known as HLA typing. That means that if Mr and Mrs Hashmi's sperm and eggs are used to create IVF embryos which are then tested for beta thalassaemia major by PGD and for tissue compatibility with Zain by HLA typing, they can know that the child Mrs Hashmi conceives will have stem cells which could cure Zain. The question in this appeal is whether this can lawfully be done in the United Kingdom.

After the birth of the first IVF child or "test tube baby" in 1978, it became clear that the new technique, together with other potential developments in embryology and genetics, could raise serious medical and ethical issues. The government appointed a committee under the chairmanship of Dame Mary Warnock DBE to advise. * * * The centrepiece of the committee's recommendations was the creation of a statutory licensing authority to regulate all research and treatment which involved the use of IVF embryos.

This recommendation was given effect by the Human Fertilisation and Embryology Act 1990, which set up the Human Fertilisation and Embryology Authority ("the authority"). Members are appointed by the Secretary of State and it has to have a lay (i e not medically qualified or engaged in IVF treatment or research) chairman and deputy chairman and a majority of lay members.* * *

The source of the authority's power is section 3(1), which makes it a criminal offence to bring about the creation of an embryo or keep or use an embryo except pursuant to a licence from the authority. The proposed treatment of Mrs Hashmi to assist her in bearing a tissue-compatible child involves the creation and use of embryos and therefore requires a licence. In this case, the authority has granted a licence which permits both PGD and HLA typing. But Ms Quintavalle, the claimant in these proceedings, who is director and founder of a group which believes in absolute respect for the human embryo, says that the authority has no power to authorise HLA typing. She brought judicial review proceedings for a declaration to that effect. It was granted * * * but an appeal was allowed and the application dismissed by the Court of Appeal.

* * *

In this case we are particularly concerned with the activities which may be authorised to be done in the course of providing treatment services. "Treatment services" are defined by section 2(1) to mean, among other things, medical services provided to the public for the purpose of assisting women to carry children. IVF is of course such a service; the proposal is to assist Mrs Hashmi to carry a child conceived by the implantation of an IVF embryo. So the question is whether PGD and HLA typing are activities which the authority can authorise to be done "in the course" of providing her with IVF treatment.

To find the answer, one must look at the list of activities in para 1 of Schedule 2. Para 1(3) provides that the authority may licence an activity on the list only if it appears to the authority to be "necessary or desirable for the purpose of providing treatment services". The activities include: "1(1) ... (d) practices designed to secure that embryos are in a suitable condition to be placed in a woman or to determine whether embryos are suitable for that purpose."

The authority's case is that both PGD and HLA typing are to determine whether an embryo would be suitable for the purpose of being placed in Mrs Hashmi. The definition of treatment services focuses upon the woman as the person to whom the services are provided. The authority says that Mrs Hashmi is entitled to regard an embryo as unsuitable unless it is both free of abnormality and tissue compatible with Zain. Without such testing, she cannot make an informed choice as to whether she wants the embryo placed in her body or not. The authority considers it desirable for the purpose of providing her with treatment services, i e IVF treatment, that she should be able to make such a choice. Mr Pannick, who appeared for the authority, pointed out that the Act does not require that PGD or HLA typing should *constitute* treatment services. They must be activities *in the course* of such services, i e in the course of providing IVF treatment.

The claimant, on the other hand, says that this gives far too wide a meaning to the notion of being suitable. It would enable the authority to authorise a single cell biopsy to test the embryo for whatever characteristics the mother might wish to know: whether the child would be male or female, dark or blonde, perhaps even, in time to come, intelligent or stupid. Suitable must therefore have a narrower meaning than suitable for that particular mother. Maurice Kay J thought that suitable meant only that the embryo would be viable. That would rule out a good deal of PGD, because many genetic abnormalities do not affect the viability of the foetus. * * * The narrower meaning is particularly difficult to support when paragraph 3(2)(e) lists, among the research projects which may be licensed, "developing methods for detecting the presence of gene or chromosome abnormalities in embryos before implantation". It would be very odd if Parliament contemplated research to develop techniques which could not lawfully be used. So Lord Brennan [representing the claimant] accepts that suitable means more than viable. Building on paragraph 3(2)(e), he says that an embryo is suitable if it is capable of becoming a healthy child, free of abnormalities. PGD to establish that the embryo is free from genetic abnormalities is therefore acceptable. But not HLA typing. A baby which is not tissue compatible with Zain would not be in any way abnormal. It just would not answer the particular needs of the Hashmi family.

"Suitable" is one of those adjectives which leaves its content to be determined entirely by context. As my noble and learned friend, Lord Scott of Foscote, put it in argument, a suitable hat for Royal Ascot is very different from a suitable hat for the Banbury cattle market. The context must be found in the scheme of the 1990 Act and the background against which it was enacted.* * *

The Warnock Report discussed possible future developments in embryology. Some of these, such as creating children in vitro or the gestation of human embryos in other species, it recommended should be unequivocally banned. On others, it made no such recommendations. One of these was embryonic biopsy, such as can now be used for PGD and HLA typing. It described, in para 12.13, the advantages of PGD in detecting abnormalities before implantation * * * and its disadvantages, namely the need to use IVF. It concluded that it was unlikely that embryonic biopsy would become a feasible method of detecting abnormal embryos for some considerable time.

For present purposes, the most relevant discussion in the Warnock Report concerned gender identification. * * * Such information could be used to select embryos to "prevent the birth of a child with a sex-linked hereditary disease". The committee saw no reason why this should not be done: para 9.11. It then went on to consider the use of gender identification to select the sex of a child "for purely social reasons". After some discussion of the social issues (population distribution, the role of women in society), the committee said that it was unable to make any positive recommendations.* * *

* * *

The conclusion which I draw is that the committee contemplated that the authority would decide the circumstances, if any, in which sex selection on social grounds should be authorised. As sex selection on social grounds is the most obvious case of selecting an embryo on grounds other than its health, I would infer that the Warnock committee did not intend that selection of IVF embryos on grounds which went beyond genetic abnormality should be altogether banned.

* * * The intention [or Parliament as evidenced by the White Paper that preceded the legislation] was therefore to define the functions of the authority in very broad terms. To ensure that the legislation was flexible enough to deal with "as yet unforeseen treatment developments which may raise new ethical issues", the Bill would "contain powers to make regulations (subject to the affirmative resolution procedure) to add to or subtract from the range of matters coming within the regulatory scope of the [authority]".

* * *

Included in the matters which were to be prohibited were what journalists commonly call "designer babies" or, as the White Paper put it, in para 37: "the artificial creation of human beings with certain predetermined characteristics through modification of an early embryo's genetic structure." Another was the cloning of individuals by nuclear substitution. But, relevantly for present purposes, there was no proposal to include in the "clearly prohibited" list the testing of embryos to enable the mother to choose to carry a child with characteristics of her choice. One infers that the White Paper intended the fundamental ethical issues which such activities might raise to be determined by the statutory authority, subject to the regulation-making power by which Parliament could impose its own decision.

* * * Section 3(3)(a) prevents, as the Warnock Committee recommended, the development of the foetus in vitro by providing that a licence may not authorise the keeping or use of an embryo after the appearance of the primitive streak. Nor may the authority authorise the placing of an embryo in an animal (subsection (3)(b)) or the cloning of an embryo (subsection (3)(d)). By para 1(4) of Schedule 2, a licence may not authorise altering the genetic structure of any cell while it forms part of an embryo.* * *

Subject to these prohibitions, the licensing power of the authority is defined in broad terms. Paragraph 1(1) of Schedule 2 enables it to authorise a variety of activities (with the possibility of others being added by regulation) provided only that they are done "in the course of" providing IVF services to the public and appear to the authority "necessary or desirable" for the purpose of providing those services. Thus, if the concept of suitability in sub-paragraph (d) of 1(1) is broad enough to include suitability for the purposes of the particular mother, it seems to me clear enough that the activity of determining the genetic characteristics of the embryo by way of PGD or HLA typing would be "in the course of" providing the mother with IVF services and that the authority would be entitled to take the view that it was necessary or desirable for the purpose of providing such services.

The chief argument of Lord Brennan [counsel for the claimant] against interpreting suitability in this sense was that, once one allowed the mother's choice to be a legitimate ground for selection, one could not stop short of allowing it to be based upon such frivolous reasons as eye or hair colour as well as more sinister eugenic practices. It was, he said, inconceivable that Parliament could have contemplated the possibility of this happening.

Let it be accepted that a broad interpretation of the concept of suitability would include activities highly unlikely to be acceptable to majority public opinion. It could nevertheless be more sensible for Parliament to confine itself to a few prohibitions which could be clearly defined but otherwise to leave the authority to decide what should be acceptable. The fact that these decisions might raise difficult ethical questions is no objection. The membership of the authority and the proposals of the Warnock committee and the White Paper make it clear that it was intended to grapple with such issues.

In this case, as I have said, Maurice Kay J thought that suitable meant no more than suitable to produce a viable foetus but Lord Brennan, understandably unwilling to argue that Parliament might have outlawed PGD, said that it meant suitable to produce a healthy foetus, free of genetic defects. But this definition is itself not free from difficulty. What amounts to a genetic defect? Marie Stopes, an enthusiastic believer in eugenics, cut off relations with her son because she considered that the woman he chose to marry suffered from a genetic defect: she was short-sighted and had to wear spectacles. Surely it would be more sensible to concentrate on whether choice on such grounds was ethically acceptable rather than to argue over whether it counted as a genetic defect. The great advantage which Parliament would have seen in using broad concepts to define the remit of the authority is that it would avoid sterile arguments over questions of definition and focus attention upon the ethical issues.

Even in cases in which one could clearly say that the ground for selection was not a genetic defect, a total prohibition might exclude cases which many people would think ethically acceptable. Mr Pannick drew attention to the facts of Leeds Teaching Hospitals

NHS Trust v A [2003] 1 FLR 1091. In the course of providing IVF treatment to a husband and wife, the hospital mixed up the sperm provided by the husband with that of another man. As a result, a woman gave birth to twins, the father of whom was a stranger. But they suffered from no genetic defects and Mr Pannick points out that if the muddle had been suspected before implantation of the embryo, Lord Brennan's construction of suitability would have prevented any tests to check the embryo's DNA. * * *

* * *

I would * * * accept Mr Pannick's argument and hold that both PGD and HLA typing could lawfully be authorised by the authority as activities to determine the suitability of the embryo for implantation within the meaning of paragraph 1(1)(d).

* * *

Another point on which the authority has shifted its position is the use of bone marrow rather than umbilical cord blood as a source of stem cells. Bone marrow may in some cases be more suitable but involves a far more intrusive operation upon the donor child than taking cord blood. The policy formulated by the authority in 2001 (under which the licence which authorised the treatment of Mrs Hashmi was granted) required a condition that "the intention" should be only to take cord blood. After a review in 2004, the authority decided to delete this condition. It was in practice unenforceable because once the embryo had been implanted and the child conceived, the case passed out of the jurisdiction of the authority. * * *

* * *

In my opinion, however, it is unnecessary to express any view about Lord Brennan's criticisms of the way the authority has exercised its jurisdiction. There has never been any suggestion that the authority acted unreasonably in granting a licence. The case has always been that it had no power to do so. In my opinion it did, and I would therefore dismiss the appeal.

* * *

Lord Brown of Eaton-Under-Heywood

* * *

* * * [S]ince that December 2001 policy decision the authority has contemplated licensing tissue typing on a less restricted basis: first, in cases where there is no need for PGD; secondly, where the intention is if necessary to use bone marrow and not just blood from the abdominal cord; and thirdly, where a parent rather than a sibling is to be benefited. All this, however, goes only to emphasise the comparative narrowness of the issue presently before the House. Your Lordships are simply not concerned with the conditions under which tissue testing should be licensed, assuming it is licensable at all—nor even, indeed, with *whether* it should be licensed. Your Lordships' sole concern is whether the Act *allows* the authority to license tissue typing were it in its discretion to think it right to do so.

* * *

[The weakness of the claimant's case] lies in the difficulty Lord Brennan himself has in establishing a satisfactory and coherent dividing line between embryo selection which is permissible and that which is not—let alone finding support for any such dividing line in the 1990 Act. * * * I was at one time attracted to Lord Brennan's dividing line between selection aimed purely at eliminating serious genetic or chromosome defects (permissible) and other selective criteria (impermissible). As, however, Lord Hoffmann points out, at para 27 of his speech, what amounts to a serious genetic defect will itself often be contentious. Still less can one find in the statutory language any basis for saying that the elimination of serious genetic or chromosome defects contributes to the process of "assisting women to carry children" whereas other embryo selection does not.

The fact is that once the concession is made (as necessarily it had to be) that PGD itself is licensable to produce not just a viable foetus but a genetically healthy child, there can be no logical basis for construing the authority's power to end at that point. PGD with a view to producing a healthy child assists a woman to carry a child only in the sense that it helps her decide whether the embryo is "suitable" and whether she will bear the child. Whereas, however, suitability is for the woman, the limits of permissible embryo selection are for the authority. In the unlikely event that the authority were to propose licensing genetic selection for purely social reasons, Parliament would surely act at once to remove that possibility, doubtless using for the purpose the regulation making power under section 3(3)(c). Failing that, in an extreme case the court's supervisory jurisdiction could be invoked.

For these reasons, most of which are more fully explained in Lord Hoffmann's speech with which I entirely agree, I too would dismiss this appeal.

Appeal dismissed.

* * *

Notes

1. In another recent controversial decision, the House of Lords upheld the jurisdiction of HEFA over cloning (cell nuclear Replacement). *R (On the Application of Quintavalle) v. Secretary of State for Health*, House of Lords, [2003] U.K.H.L. 13 and [2003] 2 All. E.R. 113.

2. Reproductive cloning has not generally been as well received as other forms of assisted reproduction. An additional protocol to the Council of Europe's Convention on Human Rights and Biomedicine states:

> 1 Any intervention seeking to create a human being genetically identical to another human being, whether living or dead, is prohibited.
>
> 2 For the purpose of this article, the term human being "genetically identical" to another human being means a human being sharing with another the same nuclear gene set.

See discussing this provision, Nati Somekh, The European Total Ban on Human Cloning: An Analysis of the Council of Europe's Action in Prohibiting Total Cloning, 17 *B.U. Int'l L.J.* 397 (1999).

3. On March 8, 2005, the United Nations General Assembly adopted resolution 29/280, the United Nations Declaration on Human Cloning, encouraging all member states to prohibit, "all forms of human cloning inasmuch as they are incompatible with human dignity and the protection of human life." The resolution in non-binding, was adopted after four years of intensive debate, and passed by a vote of 84 to 34 with 37 abstentions. See Angela Campbell and Gillian Nycum, Harmonizing the International Regulation of Embryonic Stem Cell Research: Possibilities, Promises and Potential Pitfalls, 7 *Med. L. Int.* 113 (2005). Although reproductive cloning is widely condemned, cloning for research

purposes remains very controversial, as this debate illustrates. See also, discussing the legislation of various countries dealing with cloning, Angela Campbell, Ethos and Economics: Examining the Rationale Underlying Stem Cell and Cloning Research Poicies in the United States, Germany and Japan, 31 *Am. J. L. & Med.* 47 (2005); Jason T. Corsover, The Logical Next Step? An International Perspective on the Issues of Human Cloning and Genetic Technology, 4 *ILSA J. Int'l and Comp. L.* 697 (1998).

C. The Right to Die

Although a right on the part of a patient to decide whether or not to discontinue life sustaining treatment has been recognized in the United States since the *Quinlan* case in 1976, and all of the states now have legislation governing advance directives, the right to die has developed more slowly and along different lines in most other nations. Probably the legal situation in Canada, where most of the provinces have adopted laws recognizing advance directives and several have appellate court decisions recognizing a right to die, resembles that of the United States most closely. See Decision-Making at the End of Life, in *Canadian Health Law and Policy* 501–532 (Jocelyn Downie, Timothy Caulfield, and Colleen Flood, eds., 2d. ed. (2002)). Advance directives are also recognized under Singapore law (See, Ter Kah Leng and Susanna Leong Huey Sy, Advance Medical Directives in Singapore, 5 *Med. L. Rev.* 63 (1997)), and in a number of the Australian states and territories (See Michael Eburn, Withdrawing, Withholding, and Refusing Emergency Resuscitation, 2 *J. L. & Med.* 131 (1994)). Denmark has a statute governing advance directives, and Finland and the Netherlands recognize them as well, though they do not regulate them in detail. See Herman Nys, Emerging Legislation in Europe on the Legal Status of Advance Directives and Medical Decison-Making with Respect to an Incompetent Patient ("Living-Wills"), 4 *Eur. J. Health L.* 179 (1997). See, discussing the English situation, where advance directives have common law, though not statutory, authority; David Jessop, Patients' Rights and Doctors' Responsibilities: Confluence and Conflict, 3 *Med. L. Int.* 197 (1997); Kristina Stern, Advance Directives, 2 *Med.L.Rev.* 57 (1994).

In much of the world, however, death and dying issues are governed by court decisions, often interpreting code provisions prohibiting homicide and assisted suicide, and by the ethical codes, opinions, and disciplinary decisions of medical associations and licensure boards. These decisions and opinions often vary from their United States counterparts in important respects. First, in the United States, the right to refuse life sustaining treatment seemed to follow quite directly from the right of patients to autonomous decision making, that is, the right to informed consent. In other parts of the world this connection has not seemed so obvious. Though the right to consent to treatment is recognized almost everywhere (in theory, if not in practice, see chapter 2, sec. C, above), in some countries this right is seen primarily as a right to bodily integrity—the right to not have one's body invaded without consent. It is not obvious in these countries that the right extends comprehensively to patient involvement in medical decisions generally, or that it covers interventions like the provision of artificial nutrition or hydration. See Sjef Gevers, Patient Involvement in Non-Treatment Decisions, 4 *Eur. J. Health L.* 145 (1997).

Further, in some countries the right of the doctor to determine the appropriate treatment for his or her patient is also considered important, and must be balanced with the patient's rights. One organization responding to the 1994 British Select Committee on Medical Ethics stated that "it would be bizarre in the extreme to require a skilled professional doctor to adhere to the stipulations of a living will which did not accord with his/her expert opinion of what would be in the best interests of the patient's health." (quoted in Anne Morris, Life and Death Decisions: "Die, My Dear Doctor? That's the Last Thing I Shall Do!" 3 *European J. Health L.* 9, 26 (1996). Though this statement is somewhat extreme, courts in other countries do afford much more deference than American courts do to the opinions of medical professionals as to whether or not treatment should be continued. Indeed, in some countries a doctor may be found to have violated his or her ethical obligations by withholding or withdrawing treatment and allowing a patient to die, even if the patient requested that medical interventions cease.

Other countries also seem to afford the courts a more central role in end of life decisions where the patient is incompetent. Though courts and legislatures in the United States are increasingly willing to leave these decisions to patients and their families, judicial oversight remains more prominent in other countries. Moreover, the role of the family is given less weight. See Cameron Stewart, Who Decides When I can Die? Problems Concerning Proxy Decisions to Forego Medical Treatment, 4 *J. L. & Med.* 386 (1997). Further, outside of the United States the "substituted judgment" approach to decision making—in which a surrogate decision maker attempts to make the decision the patient would have made if competent—is generally rejected in favor of a "best interests" test, under which caregivers and courts attempt to figure out what is best for the patient.

The following reading considers European international law and the contrasting law of several European countries on the right to die issue.

Physician Involvement in a Patient's Death: A Continental European Perspective

Herman Nys, (text originally from Medical Law Review, vol. 7 (1999), updated by Herman Nys, 2007)

I. Introduction

This article contains an analysis of recent legal developments in Europe (which is the supranational and international level of the Council of Europe and the European Union) and in some continental European countries regarding physician involvement in a patient's death.

Four types of physician involvement in a patient's death have been distinguished. Firstly, a physician may become involved in a patient's death because the patient refuses a treatment that may possibly save his life. Is there a legally recognised obligation for a physician to respect the right of a patient to refuse treatment when death may be the consequence of such refusal? What is the legal value of an advance refusal of such a treatment (the so-called living will)? And what is the role played by formally appointed representatives and close relatives?

Secondly, a physician may become involved in a patient's death as the result of a non-treatment decision. If this decision is the consequence of a refusal of the treatment by the patient, it falls under the first category. Non-treatment or abstinence decisions however, mainly refer to the patient whose condition is agreed to be hopeless either in the sense that the treatment has no chance of success or that it would be (or has become) disproportionate to any benefit for the patient.

Thirdly, a physician may become involved in a patient's death because of the use of drugs to alleviate pain or other symptoms even though the dose used will more or less certainly hasten the moment of death. I will refer to this category as "pain relief (decisions".

Fourthly, physician involvement in a patient's death when the physician intentionally terminates the life, at the patient's request or not. If this is done at the request of the patient I term this (mainly under the influence of Dutch jurisprudence) euthanasia. However, I am aware that this term is also used (together with adjectives as active or passive, direct or indirect) in a much broader sense in other countries. In a comparative analysis, the term euthanasia is therefore useless. I will for this reason use a more neutral term, termination of life on request. This category also covers doctor-assisted suicide although I am aware that to many people "active, voluntary euthanasia" and "doctor-assisted suicide" are distinct categories. [The author's discussion of assisted suicide and euthanasia is found in the next section.]

II. Developments in European Law

A. The Right of a Patient to Refuse a Medical Treatment

1. General remarks

A treatment against the will of a competent patient may first of all be considered as a violation of Article 8 of the European Convention for the protection of Human Rights (ECHR). This article reads as follows:

> 1. Everyone has the right to respect for his private and family life, home and correspondence.
>
> 2. There shall be no interference by a public authority with the exercise of this right except such as in accordance with the law and necessary in a democratic society in the interests of national security, public safety or the economy well-being of the country, for the prevention of disorder or crime, for the protection of health or morals, or for the protection of the rights and freedoms of others.

The right to respect for his private life protected by Article 8 ECHR is most clearly concerned with individual choices as to bodily autonomy. The European Commission on. Human Rights has decided that medical intervention against the will of the patient, even of minimal importance, violates the right to respect of privacy.

The European Court of Justice of the European Communities (established in Luxembourg and not to be confused with the European Court of Human Rights in Strasbourg) has decided that "the right for private life requires that a person's refusal (of an HIV test in the particular case) be respected in its entirety". This aspect of article 8 also includes the right not to be treated medically without consent. For this reason the Court found a violation of article 8 in the *Glass* case (2004). In the *Pretty* case (2002) the Court held as follows: "in the sphere of medical treatment, the refusal to accept a particular treatment might, inevitably, lead to a fatal outcome, yet the imposition of medical treatment, without the consent of a mentally competent adult patient, would interfere with a person's physical integrity in a manner capable of engaging the rights protected under article 8 (1) of the Convention".

Bodily autonomy is also protected by Article 2 that protects the right to life, and Article 3 that protects the right to be free from torture or inhuman, or degrading treatment, or punishment. The case law associated with Article 3, however, indicates that it is mainly concerned with punishment. Even though the article protects an individual from "degrading treatment", a term which terminally ill persons may associate with the intrusive procedures and loss of dignity accompanying their illness, it seems not applicable with respect to a medical treatment against the expressed refusal of a competent patient. With regard to refusal by an incompetent patient, in the case of *Herczegfalvy*, the Court decided that it was for the medical authorities to decide, on the basis of the recognised rules of medical science on the therapeutic methods to be used, by force if necessary, to preserve the physical and mental health of patients who are entirely incapable of deciding for themselves. In general, a medical treatment that is necessary cannot be considered as inhuman or degrading. Article 5 ECHR ("Everyone has the right to liberty and security of person") that protects personal freedom can also be of relevance although it is mainly of importance to protect a patient against illegal deprival of freedom. When the refusal of a lifesaving treatment is also inspired by religious reasons (cf. Jehovah's Witness), Article 9 ECHR that guarantees the freedom of conviction and religion is of relevance.

Nowadays, the protection of European citizens of medical treatment against their refusal cannot only be deduced from Article 8 ECHR. On 1 December 1999 the European Convention on Human Rights and Biomedicine of 4 April 1997 became effective. Article 5 of this Convention reads as follows:

> An intervention in the health field may only be carried out after the person concerned has given free and informed consent to it. This person shall before hand be given appropriate information as to the purpose and nature of the intervention as well as on its consequences and risks. The person concerned may freely withdraw consent at any time.

2. Advance refusal of a treatment (Living will)

The ECHR does not contain any direct reference to an advance refusal of a medical treatment. In this respect, Article 9 of the Convention on Human Rights and Biomedicine is of direct relevance. It reads as follows:

> The previously expressed wishes relating to a medical intervention by a patient who is not, at the time of the intervention, in a state to express his or her wishes shall be taken into account. "Taking into account" is only a weak recognition of the right to refuse medical treatment in advance. According to the Explanatory Report, taking previously expressed wishes into account does not mean that they should necessarily be followed. For example, when the wishes were expressed a long time before the intervention and science has since progressed, there may be grounds for not heeding the patient's opinion. The practitioner should thus, as far as possible, be satisfied that the wishes of the patient apply to the present situation and are still valid taking into account in particular of technical progress in medicine.

This cautious approach of the Convention reflects the lack of consensus in many European countries as to the validity of an advance refusal of treatment, especially life supporting treatment (infra).

3. Refusal by a representative

Article 6 of the Convention on Human Rights and Biomedicine contains a mechanism to protect persons not able to consent. Article 6(3) reads as follows:

> Where, according to law, an adult does not have the capacity to consent to an intervention because of a mental disability, a disease or for similar reasons, the intervention may only be carried out with the authorisation of his or her repre-

> sentative or a person or body provided for by law. The individual concerned shall as far as possible take part in the authorisation.

Article 6(5) provides that the authorisation may be withdrawn at any time in the best interests of the person concerned. Although the refusal of a treatment is not mentioned here expressly, the explanatory memorandum makes it clear that a representative may refuse a treatment: "It was not considered necessary to provide in this article for a right of appeal against the decision of the legal representative to authorise or refuse to authorise an interventions."

B. Non-treatment Decisions

The European Commission has been confronted with the question whether Article 2 ECHR (right to life) obliges a Member State to protect its citizens against non-treatment decisions. A Swiss citizen lodged a complaint before the European Commission because of what he considered as a case of "passive euthanasia" on his father who suffered from Parkinson's disease. The facts of the application do not reveal the medical treatment or under what circumstances it was withdrawn. Regardless, his complaint before the Swiss Courts was dismissed and finally the Swiss Federal Supreme Court declared his appeal inadmissible. Before the European Commission, the applicant complained that Swiss law violates the right to life (Article 2 ECHR) because it does not condemn *expressis verbis* a so-called "passive euthanasia" applied without the written and express consent of the patient. The applicant also considered this legal vacuum as a violation of Article 8 ECHR because not respecting the will of the patient constitutes a violation of his right to privacy. According to the Commission, Article 2 obliges a state not only to abstain from intentionally killing a person, but also that it takes adequate measures to protect life. The European Commission declared the complaint inadmissible because the Swiss law incriminates the fact of taking life by negligence or by guilty imprudence. By offering this protection Swiss law complies with the obligation imposed by Article 2 ECHR.

Unfortunately, the Commission has not given an answer with respect to the violation of Article 8. In the *Glass* case (2004) the Court did not consider it necessary to examine separately the applicants' complaint regarding the inclusion of a DNR notice in the first applicant's (a severely disabled child) case notes without the consent and knowledge of the second applicant (his mother). It however observed in line with its admissibility decision that the notice was only directed against the application of vigorous cardiac massage and intensive respiratory support, and did not exclude the use of other techniques, such as the provision of oxygen, to keep the first applicant alive. The participation of the patient (or his legal representative) in a non-treatment decision has also otherwise not received much attention until recently. In much of the literature, in statements by international organisations, and in many national legal documents, informed consent by the patient is not related to the concept of "medical decisions" but to the narrower concept of "intervention" or even "treatment": For example, Article 5 of the Convention on Human Rights and Biomedicine (supra) limits the right to give informed consent to such "intervention". Although the term "intervention" must be understood here in a broad sense— it covers all medical acts, in particular interventions performed for the purpose of preventive care diagnosis, treatment or rehabilitation, or in a research context—it nevertheless is limited to "acts." If informed consent is only required before a medical intervention is carried out, in fact only one albeit important aspect of patient participation in medical decision making (the possibility to refuse an intervention after adequate information has been provided) has the status of a legal obligation for the physician. This creates the risk that in other medical decisions involving the patient, such as non-treatment decisions, he may be left at the discretion of the health professional or that it may be considered only a matter of good practice to ask for the opinion of the patient, and not necessarily a legal duty.

This limited approach of patient participation in medical decisions may be explained because informed consent is viewed traditionally and essentially as a justification for unauthorised, intentional touching of another person. Moreover, in this opinion a medical intervention is only justified when the physician acts with a therapeutic intention. If, however, according to the physician the situation of the patient is such that his intervention cannot serve any therapeutic purpose, he not only has a right but a duty to withdraw the treatment. This reasoning leaves no room for an active patient (or his relatives) participation in a non-treatment decision.

C. Pain Relief

In the *Glass* case (2004) the European Court considered that the decision to impose pain relieving treatment on the severely handicapped child in defiance of his mother's objections gave rise to an interference with the first applicant's right to respect for his private life, and in particular his right to physical integrity.

D. Termination of life on request

According to the European Court, article 2 ECHR cannot be said to guarantee to anyone a right to die, and, therefore, it cannot be regarded as an avenue for challenging national legislation prohibiting termination of life on request or assisted suicide (*Pretty* case, 2002). With regard to article 3 ECHR the Court concluded that no positive obligation arises under this article to require a State to provide a lawful opportunity for any form of assisted suicide. However, the Court was not prepared to exclude the possibility that a complete ban on assisted suicide constitutes an interference with the right to respect for private life as guaranteed under Article 8 (1) ECHR.

III. Developments in National Law

A. Denmark

1. The right to refuse a medical treatment

In Denmark the right to refuse a medical treatment has explicitly been recognised by statute law. Section 25 of the of Law No. 546 of 24 June 2005 on Health that entered into force 1 January 2007 reads as follows:

> A terminal patient may reject treatment entirely aimed at delaying the time of death.

One of the implications of this disposition is that the patient can reject treatment and can thus, for example, avoid being kept alive artificially. The Danish Parliament has attached decisive emphasis to respecting the patient's right of self-determination and to avoiding the sustenance of life at any cost. Under Danish legislation, the doctor must respect the patient's autonomy with regard to foregoing treatment alternatives. If the patient makes a non-treatment decision, the doctor must comply with the patient's wishes.

Law No. 546 of 24 June 2005 has also expressly recognized the validity of advance refusals or living wills. Section 26 (1) of this act provides as follows:

> Any person over the age of 18 and not under guardianship may establish a living will. In the living will the patient may express his wishes regarding treatment, in case he experiences a condition where he is no longer able to perform his right to self-determination.

According to subsection 2 in a living will it is possible to record conditions regarding:

> a) refusal of life prolonging treatment in situations where the patient is terminally ill, and
>
> b) refusal of life prolonging treatment in case of illness, progressed decrepitude, accident, heart failure or the like leaving the patient permanently unable to take care of himself or herself physically and mentally.

Life prolonging treatment is defined in subsection 3 as treatment with no prospect of cure, improvement or relief, but only for some life prolonging. It does not include life-supporting treatment.

According to subsection 5 the wishes expressed according to subsection 2 (a) (terminally ill patient refusing life prolonging treatment) are binding for the health care provider who in other words is obliged to respect the patient's request to omit treatment. The law requires that only the assessment of the patient's medical condition may be taken into consideration, whereas other factors may not be considered relevant, e.g. the physician's personal preferences, research interests or economic motives. A wish expressed according to subsection 2 (b) (permanently severely impaired patient refusing life prolonging treatment) however is a recommendation for the health care provider and must be taken into consideration as such. The law presupposes that the request in such a living will, although legally not binding, may only be overruled due to reasons of a very substantial nature. In the physician's considerations, a number of factors might be included, e.g. the nature and progression of the illness, the treatment options, the patient's age and life situation, the relative's opinions etc. The physician's discretionary power in this respect is rather wide and vague.

Section 26 (4) stipulates that in case a health care provider, when the patient is unable to perform his right to self-determination, is planning the initiation of life-extending treatment to a terminally ill patient, or plans on continuing life prolonging treatment in a situation as described in subsection 2 (b), he must contact the living will registry established according to section 27 to check for the existence of a living will. Section 27 empowers the Interior and Health Minister to establish a living wills register and determine regulations for the issue, design, registration and withdrawal of living wills. The registration procedure currently costs about 7€. The validity of an advance directive is not limited to a set period of time. A clear statement issued in a different manner may be given legal status equivalent to an advance directive filed on the official formula, if a physician becomes aware of its existence and content. A patient may always revoke the living will by issuing a written and clear notification to the Registry. In connection with a current illness, the living will may informally be revoked by a plain statement, e.g. to the responsible physician or another health care professional.

2. Non-treatment decision

Section 25 (2) of Law N° 546 of 24 June 2005 reads as follows:

> In case a patient is no longer able to practice his right to self-determination, the health care person may refrain from initiating or proceeding with life-extending treatment.

3. Pain relief

Section 25 (3) of this Law provides:

> A terminal patient may receive pain-relieving, sedative or similar medication necessary to relieve the condition of the patient, even if this might accelerate the time of death.

B. France

1. The right to refuse a medical treatment

Article 3 of Law No. 94-653 of 29 July 1994 regarding respect for the human body (one of the so-called Bioethics laws) has amended Article 16 of the French Civil Code. Following amendments in 1999 and 2004 article 16(3) now reads as follows:

> The integrity of the human body may only be violated in case of medical necessity for the person concerned.... The consent of the person concerned has to be given beforehand except when his state of health requires a medical intervention to which he cannot give his consent.

The right to refuse a medical intervention is clearly recognised. As a consequence of this law, the French Court of Cassation has already changed its jurisprudence as to what party—the patient or the physician—has to prove whether the patient has given his informed consent. Until 1997 the Court laid the burden of proof upon the patient. In a decision of 25 February 1997 however the Court revised its position: it is now to the physician to demonstrate that he has obtained the informed consent. This change follows logically from Article 16(3) of the French Civil Code: a violation of the human body is prohibited unless for medical reasons and unless the person concerned has consented to it. A physician who violates this prohibition must demonstrate that these conditions are present. It also means that a physician has to accept the refusal of a patient because without consent of the patient, he may not violate the bodily integrity of the patient to refuse a medical treatment.

Since its amendment in 1995, article 36 of the professional ethics Code of the French Order of Physicians is also very clear with respect to the right of a patient to refuse a medical treatment. It reads as follows:

> Consent of the person concerned has to be sought before any diagnostic procedure or treatment. If a competent patient refuses a diagnostic procedure or treatment, the physician has to respect this refusal after having informed the patient of all its consequences.

Finally, in 2002 a far-reaching provision was introduced by Law N° 2002-303 of 4 March 2002 on the rights of patients in the Code of Public Health (section L1111-4). After being amended by Law N° 2005-370 of 22 April 2005 on the rights of patients and the end of life, section L1111-4 reads as follows:

> Each person takes his own decisions regarding his health, in conjunction with the healthcare professional and taking account of the information and recommendations furnished by him.

The physician must respect the will of the person after having informed him of the consequences of his choices. If the patient's decision to refuse or stop any treatment puts his life in danger, the physician must do all he can to convince him to accept the needed treatment. He can consult a colleague. In any case the patient has to reiterate his decision after a reasonable period of time. This is added to his medical file. The physician preserves the dignity of the dying patient and assures the quality of the end of life.

No medical act and no treatment can be provided without the free and informed consent of the person. This consent can be withdrawn at any time.

The obligation to help a person in danger, provided for in Article 223-6, section 2 of the French New Criminal Code (Article 63, old Criminal Code) is not an absolute one and has to yield when a competent patient has knowingly expressed a refusal to receive a treatment, according to the French Court of Cassation in a famous decision of 3 January 1973. A decision of the French Council of State nullified a disciplinary sanction imposed by the French Order of Physicians on a physician who had prescribed a palliative treatment to a woman who refused an efficient treatment for cancer. Against the background of this jurisprudence and the legislative change in 1994, the decision by the Council of State in the *Granier* case surprised most commentators. In this decision, the Council of State indeed confirmed a disciplinary sanction imposed upon a physician by the French Order of Physicians. Confronted with a patient suffering from breast cancer and who had explicitly refused a mamectomy and radiotherapy, the physician had limited himself to offer palliative care. After a complaint by a colleague the physician was sentenced by the order of physicians to a prohibition of three, and after appeal, six months of practice of medicine. After the appeal of the physician, the Council of State confirmed this severe sanction. For Dubouis, this sanction cannot be reconciled with the right of the patient to refuse a treatment and the duty of the physician to respect this refusal, the more so because in a previous decision the Council had reached an opposite conclusion. For Dunet-Larousse the practical consequences of the *Granier* decision should not be exaggerated because the palliative treatment offered to the patient was of a scientifically disputable nature. But having regard to the principles at stake, the decision is incompatible with civil law and the code of professional ethics.

The development introduced by the Council of State with the *Granier* decision, has recently been confirmed by lower administrative court decisions. The Paris Administrative Court of Appeal had to decide whether a physician could lawfully carry out a blood transfusion against the express refusal of a Jehovah's Witness. In both cases the patient had clearly expressed his refusal to undergo a blood transfusion. The widow of the patient in the first case (notwithstanding the blood transfusion the patient had died) and the patient herself in the second case argued that the treating physician had not respected obligations imposed both by European and French law. With respect to European law, they referred to Articles 3, 5, and Article 9 ECHR. Rather surprisingly they did not mention Article 8 ECHR. The Court decided that there was no violation of Articles 3 and 5. The blood transfusion could be regarded as a violation of the freedom of religion (Article 9 ECHR) but in this particular case it was justified by the duty of the physician to save the life of the patient. With respect to French law, the Court considered that Article 36 of the Code of Professional Ethics of the Order of Physicians that had been approved by decree and thus had a binding force, and Article 16(3) of the Civil Code, obliged a physician to respect the will of the patient. However, the Court added, the obligation of the physician to respect the will of the patient is limited by another obligation of the physician to save the health and life of the patient if the following three conditions are met: Firstly, the medical intervention is urgently needed; secondly, the life of the patient is in danger; and thirdly, there is no alternative solution.

Both decisions leave many questions unanswered. First, one may wonder Whether the Court would have reached the same conclusion if a life-saving treatment was refused not because of religious reasons as was the case here, but because the patient did not want to live any more. A Jehovah's Witness who refuses blood does not want to be dead, but accepts death as a consequence of refusal. The fact that no referral was made to Article 8

ECHR may be understood in this context. Although both decisions are silent on this, the advice of the Commissioner of the Government to the Court made it clear that even if the refusal was based on the right of the patient to refuse a treatment and not on religious reasons, the attending physician had not to respect the will of the patient. According to the Commissioner it is not for the Courts to recognize in a praetorian-way a right to die by refusing relatively simple and efficient medical care, whereas the legislator has not legalized euthanasia. In other words, recognizing a right to refuse life-saving treatment is considered as paving the way to a right to be killed on request and that is a matter that has to be decided by Parliament. Another important and not clearly answered question is the legal basis of the duty of a physician to save the life and health of the patient. This cannot be the obligation imposed by the Criminal Code to help a person who is in danger because it is generally accepted in French law that this obligation is limited by a refusal of the patient.

The French Council of State has confirmed both decisions. Given the *Granier* opinion it would have been surprising if the Council had nullified them. It was not clear whether this decision would survive the recognition of the right to refuse a life saving treatment as a patient right in 2002. In August 2002 the Council of State, however, confirmed its decision. Despite the numerous legislative declarations of the patient's right to self-determination the French courts are not inclined to force physicians to respect patient's refusals of life-saving treatment. It remains to be seen whether the legislative change in 2005 will be more effective.

The forgoing relates in general to the refusal of a life saving treatment by any patient. With regard to the refusal of any treatment by a terminally ill patient article L.1111-10 of the Public Health Code provides that the physician has to respect his wish after having informed him of the consequences of his choice. The decision of the patient is added to his medical file.

The law N° 2005-370 of 22 April 2005 on the rights of patients and the end of life has also created a legal basis for advance directives and proxy decisions. Article L1111-11 reads as follows.

> Every adult person may make up advance directives in case he is no longer capable to express his will. These advance directives indicate the wishes of the person concerning the conditions to limit or to stop treatment at the end of his life. They may be revoked at any time.

On the condition that they have been made up three years before the person became unconscious the physician takes them into consideration before taking a decision to diagnose, intervene or treat.

Article L.1111-12 of the Code of Public Health provides:

> If a terminally ill person who is incapable to express his will has designated a person of confidence the opinion of this person prevails, except in a case of urgency or impossibility, to any other non medical opinion, with the exclusion of advance directives, in decisions taken by a physician to diagnose, intervene or treat the incapable patient.

2. Non-treatment decisions

The Court of Appeal of Rouen on 6 March 1996 condemned an anaesthesiologist for involuntary homicide: he had decided to extubate a patient and to withdraw reanimation of that patient. According to the Court both decisions had been taken against a logic and medical ethics and against the accepted rules of good practice. The physician appealed against this decision. He argued that no causal relationship had been demonstrated between the decision to stop the reanimation and the death of the patient because the Court had itself ascertained that the patient had no chance of recovery or survival. The Court of Cassation confirmed the decision of the Court of Appeal in a judgment of 19 February 1997. According to the Court of Cassation the Court of Appeal had correctly interpreted the facts of the case.

More important than the decision of the Court of Cassation itself—after all the Court hides itself behind the sovereign appreciation of the facts by the Court of Appeal—are the comments on this decision in the literature. Both Legros and Chevallier have difficulties with the legal qualification of the decision to stop reanimating followed by the death of the patient as an involuntary homicide. They argue that the correct qualification would have been a voluntary homicide. According to Chevallier there is a deliberate policy underlying this qualification. A voluntary homicide (euthanasia) has to be judged by a jury composed of lay persons and one may fear that they would be too lenient, misled by emotions. By qualifying the withdrawal of reanimation as an involuntary homicide, it has to be judged by professional judges. This will result in a more efficient fight against euthanasia according to Chevallier who admits that the judgment of the Court of Cassation was a severe one. This severity is inspired by the desire of the Court to combat certain contemporary tendencies to deliberately end the pain and suffering of patients who are manifestly condemned to die in a short time. There is no doubt, according to Chevallier that the decision of the Court of Cassation has to be situated within a more general approach of the jurisprudence to combat immoral practices tending towards euthanasia and instead to impose, respecting the traditional Hippocratic oath, what some call incorrectly therapeutic obstination.

In 1987 the District Court of Paris was confronted with two conflicting requests by relatives of a 61-year-old cancer patient who was at that moment terminally ill. The father of the patient asked the Court to continue giving him chemotherapy while his daughter-in-law (the spouse of the patient) asked that this therapy be discontinued and replaced by an alternative treatment. The Court appointed experts who came to the conclusion that continuation of chemotherapy did not cause unbearable suffering to the patient. But before the Court had taken a decision on the request to discontinue this treatment, the patient died.

Law N° 2005-370 on the rights of patients and the end of life has also introduced some rules regarding non-treatment decisions. Article L 1111-4 (4) of the Code of Public Health provides the following:

> When the patient cannot express his will, limiting or withdrawing a treatment so that his life may be endangered may not be decided without consulting colleagues and without asking the opinion of the person of confidence appointed by the patient or his family or his relatives and taking into consideration his advance directives. The decision to limit or withdraw treatment has to be added to his medical file.

Article L 1111-13 relates to terminally ill patients who cannot express their will. If a physician wants to limit or to withdraw treatment because it is futile, disproportionate or only prolonging artificially the life of the patient he has to consult colleagues and ask the opinion of the person of confidence appointed by the patient or his family or his relatives and take into consideration his advance directives.

C. Pain relief

In 2000 the Council of State approved the decision taken by the National Council of the Order of physicians in a case where a physician had admitted injecting his terminally ill patient with potassium chloride in order to prevent her suffering atrociously during the last few hours of her life. The National Council condemned him because he had not attempted to relieve her pain by palliative care.

Law N° 2002-303 on the rights of patients has stipulated that any person has a right to receive pain relieving treatment (article L.1110-5 Code of Public Health). Law N° 2005-370 on the rights of patients and the end of life has supplemented this article by the following provision:

If a physician is convinced that he cannot relief the pain of a terminally ill patient otherwise than by applying a treatment that may have the secondary effect to shorten the life of the patient, he must inform the patient, his person of confidence, his family or his relatives. His decision has to be added to his medical file.

C. *Germany*

1. The right to refuse a medical treatment

In Germany, the citizen's right of self-determination is explicitly protected by Article 2(1) of the *GrundGesetz*. Not surprisingly, it has long been recognized in jurisprudence that a patient capable of making a decision can refuse a medical treatment, even if the treatment is vital. In a landmark case of 13 September 1994 a Criminal Panel of the German Supreme Court (re)emphasized a patient's right of self-determination, a right to be respected even in the case of a dangerously ill patient. The decision makes clear that withdrawal of treatment or care which leads to death may be done consistently with a patient's rights: indeed may be a vindication of them even where there is a constitutionally protected "right to life." As early as 1957 the Supreme Court had recognised the right to refuse a medical treatment.

The Judgment of the Supreme Court of 13 September 1994 was also important in another respect. As a consequence, the German Medical Association decided to amend its guidelines on medical *Sterbebegleitung* (aid-in-dying). The amended guideline is unambiguous as to the right of a patient to refuse a medical treatment: if a patient is competent, the physician has to respect the contemporaneously expressed will of a well informed patient, even if this will does not correspond with medically indicated measures. This is also valid for a request to end life-supporting measures that have already been started. The physician must help a patient who refuses a life-saving treatment to consider the consequences.

In the decision of 13 September 1994, the Court also laid the basis for widespread acceptance of living wills in Germany. A 70-year-old patient who suffered serious, irreversible brain damage caused by a cardiac arrest in 1990, was unable to express her wishes. She could not swallow and had to be artificially fed through a tube. Her son had been appointed as her guardian. In March 1993, her doctor and her son ordered the nursing staff to discontinue artificial feeding. The staff however refused to do so and informed the guardian Court, which in turn, informed the prosecutor. As a result, the doctor and the son were prosecuted for attempted manslaughter. The District Court found them both guilty of attempted manslaughter. The defendants appealed to the Federal Supreme Court. The Court allowed the appeal and remanded the case for retrial. According to the Court:

1. The District Court erred in holding that allowing someone with cardiac activity, respiratory activity and proper circulation to die by way of terminating medical treatment, automatically gives rise to criminal liability. Provision must be made for exceptional cases such as this where regard must be given to the pa-

> tient's right of self-determination which embraces the right to refuse life-sustaining medical treatment.
>
> 2. Where the wishes of an incompetent person must be presumed, the need to protect human life demands that a high evidential standard be satisfied. Account must be taken of the patient's written or oral indications, religious views, other value-systems and expectations of life. Objective criteria may be clues to individual hypothetical intention, but should not be accorded significant weight unless the patient's presumed intention is indeterminate.

Subsequently, the District Court (judgment of 17 May 1995) acquitted both defendants on the basis of the "presumed consent or will" test of the German Supreme Court. Applying what the Court termed "strict evidential requirements" to determine the patient's presumed will, the District Court set out its approach based upon the Supreme Court's decision as follows:

> Single utterances alone will not as a rule amount to a proper basis as they could have been made during a passing mood. Things do not depend solely on former, verbal or written declarations by the patient. Such declarations may not be assessed in isolation, but have to be looked at together with further indicia which go to reveal the patient's will. The Federal Supreme Court listed a number of indicia which are not exhaustive. What is decisive in ascertaining the patient's presumed consent are her religious beliefs, her other personal value beliefs, her expectations of life (bearing in mind her age), the pain she suffers and the burden to the patient of her pain, the reasonableness of medical intervention, as well as the individual views of the patient.

Hence, the physician and the son were declared not guilty. From the decisions of the District Court, and the Supreme Court, it follows that the presumed consent of a patient in withdrawing life supporting treatment is binding on the attending physician.

Although the expression "advance directive" or "living will" does not appear even once in the decision of the German Supreme Court, according to a German annotator "you can almost hear the sigh of the judge who wrote the judgment: 'How much easier this case would have been had the patient made use of such an advance directive.'"

As consequence of this judgment by the Supreme Court, more and more use is made in Germany of written refusals of life-supporting treatment in the event of an irreversible state of unconsciousness. Such a will is considered to be binding on the attending physician, the guardian and the guardian Court as the writer is aware that, at the moment of drawing up, he will not be able to change his mind. However a more recent decision of a Guardianship Panel of the German Supreme Court of 7 March 2003 has cast doubt on the legal validity of living wills. Unlike the Criminal Panel which relate exclusively to the declared or presumed wish of the patient, the Guardianship Panel demands "objective medical" criteria. This means that the wishes of a patient expressed in a living will are not exclusively decisive.

In its decision of 13 September 1994, the Supreme Court did not have to deal with [the question of appointing a guardian] as a guardian had already been appointed a (the son of the patient) before the problem of withdrawing life-supporting treatment had arisen. For the majority of German commentators it is obvious, however, that the intervention of a guardian is a necessity before a decision to withdraw a life supporting treatment is taken.

Another important question is whether the guardianship court must be involved in such a decision. According to Article 1904, German Civil Code, the guardian's consent concerning medical examination, treatment or surgical intervention has to be approved by the guardianship court if the envisioned procedure poses a danger to the patient's life, or a long and serious injury to his health. In its decision of 13 September 1994 the German Supreme Court argued for an application mutatis mutandis of this rule in cases of withdrawal of treatment, at least if the process of dying had not yet begun." This opinion has been confirmed in a decision of the Central District Court of Frankfurt-am-Main of 17 July 1998. Also, the revised (in 1998 and amended again in 2004) Guidelines of the German Medical Association state that the request of the guardian to end a life-supporting treatment has to be confirmed by a guardianship court when the process of dying has not yet begun. However there is no consensus on this and some District Courts (München I, Augsburg, Karlruhe/Freiburg) have taken the view that a decision to withdraw treatment is a very personal one which cannot be delegated to a guardian in any case.

3. Pain relief

In another landmark decision of 15 November 1996, the German Supreme Court decided that a medically indicated pain relief treatment, in accordance with the express or presumed consent of a dying patient, does not become an illegal act because of the unwanted but unavoidable consequence that the process of dying is accelerated.

This was the first decision by the German Supreme Court dealing with "indirekten Sterbehiffe" (indirect euthanasia). Together with the decision of 13 September 1994 it is an important determination regarding the limits of the duty to treat by a physician. It is also a significant decision because it may free physicians from the fear of prosecution for homicide when they apply pain relief treatment. According to Verrel the opposite is the case: a physician who withholds from his patient a medically indicated pain treatment violates the bodily integrity of that patient. A more recent decision of the German Supreme Court of 7 February 2001 has confirmed this case law and in more concrete terms stated that "indirect euthanasia" is jusitified through the emergency regulation of Article 34 of the German Criminal Code. The guidelines of the German Medical Association (as amended in 2004) reflect the unanimity on this: "in cases of mortal illness the alleviation of suffering may have priority to such an extent that the possibility of an unavoidable shortening of the patient's life will become acceptable".

D. *The Netherlands*

1. The right to refuse a medical treatment

In the not too distant past, Dutch physicians have tended to be rather authoritarian and the law accepted this, but now the patient's unqualified right to self-determination in this regard is no longer subject to doubt. It may be a right whose exercise is not always made easy for the patient, but as a matter of legal principle the doctor who imposes treatment on a patient without his consent is without question guilty of a number of medical disciplinary, civil and even criminal offences. Thus, a competent patient has the legal right, for whatever reason, to refuse (further) treatment, even if the treatment is in the opinion of the doctor indicated and necessary to continued life. It is not relevant that the patient exercises this right in order to shorten his life; nor is it relevant that the doctor (or anyone else) agree with the patient's decision.

With regard to an advance refusal of a medical treatment or living will, Article 450(3) of the Act on the Medical Contract provides for the following:

> In the case of an incompetent patient of 16 years or older, the physician has to follow the clearly expressed opinions of the patient in a written form at a mo-

ment that he was competent and containing a refusal of consent. The physician may override this refusal if he has well founded reasons for doing so.

It has taken much pressure from the Dutch Parliament to have this provision incorporated into the Act on Medical Contract. Against the wishes of the government, and at the last moment, a majority in Parliament approved an amendment. The main issue of discussion was the value that should be attached to written anticipatory decisions. For the government the amendment added little to the already accepted principle of informed consent whilst in the view of Parliament, the amendment was necessary to end the uncertainty that surrounded advance refusals in daily life.

The authority of the physician to override an advance refusal should not be used too extensively, otherwise the provision would become senseless. Preferably, health care providers should use this power only in situations in which the statement is apparently unspecific and/or outdated. The same legislation provides that appointed representatives and close relatives of the patient can exercise the right on his behalf. A physician who, at the request of the patient, abstains from treatment that is necessary for the preservation of life is not regarded as having killed the patient, in the sense of homicide. The patient's death is considered due to a "natural" cause, which means that no special legal controls exist.

2. Non-treatment decisions

Not initiating, or terminating, life-prolonging treatment when this is "medically futile", either in the sense that the treatment has no chance of success or that it would be (or has become) disproportionate to any benefit for the patient, is considered to fall within the scope of the "normal medical practice" that a physician is authorised to perform.

What constitutes "medical treatment" in this connection has been the subject of considerable discussion. In June 1987 Gerard Stinissen brought a civil action in the District Court of Almelo, asking for a judgment that further treatment of his wife should be stopped. She had been in coma since March 1974 as a result of a medical mistake during a Caesarean delivery. In 1976 her husband had asked the nursing home where she was being kept alive to allow her to die. The nursing home refused, initially because they were opposed to taking an "active" decision to let a patient die, but later because they were unsure of their legal position. Stinissen requested the District Court to order that the artificial feeding of his wife be stopped, that possible complications not be treated, and that the nursing home confine itself to care aimed at the relief of suffering. Stinissen argued that medical treatment was futile and that the patient could not be considered to have given consent to it. The Court ruled that the artificial feeding of Ms Stinissen should be considered medical treatment and therefore fell within the authority of a doctor to terminate futile medical treatment. But it considered the doctor's decision to keep her alive legitimate and refused to intervene. The Court of Appeal of Arnhem likewise rejected Stinissen's request that artificial feeding be stopped. The Court argued that doctors should make judgments concerning medical treatment. The Court also confirmed the ruling of the District Court that the artificial feeding should be considered medical treatment. After the Court of Appeal's decision, her physician decided to stop the artificial feeding.

With regard to patient participation in a non-treatment decision, a doctor is not required to accede to a patient's (or his representative) insistence on treatment the doctor considers futile. On general principles, it would seem that he must at least inform the patient, or in the case of a non-competent patient, the family or others responsible for the patient, of the fact that he proposes to abstain from treatment he considers futile, if only so that they can seek a second professional opinion.

Unless based on the patient's request, DNR instructions and other advance decisions, not to administer life-prolonging treatment under specific conditions also fall in this category. It has recently been argued in connection with a hospital protocol for such decisions that the greater the role that proportionality or "quality-of-life" considerations play, the greater the role of the patient (or his representative) in the decision-making should be.

IV. Conclusion: Strengths and Weaknesses of Continental European Medical Law

Comparative studies in the area of health law are rare. It is easy to identify a number of factors which have contributed to this paucity of comparative analysis. The linguistic differences have no doubt made their contribution. Also the differences in legal culture make comparative health law a difficult undertaking. With regard to the law of physician involvement in a patient's death, these difficulties are amplified by the lack of uniformity in terminology.

I will limit myself in this concluding part to draw the attention to some remarkable differences and resemblances in the legal approach of physician involvement in a patient's death in the countries I have studied.

The most interesting and surprising conclusion to me is the role played by the jurisprudence in France and Germany, and the different directions in which both countries have evolved under the influence of that jurisprudence during the last decennium.

There is, of course, one important common feature: the prohibition of termination of life by a physician at the request of a patient is considered to be an absolute limit to legally acceptable physician involvement in a patient's death. But with the same objective in mind, namely safeguarding this limit, the jurisprudence in both countries has created a totally different system. In France, the right of a patient to refuse a life-saving treatment, and the right of the physician to take a non-treatment decision, are considered as a threat to the prohibition of termination of life upon request. Admittedly, this is not said in so many words in the judgments; there are differences in approach between the Council of State and the Court of Cassation; the actual facts of the case may influence decisively a judgment and comments on these judgments are rather rare. But we cannot close our eyes to the apparent fact that the French jurisprudence has evolved during the 1990s in a direction that makes it difficult for patient and physician alike to opt for death with dignity. That the French jurisprudence prefers therapeutic obstination over dying with dignity in order to prevent the slippery slope to termination of life request may be too strong a statement because there are also signs pointing in another direction (especially in some comments on this jurisprudence). Nonetheless, there is a French model in the law of physician involvement in a patient's death. A model that aims at preventing that termination of life on request becomes an accepted practice by refusing patient and physician alike to take decisions that may eventually lead to the death of the patient. Not surprisingly, this jurisprudence expressly refers to accepted medical professional ethics that tends to be rather conservative. In 2002 and subsequently in 2005 the French legislature has intervened to strengthen the rights of patients in general (2002) and of dying patients in particular. And although the right to refuse a treatment even in an advance directive is now legally accepted, medical and legal practice still are profoundly influenced by the habits and attitudes of the last decennium of the previous century.

On the other hand, the Criminal Panel of the German Federal Supreme Court has built up during the last decennium or so a jurisprudence that lays the decisions regarding the refusal of medical treatment, non-treatment and pain relief with the patient. In interviews in legal journals, judges of the Court with a remarkable openness have explained that the right to determination is the red thread in a strategy to make termination of life on request more or less superfluous. There is also a German model in the law of physician involvement in a patient's death. A model that aims at preventing that termination of life on request becomes an accepted practice by recognising the right of the patient to refuse treatment and to participate in non-treatment and pain relief decisions. In this jurisprudence, no referral is made to existing medical professional guidelines. Just the opposite is true: these guidelines have been adjusted to the jurisprudence.

Notes

1. Though right-to-die law varies from state to state in the United States, the law has become increasingly uniform over the years. The emergence of a fairly widely held consensus on what the law should be has been led by three Supreme Court decisions, *Cruzan v. Director, Missouri Dept. of Health*, 497 U.S. 261 (1990); *Washington v. Glucksberg*, 521 U.S. 702 (1997); and *Vacco v. Quill*, 521 U.S. 793 (1997), which have laid out several basic principles. These principles are, first, that the right to make decisions at the end of life is a constitutionally protected liberty interest. Second, that right does not extend to requesting assistance with suicide or euthanasia. The Court in *Vacco* opined that refusing end of life care and requesting assistance in bringing an end to life were distinguishable both in terms of causation and intent. Third, the "right to die" survives incompetency, and decisions affecting incompetents will normally be made on a substituted judgment basis, though best interest judgments may be permissible if there is insufficient evidence of the subject's desires to ground a substituted judgment decision. States may, according to *Cruzan*, require clear and convincing evidence to permit termination of treatment. Most states do, though the vigor with which the standard is enforced varies considerably from state to state. Artificial provision of nutrition and hydration (tube feeding) is treated as a medical procedure, and may be refused like others, though some states place more stringent requirements on terminating tube feeding than on terminating other procedures. All states provide for advanced directives, usually living wills and durable powers of attorney, and these are either decisive or are given considerable weight in decision making. How does this consensus compare with the law of other jurisdictions we have studied?

2. France has effectively two Supreme Courts, the Cour de Cassation, the court of last resort for reviewing judicial decisions; and the Council of State, the final court of appeal for administrative decisions. Are the decisions of these two bodies in this instance consistent? Note the powerful role which the duty to rescue in emergencies plays in the French right to die law. The "Commissioner of the Government" who played a role in the Jehovah's Witness case is a functionary who presents the position of the state in French court cases. This role is a bit like that of the solicitor general in the United States, but is more frequently exercised. See Mitchel de S.-O.-l'E Lasser, Comparative Law and Comparative Literature: A Project in Progress, 1997 *Utah L. Rev.* 471.

3. Germany has consistently taken a strong right-to-life position in most of the issues that we have studied. It has also, however, taken a strong position supporting autonomous patient decisionmaking. Are these two positions in conflict here? Or has Germany found a way to reconcile them?

4. In the United States, the issue that Nys identifies as "non-treatment" decisions is usually discussed under the rubric of medical "futility". The issue is raised when further med-

ical care serves no purpose, and involves the obligation or right the physician has at that point to terminate care. In one well-known American case, *In the Matter of Baby K*, 16 F.3d 590 (1994), the Fourth Circuit Court of Appeals held that the Emergency Medical Treatment and Active Labor Act prohibits denial of treatment to an anencephalic newborn even when further care would be "futile". In a similar case in the United Kingdom, *In re J*, 4 All E.R. 614 (C.A. 1992), the court decided that the family could not compel the doctors to treat a baby where treatment was counterindicated. See James Munby, Rhetoric and Reality: The Limitations of Patient Self-Determination in Contemporary English Law, 14 J. *Contemp. Health L. & Pol'y* 315 (1998). See, reporting a similar more recent British Case, Margot Brazier, Commentary: An Intractable Dispute: When Parents and Professionals Disagree, 13 *Med. L. Rev.* 412 (2005).

5. Undertreatment of pain has traditionally been common throughout the world, and in particular in the United States. There has been a concerted effort in recent years to remove regulatory and law enforcement barriers to effective pain management. Special symposium issues of the Journal of Law Medicine and Ethics in 1996 and 1998 highlighted this issue. The Supreme Court in *Washington v. Glucksberg* (particularly Justice Souter and O'Connor's concurring opinions, at 521 U.S. 702, 738 and 785, n.16 (1997)), countenanced the possibility of "terminal sedation"—providing pain relief in high enough quantities to cause death, if the intent of the medical professional was to diminish pain. Other countries seem also to be increasingly aware of this problem. See on pain and end of life care, See Timothy Jost & Danuta Mendelson, A Comparative Study of the Law of Palliative Care and End of Life Treatment, 21 *J. L. Med. & Ethics* 130 (2003). A recent European Court of Human Rights case, however, held that an English court violated Article 8 of the European Convention of Human Rights guarantying a right to physical and moral integrity when it refused to block a hospital from administering morphine and coding as do not resuscitate a severely disabled child suffering postoperative complications at the insistence of the child's mother. ECHR 2004/9 *Case of Glass v. The United Kingdom*, 9 March 2004, no. 61827/00.

6. The Terri Schiavo controversy in the United States raised starkly the question of when nutrition and hydration should be removed when there is a dispute among close relatives as to what the person would have wanted, and even as to the nature of the patient's condition. See, discussing the *Schiavo* case in an international comparative perspective, Symposium, 12 *European Journal of Health Law* 317ff (2005), including articles on German, U.K. and Dutch law.

7. Note that other countries seem to give far less authority to advanced directives than do American jurisdictions. Why is this? Some American commentators have also begun to question whether advanced directives should always be given decisive weight, particularly when the mental state of the person who signed the directive has changed dramatically. See Rebecca Dresser, Missing Persons: Perceptions of Incompetent Persons, 46 *Rutgers L. Rev.* 609 (1994).

8. Why do European countries seem to prefer "best interest" to "substituted judgment" standards for making termination of treatment decisions? Might our "substituted judgement" standard be explained by our grounding "right-to-die" law heavily on the doctrine of informed consent? Is European law based more directly on therapeutic judgment?

9. See also, Hans-Georg Koch, Erwin Bernat and Alan Meisel, Self-Determination, *Privacy and the Right to Die. A Comparative Law Analysis* (Germany, United States of America, Japan), 4 *European J. Health L.* 127 (1997).

10. The leading British decision concerning the right-to-die issue with respect to incompetents remains *Airedale NHS Trust v. Bland*, [1993] All ER 275. In this case the

British House of Lords decided that discontinuance of the provision of artificial nutrition and hydration would be in the best interests of a patient in a persistent vegetative state, even though it would cause his death. The court concluded that the best interests test was appropriate for these cases, and that this standard should be applied by a court, placing considerable weight on medical opinion. See discussing this case, Ian Freckelton, Withdrawal of Life Support: The "Persistent Vegetative State" Conundrum, 1 *J.L. & Med.* 35 (1993); Andrew Grubb, The Persistent Vegetative State: A Duty (Not) to Treat and Conscientious Objection, 4 *Eur. J.Health L.* 157 (1997). The following case, from the Irish Supreme Court, addresses the same issue. The opinions of two of the five justices in the majority, Denham and O'Flaherty are reproduced, as is part of the opinion of Justice Egan in dissent.

In the Matter of A Ward of Court

2 I.L.R.M. 401 (Irish Supreme Court, 27 July 1995).

Panel: Hamilton, CJ, O'Flaherty, Egan, Blayney and Denham, JJ.

[Opinions of Hamilton, CJ, and Blayney, J. omitted]

Denham, J.:

This case concerns a patient who is a Ward of Court. It is an appeal against a judgment of the High Court delivered on 5 May, 1995; and an Order perfected on 10 May, 1995 which stated, inter alia, that Lynch J being the Judge assigned in that behalf by the President of the High Court:

> (1) Doth hereby consent on behalf of the Ward to the withdrawal and termination of the abnormal artificial means of nourishment by tube whether nasogastric or gastrostomy tube and doth declare that such withdrawal and termination are lawful
>
> (2) Doth hereby consent on behalf of the Ward to the non-treatment of infections or other pathological conditions which may affect the Ward save in a palliative way to avoid pain and suffering and doth declare such non-treatment to be lawful.

The Order was sought by the family of the Ward of Court. The decision of the High Court has been appealed by the Attorney General, the Institution wherein the Ward is being cared, and the guardian ad litem of the Ward. The family of the Ward have sought to vary the judgment (a) insofar as it determines the standard of proof, and (b) insofar as it limits the authority of the family.

The Ward has been placed in her current state by application of advanced medical science. Were it not for this application she would not have long survived a catastrophe over 20 years ago. The case illustrates the problems arising out of modern medical technology and consequent legal issues. These matters have not been addressed by the Oireachtas [the Irish parliament] so it falls to be decided by this Court in accordance with the Constitution and the common law.

Facts

The facts as found by the learned trial Judge may be summarised as follows. In 1972, when she was aged 22, the Ward suffered brain damage as a result of cardiac arrests during a minor gynaecological operation. That catastrophe has resulted in her being completely dependent on others, requiring total nursing care. She is spastic, both arms and hands are contracted and her legs and feet are extended, her jaws are clenched, and, to protect her from biting herself, her back teeth have been capped to prevent the front teeth closing fully. She cannot swallow or speak. She is incontinent. In the first few months after the catastrophe there were minimal signs of recovery which then faded.

The Ward's heart and lungs function normally. If she is given special food her body absorbs the nourishment normally, although she has to be aided with bowel movements. As she cannot swallow, and as her teeth are spastically clenched together, she cannot receive nourishment in the normal way and thus has been tube fed since the catastrophe. For approximately 20 years she was fed by a nasogastric tube which she seemed to find irritating or distressing and pulled out many times. In 1992 it was replaced under general anaesthetic by a gastrostomy tube. Since then she has been fed by this method. The gastrostomy tube became detached and was reinserted under general anaesthetic in December, 1993. Assuming she continues to be tube fed she could live for many more years, but she also might die if she developed an infection and it was not treated with antibiotics.

The Ward has no capacity to communicate. She cannot speak. A speech therapist failed to elicit any means of communication. She has a minimal capacity to recognise long established nursing staff and to react to strangers by showing distress. She tracks people with her eyes and reacts to noise although the latter is mainly, if not wholly, reflex from the brain stem. The eye tracking also represents brain stem reflex with minimal purposive content.

The Ward's family state that in over 20 years of visiting her they have never detected any signs of recognition nor efforts at communication by her. The Ward's mother disagreed with evidence that the Ward had any cognition. It was her evidence that in over two decades of visiting she got no response whatsoever from the Ward, that the Ward just stares and there is nothing in it unless it be "please let me go". It was her view that the Ward was in a horrendous situation.

* * *

In this case, the onus rests on the family to prove their case on the balance of probabilities, but the Court should not draw its conclusions lightly or without due regard to all the relevant circumstances, including the consequences for the Ward, the family and the carers involved.

Spiritual Aspect

The Ward and her family profess the Roman Catholic faith. Great care has been taken by the mother of the Ward to ensure that no steps are taken contrary to the family's faith. Evidence was given on their behalf by two theologians. This is a Court of law, and the Constitution and law are applied: not moral law. However, the religious beliefs of the Ward and her family are one of several factors for the Court to consider when evaluating the bona fides of the family and as Lynch J said:

> ... the evidence of the moral theologians is of relevance for two reasons: first, as showing that in proposing the course which they do propose the Ward's family are not contravening their own ethic (see Karen Quinlan's case) and secondly, the matter being *res integra*, the views of theologians of various faiths are of assistance in that they endeavour to apply right reason to the problems for decision by the Court and analogous problems.

* * *

Consent

Medical treatment may not be given to an adult person of full capacity without his or her consent. There are a few rare exceptions to this eg, in regard to contagious diseases; in a medical emergency where the patient is unable to communicate. This right arises out of civil, criminal and constitutional law. If medical treatment is given without consent it may be a trespass against the person in civil law, a battery in criminal law, and a breach of the individual's constitutional rights. The consent which is given by an adult of full capacity is a matter of choice. It is not necessarily a decision based on medical considerations. Thus, medical treatment may be refused for other than medical reasons. Such reasons may not be viewed as good medical reasons, or reasons most citizens would regard as rational, but the person of full age and capacity may make the decision for their own reasons.

If the patient is a minor then consent may be given on their behalf by parents or guardians. If the patient is incapacitated by reason other than age then the issue of capacity to consent arises. In this instance, where the patient is a Ward of Court, the Court makes the decision.

Bodily Integrity

The requirement of consent to medical treatment is an aspect of a person's right to bodily integrity under Article 40.3 of the Constitution. * * *

Mrs Ryan pursued her case against the State. However, the right to bodily integrity must be recognised by private individuals as well as the State.

Medical Treatment

At issue in the High Court was whether the nutrition and hydration of the Ward is medical treatment. The Ward is currently being fed a specific formula through a gastrostomy tube. The facts as found by the learned trial Judge were:

> The nasogastric tube was developed early in this century. It is uncomfortable and many patients have great difficulty in tolerating it. The gastrostomy tube was developed in the early 1980s. It is much less stressful on the patient and is now widely used where long term artificial feeding is necessary. Neither tube allows the patient the pleasures of eating and drinking: the taste and the smell of food is bypassed.
>
> It is said by the carers that the provision of nourishment by means of a tube must now be considered to be normal for the Ward since she has been so nourished for over twenty years. I cannot see, however, that a method of providing nourishment that is manifestly artificial and therefore abnormal at the outset, can change its essential nature and be regarded as and become normal or ordinary, simply because it has continued for a long time. It may be that a patient may get used to the abnormal artificial method of providing nourishment and no longer find it burdensome, but that does not make tube feeding normal. In the Ward's case, it is also clear that she never got used to the nasogastric tube. She reacted against it by pulling it out an enormous number of times, probably well over a thousand times and probably also by way of reflex reaction to an unpleasant stimulus and if there was any element of cognition in her rejection of the nasogastric tube, that makes it all the more emphatic. Its re-insertion, prior to its replacement by the gastrostomy tube in April, 1992, used to cause great distress to the Ward.
>
> The gastrostomy tube is now being used for three years. It is a far easier and more satisfactory way of delivering nourishment to the Ward and is much less

> burdensome to her. That does not, however, make it in any sense, a normal way of receiving nourishment. * * * I should also say that I see no difference in principle between the artificial provision of air by a ventilator and the artificial provision of nourishment by a tube.

The above determinations by the High Court insofar as they are fact were made on credible evidence, and are binding on this Court. I am satisfied that feeding the Ward a formula through a gastrostomy or nasogastric tube is a form of medical treatment.

A decision has now to be made whether to continue the medical treatment or not. To continue the treatment is as much a decision as not to do so. If the decision is to continue medical treatment, a consent has to be given on behalf of the Ward for the invasive medical treatment. If the decision is to cease the medical treatment, a consent on behalf of the Ward has also to be given.

Ordinary or Extraordinary Medical Treatment

It is not pertinent whether the treatment is ordinary or extraordinary medical treatment. Consent of the adult with capacity is necessary for either ordinary or extraordinary medical treatment.

However, the nature of the medical treatment here is pertinent to the Ward's condition. The medical treatment is invasive. This results in a loss of bodily integrity and dignity. It removes control of self and control of bodily functions. When medical treatment is ingested, inhaled or applied then there is a voluntary co-operative effort by the patient and each time a voluntary effort occurs the patient reveals to their carers their continuing consent to treatment which invades the integrity of the body. When the treatment is administered by a tube or a needle, the element of co-operation by the patient is lost. Normally, the benefits of such invasive treatment are clearly in a patient's best interest, but they are given to a patient in ways in which the individual has no control and are fundamentally different to non-invasive treatment. Whilst an unconscious patient in an emergency should receive all reasonable treatment pending a determination of their best interests, invasive therapy should not be continued in a casual or ill considered way.

Equality

If the Ward were of full capacity—as she is of full age—she would be required to consent before the current medical treatment were to be given to her. She is unable so to do. The issue then is whether anyone else can make the decision for her. Her family have applied to have the medical treatment stopped. Her Committee (her mother) feels this should happen in her best interests. The carers where she is at present say she should continue to be fed through the gastrostomy. The Attorney General has argued that this Court cannot make a decision to cease the nutrition and hydration through the tube process. Yet, no matter what the medical condition of the Ward, PVS, near PVS, or non PVS, she has a right of equality within the Constitution.

The Constitution specifically addresses the issue of equality in Article 40 stating:

> 1. All citizens shall, as human persons, be held equal before the law.
>
> This shall not be held to mean that the State shall not in its enactments have due regard to differences of capacity, physical and moral, and of social function.

Thus, all citizens as human persons are equal before the law. This is not a restricted concept, it does not mean solely that legislation should not be discriminatory. It is a positive proposition.

The right to equality arises in recognition that citizens are human persons. It exists as long as they are human persons. A citizen is a human person until death.

Due regard may be had to differences. It may be that in certain instances a person may not be able to exercise a right. But the right exists. The State has due regard to the difference of capacity and may envisage a different process to protect the rights of the incapacitated. It is the duty of the Court to uphold equality before the law. It is thus appropriate to consider if a method exists to give to the insentient person, the Ward, equal rights with those who are sentient.

The Right to Life

Article 40.3 of Bunreacht na hÉireann [the Constitution] states:

> 1. The State guarantees in its laws to respect, and, as far as practicable, by its laws to defend and vindicate the personal rights of the citizen.
>
> 2. The State shall, in particular, by its laws protect as best it may from unjust attack and, in the case of injustice done, vindicate the life, person, good name, and property rights of every citizen.

The right to life is the preeminent personal right. The State has guaranteed in its laws to respect this right. The respect is absolute. This right refers to all lives: all lives are respected for the benefit of the individual and for the common good. The State's respect for the life of the individual encompasses the right of the individual to, for example, refuse a blood transfusion for religious reasons. In the recognition of the individual's autonomy life is respected.

The requirement to defend and vindicate the life is a requirement "as far as practicable", it is not an absolute. Life itself is not an absolute.

The State stands firmly committed to protect personal rights. These are the rights personal to the individual. Some of them are enumerated eg, life, person, good name and property. Some are unenumerated eg, right to bodily integrity, right to work, right to earn a livelihood, right to marital privacy, right of access to the courts, right to travel.

In this case, the right to life is in issue. The State, under the Constitution, must protect "as best it may" that life from unjust attack. Thus, it also is not an absolute right, it is qualified.

Respect is given to the life of the Ward. Her life is no less protected or guarded than any other person's. Her rights as a citizen stand.

As she herself cannot make the necessary decision as to the medical treatment, an easy way to deal with the matter would be to say that no decision can then be made. However, that would not be to respect her life. That would be to refuse to her the rights given to other persons. That would be to say effectively that by her incapacity to make a decision she has lost that right. It would be to regard her life as less worthy of decision. Therefore, in order to respect her life a decision should be made.

In taking that decision it must be made so as to preserve, defend and vindicate her life. In view of the constitutional requirement that life be respected, that it be protected as best it may from unjust attack and that it be defended and vindicated as far as practicable, there is a clear constitutional presumption that the status quo in this case should continue. It is for the applicant on the balance of probabilities to establish that the life of the Ward is best respected, protected and vindicated by the Court acceding to the application.

Sanctity of Life

The right to life also encompasses the concept of the sanctity of life. It is a concept fundamental to our society. Life has a sacred value, an intrinsic worth. As Walsh J said in Ouinn's Supermarket v Attorney General, the Constitution:

"reflects a firm conviction that we are a religious people."

That foundation is an aid in interpreting the law and the Constitution. In regard specifically to the right to life it enables the interpretation to be inclusive of a spiritual or religious component. This approach is signalled in the first words of Article 40.3.1 where the unqualified "respect" for life is stated. In respecting a person's death we are also respecting their life—giving to it sanctity. That concept of sanctity is an inclusive view which recognises that in our society persons, whether members of a religion, or not, all under the Constitution are protected by respect for human life. A view that life must be preserved at all costs does not sanctify life. A person, and/or her family, who have a view as to the intrinsic sanctity of the life in question are, in fact, encompassed in the constitutional mandate to protect life for the common good, what is being protected (and not denied or ignored or overruled), is the sanctity of that person's life. To care for the dying, to love and cherish them, and to free them from suffering rather than simply to postpone death, is to have fundamental respect for the sanctity of life and its end.

Common Good

In analysing the right to life attention must be given to the person's right to life, privacy, autonomy and bodily integrity. Also, the common good, the interest of the community, in the protection of life, must be considered. It is an area where the two interests may appear to conflict.

The common good is achieved by the protection of life within the community. However, we recognise that a competent adult may decide that they do not consent to medical treatment. The State's respect for the life of the person encompasses the right of the person to hold views such that for religious or other reasons they refuse medical treatment. In the acceptance of the person's decision, their life is respected.

If that person is incapacitated and cannot make the decision is it appropriate to keep them alive in a manner which their family finds horrendous? Is it right for the decisions of doctors and carers or the State to override the family's view? Is the right to life such that it must be maintained at all costs, in all circumstances, if the facilities exist? Does it become a question of whether the care can be given?

The primary constitutional concept is to protect life within the community. The State has an interest in the moral aspect of society—for the common good. But, balanced against that is the person's right to life—which encompasses a right to die naturally and in the privacy of the family and with minimum suffering.

Right to Privacy

The right to privacy is an unenumerated right under the Constitution. * * *

* * *

Part of the right to privacy is the giving or refusing of consent to medical treatment. Merely because medical treatment becomes necessary to sustain life does not mean that the right to privacy is lost, neither is the right lost by a person becoming insentient. Nor is the right lost if a person becomes insentient and needs medical treatment to sustain life and is cared for by people who can and wish to continue taking care of the person. Simply it means that the right may be exercised by a different process. The individual retains their personal rights.

The right to privacy is not absolute. It has to be balanced against the State's duty to protect and vindicate life. However,

> the individual's right to privacy grows as the degree of bodily invasion increases. See *In Re Quinlan.*

The increasing personal right to privacy in such a situation is consistent with the defence and vindication of life being "as far as practicable".

A constituent of the right of privacy is the right to die naturally, with dignity and with minimum suffering. This right is not lost to a person if they become incapacitated or insentient.

Dignity

An unspecified right under the Constitution to all persons as human persons is dignity—to be treated with dignity. Such right is not lost by illness or accident. As long as a person is alive they have this right. Thus, the Ward in this case has a right to dignity. Decision-making in relation to medical treatment is an aspect of the right to privacy, however, a component in the decision may relate to personal dignity. Is the Ward, as described by Brennan J in his dissenting judgment in *Cruzan v Director, Missouri Department of Health,* a "passive prisoner of medical techno1ogy"? If that be so, is it in keeping with her right as a human person to dignity? Just as "the individual's right to privacy grows as the degree of bodily invasion increases" (*In Re Quinlan*) so too the dignity of a person is progressively diminished by increasingly invasive medicine.

Right of Choice

As part and parcel of their constitutional rights, a patient has a right to choose whether she will or will not accept medical treatment. This concept is the requirement of consent to medical treatment seen from another aspect.

* * *

Causation

Twenty three years ago, the Ward suffered major injury to her brain during a minor gynaecological operation. If it were not for modern medical technology, utilised after the catastrophe, she would have died long since. She has been kept alive by modern medical science and the dedicated care and skill of the medical and nursing professions.

The cause of the original brain injury has cast a shadow over this whole case. Originally, communication between the family and the carers was neither open nor easy.

The evidence presents illustrations of a lack of communication between the medical profession and the family evocative of the Victorian era. This lack of communication stemmed from the long shadow of the original catastrophe and the subsequent Court action. It was a difficult situation not only for the family but also for the doctors and carers. However, that situation has long since changed. Apart from the Ward and the family, the personnel are different.

If this Court determines that the Order of the High Court be upheld then, those acts so ordered being lawful, the Ward would die shortly as a result of the medical catastrophe which occurred 23 years ago. This fact must not now cloud the decision to be made by the Court.

Duty of Doctor

The doctors have a duty to the patient, the Ward. The decision of the Court is a decision in accordance with the Constitution and the law and is wider than the doctor's clinical judgment. It takes into account other factors.

* * *

Decision

The decision at issue is not a clinical medical decision. Nor is it grounded on whether the doctors and/or carers can keep the Ward alive. Nor is it based on the availability or not of facilities. It is the test of what is the best interest of the Ward within constitutional parameters taking factors including those enumerated previously into account.

I shall consider each of the stated factors in the same order as set forth above and relate them to the Ward's situation.

(1) The Ward's current condition as found by the learned trial Judge has been set out previously in this judgment. * * *

(2) The current medical treatment includes nutrition and hydration by way of gastrostomy; and daily medication of morphine, dysparnet, melleril and valium.

The Ward receives total nursing care on a twenty four hour basis, being turned every few hours, washed, fed via the gastrostomy tube, aided with bowel movements.

(3) The medical treatment of the Ward is invasive. It is delivered to her in a manner whereby no free will can be exercised.

(4) The legal and constitutional process to be carried out in this case is that as the patient is a Ward of Court the Court must make the decision as to the medical treatment. In reaching that decision the Court should apply the test as set out herein.

(5) The Ward's life history has been set out in the judgment of the High Court and summarised in this judgment. She is in a, or near, persistent or permanent vegetative state in which she has remained for 23 years. No further time is required to increase diagnostic accuracy.

(6) The prognosis for the Ward is that her condition is irreversible. There is no possibility of return from her current condition. She is being kept alive by the medical treatment. If she does not receive the medical treatment she will die within two weeks. If she continues to receive the medical treatment she may live for a further 20 years.

(7) The Ward expressed no proved views as to what she would wish in such a situation. However, I am satisfied that she had a marked dislike of hospitals, medical procedures and she could not even bear the smell of hospital.

(8) The mother, Committee, of the Ward, has taken great care, sought medical, theological and legal advice, and has a very strong view that the Ward should not receive this medical treatment. The entire family agree with her view.

(9) The medical personnel who care for the Ward in the Institution consider that the medical treatment should continue.

(10) The nursing staff who care for the Ward regard it as a privilege to care for her and would continue the medical treatment in issue.

(11) The Ward is a member of the Roman Catholic Church, as are her family. Great care has been taken by the family to reach a decision in accordance with the family ethic.

(12) The Ward retains her constitutional rights. At issue are her personal constitutional rights, within the framework of the Common Good. The Ward has rights of life, privacy, bodily integrity, autonomy and dignity in life and death.

(13) The Ward's life is respected, this is an absolute, and the making of a decision on her medical treatment is indicative that her rights exist, though enforced through a process different to that of a competent person.

(14) Deliberations on the issue commence with the constitutional presumption that the Ward's life be protected.

(15) The burden of proof is on the Appellants.

Applying the test of the best interests of the Ward, the mother and family arrived at a decision not to consent to the medical treatment.

The High Court in acceding to the application of the mother of the Ward applied to the facts a test of the best interests of the Ward. Lynch J stated:

> The test is whether having heard and considered the whole case and the authorities cited to me, I am of opinion that it is or it is not in the best interests of the Ward that her life should be prolonged by the continuance of the abnormal artificial means of nourishment whether by nasogastric or gastrostomy tube.

This is the correct test which I have had the opportunity of setting out in further detail. Applying the factors recited herein, as a prudent, good and caring parent, in the best interests of the Ward, the learned trial Judge did not err in his Order which is, in effect, not to consent to the medical treatment for the Ward.

I would dismiss the appeal and uphold the Order of the High Court.

O'Flaherty J.:

* * *

In resolving that issue it is of the utmost importance to state that we are deciding this case on a specific set of facts. It must be clear that our decision should not be regarded as authority for anything wider than the case with which we are confronted. It is essential, therefore, to state what the case is not about.

This case is not about euthanasia; euthanasia in the strict and proper sense relates to the termination of life by a positive act. The declarations sought in this case concern the withdrawal of invasive medical treatment in order to allow nature to take its course.

The Ward may be alive but she has no life at all. Lynch J found as a fact that although the Ward is not fully PVS, she is very nearly so and such cognitive capacity as she possesses is extremely minimal. * * *

Thus, the circumstances of the current case are clearly distinguishable from the position as regards, for example, a seriously mentally handicapped person. A mentally handicapped person is conscious of his or her situation and is capable of obtaining pleasure and enjoyment from life. It is fanciful to attempt to equate the position of the Ward in this case with that of a person whose life has been impaired by handicap. The analogy is both false and misleading; the quality of the Ward's life was never in issue; she is not living a life in any meaningful sense. We are concerned here only with allowing nature to take its course and for the Ward to die with dignity. We are not thereby going down any slippery slope or stepping into any abyss.

It is the fact that indubitably the Ward is alive. All life is sacred. When much emphasis was placed on the importance our Constitution places on the right to life in the course of the debate here I suggested that courts throughout the civilised world would regard their responsibilities as gravely as we do whether or not constitutional provisions were as explicit in various jurisdictions. And see Article 2 of the Convention for the Protection of Human Rights and Fundamental Freedoms [Rome, 4 November 1950] and Article 6 of the International Covenant on Civil and Political Rights [New York, 19 December 1966].

I move to the concept of death. For those of religious belief death is not an end but a beginning. In the submissions at Bar on behalf of the committee of the Ward death was said to be part of life—indeed the only certainty in life. Although, as Bryan MacMahon has written "each person attempts to mute or cancel the terror of impending death" (The Storyman—by Bryan MacMahon (1994)) nonetheless, in everyone's sub-conscious there is a hope of a peaceful and dignified death. We console the bereaved when a death occurs unexpectedly if the deceased was spared suffering.

In my judgment, this case is not about terminating a life but only to allow nature to take its course which would have happened even a short number of years ago and still does in places where medical technology has not advanced as far as it has in this country, for example. But now the advance of medical science may result in rendering a patient a prisoner in a ward from which there may be no release for many years without any enjoyment or quality of life: indeed without life in any acceptable meaning of that concept except in the sense that by means of various mechanisms life is kept in the body. * * *

The stark dilemma that presents itself for resolution is: given the sanctity of life, given the right to self-determination and given an incompetent who cannot herself make a choice, since I hold that an incompetent does not lose the constitutional right of self-determination she would otherwise have had, how should the Court exercise the choice for her because, as already indicated, a choice has to be made one way or the other.

What formula should the Court use in making the choice?

In the United States of America this matter has been much litigated throughout the States. * * *

Absent the existence of a statute on the subject, the various legal precepts relied upon to authorise the withdrawal of sustenance from a person in a persistent vegetative state have been reduced to a "best interest" analysis, "substituted judgment" criterion or a "clear and convincing" evidence standard of proof which draw their strengths from the federal or state constitutional rights of privacy.

Equally applicable to the right of an individual to forego life-sustaining medical treatment is the common law right to freedom from unwanted interference with bodily integrity ("self-determination").

As noted by one commentator with regard to the "right of self-determination":

> Since the right of self-determination can only be exercised by a person competent to evaluate her condition, a patient lacking this capacity forfeits her right of self-determination unless the surrogate decision-maker, standing in the place of the incompetent, asserts the patient's preference. This surrogate decision-making is embodied in this doctrine of substitute judgment. Courts will rely on the substitute judgment doctrine only when the surrogate decision-maker demonstrates the incompetent person's preferences with reasonable certainty. When the patient expresses a treatment preference prior to her loss of competence, the court views the surrogate as merely supplying the capacity to enforce the incompetent's choice. * * *

For myself, I find it impossible to adapt the idea of the "substituted judgment" to the circumstances of this case and, it may be, that it is only appropriate where the person has had the foresight to provide for future eventualities. That must be unusual (if it ever happens) at the present time; with increased publicity in regard to these type of cases it may get more common. For now, I prefer to rest my judgment by deciding what is in the best interests of the Ward.

That means I come back to deal with the choice that must be made between continuing life or allowing nature to take its course. * * *

* * *

The learned trial judge concluded that the State undoubtedly has an interest in preserving life but this interest is not absolute in the sense that life must be preserved and prolonged at all costs and no matter what the circumstances. He went on to say:

> Death is a natural part of life. All humanity is mortal and death comes in the ordinary course of nature and this aspect of nature must be respected as well as its life-giving aspect. Not infrequently, death is welcomed and desired by the patient and there is nothing legally or morally wrong in such an attitude. A person has a right to be allowed to die in accordance with nature and with all such palliative care as is necessary to ensure a peaceful and dignified death.

I agree with this reasoning and with the importance the judge accorded to the wishes of the Ward's family (and in which regard I endorse everything he had to say about the extraordinary love and devotion that they have lavished on the Ward) and for the reasons that I have set out I would regard the best interests of the Ward to be that the choice that should be made is that nature should take its course in this case without artificial means of preserving what technically is life but life without purpose, meaning or dignity.

I would dismiss the appeals.

* * *

Egan, J.:

* * *

What principles or factors should guide the Court in determining the best interests of the Ward? It appeared to be tacitly accepted that a cessation of the method of nutrition and hydration would be wholly permissible if the Ward had not cognitive function. In truth, she has almost none. The learned trial Judge found that she was "in a condition which is nearly, but not quite, what is known as persistent or permanent vegetative state (PVS)". His actual finding in this regard was as follows:

> She has a minimal capacity to recognise, for example, the long established nursing staff and to react to strangers by showing distress. She also follows or tracks people with her eyes and reacts to noise, although the latter is mainly, if not indeed, wholly reflex from the brain stem and a large element of reflex eye tracking is also present in the former which, however, also has some minimal purposive content.

It was not contended that a degree of cognitive function, however minimal, ought to preclude the Court from consenting to the withdrawal of the tube. It appeared to be conceded that consent could properly be given if the intrusive method was painful and burdensome. The evidence, however, would not justify such a finding nor was such a finding made. I also reject any argument based on an allegation that the Ward is terminally ill. Unless the tube is removed there is an undisputed possibility that she may live for many years.

The removal of the tube would, as already, stated, result in death within a short period of time. It matters not how euphemistically it is worded. The inevitable result of removal would be to kill a human being. In view of the Constitutional guarantees it would require (and I deem the right to life to be highest in the hierarchy of rights) a strong and cogent reason to justify the taking of a life.

As previously stated, this is not a case of no cognitive function. Such function is present, however minimal and however close to PVS. If slightly more cognitive function existed, would a right to withdraw sustenance still be claimed to be permissible? Where would the line be drawn? Cognition in a human being is something which is either present or absent and should, in my opinion, be so recognised and treated. Any effort to measure its value would be dangerous.

The Ward's condition has been described as "horrendous" and has been a source of deep distress to her family for a long period of time. Many other families endure great distress when a member continues to survive notwithstanding great physical or mental handicaps. This in no way lessens the sympathy which one inevitably feels for this particular family but regretfully, in my opinion, does not justify the Orders made in the case.

Appeal dismissed

Note

Is there any inconsistency between the Irish view of abortion and of end-of-life decision making? Note that Germany also takes a very conservative position on abortion, but is generally open to termination of life support at the end of life. See, discussing this case, Dermot Feenan, A "Terrible Beauty," the Irish Supreme Court, and Dying, 3 *Eur.J.Health L.* 29 (1996).

D. Assisted Suicide and Euthanasia

Though withholding or withdrawal of life-sustaining treatment for the terminally ill or persons in a persistent vegetative state is now generally accepted everywhere, virtually all nations still refuse to permit medical personnel to assist their patients in a terminal condition or in extreme suffering to commit suicide (assisted suicide) or to themselves cause the death of such patients (euthanasia). Few health law issues provoke such strongly and emotionally held opinions as assisted suicide and euthanasia. This fervor tends to express itself in the scholarship on this issue, which is voluminous and much of which is quite tendentious.

In a number of countries the argument has been put forward that the generally recognized "right to die" includes a right to receive euthanasia or assistance with suicide, and that the refusal to extend the right to die to this extent constitutes illegal discrimination against those who wish to die because of their medical condition, but cannot do so naturally or without assistance. These arguments were rejected in the United States in *Cruzan v. Director, Missouri Department of Health*, 497 U.S. 261 (1990). They were also rejected by the Canadian Supreme Court's *Rodriguez* decision, which follows:

Sue Rodriguez, Appellant v. The Attorney General of Canada and the Attorney General of British Columbia Respondents

[1993] 107 D.L.R. 4th 342 (Supreme Court of Canada).

Panel: Lamer C.J. and La Forest, L'Heureux-Dube, Sopinka, Gonthier, Cory, McLachlin, Iacobucci and Major JJ.

[The dissenting opinions of Chief Justice Lamer and of Cory and McLachlin J. are omitted.]

Sopinka, J.—I have read the reasons of the Chief Justice and those of McLachlin J. herein. The result of the reasons of my colleagues is that all persons who by reason of disability are unable to commit suicide have a right under the Canadian Charter of Rights and Freedoms to be free from government interference in procuring the assistance of others to take their life. They are entitled to a constitutional exemption from the operation of s. 241 of the Criminal Code, which prohibits the giving of assistance to commit suicide (hereinafter referred to as "assisted suicide"). The exemption would apply during the period that this Court's order would be suspended and thereafter Parliament could only replace the legislation subject to this right. I must respectfully disagree with the conclusion reached by my colleagues and with their reasons. In my view, nothing in the Charter mandates this result which raises the following serious concerns:

It recognizes a constitutional right to legally assisted suicide beyond that of any country in the western world, beyond any serious proposal for reform in the western world and beyond the claim made in this very case. The apparent reason for the expansion beyond the claim in this case is that restriction of the right to the terminally ill could not be justified under s. 15.

It fails to provide the safeguards which are required either under the Dutch guidelines or the recent proposals for reform in the states of Washington and California which were defeated by voters in those states principally because comparable and even more stringent safeguards were considered inadequate.

The conditions imposed are vague and in some respects unenforceable. * * * [T]he conditions imposed by my colleagues do not require that the person assisting be a physician or impose any restriction in this regard. Since much of the medical profession is opposed to being involved in assisting suicide because it is antithetical to their role as healers of the sick, many doctors will refuse to assist, leaving open the potential for the growth of a macabre specialty in this area reminiscent of Dr. Kervorkian and his suicide machine.

To add to the uncertainty of the conditions, they are to serve merely as guidelines, leaving it to individual judges to decide upon application whether to grant or withhold the right to commit suicide. In the case of the appellant, the remedy proposed by the Chief Justice, concurred in by McLachlin J., would not require such an application. She alone is to decide that the conditions or guidelines are complied with. Any judicial review of this decision would only occur if she were to commit suicide and a charge were laid against the person who assisted her. The reasons of McLachlin J. remove any requirement to monitor the choice made by the appellant to commit suicide so that the act might occur after the last expression of the desire to commit suicide is stale-dated.

I have concluded that the conclusion of my colleagues cannot be supported under the provisions of the Charter. Reliance was placed on ss. 7, 12 and 15 and I will examine each in turn.

I. Section 7

The most substantial issue in this appeal is whether s. 241(b) infringes s. 7 in that it inhibits the appellant in controlling the timing and manner of her death. I conclude that while the section impinges on the security interest of the appellant, any resulting deprivation is not contrary to the principles of fundamental justice. I would come to the same conclusion with respect to any liberty interest which may be involved.

Section 7 of the Charter provides as follows:

> 7. Everyone has the right to life, liberty and security of the person and the right not to be deprived thereof except in accordance with the principles of fundamental justice.

The appellant argues that, by prohibiting anyone from assisting her to end her life when her illness has rendered her incapable of terminating her life without such assistance, by threat of criminal sanction, s. 241(b) deprives her of both her liberty and her security of the person. The appellant asserts that her application is based upon (a) the right to live her remaining life with the inherent dignity of a human person, (b) the right to control what happens to her body while she is living, and (c) the right to be free from governmental interference in making fundamental personal decisions concerning the terminal stages of her life. The first two of these asserted rights can be seen to invoke both liberty and security of the person; the latter is more closely associated with only the liberty interest.

(a) Life, Liberty and Security of the Person

The appellant seeks a remedy which would assure her some control over the time and manner of her death. While she supports her claim on the ground that her liberty and security of the person interests are engaged, a consideration of these interests cannot be divorced from the sanctity of life, which is one of the three Charter values protected by s. 7.

None of these values prevail a priori over the others. All must be taken into account in determining the content of the principles of fundamental justice and there is no basis for imposing a greater burden on the propounder of one value as against that imposed on another.

Section 7 involves two stages of analysis. The first is as to the values at stake with respect to the individual. The second is concerned with possible limitations of those values when considered in conformity with fundamental justice. In assessing the first aspect, we may do so by considering whether there has been a violation of Ms. Rodriguez's security of the person and we must consider this in light of the other values I have mentioned.

As a threshold issue, I do not accept the submission that the appellant's problems are due to her physical disabilities caused by her terminal illness, and not by governmental action. There is no doubt that the prohibition in s. 241(b) will contribute to the appellant's distress if she is prevented from managing her death in the circumstances which she fears will occur. Nor do I accept the submission that the appellant cannot avail herself of s. 7 because she is not presently engaged in interaction with the criminal justice system, and that she will likely never be so engaged. It was argued that the comments concerning security of the person found in *R. v. Morgentaler* * * *, were not applicable to this case and that the appellant could not seek the protection of s. 7 at all, as that section is concerned with the interaction of the individual with the justice system. In my view, the fact that it is the criminal prohibition in s. 241(b) which has the effect of depriving the appellant of the ability to end her life when she is no longer able to do so without assistance is a sufficient interaction with the justice system to engage the provisions of s. 7 assuming a security interest is otherwise involved.

I find more merit in the argument that security of the person, by its nature, cannot encompass a right to take action that will end one's life as security of the person is intrinsically concerned with the well-being of the living person. This argument focuses on the generally held and deeply rooted belief in our society that human life is sacred or inviolable (which terms I use in the non-religious sense described by Dworkin (*Life's Dominion: An Argument About Abortion, Euthanasia, and Individual Freedom* (1993)) to mean that human life is seen to have a deep intrinsic value of its own). As members of a society based upon respect for the intrinsic value of human life and on the inherent dignity of every human being, can we incorporate within the Constitution which embodies our most fundamental values a right to terminate one's own life in any circumstances? This question in turn evokes other queries of fundamental importance such as the degree to which our conception of the sanctity of life includes notions of quality of life as well.

Sanctity of life, as we will see, has been understood historically as excluding freedom of choice in the self-infliction of death and certainly in the involvement of others in carrying out that choice. At the very least, no new consensus has emerged in society opposing the right of the state to regulate the involvement of others in exercising power over individuals ending their lives.

The appellant suggests that for the terminally ill, the choice is one of time and manner of death rather than death itself since the latter is inevitable. I disagree. Rather it is one of choosing death instead of allowing natural forces to run their course. The time and precise manner of death remain unknown until death actually occurs. There can be no certainty in forecasting the precise circumstances of a death. Death is, for all mortals, inevitable. Even when death appears imminent, seeking to control the manner and timing of one's death constitutes a conscious choice of death over life. It follows that life as a value is engaged even in the case of the terminally ill who seek to choose death over life.

Indeed, it has been abundantly pointed out that such persons are particularly vulnerable as to their life and will to live and great concern has been expressed as to their adequate protection, as will be further set forth.

I do not draw from this that in such circumstances life as a value must prevail over security of person or liberty as these have been understood under the Charter, but that it is one of the values engaged in the present case.

What, then, can security of the person be said to encompass in the context of this case? The starting point for the answer to this question is *Morgentaler*, in which this Court struck down Criminal Code provisions which had the effect of preventing women access to therapeutic abortion unless they complied with an administrative scheme found to be contrary to principles of fundamental justice. In finding a violation of security of the person, Beetz J. held, that:

> "Security of the person" must include a right of access to medical treatment for a condition representing a danger to life or health without fear of criminal sanction. * * *

* * *

In my view, then, the judgments of this Court in *Morgentaler* can be seen to encompass a notion of personal autonomy involving, at the very least, control over one's bodily integrity free from state interference and freedom from state-imposed psychological and emotional stress. * * * There is no question, * * * that personal autonomy, at least with respect to the right to make choices concerning one's own body, control over one's physical and psychological integrity, and basic human dignity are encompassed within security of the person, at least to the extent of freedom from criminal prohibitions which interfere with these.

The effect of the prohibition in s. 241(b) is to prevent the appellant from having assistance to commit suicide when she is no longer able to do so on her own. She fears that she will be required to live until the deterioration from her disease is such that she will die as a result of choking, suffocation or pneumonia caused by aspiration of food or secretions. She will be totally dependent upon machines to perform her bodily functions and completely dependent upon others. Throughout this time, she will remain mentally competent and able to appreciate all that is happening to her. Although palliative care may be available to ease the pain and other physical discomfort which she will experience, the appellant fears the sedating effects of such drugs and argues, in any event, that they will not prevent the psychological and emotional distress which will result from being in a situation of utter dependence and loss of dignity. That there is a right to choose how one's body will be dealt with, even in the context of beneficial medical treatment, has long been recognized by the common law. To impose medical treatment on one who refuses it constitutes battery, and our common law has recognized the right to demand that medical treatment which would extend life be withheld or withdrawn. In my view, these considerations lead to the conclusion that the prohibition in s. 241(b) deprives the appellant of autonomy over her person and causes her physical pain and psychological stress in a manner which impinges on the security of her person. The appellant's security interest (considered in the context of the life and liberty interest) is therefore engaged, and it is necessary to determine whether there has been any deprivation thereof that is not in accordance with the principles of fundamental justice.

(b) The Principles of Fundamental Justice

* * *

In this case, it is not disputed that in general s. 241(b) is valid and desirable legislation which fulfils the government's objectives of preserving life and protecting the vulnerable. The complaint is that the legislation is over-inclusive because it does not exclude from the reach of the prohibition those in the situation of the appellant who are terminally ill, mentally competent, but cannot commit suicide on their own. It is also argued that the extension of the prohibition to the appellant is arbitrary and unfair as suicide itself is not unlawful, and the common law allows a physician to withhold or withdraw life-saving or life-maintaining treatment on the patient's instructions and to administer palliative care which has the effect of hastening death. The issue is whether, given this legal context, the existence of a criminal prohibition on assisting suicide for one in the appellant's situation is contrary to principles of fundamental justice.

Discerning the principles of fundamental justice with which deprivation of life, liberty or security of the person must accord, in order to withstand constitutional scrutiny, is not an easy task. A mere common law rule does not suffice to constitute a principle of fundamental justice, rather, as the term implies, principles upon which there is some consensus that they are vital or fundamental to our societal notion of justice are required. Principles of fundamental justice must not, however, be so broad as to be no more than vague generalizations about what our society considers to be ethical or moral. They must be capable of being identified with some precision and applied to situations in a manner which yields an understandable result. They must also, in my view, be legal principles. The now familiar words of Lamer J. * * * are as follows:

> Consequently, the principles of fundamental justice are to be found in the basic tenets and principles, not only of our judicial process, but also of the other components of our legal system.

* * *

> Whether any given principle may be said to be a principle of fundamental justice within the meaning of s. 7 will rest upon an analysis of the nature, sources, rationale and essential role of that principle within the judicial process and in our legal system, as it evolves.

This Court has often stated that in discerning the principles of fundamental justice governing a particular case, it is helpful to look at the common law and legislative history of the offence in question. It is not sufficient, however, merely to conduct a historical review and conclude that because neither Parliament nor the various medical associations had ever expressed a view that assisted suicide should be decriminalized, that to prohibit it could not be said to be contrary to the principles of fundamental justice. Such an approach would be problematic for two reasons. First, a strictly historical analysis will always lead to the conclusion in a case such as this that the deprivation is in accordance with fundamental justice as the legislation will not have kept pace with advances in medical technology. Second, such reasoning is somewhat circular, in that it relies on the continuing existence of the prohibition to find the prohibition to be fundamentally just.

The way to resolve these problems is not to avoid the historical analysis, but to make sure that one is looking not just at the existence of the practice itself (i.e., the continued criminalization of assisted suicide) but at the rationale behind that practice and the principles which underlie it.

The appellant asserts that it is a principle of fundamental justice that the human dignity and autonomy of individuals be respected, and that to subject her to needless suffering in this manner is to rob her of her dignity. * * *

That respect for human dignity is one of the underlying principles upon which our society is based is unquestioned. I have difficulty, however, in characterizing this in itself as a principle of fundamental justice within the meaning of s. 7. While respect for human dignity is the genesis for many principles of fundamental justice, not every law that fails to accord such respect runs afoul of these principles. To state that "respect for human dignity and autonomy" is a principle of fundamental justice, then, is essentially to state that the deprivation of the appellant's security of the person is contrary to principles of fundamental justice because it deprives her of security of the person. This interpretation would equate security of the person with a principle of fundamental justice and render the latter redundant.

I cannot subscribe to the opinion expressed by my colleague, McLachlin J., that the state interest is an inappropriate consideration in recognizing the principles of fundamental justice in this case. This Court has affirmed that in arriving at these principles, a balancing of the interest of the state and the individual is required. * * *

* * *

Where the deprivation of the right in question does little or nothing to enhance the state's interest (whatever it may be), it seems to me that a breach of fundamental justice will be made out. * * * It follows that before one can determine that a statutory provision is contrary to fundamental justice, the relationship between the provision and the state interest must be considered. One cannot conclude that a particular limit is arbitrary because (in the words of my colleague, McLachlin J.) "it bears no relation to, or is inconsistent with, the objective that lies behind the legislation" without considering the state interest and the societal concerns which it reflects.

The issue here, then, can be characterized as being whether the blanket prohibition on assisted suicide is arbitrary or unfair in that it is unrelated to the state's interest in protecting the vulnerable, and that it lacks a foundation in the legal tradition and societal beliefs which are said to be represented by the prohibition.

Section 241(b) has as its purpose the protection of the vulnerable who might be induced in moments of weakness to commit suicide. This purpose is grounded in the state interest in protecting life and reflects the policy of the state that human life should not be depreciated by allowing life to be taken. This policy finds expression not only in the provisions of our Criminal Code which prohibit murder and other violent acts against others notwithstanding the consent of the victim, but also in the policy against capital punishment and, until its repeal, attempted suicide. This is not only a policy of the state, however, but is part of our fundamental conception of the sanctity of human life. * * *

As is noted in the above passage, the principle of sanctity of life is no longer seen to require that all human life be preserved at all costs. Rather, it has come to be understood, at least by some, as encompassing quality of life considerations, and to be subject to certain limitations and qualifications reflective of personal autonomy and dignity. An analysis of our legislative and social policy in this area is necessary in order to determine whether fundamental principles have evolved such that they conflict with the validity of the balancing of interests undertaken by Parliament.

(i) History of the Suicide Provisions

At common law, suicide was seen as a form of felonious homicide that offended both against God and the King's interest in the life of his citizens. As Blackstone noted in *Commentaries on the Laws of England* (1769):

> ... the law of England wisely and religiously considers, that no man hath a power to destroy life, but by commission from God, the author of it: and, as the suicide is guilty of a double offence; one spiritual, in invading the prerogative of the Almighty, and rushing into his immediate presence uncalled for; the other temporal, against the king, who hath an interest in the preservation of all his subjects; the law has therefore ranked this among the highest crimes, making it a peculiar species of felony, a felony committed on oneself.
>
> This is essentially the view first propounded by Plato and Aristotle that suicide was "an offence against the gods or the state".

However, the contrary school of thought has always existed and is premised on notions of both freedom and compassion. The Roman Stoics, for example, "tended to condone suicide as a lawful and rational exercise of individual freedom and even wise in the cases of old age, disease, or dishonor". There has never been a consensus with respect to this contrary school of thought.

Thus, until 1823, English law provided that the property of the suicide be forfeited and his body placed at the cross-roads of two highways with a stake driven through it. Burial indignities were also imposed in ancien regime France where the body of the suicide was often put on trial before being crucified.

However, given the practical difficulties of prosecuting the successful suicide, most prohibitions centred on attempted suicide; it was considered an offence and accessory liability for assisted suicide was made punishable. In England, this took the form of a charge of accessory before the fact to murder or murder itself until the passage of the Suicide Act, 1961, which created an offence of assisting suicide which reads much like our s. 241. In Canada, the common law recognized that aiding suicide was criminal and this was enshrined in the first Criminal Code. * * *

* * *

(ii) Medical Care at the End of Life

Canadian courts have recognized a common law right of patients to refuse consent to medical treatment, or to demand that treatment, once commenced, be withdrawn or discontinued. The United States Supreme Court has also recently recognized that the right to refuse life-sustaining medical treatment is an aspect of the liberty interest protected by the Fourteenth Amendment in *Cruzan v. Director, Missouri Health Department* (1990). However, that Court also enunciated the view that when a patient was unconscious and thus unable to express her own views, the state was justified in requiring compelling evidence that withdrawal of treatment was in fact what the patient would have requested had she been competent.

The House of Lords has also had occasion very recently to address the matter of withdrawal of treatment. In *Airedale N.H.S. Trust v. Bland*, [1993], their Lordships authorized the withdrawal of artificial feeding from a 17-year-old boy who was in a persistent vegetative state as a result of injuries suffered in soccer riots, upon the consent of his parents. Persistence in a vegetative state was found not to be beneficial to the patient and the principle of sanctity of life, which was not absolute, was therefore found not to be violated by the withdrawal of treatment.

Although the issue was not before them, their Lordships nevertheless commented on the distinction between withdrawal of treatment and active euthanasia. Lord Keith stated that though the principle of sanctity of life is not an absolute one, "it forbids the taking of active measures to cut short the life of a terminally ill patient".

* * *

The probable reason why legislation has not made an exception for the terminally ill lies in the fear of the excesses or abuses to which liberalization of the existing law could lead. As in the case of "compassionate murder", decriminalization of aiding suicide would be based on the humanitarian nature of the motive leading the person to provide such aid, counsel or encouragement. As in the case of compassionate murder, moreover, the law may legitimately fear the difficulties involved in determining the true motivation of the person committing the act.

Aiding or counselling a person to commit suicide, on the one hand, and homicide, on the other, are sometimes extremely closely related. Consider, for example, the doctor who holds the glass of poison and pours the contents into the patient's mouth. Is he aiding him to commit suicide? Or is he committing homicide, since the victim's willingness to die is legally immaterial? There is reason to fear that homicide of the terminally ill for ignoble motives may readily be disguised as aiding suicide.

* * *

It can be seen, therefore, that while both the House of Lords, and the Law Reform Commission of Canada have great sympathy for the plight of those who wish to end their lives so as to avoid significant suffering, neither has been prepared to recognize that the active assistance of a third party in carrying out this desire should be condoned, even for the terminally ill. The basis for this refusal is twofold it seems—first, the active participation by one individual in the death of another is intrinsically morally and legally wrong, and second, there is no certainty that abuses can be prevented by anything less than a complete prohibition. Creating an exception for the terminally ill might therefore frustrate the purpose of the legislation of protecting the vulnerable because adequate guidelines to control abuse are difficult or impossible to develop.

(iii) Review of Legislation in other Countries

A brief review of the legislative situation in other Western democracies demonstrates that in general, the approach taken is very similar to that which currently exists in Canada. Nowhere is assisted suicide expressly permitted, and most countries have provisions expressly dealing with assisted suicide which are at least as restrictive as our s. 241. For example, the Austrian Penal Act 1945, s. 139b, and the Spanish Penal Code, art. 409, have provisions virtually identical to our own, while the Italian Penal Code of 1930, art. 580, is even more broadly drafted, reading as follows:

> Whoever brings about another's suicide or reinforces his determination to commit suicide, or *in any way facilitates its commission,* shall be punished.... [Emphasis added.]

The relevant provision of the Suicide Act, 1961 of the United Kingdom punishes a "person who aids, abets, counsels or procures the suicide of another, or an attempt by another to commit suicide", and this form of prohibition is echoed in the criminal statutes of all state and territorial jurisdictions in Australia. The U.K. provision is apparently the only prohibition on assisted suicide which has been subjected to judicial scrutiny for its impact on human rights prior to the present case. In the Application No. 10083/82, *R. v. United Kingdom*, the European Commission of Human Rights considered whether s. 2 of the Suicide Act, 1961 violated either the right to privacy in Article 8 or freedom of expression in Article 10 of the Convention for the Protection of Human Rights and Fundamental Freedoms. The applicant, who was a member of a voluntary euthanasia association, had been convicted of several counts of conspiracy to aid and abet a suicide for his actions in placing persons with a desire to kill themselves in touch with his co-accused who then assisted them in committing suicide. The European Commission held that the acts of aiding, abetting, counselling or procuring suicide were "excluded from the concept of privacy by virtue of their trespass on the public interest of protecting life, as reflected in the criminal provisions of the 1961 Act", and upheld the applicant's conviction for the offence. Further, the Commission upheld the restriction on the applicant's freedom of expression.

* * *

Some European countries have mitigated prohibitions on assisted suicide which might render assistance in a case similar to that before us legal in those countries. In the Netherlands, although assisted suicide and voluntary active euthanasia are officially illegal, prosecutions will not be laid so long as there is compliance with medically established guidelines. Critics of the Dutch approach point to evidence suggesting that involuntary active euthanasia (which is not permitted by the guidelines) is being practised to an increasing degree. This worrisome trend supports the view that a relaxation of the absolute prohibition takes us down "the slippery slope". Certain other European countries, such as Switzerland and Denmark, emphasize the motive of the assistor in suicide, such that the Swiss Penal Code, art. 115, criminalizes only those who incite or assist a suicide for a selfish motive, and the Danish Penal Code, art. 240, while punishing all assistance, imposes a greater penalty upon those who act out of self-interest. In France, while no provision of the Penal Code addresses specifically the issue of assisted suicide, failure to seek to prevent someone from committing suicide may still lead to criminal sanctions under art. 63, para. 2 (omission to provide assistance to a person in danger) or art. 319 (involuntary homicide by negligence or carelessness) of that Code. * * *

* * *

Overall, then, it appears that a blanket prohibition on assisted suicide similar to that in s. 241 is the norm among Western democracies, and such a prohibition has never been adjudged to be unconstitutional or contrary to fundamental human rights. Recent attempts to alter the status quo in our neighbour to the south have been defeated by the electorate, suggesting that despite a recognition that a blanket prohibition causes suffering in certain cases, the societal concern with preserving life and protecting the vulnerable rendered the blanket prohibition preferable to a law which might not adequately prevent abuse.

(iv) Conclusion on Principles of Fundamental Justice

What the preceding review demonstrates is that Canada and other Western democracies recognize and apply the principle of the sanctity of life as a general principle which is subject to limited and narrow exceptions in situations in which notions of personal autonomy and dignity must prevail. However, these same societies continue to draw distinctions between passive and active forms of intervention in the dying process, and with very few exceptions, prohibit assisted suicide in situations akin to that of the appellant. The task then becomes to identify the rationales upon which these distinctions are based and to determine whether they are constitutionally supportable.

The distinction between withdrawing treatment upon a patient's request, such as occurred in the *Nancy B.* case, on the one hand, and assisted suicide on the other has been criticized as resting on a legal fiction—that is, the distinction between active and passive forms of treatment. The criticism is based on the fact that the withdrawal of life supportive measures is done with the knowledge that death will ensue, just as is assisting suicide, and that death does in fact ensue as a result of the action taken.

Other commentators, however, uphold the distinction on the basis that in the case of withdrawal of treatment, the death is "natural"—the artificial forces of medical technology which have kept the patient alive are removed and nature takes its course. In the case of assisted suicide or euthanasia, however, the course of nature is interrupted, and death results directly from the human action taken.

Whether or not one agrees that the active vs. passive distinction is maintainable, however, the fact remains that under our common law, the physician has no choice but to accept the patient's instructions to discontinue treatment. To continue to treat the patient when the patient has withdrawn consent to that treatment constitutes battery. The doctor is therefore not required to make a choice which will result in the patient's death as he would be if he chose to assist a suicide or to perform active euthanasia.

The fact that doctors may deliver palliative care to terminally ill patients without fear of sanction, it is argued, attenuates to an even greater degree any legitimate distinction which can be drawn between assisted suicide and what are currently acceptable forms of medical treatment. The administration of drugs designed for pain control in dosages which the physician knows will hasten death constitutes active contribution to death by any standard. However, the distinction drawn here is one based upon intention—in the case of palliative care the intention is to ease pain, which has the effect of hastening death, while in the case of assisted suicide, the intention is undeniably to cause death.*** In my view, distinctions based upon intent are important, and in fact form the basis of our criminal law. While factually the distinction may, at times, be difficult to draw, legally it is clear. The fact that in some cases, the third party will, under the guise of palliative care, commit euthanasia or assist in suicide and go unsanctioned due to the difficulty of proof cannot be said to render the existence of the prohibition fundamentally unjust.

The principles of fundamental justice cannot be created for the occasion to reflect the court's dislike or distaste of a particular statute. While the principles of fundamental justice are concerned with more than process, reference must be made to principles which are "fundamental" in the sense that they would have general acceptance among reasonable people. From the review that I have conducted above, I am unable to discern anything approaching unanimity with respect to the issue before us. Regardless of one's personal views as to whether the distinctions drawn between withdrawal of treatment and palliative care, on the one hand, and assisted suicide on the other are practically compelling, the fact remains that these distinctions are maintained and can be persuasively defended. To the extent that there is a consensus, it is that human life must be respected and we must be careful not to undermine the institutions that protect it.

* * *

III. Section 15

The Chief Justice concludes that disabled persons who are unable to commit suicide without assistance are discriminated against contrary to s. 15 in that they are deprived of a benefit or subjected to a burden by virtue of s. 241(b) of the Criminal Code. * * *

* * *

* * * Since I am of the opinion that any infringement is clearly saved under s. 1 of the Charter, I prefer not to decide these issues in this case. They are better left to a case in which they are essential to its resolution. Rather, I will assume that s. 15 of the Charter is infringed and consider the application of s. 1.

IV. Section 1

I agree with the Chief Justice that s. 241(b) has "a clearly pressing and substantial legislative objective" grounded in the respect for and the desire to protect human life, a fundamental Charter value. * * *

On the issue of proportionality, which is the second factor to be considered under s. 1, it could hardly be suggested that a prohibition on giving assistance to commit suicide is not rationally connected to the purpose of s. 241(b). The Chief Justice does not suggest otherwise. Section 241(b) protects all individuals against the control of others over their lives. To introduce an exception to this blanket protection for certain groups would create an inequality. As I have sought to demonstrate in my discussion of s. 7, this protection is grounded on a substantial consensus among western countries, medical organizations and our own Law Reform Commission that in order to effectively protect life and those who are vulnerable in society, a prohibition without exception on the giving of assistance to commit suicide is the best approach. Attempts to fine tune this approach by creating exceptions have been unsatisfactory and have tended to support the theory of the "slippery slope". The formulation of safeguards to prevent excesses has been unsatisfactory and has failed to allay fears that a relaxation of the clear standard set by the law will undermine the protection of life and will lead to abuses of the exception. The recent Working Paper of the Law Reform Commission, quoted above, bears repeating here:

> The probable reason why legislation has not made an exception for the terminally ill lies in the fear of the excesses or abuses to which liberalization of the existing law could lead. As in the case of "compassionate murder", decriminalization of aiding suicide would be based on the humanitarian nature of the motive leading the person to provide such aid, counsel or encouragement. As in the case of compassionate murder, moreover, the law may legitimately fear the

> difficulties involved in determining the true motivation of the person committing the act.

The foregoing is also the answer to the submission that the impugned legislation is overbroad. There is no halfway measure that could be relied upon with assurance to fully achieve the legislation's purpose; first, because the purpose extends to the protection of the life of the terminally ill. Part of this purpose, as I have explained above, is to discourage the terminally ill from choosing death over life. Secondly, even if the latter consideration can be stripped from the legislative purpose, we have no assurance that the exception can be made to limit the taking of life to those who are terminally ill and genuinely desire death.

I wholeheartedly agree with the Chief Justice that in dealing with this "contentious" and "morally laden" issue, Parliament must be accorded some flexibility. In these circumstances, the question to be answered is, to repeat the words of La Forest J., quoted by the Chief Justice, whether the government can "show that it had a reasonable basis for concluding that it has complied with the requirement of minimal impairment". In light of the significant support for the type of legislation under attack in this case and the contentious and complex nature of the issues, I find that the government had a reasonable basis for concluding that it had complied with the requirement of minimum impairment. This satisfies this branch of the proportionality test and it is not the proper function of this Court to speculate as to whether other alternatives available to Parliament might have been preferable.

It follows from the above that I am satisfied that the final aspect of the proportionality test, balance between the restriction and the government objective, is also met. I conclude, therefore, that any infringement of s. 15 is clearly justified under s. 1 of the Charter.

* * *

Notes

1. While the right to die is well recognized in the United States, euthansia and assisted suicide are almost uniformly illegal. The Supreme Court in *Glucksberg* and *Vacco* soundly rejected, with no dissents, arguments that a right to assistance in committing suicide was protected by the due process or equal protection clause, though several concurring opinions left open the possibility that such a right might arise under some circumstances. Only in Oregon is a right to assisted suicide recognized by law. The Oregon law was adopted by initiative and upheld by a subsequent referendum. An attempt by the United States Attorney General to block the operation of the Oregon law as in violation of the federal drug laws was rejected on statutory grounds by the United States Supreme Court in *Gonzales v. Oregon*, 546 U.S. 243 (2006).

2. In contrast to the U.S. Supreme Court's 9–0 decisions in *Glucksberg* and *Vacco*, the Canadian Supreme Court was split 5–4 in *Rodriguez*, with three dissenting opinions. Two of the dissents concluded that the statute violates section 7, which protects the right to personal autonomy and human dignity, and two that it violated the right to equality of section 15, insofar as the law permitted withdrawal of treatment but not assisted suicide. See, discussing *Rodriguez* in comparative perspective, Patrick Thompson, The Law and Active Euthanasia: Whose Life is it Anyway? 2 *J. L. & Med.* 233 (1995).

The law with respect to European nations on euthanasia and assisted suicide is discussed in the following excerpts from the Nys article, also excerpted above:

Physician Involvement in a Patient's Death: A Continental European Perspective

Herman Nys, Medical Law Review, vol. 7, 208 (1999), updated by Herman Nys, 2007

European Law

D. Termination of Life on Request and Assisted Suicide

1. The right to request death

Articles 2 and 3 ECHR

For obvious reasons, especially in the Netherlands, the question has arisen as to whether legal regulation (in the sense of legalisation) of euthanasia or killing another at his request is compatible with Article 2 ECHR that protects human life. In the explanatory memorandum to the Act on termination of life on request and assisted suicide it is recognised that Article 2 ties a duty upon the government to protect life. The question whether this implies that a regulation of euthanasia ("careful termination of life on request") is in breach of this duty and Article 2 ECHR is answered negatively. According to the Memorandum, "it must be borne in mind that individual rights, of which Article 2 ECHR is one, are concerned with protection from third-parties. The need for protection from third parties has caused the creation of individual civil rights. It is not the intention that individual rights strip those involved of their freedom to make their own decisions on their personal matters. Bearing in mind that euthanasia demands an express request from the person involved, and that it is his own life, a regulation of euthanasia is not in breach of Article 2 ECHR".

This is clearly not the viewpoint of the European Court of Human Rights. According to the European Court, article 2 ECHR cannot be said to guarantee to anyone a right to die, and, therefore, it cannot be regarded as an avenue for challenging national legislation prohibiting termination of life on request or assisted suicide (*Pretty* case, 2002). With regard to article 3 ECHR the Court concluded that no positive obligation arises under this article to require a State to provide a lawful opportunity for any form of assisted suicide. However, the Court was not prepared to exclude the possibility that a complete ban on assisted suicide constitutes an interference with the right to respect for private life as guaranteed under Article 8 (1) ECHR.

The difficult question is how far the consent of a "victim" may negate what would otherwise be a violation of the Convention. In principle, it would seem that the fundamental character of the rights guaranteed by the ECHR and the element of public interest, would exclude the possibility of any form of waiver of those rights. Some commentators suggest that a person's consent to the termination of their own life takes the matter outside Article 2, but others suggest that the right to life may be inalienable although "in this respect too, a certain trend may be discerned, but not yet a *communis opinio*."

The same authors also suggest that euthanasia does not *per se* conflict with the Convention. In fact, the value of life to be protected can and must be weighed against other rights in question, particularly his right, laid down in Article 3, to be protected from inhuman and degrading treatment. At first sight one is inclined to argue that Article 3 is not of relevance because the suffering of an incurable patient cannot be considered as an inhuman or degrading treatment attributable to the State. To consider the absolute prohibition of euthanasia in all circumstances and without any legal exception as an inhuman and degrading treatment by the State surely is based on a broad understanding of Article 3. Until now there is no jurisprudence supporting this interpretation. However, in the exceptional case that this prohibition brings with it that a patient who suffers inhumanly and where pain medication offers no relief, cannot be released from his pain and suffering, one could argue that the prohibition creates an inhuman and degrading situation. The State is then confronted with a conflict between two basic rights protected by Articles 2 and 3 ECHR. Curiously, the ECHR itself does not contain a mechanism to solve such a conflict. The right to life has not a principal priority over the other rights protected by the ECHR. This leaves margin to the member states to solve the conflict between two basic rights in their own way.

Termination of life without request

With regard to unrequested termination of life (e.g. in the case of a comatose, or mentally handicapped patient, or a severely handicapped child), in the Netherlands until now it has been generally accepted that legal regulation of termination without request does not comply with Article 2 ECHR. This does not necessarily mean that termination of life without request is always in conflict with the Convention. The conflict between Articles 2 and 3 may also arise when a patient is not able to request death. Because of the danger of abuse, Article 2 brings with it the obligation to consider such cases with even more suspicion than when there is a request by the patient.

On 10 December 2004 paediatricians at academic hospitals in the Netherlands have called for the formation of a national committee to draw up a nationwide protocol for life ending treatment for newborns who are so ill and suffering so severely that they have no prospect of a future. The issue expressly relates to exceptional cases, around 600 newborns a year worldwide. The call to set up a national committee has been prompted by the discussions that erupted worldwide after paediatricians from Groningen University Hospital announced that they had drawn up a protocol for such cases in association with the Dutch public prosecutors, called the Board of Procurators General. The so called "Groningen Protocol" has five criteria: the suffering must be so severe that the newborn has no prospects of a future; there is no possibility of a cure or alleviation with medication or surgery; the parents must always give their consent; a second opinion must be provided by an independent doctor who has not been involved with the child's treatment; and the deliberate ending of life must be meticulously carried out with the emphasis on aftercare. In November 2005 the Dutch Government has decided to establish such a national committee. It is composed of one lawyer, one ethicist and three physicians. Any case of termination of life of a severely handicapped new born has to be notified to this committee. In a resolution on respect for human rights in the European Union, the European Parliament called "for a ban on euthanasia to the detriment of the disabled, patients in long-term coma, disabled newborn infants and the elderly" and called on "the Member States to give priority to setting up units to provide palliative care for the terminally ill so they can die with dignity".

Assisting suicide

In the Netherlands euthanasia and aiding suicide are considered to be comparable acts. The "Dutch" reasoning as to the conformity of a regulation on euthanasia with Article 2 ECHR is also valid for physician-assisted suicide. This reasoning does not correspond however to the judgement of the European Court of Human Rights in the *Pretty* case (2002).

Denmark

4. Termination of life on request and assisting suicide

Both assisting suicide and killing someone on his request are actually prohibited in Denmark. In an advice published in 1997 the members of the Council of Ethics were divided on the question of whether (active) euthanasia should to some degree be legalised in Denmark. A majority of 16 members recommended maintaining the prohibition on (active) euthanasia. One of the members however, felt that the law must be changed to open the way for (active) euthanasia. In 2003 the Council reiterated its opposition to legalization of euthanasia.

For the majority, there are many reasons for being unable to recommend that (active) euthanasia be made legal in Denmark. There is more than just the individual's right of autonomy over his or her own life at stake in the opinion of the majority. Virtually all patients' requirements in respect of pain control, psycho-social support, and care and nursing can be accommodated to a reasonable degree. It is frightening that there are cases where even optimal efforts cannot alleviate severe pain or other overwhelming suffering. With these cases in mind, the majority on the Council of Ethics also realises that keeping up the ban on (active) euthanasia has its price. However, legalising active euthanasia in order to help such patients would involve serious and unacceptable risks for many other patients.

France

3. Euthanasia and aiding suicide

Assisting suicide is not formally prohibited in France. However, procuring a patient the means to kill himself is regarded as a failure to help a person who is in danger. In the 1980s, the publication *Suicide, Mode d'Emploi,* and the apparent lack of legal grounds to prohibit such books, led the French legislature to adopt Law No. 87-1133 of 31 December 1987 to prohibit the encouragement of suicide. Interestingly, this law does not cover aiding suicide as the legislature wanted in no way to give the impression of regulating "euthanasia".

Killing someone on his request is a homicide. In 1991 the French National Consultative Ethics Committee for Health and Life Sciences issued an opinion on the Schwartzenberg resolution. In this advice, the Committee expressed the opinion that legalised euthanasia, even in exceptional cases, would be open to abuse and uncontrollable interpretation: the decision on death would be taken at the request of the patient—a respectable request no doubt—but highly ambivalent. Accordingly, the Committee expressed its disapproval of legislation or regulations that legitimise the act of taking the life of a patient. However in January 2000 the French National Consultative Ethics Committee published an advice that to the surprise of many in and outside France contained "a plea of defence of euthanasia" that in exceptional cases would allow a court not to sanction a physician who at the request of his patient would have terminated his life. The French legislature did not follow this advice and instead has approved in 2005 an Act on the rights of patients and the end of life. [The 2005 law is discussed in the previous section].

The revised (1995) Code of Professional Ethics of the French Order of Physicians stipulates that a physician has no right to intentionally provoke the death of a patient (Article 38, last subsection). In his comments, René writes that one has deliberately avoided to use the notion "euthanasia" because it has lost its original meaning of "good death".

Germany

4. Termination of life and aiding suicide

Assisting suicide is not a crime in Germany, provided that the person about to commit suicide is "*taterschaftsfähig*", that is capable of exercising control over his actions and also that he acts out of freely responsible choice. In other words, aiding an informed, voluntary suicide is permitted. On the other hand, German law imposes an obligation to a physician to rescue a suicide in progress. Thus, although the physician is not prohibited from giving a lethal drug to a patient, once that patient has taken the drug and becomes unconscious, the physician incurs a duty to rescue him.

In the *Wittig* case of 4 July 1984 the German Supreme Court confirmed its position that a physician who does not try his best to avert the consequences of an apparent attempt by a patient to kill himself, may be liable at criminal law.

Later, however, in the so-called *Hackethal* case (1988), the Supreme Court demonstrated a more flexible attitude to the legal value of a "*Selbsttötungsentschluss.*" An important difference with the *Wittig* case (not providing help after a suicide attempt) is that in the *Hackethal* case a physician had provided a lethal drug to a patient who seriously suffered so that she could kill herself. The Supreme Court confirmed a judgment of the Central District Court of Munich. According to the Court, the duty of a physician to save the life of a patient may be limited in a specific case when the patient himself only experiences his life as a burden and wants to be freed from it ("*wenn der Kranke selber sein Leben nur noch als quälende Last erleidet und es preisgeben will*").

The 1998 and 2004 amended guidelines on aid-in-dying of the German Medical Association, however, have not integrated this development: a physician who gives assistance to a suicide contravenes medical ethics and may be held criminally liable ("*Die Mitwirkung des Arztes bei der Selbsttötung widerspricht dem ärztlichen Ethos und kann strafbar sein*").

Killing upon request is prohibited specifically under German law. The amended guidelines of the German Medical Association have confirmed this prohibition ("*Active Sterbehilfe ist unzulässig und mit Strafe bedroht, auch dann, wenn sie auf verlangen des Patienten geschieht*").

The Netherlands

4. Termination of life and aiding suicide

Legal situation

One of the most important contributions of the Report of the State Commission on Euthanasia (1985) was to clarify the definition of "euthanasia". In the Netherlands (and in other countries such as Belgium * * *) "euthanasia" now refers exclusively to behaviour that terminates the life of another at the request of the person concerned.

Two Articles of the Dutch Criminal Code explicitly prohibit euthanasia and aiding suicide. Article 293 prohibits killing a person at his request whilst Article 294 prohibits assisting a suicide. Despite their distinct treatment in the Criminal Code and the fact that they carry rather different penalties, Dutch law generally makes no distinction between the two as far as the justification to a doctor available is concerned.

Unlike the situation elsewhere, one of the most characteristic features of euthanasia practice in the Netherlands is that from the beginning of public discussion until very recently there has been no suggestion of a legal preference for assistance with suicide above euthanasia. On the contrary, killing on request is more common than assistance with suicide. Griffiths suggests a very interesting explanation for the Dutch preference for killing on request. By contrast with the situation in, for example, the United States, the development of euthanasia law began not so much with a demand for "patient's rights" as with the insistence by doctors, supported after some initial hesitation by the Medical Association, that under limited circumstances euthanasia is a legitimate medical procedure. The issue was legally formulated not so much in terms of what patients have a right to demand as in terms of what doctors are authorised to do.

Despite the apparently forbidding text of the provisions of the Criminal Code the courts have held that Article 40 of the Criminal Code makes a defense of justification available to a physician charged under Articles 293 or 294. The first acquittal took place in 1983 and this was upheld by the Dutch Supreme Court in the *Schoonheim* case in 1984. The Supreme Court held that a physician could invoke the defense of justification due to necessity if, confronted by a conflict between the duty to his patient whose suffering is "unbearable and hopeless" and the requirements of the Criminal Code, and exercising the care required of a medical professional, his choice was "objectively justified". It is remarkable that the Supreme Court explicitly referred to "responsible medical opinion, subject to the applicable norms of medical ethics" as the criterion to decide on a situation of necessity. The decision in *Schoonheim* led to a series of judicial decisions in which the conditions and limitations of the defense were gradually worked out.

The requirements of a substantive and of a procedural or professional character that must be met by a doctor who carries out euthanasia or gives assistance with suicide have become fairly clear. The essential substantive conditions of euthanasia concern the patient's request, the patient's suffering and the doctor-patient relationship. The patient's request must be "express and earnest". The patient's suffering must be "unbearable" and "hopeless". In light of the decision in *Chabot* it seems clear that the suffering need not be physical (pain, etc.) nor is a somatic basis required. It is also clear since the *Chabot* decision that the patient must not be in the "terminal phase" of his illness. Finally, only a doctor may legally perform euthanasia. In principle this should be a doctor who has an established treatment relationship with the patient.

In addition to these substantive conditions, the doctor who performs euthanasia must meet a number of procedural requirements: (a) The physician must formally consult at least one doctor with respect to the patient's condition and life expectancy, the available alternatives and the adequacy of the request. Part of the consultation requirement is that the consultant agrees with the decision of the responsible doctor. (b) The doctor should discuss the matter with the immediate family and intimate friends of the patient (unless the patient does not want this or there other good reasons for not doing so). (c) The doctor should discuss the matter with nursing personnel responsible for the patient's care and, if the nurse is involved in the request for euthanasia, she should be included in the decision-making. (d) The doctor should keep a full written record of the case. (e) The termination of life should be carried out in a professionally responsible way and the doctor should stay with the patient continuously—or be immediately available—until the patient dies. (f) Death due to euthanasia may not be reported as a "natural death".

The euthanasia statute

As far as the legal norms concerning euthanasia are concerned, the process of legalisation has been completed in 2001, and there is little controversy over the results reached.

These results have been codified in the Termination of Life on Request and Assisted Suicide (Review procedures) Act 2001.

The Act contains amendments to Article 293 and Article 294 of the Criminal Code and the Burial and Cremation Act in relation to the termination of life on request and suicide assistance. Article 293 is enlarged with a new section 2 which stipulates that termination of life on request is not an offence if it is committed by a physician who fulfills the due care criteria set out in Article 2 of the Termination of Life on Request and Assisted Suicide (Review procedures) Act 2001. These due care criteria hold that the medical doctor:

(a) has been convinced that the patient has requested a termination of his life voluntarily and deliberately;

(b) has provided the patient with information on the situation in which the patient finds himself and the prospects with reference to this situation of distress;

(c) together with the patient has been convinced that there is no reasonable alternative solution for the situation of distress;

(d) has consulted an independent medical doctor, who has formed a judgment on the hopeless situation of distress, and has visited the patient in the event that careful judgment so requires.

Adolescents between 16 to 18 years old may request and receive euthanasia or assisted suicide. A parent or guardian must "have been involved in decision process," but need not agree or approve. Children between to 12 to 15 years old may request and receive euthanasia or assisted suicide. A parent or guardian must "agree with the termination of life or the assisted suicide."

Article 7(2) of the amended Burial and Cremation Act stipulates that in the event of death occurring as a result of termination of life on request or suicide assistance, the attending physician shall not issue any death certificate but shall inform the municipal coroner of the cause of death without delay by means of a completed form. In doing so, the attending physician shall enclose an annotated report in relation to the observance of the requirements of due care. According to Article 10 (2) the municipal coroner shall report to one of the five regional commissions by means of a completed form and enclose the annotated report made up by the attending physician.

Chapter III of Termination of Life on Request and Assisted Suicide (Review procedures) Act 2001 establishes the regional review commissions. It is the task of a commission to judge whether the attending physician in the case of termination of life on request or assisting suicide has fulfilled all requirements of due care. It has to make known its motivated evaluation within six weeks after receipt of the report to the attending physician in writing. If according to this evaluation, the medical doctor has failed to act in accordance with the requirements of due care, the regional review commission shall make known its judgment to the Public Prosecutor and the Inspector for Public Health.

Notes

1. The experience of the Netherlands with assisted suicide has played a major role in the development of American law. In *Glucksberg* and *Vacco*, several justices described the Dutch experience, generally as providing a basis for proceeding cautiously in recognizing assisted suicide. American debate has used the Dutch experience as both supporting and undermining the arguments for legalizing assisted suicide or euthanasia.

2. Discussion in the United States has by and large been limited to the issue of assisted suicide, with euthanasia viewed much more skeptically. In the Netherlands, on the other hand, euthanasia is much more common than assisted suicide. What explains the difference?

3. Note the role of the duty of physicians to rescue persons in emergencies in France and Germany in the assisted suicide/euthanasia debate. A general duty to rescue enforced through the criminal law is absent in the United States but exists generally in Europe. How does this affect the nature of the debate in these countries?

4. Currently the Netherlands and Belgium are only nations that officially sanction euthanasia and assisted suicide and make provision for it. The Northern Territory of Australia also legalized assisted suicide and voluntary euthanasia in 1995, but the legislation was invalidated by the Australian national parliament in 1997 as being inconsistent with Commonwealth law, after it had been in effect for only six months. See Symposium Euthanasia and the Northern Territory Initiative, 3 *J. L. & Med.* 99–111, 121–191 (1995); and Suzanne Trollope, Legislating a Right to Die: The Rights of the Terminally Ill Act 1995 (NT), 3 *J. L. & Med.* 19 (1995). Assisted suicide is also legal in the United States state of Oregon. "Euthanasia" was widely practiced in Nazi Germany, where handicapped persons were executed in large numbers. This experience, of course, continues to influence the debate on this issue. The laws of several other nations either do not explicitly prohibit assisted suicide or, alternatively, recognize a defense of necessity in some assisted suicide cases, though they do not, as in the Netherlands, provide an official procedure for carrying out assisted suicide. The laws of a selection of European nations is discussed in portions of the Nys excerpt above that were edited out. See also, comparing the approaches of various nations to these issues, Raphael Cohen-Almagor, Euthanasia and Physician-Assisted Suicide in the Democratic World: Legal Overview, 16 *N.Y. Int. L. Rev.* 1 (2003); Hazel E. McHaffie, et al., Withholding/Withdrawing Treatment from Neonates: Legislation and Official Guidelines Across Europe, 25 *J. Med. Ethics* 440 (1999); Michael Ashby, Of Life and Death: The Canadian and Australian Senates on Palliative Care and Euthanasia, 6 *J. L. & Med.* 40 (1997); Meredith Blake, Physician-Assisted Suicide: A Criminal Offence or a Patient's Right? 5 *Med. L. Rev.* 294 (1997); and Roger S. Magnusson, The Sanctity of Life and the Right to Die: Social and Jurisprudential Aspects of the Euthanasia Debate in Australia and the United States, 6 *Pac. Rim L. & Pol'y J.* 1 (1997). See also, considering the status of assisted suicide under British law, John Keown, Euthanasia in England: Courts, Committees and Consistency, 16 *Medicine and Law* 805 (1997); and David P.T. Price, Assisted Suicide and Refusing Medical Treatment: Linguistics, Morals and Legal Contortions, 4 *Med. L. Rev.* 270 (1996); under Belgian law, Herman Nys, A Presentation of the Belgian Act on Euthanasia Against the Background of Dutch Euthanasia Law, 10 *Eur. J. Health L.* 239 (2003); Eva Strubbe, Toward a Legal Recognition for Termination of Life without Request, 7 *Eur. J. Health L.* 57 (2000); and under Canadian law, Michael Stingl, Euthanasia and Health Reform in Canada, 7 *Cambridge Q. Healthcare Ethics*, 348 (1998).

5. The Dutch situation has been extensively studied. In particular, a series of empirical studies have been conducted on practice under the statute. See, e.g. Bregje Onwuteaka-Philipsen, et al, Taking the Final Step: Changing the Law on Euthanasia and Physician-Assisted Suicide: Dutch Experience of Monitoring Euthanasia, 331 *BMJ* 691 (2005); Jacqueline M. Cuperus-Bosma, Physician-Assisted Death: Policy-Making by the Assembly of Prosecutors General in the Netherlands, 4 *Eur.J.Health L.* 225 (1997); Robert J.M. Dillman, Euthanasia in the Netherlands: The State of Legal Debate, 1 *Eur. J. Health L.* 81 (1994); Johanna H. Groenewoud, et al., Clinical Problems with the Performance

of Euthanasia and Physician-Assisted Suicide in the Netherlands, 342 *New Eng. J. Med.* 551 (2000); Johanna H. Groenewoud, Physician-Assisted Death in Psychiatric Practice in the Netherlands, 336 *New Eng. J. Med.* 1795 (1997); and Paul J. van der Maas, Euthanasia, Physician-Assisted Suicide, and Other Medical Practices Involving End of Life in the Netherlands, 1990–1995, 335 *New Eng. J. Med.* 1699 (1996). Depending on one's point of view, these studies demonstrate either that the Netherlands are well down the slippery slope toward the Nazi experience, or that the practice is being carried out responsibly under the Dutch procedures. There is, in particular, a concern that assisted suicide and euthanasia are widely underreported. A number of commentators, however, have pointed out that these practices are probably being carried out in many other nations secretly, and are never reported. For example, a number of nations, including the United States, permit the practice of terminal sedation—increasing dosages of medication for persons in severe pain to the point where the medication may result in death. There is often a thin line between officially permitted terminal sedation or withdrawal of treatment on the one hand, and assistance in suicide or provision of euthanasia on the other.

6. A comprehensive discussion of the Dutch experience is found in John Griffiths, Alex Bood and Heleen Weyers, *Euthanasia and Law in the Netherlands* (1998). See also, presenting the full range of perspectives on the Netherlands experience, Raphael Cohen-Almagor, Non-voluntary and Involuntary Euthansia in the Netherlands: Dutch Perspectives, 18 *Issues in Law and Medicine* 239 (2003); Raphael Cohen-Almagor, The Guidelines for Euthanasia in the Netherlands: Reflection on Dutch Perspectives, 9 *Ethical Perspectives* 3 (2002); Margaret Pabst Battin, A Dozen Caveats Concerning Discussion of Euthanasia in the Netherlands, in M.P. Battin, *The Least Worst Death*, 130 (1994); Sherwin B. Nuland, Physician-Assisted Suicide and Euthanasia in Practice, 342 *New Eng. J. Med.* 583 (2000); National Legal Center for the Medically Dependent and Disabled, Physician-Assisted Suicide and Euthanasia in the Netherlands: A Report to the House Judiciary Subcommittee on the Constitution, 14 *Issues L. & Med.* 301 (1998); Simon Chesterman, Last Rights: Euthanasia, The Sanctity of Life, and the Law in the Netherlands and the Northern Territory of Australia, 47 *Int. & Comp.L.Q.* 362 (1998); Timothy Quill and Gerrit Kimsa, End-of-Life Care in the Netherlands and the United States: A Comparison of Values, Justifications, and Practices, 6 *Cambridge Quarterly of Healthcare Ethics* 189 (1997); Marcia Angell, Euthanasia in the Netherlands-Good News or Bad? 335 New Eng. J. Med. 1676 (1996); John Griffiths, Recent Developments in the Netherlands Concerning Euthanasia and Other Medical Behavior that Shortens Life, 1 *Med. L. Int.* 347 (1995); John Keown, Euthanasia in the Netherlands: Sliding Down the Slippery Slope? 9 *Notre Dame J.L. & Ethics & Pub. Pol'y* 407 (1995); and John Griffiths, The Regulation of Euthanasia and Related Medical Procedures that Shorten Life in the Netherlands, 1 *Med. L. Rev.* 137 (1994).

7. Some have argued that euthanasia and assisted suicide enjoy widespread support in the Netherlands because the role of the medical profession is understood there somewhat differently than in other countries. The Dutch medical profession believes that its task is not simply to preserve life, but also to combat pain and suffering. When these values come in conflict, the priority of preserving life is not a foregone conclusion. The circumstances under which preventing suffering can trump preserving life remain controversial, however. One of the most controversial cases in recent years was the *Chabot* case, in which a patient who was severely depressed because of her life circumstances—but not in serious physical ill health—requested and obtained assistance in suicide.

Chabot

Supreme Court of the Netherlands, Criminal Chamber, 21 June 1994, no. 96.972. Judges Haak (vice-president), Mout, Davids, Van Erp Taalman Kip-Nieuwenkamp, Schipper. [*Nederlandse Jurisprudentie* 1994, no. 656; *Tijdschrift voor Gezondheidsrecht* 1994, no. 47], from John Griffiths, Alex Bood, and Haleen Weyers, Euthansia and the Law in the Netherlands 329–38 (1998).

1. *Procedure*

The appeal is from the Court of Appeals, Leeuwarden (30 September 1993), which (like the District court, Assen, 21 April 1993) found the defendant not guilty of the offence charged: "Intentionally assisting another person to commit suicide" as prohibited by article 294 of the Criminal Code. The Court of Appeals found the defense of justification due to necessity well-founded and the question on appeal is whether the Court's interpretation of the scope of the defense was legally correct and whether the facts as found support the decision.

* * *

2. *Facts*

The following facts were established by the Court of Appeals.

Defendant is a psychiatrist who on 28 September 1991 supplied to Ms. B, at her request, lethal drugs that she consumed in the presence of defendant, a GP, and her friend Ms. H. She died half an hour later. Defendant reported her death the same day to the local coroner as a suicide which he had assisted. He included what the Court of Appeals characterizes as an "extensive report" of the case, with "a very detailed account of the discussions with Ms. B (and her sister and brother-in-law), a report of the psychiatric investigation and defendant's diagnosis, his considerations concerning Ms. B's bereavement process and her refusal of treatment."

Ms. B was 50 years old. She had married at the age of 22 but the marriage was from the beginning not a happy one. She had two sons, Patrick and Rodney. In 1986 her older son, Patrick, committed suicide while in military service in Germany. From that time on her marital problems grew worse and the relationship more violent, and her wish to end her life began to manifest itself. According to her own statements, she only remained alive to care for her other son Rodney. These circumstances led to a brief admission to the psychiatric ward of a local hospital in October of 1986, followed by polyclinical psychiatric treatment, neither of which had an effect on her situation: according to the psychiatrist at the time, she was not open to any suggestion of working toward an acceptance of Patrick's death.

In December 1988, shortly after the death of her father, Ms. B left her husband, taking Rodney with her; the divorce followed in February 1990. In November 1990 Rodney was admitted to hospital in connection with a traffic accident. In the hospital he was found to be suffering from cancer, from which he died on 3 May 1991. That evening Ms. B attempted suicide with drugs that she had received from her psychiatrist in 1986 but had saved. The attempt was unsuccessful, and to her great disappointment she recovered consciousness a day and a half later. She immediately began to save drugs again with the intention of committing suicide.

Finding a way to die came to dominate her thoughts. She discussed various methods with her sister; she gave an old friend a letter that was to be opened only after her death;

she arranged for cemetery plots for herself, her two sons and her former husband and had her first son reburied so that there was space for her between the graves of her two sons. She attempted to get effective drugs for committing suicide and considered other methods as well, which she discussed with various people. However, she was afraid that a second failure might lead either to an involuntary committal to a mental institution or to continued life with a serious disability. She made it known to others that she wished to die, but in a humane way that would not involuntarily confront others with her suicide.

Ms. B approached the Dutch Association for Voluntary Euthanasia and in this way came in contact with defendant, who had indicated his willingness to give psychiatric support to persons who might approach the Association for help. Between 2 August and 7 September 1991 defendant had four series of discussions with Ms. B, totalling some 24 hours. He also spoke with Ms. B's sister and brother-in-law. Beginning on 11 August, after the second series of discussions with Ms. B, defendant approached 4 consultants. He furnished them with an extensive account of his findings and requested suggestions concerning matters that he might have overlooked in the psychiatric investigation of Ms. B or that required further clarification. He also asked whether they were in agreement with his diagnosis. Later, after the third series of discussions, he approached 3 more consultants.

In considering the question "whether Ms. B was suffering from any illness" the Court of Appeals concluded that there was no indication of any somatic condition that might have been the source of Ms. B's wish to die. From the beginning of defendant's contacts with her it was clear that she was suffering from psychic traumas that in principle lent themselves to psychiatric treatment, so that defendant was justified in entering into a doctor-patient relationship with her even though that might ultimately expose him to a conflict of duties.

Defendant's professional judgment of Ms. B was that there was no question in her case of a psychiatric illness or major depressive episode, but that according to the classification system of the American Psychiatric Association (D.S.M.-III-R), she was suffering from an adjustment disorder consisting of a depressed mood, without psychotic signs, in the context of a complicated bereavement process. In his opinion, she was experiencing intense, long-term psychic suffering that, for her, was unbearable and without prospect of improvement. Her request for assistance with suicide was well-considered: in letters and discussions with him she presented the reasons for her decision clearly and consistently and showed that she understood her situation and the consequences of her decision. In his judgment, her rejection of therapy was also well-considered.

The Court of Appeals found that defendant was an experienced psychiatrist who made his diagnosis in a very careful way. The experts consulted by him were agreed that Ms. B's decision was well-considered and her suffering long-term and unbearable, and that in the circumstances there was no "concrete treatment perspective"; the majority agreed without reservation with the way he had handled the case. Several of them observed that it was highly likely that, if not given expert assistance, Ms. B would have continued her efforts to commit suicide, using increasingly violent means. Although her condition was in principle treatable, treatment would probably have been long and the chance of success was small. None of the experts consulted considered that there was in fact any realistic treatment perspective, in light of her well-established refusal of treatment. Defendant had repeatedly tried to persuade Ms. B to accept some form of therapy and the Court of Appeals accepted defendant's testimony to the effect that if there had been an available treatment with a realistic chance of success within a reasonable period, he would have continued to pressure Ms. B to accept it and, if she continued to refuse, would not have given her the requested assistance.

The experts consulted in this case, a discussion paper of the Medical Association on the subject, a discussion paper of the Inspectorate for Mental Health, and a position paper of the Dutch Association for Psychiatry all agree that from the point of view of medical ethics, there may be circumstances in which assistance with suicide is legitimate in the case of persons whose suffering does not have a somatic origin and who are not in the terminal phase of their disease.

3. *The opinion of the Supreme Court*

3.1 General Considerations

* * *

* * * [T]he circumstances of an individual case may be such that rendering assistance with suicide, like performing euthanasia, can be considered justifiable. This is the case when it is proved that the defendant acted in a situation of necessity, that is to say—speaking generally—that confronted with a choice between mutually conflicting duties, he chose to perform the one of greater weight. In particular, a doctor may be in a situation of necessity if he had to choose between the duty to preserve life and the duty as a doctor to do everything possible to relieve the unbearable and hopeless suffering [*ondraaglijk en uizichtloos lijden*] of a patient committed to his care.

When a doctor who has performed euthanasia or furnished the means for suicide claims that he acted in a situation of necessity, the trial court must investigate—this task is *par excellence* that of the trial court—whether the doctor, especially in the light of scientifically responsible medical opinion and according to the norms recognized in medical ethics, made a choice between mutually conflicting duties that, considered objectively and in the context of the specific circumstances of the case, can be considered justifiable. In this connection it should be observed that the procedure by which the doctor responsible for treatment [*behandelende arts*] is to report cases of euthanasia and assistance with suicide, including thereby information on a number of specified items—a procedure that has been in effect in practice since 1 November 1990 and has recently received a legislative foundation ... —contains no substantive criteria which, if met by a doctor who performs euthanasia or renders assistance with suicide, entail that his behavior is justifiable. The reporting procedure offers a procedural structure within which the responsible doctor can render account of his behavior and the prosecutorial authorities or the trial court can assess it.

3.2 The Justifiability of Assistance With Suicide in the Case of Non-Somatic Suffering and a Patient Who is Not in the Terminal Phase

The first ground of appeal depends on the view that assistance with suicide by a doctor, in the case of a patient like Ms. B whose suffering is not somatic and who is not in the terminal phase, cannot [as a matter of law] be justifiable.

This view cannot be considered correct. The specific nature of the defense of necessity, which, depending upon the trial court's weighing and evaluation after the fact of the particular circumstances of the case can lead it to decide that the act was justified, does not allow for any such general limitation. A claim of necessity can therefore not be excluded simply on the ground that the patient's unbearable suffering, without prospect of improvement, does not have a somatic cause and that the patient is not in the terminal phase. The Court of Appeals found, and this is not challenged on appeal, that from the point of view of medical ethics the legitimacy of euthanasia or assistance with suicide in such circumstances is not categorically excluded. In answering the question whether in a particular case a person's suffering must be regarded as so unbearable and hopeless that an act that violates article 294 must be considered justified because performed in a situation of necessity, the suffering must be distinguished from its cause, in the sense that the cause of the suffering does not detract from the extent to which suffering is experienced. But the fact remains that when the suffering of a patient does not demonstrably follow from a somatic illness or condition, consisting simply of the experience of pain and loss of bodily functions, it is more difficult objectively to establish the fact of suffering and in particular its seriousness and lack of prospect of improvement. For this reason the trial court must in such cases approach the question whether there was a situation of necessity with exceptional care.

3.3 The Voluntariness of the Request in the Case of a Psychiatric Patient

[The second ground of appeal challenges the Court of Appeals' holding that it is possible for a psychiatric patient voluntarily to request assistance with suicide; alternatively, it is argued that the judgment of the Court of Appeals that the request was voluntary is not based on sufficient evidence. The third ground of appeal challenges the Court of Appeals' holding that the fact that a second psychiatrist had not examined Ms. B is not an obstacle to accepting the defense of necessity. The Supreme Court deals with these various contentions together.

The Court holds that the prosecution's assertion that the request for assistance with suicide of a psychiatric patient cannot be voluntary "is as a general [legal] proposition incorrect." The Court of Appeals held "that the wish to die of a person whose suffering is psychic can be based on an autonomous judgment. That holding is in itself not incorrect."

The alternative challenge—to the sufficiency of the evidence—is, however, well founded, among other things in light of the fact that Ms. B had not been examined by a second psychiatrist.]

As stated above, in a case in which the suffering of a patient is not based on a somatic disease or condition, the trial court must approach the question whether under the circumstances of the case assistance with suicide can be justified as having occurred in a situation of necessity with exceptional care.

If a doctor who affords his patient assistance with suicide has neglected before acting to check his judgment concerning the situation with which he is confronted against that of an independent colleague, whether or not the latter conducts his own examination of the patient, this need not in general preclude the possibility that the trial court, based on its own investigation of the circumstances of the case, comes to the conclusion that the doctor acted in a situation of necessity and therefore must be considered not guilty. However, the situation is different in a case like the present one.

[When the case involves] a patient whose suffering is not based on a somatic disease or condition ... the trial court, in considering whether the claim of necessity is well-founded, must—considering the exceptional care with which it is to approach this matter—base its decision among other things on the judgment of an independent medical expert who has at least seen and examined the patient himself. Since the trial court must decide whether the defense of necessity is compatible with the requirement that the course of conduct chosen be proportional to the harm to be avoided and also the least harmful choice available, the judgment of the independent colleague of the defendant, based partly on his own examination, should deal with the seriousness of the suffering and the lack of prospect for improvement, and in that connection also with other possibilities of providing help. This is because in assessing whether suffering is so unbearable and hopeless that assistance with suicide can be deemed a choice justified by a situation of necessity, there can in principle be no question of hopelessness if there is a realistic alternative to relieve the suffering which the patient has in complete freedom rejected. The independent expert must also include in his examination the question, whether the patient has made a voluntary and well-considered request, without his competence being influenced by his sickness or condition.

Absent the judgment of an expert who saw and examined Ms. B, the Court of Appeals could not properly come to the conclusion that defendant as the responsible psychiatrist was confronted with an unavoidable conflict of duties and in that situation made a justifiable choice. In such a situation, the Court of Appeals should have rejected the defense.

3.4 Judgment

[The judgment below must be reversed. In general, this would lead to referral of the case to another Court of Appeals. In the circumstances of this case such a referral—considering the absence of the essential report of an independent expert who himself examined Ms. B—could only lead to the conclusion that the defense of necessity must be rejected. In such a case it is more efficient for the Supreme Court to give final judgment itself.

The defense of necessity is rejected, and the defendant, not having made any other defense, is found guilty of the offence as charged.

However, "the person of the defendant and the circumstances in which the offence was committed ... have led the Supreme Court to apply article 9a of the Criminal Code and not to impose any punishment or other measure."]

Following the decision, further disciplinary actions were taken, described in the following excerpt from Griffiths, Bood, and Weyers, supra, at 338–39.

The medical disciplinary proceedings against Chabot

The prosecution in the criminal case had requested the responsible Medical Inspector, who was contemplating a medical disciplinary proceeding, not to go ahead with it while the criminal case was pending. When, with the decision of the Supreme Court on 21 June 1994, the criminal case was over, the disciplinary proceedings against Chabot got under way. The regional Medical Disciplinary Tribunal rendered a decision on 6 February 1995. It concluded that Chabot had "undermined confidence in the medical profession" (the basic disciplinary norm). Chabot received a relatively severe sanction: "Reprimand." On 19 April 1995 Chabot announced that he had had enough of legal proceedings and would not appeal this decision, so that the case was finally closed.

The Medical Disciplinary Tribunal held, as had the Supreme Court, that assistance with suicide can be legitimate in the case of a person whose suffering is of non-somatic origin and who is not in the terminal phase. The request must be the result of an "autonomous decision" and not of a treatable disorder. The consulted doctors must have personally examined the person concerned (the Tribunal is not entirely clear whether more than one doctor must be consulted nor whether this must be a psychiatrist).

The Tribunal considered that in the specific circumstances of the case Chabot had not adequately preserved his professional distance, particularly in light of the frequency and length of his sessions with Ms. B and the fact that these took place at Chabot's house in the countryside (where Ms. B, together with a couple who accompanied her, resided in a guest cottage on Chabot's property).

Finally, the Tribunal seems to have taken a more restrictive view than the Supreme Court on one crucial aspect of the case: the extent to which a doctor must insist on treatment as an alternative to assistance with suicide. The Supreme Court's opinion refers to a "realistic alternative," leaving room for the possibility that available treatment possibilities may not be considered "realistic." The Tribunal, on the other hand, takes the position that Chabot could not properly conclude that Ms. B's condition was untreatable until after treatment had in fact been tried. "The patient's refusal of treatment should have been a reason for [Chabot] to refuse the requested assistance with suicide, at least for the time being."

This difference between the two decisions reflects the fundamental difference of opinion between the experts called by the Tribunal in the disciplinary proceeding. The Tribunal adopted the latter's view that treatment ought not to have been honored.

* * *

Notes

1. See, commenting on Chabot, Raphael Cohen-Almagor, The Chabot Case: Analysis and Account of Dutch Perspectives, 5 *Med. L. Int.* 141 (2002); H.J.J. Leenan, Dutch Supreme Court about Assistance to Suicide in the Case of Severe Mental Suffering, 1 *Eur. J. Health L.* 377 (1994); Johan Legemaate & J.K.M. Gevers, Physician-Assisted Suicide in Psychiatry: Developments in the Netherlands, 6 *Cambridge Q. in Healthcare Ethics* 175 (1997); and Johanna H. Groenewoud, Physician-Assisted Death in Psychiatric Practice in the Netherlands, 336 *New Eng. J. Med.* 1795 (1997).

2. We have noted a number of times, euthanasia is generally prohibited in the West (outside of the Netherlands, Belgium, and Oregon), while withdrawal of treatment is generally permitted. It is not, of course, necessary to observe this distinction. The Japanese case that follows both accepts active euthanasia, in principle, and takes a very conservative view (by Western standards) of withdrawal of treatment.

Tōkai University Hospital — Euthanasia Case

Judgment of Yokohama District Court, March 28, 1995, 1530 *Hanrei Jihō* 28 (Japan v. Tokunaga), (Tōkai University Hospital euthanasia case)
Translated and edited by Robert B Leflar

[Translator's note: This case was the first case in Japan in which a physician was prosecuted for an act of euthanasia. The patient, Mr. Katsuhara, age 57, was terminally ill with bone marrow cancer. He was hospitalized in Tōkai University Hospital at the end of 1990. His three physicians were Dr. Nozaki, Dr. Noguchi, and the defendant, Dr. Tokunaga.]

Facts

Dr. Nozaki, the original attending physician, informed the patient's son and wife that the patient, Mr. Katsuhara, had untreatable bone marrow cancer. The son strongly requested that his father not be informed of the cancer diagnosis; so the patient was told there was an "insufficiency of bone marrow function."

The patient's condition worsened in late March 1991. The defendant, Dr. Tokunaga, was told by Drs. Nozaki and Noguchi about Mr. Katsuhara's condition and prognosis, and about the family's request that the patient not be informed of his diagnosis. On April 5, the patient began vomiting blood, and on April 8 a plasma exchange was commenced. [There follows a day-by-day account, somewhat excerpted, of his last illness.]

April 9: The patient was scarcely conscious, and could respond only to simple commands. At 9 am his wife and son said to Dr. Noguchi: "The patient didn't sleep at all last night. He is complaining of pain from the Foley catheter. He's suffering so much we can't watch. We want the plasma exchange stopped. Take out the I.V. and the Foley catheter, and stop all treatment. The patient understands what's happening. This is an incurable illness, there's no point in treating it any more; please don't keep him suffering."

Dr. Noguchi told Dr. Tokunaga of this request by the family to cease treatment; Dr. Noguchi also presented it to the senior physician on his rounds. But the family withdrew the request later after hearing an explanation from the senior physician.

April 10: The patient could not respond when spoken to, but his condition had stabilized. At 6:30 pm the wife and son asked Dr. Noguchi again to stop treatment and to discontinue the I.V. and catheter. Despite his attempts at persuading them to continue treatment, they tenaciously refused to acquiesce. After an hour of his persuasion, though, they finally acquiesced in the continuation of treatment. But at 9 pm Mrs. Katsuhara called Dr. Noguchi at home, angry that his promise that sedative drugs would not be injected had been broken. Dr. Noguchi was at a loss to respond to the family; he lost confidence in his ability to relate to them.

April 11: * * * 9 am: Dr. Noguchi told the defendant of the family's request to cease treatment, and of the angry phone conversation the previous evening. Drs. Noguchi, Nozaki and Tokunaga conferred, and decided that Dr. Noguchi would henceforth be in the background, and Dr. Tokunaga would deal with the family. They also agreed that the plasma exchange, which carried some risk, would be discontinued.

Defendant, thinking the family's attitude might be changed a little, met with the wife at 9:30, saying: "It's a critical situation. But as a physician, as long as there's any possibility [of cure], of course we'll keep treating the patient. I believe there's some hope, so I'll continue treatment. So please grit it out with me. If we stopped all treatment, you'd regret it afterward."

The son said, "When the time comes, let him face death naturally. Withdraw the I.V. and the catheter." Dr. Tokunaga responded: "*Even when the patient is facing death, I believe a physician must not cease treatment. So I must refuse your request. It's the physician's job to continue treatment right up to the end.*" (Emphasis by the court)

But the son said, "Don't make my father suffer. When death is near, don't use meaningless treatment. I want him to be able to face death easily, without pain." Dr. Tokunaga responded, "Well anyway, we won't use CPR at the end." But Tokunaga was wondering, how much does this patient really mean to his family?

April 12: The patient's condition worsened; lung inflammation had set in. Antibiotics were started and a breathing tube put in. The patient's level of consciousness slipped further, and he had difficulty breathing.

* * *

The son and wife spent the night at the hospital. The son brought a photo of the patient's oldest daughter (his sister); the patient showed no response. The son, thinking that he had lied to his father about his disease and given him false hope of an impossible cure, was filled with regret.

* * *

April 13: The patient declined through the day. Breathing was more difficult; consciousness declined to level 6 (no reaction to painful stimuli); cyanosis of the fingers with light pressure.

The son said, "My mother and I can't take this any more. Stop all treatment; liberate him from this suffering and let him die naturally; even if death comes a little sooner, it's all right." Later that morning, the wife happened to meet Dr. Nozaki in the corridor. "I've been with him without sleeping for a week now, and I'm tired," she exclaimed. "If it's incurable, stop the treatments. I'm going to say this to Dr. Tokunaga too."

About 10 am, the son and wife said to a nurse, "You've done everything you can do. We want you to take him off the I.V. and the Foley catheter." Dr. Tokunaga, hearing this, came in about 11. The family told him: "You've done everything you can. We want you to take him off the I.V. and the catheter. We want to take him home quickly. We can't stand to see him suffer like this any more. We want you to let him be comfortable. We've thought about this and decided."

Dr. Tokunaga said, "Taking him off the I.V. means stopping nutrition and hydration, and that would shorten his life. Wouldn't that be too selfish, to let him die? I can't do that. As a doctor I'm going to fight it to the end."

Defendant on the one hand as a doctor believed he couldn't stop treatment. On the other hand, he understood the family's feeling that with death only a day or two away, advancing that death by removing the I.V. and Foley catheter that the patient seemed to dislike and permitting him to die naturally, probably wouldn't contravene the patient's own wishes. All these things flitted through the doctor's mind. [Translator's comment: The judge is exercising a good deal of creativity in setting out these facts.]

So Dr. Tokunaga finally reached the conclusion that removing the life-sustaining treatment and speeding up the patient's death would be acceptable, and he answered the family: "All right. I understand." He went back to the nurse station, and said to Head Nurse Itō, "I've been told by the family that they want all treatment stopped. I've tried over and over to persuade them otherwise, but they won't listen. So we'll stop all treatment, and remove the I.V. and Foley catheter." Hearing this, Nurse Itō said, "Let me try to talk with them." She did so, but to no avail.

At 11:20 am defendant Tokunaga told a nurse to stop all treatment, and wrote the order in the chart. About 1:30 pm, the nurse disconnected all the equipment.

The son thought that the father would die naturally as though in his sleep that night. He stayed in the hospital room with him. But the father's breathing became more labored still, weighing on the son's mind. (The wife, at the son's suggestion, had gone home in the afternoon to rest.)

About 2 pm, Dr. Nozaki came by and was surprised to find the I.V. and catheter out. Thinking that Dr. Tokunaga, to whom he had turned over the patient's care, had given in to the family's requests, he called out to Dr. Tokunaga at the nurse station, "I see you've stopped the I.V." Dr. Tokunaga responded: "I tried to persuade them, but they wouldn't listen, so I stopped it." Dr. Nozaki, acquiescing, then left for a conference in Kyoto.

About 3 pm, Dr. Tokunaga checked the patient. The breathing tube was in, and the EKG monitor was attached. The patient's level of consciousness was Level 6: no reaction to pain stimuli, no consciousness. He thought the patient probably would die that day or the next. At about 4 pm, he met Dr. Mishima of the same department and rank as he; he told Mishima that he had stopped treatment. Mishima replied, "That ought to shut the family up."

The son, seeing his father apparently suffering with heavy breathing and wanting him to die quietly as though in his sleep, called Dr. Tokunaga to the room about 5 pm. "He's suffering. I want you to take out the breathing tube." Dr. Tokunaga replied, "I can't do that. There's a danger that his tongue will block his throat and he'll stop breathing." The son renewed the request. Dr. Tokunaga thought, it's all right with the son if his father dies. I've already agreed to his request to disconnect the I.V. and catheter. So at 5:45 pm, he took out the breathing tube.

The patient's labored breathing continued. About 6 pm the son called Dr. Tokunaga to the bedside again. "I can't stand to listen to his breathing, and see him suffering like this. Please put him to rest. Please let me take him home quickly." Dr. Tokunaga, thinking that at least he could quiet the father's breathing, said "I understand." He went back to the nurse station, considering what drug would suppress this labored breathing.

He decided on Horizon, an analgesic with the side effect of suppressing breathing, knowing the drug might hasten the patient's death. He had Nurse Kadogawa prepare twice the usual dose: 4 ml. At 6:15 he injected it into the patient's left arm. The son silently watched him from the bedside.

After watching for nearly an hour after this injection, the son, seeing that his father's labored breathing continued unchanged, called loudly for Dr. Tokunaga: "He's still breathing. I want to take him home quickly." Dr. Tokunaga went back to the nurse station, filled a syringe himself with double the normal dose of the drug Sereneisu, and at about 7 pm injected it into the patient's left arm. (Sereneisu also has the side effect of suppressing breathing.)

The son, after watching the injection, asked "How long will it take?" Dr. Tokunaga replied: "His heart's really strong. Maybe an hour or two."

After the Sereneisu injection, Dr. Tokunaga, seeking to forestall any more requests from the son, called him out of the hospital room. "You're asking me to kill him with these drugs. Well, the law doesn't allow it, and as a physician I can't do it." The son just listened silently.

The son, seeing the father unchanged after the second injection, suspected Dr. Tokunaga of trying to fool him with meaningless injections. He paged Dr. Tokunaga, who was in his car to get some dinner outside the hospital. Dr. Tokunaga turned and came back without getting dinner. The son confronted him at the nurse station angrily. "What are you up to, doctor? He's still breathing! I want to take him home before this day is over."

Dr. Tokunaga felt that he could not escape from the unusually persistent demands of the son. He went into the nurse station without answering, worried about what to do. He felt as though as much as he tried to refuse the son's requests, he couldn't keep doing so forever. He was physically and mentally exhausted. Finally he decided to do the son's bidding, and make the patient die.

He decided to use a drug that would make the patient's heart stop. Looking in the bookcase at the nurse station, he saw in a drug compendium that Wasoran, used for circulatory conditions, had the side effect of transient heart stoppage. He decided to use it. But that alone might not kill the patient immediately. So he decided to add KCl (potassium chloride), which causes damage to the heart's electrical function, to the mix.

Usually potassium chloride is diluted and given patients intravenously. But Dr. Tokunaga decided to inject it in undiluted form. He asked Nurse Miyoko Takanishi if they had potassium chloride and Wasoran available. She said "There's some potassium chloride, but no Wasoran." But she knew about his trying the other two drugs, and she acceded to his request. She wrote up an order for Wasoran to the hospital pharmacy, and gave it to Dr. Tokunaga. He got it from the pharmacy.

Dr. Tokunaga put 5 ml of Wasoran—twice the usual dose—into a syringe. He put 20 ml of potassium chloride in another. He went to the patient's room. The patient was breathing laboriously. The son watched him silently.

Facts Constituting the Crime

The defendant, on April 13, 1991 at about 8:35 pm, in Isehara City, Kanagawa-ken, at Tōkai University Affiliated Hospital, 6th floor Room 14, injected the patient first with Wasoran; upon seeing that had no effect, he injected 20 ml of undiluted potassium chloride into the patient's left arm. Nurse Kadogawa immediately noticed an abnormality on the heart monitor and shouted, "There's a ventricular narrowing." But Dr. Tokunaga kept on with the injection. He confirmed the patient's heart stoppage on the monitor, checking for lack of a heartbeat and pulse. He said to the son "It's over." At about 8:46 pm, the patient died of heart stoppage caused by an acute high level of potassium in the blood.

Judgment of the Court

Part I. Introduction

[The court makes general observations about medical progress, euthanasia, and how this case forces us to define the legal limits; what's important about the case; the consequences of the decision.]

Part II. Requirements for Cessation of Treatment

Death must be unavoidable; the patient must be in the last stages of an incurable disease with no prospect of recovery. The cessation of treatment originates in the patient's right of self-determination and the limit of a physician's duty in cases of medical futility. This is not to recognize the patient's right to die as such, or right to choose death. It simply recognizes a right to choose the method or process of facing death. This is to prevent us from viewing death too lightly. It is desirable that more than one physician make the judgment that recovery is impossible. Also, if the treatment in question is one that has only a small influence on the patient's continued life, it should be easier to terminate the treatment than if it ties in directly with the patient's death—in which latter case the patient should be actually facing death before the treatment is terminated.

It is necessary for the patient to have made an expression of intent that treatment cease, and that that intent [not be revoked] at the time of the cessation of treatment. It goes without saying that it is most desirable for the patient himself to have clearly expressed that intention. The expression of intention should be based on the patient's own accurate knowledge of his disease, nature of treatment, and prognosis. For this reason the importance of informing the patient of his diagnosis and of informed consent is indicated.

However, in the great majority of cases, patients will be unable to express their intention about cessation of treatment at the time the decision must be made. Most Japanese today, we expect, would want meaningless treatment stopped, and we can expect that in future, living wills will become more prevalent. But we must consider whether substituted consent [lit. "inferred intent"—*suiteiteki ishi*] should be recognized.

If there is a prior expression of will by the patient, whether written or oral, it is powerful proof—if near in time. But if remote in time, or vague, then the case should be treated like situations where no expression of will by the patient exists. Where no reliable expression of the patient's intent exists, it is best to rely on the family to state the patient's "inferred intent." Better this, than digging into fragmentary evidence of what the patient might have said in passing. The family is likely to know the patient's character, values, and view of human existence. The family, like the patient, should be given accurate information about the patient's condition, nature of treatment, prognosis, etc. To judge the family's ability to speak for the patient, it is necessary for the physician to know about the patient's relationship to his family, how close they are, and so forth.

The treatments that may be terminated include drugs, chemical treatment, artificial respiration, blood transfusion, nutrition and hydration—both measures for treatment of disease and life support measures. However, what treatments should be stopped, and when, are medical judgments about when the treatments are meaningless.

Part III. Requirements for Euthanasia

Conditions for active euthanasia by a physician:

a. Physical pain difficult to bear.

b. The time of unavoidable death is drawing near.

c. Methods of eliminating or easing physical pain are exhausted, and no substitute means remain.

d. There is a clear expression of intent to accept the shortening of life.

Conditions for cessation of treatment: An expression of intent by family members who can infer the patient's will, will suffice. [Moreover, cessation must be medically appropriate.]

Defendant's acts here did not meet the conditions allowing either "cessation of treatment" or "active euthanasia."

The patient had bone marrow cancer. A doctor at Tōkai University Hospital received a request from the patient's son to "put him to rest," saying "I want to take him home quickly" [i.e., as a corpse].

A distinction must be made between physical suffering (whether existing or probable in the future), which can serve as a justification for active euthanasia, and mental suffering, which cannot. Judging mental suffering is too subjective; we could start to view death too lightly.

Active euthanasia is permitted as long as death is imminent. But if it is not, "indirect euthanasia" [*kansetsu-teki anrakushi*], in the sense of pain relief treatment with the possibility of hastening death, can be used.

The idea of allowing euthanasia is based in part on the concept of patient autonomy: the patient must choose whether to undergo suffering or shorten life. So an indication of the patient's will is essential. Whether a clear indication of the patient's will is required, or whether merely an inference of the patient's intent will suffice, depends on the method of euthanasia.

[The court sets out three types of euthanasia:

Passive (*shōkyokuteki*): the cessation of life-prolonging treatment, a non-deliberate (*fusakui*) act

Indirect (*kansetsuteki*): giving pain relief treatment with the possibility of hastening death

Active (*sekkyokuteki*): treatment deliberately inviting death in order to free the patient from suffering]

The permissibility of euthanasia differs according to which of the three types is in question.

The permissibility of passive euthanasia is to be judged merely as a matter of whether it is medically appropriate to cease treatment. Indirect euthanasia is permitted in accordance with the principle of patient autonomy. An inference of the patient's intent will suffice; and this can be inferred from the family's expression of intent. Active euthanasia is permissible only when all means of removing or easing pain have been exhausted, and no other alternate methods exist. Then as the Nagoya High Court said in its December 22, 1962 judgment (Hanrei Jihō 324:1): "It must be performed by a physician."

Active euthanasia is based on the principles of emergency refuge [*kinky ū hinan*] and patients' self-determination; so it is permissible only with a clear expression of intent by the patient. Passive euthanasia is permissible only if the patient is in an incurable state, nearing death, with no prospect of recovery. Some evidence of the patient's intent is required for passive euthanasia. Clear evidence of the patient's will at the time of the decision to cease treatment is desirable. It should be based on continuing consideration and accurate information concerning prognosis, accurately understood.

However, clear evidence of the patient's will is not necessary for cessation of treatment. Passive euthanasia is also allowed based on inferences from the patient's own previous expression of will, or from the family's statement of intent. Still, to recognize that the family is properly inferring the patient's will, the family must know the patient's character and values, and must have full and accurate information on the nature of the disease, treatment, and prognosis. Moreover, the physician assessing the family's expression of will must be in a position to know both the patient's own thoughts and position concerning his disease and treatment, and the level of the patient's relationship with his family.

The conditions justifying active [or indirect] euthanasia were not met here. The fatal injection was not for the purpose of relieving physical pain, since at that time the patient was not suffering; and since the patient had never been told he was suffering from cancer, there was no clear statement available as to the patient's own intent.

Part IV. Evaluation of Defendant's Specific Acts

Removal of I.V., Foley Catheter & Breathing Tube: Both Dr. Tokunaga and Dr. Nozaki judged that the patient, as of April 13, 1991, had only a day or two to live. Other physicians said the same; even with aggressive treatment, the patient could at most have survived 4–5 days. So objectively, the patient's condition was at the stage appropriate for consideration of termination of treatment.

As for the expression of the patient's will, this patient had not been informed of his diagnosis, and had not received an accurate explanation of his condition and prognosis. At the time of decision, he was incapable of expressing his will. So we must determine whether the family could properly speak for the patient. Both the wife and son had lived with the patient for many years, and knew his character, values, and outlook on life. They kept insisting on cessation of treatment over several days. We can conclude that they were capable of expressing the patient's inferred intent. However, the family were not properly informed of the patient's inability to feel pain. On April 13, when they asked that the I.V. and Foley catheter be discontinued, they were not told that he had no response to painful stimuli. So their request cannot be considered to be properly grounded, inferred expressions of the patient's intent.

This defendant had only known the family for a short time—less than two weeks—at the time he became attending physician for this patient. There is doubt whether he really understood their position. He was not in a position to judge whether their decisions were a proper expression of the patient's intent. The patient's intent was neither expressed nor could be inferred from the family. Therefore the withdrawal of the I.V. etc. was not permitted by law.

2. The Injections of Horizon and Sereneisu

Not being premised either on the patient's own expression of intention nor on the patient's inferred intent stated by a properly informed family, these injections do not fall within the permitted indirect euthanasia.

3. The Injections of Wasoran and Potassium Chloride

Since the patient was feeling no pain at the time, the prerequisite for legal active euthanasia—intractible physical pain—was not met. Nor was there a finding that alternative measures were not available. Neither did the patient give express consent. The conditions for legally permissible active euthanasia were not fulfilled. Defendant pleaded that the son was an "instigator." But the court considered the doctor's higher status and position, and rejected the argument.

Reasons for Punishment

[The court concluded these illegal acts undercut trust in medicine, and speculated that doctors might start shortening the lives of patients who are not facing immediate death.]

Even though the hospital at which defendant was employed has high standards, its system for end-of-life care was deficient. The "team concept" did not function well, because of the shuffling around of staff.

The family's influence on end-of-life decisions is great. This doctor's training and experience in dealing with such situations was poor. [The court gave reasons for leniency with the punishment: e.g. the family does not hold bad feelings toward the defendant.]

Sentence: Two years, suspended. [The sentence was not appealed.]

Note

The Tokai University case has been quite influential among legal and medical scholars and practitioners. However, the decision has by no means ended debate on the subject in Japan: it was just a district court case; most of the court's analytical framework was not necessary to the decision in the case; and subsequent court decisions raising similar issues are few. (In one other case the same court generally followed the same analytical framework, also holding a physician criminally liable for his part in bringing about a terminally ill patient's death. *Judgment of Yokohama District Court,* March 25, 2005, 1909 Hanrei Jiho 130.) Thus, the court's analytical framework lacks authoritative support. Absent authoritative guidance and fearing criminal liability, many physicians simply refuse families' requests to remove life support from comatose terminal patients. Other physicians will halt medications but will not remove a respirator. Aiming at clarification of this controversial area, in early 2007 the health ministry named a blue-ribbon committee to propose authoritative guidelines for end-of-life care—or at least to propose procedures for making the decisions. The committee's recommendations are not yet available as this book goes to press. (This note provided by Robert Leflar and Norio Higuchi).

Chapter 4

The Rights of the Individual and the Interests of Society

A. Public Health Law: Legal Approaches to HIV/AIDS

The first three chapters of this book have dealt primarily with the rights of private patients and consumers in their relationships with professionals, institutions, or the government in matters pertaining to health care. The law also plays a role in protecting the health of the public. The topic of public health law is the subject of this final chapter.

Public health law came into its own in the late 19th century, as the law was used as a tool to impede the spread of infectious diseases, promote sanitation, protect workers from threats to their health and safety, combat environmental nuisances, and defend the public from unsafe food or drugs. Indeed, the late 19th century was not only a time of the spread of national public health legislation, but also of international. See David Fidler. International Law and Global Public Health, 40 *U.Kan.L.Rev.* 1 (1999). In the 20th century, public health law has continued to address these concerns, and has broadened to address other health promotion and prevention concerns, such as tobacco advertising and sales. See, Christopher Reynolds, The Promise of Public Health Law, 1 *J.Law and Med.* 212 (1994). At the same time, environmental law, traditionally a field within public health law, has become a largely independent body of law.

One of the greatest challenge to confront public health law in recent decades has been the spread of HIV/AIDS. HIV/AIDS emerged in the 1980s, at a time when the developed nations had become quite complacent about infectious diseases. The disease emerged quite suddenly; seemed to be incurable and invariably fatal; and appeared initially in marginalized groups such as homosexuals, intravenous drug users, and prostitutes. For all of these reasons, there was in some countries a push to adopt laws that would treat HIV/AIDS differently than other infectious diseases. In particular there was a tendency on the part of some policy-makers to argue for the use of traditional public health tools such as screening, quarantine, and contact tracing, rather than more modern approaches of education and persuasion. The following excerpt discusses the contrasting approaches taken by various European jurisdictions to the HIV/AIDS crisis:

AIDS, Public Health and the Law: A Case of Structural Coupling?

John A. Harrington, European J. Health Law, vol. 6, pp. 213, 213–26 (1999)

1. Introduction

AIDS has been a focus of health care policy and medical law in Europe for almost two decades now. In its early years AIDS represented the greatest challenge to public health since the pre-World War II era when tuberculosis was prevalent. The sense of panic or crisis which affected policy makers as well as the general public was caused not primarily by the numbers of persons affected, but by the potential for huge and rapid spread of the disease in the population. The risk of future catastrophe, even more than the reality of present disaster, was the significant object of public policy. It was this future-orientation which marked AIDS out as typically a public health issue: that is, measures proposed and measures taken were preventive in purpose and design. Given the passing of time it is now appropriate to speak of a history of AIDS in Europe. This history is at least partly one of public health responses to the disease. A history, that is, of competing predictions, proposals and measures implemented to combat the spread of AIDS.

Each model of disease control envisaged a very specific, but variable role for the law. The imposition of legal sanctions for disapproved behaviour, the application of coercive control to high risk groups and the availability of legal remedies for infected persons were all thus significantly dependent upon differing public health understandings. An examination of the history of AIDS can therefore be expected to reveal the varying incidence and intensity of links between public health medicine and the law. It can, in other words, demonstrate a positive correlation between specific medical theories and recommendations on the one hand, and specific legal change on the other.

* * *

2. Public Health—"Old and New"

Although public health and other medical experts, often liaising with gay activists and other interest groups, were at the heart of policy making on AIDS across Europe, there was no unanimity in their recommendations. Science does not necessarily give an unambiguous, clear-cut message to policy makers, and the case of AIDS illustrates the scope for conflicting signals from experts. These distinct responses to HIV/AIDS may be related to what has been termed the "old" and the "new" public health. * * *

The old public health evolved in the nineteenth century as a response to the spread of infectious disease. Epidemics of cholera, typhus, tuberculosis and scarlet fever had devastating effects in the massively expanded industrial cities of Europe. * * * As the century progressed, scientific breakthroughs, such as those of Louis Pasteur and Robert Koch, showed that prevalent diseases were very frequently caused by the transmission of viruses from person to person and that this process of infection was intensified by the social conditions [of the time]. In the absence of effective vaccines for most conditions and before the development of "miracle" drugs such as penicillin, the chief recommendation of epidemiologists and other public health specialists was that in each case the chain of infection should be broken, thus stopping the spread of the disease. To achieve this local and state health authorities implemented programmes of quarantine, isolation, testing and compulsory treatment on the outbreak of infectious disease in their areas. * * * Importantly, these measures were cast in legal form: they empowered officials acting on the advice of doctors to impose drastic restrictions upon the freedom of movement of individuals and upon economic activity in affected areas.

With the abatement of the great epidemics, these powers, though remaining in force, were used more and more infrequently. Their coercive approach was displaced in orthodox public health medicine in response to changing patterns of morbidity and mortality in Europe, especially after the Second World War. This "new" public health sought to combat much more prevalent conditions such as cancer, heart disease and obesity with strategies of persuasion, education and behaviour modification. * * * The obvious distinction with the major nineteenth century illnesses was that none of the more recently occurring conditions is contagious. The issue of whether and how to break chains of infection did not arise. Neither, therefore, did the question of whether to reactivate the inherited corpus of draconian health legislation. All this was to change with the advent of AIDS in the early 1980s.

3. Policy Responses to HIV/AIDS

Soon after the diagnosis of the first cases of AIDS, epidemiological studies indicated a concentration of cases among two main social groups: homosexual men and intravenous drug users. Subsequently it became clear that members of other groups could also be infected. In 1983–4 French and American scientists, working independently of each other, demonstrated that the immune weakness, which lead ultimately to the complex of illness known as "full-blown" AIDS, was caused by the so-called Human Immunodeficiency Virus (HIV). Further studies showed that the virus is passed from person to person by certain, rather limited forms of human contact, in particular by the exchange of body fluids such as blood, semen and breastmilk. Although the main aetiological questions were settled, two outstanding issues remained: the fact that AIDS was an incurable condition leading to the death of almost all those infected with HIV; and, in the light of this, the question of how to stop or at least slow the spread of the virus in the population. * * *

Two main approaches to the control of AIDS were recommended, one non-coercive and broadly in line with the new public health, the other coercive and in line with the old public health. In essence the non-coercive strategy sought to mobilize infected persons and the general public to change their behaviour in order to reduce the spread of infection. As the United Kingdom Chief Medical Officer put it in 1986, "[i]n the absence of a vaccine or effective anti-viral agent, public education to help people avoid risky sexual behaviour and drug abuse is the mainstay of a policy for controlling the spread of infection." Consequently a strong message was conveyed that the use of condoms in sexual intercourse and of sterile equipment in intravenous drug-taking was the best means of protecting oneself and others. These education campaigns were essentially based upon the utilitarian assumption that, once the risks of certain behaviours were explained to them, individuals would act rationally in their own best interests.

There is a further, less immediate sense in which general education campaigns were intended to reduce the spread of AIDS. It was widely recognized that those groups at highest risk of infection had suffered from discrimination before the advent of AIDS solely by reason of their choice of lifestyle. Activists and public health specialists repeatedly emphasized that the new association of these stigmatized lifestyles with a fatal, incurable disease would further distance high risk groups from both the wider society and the state medical system. Without these contacts behaviour modification among those most at risk of being infected and of infecting others would be very difficult to achieve. Thus, homosexual men, drug users and prostitutes were intended to understand public health campaigns in a further indirect sense: as indicating a tolerant and inclusive attitude on the part of the authorities, and as creating a less hostile attitude toward them among the heterosexual and non-drug taking population. This distinctive approach to public health is sometimes formulated as "the AIDS-paradox": only by protecting at risk persons from discrimination and coercion could the state protect the interests of the uninfected majority of the population. In other words to respect the human rights of persons immediately affected by the epidemic was at the same time to promote the health of all. AIDS was, therefore, constructed in these campaigns as a "national" problem, a condition which could and did affect everyone. Gay groups in particular met with a largely positive response on initiating contact with and making proposals for action to national health authorities. Partly pro-active, partly co-opted, they were used by the medical establishment to organize information campaigns as well as practical help for their constituencies.

As has been noted, the coercive response to HIV/AIDS was typically founded upon older notions of public health medicine outlined above. In particular it remained true to the initial epidemiological emphasis upon high risk groups, as opposed to high risk activities. * * * On the basis of this methodology, homosexuals, drug users and prostitutes, were defined as being outside and "other than" the largely unaffected heterosexual population. The task of medicine and law was, therefore, to protect the "majority" by preventing the epidemic from crossing this notional divide. It is clear that this recommendation of public health was reciprocally linked with common moral and political responses to epidemics. Right-wing cultural critics promoted a view of AIDS as an inevitable consequence of, if not a punishment for, decadent forms of life. By contrast with the non-coercive approach, this model of disease prevention did not attribute to high risk groups the same self-interested rationality as that of the rest of the population. They were assumed instead to be typically irrational and heedless of the danger presented to themselves and others by their "hedonistic" pursuits. Consequently they could not be reached in the first instance by education, that is by rational persuasion. Neither were they seen as likely to respond to a more tolerant climate by modifying their behaviour. Control strategies were to be directed rather more at the bodies than the minds of infected or potentially infected persons, identified by their status as members of high risk groups. It was thus clear that, in attempting to break the chain of infection, the authorities would resort to techniques of surveillance, testing and isolation, i.e. legally sanctioned coercion. The only reflective response on the part of targeted groups and individuals contemplated was one of fear. * * *

The chief examples of the non-coercive strategy in Western Europe are provided by the United Kingdom and all but one of the German federal states; those of the coercive strategy by the German state of Bavaria and Sweden. * * *

4. The Non-Coercive Approach

4.1 United Kingdom

United Kingdom governmental policy on AIDS was shaped by a high degree of agreement between ministers, public health specialists and representatives of affected groups. Challenges to the overridingly non-coercive policy adopted came most frequently not from rival schools of public health, but from social conservatives on the right wing of the political spectrum. More than a policy, non-coercion became a culture which spread, admittedly not without local resistance, from political and professional elites to volunteer and health service workers involved in treating and counselling people with HIV. The latter group was significantly comprised of doctors and nurses. * * *

In Britain the main legislation relating to contagious diseases is the Public Health (Control of Diseases) Act 1984, a consolidation of measures which date from the Victorian era. It provides local authorities with powers to deal with certain listed conditions. These include the classic targets of nineteenth century public health: cholera, plague, tuberculosis, small pox, scarlet fever, etc. Most, though not all, of these conditions are notifiable under s. 11 of the Act, i.e. a doctor encountering them in a patient must inform the local authority or face criminal sanction. Further permissible measures include detention and isolation of sufferers or suspected sufferers, compulsory examination and testing, prohibition of employment and upon the use of public facilities such as buses, libraries and swimming pools. At the beginning of the epidemic there was pressure in Britain to make AIDS and HIV notifiable conditions, but this was successfully resisted. (The AIDS (Control) Act 1987 does provide for the collection of data on the prevalence of the disease in the United Kingdom, but this is done on an anonymous basis.) Admittedly, AIDS was added to the list of infectious conditions for which some of the other, aforementioned coercive measures might be taken. Local authorities and medical practitioners, therefore, still have the power to adopt an authoritarian approach to persons with AIDS. However, the liberal policy consensus prevailed. It was generally accepted that "AIDS" within the terms of the Act does not include the condition of being asymptomatically infected with HIV. This restricts the applicability of coercive measures in the case of an individual sufferer to the last year or so of their lives when they are in any case usually subject to treatment (and therefore supervision) in hospital. Furthermore even in relation to AIDS itself the powers provided were used only once: a patient being subjected to compulsory detention in Manchester in 1985.

One of the most controversial issues in this area, throughout Europe, and indeed elsewhere, has been that of non-voluntary testing for HIV (whether against the express wishes of the patient or secretly, without their consent). Since 1990 blood taken from patients at ante-natal and genito-urinary medicine clinics in Britain has been tested for HIV. Test results are "anonymized" and the data obtained are used solely for epidemiological purposes. * * *

Even though anonymized testing continues to be carried out, academic constructions of the relevant law have had a restraining effect upon policy makers and medical professionals alike. In 1988, for example, the British Medical Association was forced to overturn a resolution of its annual representative meeting to the effect that unconsented to testing for HIV be left entirely to the discretion of the individual doctor. Legal advice indicated that action in accordance with the resolution would be in breach of civil and possibly criminal law. Furthermore a series of guidelines on ethically permissible testing was issued in 1987 by United Kingdom General Medical Council (GMC), the profession's own disciplinary body. These stated that secret testing was only allowed, as a matter of professional ethics, where it was necessary to avert a clear and immediate danger to others, in particular health care workers carrying out risky procedures on a patient. * * *

The approach of the medical and governmental authorities to the testing of health care workers has been similarly non-coercive. Admittedly there have been frequent outbursts of panic regarding HIV-infected doctors and nurses in Britain and tracing of patients has been conducted in several cases. The authorities have, however, forgone recourse to compulsory screening of hospital staff. Furthermore, there has in the recent past been only a single prosecution of a health worker in connection with infectious disease. Instead of a widespread use of the criminal law, regulation has again been left to the GMC. Its 1987 guidelines also contained ethical advice directed to practitioners who are or might be infected with HIV or other contagious diseases. This embodies a voluntary approach: advising doctors who suspect that they might be carrying the virus to come forward for testing and, if found to be HIV positive, to desist from working in situations where they pose a risk to their patients.

Closely linked to testing is the generally recognized obligation of confidentiality. Again the law in England on this issue is unclear. In the case of *X v Y*, it was held that no exception was available to allow publication of an identified doctor's HIV positive status by the press. * * * Rose J noted that:

> Confidentiality is of paramount importance to [HIV-infected] patients including doctors ... If it is breached, or if patients have grounds for believing that it may be or has been breached they will be reluctant to come forward for and to continue treatment and, in particular, counselling. If the actual or apprehended breach is to the press that reluctance is likely to be very great. If treatment is not provided or continued the individual will be deprived of its benefit and the public are likely to suffer from an increase in the rate of spread of the disease. The preservation of confidentiality is therefore in the public interest.

In this respect, his judgement is clearly based upon the public health consensus already outlined.

* * *

4.2 Germany

As in the United Kingdom, the central issue in the German debate on HIV/AIDS was whether a coercive, legally backed campaign should be waged against the disease, or whether a non-coercive, voluntaristic approach should be taken. The main German legislation in this area is the Federal Law on Contagious diseases. This is rather similar to the British Public Health (Control of Diseases) Act 1984 in the conditions it is aimed at and in the powers which it confers upon health officials. It is important to note that the requirement of notification under para. 3 of the Law is limited to a list of seventeen specific conditions. Discussion and commentary in Germany focused *inter alia* on whether legislation should be passed to include HIV and AIDS in this list. The authorities in all the federal states apart from Bavaria, agreed that they would not be so included. As in the United Kingdom, however, a system of anonymous collection of data on the incidence of HIV/AIDS was put in place under the Laboratory Notification Ordinance 1987. A declaration issued by their Health Ministers together with Federal Minister for Youth, Family and Health testifies to a general policy consensus in Germany similar to that which emerged in the United Kingdom. It accepted that:

> the availability of voluntary testing, advice and social assistance in various forms would be more effective in controlling the disease than the introduction of a legal duty of notification under the infectious disease legislation. The transmission of disease by way of sexual contact cannot be subject to control by the state. The state cannot take away the highly personal responsibility of each citizen for his or her own sexual behaviour and therefore cannot ensure absolute protection in this regard.

By contrast with the requirement of notification, the other powers under the Federal Law on Contagious Diseases are not limited to specifically enumerated conditions. For these purposes, para. 1 of the Law defines as "contagious diseases" those which are caused by pathogenic agents capable of being transmitted from one human being to another.

Whether a disease or condition comes within para. 1 is, therefore, a matter of interpretation. In so far as it does, para. 34 of the Law allows the following measures to be taken: compulsory testing, exclusion from employment, quarantining and supervision by the authorities. * * * In their declaration, however, the health ministers considered that the powers contained in para. 34 would rarely be needed, if at all, owing to the manner in which HIV is transmitted and the ease with which individuals can protect themselves. In addition, because such measures would severely abrogate the fundamental, constitutionally guaranteed rights of persons with HIV or AIDS they would come under scrutiny in accordance with the general administrative and constitutional law requirement of proportionality. Academic commentary largely took the view that coercive measures taken under para. 34 would not withstand such scrutiny, especially given their relative inefficacy as means of reducing the spread of HIV.

Instead, in implementation of a non-coercive programme, federal and state authorities have spent sums in excess of DM 150 million on information and education campaigns since 1987. A special commission of the Federal Lower Chamber of Parliament on AIDS reported in 1990 that the chief aim of this campaign was and should be: 1) to inform the public; 2) to encourage responsible, self-protective behaviour; 3) to reduce irrational anxiety; 4) to promote solidarity with the victims of AIDS; and 5) to counter discrimination against high risk groups. A nationwide confidential telephone counselling service was established. An important dimension of the AIDS campaign in Germany, with parallels in the United Kingdom, has been the encouragement and financial support given to voluntary and self-help organizations active in the field. These groups, largely federated under the umbrella of the Deutsche AIDS-Hilfe eV, include gay groups, prostitute organizations and others active in providing social and health services and in political campaigning. * * *

A certain amount of "wild" or speculative testing was carried out, particularly in hospitals, in the early years of the epidemic in Germany. This has become much less frequent in the light of both the public health consensus outlined above, and an increased awareness of how medical professionals can protect themselves. The latter especially has led to a restrictive interpretation of the relevant law, as in the United Kingdom. There is no dispute that an AIDS test, carried out against the express wishes of a patient, would give rise to criminal liability for invasion of bodily integrity under para. 223 of the German Criminal Code. The issue of implied consent, particularly where the patient presents for a general check-up, has been more controversial. Concern has been expressed that consent might be too easily implied due to the wide variety of symptoms associated with AIDS, e.g. tuberculosis. It has even been suggested that membership of a high risk group would be sufficient to justify testing were this ground recognized. Given the individual's constitutionally guaranteed right to self-determination, it has been argued strongly that consent to the carrying out of secret tests is not readily to be implied even where the patient has not openly ruled them out. * * * Finally it should be noted that breach of medical confidentiality is a criminal offence in Germany, under para. 203 I 1 of the Criminal Code, albeit with some exceptions. The sharing of information between members of a health care team is viewed as de minimis for instance. In addition it maybe permissible to make disclosure of a patient's HIV status to a third party at risk of infection under the defence of emergency. In each case, however, the rights to life and bodily integrity of the third party must be balanced with the rights to privacy and self-determination of the patient and with the general interest in maintaining the confidentiality of the doctor-patient relationship. * * *

* * *

5. The Coercive Approach

5.1. Bavaria

By contrast with the German Federal government and all the other states, Bavaria implemented a coercive programme of measures to prevent the spread of HIV/AIDS in its population. In essence it understood itself to be subject to a constitutional obligation to take such measures for the protection of its citizens' health. In a 1987 decision, however, the Federal Constitutional Court rejected the claim of a plaintiff who had been infected with contaminated blood that there was such a constitutional imperative. The Court agreed with his contention that the authorities were obliged to respond to the epidemic; but it held that judgments as to the broad policy of such campaigns as well as their fine detail were not appropriate to the judicial function. Decisions about timing, method and expenditure were contingent upon ever changing empirical data, more readily available to the legislative and executive organs of government. Only if the Federal Health Ministry had been completely inactive could the Court issue a declaration compelling legislative or other measures. As has already been seen, this was not the case.

In a piece written in 1988 Peter Gauweiler, the Interior Minister responsible for introducing and implementing the Bavarian Catalogue of Measures for the combat of AIDS, outlined the three public health principles on which it was based. These were: 1) the earlier and more intensive the intervention against the epidemic the better; 2) sources of infection must be dealt with without exception; 3) suitable measures must be taken to break the chain of infection. These clearly represented a prioritization of the dangerousness approach over that focused upon voluntarism and personal autonomy. Instead of education and information aimed in the first instance at the general population and seeking to persuade them, as rational agents to alter their behaviour, emphasis was laid upon identifying high risk groups and more or less coercing them to act in the interests of general well-being. The Catalogue of Measures was legally based for the greater part upon the powers contained in the Federal Law on Contagious Diseases. In the first six months of its implementation in Bavaria 1047 individuals were investigated by the authorities of whom 492 were tested for HIV. In three instances the blood had to be obtained by application of direct physical force. Police raids were carried out on sauna clubs and other establishments known to be frequented by homosexual men. Many were shut down. More generally the grant of residence permits in Bavaria to nationals of certain, non-EC countries, is made conditional upon their testing negative for HIV. Prostitutes and intravenous drug users are classified as "suspected infectious" within the Federal Law on Contagious Diseases and are subjected to routine testing. In the case of registered prostitutes this means every quarter. They are then granted a certificate of good health for the "reassurance" of their customers. Those testing positive are forbidden to continue with their work. All prostitutes are under an obligation, breach of which is punishable, to ensure condom use. Normally a positive test result leads to an obligation to notify sexual partners and medical authorities. The individual concerned can also be supervised by the Bavarian health authorities and there is also provision for the quarantining of the uncooperative, or "AIDS-desperados" as Minister Gauweiler labelled them. A challenge to compulsory testing was rejected by the Bavarian Administrative Court. Inevitably these measures, among the most coercive in Europe, provoked fierce criticism from activists and academic commentators. It was noted that the Bavarian authorities had applied the Federal Law on Contagious Diseases in this draconian and controversial manner merely on the basis of an administrative decree. Such measures should instead have been sanctioned by legislation, preferably at federal level. In practice, it soon became clear that the measures adopted were highly inefficient relative to the cost of their implementation. There is, for instance, some anecdotal evidence that members of high-risk groups were driven underground and therefore out of reach of counselling and therapy. Munich prostitutes, for example, were reported to have sought medical treatment in the city of Ulm which lies just over the border from Bavaria, so to speak, in the neighbouring state of Baden-Wuerttemberg. It should be remarked that, over a decade after their enactment, many of the powers contained in the Catalogue of Measures, though still "on the books" are no longer enforced.

5.2 *Sweden*

A coercive AIDS policy was also adopted in Sweden, a country long known for its distinctive mix of social democracy and state paternalism. Under an order of 1985, the Communicable Diseases Law (No. 231) of 1968 was amended to include infection with HIV among the venereal diseases in respect of which measures under the law could be taken. The latter include: registration of infected people; contact tracing; and isolation of a patient in hospital when they are believed by their physician not to be following instructions necessary to stop the spread of the disease. Anyone who believes that they have been exposed to infection must report this to a physician and must facilitate contact tracing. In addition the National Board of Health and Welfare promulgated regulations regarding the behaviour of HIV positive individuals. The latter must seek regular medical examinations, inform all sexual partners about their HIV status, and inform physicians and dentists of any condition for which they are being treated. If the patient fails, or is suspected of failing to comply with these norms of behaviour, the doctor must inform the local contagious diseases officer. On investigation of the patient's case, including inspection of all relevant files, the officer may engage the support of social workers and the police in order to enforce compliance. Although there has been a certain amount of flexibility on the part of the authorities in using these powers, there is no doubting the coercive thrust of Swedish AIDS policy. One power under the Communicable Diseases Law which has been deployed is that of isolation. Use of this measure has been criticized from the non-coercive public health perspective as "arbitrarily cruel, astronomically dear, and epidemiologically inefficient." 1987 saw a parliamentary decision forcibly to shut down gay saunas and bathhouses. Admittedly, in Sweden a vigorous educational campaign was waged to inform people of how to protect themselves against infection with HIV. However, moralistic advertising always went hand in hand with the ultimate and very real threat of coercive sanctions.

* * *

Notes

1. The United States has by and large embraced the non-coercive approach to AIDS prevention, although some states have adopted elements of more coercive approaches. In particular, laws requiring reporting of AIDS/HIV infection are quite common, and contact tracing is required in some states. Compulsory testing is rare, and state laws protecting confidentiality are generally quite strict. There are some cases, however, recognizing an obligation on the part of HIV-infected health care employees to notify their patients. Also the laws of some states authorize disclosure of HIV tests under some circumstances, for example to emergency care workers or corrections officers who have been exposed to blood.

2. See also, Margaret Brazier and John Harris, Public Health and Private Lives, 4 *Med. L. Rev.* 171 (1996); Gunter Frankenberg, "In the beginning of all the world was Amer-

ica": AIDS Policy and Law in West Germany, 23 *New York U. J. of Int. L. & Pol.*, 1079 (1991); Helen Watchirs, HIV/AIDS and the Law: The Need for Reform in Australia, 1 *J. L. & Med.* 9 (1993).

3. At the beginning of the twenty-first century, HIV/AIDS is having its most devastating impact on Africa. The fact that Africa lacks the health resources available in North America and Europe for combating this epidemic makes the effect of the epidemic all the more disastrous. African nations are, however, adopting laws to address this crisis. The approach that various nations take depends to some extent on which of the multitude of legal traditions found within Africa is dominant in a particular nation. The following excerpt discusses the various approaches African countries are taking:

HIV and AIDS in Africa: African Policies in Response to AIDS in Relation to Various National Legal Traditions,

Peri H. Alkas, J.D. and Wayne X. Shandera, M.D.
17 J. Legal Med. 527, 527–29, 538–43 (1996)

AIDS is a major health crisis whose resolution depends on global cooperation in control and prevention. Although the full extent of the outbreak is unknown, it is estimated that perhaps one in 275 persons worldwide is infected with the human immunodeficiency virus (HIV), with even higher rates in the Caribbean, the United States, sub-Saharan Africa, Europe, urban Asia, and Latin America. In the first 15 years of the outbreak, Africa has suffered more than any other geographic area. While the future outbreak may selectively involve Asia, due to its large population base, about two-thirds of cases to date are estimated to have occurred in Africa.

Reported African AIDS cases notoriously underestimate the size of the outbreak; for years certain nations were reluctant to admit any AIDS cases. Data gathering also is problematic, and extrapolations to large areas based on small sample sizes may not be valid. In addition, the clinical definition of AIDS used in Africa (the "Bangui" definition), is nonspecific in contrast to the Caracas and Centers for Disease Control (CDC) definitions used in Westernized countries but not useful in countries where limited resources prevent sophisticated diagnosis. The former diagnostic difficulty in distinguishing HIV-1 and HIV-2 also complicates the analysis of early data, especially from West Africa.

Nonetheless, available data can be used to assess the size of the AIDS outbreak in high prevalence areas of central and southern Africa. Recent estimates are that up to 10 million sub-Saharan Africans, or 1 in 40 adults, are infected with HIV. Models have been developed predicting a decline in life expectancy among sub-Saharan Africans by more than 12 years, by 2010. The projected increase in pediatric AIDS mortality may negate the achievements made in infant survival over the last 20 years.

Other statistics are equally staggering. In association with 40% of cases occurring in women, AIDS will result this decade in over 10 million infants being orphaned. Agriculture will be significantly affected because the primary workers are young women who have the highest infection rate. Because infected people are often the economically and educationally elite of an African nation, the ultimate repercussions on the political and economic aspects of national development are unknown.

The prompt response of African nations to the AIDS crisis has included assorted policies and laws determined in part by the legal background of reporting nations and in part by the size of the national outbreak. The responses of African countries may be useful to African nations now establishing policies and to the Asian nations whose policies are under consideration.

* * *

II. Survey Results of HIV and AIDS Policies

Forty of the fifty-two African countries surveyed responded. The countries responding were grouped into the following classifications: civil; common; civil/common; civil/Islamic; and common/Islamic. As with any system of categorization, the danger inheres that the legal traditions of some countries are not clearly identifiable from their history. However, for the purposes of this analysis, bright lines had to be drawn.

Those responding countries which fell into the civil law class were Benin, Burkina Faso, Burundi, Cape Verde, Equatorial Guinea, Gabon, Guinea-Bissau, Ivory Coast, Madagascar, Mozambique, Niger, Rwanda, Sao Tome & Principe, Seychelles, Togo, and Zaire. Those in the common-law group were Liberia, Uganda, Zambia, and Zimbabwe. Those that were civil/common mixed included Botswana, Cameroon, Mauritius, Namibia, South Africa, and Swaziland. Those falling into a civil/Islamic legal tradition were Algeria, Chad, Djibouti, Guinea, Libya, Mali, Mauritania, Morocco, Senegal, Sudan, and Tunisia. Finally, those grouped as common/Islamic included The Gambia and Nigeria. Ethiopia, uniquely not having been colonized, has a history of socialist traditions, traditions also to be found in Angola and The Congo (nonrespondents), and Libya. Countries were asked about reporting, notification, antidiscrimination policies, immigration policies, and blood banking. The most significant correlations by types of legal traditions were found in the areas of antidiscrimination policies, immigration, and blood screening.* * *

A. Antidiscrimination Policies

Prejudice against those persons infected with HIV or suffering from AIDS merely because of their seropositive status is generally deemed counterproductive throughout Africa. Discriminatory practices are recognized to delay or defer testing or seeking of treatment, thereby increasing the risk of transmission to others. Discrimination unfortunately may occur, either overtly or subtly, in a myriad of circumstances. Many concerns of antidiscrimination policies in the West are irrelevant in Africa. For example, a law enforcing the right of infected children to attend school is useless in a rural area where few children attend school. Similarly, laws prohibiting the denial of insurance have no relevance because few Africans, especially in rural areas, have health insurance. Further, even antidiscrimination policies that allow universal access to health care are of limited utility considering the underfunded nature of the health care systems.

Nonetheless, countries without antidiscrimination policies need to enact them, in an effort to counter remaining discrimination. Nations without such policies are in contravention of a World Health Organization (WHO) resolution calling on all countries to prohibit discrimination against those with AIDS. This resolution states that the WHO:

> 1. urges Member States, particularly in devising and carrying out national programmes for the prevention and control of HIV infection and AIDS:
>
> (1) to foster a spirit of understanding and compassion for HIV-infected people and people with AIDS …
>
> (2) to protect the human rights and dignity of HIV-infected people and people with AIDS, and of members of population groups, and to avoid discriminatory

> action against and stigmatization of them in the provision of services, employment and travel....

This WHO resolution is supplemented by the African regional human rights system. The Organization of African Unity (OAU) drafted an African Charter on Human and Peoples' Rights (also known as the Banjul Charter) in 1981, which became effective in 1986. The Charter had more than 30 signatories. It stated that every person shall enjoy personal rights fully without regard to distinctions of status; it guaranteed medical service to anyone in need; and it prohibited discrimination against AIDS patients.

No African nation has established a quarantine, and most African nations have commendably enacted legislation in their countries prohibiting discrimination toward HIV-infected persons. Among nations who responded to the survey, civil and mixed civil/Islamic or civil/common-law countries most commonly enacted antidiscrimination legislation. Two countries, Rwanda (civil) and Cameroon (civil/common), responded that nondiscrimination policies, without legislation, were in place. Among the nations with antidiscrimination measures, typically all areas were regulated—housing, occupation, insurance, and research protocols.

The civil law reliance on codes may explain the abundance of such legislation in civil-law countries. Codes can be generalized as a guide to future conduct. Also, civil-law countries tend to consider equity interests by law rather than by court.

Three civil/Islamic countries with antidiscrimination measures discriminated in other areas, specifically screening and immigration. Libya limits immigration of the HIV-infected and has mandatory screening for high-risk groups such as prostitutes, drug users, homosexual/bisexual men, and hemophiliacs. Tunisia and Senegal also screen high-risk groups. Such screening may be a consequence of Moslem attitudes toward HIV-infected persons, a group often disfavored in the Moslem religion. Because African AIDS is, by exclusion, a heterosexual disease, the stigma of promiscuity may attach to being HIV-infected.

Common-law countries, by contrast, did the least to establish antidiscrimination measures. None of the surveyed common or common/Islamic law nations had enacted any antidiscrimination policies. This may support the idea that common-law countries intend to handle problems on a case-by-case basis as they arise. Also, the mutability of the common-law tradition may allow for greater applicability of African customary law philosophy, in which the collective good is emphasized over the protection of an infected individual's rights.

B. Immigration

The reasons why nations set up immigration policies that bar entry of HIV-infected persons are diverse—a desire to do something to contain infection, the presence of strong nationalistic tendencies, limited concern regarding individual rights, and monetary worries about straining national health care resources. Among the many countries that have maintained policies limiting immigration and travel include China, Costa Rica, Cuba, Iraq, Republic of Korea, Russia, Syria, and the United States. Such policies have little support in international agencies.

Since 1951, the WHO, for example, maintained a philosophy of maximizing security against the spread of disease while minimizing interference with international travel. The AIDS epidemic has not altered WHO policy that quarantines should be disregarded in favor of epidemiologic surveillance and improved health services in member countries. When member states sought advice from the WHO regarding certifications from international travelers of HIV status, the WHO responded that certification and border testing are unwarranted. Further, in 1987, the WHO, the Council of Europe, and the European Community all agreed that mandatory testing of international travelers at borders be prohibited.

WHO officials have concluded that no program of certification for foreigners can control the spread of HIV effectively, and that mandatory testing, in a very cost-ineffective fashion, only briefly retards the influx of HIV. Limited resources are deemed better spent on preventive education of citizenry and protection of blood supplies. Border testing also runs the risk of infusing a false sense of security regarding prevention programs.

In response to survey questions with regard to entry of HIV-infected persons for purposes of tourism, employment, and permanent residence among African nations, only Libya and Mauritius excluded such persons outright. Additionally, South African immigration authorities reserve the right to refuse entry to anyone on grounds of health status. Initially, Chad responded that it did ban entry of HIV-infected persons, but in a later survey changed its response. The limited number of such responses prevented making any analysis of legal systems in response to immigration.

C. Reporting and Notification

Surveyed African countries were asked if physicians were required to report both HIV infection and incidence of AIDS to government authorities. While more countries required the reporting of AIDS than they did HIV, the majority of respondents required both. Namibia was the only country that required reporting for HIV, but not for AIDS.

All of the countries that did not require AIDS reporting were civil in nature, largely of either civil/common or civil/Islamic legal tradition. Countries that did not require HIV reporting were from a variety of legal heritages (3 of the 14 with common law, 9 of the 32 with civil law, and 5 of the 13 with Islamic law heritage).

Countries also were asked if notification of spouses or sex partners of persons with AIDS was required by law. Only four countries required such notification of partners regarding possible HIV exposure. Two out of the four respondents were of the common legal tradition. This number was too small to allow any correlations to be made.

As for the question whether an HIV-infected physician is required to warn patients, only one country, Ethiopia, answered in the affirmative * * *. Two countries, Tunisia and Cape Verde, both responded that this situation had yet to be encountered.

D. Safety of the Blood Supply

Early epidemiologic studies showed that African children with AIDS were more likely to have received blood transfusions than the uninfected. Already by 1986, a WHO survey found that 56% of African countries reported at least some HIV screening of blood for transfusion. This figure has increased despite all the difficulties involved in maintaining a safe blood supply. Still, HIV infection from receiving blood products in the past accounted for five percent of all AIDS cases.

A fully integrated system for blood supplies, as exists in industrialized countries, is not affordable for most developing countries. The cost of a unit of blood in the United States averages $70 to $100. In several African countries, such as Zimbabwe, Ethiopia, Ivory Coast, and Senegal, the cost averages $30 to $50 U.S. dollars, a figure in excess of the per capita health care budgets for these nations.

Seventy-three percent (29/40) of nations reported legislation mandating blood supply testing. The 11 nations without such policies reflected the full diversity of legal traditions—common, civil/common, civil/Islamic, and common/Islamic classifications. Nations that did not mandate blood testing were largely from low (Algeria, Morocco, Sao Tome & Principe, Botswana, Mauritius, Seychelles, Sudan) or medium (The Gambia, Guinea-Bissau, Nigeria) seroprevalence areas of infection. Only Zambia was represented among high prevalence areas, although Zambia has reported progress in the development of clean blood supplies.

Only 12 (37.5%) of the 32 respondents to this question had policies prohibiting HIV-infected individuals from donating blood. Nations with such policies largely had some exposure to a civil-law tradition (Ethiopia being the exception). This may be due to the established codes of a civil tradition. Twelve of 20 countries (60%) that did not report measures prohibiting HIV-infected donation had policies requiring testing of the blood supplies in general. However, among countries that lacked mandatory testing of the blood supply, none had policies prohibiting the donation of HIV-infected blood.

Such policies are most effective when combined with measures that encourage selective screening and counseling of donors, decentralized, well-financed transfusion resources, and the judicious use of blood supplies.

* * *

Notes

1. See also, Florence Shu-Acquaye, The Legal Implications of Living with HIV/AIDS in a Developing Country: The African Story, 32 *Syracuse J. Int'l L & Com.* 51 (2004); Kenneth J. Bartschi, Legislative Responses to HIV/AIDS in Africa, 11 *Conn. J. Int'l L.* 169 (1995).

2. Since this report, conditions have continued to worsen in Africa. Over 24 million Sub-Saharan Africans were infected with HIV in 2005. Two million died during that year, while fourteen million have died of AIDS and over twelve million children have been orphaned since the epidemic began.

3. Among the most controversial legal issues in recent years relating to AIDS in the developing world has been that of restrictions on access to patented anti-retroviral drugs under the International Trade Laws. The Trade Related Aspects of Intellectual Property Rights (TRIPS) agreement obligates members of the World Trade Organization to respect intellectual property rights, including patents for pharmaceutical products and processes. TRIPS limits the ability of developing nations to manufacture or import generic copies of patented drugs under compulsory licenses or without the permission of patent holders. TRIPS gave pharmaceutical companies the power to insist on prices for patented drugs that would have made them unaffordable for developing countries, but after embarrassing trade disputes, the WTO adopted the Doha Declaration in 2001 recognizing the need for flexibility on this issue to permit WTO members to protect the public health of their people. This topic is beyond the scope of this book, but for an introduction to the issues see, Frederick M.Abbott, The WTO Medicines Decison: World Pharmaceutical Trade and the Protection of Public Health, 99 *Am.J. Int. L.* 317 (2005); Kevin Outterson, Pharmaceutical Arbitrage: Balancing Access and Innovation in International Prescription Drug Markets, 5 *Yale J. Health Pol'y, L. & Ethics* 193 (2005); and M. Gregg Bloche and Elizabeth R. Jungman, Health Policy and the WTO, 31 *J. L. Med. & Ethics* 529 (2003). Access to AIDS medications has also raised constitutional human rights issues in a number of countries, including South Africa and Venezuela, See Chapter 1 for a discussion of these issues.

4. At the international level the United Nation's World Health Organization has responsibility for public health issues. Though the WHO has legal competency, it has historically relied on education and assistance rather than on legal mandates. See David Fidler, The Future of the World Health Organization: What Role for International Law, 31 *Vanderbilt J. Trans. L.* 1079 (199). See, however, Alison Lakin, The Legal Powers of the World Health Organization, 3 *Med. L. Int.* 23 (1997). The United Nations Commission on Human Rights has published guidelines with respect to AIDS legislation, Commission on Human Rights, The Protection of Human Rights in the Context of the Human Immunodeficiency Virus (HIV) and *Acquired Immune Deficiency Syndrome (AIDS), Commission on Human Rights Resolution 1997/33.* Compliance with these guidelines is monitored by the WHO.

5. African nations are rich in the diversity of their legal systems. Many inherited a common law or civil law system from the colonial powers, while others have adopted Muslim or socialist law. Traditional customary law is also usually present. Often the civil or common law affects a relatively small proportion of the population, with local disputes being settled through customary law and alternative dispute resolution fora. In this context, the existence of a statute directing or proscribing a certain form of behavior may not necessarily have a direct and immediate effect on conduct, though this is, of course, true in Western countries as well.

B. Public Health Law, Infectious Diseases: SARS

The first major new epidemic of the twenty-first century was Severe Acute Respiratory Syndrome, or SARS. Although SARS, like HIV/AIDS is an infectious disease for which there is no vaccine, the characteristics of SARS are quite different from those of HIV/AIDS. It thus posed a different public health threat warranting a different public health response. HIV is spread primarily through sexual contact or blood exchange. Although it is not fully understood exactly how SARS spreads, it can be spread through close contact not involving exchanges of bodily fluids, involving probably airborne spread through large droplets. SARS was thus perceived as posing a more general risk of infection through random contact. SARS is also unlike HIV/AIDS in that it manifests itself very quickly, allowing more rapid containment of an epidemic through isolating infected persons. The rate of mortality from SARS is lower than that of AIDS (probably 8% to 15%), although it is much higher among the elderly than among young people. On the other hand, death comes much more rapidly with SARS, limiting the spread of the disease. The two readings that follow address the public health response to the SARS epidemic of China, the country where SARS first appeared, and of other countries to which SARS spread, focusing on legal approaches.

Regulating Sars in China: Law as an Antidote?

Chenglin Liu, Washington University Global Studies Review, vol. 4, pp. 81, 82–101, 103–09, 115–17 (2005)

* * *

SARS was first identified in a southern province of China on November 16, 2002. It quickly spread to twenty-seven countries. * * * During the 2003 outbreak, 8,096 people worldwide were infected with SARS, 774 of whom fell victim to the disease. In China, the economic and social costs of the outbreak were enormous. 5,327 people were infected with SARS in China by June of 2003. 329 died as a result of these infections. The direct economic loss of the outbreak over three months was approximately $18 billion. In addition, the public lost an inordinate amount of confidence in the Chinese health care system.

* * *

In the 2003 outbreak, the global effort to combat the SARS epidemic hinged on how effectively China dealt with the crisis. * * * Unfortunately, initial information about the outbreak in China was concealed for fear of damaging local image and trade. As a result, the epidemic quickly gained momentum and erupted into a national health threat. After the SARS epidemic devastated Beijing in April of 2003, the Chinese government began a transparent approach and openly launched a national campaign against SARS. Newly enacted SARS laws and regulations played a crucial role in establishing the SARS reporting system, allocating medical resources, and administering massive quarantine and isolation. The epidemic was brought under control in June of 2003.

* * *

According to the World Health Organization (WHO), the first SARS case was identified on November 16, 2002, in Guangdong Province, China. The patient was treated in a local hospital where several medical workers were infected with the same disease. * * *

Two months later, in response to an increase in the number of reported SARS cases, the Health Department of Guangdong sent a task force on January 21, 2003 to three local hospitals that admitted SARS patients. The task force produced an internal report that confirmed the outbreak of SARS and detailed the symptoms of the disease. The report also provided several rules on how hospitals should handle SARS cases. Unfortunately, the internal report was not released to the public until February 11, 2003.

Among the many SARS cases, the most notable was that of Mr. Zhou, the "super spreader." During his treatment at Zhongshan No. 2 hospital, Mr. Zhou infected more than thirty people, including attending doctors, nurses, and other health care personnel. * * * Mr. Zhou's case was well recorded by the local news, but was withheld from the public for several weeks before being published.

While local hospitals were overwhelmed by the highly contagious disease, the public was kept in the dark. No public announcements or news releases detailed the outbreak. Speculation soon began to circulate among the uninformed public that a strange, incurable disease had rapidly developed in Guangzhou. The public, lacking official guidance, panicked in reaction to the outbreak. Local residents rushed to purchase Ban Lan Gen (BLG, a Chinese herb medicine), antibiotics, white vinegar, and even iodized salt, all of which were rumored to be effective against SARS. Cunning merchants took advantage of the opportunity and used the false information to exploit the crisis.

Under mounting public pressure, the government, on February 11, 2003, finally acknowledged that there had been 305 SARS cases and five deaths in Guangdong. It authorized a local newspaper to release the information to the public. Nearly three months transpired between the first identified case and the initial public announcement of the outbreak. By the time the government dealt publicly with the outbreak, SARS had garnered significant momentum and was on its way to other regions.

When Guangzhou health officials admitted to the SARS outbreak in February, they made it clear that the city was safe to live in and visit. As a result, the public panic in the province received little attention in Hong Kong, which is only 174 kilometers (108 miles) away. * * *

While one cannot reconstruct the exact route by which the deadly virus was transmitted to Hong Kong, Dr. Liu is widely believed to have set off the SARS epidemic there. Dr. Liu was one of the physicians who treated SARS patients. * * * On February 21, 2003, Dr. Liu traveled to Hong Kong to attend a wedding. * * *

When Dr. Liu checked into the hotel, he already had a fever and a dry cough, and experts believed that Dr. Liu left a trail of the deadly virus on the ninth floor. At least sixteen people staying at the hotel were infected with SARS the same day. Those people eventually carried the virus to Vancouver, Toronto, Singapore and Hanoi. Dr. Liu was later admitted to the Kwong Wah Hospital. Although he told doctors and nurses at the hospital that he was highly contagious and asked to be isolated, the doctors did not heed his advice. By the time doctors placed Dr. Liu in isolation, seventy hospital workers and seventeen students were infected. Dr. Liu died of SARS on March 4, 2003. In the end, 1755 people in Hong Kong were infected with SARS, of whom 299 died.

It was a bold step for the government of Guangdong, in the midst of mounting domestic and international criticism, to reveal the SARS outbreak. However, the epidemic at that point was far from controlled. The government tried to downplay the seriousness of the outbreak in order to rebuild Guangdong's tarnished image and minimize damage to the local economy. Most people outside Guangdong were convinced that the disease was mild with a minute fatality rate. As a result, no preventive measures were taken in Beijing and other Northern cities. Train travel between Guangzhou, Hong Kong and other domestic cities remained unrestricted.

Ms. Xu reportedly spread the SARS epidemic to Shanxi Province and the city of Beijing. * * *

On February 28, 2003, Ms. Xu was transferred to the 301 Military Hospital in Beijing, one of the most highly regarded hospitals in China. * * * Ms. Xu was first put in an observation ward where three patients were being treated for other diseases. By the time a respiratory expert realized the unusual nature of her illness and put Ms. Xu under quarantine, a number of health workers and co-patients had been infected. * * *

Unfortunately, the virus did not stop at the military hospitals. SARS cases were soon found in other hospitals in Beijing. * * * The SARS epidemic spread rapidly; by the end of April, it took the entire city of Beijing hostage.

April 20, 2003 was the turning point in the battle against SARS in China. Prior to this date, the SARS epidemic was taboo in the Chinese news media. Both the local government in Guangdong and the highest health department in Beijing denied that SARS was a serious threat to public health. Both assured the public that SARS was a regional problem, confined to the southern part of China, and it was under control. The words "epidemic" and "outbreak" rarely appeared in the media. After April 20 the Chinese government took a completely different approach. Minister Zhang of the State Health Ministry and the Mayor of Beijing were removed from office, the national media was full of SARS reports, a daily SARS reporting system was established, and a national campaign against SARS was officially and openly launched. In short, the SARS outbreak was no longer a secret. However, winning the battle over the release of the information was not easy.

* * *

In an effort to defuse speculation that the number of SARS cases was underreported, the Health Ministry of China held its first news conference about SARS on April 3, 2003. News reporters from China and abroad were invited to the conference. Mr. Zhang, the Minister of Health, assured the public that SARS was under control, going so far as to tease a foreign cameraman who was wearing a facemask at the conference, saying, "China is safe to live in and travel to, ... with or without a mask!" Mr. Zhang's calm demeanor and humorous disposition convinced the public that SARS was not serious and would soon fade away. * * * Minister Zhang's message convinced not only to the public, but also the WHO, which, after the news conference, took Beijing off its list of SARS-affected areas.

* * *

Dr. Jiang, a seventy-two-year-old retired surgeon, finally broke the silence about SARS. After his best friend contracted SARS at the 301 Military Hospital, he conducted a preliminary investigation and discovered 146 SARS cases in the three military hospitals alone; this was more than ten times the figure Minister Zhang had released at the news conference. On April 4, 2003, Dr. Jiang wrote a letter to China Central Television (CCTV-4) and to Phoenix, a Hong Kong-based television station. In his letter, Dr. Jiang revealed that the SARS epidemic was far more serious than Minister Zhang had suggested. In a separate letter, Dr. Jiang called on the Minister to resign for covering up SARS information in Beijing. After the stations refused to publish the letters, Time Magazine released Dr. Jiang's findings on the Internet in Susan Jakes's article, Beijing's SARS Attack.

Whistle-blowers in China are rare and usually face extreme government opposition. It took extraordinary courage for Dr. Jiang to disclose this information to the media. Many doctors, experts, and health officials were also aware of the severe situation in Beijing when Dr. Jiang challenged the underreported figures. However, Dr. Jiang was the only one who spoke out. In the Chinese political system, it is unwise to reveal top-secret information to the foreign press. * * *

Dr. Jiang's letter played a crucial role in getting the information to the domestic public as well as to the international community. The WHO publicly criticized the Government of Beijing for its poor cooperation after the actual facts regarding SARS in Beijing were released. * * *On April 20, Minister Zhang was removed from his post and a National Campaign against SARS was launched. Dr. Jiang became an instant hero.

* * *

* * * The SARS outbreak presented two options [to the Chinese government]: keep quiet and handle the crisis behind closed doors, or take an open and transparent approach. In the past, national emergencies, such as earthquakes, floods, and mining accidents, were handled quietly by the government. Some scholars have referred to this as a "black box" approach, under which the public becomes aware of the situation only after the government has emerged victorious over the catastrophe. * * *

In attempting to balance between economic loss and public health and safety, the new government chose to emphasize public health.* * * Choosing a transparent approach required the government to forego economic gains and even suffer losses. For a nation accustomed to the "black box" approach, openly dealing with the SARS epidemic was a milestone. The new approach proved a tremendous success. The new government earned a reputation as a people-loving government that candidly addresses the serious social issues left over from the economic boom of the 1990s.

The SARS campaign took place from April 20 until June 24, 2003, during which time two major pieces of legislation were enacted: (1) Regulations on Dealing with the Outbreak of Public Health Emergencies (Regulations), which was enacted by the State Council on May 9, 2003 and took effect on May 12, 2003, and (2) Measures on the Prevention and Treatment of Infectious Atypical Pneumonia (Measures), which was promulgated by the Ministry of Health and took effect on May 12, 2003. In addition, The Laws of the

People's Republic of China on the Prevention and Treatment of Infectious Diseases (PTID), which was originally passed by the NPC Standing Committee in 1989, was republished on April 26, 2003 by the State Council. In summary, these laws and regulations addressed three issues: emergency information reporting, treatment, and prevention.

* * *

* * * To disseminate information effectively, the new laws specifically delineate when to report, how to report, to whom the original report should go, and how the department receiving a report should deal with the information.

Article 19 of the Regulations specifies that the Health Department of the State Council shall be in charge of establishing an emergency reporting system. Not more than nine hours may elapse from discovery to the reporting of a case to the State Council, the highest authority. * * *

First, according to article 19, if a public health emergency occurs a provincial government that has received epidemic information has one hour to report it to the Health Department of the State Council. The law also requires the Health Department to report to the State Council when an emergency is of a significant danger to the public.

Second, article 20 requires medical institutions that have a confirmed or suspected case of SARS promptly report this to the local county government. After receiving the report, the local government and its health department must forward it to higher levels of the government. This transfer of information should not take more than two hours.

* * *

While reporting relevant information is important, it is only the first step toward establishing a transparent system. If information stops at a higher level, the system ceases to function. The flow of information should be vertical toward governments at higher levels and horizontal toward related departments, neighboring regions, and the public.

* * *

Lawmakers were aware of the problems caused by the lack of horizontal flow of information in the beginning of the outbreak. Article 23 of the Regulations requires the State Council to promptly release information to other related departments including hospitals and health departments of the Army. The provision also stipulates that the Head Official of any province experiencing an epidemic should inform neighboring provinces or regions of the outbreak.

However, article 23 is difficult to implement in practice. Under the centralized system, emphasis is placed more on vertical subordination of the local governments to the Central Government, rather than on cooperation between local governments at the same level. * * * Thus, it should not be surprising that, during the SARS outbreak, the spread of the virus was largely attributable to a lack of cooperation and coordination among various regions.

A system of making information public is described in article 25. The Central Government must inform the public of any epidemic information that provincial level governments report. The local government may then be authorized by the Central Government to publicly announce possible outbreaks independently. Article 25 states that the "announcement should be up-to-date, accurate, and comprehensive." However, article 25 does not provide guidance on interpreting the phrase "up-to-date, accurate, and comprehensive." It is thus unclear how soon the public should be informed after an epidemic is reported to the Central Government.* * * In practice, article 25 gives the Central Government vast discretion in deciding whether or when to release information about an epidemic that was reported from lower governments or health departments.

Lawmakers drafting the Regulations were concerned that the entire reporting system would fail if any level of government did not promptly pass along information. The situation in Beijing proved that an individual can make a real difference in dispersing information and can in this sense, help ensure that the transfer of information is maintained. In this regard, Dr. Jiang served as a great example of individual reporting by releasing vital information that Health Ministry grossly underreported.

In the Regulations, the lawmakers embedded an important provision for protecting whistleblowers. Article 24 provides that any unit or individual has the right to report an outbreak of an epidemic to the relevant government department, which in turn must conduct a thorough investigation of the situation. The unit or individual who has informed the government of an outbreak should be rewarded.

While the law provides that the informers should be rewarded, it does not specify or refer to punishment for retaliation by the local government. The major concern for most people is how to go about life after revealing the government's failure. Informers who continue to live under the same authority will be under constant pressure from the local government. Therefore, even with the rights conferred by the Regulations, most potential informers will likely choose to stay silent in the face of government irregularities.

Although the law allows an individual to report a local government's failure to the government at higher levels, it does not specify whether the individual enjoys the right to release related information to the media. According to a notice issued by the Health Department in 1989 that is still in force, no unit or individual may release and announce epidemic information to foreign media or publish unannounced epidemic information without the authorization of the Health Department.

Without adequate sanctions on those who impede the flow of information, the reporting system would not be effective. Article 22 states that any unit or individual should not conceal, delay, or falsely report emergency information, or direct others to do so. The sanctions are set forth in article 45 of the Regulations, which also states that the head of the department is required to take all responsibility for a failure to report. These penalties range from demotion to a lower administrative rank to removal from one's administrative position, depending on the seriousness of the concealment. The article also leaves the door open for criminal charges against the leader of a department if late reporting causes a massive spread of the disease. * * *

* * *

Before the new laws were enacted, health departments issued a number of guidelines to hospitals on the treatment and prevention of SARS. These guidelines were issued in great haste and produced mixed results. Nevertheless, these guidelines shaped many of the relevant provisions of the new laws on SARS.

To deflect social attention away from SARS, especially during the congressional session, the Health Ministry required all SARS patients to be treated at the hospitals where they were admitted. This method was referred to as the "absorb" method. Officials hoped that hospitals could treat SARS cases and eliminate the disease without causing public panic like that in Guangzhou. The "absorb" method was consistent with the "black box" approach.

The "absorb" requirement was a complete failure. Hospitals not only failed to provide proper care to SARS patients, but the hospitals themselves became a source of infection.* * *

* * *

The catastrophe in the People's Hospital and other hospitals caused health officials to revisit the so-called "absorb" method. Based on the experience in Guangdong, some experts proposed designating a few hospitals with good medical facilities as SARS-designated hospitals suitable for treating infectious diseases. These designated hospitals played an important role in lowering the cross-infection rate at the start of the outbreak; however, the sharp increase of SARS patients soon caused these hospitals to be overwhelmed. The government decided to construct a specialized SARS hospital in a suburb of Beijing. This new hospital, containing 1,000 beds, was built in only seven days and accepted the first group of patients on May 1, 2003. By the time the last patients were discharged less than two months later, the new hospital had admitted 680 patients, of whom only eight died of SARS. As a result, the new hospital substantially reduced the pressure that hospitals in the urban areas faced.

* * *

The new laws also specify that hospitals should provide free treatment to SARS patients who cannot afford medical expenses. In some reported cases, hospitals refused or delayed admission to SARS patients. * * *

Refusing to accept SARS patients jeopardizes the patient's health and safety and puts the public at a higher risk because the disease is extremely infectious. Citing the law on infectious disease, the Health Ministry issued an urgent notice on April 22, 2003 that required all hospitals to accept SARS patients without exception. * * *

The government encountered enormous challenges in implementing the above rules. There are several reasons that hospitals were reluctant to admit SARS patients. First, they were afraid that the spread of the virus would put doctors, nurses, and patients in great danger because medical workers were among the very first victims of the outbreak. Second, after the economic reform in the 1980s, hospitals were pushed into market reliance. Many of the hospitals heavily relied on the revenue coming from patients. High cross-infection rates would hurt a hospital's reputation, thus reducing the volume of patient visits. Third, SARS treatment could be extremely expensive, costing hospitals up to RMB 100,000 ($12,000) per patient. To conform to the laws, hospitals had to cover the costs for patients without health insurance. * * *

To solve the financial pressure facing both patients and hospitals, the Ministry of Finance allocated RMB 2 billion ($242 million) for SARS prevention and treatment, a considerable portion of which was used for covering the treatment of the uninsured SARS patients. * * *

* * *

As the SARS situation worsened, many migrant workers in Beijing began to flee the city and return to their hometowns. In some cases, migrant workers escaped mandatory quarantine in Beijing and took a train home. * * *

The wave of migration was of great concern to the government because these migrant workers could bring the virus back to their home provinces. These workers usually came from poor rural regions where medical networks barely existed. Though SARS has no cure, high quality medical care plays an important role in treating the complications resulting from a SARS infection. If workers set off an epidemic back home, the consequences would be unimaginable.

* * *

In the meantime, local governments took measures to monitor the returning migrant workers closely to keep the virus out of their regions. Screening measures included setting up checkpoints at local train stations and bus stops, and imposing quarantine on all the returnees for two weeks.

Also, to reduce the danger of spreading SARS to those migrant workers' hometowns, the government required all the companies that employed migrant workers to comply strictly with the so-called "three-local principles": First, the prevention work for healthy workers must be carried out locally. Second, epidemiological observation of the workers in close contact with SARS patients must be conducted locally. Third, confirmed cases must be treated locally. If any company failed to do so, various sanctions would be imposed.* * *

* * *

There were several reported cases where SARS patients or persons suspected to be infected with SARS escaped quarantine and caused SARS to spread. On rare occasions, the patients were believed to have spread SARS deliberately.

On May 5, 2003, Li Song was arrested on charges of obstructing the prevention of infectious disease and treatment, and endangering public security through dangerous means, in violation of the Criminal Law.* * *

Li's case was regarded as the first in which the government resorted to criminal sanctions in order to impose compulsory quarantine on a SARS patient. It was widely believed that Li's case directly led to the promulgation of the interpretation of the relevant articles of the Criminal Law regarding public safety jointly issued by the Supreme People's Court and Supreme People's Procuratorate (Interpretation). According to this Interpretation, those who cause death or serious injury by deliberately spreading the virus can be sentenced to a fixed prison term ranging from ten years to life imprisonment. They may even face the death penalty.

* * *

On April 12, 2003, the Transportation Ministry, Railroad Ministry, Airline Bureau, Health Ministry, and Finance Ministry jointly issued a notice requiring that their related departments take measures to prevent SARS from spreading through public transportation, including trains, boats, long distance buses, and airplanes. This notice required that "stay stations" be set up in the cities where transportation stations are located to provide a place where SARS patients or suspected cases found on the carriers can be accepted. To establish the "stay stations", the local government was to provide financial aid, technical support and the necessary equipment. Once a SARS patient (or suspected patient) was discovered on public transportation, the responsible head of the carrier was required to promptly contact the next closest "stay station" and arrange a drop-off for those patients to receive medical observation, quarantine, and treatment. All "stay stations" were obligated to accept these patients. The carrier was also to take measures necessary to enhance air circulation, and trace and record the identities of persons who have been in close contact with SARS patients. The notice also authorized the departments of transportation to persuade persons showing SARS symptoms not to use public transportation. * * *

* * *

On August 28, 2004, the eleventh session of the Tenth NPC passed sweeping amendments to the PTID. [Law of the People's Republic of China on the Prevention and Treatment of Infectious Diseases]. * * *

First, the new amendments adjust the disease classifications of the PTID. SARS, Avian Flu and tuberculosis are now included as Class B diseases, and the new law authorizes the State Council to add previously unknown diseases to the list. * * *

Second, the new law revamps the epidemic reporting system. In addition to reiterating the vertical reporting schemes, the new law stresses the importance of releasing information horizontally to neighboring regions. The new law also requires the government to announce epidemic situations periodically. Unlike SARS regulations, however, the new law does not prescribe a fixed time frame for reporting, releasing, and announcing information about an outbreak.

Third, the new law emphasizes the government's role in coping with future epidemics. The law requires that infectious disease prevention be a part of the government's social and economic development plan. The purpose of adding this article is to show that epidemic prevention is an integral and permanent part of the government's regular responsibilities. Under the new law, the various levels of government are required to establish and maintain a functional epidemic surveillance system and routinely evaluate the epidemic situation in their respective regions. The central government is required to provide financial assistance to inner regions where the economy lags far behind, and provide adequate training to the medical personnel there to increase the capability of those regions to handle sudden epidemics. The law also requires hospitals to accept infectious disease patients and provide free treatment to those who can not afford their medical expenses.

Fourth, the new law strikes a balance between the protection of the rights of individuals and the public interest. To protect patients' privacy, the new law prohibits hospitals from releasing patients' medical records. * * * In order to increase cooperation from patients, the new law requires that patients be continuously paid by their employers during quarantine or isolation. On the other hand, the new law provides stricter rules on quarantine and isolation. For example, under the previous law, suspected carriers of Class A diseases were only subject to epidemiological observation at appointed facilities. The new law provides that suspect patients be placed in isolation, which is more restrictive.

* * *

Although SARS began in China, it quickly spread to other countries. A discussion of the responses of those countries follows.

SARS and International Legal Preparedness

Jason W. Sapsin, Lawrence O. Gostin, Jon S. Vernick, Scott Burris, and Stephen P. Teret

Temple Law Review, vol 77, pp. 155, 155–165, 167–68 (2004).

The disease known now as severe acute respiratory syndrome ("SARS") first emerged in November 2002 in China's Guangdong Province and has since been described as the first severe, readily transmissible new disease of the twenty-first century. Its relatively rapid dissemination across the globe left biomedical researchers and public health authorities struggling to maintain pace with the disease in the face of scientific uncertainties and difficult policy choices. This article focuses on the earliest stage of the epidemic. We discuss examples of how regions faced with SARS turned to disease control strategies based on public health law, such as "personal control measures" like quarantine and isolation; weaknesses in the ability of nations' legal systems to frame balanced, coordinated and well-executed public health programs for rapid disease containment; and the responses of diverse populations to restrictive personal control measures.

* * * [W]e highlight the legal aspects of personal control measures employed against SARS in order to emphasize the importance of understanding public health law's role in authorizing and constraining disease control strategies, as well as the importance of legal preparedness in nations governed under the rule of law. In the contemporary international environment, one nation's failure in legal preparedness can affect global public health and, simultaneously, damage perceptions of that nation's ability to engage in cooperative disease control efforts and commitment to the protection of domestic civil rights. * * *

* * *

SARS' public health characteristics motivated authorities' choices of disease control strategies which, in nations governed under the rule of law, depend on effective legal systems. These included: (1) the novelty of the disease, resulting in the absence of rapid diagnostic tests to confirm infection and the current lack of a vaccine; (2) an unusual pattern of comparatively low viral shedding during the initial phase of the illness, posing further obstacles to the swift development of adequate diagnostic tools; (3) SARS' subclinical or atypical presentation in some patients; (4) the lack of effective treatment; (5) the disease's relative severity (an approximate overall case fatality rate of fourteen to fifteen percent); and (6) its mode of transmission, including the phenomenon of superspreading events. Each of these characteristics provided incentives to use nonmedical control strategies such as mandatory examination and testing, quarantine, and isolation. In the absence of effective therapy or a vaccine, health authorities' ability to control infectious disease necessarily depends upon preventing transmission by appropriately restricting the movement of exposed or infected people. Lack of adequate diagnostics limits public health authorities' ability to control transmission by impeding identification of mildly symptomatic or asymptomatic carriers and promotes reliance on contact history. Some SARS cases with atypical presentations or lacking history of direct contact with known SARS patients went undiagnosed and became "hidden reservoirs of infection on the wards of health-care facilities or in the community." To address this threat, some public health authorities chose to employ aggressive, legally based surveillance and quarantine measures. Researchers and clinicians also recommended exercising precautions in all cases of undifferentiated respiratory conditions, including isolation of health care workers and household contacts of cases.

SARS also appeared vulnerable to control measures such as quarantine and isolation: officials initially believed it to be transmitted through personal contact, possibly by air and also by fomites. In addition, "superspreading" events, by increasing the perceived risk resulting from failures to contain all cases, likely created greater incentives to implement aggressive control strategies. Five probable SARS patients in Singapore were each linked to events resulting in the apparent infection of ten or more health care workers, family or social contacts, or unrelated hospital visitors, accounting for 103 of the 205 probable SARS cases. Finally, effective isolation and quarantine become more difficult as cases accumulate, so public health authorities may more aggressively apply quarantine and isolation for a disease like SARS on the principle that "stringent measures implemented early in the course of the epidemic prevent the need for more stringent measures as the epidemic spreads."

The recommendations of the World Health Organization ("WHO") for the control of SARS provided a backdrop for national efforts * * *. By March 26th, 2003, however, governments had begun independently introducing more stringent personal control measures than those recommended by WHO—an indication both of the challenge of effectively unifying international action, and of some authorities' willingness and perceived need to implement mandatory personal control measures. In the process, many governments examined and revised their disease control laws. * * *

The first, still undiagnosed SARS patients were admitted to Singaporean hospitals from March 1st through 3rd, 2003; on March 6th, the Ministry of Health was notified of three cases of atypical pneumonia, following travel to Hong Kong. * * * As control efforts advanced (March 3rd–April 27th), the average time from onset of SARS symptoms to isolation of probable cases declined in Singapore from 6.8 to 1.3 days. Officials from the Singapore Ministry of Health maintain that broad and sensitive surveillance, rapid and effective contact tracing, and early use of enforced quarantine during the outbreak were crucial in containing SARS.

Singapore's public health response included important legal components. Authorities declared SARS a notifiable disease under the Infectious Disease Act ("IDA") on March 17th, allowing mandatory examination, treatment, medical information exchange, health care provider/institutional cooperation, use of facilities, quarantine, and isolation for SARS. The IDA was officially invoked for SARS on March 24th (quarantining contacts and closing hospitals to visitors two weeks before the WHO recommendation). By March 25th, approximately 740 people were in home quarantine under the IDA (with fines for noncompliance). They were legally required, among other things, to restrict visitors and maintain visitor registries; to respond immediately to health department communications; and to keep children under eighteen years of age at home. Private sector nurses and physicians were temporarily restricted from working in more than one medical facility. Further, in contrast to some other countries, Singapore concentrated all SARS patients into one facility and ultimately achieved containment more rapidly.

On April 24th, Singapore amended the IDA to: require persons with possibly infectious diseases to report to designated treatment centers; prohibit SARS contacts from going to public places; enforce home quarantine with electronic tagging and forced detention; and allow the quarantine and destruction of SARS-contaminated property. Section 21A of the Act imposed the affirmative obligation to avoid exposing others (outside immediate family) on any person knowing, or having reason to suspect, that he was a case, carrier or contact of SARS. To mitigate the effects of its aggressive containment strategy, Singapore provided economic assistance to people and businesses affected by home quarantine orders through a "Home Quarantine Order Allowance Scheme". While officials from Singapore's Ministry of Health maintained that broad surveillance, rapid and effective contact tracing, and early enforced quarantine were crucial in containing SARS, their actions were built upon a strong foundation of accessible, high-quality health and social services.

Hong Kong's SARS index case, a twenty-six year-old ethnic Chinese man, was admitted to the Prince of Wales Hospital on March 4th, 2003 (the Hong Kong Department of Health received notice on March 10th). * * * Ultimately, sixty-nine health workers and sixteen medical students developed SARS directly attributable to workplace exposure to the index case; the disease then spread to family members (and other contacts) of the affected workers. * * * As of May 5th, 2003, 1,080 contacts (from 425 households) of SARS patients had been confined and placed under medical surveillance, with the government providing daily material and financial assistance to 738 of these contacts (283 households). By June 15th, 2003, the total number of people served home quarantine notices in Hong Kong was 1,262.

Hong Kong's control measures also initiated the use and review of public health law. Like Singapore, Hong Kong added SARS to its disease control statutes (March 27th, 2003) and notified physicians that SARS was reportable. On April 15th, in order to establish a legal basis for further disease control measures, Hong Kong authorities amended the Prevention of the Spread of Infectious Diseases Regulations to allow health officers to prevent travelers from leaving the region; to permit authorized persons to measure travelers' body temperatures; and to examine travelers for SARS. At least one subsequent analysis of public health approaches in Hong Kong suggests that reductions in time from symptom onset to hospitalization, population contact rate, and incidence of nosocomial infection were jointly significant in bringing the epidemic under control. * * *

Toronto's SARS outbreak was the largest outside of Asia and carried economic effects estimated at one billion Canadian dollars in gross domestic product for 2003. A SARS patient was admitted to a local community hospital shortly after March 5th; this hospital became the epicenter of the Toronto outbreak. The disease was transmitted within the hospital to patients and healthcare workers prior to the implementation of control measures. Transfer of patients between health care institutions resulted in further dissemination of the virus. * * *

The legal components of Canada's response included the closure of hospitals, the declaration of a public health emergency, the compulsory quarantine of recalcitrant citizens, and the imposition of mandatory self-quarantine. Canada's Quarantine Act and Regulations were amended to list SARS in the schedule of diseases; authorize detention of travelers with suspected SARS for up to twenty days; allow national quarantine officers to compel air carriers to distribute SARS information and questionnaires on flights; and require aircraft to report en route illnesses and deaths at Canadian airports. Health is a joint responsibility of the Canadian Federal and Provincial governments, and federal responses included lending personnel and equipment, coordinating strategy to boost the health workforce, screening travelers at borders, making employment insurance benefits available for quarantined citizens, and arranging tax relief for affected individuals.

Canada also provides an example of WHO's difficulty in coordinating health policies across independent, but inter-dependent, regions. Canada officially challenged WHO's April 23rd Toronto travel advisory and promised at least ten million Canadian dollars to promote Toronto as a safe destination. Even as late as May 2nd, a WHO official noted the failure to receive "good, fast information from Canada," further stating that "[c]ountries are not very good about reporting new cases, even the United States."

The United States' federal government has authority over public health measures at national borders and in matters affecting interstate transmission of disease, but assumes direction of states' internal health affairs only under extraordinary circumstances. * * * By April 2003, the United States' Centers for Disease Control and Prevention ("U.S. CDC") had deployed more than 40 public health professionals and scientists worldwide and assigned more than 400 staff members to SARS; as of June 18th, 2003, the United had 334 suspected and 75 probable cases of SARS.

SARS provoked at least one significant change in the United States' national legal structure for disease control. Early in the worldwide outbreak, federal authorities found themselves legally powerless to detain a noncompliant traveler from China and so federal regulations were amended in order to address failures to cooperate with SARS control measures. While the amendment brought SARS within the scope of "national" legislation (section 361(b) of the Public Health Service Act) it could not, however, redress the decentralization of public health authority across the United States. State and local authorities continued to be able to withhold or delay SARS reports to the federal government. Also, at least through the middle of April 2003, U.S. CDC relied on state and local health department resources to develop the necessary methods for actively monitoring exposed persons. But facing a smaller outbreak than those of other countries, policymakers in the United States generally avoided using compulsory personal control measures for disease containment and such powers were used infrequently. Only five aircraft arriving from SARS-affected regions were sequestered, and quarantine and isolation tended to be voluntary or quasi-voluntary, although there were some cases of compulsory confinement.

Overall, SARS quarantine and isolation events illustrate both general compliance with public health measures and the difficulties posed by even a relatively few, noncompliant individuals. Officials in Ontario prosecuted at least one recalcitrant individual and threatened unknown numbers of others with forced confinement. Ontario's Commissioner of Public Security perceived noncompliance as the greatest threat to controlling SARS. By April 19th, however, Toronto health officials had pursued legal measures against only fifteen people. Singapore enacted penalties for quarantine violation, utilized its Security Services and electronic, in-home cameras, and arrested at least one man violating a home quarantine order. Violations of quarantine led to calls in Hong Kong for stricter enforcement of orders with implementation of fines and detentions. In comparison, Taiwan apparently suffered serious difficulties in obtaining public cooperation, including citizens' refusal to register with local health authorities before traveling; large scale failures to cooperate with epidemiological contact tracing; mass disobedience of quarantine orders; and hospital concealment of SARS cases. The United States did not implement widespread quarantine. However, polling studies forecast U.S. voluntary quarantine noncompliance rates ranging from eight percent to twenty-five percent. Given the wide range of population responses internationally, the risk and consequences of noncompliance must also be considered when planning U.S. disease containment strategies.

* * *

Nationally effective health care and public health systems are crucial to effective disease control in modern societies.* * * Adequate preparation for widespread outbreaks of dangerous, communicable diseases necessarily is built on a foundation of accessible health care and competent, properly funded public health agencies regardless of the approach used. In societies such as the United States, which have chronically neglected public health infrastructures, this entails the swift expenditure of considerable public resources to overcome existing weaknesses in the nation's health system. Traditional U.S. market-based patterns of health care financing and delivery contribute heavily to this problem. Chronic underfunding of public hospitals and the lack of surge capacity to handle health emergencies are extensively documented and threaten U.S. public health preparedness. A recent study of urban U.S. hospitals concluded that while most had conducted basic planning and coordination activities for bioterrorism response (also relevant to a large-scale outbreak of a naturally occurring infectious disease such as SARS), "[m]ost hospitals, however, still lack equipment, medical stockpiles, and quarantine and isolation facilities for even a small scale response." Staffing shortages remain a major concern in public health departments, laboratories and hospitals across the country. * * *

* * *

Governing authorities in Singapore, Hong Kong, and Canada each furnished, to varying degrees, financial and material support to quarantined populations. Interestingly, in Beijing, China, it is reported that only some employers continued to pay salary to quarantined individuals (though all were provided food and medicine). Societies attempting to follow democratic principles and utilizing disease control measures such as quarantine and isolation must recognize the extraordinary responsibility necessarily undertaken by governments employing these measures. As acknowledged by the Canadian government, "[a]pplying the principle of reciprocity, society has a duty to provide support and other alternatives to those whose rights have been infringed under quarantine." Singapore, the Hong Kong Special Administrative Region, and Canada each recognized this duty. In nations which have only incompletely addressed this problem, quarantine and isolation regulations should legally require confined persons to be provided with: (1) safe, habitable, and medically appropriate housing during confinement, (2) necessary food, clothing, and medical care, (3) means of communication with family, friends, and personal representatives, (4) necessary social services (e.g., childcare and mental health services), (5) appropriate legal review; and (6) protection from adverse social and economic consequences, such as lost income or employment or insurance discrimination during confinement. * * *

Notes

1. See also, David Fidler, SARS: Governance and the Globalization of Disease (2004); Andreas Schloenhardt, From Black Death to Bird Flu: Infectious Diseases and Immigration Restrictions in Asia, 12 *New Eng. J. Int'l & Comp. L.* 263 (2006); Jacques deLisle, Atypical Pneumonia and Ambivalent Law and Politics: SARS and the Response to SARS in China, 77 *Temp. L. Rev.* 193 (2004); Lawrence Gostin, Pandemic Influenza: Public Health Preparedness for the Next Global Emergency, 32 *J. L., Med.& Ethics* 564 (2004); Lawrence Gostin, Ronald Bayer, & Amy Fairchild, Ethical and Legal Challenges Posed by Severe Acute Respiratory Syndrome: Implications for the Control of Severe Infectious Disease Threats, 290 *JAMA* 3229 (2003).

2. Not surprisingly, international law and international organizations play a more significant role in responding to infectious diseases than they do in most other areas of health law. Among the most important authorities here are the recently revised International Health Regulations (IHR) adopted by the World Health Assembly in 2005. The goal of the revised IHR, which replaced regulations that had been in place for half a century, was to balance the right of states to protect the health of their residents with the goal of minimizing interference with international trade, while also protecting human rights. Unlike the old Regulations, which applied only to a short list of traditional infectious diseases, the IHR apply comprehensively to infectious diseases and also to disease-causing hazardous substances and the intentional or negligent release of harmful biological, chemical, or radioactive agents. The IHR require states to develop surveillance and response capacities, and to report public health emergencies of international concern to the World Health Orgnization. The IHR also allows the WHO to receive reports from non-governmental sources, to request verification of this information from governments, and to share this information with the international community, thus opening the door to whistle-blowers. The WHO is empowered by the IHR to determine if international public health emergencies exist, and to issue temporary, non-binding recommendations for addressing emergencies. The IHR obligates governments to incorporate human rights principles respecting rights to privacy and informed consent, and specifically limits the ways in which governments can limit international traffic. See, describing the IHR, David Fidler and Lawrence Gostin, The New International Health Regulations: An Historic Development for International Law and Public Health. 34 *J. L. Med. & Ethics* 85 (2006).

3. The past half century has been marked by a growing influence of globalization, and in particular with a concern that national public health measures not unduly restrain international trade. The General Agreement on Tariffs and Trade (GATT), the Agreement on the Application of Sanitary and Phytosanitary Measures (SPS), and the Agreement on Technical Barriers to Trade all limit the ability of World Trade Organization member states to unnecessarily limit international trade for public health reasons. GATT's Article XX(b) permits measures "necessary to protect human, animal and plant life or health" if they are not applied in a discriminatory or arbitrary fashion. The SPS also permits sanitary controls, but they must be based on scientific risk assessment. The General Agreement on Trade in Services is also leading to the deregulation of the international flow of health services. Finally, regional agreements such as the North American Free Trade Agreement (NAFTA) impose separate, perhaps greater, limitations on the ability of signatory states to limit trade in health care goods and services for public health reasons. See Jason Sapsin, et al., International Trade Law and Public Health Advocacy, 31 *J. L. Med. & Ethics* 546 (2003): David Fidler, Emerging Trends in International Law Concerning Global Infectious Disease Control, 9 *Emerging Infections Diseases* 285 (2003).

C. Public Health Law: Tobacco Regulation

While AIDS and SARS post obvious threats to the public health as infectious diseases, tobacco and other dangerous products such as asbestos or pesticides pose a public health threat of a different sort. They are also subject to legal regulation. Tobacco provides a fascinating subject for comparative study because of the conflict that it poses between the rights of individuals to enjoy their private pleasures and the rights of others to be free from the annoyance (and, as has become increasingly obvious, the health hazards) of breathing the smoke of others. It also poses a conflict between the right of the state to intervene paternalistically to restrict the use of substances that are dangerous and addictive and the autonomy of individuals to risk destruction of their health if they choose to do so. Smoking is also important culturally in some countries, as is noted in excerpts below. Finally, the regulation of tobacco has very important financial implications. On the one hand, tobacco is heavily taxed and is thus an important source of revenue in most counties; indeed, in some countries is sold through a lucrative public monopoly. On the other, public health insurance programs bear a heavy cost for paying for the diseases tobacco causes (although tobacco also causes early death and thus may free public pension programs from considerable expense). Each country weighs these considerations differently, as the three excerpts that follow illustrate:

The Culture of Legal Change: A Case Study of Tobacco Control in Twenty-First Century Japan

Eric A. Feldman, 27 Mich J. Int' L 743, 746–50, 769, 771–83, 797, 799, 803–04, 806, 815–17 (2006).

* * *

* * *After almost half a millennium of tobacco cultivation, nearly a century of government monopolization of tobacco growth, manufacture, and sale, and the highest rate of tobacco consumption in the industrialized world, Japan at the end of the twentieth cen-

tury had few laws regarding tobacco consumption. The political economy of tobacco, in the view of most commentators, was the reason for the absence of laws. The ruling Liberal Democratic Party (LDP) depended upon the electoral support of tobacco farmers and retailers, and the Ministry of Finance (MoF) was the majority shareholder in Japan's only tobacco company and enjoyed the income from tobacco sales (both tax and profit)—thus the LDP and MoF together ensured that the sale and use of tobacco products was largely unencumbered by legal restrictions. In the first years of the new millennium, however, both the national and local governments rapidly passed a cascade of tobacco-related laws. * * * The rapid and seismic shift in Japan's legal control of tobacco, a legal change unanticipated and so far unexplained, is the puzzle this Article seeks to unravel. It does so by identifying specific cultural attitudes and agents and presenting evidence of their causal role in bringing about change.

* * *

This Article * * * suggest[s] that the legal changes reshaping the landscape of tobacco in Japan since 2000 started with the normative transformation of smoking in the West. Over the past several decades, citizens in the United States and other Western nations have steadily condemned the act of smoking. Once an activity of the upper class, it has come to be seen as a socially unacceptable habit favored by the poor, the uneducated, and the unwise. The denormalization of smoking in the West has been duly noted in Japan; the print media regularly highlights the contrast between smoking practices and perceptions in the West and Japan; fiction writers have popularized it; Japanese overseas travelers have witnessed it; Japanese and non-Japanese companies have built their businesses around the association of smoke-free spaces with Western chic; those who associate with Western tourists in Japan have been made aware of it; television dramas and documentaries have portrayed it; and lawmakers have discussed it.

Why does the increasingly powerful social condemnation of smoking in the United States and elsewhere have an influence in Japan? Because, this Article argues, it highlights the gap between Japan and Western states and implicates a broadly-held social norm—the norm of conformity with the West. The conformity norm does not trigger blind or random copying; it neither presupposes that the "West is best" nor results in the importation of unaltered Western laws or practices. With regard to tobacco, this Article argues that the conformity norm catalyzed law-making behavior; it moved elites (and some in the general populace) to reassess their tolerance of tobacco and caused lawmakers to create laws that expressed the approbation of smoking. No single factor can fully explain something as complex and multi-causal as legal change, and this Article emphasizes that the interaction of a number of forces was critical in bringing about Japan's new legal regime of tobacco control. But as it demonstrates, the conformity norm is a crucial variable in explaining the timing and intensity of tobacco-related legal changes in Japan.

* * *

Only a few decades ago, smokers in the United States could light up at will. As Emily Post so sharply scolded her readers in 1940, "those who do not smoke cannot live apart, and when they come in contact with smokers, it is scarcely fair that the few should be allowed to prohibit the many from the pursuit of their comforts and their pleasure." By the end of the twentieth century, the norms of acceptable smoking behavior had been fundamentally altered, first through the norm of asking permission to smoke and ultimately by the re-zoning of both public and private space to exclude smoking. It was a remarkable change, not only for the rapidity with which smoking went from a quotidian act to a deviant habit but also for the thoroughness of the transformation. * * *

* * *

Scientific studies and government reports about the health harms of smoking, anti-tobacco activism, the public release of previously confidential tobacco industry documents, Congressional hearings, the settlement between the industry and state attorneys general, tort litigation, and debate over tobacco control laws, together with cultural assumptions about risk and temperance, all contributed to the denormalization of smokers and smoking in the United States. By the 1980s and 1990s, according to social historian Allan Brandt, a "radical transformation" made smoking "an increasingly unacceptable behavior in public settings." Robert Kagan and Jerome Skolnick make a similar observation: "Throughout the United States, in universities, in other workplaces, in restaurants, there has been a dramatic change in the social acceptability of tobacco smoking. Smokers feel condemned, isolated, disenfranchised, alienated." By the 1990s, Joseph Gusfield writes, "the smoker was not only a foolish victim of his or her habit but also an obnoxious and uncivil source of danger, pollution, and illness to others."

International events amplified the shift in attitudes toward smoking in the United States. In addition to changes within particular states, and perhaps more importantly, the World Health Organization (WHO) has been increasingly active in changing attitudes toward smoking. In 1996, the World Health Assembly adopted a resolution requesting the WHO to initiate the development of an international tobacco control agreement. * * * [T]he UN Ad Hoc Inter-Agency Task Force on Tobacco Control, created the Tobacco Free Initiative, and began working on the WHO's first-ever binding convention, the Framework Convention on Tobacco Control (FCTC), in 1999.

Among the areas the FCTC addresses are restrictions on tobacco advertising, sponsorship, and promotion; the creation of new packet warnings for tobacco products; and the zoning of public space to limit the harms of ETS. Because the WHO's regulatory powers are limited, however, the FCTC's provisions are aspirational, and national laws remain the most important factor in determining tobacco control policy. The FCTC's significance is thus more symbolic than practical; it indicates the premier international health organization has made the elimination of smoking a core policy objective.* * *

* * *

Thus, most strongly in the United States but also in other nations and the WHO, smoking is increasingly seen as an individual moral failing. In some cases, particular nations have embedded this new view in specific tobacco control laws. In addition, the social climate surrounding smoking has undergone a fundamental change. Stated most starkly, by the early twenty-first century the unquestioned acceptability of smoking in the West had vanished. In place of the rugged individualist was the addict, wedded to an increasingly expensive habit that was a source of annoyance to others and a threat to public health. Denormalization was not uniform across the range of Western nations—it was most apparent in the United States and WHO. Together, and supplemented by new policies, practices, and outlooks on smoking in other Western industrialized democracies, they provide the context for the rapid changes that would soon emerge in Japan.

Until the beginning of the twenty-first century, smoking in Japan was rarely the subject of regulatory concern, and rates of smoking among Japanese men were the highest in the industrialized world. * * * Japan enacted its first tobacco tax in 1624, and by the early twentieth century the government had monopolized the tobacco business and placed it under the control of MoF. * * * The Japanese government's tobacco monopoly lasted for almost a century. * * *

In 1985, yielding to U.S. pressure to eliminate trade barriers against U.S. tobacco companies, the Japanese government prepared for competition from foreign tobacco products by formally creating Japan Tobacco, Inc. (JT), a domestic tobacco company that could compete with foreign tobacco corporations. * * * Under the terms of the Tobacco Enterprise Law, MoF must continue to own a majority of JT's stock (until recently it owned 66.7 percent, and since summer 2004 it has owned 50 percent), and it retained control of key aspects of tobacco policy, such as advertising, packet warnings, price, and taxation. The legislation also made clear MoF's regulatory goal: to foster Japan's tobacco industry in order to improve the national economy and increase tax revenues. * * * At the close of the twentieth century, Japanese tobacco policy was primarily focused on the business of tobacco.

Beginning in 2000, however, the legal control of tobacco in Japan took a dramatic turn. Elected politicians in the national Diet debated and passed legislation aimed at limiting tobacco-related morbidity and mortality. Local governments enacted laws that controlled the use of cigarettes. Even MoF officials took a new approach to smoking, using their policy powers in ways more likely to reduce tobacco consumption than ensure "the development of the national tobacco industry." The laws they created were not, in most cases, transplants; neither individually nor as a group could similar legal restrictions be found in other jurisdictions. Instead, inspired by foreign changes and informed about them, Japanese lawmakers created a distinctive set of legal interventions. * * *

Japan's most significant national tobacco control legislation, the Health Promotion Law (HPL), went into effect on May 1, 2003. Three years earlier, in February 2000, the MHLW had issued the final version of its blueprint for Japan's health, "Healthy Japan 21." * * * The MHLW had not previously been active in the public health aspects of smoking; it had limited resources to devote to tobacco control (due to its dependence on MoF for its operating budget) and no political support for such activities. But emboldened perhaps by the international focus on tobacco-related morbidity and mortality and sensing a domestic political opportunity, the MHLW included in its first draft of the "Healthy Japan 21" a set of specific numerical goals for the reduction of smoking. After clashing with MoF, JT, and senior Liberal Democratic Party (LDP, the ruling conservative party) politicians over the contents of the report, officials at the MHLW abandoned their plan. Beyond platitudes about the importance of reducing tobacco-related disease, eliminating smoking among minors and educating the public about the health consequences of smoking, when "Healthy Japan 21" emerged in 2000 it contained no legal restrictions on smoking.

The HPL, submitted to the Diet on March 1, 2002, as part of a legislative package that included amendments to the Health Insurance Law, was meant to provide a legislative basis for the various goals announced in the final report of "Healthy Japan 21." Central to that report was a focus on reducing "lifestyle-related disease," defined as "a group of diseases whose symptomatic appearance and progress are affected by living practices including eating, exercising, rest, smoking, and drinking." Harms to nonsmokers from environmental tobacco smoke (ETS) were included in that grouping, so the report suggested that workplaces and public facilities contain smoke free areas. Because of the conflict between MoF and MHLW, the ETS-related recommendations in "Healthy Japan 21" were vaguely worded and demanded no specific actions by the government or private parties. As a result, they seemed unlikely to have a significant impact on tobacco policy or the public health impact of ETS.

* * *

Despite its weak wording, the HPL has spurred a wide range of actions. Soon after it went into effect, 10 private railway companies in the Tokyo metropolitan area banned smoking at all of their 730 stations. Eighteen of forty-seven prefectures banned smoking at prefectural schools, even though they could have created no-smoking areas or designated particular buildings as smoke-free. West Japan Railway, a major carrier, banned smoking at all 1200 of its stations, and the number of smoking cars on the bullet trains has dwindled to just one or two cars per train. The National Personnel Agency issued new guidelines for all central government offices in Tokyo aimed at reducing smoking among public employees. * * *

A number of other HPL-related changes have been made or are under discussion. The National Personnel Authority, for example, issued guidelines in July 2003 that established a goal of eliminating smoking from all central government office buildings. Despite lacking a concrete timetable, the guidelines have had an impact.* * *

In addition to the concrete responses the HPL provoked, the legislation itself represents an important practical and symbolic change in the approach of nationally-elected representatives to tobacco policy. For the first time since 1900, the Japanese government had endorsed legislation with the potential to limit tobacco consumption. Despite the cozy relationship between the ruling LDP, tobacco farmers, tobacco sellers, MoF, and JT, which had long subdued any enthusiasm for smoking controls, the Diet's HPL broke with the past and endorsed a legal strategy that has started to marginalize the use of tobacco.

Japanese law has since 1900 prohibited minors from using tobacco products. In December 2000, the Diet revised the law for the first time since its passage a century ago. The new provisions, which took effect in September 2001, forbid retailers to sell tobacco products to those below the age of 20 * * *. In addition, the tobacco industry has been experimenting with vending machine identification cards that limit access to those over the age of 20.

* * *

Since 1980, smokers suffering from allegedly tobacco-related illnesses have been suing the government—and after 1985, JT—demanding compensation for their harms. Courts have uniformly rejected the lawsuits, questioning the link between smoking and lung cancer, considering the externalities of smoking a tolerable risk, and rejecting claims about the addictiveness of nicotine. Despite this record of failure, litigation is now beginning to percolate in settings where tobacco-related lawsuits would have previously been unthinkable. * * *

In July 2004, in a case involving a local government employee, a plaintiff in a tobacco case finally prevailed. The pro se plaintiff, who had worked in the Urban Renewal Department of Tokyo's Edogawa Ward since 1985, claimed to suffer from headaches and sore throats as a result of smoke from his co-workers' cigarettes. He complained to his boss and asked for the creation of a no-smoking section in his office or the installation of effective ventilation equipment, but no action was taken. After the plaintiff's physician informed him that he was suffering from damage to his larynx and his employer denied his request for the reimbursement of his medical expenses, he sued the Edogawa Ward government in the Tokyo District Court. The resulting judgment carefully avoids the issue of causation; it says nothing about whether the plaintiff's harm was the consequence of his exposure to workplace tobacco smoke. Instead, it asserts that the Ward had a duty to make an effort to attend to the health problems of the plaintiff, and its failure to quickly transfer him to another section of the office makes it in part responsible for paying the costs of his health insurance. * * *

In March 2004, Japan became the 98th state to sign the WHO's Framework Convention on Tobacco Control, and the Diet subsequently approved the Convention in June 2004. * * *

Because the FCTC's provisions were fundamentally hortatory, signing the document did not obligate the Japanese government to make any changes to its tobacco control policy. But in the period prior to Japan's signing, MoF initiated a number of changes. Under the Tobacco Enterprise Law, for example, MoF has the authority to regulate the advertising of tobacco products. It did so in 1989 when it issued guidelines restricting television ads during daytime programming, apparently in an effort to protect JT's cigarette market share from foreign companies that had recently started to sell their full range of products in Japan. In most cases, MoF relied on voluntary agreements between key industry actors to limit tobacco advertising. It was not until 2003 that MoF and the Tobacco Institute of Japan (TIOJ), a private group which represents the industry, began to discuss more rigorous advertising controls.

MoF's new advertising restrictions eliminated tobacco ads on buses and trains in October 2004 and prohibited new outdoor advertising as of April 1, 2005 (existing ads must be removed by September 2005). The MoF permits newspaper advertising, but it limits tobacco manufacturers to twelve ads each year and a maximum of three per month. Tobacco industry sponsorship is now restricted to events in which participants and organizers are over the age of 20. The MoF allows tobacco advertising in the smoking areas of train stations, as well as ads that urge smokers to exercise good "manners" and those aimed at preventing youth smoking. * * *

Further, MoF has taken action on a new set of cigarette packet warnings, which are turning what has been a whisper of caution into more of a shout. Current warnings, dating from 1990, are benign, suggesting to smokers that they should "take care not to smoke too much" because it is bad for their health. Effective July 2005, manufacturers are required to select two of MoF's eight authorized warnings and to place a different warning on the front and back of each pack of cigarettes. * * *

Although the messages are less direct than those now found in the EU and elsewhere, which bluntly state that "smoking kills," the new Japanese warnings are far clearer and stronger than what preceded them. Included among the eight warnings, for example, are "smoking can be one of the causes of lung cancer;" "if pregnant women smoke, it could adversely affect the development of their fetus and cause premature birth;" and "smoke from your cigarettes could adversely affect the health of people around you, particularly children and the elderly." * * *

* * *

A variety of agents have widely disseminated information about Western anti-smoking norms and the contrast they provide with smoking in Japan. First, in a large volume of articles and reports about tobacco litigation and policy in the West, the Japanese media has consistently drawn unfavorable comparisons with the situation in Japan. * * * All of the major Japanese newspapers devote extensive coverage to tobacco-related changes in the West—the banning of smoking in New York's restaurants and bars, the elimination of smoking in Irish pubs, the jury verdicts for U.S. smokers, and the no-smoking beaches of Santa Monica, California, to cite only a fraction of the coverage of foreign tobacco-related issues. In many instances, articles explicitly compare the smoking situation in the West and Japan and conclude, as did one article in the Asahi Newspaper, that "Japan is obviously a smokers' paradise (*kitsuensha no tengoku*) in the developed world." * * *

* * *

Coverage of tobacco and smoking has also increased on television, with frequent discussions of smoking on so-called "variety" shows, some of which have created a "smokers' corner" on the set for those who want to light up. Some TV documentaries have been particularly pointed in discussing the gap between smoking norms and law in the West and Japan.* * *

* * *

The FCTC presented a particularly complex dilemma to Japanese lawmakers. On the one hand, they were united with the United States and Germany in opposing many aspects of the document. * * *

On the other hand, the NGOs that were a constant presence outside the negotiating chambers subjected Japan's involvement in the FCTC [i.e. its resistence to strong international tobacco controls] to withering criticism. * * *

* * *

* * * Western smoking norms have made themselves felt in Japan through the presence of foreign corporations. The most vivid example is the Starbucks chain of coffee shops, brought to Japan as a joint venture with the Japanese company Sazaby. * * * When the first Starbucks store opened in the Ginza in 1996, it was billed as "bringing to Japan the Starbucks Coffee store experience and the new coffee and espresso culture that had proved so successful in North America." Part of that culture was the decoupling of coffee and cigarettes; the first two Starbucks had smoking sections on the second floor, but they were quickly eliminated and all successive stores have been smoke free. The strategy appears to have worked. By 1998 there were 12 Starbucks in Japan, a number that grew to 97 in 1999, 321 in 2002, and 503 in 2003.

* * *

This Article argues that the denormalization of smoking in the West was a critical factor in causing the emergence of newly robust legal controls of smoking in Japan. The relationship between Western norms and Japanese law, it asserts, is mediated by a conformity norm that facilitates the translation of Western smoking norms into Japanese laws. * * *

Given the plethora of norms that govern behavior in the United States and other Western nations, how does one account for the fact that some norms appear to have a powerful influence in Japan while others are ineffective? * * * [T]hree criteria are particularly important: the substance and content of a norm, the availability of local agents to introduce and promote the norm, and the degree to which domestic conditions are receptive to the norm. The substance of the anti-smoking norms fits well in Japan, * * * both because the consequence of adopting the norm involves obvious health benefits and because it implicates a set of behaviors involving manners and propriety that have long served as markers of Japan's "civilized" status. Local agents, * * * were active and diverse. They included the media, government officials who negotiated the WHO's international tobacco treaty, foreign companies operating in Japan, anti-tobacco activists, some politicians and finance ministry officials, and others. Those agents were critical to the transmission of Western tobacco-related norms; * * *. Domestic conditions, * * * discusses, were receptive to the influence of the new tobacco-related norms. Most importantly, the power and resolve of the tobacco lobby, which had for decades defeated all efforts to create a more robust set of controls for tobacco, had waned, defanging what had been a powerful opposition to robust tobacco policy.

* * *

As the Diet and local authorities enacted new laws that emphasized who can smoke, created limited smoking zones, and regulated the disposal of cigarette butts (among other measures), they sent a clear message to the Japanese citizenry and the international community: Smoking is no longer the unquestioned, "natural," assumed state of affairs. In place of smoking normalcy, the new legal regime draws attention to the smoker as outcast * * *. Together with a newly robust legal framework for tobacco, therefore, Japan is experiencing another equally far-reaching set of changes—a reshaping of informal smoking norms.

* * *

Liberte, Egalité, Fumée: Smoking and Tobacco Control in France

Constance A. Nathanson, from Unfiltered, Eric Feldman and Ronald Bayer, eds., pp. 138, 141–45, 149–50, 152–53, 155, 159–60 (2004)

The left-bank intellectual with a Gauloise drooping from the corner of his mouth has virtual iconic status as a symbol—if not to the French themselves, at least to the tourist soaking up culture and smoke in equal parts at every café and on every street corner. This image is, nevertheless, of relatively recent date and, in some sense, misleading. Not until after the Second World War did cigarettes become the dominant form of tobacco consumption in France, and it is only very recently that the prevalence of smoking has come close to that in the United States. Even more counterintuitive, perhaps, is that France was among the first countries to pass, in 1976, stringent tobacco-control legislation, including controls both on advertising and on smoking in places "open to the public." Reflected here are multiple contradictions: not only do symbol and reality collide, but what is symbol and what is reality are often unclear. * * *

* * *

By the end of the eighteenth century, the French tobacco monopoly yielded 7 percent of total state revenues. This figure was a weighty one "in that it created both a state interest and private interests that could not readily be ignored when relevant policy questions came to be decided." This state of affairs remained relatively stable until about 1970. In the past thirty years, the interrelated pressures of market, consumer, and regulatory change have led to the monopoly's gradual privatization and, in 1999, to a merger between the tobacco industries of France and Spain. Tobacco nevertheless continues to be an important source of revenue for the French state, and to engage substantial public and private interests.

The *Societé nationale d'exploitation industrielle des tabacs et allumettes,* or SEITA—best known as the manufacturer of Gauloises and Gitanes—was created in 1926. SEITA had the monopoly not only on the manufacture and wholesale distribution of tobacco products and matches, but also on tobacco farming; further, the state was under an obligation to purchase the tobacco harvest. * * *

* * *

Under the French tobacco regime, both tobacco taxes and the total price of cigarettes to the consumer were controlled by the state. Taxes have consistently hovered around 75 percent of the total price (a percentage not atypical for Europe). Until 1991, however, the overall price of cigarettes was about half their cost in other countries of the European Union. The Finance Ministry's interest in holding down the price of cigarettes was dictated by tobacco's inclusion in the cost-of-living index. The index played a major role in employer-employee negotiations over wages and salaries. As long as the index included tobacco, any price increase would immediately have been reflected in demands for higher salaries contributing—from the ministry's perspective—to the threat of inflation. In 1992, as part of a broader legislative initiative to regulate both tobacco and alcohol (see below), tobacco was removed from the cost-of-living index. In the ensuing nine years, cigarette prices have been increased eleven times, by a total of 122 percent. The parallel, if not wholly commensurate, decline in smoking has been attributed to these increases. Higher prices have, of course, redounded to the benefit of the French treasury (tax revenue from tobacco sales doubled between 1991 and 2000) and contributed to the health of the French tobacco industry.

* * *

* * * France's first tobacco legislation, the *loi Veil*—as it became known, after its principal sponsor—was passed with relatively little fanfare in June 1976. The gist of its provisions, described below in greater detail, was to restrict tobacco advertising and to place limitations on smoking in places *affectés à un usage collectif* (open to the public).

As in other parliamentary democracies, legislative proposals come to the French Parliament in the form of government or private bills. The *loi Veil* was a government bill and, as such, had the support of members of the (center-right) party in power. Nevertheless, the government appears to have done its best to minimize what opposition there might have been. The bill was sprung on the General Assembly on a Friday evening with many members absent (a tactic that elicited relatively mild complaint). Government spokespersons took what appears in retrospect to be extraordinary pains to reassure members present that the law would have no adverse economic consequences for tobacco growers and retail outlets, and that there was no intention of "discriminating" against smokers. Parliamentarians congratulated themselves that *tabagisme* was an issue that crossed party lines, since so many members smoked. The most contentious issue was the government's proposal to end tobacco sponsorship of sporting events, resolved by the inclusion of an exception for auto racing. Indeed, the only organized opposition to the government's bill was from the *groupe communiste* on the ground that this "preventive" legislation was largely cosmetic in the face of the real problems facing the country.

Specifically, the *loi Veil* prohibited advertising for tobacco or tobacco products on radio and television, in theaters and movie houses, and, with some exceptions, on posters and billboards. Tobacco sponsorship of sporting events was prohibited, with the exception noted above. Advertising was allowed in retail tobacco sales outlets (small, mom-and-pop stores) and in the print media under specified conditions. Package warnings *(abus dangereux)* and requirements for content labeling (specifics to be determined) were imposed, and pertinent health information was to be provided for schools and the army. Both in the government's presentations to Parliament and in the wording of the foregoing legislative provisions, primary emphasis was on the protection of youth from industry blandishments.

Among the many curious aspects of this legislation (for example, a warning limited to tobacco "abuse"), none are more so than the provisions that refer to smoking in places "open to the public." These provisions consist of two sentences under the heading *"dispositions diverses"* (more or less equivalent to "miscellaneous"). The first sentence reads, "Without prejudice to measures that may be taken by the police to preserve public order and tranquility, decrees of the *Conseil d'etat* will determine the conditions under which smoking prohibitions will be established in places open to the public where this practice can have consequences dangerous to health." The second sentence states that in locations and in vehicles where smokers and nonsmokers might be differently affected, the space designated for the non-smokers cannot be less than half of the total space.

The *loi Veil* was implemented by a series of *décrets* (by the *Conseil d'état,* with the force of law) and *arrêtés* (administrative regulations issued by the Ministry of Health) in 1977 and 1978. The first *décret,* published in September 1977, dealt with smoking in places "open to the public," for the first time making clear (or clearer) what was meant by places *affectés à un usage collectif.* Under the *loi Veil* this phrase referred to educational establishments, hospitals, kitchens where food was *prepared* for sale, and laboratories that dealt with germs or "toxic substances." Also included were modes of public transportation: buses, trains, airplanes, and ships. There was no mention of restaurants and bars, or places of employment. They were excluded by omission. Even within the "places" that were included, however, the rules were far from simple. For example, smoking in schools and colleges was prohibited only where and when students were present. Smoking in hospitals was prohibited only where there were patients. Unless used primarily by students, modes of public transportation were subject to the rule of "no more than one-half:" no more than one-half of the places in buses, trains, airplanes, and so on could be given over to smokers.

* * *

As a piece of legislation, the *loi Veil* law was ahead of its time, banning most outdoor advertising and restricting smoking in places of public accommodation years before anything comparable was passed elsewhere. In practice, however, the Veil law amounted to little more than an intellectual exercise, honored far more in the breach than the observance. The law was the work of one person, Simone Veil. While it had the support of President Valéry Giscard d'Estaing, the powerful Finance Ministry—ever mindful of tobacco's contribution to the treasury and fearful of what any increase in tobacco prices might do to the cost-of-living index—was opposed. French authorities took few or no steps to enforce the law; industry evasion of its provisions with respect to advertising was widespread; and the law's limitations on smoking in places open to the public were essentially ignored.

The pattern I describe—a law is passed but neither implemented nor enforced with any rigor—is not unusual in France. Indeed, I was told more than once that the French "don't have much respect for law." This statement is something of an oversimplification, however. The law in France has a tutelary function: it is a statement of the norms to which French citizens are expected to adhere, much as a parent sets normative boundaries—"behave respectfully to your elders," "come home before midnight"—for a child. It is not only understood, but expected, that reality may not conform to the norm, but the norm itself is no less valid.

* * *

The *loi Veil* was replaced in 1991 by the *loi Evin,* named for the health minister who shepherded its adoption, Claude Evin. Credit for this law belongs in large part to a group of five physicians—the *cinq sages* as they came to be known—who came together out of common frustration with what they saw as government complicity to weaken or evade existing laws for the protection of public health. * * *

* * *

Parliamentary debate focused almost entirely on the potential threat of these advertising restrictions to French economic interests—the tobacco industry, mass media, and automobile racing. From the public's perspective, however, the law's principal innovation was not in its strengthened advertising bans, but in a single sentence (pithier even than comparable provisions of the *loi Veil)* that, for the first time, privileged the rights of nonsmokers over those of smokers: "Smoking is prohibited in places open to the public, including educational institutions, and in public transport—*except* in locations expressly designated for smokers." In comments in the course of parliamentary debate, Evin made his intentions explicit: "Our aim is the reversal of current logic. Smoking [now] is allowed everywhere except in places reserved for nonsmokers. Henceforth it will be forbidden to smoke except in places reserved for smokers." * * *

Given the vagueness of this regulatory framework and the government's reliance for its implementation on a multitude of unspecified authorities with, by and large, little to gain from compliance, it is unsurprising that on June 1, 2000, marking the occasion of France's annual "day without tobacco." The headline in *Le Monde* proclaimed that the "Evin law is badly applied." The article goes on to explain that "while advertising is markedly reduced, the division of space between smokers and non-smokers is poorly respected." The commission constituted to evaluate the law's operation reached much the same conclusions. Where smoking prohibitions exist, and where their implementation is required, compliance is variable, at best. Restrictions on smoking in trains and airplanes are largely observed (not, however, in stations and waiting rooms). Bars and restaurants are another matter altogether. Perhaps most striking to the American observer is the absence of enforcement in hospitals, not to speak of educational institutions, where smoking goes on in corridors, classrooms, and private offices. Workplace restrictions are not uniform and (at least as reflected in newspaper accounts and in complaints by nonsmokers to anti-tobacco groups such as the Comité national contre le tabagisme (CNCT)) have, indeed, encountered the greatest resistance. Nonsmokers have generally been reluctant to assert their right to protection (repeated several times in the 1992 *décret),* and it was not until 1997 that CNCT began a systematic effort to bring these complaints to the attention of the courts, with some success.

* * *

Perhaps the most interesting road not taken in France is prohibition of cigarette sales to minors. The need to protect "our children" from the dangers of tobacco was a major theme in the parliamentary debates surrounding both the *loi Veil* and the *loi Evin,* and the percentage of smokers among adolescents is high (among eighteen-year-olds, 60 percent report that they smoke). Nevertheless, restriction of sales to persons seventeen and over was considered and rejected on both occasions. Many of the arguments are familiar: for adolescents, prohibition will be an additional incentive to smoke; restrictions "don't work" and will be evaded. At least two other arguments are less familiar, at least to those not living in France: a prohibition limited to children might imply that smoking is not dangerous for adults, and the government should not impose regulations that it fears will not be enforced. * * *

* * *

Given this background, what accounts for the (relative) success achieved by the *cinq sages?* Their strategy had four elements critical to what they were able to accomplish. First was their discovery of "outsider," media-based lobbying. British physicians played an equally key role in that country's tobacco story, but their strategy relied much more heavily on Britain's long tradition of "insider" negotiations between civil servants and the medical elite. The second crucial element in the French doctors' strategy was their use of medical luminaries (Nobel Prize winners and the like) as props to reinforce the scientific authority and legitimacy of their case. Third was the link created between tobacco and alcohol, a strategy difficult to understand outside of France: tobacco was employed as a stalking horse to get legislation limiting alcohol advertising. As explained by Hirsch, referring to the notorious failure of Mendés-France's campaign in favor of milk, "In this country it was absolutely impossible to do anything in alcohol . . . So, we decided to mask the wine problem behind the tobacco problem." The final element and, indeed, the coup de grace for a Socialist government, according to Hirsch, was the social inequality of sickness and death (that is, higher morbidity and mortality among the poor than the rich)—an inequality, stated the *cinq sages,* created by diseases associated with tobacco and alcohol. For a "government of the left," this inequality was an argument impossible to ignore.

* * *

The American left is friendly to public health, identifying it as among the few government-financed and -run programs that directly serve the poorest and most vulnerable members of the population (poor mothers and children, drug users, persons with sexually transmitted infections, and so on). "No smoking" rules, furthermore, are largely self-enforcing. The French left, by contrast, sees public health—and, in particular, the "new" public health focused on what are perceived to be "lifestyle" choices—as requiring unacceptable intervention by the "hygienic" state into individuals' most personal decisions. "Medicine wants to direct our life, dictate our conduct, rule over us by 'the medical light.'" Invasion of privacy, health "fascism," discrimination, setting smokers and nonsmokers at one another's throats, and victim blaming are among the major themes of this discourse. In these polemics, the United States serves as an all-purpose *bête noire.* It is used by the left as a horrible example of what is in store for France—not only "a new prohibition," but also new forms of segregation reminiscent of Jim Crow. And it is used by public health advocates as an instructive example of what not to do: the unreconstructed smoker will not, in France, be pushed outside the social pale.

Not far beneath the surface of this debate are conceptions of the nonsmoker and of the relation between smokers and nonsmokers that are very different from those in the United States. Advocates of smoking restrictions portray nonsmokers as victims especially in need of the state's protection. "Legislation must above all protect nonsmokers ... [T]he right of the most vulnerable [e.g., children, pregnant women] to breathe clean air must be respected." By the same token, to protest against another's smoke is to cast *oneself* in the role of victim—a victim, furthermore, who is prepared to interfere with another's "small pleasures" for what are perceived by smokers and many others to be specious reasons: "The smoker—I know, I've been there—does not for a moment believe that the non-smoker is truly bothered. No, he simply wants to annoy, to, deprive the smoker of a little pleasure." * * * This construction of smoking as *tin petit plaisir* with which it is simply churlish to interfere largely explains why smoking restrictions are more readily respected aboard buses, trains, and airplanes than in cafés and restaurants. The latter are defined as zones of pleasure, whereas the former are not.

Just as the principle of *solidarité* dictates that children should not be discriminated against, so—and even more powerfully—it dictates that smokers should, insofar as possible, not be segregated. Images of the smoker out in the cold, of "civil war between smokers and nonsmokers" are invoked to argue against any overzealous enforcement of restrictions on when and where smoking will be allowed. Ideally, smokers and nonsmokers will resolve their disagreements through dialogue and negotiation, and will arrive at a solution equally satisfying to all parties. This process is likely to take a while, however, and there is no guarantee that it will be continuous. "In the end, France will change like everyone else: the whole world has come to know that the Marlboro cowboy died of smoker's cancer. But we have a long way still to go."

* * *

Holy Smoke, No More? Tobacco Control in Denmark

Erik Aibtek, from Eric Feldman and Ronald Bayer (eds.) Unfiltered, pp. 190–91, 193, 209, 215–16 (2004)

Foreigners visiting Denmark often find the country's tobacco-control policies appallingly lax. When they arrive at Copenhagen International Airport, they find the designated smoking areas to be a joke, separated from nonsmoking areas by nothing but (impure) air; they find it virtually impossible to find a smoke-free section even in Denmark's most upscale French restaurant, let alone cafés or bars; and they learn with disbelief that nonsmoking employees in Danish private workplaces are not even protected from smoke during lunch. Many Danish health policymakers share this gloomy view that Danish tobacco-control policies lag behind those of most "civilized" countries.

It is debatable, however, whether Danish tobacco-control policies, in general, lag behind policies in comparable countries. It may appear so when one focuses exclusively on Denmark's weak restrictions on public smoking, but the country's tobacco-control policymakers use all of the available policy instruments in efforts to reduce smoking: carrot (economic incentives), stick (regulations), and sermon (information). If the whole spectrum of policy instruments is considered, Denmark does not fare badly. In fact, the country has for decades been a front-runner in tobacco-control policies, and it still has some of the world's toughest policies. For instance, in the late 1920s, when Denmark dramatically increased its excise duty on tobacco products (a duty first imposed in 1912), the country became a world leader in tobacco taxation. Moreover, it remains a leader today; its taxes on tobacco are the third highest in the European Union (EU). Also noteworthy is that the country has never permitted tobacco advertisements on the broadcast media.

* * * New tobacco-control policies were accepted as long as they were based on two fundamental principles implicitly informing the initial. Danish introduction of excise duty on tobacco products: tobacco consumption is considered a private matter, and voluntary agreement is preferred to legal regulation. On the one hand, the acceptance of these principles allowed for the introduction of ever more restrictive policies to reduce active smoking. On the other, these same two principles would effectively preempt any attempts to introduce policies intended to protect nonsmokers from involuntary exposure to smoke—that is, passive smoking.

Nevertheless, Danish policies on passive smoking have become more restrictive, and the proposals for tobacco control put forward by the Danish health authorities during the last decade suggest a shift in policy over a very short period of time. We are thus faced with a second paradox, since conventional wisdom has it that once a policy path has been staked out, it is very difficult to change.

* * *

Throughout the twentieth century, smoking and alcohol consumption (from 1917) were viewed as private matters. During the past forty years, while Denmark's welfare state expanded, Danish decision makers abandoned restrictive legislation by "privatizing" decision making about a small but important set of issues like abortion, pornography, and domestic partnership arrangements. The Danes take pride in this liberal feature of Danish politics and look skeptically at countries where they think moralism informs political decisions, as in the United States or neighboring "Prohibition Sweden," so nicknamed because of its restrictive alcohol policies.

A 1992 survey showed that Danes were less inclined to favor restrictions on smoking in public areas than citizens of other EU countries. With two out of three Danes indicating in 2000 that smokers should be allowed to smoke as long as they do so "considerately," Denmark has a far more tolerant attitude toward smoking than other Nordic countries. Danes are also more likely than citizens of other Nordic countries to find the talk about passive smoking exaggerated. When the *Lancet* in 2001 accused Denmark's Queen Margrethe II of causing the high prevalence of smoking among Danish women, Danes almost unanimously defended their queen's right to smoke.

In both the public and private sectors, Denmark prefers voluntary alternatives over legal regulation. If the state wants to change people's behavior, one legitimate policy instrument is information. If that fails, the next option is voluntary agreement. * * *

* * *

The tobacco-control strategy that has caused the most controversy in Denmark is the restriction of when and where smoking is permitted. Taxation, regulation of advertising, labeling requirements, tar and nicotine yields, and other measures have been accepted by Danes as fully legitimate means to improve and promote public health, whereas restrictions on smoking have been seen as an infringement on the individual citizen's right to free choice. There have always been restrictions on smoking for hygienic reasons, but only in the late 1970s and early 1980s did the idea begin to emerge that nonsmokers had a right to protection against smoke. The Danes only hesitantly accepted the idea, but today there is widespread agreement that nonsmokers must be protected. Disagreements arise over whether protection for nonsmokers can be accomplished only by bans on smoking in public areas.

* * *

Smoking has also moved from the private to the public arena in quite another sense, and here, too, has become a moral issue. The individual's decision to smoke is not (yet) considered morally objectionable. Nevertheless, profiting from tobacco production and trade *is*. In 2000 Danish newspapers ran numerous articles critical of tobacco production, trade, consumption, and policy, and one newspaper launched what appeared to be a well-orchestrated campaign to discredit both the industry and the minister of health. As its point of departure, the newspaper campaign defined tobacco production as morally objectionable. As a matter of logic, representatives of the tobacco industry were therefore morally corrupt, and steps by the industry to defend its interests, morally repugnant. Included in this judgment were efforts to approach politicians or civil servants in the manner that any other Danish industry would do in order to protect its own interests. Another target was the Danish Doctors' Pension Fund, which had to sell its shares in Scandinavian Tobacco Company after critical press coverage. Even the Danish government came under attack; it had to withdraw its financial support to House of Prince for the company to begin manufacturing tobacco in the Baltic countries. It was deemed irrelevant that the company had applied and obtained government support on the exact same conditions as other Danish companies. In these and other cases, the press coverage came close to a moral crusade of the type to which the Danes usually think themselves immune.

There is no longer anything sacred about smoking in Denmark. From having been a private matter—the scope of which the government, by indirect means, might legitimately attempt to reduce—tobacco consumption has not just become one public health concern among others, but arguably what is felt by many to be the single most urgent health concern for the Danish people. As a result, there is little moral room for arguments in favor of tobacco consumption. Smoking has almost become a "valence" issue—that is, an issue to which there is essentially only one side in the public debate. One may still argue that, as a matter of principle, the state should not make decisions on behalf of its citizens and therefore should not deprive smokers of a choice. Or one may argue in utilitarian terms that, for instance, restrictions on smoking in youth clubs might be detrimental to the clubs' efforts to reach out to socially disadvantaged youngsters. Apart from these arguments, there are few left.

It is worth noting that alcohol consumption has not become a morally one-sided issue. Although the estimated annual mortality due to alcohol is far below the mortality related to tobacco, Danes do drink more than people in most other Western countries, and there are severe health problems related to alcohol consumption. Not nearly as many people are exposed to passive drinking as to passive smoking, but fetuses, children, and spouses of alcoholics all experience the harmful consequences—whether physical, psychological, economic, or social—of that particular form of substance abuse. Nevertheless, the harmful effects of alcohol consumption get little attention in the Danish media, and media coverage of alcohol is void of the moral objections made to tobacco. The social constructions of tobacco and alcohol at the beginning of the twenty-first century are thus almost the reverse of what they were at the beginning of the twentieth century. One explanatory factor may be that early in the twentieth century, alcohol consumption was clearly more prevalent in the lower classes and tobacco consumption more prevalent in the upper classes; whereas today, tobacco consumption has become a lower-class phenomenon, while education and income level are positively correlated with alcohol consumption (and negatively correlated with attitudes toward more restrictive alcohol policies).

Why did popular opinion and tobacco-control policies in Denmark shift toward ever more restrictive measures even though the configuration of interests and policy history would suggest that just the opposite would occur? * * * [I]nternational scientists, experts, and policymakers have managed with great authority to promote the view that smoking is a serious public health problem, and that tough measures must be taken to control it.

* * *

One of the strategies that many countries have used to limit tobacco use is to control tobacco advertising. In a number of countries, however, this raises significant issues of freedom of expression. The following case explores these issues.

RJR-MacDonald Inc. v. Canada

[1995] 3 S.C.R. 199, 127 D.L.R. (4th) 1, 100 C.C.C. (3d) 449, 62 C.P.R. (3d) 417, 31 C.R.R. (2d) 189, 187 N.R. 1, Supreme Court of Canada (1995)

* * *

The following is the judgment delivered by *McLachlin J.*:

At issue in these cases is the validity of the *Tobacco Products Control Act*, S.C. 1988, c. 20 (the "Act"), a law which imposes a ban on all advertising of tobacco products in the Canadian media and requires tobacco manufacturers to print unattributed health warnings on the packages of all tobacco products [i.e. warnings not attributed to a government official or agency].

The first issue is whether Parliament had the power to enact the ban and warning requirements, given that advertising and promotion of particular industries generally are matters of provincial competence. I agree * * *, that Parliament may impose advertising bans and require health warnings on tobacco products under its criminal law power.

The second issue is whether the ban and warning requirements violate the *Canadian Charter of Rights and Freedoms.* The *Charter* guarantees free expression, a guarantee which has been held to extend to commercial speech such as advertising * * *. [T]he prohibition on advertising and promotion of tobacco products constitutes a violation of the right to free expression * * * I take the view that s. 9 of the Act, which requires tobacco manufacturers to place an unattributed health warning on tobacco packages, also infringes the right of free expression. * * * "[F]reedom of expression necessarily entails the right to say nothing or the right not to say certain things". Under s. 9(2), tobacco manufacturers are prohibited from displaying on their packages any writing other than the name, brand name, trade mark, and other information required by legislation. The combination of the unattributed health warnings and the prohibition against displaying any other information which would allow tobacco manufacturers to express their own views, constitutes an infringement of the right to free expression guaranteed by s. 2(*b*) of the *Charter.*

The only remaining question is whether these infringements of the right of free expression are saved under s. 1 of the *Charter*, as being reasonable and "demonstrably justified in a free and democratic society". Acknowledging that the evidence of justification is problematic, La Forest J. concludes that it nevertheless suffices to justify the infringement of the right of free expression, given the importance of the legislative goal, the context of the law and the need to defer to Parliament on such an important and difficult issue. With respect, I cannot agree. I share the trial judge's view that the Attorney General of Canada has failed to establish justification under s. 1 for ss. 4, 8 and 9 of the Act, those provisions which impose a total advertising ban, prohibit trade mark usage on articles other than tobacco products and mandate the use of unattributed health warnings on tobacco packaging. * * * I find ss. 4, 5, 6, 8, and 9 to be invalid, leaving the remainder of the Act intact except in so far as it relates to the invalid provisions.

* * * The ultimate issue [under section 1] is whether the infringement is reasonable and "demonstrably justified in a free and democratic society". The jurisprudence laying down the dual considerations of importance of objective and proportionality between the good which may be achieved by the law and the infringement of rights it works, may be seen as articulating the factors which must be considered in determining whether a law that violates constitutional rights is nevertheless "reasonable" and "demonstrably justified". If the objective of a law which limits constitutional rights lacks sufficient importance, the infringement cannot be reasonable or justified. Similarly, if the good which may be achieved by the law pales beside the seriousness of the infringement of rights which it works, that law cannot be considered reasonable or justified. * * *

This said, there is merit in reminding ourselves of the words chosen by those who framed and agreed upon s. 1 of the *Charter*. First, to be saved under s. 1 the party defending the law (here the Attorney General of Canada) must show that the law which violates the right or freedom guaranteed by the *Charter* is "reasonable". In other words, the infringing measure must be justifiable by the processes of reason and rationality. The question is not whether the measure is popular or accords with the current public opinion polls. The question is rather whether it can be justified by application of the processes of reason. In the legal context, reason imports the notion of inference from evidence or established truths. This is not to deny intuition its role, or to require proof to the standards required by science in every case, but it is to insist on a rational, reasoned defensibility.

Second, to meet its burden under s. 1 of the *Charter*, the state must show that the violative law is "demonstrably justified". The choice of the word "demonstrably" is critical. The process is not one of mere intuition, nor is it one of deference to Parliament's choice. It is a process of *demonstration.* * * *

The bottom line is this. While remaining sensitive to the social and political context of the impugned law and allowing for difficulties of proof inherent in that context, the courts must nevertheless insist that before the state can override constitutional rights, there be a reasoned demonstration of the good which the law may achieve in relation to the seriousness of the infringement. * * *

The factors generally relevant to determining whether a violative law is reasonable and demonstrably justified in a free and democratic society remain those set out in *Oakes*. The first requirement is that the objective of the law limiting the *Charter* right or freedom must be of sufficient importance to warrant overriding it. The second is that the means chosen to achieve the objective must be proportional to the objective and the effect of the law —proportionate, in short, to the good which it may produce. Three matters are considered in determining proportionality: the measures chosen must be rationally connected to the objective; they must impair the guaranteed right or freedom as little as reasonably possible (minimal impairment); and there must be overall proportionality between the deleterious effects of the measures and the salutary effects of the law.

* * *

The question at this stage is whether the objective of the infringing measure is sufficiently important to be capable in principle of justifying a limitation on the rights and freedoms guaranteed by the constitution. Given the importance of the *Charter* guarantees, this is not easily done. To meet the test, the objective must be one of pressing and substantial importance.

* * * The objective of the advertising ban and trade mark usage restrictions must be to prevent people in Canada from being persuaded by advertising and promotion to use tobacco products. The objective of the mandatory package warning must be to discourage people who see the package from tobacco use. Both constitute important objectives, although the significance of the targeted decrease in consumption is reduced by the government's estimate that despite the ban, 65 percent of the Canadian magazine market will contain tobacco advertisements, given that the ban applies only to Canadian media and not to imported publications.

* * * The critical question is not the evil tobacco works generally in our society, but the evil which the legislation addresses.

While the limited objective of reducing tobacco-associated health risks by reducing advertising-related consumption and providing warnings of dangers is less significant than the broad objective of protecting Canadians generally from the risks associated with tobacco use, it nevertheless constitutes an objective of sufficient importance to justify overriding the right of free expression guaranteed by the *Charter*. Even a small reduction in tobacco use may work a significant benefit to the health of Canadians and justify a properly proportioned limitation of right of free expression.

* * *

As a first step in the proportionality analysis, the government must demonstrate that the infringements of the right of free expression worked by the law are rationally connected to the legislative goal of reducing tobacco consumption. * * *

The causal relationship between the infringement of rights and the benefit sought may sometimes be proved by scientific evidence showing that as a matter of repeated observation, one affects the other. Where, however, legislation is directed at changing human behaviour, as in the case of the *Tobacco Products Control Act*, the causal relationship may not be scientifically measurable. In such cases, this Court has been prepared to find a causal connection between the infringement and benefit sought on the basis of reason or logic, without insisting on direct proof of a relationship between the infringing measure and the legislative objective. * * *

The trial judge in the cases at bar found that the government had not established a rational connection between the advertising ban and unattributed warnings and a reduction in tobacco use in the first, scientific sense. The only direct or scientific evidence offered of the link between advertising bans and smoking reduction consisted of a report of the New Zealand Toxic Substances Board entitled *Health or Tobacco: An End to Tobacco Advertising and Promotion* (1989), which reviewed the effect of advertising restrictions in 33 countries and concluded that there was a correlation between the degree of restrictions imposed in each country and decline in tobacco use. * * * The trial judge, after lengthy consideration, rejected this evidence. The report was found to contain serious methodological errors which rendered it "for all intents and purposes devoid of any probative value". * * *

This leaves the question of whether there is less direct evidence that suggests as a matter of "reason" or "logic" that advertising bans and package warnings lead to a reduction in tobacco use. * * *

The question is whether this evidence establishes that it is reasonable or logical to conclude that there is a causal link between tobacco advertising and unattributed health warnings and tobacco use. * * * Why would tobacco companies spend great sums on advertising if not to increase the consumption of tobacco, it asks?

To this the tobacco companies reply that their advertising is directed not at increasing the size of the total market but at obtaining a larger share of the existing market. The evidence indicates that one of the thrusts of the advertising programs of tobacco companies is securing a larger market share, but there is also evidence suggesting that advertising is used to increase the total market. * * *

On the other hand, there does not appear to be any causal connection between the objective of decreasing tobacco consumption and the absolute prohibition on the use of a tobacco trade mark on articles other than tobacco products which is mandated by s. 8 of the Act. * * * I find that s. 8 of the Act fails the rational connection test.

As the second step in the proportionality analysis, the government must show that the measures at issue impair the right of free expression as little as reasonably possible in order to achieve the legislative objective. * * *

* * *

I turn first to the prohibition on advertising contained in s. 4 of the Act. It is, as has been observed, complete. It bans all forms of advertising of Canadian tobacco products while explicitly exempting all foreign advertising of non-Canadian products which are sold in Canada. * * * Smoking is a legal activity yet consumers are deprived of an important means of learning about product availability to suit their preferences and to compare brand content with an aim to reducing the risk to their health.

* * * A full prohibition will only be constitutionally acceptable under the minimal impairment stage of the analysis where the government can show that only a full prohibi-

tion will enable it to achieve its objective. Where, as here, no evidence is adduced to show that a partial ban would be less effective than a total ban, the justification required by s. 1 to save the violation of free speech is not established.

As noted in my analysis of rational connection, while one may conclude as a matter of reason and logic that lifestyle advertising is designed to increase consumption, there is no indication that purely informational or brand preference advertising would have this effect. The government had before it a variety of less intrusive measures when it enacted the total ban on advertising, including: a partial ban which would allow information and brand preference advertising; a ban on lifestyle advertising only; measures such as those in Quebec's *Consumer Protection Act*, R.S.Q., c. P-40.1, to prohibit advertising aimed at children and adolescents; and labelling requirements only. * * *

* * * The government presented no evidence in defence of the total ban, no evidence comparing its effects to less invasive bans.

* * *

The government is clearly justified in requiring the appellants to place warnings on tobacco packaging. The question is whether it was necessary to prohibit the appellants from attributing the message to the government and whether it was necessary to prevent the appellants from placing on their packaging any information other than that allowed by the regulations.

As with the advertising ban, it was for the government to show that the unattributed warning, as opposed to an attributed warning, was required to achieve its objective of reducing tobacco consumption among those who might read the warning. Similarly, it was for the government to show why permitting tobacco companies to place additional information on tobacco packaging, such as a statement announcing lower tar levels, would defeat the government's objective. * * *

* * *

I have found ss. 4, 8 and 9 of the *Tobacco Products Control Act* constitute unjustified infringements on free expression. These provisions spearhead the scheme under the Act and cannot be severed cleanly from other provisions dealing with promotion and trade mark usage, ss. 5 and 6. I would consequently hold that ss. 4, 5, 6, 8, and 9 are inconsistent with the *Charter* and hence are of no force or effect by reason of s. 52 of the *Constitution Act, 1982*.

The reasons of La Forest, L'Heureux-Dube and Gonthier JJ. were delivered by *La Forest J.* (dissenting) [In the original the dissent precedes the majority opinion. The dissenting justices set out at length and in detail evidence from Canadian and international sources documenting the health hazards of tobacco].

* * *

Why, then, has Parliament chosen to prohibit tobacco advertising, and not tobacco consumption itself? In my view, there is a compelling explanation for this choice. It is not that Parliament was attempting to intrude colourably upon provincial jurisdiction but that a prohibition upon the sale or consumption of tobacco is not a practical policy option at this time. It must be kept in mind that the very nature of tobacco consumption makes government action problematic. Many scientists agree that the nicotine found in tobacco is a powerfully addictive drug. * * * Given the addictive nature of tobacco products, and the fact that over one-third of Canadians smoke, it is clear that a legislative prohibition on the sale and use of tobacco products would be highly impractical. Indeed a prohibition on the manufacture and sale of tobacco products would likely lead many smokers to resort to alternative, and illegal, sources of supply. As legislators in this country discovered earlier in the century, the prohibition of a social drug such as tobacco or alcohol leads almost inevitably to an increase in smuggling and crime.

However, the mere fact that it is not practical or realistic to implement a prohibition on the use or manufacture of tobacco products does not mean that Parliament cannot, or should not, resort to other intermediate policy options. * * * If we are stopping short of actually banning the sale of this hazardous product, what steps are we prepared to take to cut down on its use over the next number of years? Certainly, a ban on tobacco advertising is one strategy which is supportable in the move to cut down on the consumption of tobacco.

* * *

While it is clear that cigarette sales cannot be banned at this time, it is equally clear that the production, distribution and sale of cigarettes should no longer be considered in the same light as the production, distribution and sale of other products. It seems reasonable to introduce whatever steps are feasible to progressively eliminate the promotion of cigarette sales and preparations should be made to assist growers and others affected by reductions in cigarette sales. It is also desirable to increase educational efforts to discourage cigarette smoking and to expand activities to make cigarette smoking less hazardous for those who continue to smoke.

* * *

* * * [I]t is difficult to believe that Canadian tobacco companies would spend over 75 million dollars every year on advertising if they did not know that advertising increases the consumption of their product. In response to this observation, the appellants insist that their advertising is directed solely toward preserving and expanding brand loyalty among smokers, and not toward expanding the tobacco market by inducing non-smokers to start. In my view, the appellants' claim is untenable for two principal reasons. First, brand loyalty alone will not, and logically cannot, maintain the profit levels of these companies if the overall number of smokers declines. A proportionate piece of a smaller pie is still a smaller piece. * * *

Second, even if this Court were to accept the appellants' brand loyalty argument, the appellants have not adequately addressed the further problem that even commercials targeted solely at brand loyalty may also serve as inducements for smokers not to quit. The government's concern with the health effects of tobacco can quite reasonably extend not only to potential smokers who are considering starting, but also to current smokers who would prefer to quit but cannot.

* * *

However, it is not necessary to rely solely upon common sense to reach this conclusion because there was, in any event, sufficient evidence adduced at trial to bear out the rational connection between advertising and consumption. * * *

* * *

Perhaps the most compelling evidence concerning the connection between advertising and consumption can be found in the internal marketing documents prepared by the tobacco manufacturers themselves. Although the appellants steadfastly argue that their marketing efforts are directed solely at maintaining and expanding brand loyalty among adult smokers, these documents show otherwise. In particular, the following general conclusions can be drawn from these documents: the tobacco companies are concerned about a shrinking tobacco market and recognize that an "advocacy thrust" is necessary to maintain the size of the overall market; the companies understand that, in order to maintain the overall numbers of smokers, they must reassure current smokers and make their product attractive to the young and to non-smokers; they also recognize that advertising is critical to maintaining the size of the market because it serves to reinforce the social acceptability of smoking by identifying it with glamour, affluence, youthfulness and vitality.

* * *

The internal marketing documents introduced at trial strongly suggest that the tobacco companies perceive advertising to be a cornerstone of their strategy to reassure current smokers and expand the market by attracting new smokers, primarily among the young. * * *

* * *

Taking into account the legislative context, it is my view that the measures adopted under the Act satisfy the *Oakes* minimal impairment requirement. It must be kept in mind that the infringed right at issue in these cases is the right of tobacco corporations to advertise the only legal product sold in Canada which, when used precisely as directed, harms and often kills those who use it. As I discussed above, I have no doubt that Parliament could validly have employed the criminal law power to prohibit the manufacture and sale of tobacco products, and that such a prohibition would have been fully justifiable under the *Charter*. There is no right to sell harmful products in Canada, nor should there be. Thus, in choosing to prohibit solely the advertisement of tobacco products, it is clear that Parliament in fact adopted a relatively *unintrusive* legislative approach to the control of tobacco products. Indeed, the scope of conduct prohibited under the Act is narrow. * * * The prohibition under this Act serves only to prevent these companies from employing sophisticated marketing and social psychology techniques to induce consumers to purchase their products. * * *

* * *

The reasonableness of Parliament's decision to prohibit tobacco advertising has been amply borne out by parallel developments in the international community before and after the passage of the Act. It is of great significance, in my view, that over 20 democratic nations have, in recent years, adopted complete prohibitions on tobacco advertising similar to those adopted under the Act, including Australia, New Zealand, Norway, Finland and France. It is also of significance that the constitutionality of full advertising prohibitions have been upheld by the French *Conseil constitutionnel* to be constitutionally valid and by American courts. The decisions of the American courts, which have traditionally been jealous guardians of the right to freedom of expression, are particularly instructive in this context because they demonstrate that the adoption of a full prohibition upon tobacco advertising is perceived as neither novel nor radical in other democratic nations. * * *

* * *

Notes

1. Following its defeat in this case, the Canadian government in 1997 reenacted advertising legislation aimed at lifestyle rather than brand-name advertising. In litigation challenging this legislation, it introduced evidence totalling nearly 10,000 pages of transcript and 988 exhibits, a step it had not taken in the first round of litigation. Challenges to the new legislation were rejected. Currently Canada has one the most restrictive ap-

proaches to tobacco of any country in the world, including very high (by US standards) excise taxes. Canada has not had successful tobacco class action cases like those in the United States; indeed no other country has. See Jeff Berryman, Canadian Reflections on the Tobacco Wars: Some Unintended Condquences of Mass Tort Litigation, 53 *Int. & Comp. L. Q.* 579 (2004). See also, Andrei Sirabionian, Why Tobacco Litigation has not Been Successful in the United Kingdom: A Comparative Analysis of Tobacco Litigation in the United States and the United Kingdom, 25 *Nw.J. Int'l L. & Bus.* 485 (2005).

2. In 2000, the European Court of Justice struck down the EU Tobacco Advertising Directive, which banned tobacco television advertising and sponsorship. Case C-376/98, *Federal Republic of Germany v. Parliament and Council*, 2000 E.C.R. I-8419. It did so primarily for federalism reasons. The Court held that the primary goal of the legislation was to protect public health, and that the EU had not jurisdiction over public health, which was the province of the separate states, and that television advertising was primarily local, and thus free trade was not involved. The ECJ, on the other hand, upheld the EU Tobacco Products Directive, which regulated tar, nicotine, and carbon monoxide and label warnings regarding these toxins and prohibited the use of terms like "mild" or "light" for tobacco products. Case 491/01, *The Queen v. Sec'y of State for Health ex parte British American Tobacco (Investments) Ltd.*, 2002 E.C.R. I-11453. The Court held that the Directive was legitimately aimed at trade. The EU subsequently adopted an advertising ban covering print media, the internet, radio and international sporting events, which seems likely, as of this writing, to be upheld. See Fernanda Nicola & Fabio Marchetti, Constitutionalizing Tobacco: The Ambivalence of European Federalism, 46 *Harv. Int'l L. J.* 507 (2005).

3. Tobacco use is clearly on the decline in the world's wealthy countries. Tobacco use among males age 15 and over in the United States declined from 52% in 1965 to 26% in 1999, in the U.K. from 61% in 1960 to 28% in 1998. Even in Japan, it has declined from 81% in 1960 to 54% in 2000. See, World Health Organization, *The Tobacco Atlas*, http://www.who.int/tobacco/statistics/tobacco_atlas/en/. To what is this decline attributable? Legal regulation? Cultural changes? Public health education? In much of the developing world, on the other hand, smoking rates are high and rising. All ten of the countries with the highest combined rates of male and female smoking are now in Eastern Europe, Asia, and Africa. Indeed, western tobacco companies are making up much of the profits they have lost in the West in the developing world. What, if any, legal response to this issue is appropriate?

D. Research Involving Human Subjects

Another context in which the rights of the individual and the interests of society can come in conflict is research. Biomedical research is essential if the scientific development of medicine is to continue, and valid research is sometimes only possible if human "guinea pigs" are available. But even before the Nuremberg trials exposed the horrors that resulted from unethical human experimentation in Nazi Germany, research involving human subjects had already resulted in abuses of the rights of research subjects elsewhere as well.

Biomedical research is regulated first and foremost at the national level. Research is often funded by governments, which in turn take responsibility for protecting research subjects. In the United States, for example, the Common Rule (46 C.F.R. §§45.101–46.409) governs research funded by the federal government. Drugs and medical devices developed through research must also be approved by national governments before they can be sold. These authorities usually require that research relied on in developing the drugs meet certain standards of conduct. Food and Drug Administration Regulations in the United States, for example, impose requirements similar to the federal common rule. (See 21 C.F.R. Parts 50 and 56.).

Increasingly, however, research takes place on an international scale. Drug and device manufacturers are not satisfied to market in only a single country, but want to sell to the entire world. They also do not want to have to conduct separate drug trials for every approving authority, but rather want to carry out their research once, and then have it accepted everywhere. The European Union has already established the European Agency for Evaluation of Medicinal Products, which offers "one stop shopping" to pharmaceutical companies that want to sell to the European Community. Beyond this, the International Conference of Harmonization is attempting to harmonize pharmaceutical regulations for the world's three largest markets, the United States, Europe, and Japan, so that manufacturer has one set of regulations with which to comply. See Ileana Dominguez-Urban, Harmonization in the Regulation of Pharmaceutical Research and Human Rights: The Need to Think Globally, 30 *Cornell Int'l L. J.* 245 (1997).

Though regulation of biomedical research is only now being harmonized, international statements on research ethics have long been available. Among the earliest of these was the Nuremberg Code itself, which begins "The voluntary consent of the human subject is absolutely essential." Such consent could only be obtained after the research subject is fully informed about the nature and risks of the experiment. See George J. Annas and Michael A. Grodin, *The Nazi Doctors and the Nuremberg Code* (1992).

The Nuremberg Code, with its emphasis on the protection of patients, has been largely eclipsed as an international reference point by the World Medical Association's Declaration of Helsinki, first promulgated in 1964, and revised several times since. Though the Declaration is in fact the statement of a professional association, and not law in any sense, it is widely regarded throughout the world as a foundational document of research ethics.

World Medical Association, Declaration of Helsinki, Ethical Principles for Medical Research Involving Human Subjects

Adopted by the 18th WMA General Assembly, Helsinki, Finland, June 1964, as revised 1975, 1983, 1989, 1996 and 2000.

A. Introduction

1. The World Medical Association has developed the Declaration of Helsinki as a statement of ethical principles to provide guidance to physicians and other participants in medical research involving human subjects. Medical research involving human subjects includes research on identifiable human material or identifiable data.

2. It is the duty of the physician to promote and safeguard the health of the people. The physician's knowledge and conscience are dedicated to the fulfillment of this duty.

3. The Declaration of Geneva of the World Medical Association binds the physician with the words, "The health of my patient will be my first consideration," and the International Code of Medical Ethics declares that, "A physician shall act only in the patient's interest when providing medical care which might have the effect of weakening the physical and mental condition of the patient."

4. Medical progress is based on research which ultimately must rest in part on experimentation involving human subjects.

5. In medical research on human subjects, considerations related to the well-being of the human subject should take precedence over the interests of science and society.

* * *

8. Medical research is subject to ethical standards that promote respect for all human beings and protect their health and rights. Some research populations are vulnerable and need special protection. The particular needs of the economically and medically disadvantaged must be recognized. Special attention is also required for those who cannot give or refuse consent for themselves, for those who may be subject to giving consent under duress, for those who will not benefit personally from the research and for those for whom the research is combined with care.

9. Research Investigators should be aware of the ethical, legal and regulatory requirements for research on human subjects in their own countries as well as applicable international requirements. No national ethical, legal or regulatory requirement should be allowed to reduce or eliminate any of the protections for human subjects set forth in this Declaration.

B. Basic Principles for all Medical Research

10. It is the duty of the physician in medical research to protect the life, health, privacy, and dignity of the human subject.

11. Medical research involving human subjects must conform to generally accepted scientific principles, be based on a thorough knowledge of the scientific literature, other relevant sources of information, and on adequate laboratory and, where appropriate, animal experimentation.

* * *

13. The design and performance of each experimental procedure involving human subjects should be clearly formulated in an experimental protocol. This protocol should be submitted for consideration, comment, guidance, and where appropriate, approval to a specially appointed ethical review committee, which must be independent of the investigator, the sponsor or any other kind of undue influence. This independent committee should be in conformity with the laws and regulations of the country in which the research experiment is performed. The committee has the right to monitor ongoing trials. The researcher has the obligation to provide monitoring information to the committee, especially any serious adverse events. The researcher should also submit to the committee, for review, information regarding funding, sponsors, institutional affiliations, other potential conflicts of interest and incentives for subjects.

* * *

15. Medical research involving human subjects should be conducted only by scientifically qualified persons and under the supervision of a clinically competent medical person. The responsibility for the human subject must always rest with a medically qualified person and never rest on the subject of the research, even though the subject has given consent.

16. Every medical research project involving human subjects should be preceded by careful assessment of predictable risks and burdens in comparison with foreseeable benefits to the subject or to others. This does not preclude the participation of healthy volunteers in medical research. The design of all studies should be publicly available.

17. Physicians should abstain from engaging in research projects involving human subjects unless they are confident that the risks involved have been adequately assessed and can be satisfactorily managed. Physicians should cease any investigation if the risks are found to outweigh the potential benefits or if there is conclusive proof of positive and beneficial results.

18. Medical research involving human subjects should only be conducted if the importance of the objective outweighs the inherent risks and burdens to the subject. This is especially important when the human subjects are healthy volunteers.

19. Medical research is only justified if there is a reasonable likelihood that the populations in which the research is carried out stand to benefit from the results of the research.

20. The subjects must be volunteers and informed participants in the research project.

21. The right of research subjects to safeguard their integrity must always be respected. Every precaution should be taken to respect the privacy of the subject, the confidentiality of the patient's information and to minimize the impact of the study on the subject's physical and mental integrity and on the personality of the subject.

22. In any research on human beings, each potential subject must be adequately informed of the aims, methods, sources of funding, any possible conflicts of interest, institutional affiliations of the researcher, the anticipated benefits and potential risks of the study and the discomfort it may entail. The subject should be informed of the right to abstain from participation in the study or to withdraw consent to participate at any time without reprisal. After ensuring that the subject has understood the information, the physician should then obtain the subject's freely-given informed consent, preferably in writing. If the consent cannot be obtained in writing, the non-written consent must be formally documented and witnessed.

23. When obtaining informed consent for the research project the physician should be particularly cautious if the subject is in a dependent relationship with the physician or may consent under duress. In that case the informed consent should be obtained by a well-informed physician who is not engaged in the investigation and who is completely independent of this relationship.

24. For a research subject who is legally incompetent, physically or mentally incapable of giving consent or is a legally incompetent minor, the investigator must obtain informed consent from the legally authorized representative in accordance with applicable law. These groups should not be included in research unless the research is necessary to promote the health of the population represented and this research cannot instead be performed on legally competent persons.

25. When a subject deemed legally incompetent, such as a minor child, is able to give assent to decisions about participation in research, the investigator must obtain that assent in addition to the consent of the legally authorized representative.

26. Research on individuals from whom it is not possible to obtain consent, including proxy or advance consent, should be done only if the physical/mental condition that prevents obtaining informed consent is a necessary characteristic of the research population. The specific reasons for involving research subjects with a condition that renders them unable to give informed consent should be stated in the experimental protocol for consideration and approval of the review committee. The protocol should state that consent to remain in the research should be obtained as soon as possible from the individual or a legally authorized surrogate.

27. Both authors and publishers have ethical obligations. In publication of the results of research, the investigators are obliged to preserve the accuracy of the results. Negative as

well as positive results should be published or otherwise publicly available. Sources of funding, institutional affiliations and any possible conflicts of interest should be declared in the publication. Reports of experimentation not in accordance with the principles laid down in this Declaration should not be accepted for publication.

C. Additional Principles for Medical Research Combined with Medical Care

28. The physician may combine medical research with medical care, only to the extent that the research is justified by its potential prophylactic, diagnostic or therapeutic value. When medical research is combined with medical care, additional standards apply to protect the patients who are research subjects.

29. The benefits, risks, burdens and effectiveness of a new method should be tested against those of the best current prophylactic, diagnostic, and therapeutic methods. This does not exclude the use of placebo, or no treatment, in studies where no proven prophylactic, diagnostic or therapeutic method exists.

30. At the conclusion of the study, every patient entered into the study should be assured of access to the best proven prophylactic, diagnostic and therapeutic methods identified by the study.

31. The physician should fully inform the patient which aspects of the care are related to the research. The refusal of a patient to participate in a study must never interfere with the patient-physician relationship.

32. In the treatment of a patient, where proven prophylactic, diagnostic and therapeutic methods do not exist or have been ineffective, the physician, with informed consent from the patient, must be free to use unproven or new prophylactic, diagnostic and therapeutic measures, if in the physician's judgement it offers hope of saving life, re-establishing health or alleviating suffering. Where possible, these measures should be made the object of research, designed to evaluate their safety and efficacy. In all cases, new information should be recorded and, where appropriate, published. The other relevant guidelines of this Declaration should be followed.

* * *

Note

The Helsinki Declaration has been roundly criticized as having "endorsed shifting the focus of protection of the human subjects in medical research from the protection of human rights through informed consent to the protection of patient welfare through physician responsibility," and as having "attempted to undermine the primacy of subject consent in the Nuremberg Code and displace it with the paternalistic values of the traditional doctor-patient relationship." George J. Annas & Michael A. Grodin, Medical Ethics and Human Rights: Legacies of Nuremberg, 3 *Hofstra L. & Pol'y Symp.* 111, 116 (1999). Do you read the Declaration in this way? See also, *Freedom and Control of Biomedical Research: The Planned Revision of the Declaration of Helsinki* (Erwin Deutsch and Jochen Taupitz, eds., 2000).

Another recent statement on research ethics is the European Convention on Human Rights and Biomedicine. This document, promulgated by the Council of Europe (again, not to be confused with the European Union), is binding upon signators, though to date many European nations (including Germany and the United Kingdom) have not signed it. How does it resemble and differ from the Helsinki declaration? Is it more or less protective of research subjects?

European Convention on Human Rights and Biomedicine, Oviedo, 1997

Council of Europe, Convention for the Protection of Human Rights and Dignity of the Human Being with Regard to the Application of Biology and Medicine

Chapter I—General provisions

1. Parties to this Convention shall protect the dignity and identity of all human beings and guarantee everyone, without discrimination, respect for their integrity and other rights and fundamental freedoms with regard to the application of biology and medicine.

Each Party shall take in its internal law the necessary measures to give effect to the provisions of this Convention.

2. The interests and welfare of the human being shall prevail over the sole interest of society or science.

* * *

Chapter II—Consent

5. An intervention in the health field may only be carried out after the person concerned has given free and informed consent to it.

* * *

Chapter IV—Human genome

* * *

13. An intervention seeking to modify the human genome may only be undertaken for preventive, diagnostic or therapeutic purposes and only if its aim is not to introduce any modification in the genome of any descendants.

* * *

Chapter V—Scientific research

15. Scientific research in the field of biology and medicine shall be carried out freely, subject to the provisions of this Convention and the other legal provisions ensuring the protection of the human being.

16. Research on a person may only be undertaken if all the following conditions are met:

i. there is no alternative of comparable effectiveness to research on humans;

ii. the risks which may be incurred by that person are not disproportionate to the potential benefits of the research;

iii. the research project has been approved by the competent body after independent examination of its scientific merit, including assessment of the importance of the aim of the research, and multidisciplinary review of its ethical acceptability;

iv. the persons undergoing research have been informed of their rights and the safeguards prescribed by law for their protection;

v. the necessary consent as provided for under Article 5 has been given expressly, specifically and is documented. Such consent may be freely withdrawn at any time.

17.1. Research on a person without the capacity to consent as stipulated in Article 5 may be undertaken only if all the following conditions are met:

i. the conditions laid down in Article 16, sub-paragraphs i to iv, are fulfilled;

ii. the results of the research have the potential to produce real and direct benefit to his or her health;

iii. research of comparable effectiveness cannot be carried out on individuals capable of giving consent;

iv. the necessary authorisation provided for under Article 6 has been given specifically and in writing; and

v. the person concerned does not object.

2. Exceptionally and under the protective conditions prescribed by law, where the research has not the potential to produce results of direct benefit to the health of the person concerned, such research may be authorised subject to the conditions laid down in paragraph 1, sub-paragraphs i, iii, iv and v above, and to the following additional conditions:

i. the research has the aim of contributing, through significant improvement in the scientific understanding of the individual's condition, disease or disorder, to the ultimate attainment of results capable of conferring benefit to the person concerned or to other persons in the same age category or afflicted with the same disease or disorder or having the same condition.

ii. the research entails only minimal risk and minimal burden for the individual concerned.

18.1. Where the law allows research on embryos *in vitro*, it shall ensure adequate protection of the embryo.

2. The creation of human embryos for research purposes is prohibited.

* * *

Notes

1. See on the European Convention, Henriette D.C. Roscam Abbing, The Convention on Human Rights and Biomedicine, An Appraisal of the Council of Europe Convention, 5 *European J. Health L.* 377 (1998). See generally, considering regulation of human subjects research in Europe, Dominique Sprumont, Legal Protection of Human Research Subjects in Europe, 6 *European J. Health L.* 25 (1999), and in Spain, Jaime Vidal-Martínez, The Protection of the Peson in Medical Research in the Spanish Law, 6 *European J. Health L.* 249 (1999).

2. Another important statement of research ethics is the International Guidelines for Biomedical Research Involving Human Subjects, published by the World Health Organization and the Council for International Organizations of Medical Sciences, usually referred to as the CIOMS Guidelines. These Guidelines focus particularly on research carried out in Developing Nations. The CIOMS Guidelines are reproduced in an excellent

overview of ethical issues in research, with an international focus: *The Ethics of Research Involving Human Subjects: Facing the 21st Century* (Harold Y. Vanderpool, ed., 1996).

3. Though research ethical codes and regulations often look quite similar on their face, subtle differences in emphasis often become important in practice. The following excerpt examines differences in the context of one particular problem, the use of placebos in biomedical research.

The Globalization of Health Law: The Case of Placebo-based Research

Timothy Stoltzfus Jost, American Journal of Law & Medicine, vol. 26, pp. 175–84 (2000)

* * *

The research that grounds the development of new drugs necessarily requires the use of human subjects. This research thus raises important ethical issues, indeed human rights issues. Research is increasingly taking place on an international basis as large, multicenter, trials become more common. Though there are international expressions of principle that address these issues, most notably the Revised Declaration of Helsinki on Research Involving Human Subjects, research, including international research, is also addressed by substantive regulations governing research at the national level. These regulatory instruments reflect different approaches to the ethical issues grounding human subjects research.

* * *

An ideal case study for understanding the globalization of health law is the regulation of placebo-controlled human subjects research. The word placebo comes from the ecclesiastical Latin, meaning "I shall please." It came to be used in medical practice as a term describing "all medicine prescribed more to please the patient than for its therapeutic effectiveness." In modern clinical research, placebos are inert substances, prepared so as to appear identical to the active substances being tested, which are provided to a control group in a randomized trial to give the control group an experience as similar as possible to that of the investigational group, except for the presence of the active ingredients being tested. In theory, any differences in response between the placebo control and investigational group (if the members of the two groups are assigned randomly and their identity is blinded both to the researchers and to the participants) is due to the active ingredients tested and not to a placebo effect or to chance.

Placebo-controlled studies are often championed by drug or medical device companies, who are often more interested in demonstrating that their product works than in comparing its effectiveness with that of existing drugs or devices. Placebo-controlled studies are also, however, often demanded by regulatory agencies, who believe that placebo-controlled studies offer the most unassailable evidence of the effectiveness of a product.

Those who oppose the use of placebos in clinical trials argue that use of placebos violates all four of the principles generally thought to underlie bioethics—beneficence, nonmaleficence, respect for personal autonomy, and justice. First (and this is the argument that flows most directly from the Helsinki declaration) controlled trials in which placebos are administered to the control group deny potentially beneficial treatment to that group. It is only ethically permissible to test a new drug or procedure on humans if there is some reason to believe that it is efficacious. But if this is true, intentionally denying a potentially beneficial treatment to one arm of the research study is at least potentially problematic. * * *

If the control group is not only administered a placebo, but is also first deprived of standard treatment (i.e. subjected to a wash-out period), the research might not only violate the principle of beneficence, but also the nonmaleficence (do no harm) principle. This may also be true if a clinical trial is permitted to continue beyond the point where it becomes clear that the proposed treatment is in fact efficacious, or if participants in the trial are not "rescued" if their health deteriorates dramatically while under placebo treatment. Administering potentially effective treatment to one group, while intentionally denying it to another, also raises justice issues.

The final cluster of arguments against the use of placebos in controlled trials are based on the principle of autonomy. A general argument against placebos in treatment is that their use is deceptive. It is commonly argued that this is not true when the placebo is used for research, because participants in placebo-controlled clinical trials are informed at the outset that they may be receiving a placebo. Though the research subjects are deceived, they are partners in the deception. Nonetheless, there is often a question as to whether participants in clinical trials who receive placebos fully understand and accept the possibility that this will be the case. * * * There is also an element of duress that makes consent questionable in situations where participating in a placebo-controlled trial is the only chance a subject has to obtain potentially helpful treatment. * * * Some of the worst abuses of placebo-controlled research have occurred in the context of research involving psychiatric conditions. Finally, autonomy cannot be a complete justification for pursuing hazardous research. It is the responsibility of researchers not to put research subjects in a position where their health or well-being would be compromised, even if the subject consents.

Ethical arguments in support of placebo-based research tend to be less principled and more pragmatic. They often begin with the assertion that in many—perhaps most—situations, placebo-controlled research is the most valid and efficient means to establishing the efficacy of a drug or procedure. * * * Placebo-controlled clinical trials can often be conducted more rapidly and using smaller populations than clinical trials using other controls, such as active controls.

Moreover, advocates argue, the statistical difficulties confronting active-control equivalency studies render placebo-controlled superiority studies the only feasible approach to clinical trials in many cases. As one can only ethically ask human subjects to participate in research if the research shows promise of establishing the effectiveness of treatments, non-placebo-controlled research is by definition unethical if it cannot scientifically establish the validity of its results. * * *

Those who argue that placebo-based research is necessary also contend that it is rarely harmful. For conditions for which there is no preexisting standard treatment, or (as is often the case) for which the standard treatment has not been validated, treatment by placebo may be as good as any other treatment, perhaps better. If the treatment provided to the investigational arm of the study turns out to be harmful, moreover, the subjects who received placebos will be the lucky ones. In any event, they argue, it is inaccurate to assert that subjects who receive investigational treatments are provided with "effective treatments" denied to those who find themselves in the placebo group—by definition the investigation is being done because we do not know whether a treatment is effective or not. A final argument that placebo-controlled investigations are ethically permissible is based on consent—each subject in such trials understands that he or she might be receiving a placebo rather than an active agent, and yet has consented to participate. To deny subjects the right to participate in a placebo-controlled trial that might assist in the development of treatments that might improve their own health and the health of others, is to deny them autonomy.

* * *

Placebo-controlled research is recognized as potentially legitimate under the Helsinki Declaration (and by other international statements of principles governing research). Since 1975, however the Revised Declaration has provided that "In any medical study, every patient—including those of a control group, if any—should be assured of the best proven diagnostic and therapeutic method." It further states: "This does not exclude the use of inert placebo in studies where no proven diagnostic or therapeutic method exists." These provisions have been widely interpreted to place strict limits on the possibilities of placebo-based research. The commentary to Guideline 14 of the Council for International Organizations of Medical Science, interprets the provision to mean "if there is already an approved and accepted drug for the condition that a candidate drug is designed to treat, placebo for controls usually cannot be justified."

* * *

Most authorities who have examined the issue of placebo-controlled studies conclude that they are ethically permissible in at least some situations. The American Medical Association, in Ethical Opinion E-2.075, states that "Used appropriately, placebo controls can safely provide valuable data and should continue to be considered in design of clinical trials." The AMA recommended, however that researchers initiating placebo-controlled studies: 1) be extremely thorough in obtaining informed consent from patients in such trials, 2) carefully evaluate study protocols to determine whether placebo controls are necessary or whether alternative study designs would be appropriate, and 3) minimize the time patients are given placebos, and monitor the study and terminate it early where indicated by positive or negative results. The AMA also acknowledged that placebo controls would generally not be appropriate where protocols involved conditions causing death or irreversible damage or severe or painful symptoms, and that there were conditions where placebo controls could not be ethically justified. It also stated, however, that the use of placebo controls could more easily be justified where standard therapies were attended by severe side effects. The AMA's position on placebo-controlled research is generally held by American authors, though some would opt for a more rigorous standard.

Authorities from outside the United States, however, tend to be more conservative. Professor Deutsch states in his standard German treatise, *Medizinrecht:* "The use of placebos is only permitted if either a minor problem is involved, perhaps headaches or insomnia, or where a standard treatment is not available." and "Placebo experiments are ... not permitted when a subject suffers from a serious disease for which there is an effective medication."

This difference in approach was amply demonstrated by country reports submitted at a conference on revision of the Declaration of Helsinki held in Goettingen Germany in 1999. Dr. Rosenau's German report concurred that "in Germany the placebo-controlled study is the exception." Prof. Angelo stated in his country report from New Zealand that "placebo-controlled trials are permitted by ethics committees only if there is no treatment available or there is merely minor discomfort." Dr. Wildhaber's report stated that the Swiss law, like the American, places considerable emphasis on fully informed consent, but also requires that the ethical obligation of the treating physician to the interests of the patient take precedence over research interests, which would normally preclude the withdrawal or withholding of effective diagnostic or treatment measures. Prof. Monteiro stated that in Portugal placebo-based research is permitted in the therapeutic context, but that it is only possible if consent is obtained, and there are either doubts about the real efficacy of treatment or the symptoms of the treated condition do not cause undue discomfort and the course of treatment is not excessively long. Prof. Romeo-Casabona related that Spain permits placebo-controlled research, but only where treatment by a placebo would not "interfere unnecessarily with the course of the illness by prolonging or aggravating it or that would result in irreversible injury." Prof. Mémeteau related that France rejects double-blind placebo-controlled research protocols because it is impossible to obtain informed consent from a patient if neither the patient nor the researcher know whether the patient will be receiving the investigational intervention or not. Prof. Blackie reported that in the United Kingdom, placebo-controlled studies are permitted, but only if there is genuine uncertainty over whether the investigational treatment is better than a placebo, there is not agreed alternative treatment of greater therapeutic value, the investigational intervention is "of significant importance," it is reasonably possible that the proposed treatment is better than placebo, and seriously ill patients will not be left untreated. Finally, Prof. Urakaw's report stated that in Japan placebo-controlled research is only permitted "When either no standard treatment existed or no harm to the patient is anticipated. If these conditions are breached, civil and criminal liability are possible." * * *

The legal situation with respect to the role of placebo-controlled research in securing approvals for new pharmaceuticals also varies somewhat from country to country. In the United States, new drugs and medical devices must be approved by the federal Food and Drug Administration before they can be marketed. The federal Food and Drug law requires that "substantial evidence" of the effectiveness of new drugs must be established by "adequate and well-controlled investigations." Federal regulations defining "adequate and well controlled studies" provide that such studies "must use a design that permits a valid comparison with a control to provide a quantitative assessment of drug effect," and "placebo concurrent control" appears first on the subsequent list of "recognized" types of controls. * * * Dr. Robert Temple, who for years has been regarded to be a spokesperson for the Food and Drug Administration (FDA) on the issue, has on several occasions taken the position that "Placebo Controls are often necessary to get a true measure of a drug's effectiveness." Indeed, the FDA's position is understood to be that placebo controls are the "gold standard" for clinical trials. * * *

European Community Law seems less attached to placebo-controlled trials. Council Directive 75/318/EEC of 20 May 1975, relating to "analytical, pharmaco-toxicological and clinical standards and protocols in respect of the testing of proprietary medicines" specified, with respect to the conduct of clinical trials, that "The design of the trials will vary from case to case and also will depend on ethical considerations; thus it may in some instances, be more pertinent to compare the therapeutic effect of a new proprietary medicinal product with that of an established medicinal product of proven therapeutic value rather than with the effect of a placebo." This suggests that placebo-controlled tests are the norm, active-control tests the exception. Commission Directive 91/507/EEC of 19 July 1991, modifying Council Directive 75/318/EEC drops this language, providing that "All clinical trials shall be carried out in accordance with the ethical principles laid down in the current revision of the Declaration of Helsinki" and listing placebo controls as one of several forms of control groups for controlled trials. Council Recommendation 87/176/EEC, which incorporates Guidelines for procedures for establishing the efficacy of several specific types of medications, advises the use of placebo-controlled studies under certain circumstances. Council Recommendation 2309/93 of 22 July 1993, establishing the European Agency for Evaluation of Medicinal Products does not address the issue of placebo-controlled clinical trials.

* * *

Notes

1. Does informed consent offer adequate protection for research subjects, or is some measure of "paternalistic" oversight of the conduct of research also necessary to afford full protection? Should certain kinds of research be always prohibited, such as placebo research to develop new products where treatments are available that are well established as effective, or research with life-threatening risks? Should certain populations—children, the mentally disabled, or prisoners—be off-limits for research? To what extent should research be permitted with fetuses or embryos? Why might different countries have different answers to these questions?

2. Research is increasingly being carried out on a global basis. Particularly problematic has been research in developing countries. On occasion there has been suspicion that research has been carried out in these countries to avoid the strict oversight imposed in developed nations. On other occasions, however, research has been conducted in developing nations because the products or procedures being developed are allegedly of value to the populations of these nations. When research is carried out, however, on populations with radically different cultures there are ample opportunities for misunderstanding. Where research is carried out on illiterate, or poor, or socially marginalized populations, there are also ample opportunities for exploitation. The following reading discusses these issues.

Towards Progress in Resolving Dilemmas in International Research Ethics

Solomon R. Benatar, Journal of Law, Medicine and Ethics, vol. 32, pp. 574, 574–75, 579–81 Winter 2004

* * *

In her recent review of agreements and controversies in international research ethics, Ruth Macklin has concluded that, despite seeming agreement on several issues, many different viewpoints persist. In her view it is unlikely that these will be resolved easily. I begin by listing the issues on which Macklin notes broad agreement, followed by a brief reference to the nature of remaining controversies (in italics).

• Research must be responsive to the needs of people in the community being studied. *How are decisions taken about what research to undertake in developing countries and how are these prioritized?*

• Research is needed on diseases that occur frequently in poor countries, especially when these cause high morbidity and mortality. *What sorts of study designs are acceptable? Can placebos be used and what comparative arms should be included?*

• It is unethical to exploit the vulnerable. *What specifically does it mean not to exploit people?*

• It is unacceptable to lower the ethical standards for research in developing countries. *What is the standard of care that should apply in research in developing countries? How is this defined and justified?*

* * * Researchers largely share a common scientific world-view and have a primary, if not exclusive interest in advancing knowledge. Underprivileged and deprived research subjects within traditional cultures tend to share a non-scientific world-view and have a predominant, and often even exclusive interest in receiving care for their illnesses. Although these differences in how people view medical research and access to health care lie along a spectrum and there may be much that is shared, the extent of such differences is not trivial and they are of practical importance in developing ethical policies for research. * * *

Anthropologists and social scientists have been critical of modern bioethics on the grounds that it is based on Western moral philosophy and western biomedical perspectives. An additional criticism is that bioethics is applied within a theoretical framework that emphasizes the application of scientifically rigorous medical care to people who are sufficiently autonomous to make self-interested decisions about themselves in a context of minimal social connectedness. Such a highly reductionist and individualistic approach takes insufficient consideration of the social and cultural context of illness or associated ethical dilemmas, isolates bioethical issues from spiritual perspectives and neglects the dynamic nature of relationships between individuals, their families and their community.

Some critics of modern bioethics favor a more embracing communitarian conception of the individual that acknowledges and values closer links with other people. As an example, the African notion of a person values links with the past (ancestors), the present (family and community), and with other animate beings within a "web of relations" that has been labeled as an "Eco-bio-communitarian perspective." Within this more embracing context of many traditional cultures, illness represents more than mechanical dysfunction, and understanding and dealing with illness requires an explanatory model with greater attention to the influence of external social interactions, luck, fate and magico-religious considerations.

These two views of people, within social relationships defined in a polarized manner either as individualistic or communitarian along a single dimension, have generated much debate in relation to cross-cultural research ethics. Some insist that the individualistic approach is the best universal model and that it must be rigorously applied in the research context. Others argue that this is a "particular rationality" about human life, one that is attractive in its abstract form but lacks resemblance to the real world in which people live. In addition it is argued that more attention should be paid to complex notions of social relationships, and in particular to potential exploitation of vulnerable subjects.

* * *

How are decisions taken about what research to undertake in developing countries and how are these prioritized?

In keeping with an approach that acknowledges that there are different forms of social relations and that understanding these and working with them offers greater prospects for resolving conflicting views the following could be advised. First, clinical trials in developing countries should be relevant to the health needs of the host country. Second, the design and conduct of trials should involve members of the host country in participatory partnerships of an emancipating nature. Third, prior evaluation should be made of whether study findings can, and will, be incorporated into local health care systems. These processes, involving dialogue and collaboration from the earliest stages of research design, are in a sense analogous to the idea of democratic deliberation, and could assist in explicating and justifying priorities in particular contexts.

What sorts of study designs are acceptable? Can placebos be used and what comparative arms should be included?

In my view it will not be possible to resolve the current debate about the use of placebos unless the different motives and world-views of those who argue for differing regulations regarding their use are considered. In addition, while general statements can be made about the use of placebos in research, their valid use in every conceivable setting cannot be deduced simply from a few sentences in research ethics guidelines. If we accept that abstract universal principles are valid; if we consider local factors to be relevant to the application of universal principles; and if we value the process of moral reasoning, then we must agree that in order to determine whether or not a placebo arm is justified, then careful consideration is required of potential harms and benefits in relation to studies designed to ask and answer specific questions in specific contexts. In those situations where morally valid reasons can be mounted for placebo-controlled trials, and where such studies are designed specifically for the benefit of local populations rather than as surrogates for acquiring information for wealthy countries (for example studies of "me too" drugs, the use of a placebo may be justified on rational grounds. The proviso is that utilitarian calculations for the benefit of whole groups of people (and with their agreement) should be constrained by the need to prevent harm to individuals, and to avoid the use of placebo when this may result in unnecessary suffering, avoidable injuries or death. Each study in which a placebo arm is anticipated should thus be considered on its merits, rather than precluded or allowed entirely on the basis of a bluntly designed clause in a declaration. Considerations of context are required aspects of moral reasoning in the application of universal principles in specific situations, and taking relevant moral factors into consideration does not entail moral relativism.

A simple definition of exploitation in the research context would include the following:

• Taking advantage of power differentials to do what researchers want to do and in any way they wish without consideration of the harms that may be perceived by research participants.

• Using research subjects as a means to achieving the ends of researchers (advancing knowledge) when the benefits of the research will not be fairly available to research participants and their communities.

• Undertaking studies in which minimal benefits accrue to participants and large benefits, especially financial, may accrue in the long term to research sponsors, thus failing to ensure fair balance of benefits and burdens to sponsors/researchers and research participants in the longer term.

• Denying participants post-trial use of therapies identified as beneficial in the trial in environments where such treatments would not otherwise be available.

To avoid exploitation priority should be given to trials that will provide useful knowledge for the host country, the balance of benefits and burdens should be fairly distributed and the benefits of research should be seen to flow into health care settings. Efforts should also be made to ensure that existing disparities are not entrenched by deflecting local human or material resources away from healthcare systems in host countries towards research.

What is the standard of care? How is this defined and how can it be justified?

The idea of a global universally applicable ethical framework for the standard of care in international research would be inclusive of at least the following features:

• Conducting research with the same respect for the dignity of all subjects wherever they are in the world—as reflected in treating them as ends in their own right and not using them merely to acquire knowledge that could be of benefit to others.

• Obtaining meaningful informed consent by structuring the process of obtaining consent within the linguistic and cultural framework of research subjects. Providing care for other diseases concomitantly afflicting research subjects for which treatment would not otherwise be available in impoverished settings and in this way enhancing the potential for community benefit to flow from research.

• The avoidance of exploitation as indicated above.

It has been further argued that such a globally reasoned universal standard of care can be translated into feasible local practices (reasoned contextual universalism). This would require the shaping an acceptable standard of care for a particular study through a deliberative scholarly process (not merely political haggling) among researchers and the community of research participants within respectful partnerships. Making progress on a continuous basis through successive research projects in local contexts could in this way improve health care and move the standard of care in research towards the reasoned global universal level.

Attempts to resolve the vexed question of the "standard of care" for research in developing countries by utilizing arguments totally within a single world-view are unlikely to convince those who have a different perspective on social relations and how these should influence social policy in research. Making progress towards narrowing the differences identified by Macklin requires giving due moral weight to morally significant contextual considerations, including the values of research participants, where these are not harmful and do not infringe on the physical and emotional integrity of others.

With regard to justification for a broader overall standard of care, several arguments have been offered. These include moral arguments that embrace concerns not to do harm, to do good and to be fair. There should be respect for harmless practices within other cultures, while rejecting those that infringe human rights. There should also be sensitivity to the adverse invasive social impact of itinerant researchers from developed countries. Strategically it can also be argued that an improved standard of care could enhance participation in research and the achievement of research goals. Not least, an operational argument can be mounted in support of the idea that research coupled to improved standards of care facilitates improvements in the delivery of health care. As the goal of medical research is to improve health care there should be greater support for encouraging closer links between research and its application at sites where the research is being undertaken. These justifications and examples of how they have been applied in practice have been described in detail elsewhere.

While dual standards of care will ensue from implementing a broader standard of care in poor countries, this is an inevitable aspect of progress. Inability to achieve immediate equity should not be an impediment to making improvements that could spread more widely with time and effort. It could be argued that it is more unethical to be satisfied with existing low or non-existent standards than to create dual standards as part of a progressive means of improving care. Of course a higher standard of care will be an inducement. But inducements are only morally wrong if they result in participants taking risks with their health and lives. What is wrong with an inducement that enables access to otherwise unavailable care and continues after the trial is over? Inability to achieve immediate equity should not be an impediment to achieving progressive reductions in inequity.

* * *

Making * * * progress will require new paradigms of thinking. Firstly, it must be acknowledged that research does not take place in a vacuum but rather in a world with wide disparities in which much research on vulnerable people has never been applied for their benefit. Secondly, researchers should increasingly view continuation of current patterns of exploitative research as ethically unacceptable. Thirdly, the need to link moral progress to scientific progress should become a high priority. Progress could be made towards such goals by coupling research to improvements in health through a broader conception of the standard of care and by linking research to development through partnerships and strategic alliances that could promote sustainability.

Notes

1. Perhaps the most famous incidents involving research in developing countries were the HIV transmission trials carried out in a number of nations in the mid-1990s. See, discussing these, Symposium, 88 *Am. J. Pub. Health* 548ff , including articles by Ruth Fadin and Nancy Kass, Isabelle De Zoysa, et al., Quarraisha Abdool Karim, et al., George Annas and Michael Grodin, Salim S. Abdool Karim, and Ronald Bayer. Among many other articles on vertical transmission HIV trials, see, criticizing the tests, M. Angell, The Ethics of Clinical Research in the Third World, 337 *New Eng. J. Med.* 847 (1997) and P. Lurie and S. Wolfe, Unethical Trials of Interventions to Reduce the Perinatal Transmission of the Human Immunodeficiency Virus in Developing Countries, 337 *New Eng. J. Med.* 853 (1997); and, defending the trials, H. Varmus and D. Satcher, Ethical Complexities of Conducting Research in Developing Countries, 337 *New Eng. J. Med.* 1000 (1997). Among the other articles discussing this controversy, see, Symposium, HIV Research in Developing Countries, 12 *Bioethics* 286 (1998); Symposium, A World of Research Subjects, 28 *Hastings Ctr. Rep.*, November/December 1998 at 25; and H. Varmus & D. Satcher, *The Conduct of Clinical Trials of Maternal-Infant Transmission of HIV Supported by the United States Department of Health and Human Services in Developing Countries, http://www.nih.gov/news/mathiv/mathiv.htm*. See also, generally, Ruth Macklin, *Double Standards in Medical Research in Developing Countries* (2004); and, specifically on the question of compensating victims of such trials, Charles Weijer, Guy J. LeBlanc, The Balm of Gilead: Is the Provision of Treatment to Those Who Seroconvert in HIV Prevention Trials a Matter of Moral Obligation or Moral Negotiations? 34 *J. L. Med. & Ethics* 793 (2006).

2. Among the many issues raised by research in developing countries is whether international Guidelines like the Declaration of Helsinki or the CIOMS Guidelines should govern research in radically different cultures. One particular issue, for example, is whether the notion of informed consent endorsed by these guidelines is in fact an artifact of Western notions of autonomous individuality, and thus inappropriate for cultures where the concept of individuality is much weaker, and where, perhaps it might be more culturally sensitive to seek consent from a subject's family or social group. Opponents of this position defend these ethical guidelines as universal, and suggest that varying these principles to fit different cultures might result in "ethical apartheid." See, espousing a principle of "ethical pluralism," Nicolas A. Christakis, The Distinction Between Ethical Pluralism and Ethical Relativism: Implications for the Conduct of Transcultural Clinical Research, and arguing for ethical universalism, Medical Research and the Principle of Respect for Persons in Non-Western Culture, both in *The Ethics of Research Involving Human Subjects: Facing the 21st Century* (Harold Y. Vanderpool, ed., 1996).

Index